Visions

Earth's Elements in Bird and Nature Photography

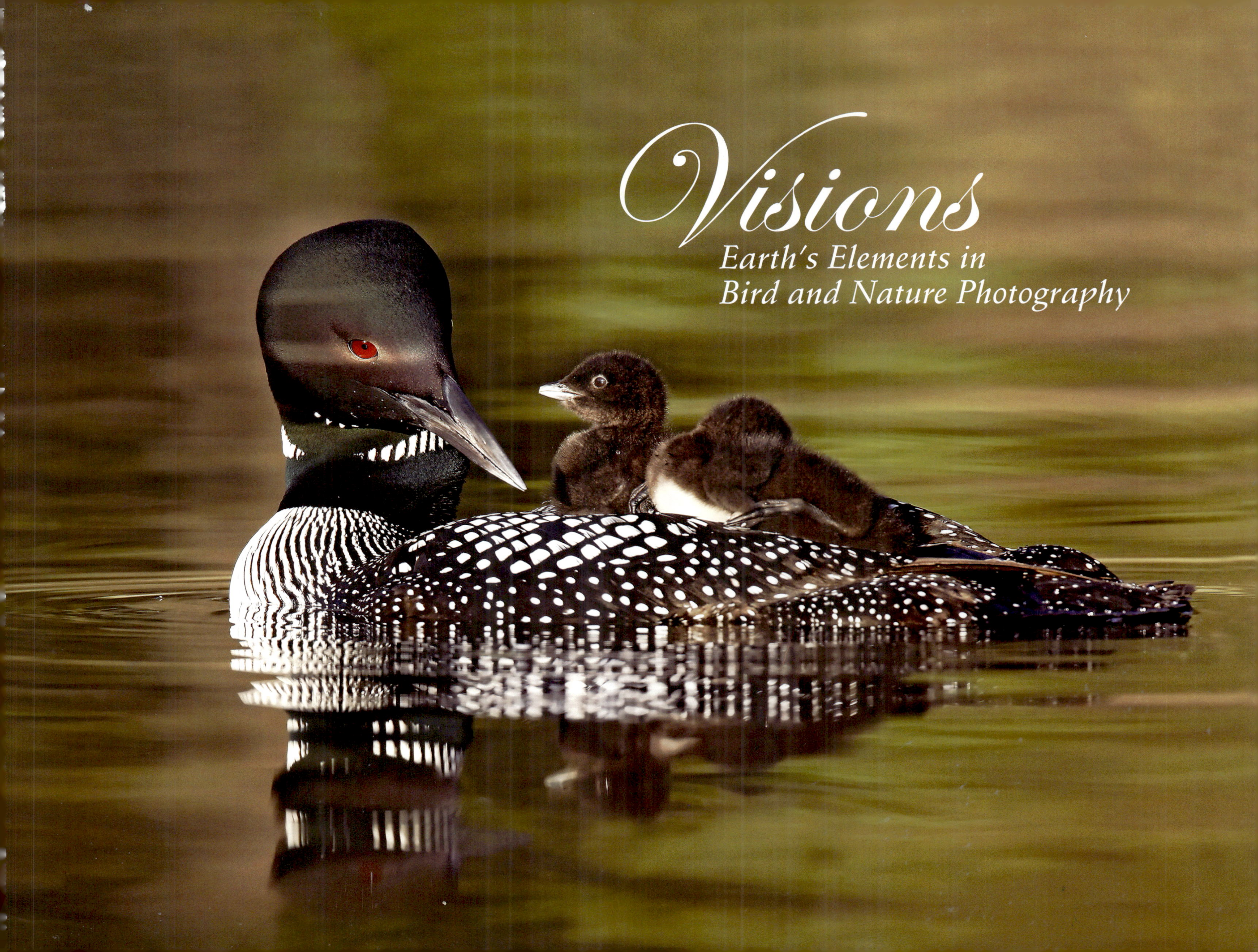

Dedications

Kevin T. Karlson: I would like to dedicate this book to two special family members: my wife Dale Rosselet and sister Patrice Karlson Brierty. Also to a dear friend Michelle Matson, who recently lost her long, courageous battle with cancer, and who inspired me and countless others with a special "vision" of life and positive outlook throughout her ordeal.

Lloyd Spitalnik: This book is dedicated to my wife Sandy who inspires me in so many ways and is the love of my life.

Scott Elowitz: I would like to dedicate this book to the love of my life, Cyndi, my beautiful wife and mother of our amazing son, Ian. Without your support and encouragement the pursuit of my passions would not be possible.

Library of Congress Control Number: 2012936064

Type set in Minion Pro

ISBN: 978-0-7643-4075-8
Printed in Hong Kong

Schiffer Books are available at special discounts for bulk purchases for sales promotions or premiums. Special editions, including personalized covers, corporate imprints, and excerpts can be created in large quantities for special needs. For more information contact the publisher:

Published by Schiffer Publishing Ltd.
4880 Lower Valley Road
Atglen, PA 19310
Phone: (610) 593-1777; Fax: (610) 593-2002
E-mail: Info@schifferbooks.com

For the largest selection of fine reference books on this and related subjects, please visit our website at **www.schifferbooks.com**
We are always looking for people to write books on new and related subjects. If you have an idea for a book, please contact us at
proposals@schifferbooks.com

This book may be purchased from the publisher.
Please try your bookstore first.
You may write for a free catalog.

In Europe, Schiffer books are distributed by
Bushwood Books
6 Marksbury Ave.
Kew Gardens
Surrey TW9 4JF England
Phone: 44 (0) 20 8392 8585; Fax: 44 (0) 20 8392 9876
E-mail: info@bushwoodbooks.co.uk
Website: www.bushwoodbooks.co.uk

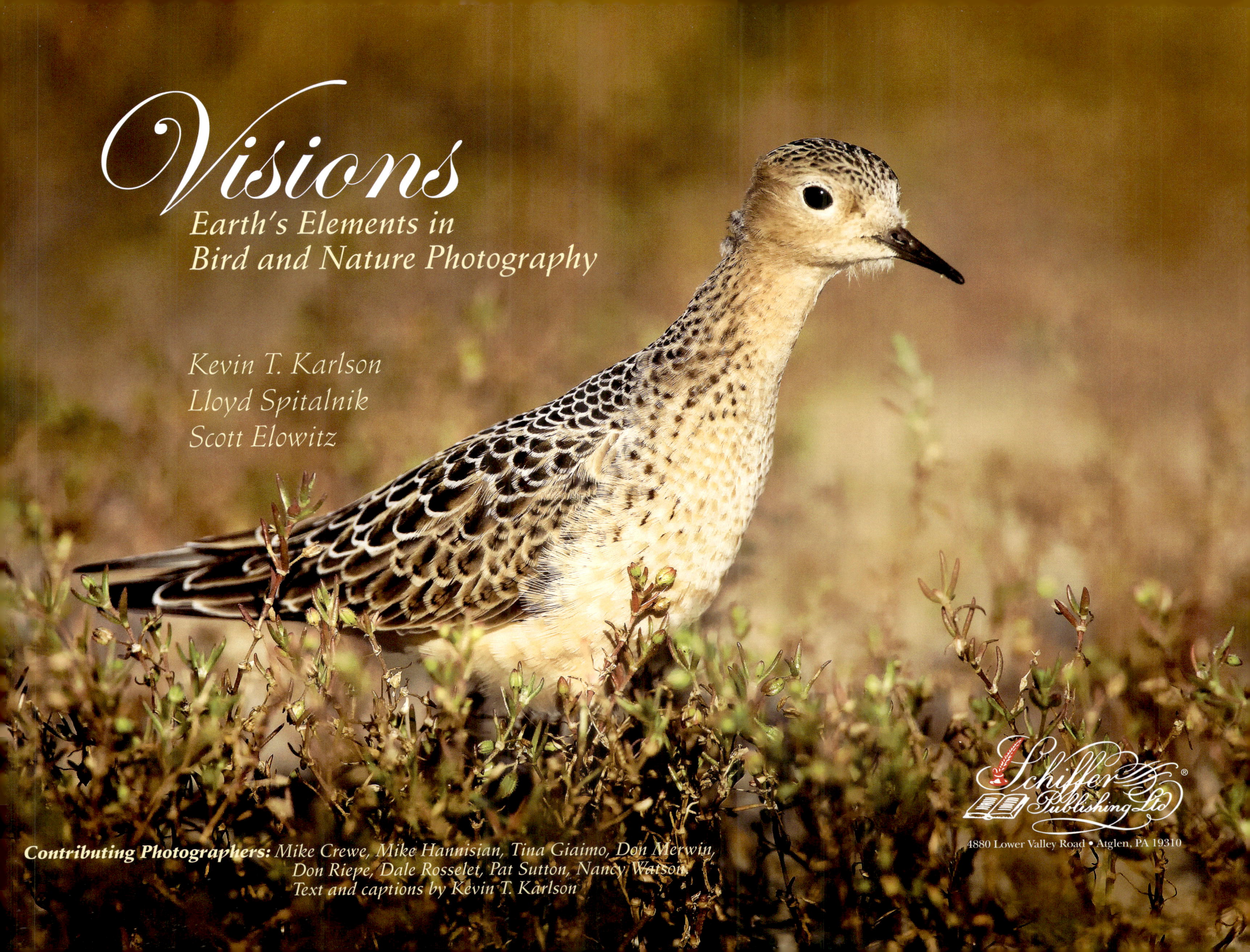

Visions

Earth's Elements in Bird and Nature Photography

Kevin T. Karlson
Lloyd Spitalnik
Scott Elowitz

Contributing Photographers: *Mike Crewe, Mike Hannisian, Tina Giaimo, Don Merwin, Don Riepe, Dale Rosselet, Pat Sutton, Nancy Watson*

Text and captions by Kevin T. Karlson

Schiffer Publishing Ltd®
4880 Lower Valley Road • Atglen, PA 19310

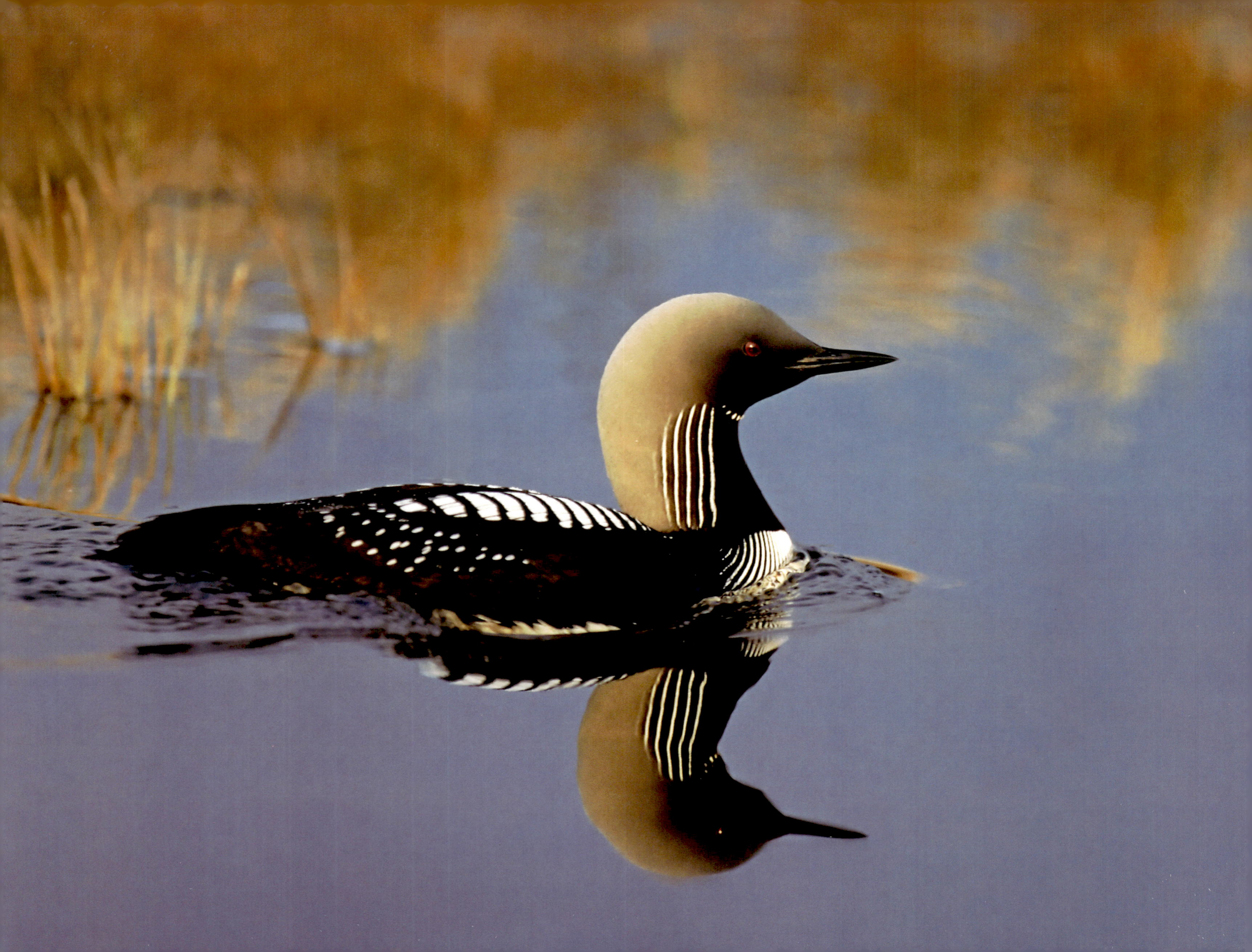

Acknowledgments

Kevin Karlson: I would like to acknowledge some people who are responsible for my development as a photographer, and who helped to mold my vision of life and nature. First, my wife Dale Rosselet, who reviews my publications, suggests alternative approaches, and adds gentle balance to the entire project. Also to my late parents, Margaret and Henry Karlson, who gave me the opportunity to pursue my dreams with gentle guidance and support for whatever I chose to do.

I would like to thank the contributing photographers of this book for donating their stunning and inspirational images of nature, especially my dear friends Scott Elowitz and Lloyd Spitalnik. Other notable photographers and people that inspire me are: Milo Burcham, Greg Downing, Maxis Gamez, Chas Glatzer, Lewis Kemper, Jerry Liguori, Erin Masters, John Moran, Arthur Morris, Alan Murphy, Jim Neiger, Don Riepe, Deb Sandidge, Rob Sheppard, Jim Zipp, and the late Tom Vezo, whose passing came way too soon. Lastly, I would like to give special thanks to Susan Zipper for her artistic advice with this project.

Lloyd Spitalnik: I want to thank several people who have helped me along the way to be a better naturalist and photographer. First and foremost, my wife Sandy. Without her I would never have gotten into birding and wildlife photography. She keeps me totally grounded and never lets my ego get the better of me. She keeps me organized, helps with photo selections, and maintains my website for me. I couldn't have asked for anyone better.

To Kevin Karlson and Scott Elowitz, my co-authors, who are fabulous photographers and even better friends. Tom Vezo, who is dearly missed and was an inspiration to me to become a decent wildlife photographer. To David Speiser, Harry Maas and Dick Gershon, "the guys" who I spend the most time with in the field. To Don Riepe, my good friend and one of the most generous people you'll ever meet. To Eliot Kutner who first got me excited to learn about birds. To my dear departed friend, Marty Sohmer, who taught me more about bird ID and bird behavior than anybody else through the years. And in no particular order, Marie Winn, for showcasing my photos on her very popular blog, Nick Wagerick, who taught me to appreciate the bug world, and Brian St. Clair. To my Central Park friends, Max and Nellie Larson, Elliott Zichlinsky, Peter Post, and Lew and Sheila Rosenberg. To all my good friends at NWPLI, a great group of photographers from Long Island. To the NY birding community including Tom Burke, Gail Benson, Shai Mitra, Pat Lindsay, Shane Blodgett and Doug Gochfeld. There are so many more people I could mention so forgive me if I left you out.

Scott Elowitz: I would like to extend a special thanks to my friend and co-author, Lloyd, for always challenging, encouraging, and inspiring me, as well as for his friendship, and to my friend and co-author, Kevin, who made this opportunity, along with countless others, possible. Kevin is one of the most giving people I know and I want to thank him for all his guidance and friendship. I would also like to thank my good friend and mentor, Alan Murphy, who has opened up my eyes like no other photographer or artist and has been one of the greatest influences on my work. But more than sharing his photographic talents with me, I want to thank him for his friendship which I will always cherish.

There are many other individuals in my life who have nurtured, guided, and influenced me. Some have shared their knowledge while others have shared friendship and love, and I could not have accomplished this milestone without each and every one of them. I would like to thank and acknowledge them here. Undoubtedly I will have omitted someone, but know you are no less important to me.

These instrumental people include: my son, Ian; my best friend Stu Rosenstein; my parents Joyce and Roger; Charles and Helen Bertsch; Craig Elowitz; Harry Rosenstein; Sue Lederman; Arthur Morris; Chas Glatzer; Greg Downing; Tom Vezo; E.J. Peiker; Jim Zipp; Joe Zugcic; Art Peslak; Chris Klapheke; Allen Leichter; George Decamp; Julian Hough; Dena Temple; Pete and Gretchen Pederson; Richard Crossley; George Wenzelburger; Omar Yamout; Sol Salamon; Shimon Halpert; and Pasquale Pascullo.

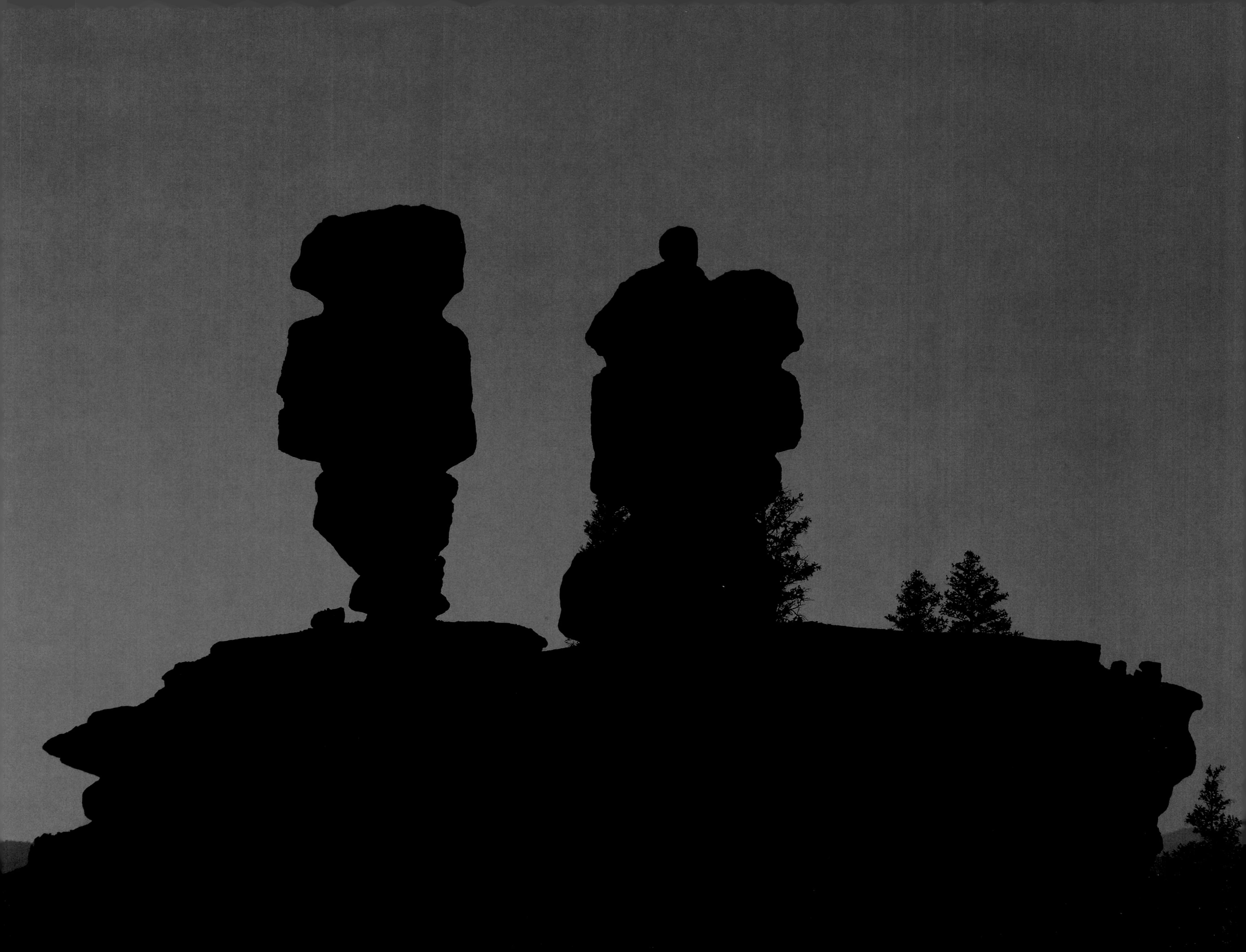

Quotes about nature were taken from various websites, especially www.quotegarden.com. They are in the public domain.

Text and captions by Kevin T. Karlson
Front cover photographs by Kevin T. Karlson
Rear cover photograph by Scott Elowitz

"The best and most beautiful things in life cannot be seen or touched. They must be felt with the heart."

Helen Keller

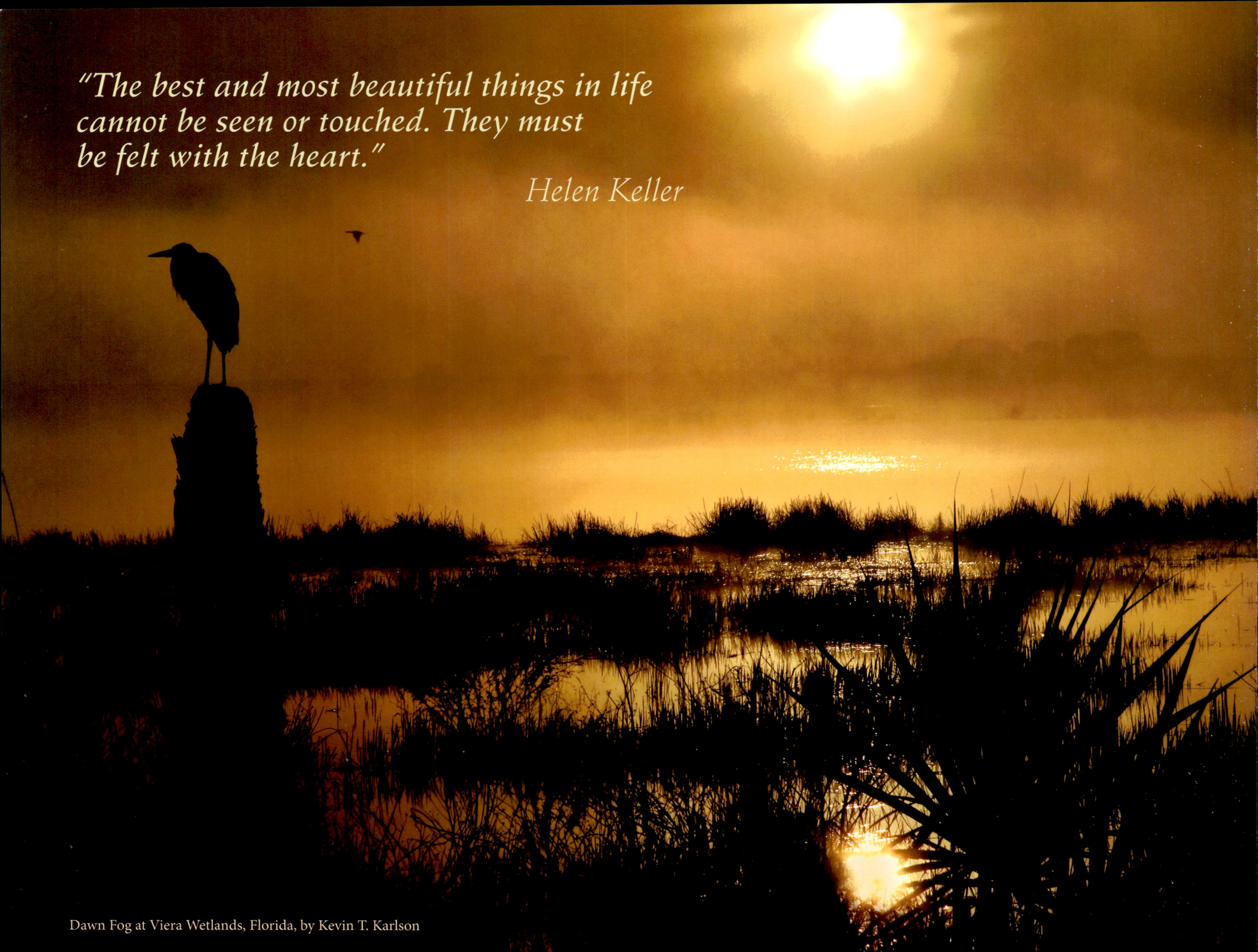

Dawn Fog at Viera Wetlands, Florida, by Kevin T. Karlson

Introduction

Everyone has visions, and some of these have the power to transform our lives. As humans, we envision how the world can be a better place for everyone, or we enjoy visions of a personal nature that include hopes, goals or inspirations that come from deep inside our being. These special insights reflect an introspective nature, and sometimes we are fortunate to see them come to life and positively affect others.

This book includes unique visions of nature offered by eleven contributing photographers. The three main photographers have long been inspired by the majesty of birds, which represent the most visible part of our natural world. For this reason, a good number of photos include birds in their typical habitats and their interactions with each other. Others reflect the many faces of nature, including flowers, landscapes, assorted creatures, and a variety of compelling visual patterns that are often overlooked in the hurry of everyday life.

Since nature represents the only true constant in an ever-changing, artificial world, I have chosen to present the photographs using the four basic elements of our planet: earth, fire, air, and water. These elements are the foundation of our natural world, and have long been considered by native peoples to be sacred and overseen by a higher power. We share these images according to the earth's elements, but often in ways that you might not expect.

For example, a photo included in the fire section may only show a red or orange highlight in a small portion of the frame, but it still invokes the mood of fire in our minds. A flying bird in the air section is placed there because birds use the magic of flight to define their lives. So you see how broadly the earth's elements can be depicted in a photographic context if you allow your imagination to run free. This artistic freedom allowed me to visualize the elemental connections in our photos.

Nature photography is undergoing major changes because of advanced digital imaging software. Many of today's images are not true representations of what was originally photographed, but a compilation of several images grouped together. Our book contains photos that are not altered and compromised by Photoshop tricks, but truly show what nature offers in real life. Minor corrections and preparations have been made to some images, but nothing artificial or external has been added to any photo.

This book is a celebration of our collective passion for nature and how we perceive it differently through the camera's eye. Our visions truly come to life when our photos touch a part of you that is connected to the universal thread of life, and one that transcends the limitations of the human condition. Enjoy the journey!

—Kevin T. Karlson

Earth

Earth is the most grounded of all the planet's elements. It has its roots in the soil, rocks, trees and grasses, and is usually represented by warm tones of color, including yellow, brown, buff, rust, and green. Some cultures envision a guiding spirit that looks after the planet, and may refer to this entity as the Earth Mother. This benevolent spirit provides balance to the everyday drama of earth's passion play.

This section highlights photos that directly relate to the earth: rocky landscapes, beaches, or terrestrial habitats and animals that rely on its bounty for their survival. Other images are included because their color scheme or overall moods are rich with earth tones. Animals that are strongly connected to the earth's ecosystems, including forests or grasslands, are also presented. Earth is a base element, and a broad range of images connected to its essence are included here.

Those who contemplate the beauty of the earth find reserves of strength that will endure as long as life lasts. There is something infinitely healing in the repeated refrains of nature— the assurance that dawn comes after night, and spring after winter.

— Rachel Carson

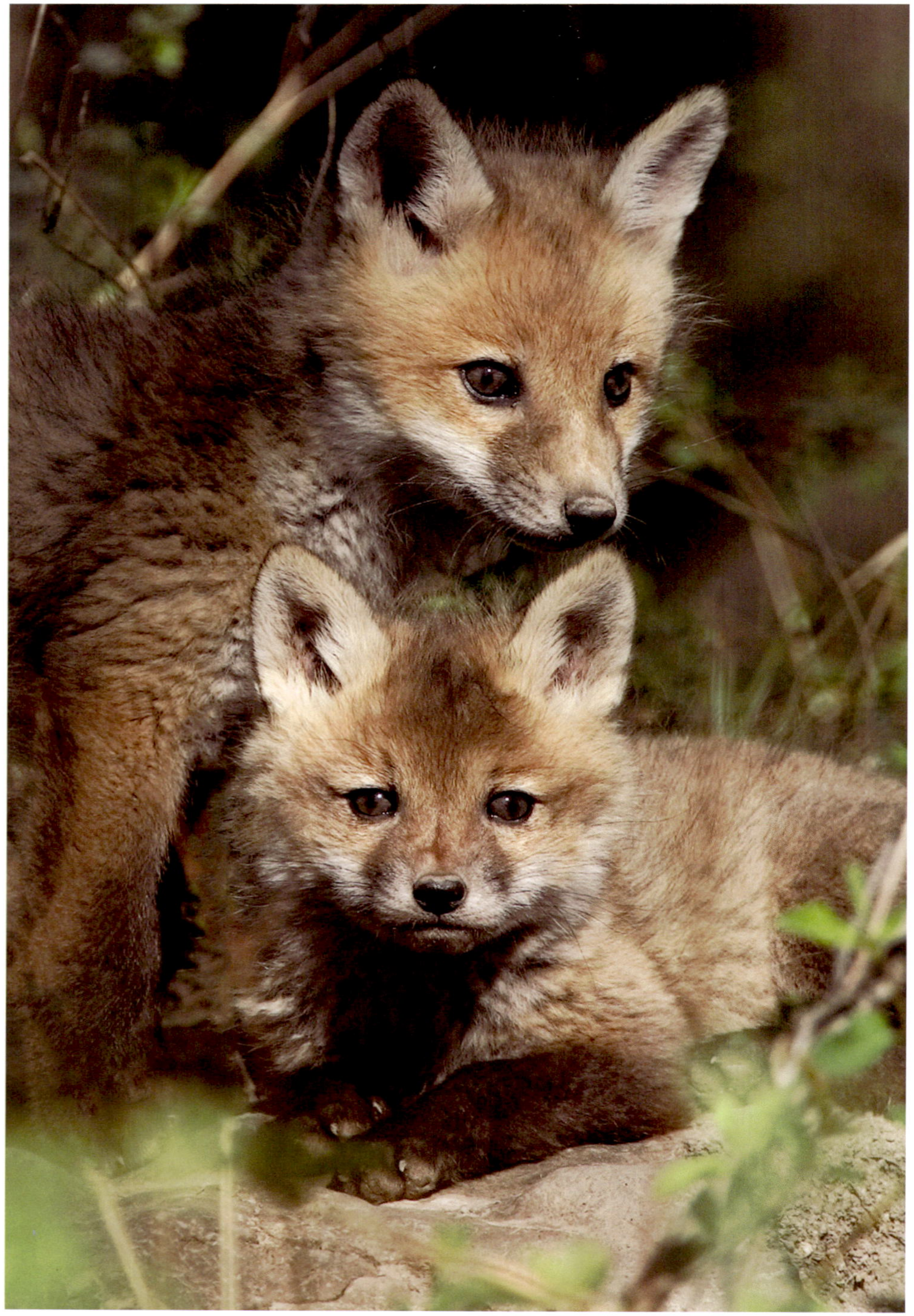

Two very young fox kits show a combination of curiosity and fear as they cautiously observe the photographer. *Photo by Scott Elowitz*

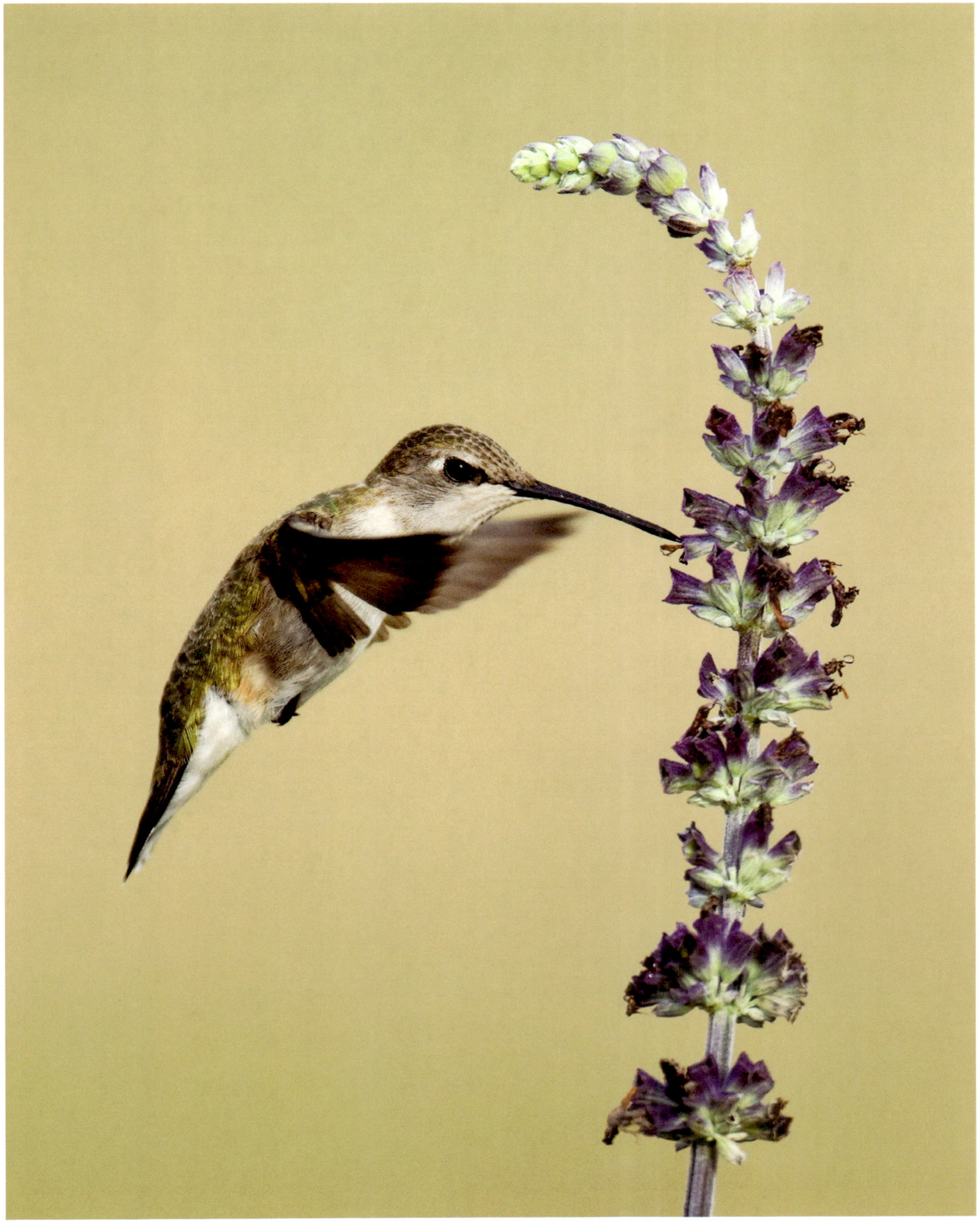

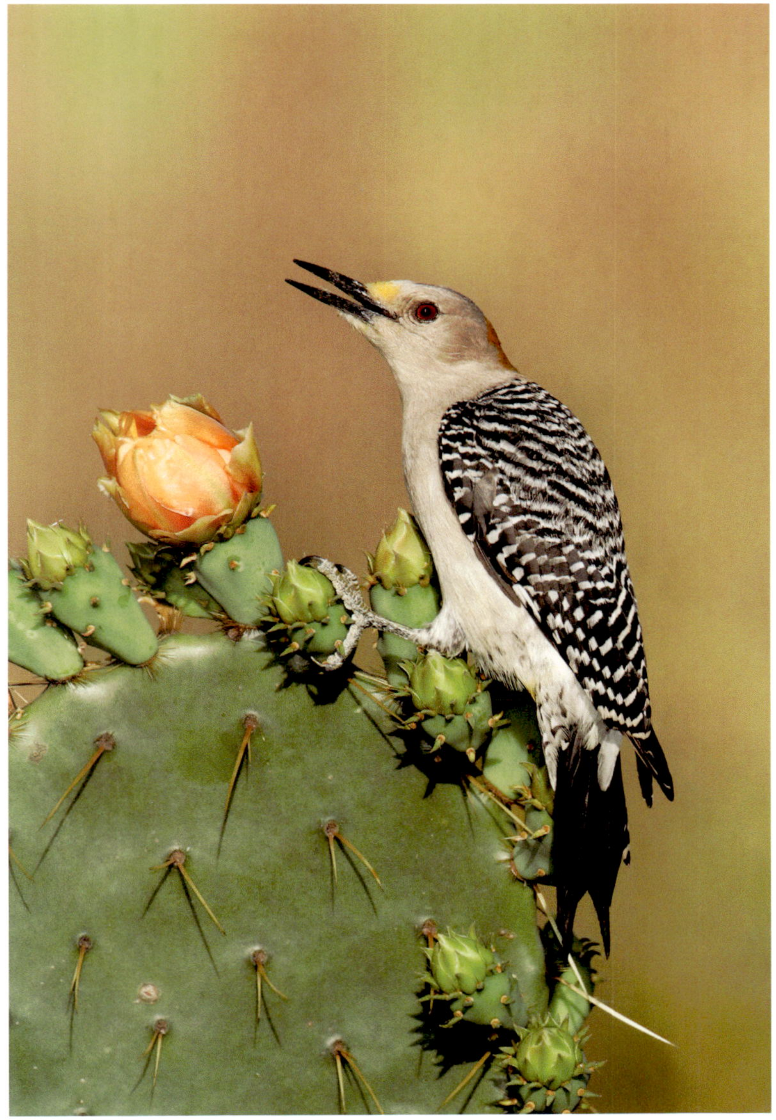

A female Black-chinned Hummingbird (left) nectars on a desert flower while a Golden-fronted Woodpecker perches tenuously on a spiny cactus. These birds eke out an existence in arid habitats with strong earth tones.

Photos by Scott Elowitz

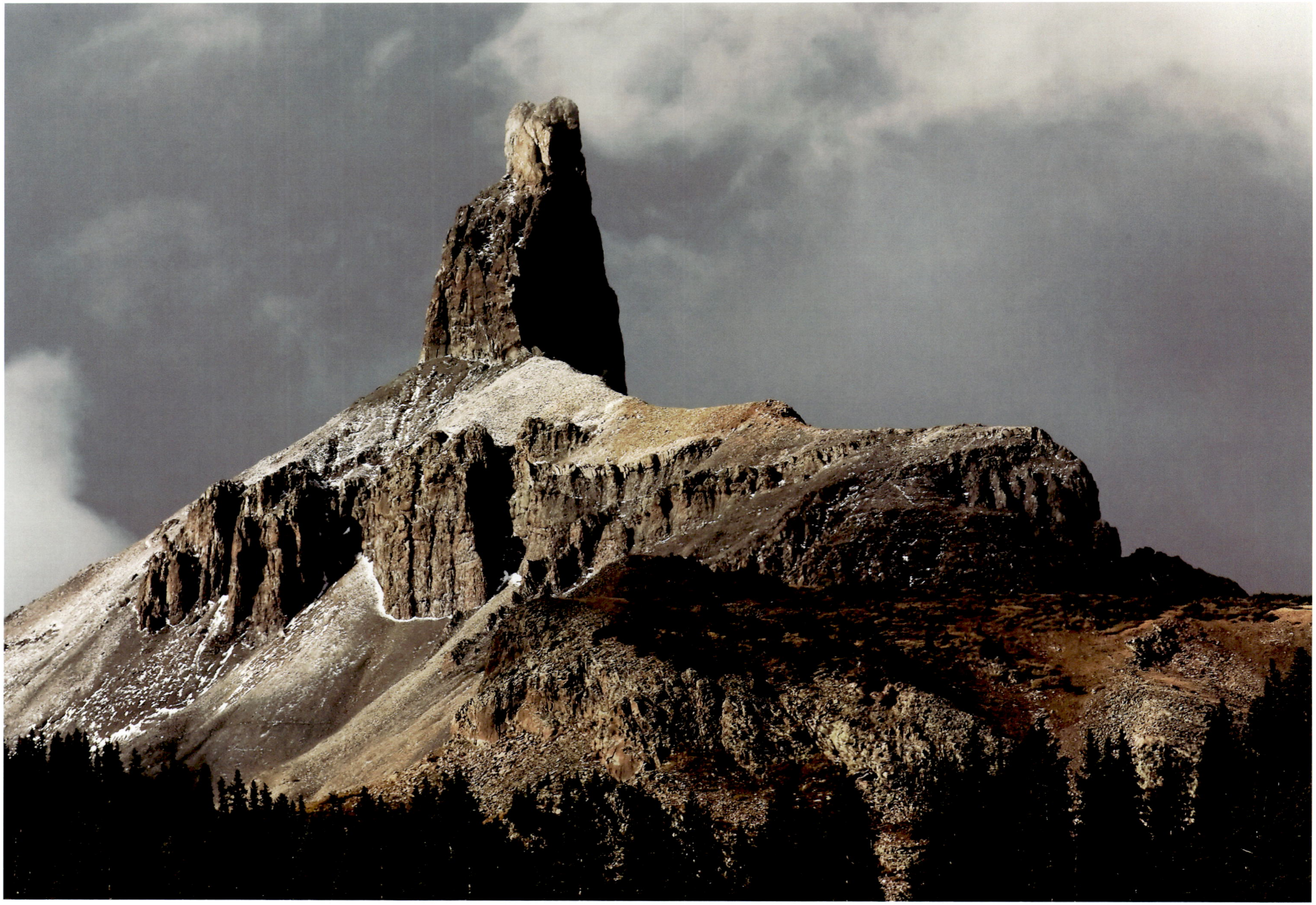

A moody, stormy day sets the scene for this dramatic rock formation on the west slope of the Rocky Mountains near Telluride, Colorado.
Photo by Kevin T. Karlson

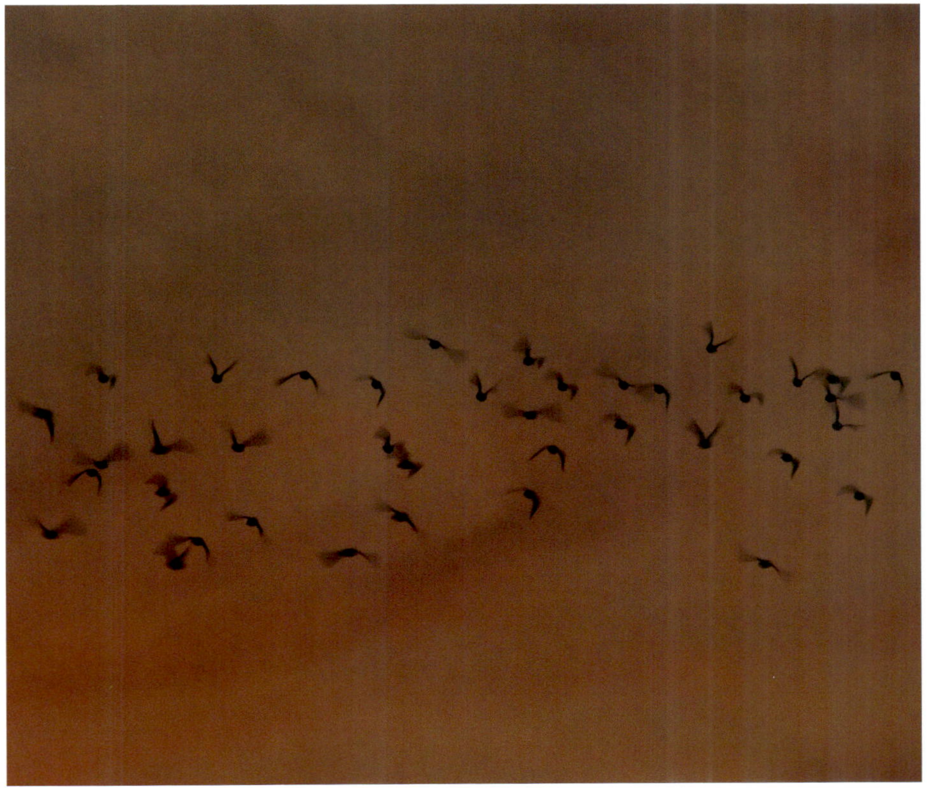

A flock of migrating shorebirds rises into a rusty sunset on their way to Arctic breeding sites. *Photo by Kevin T. Karlson*

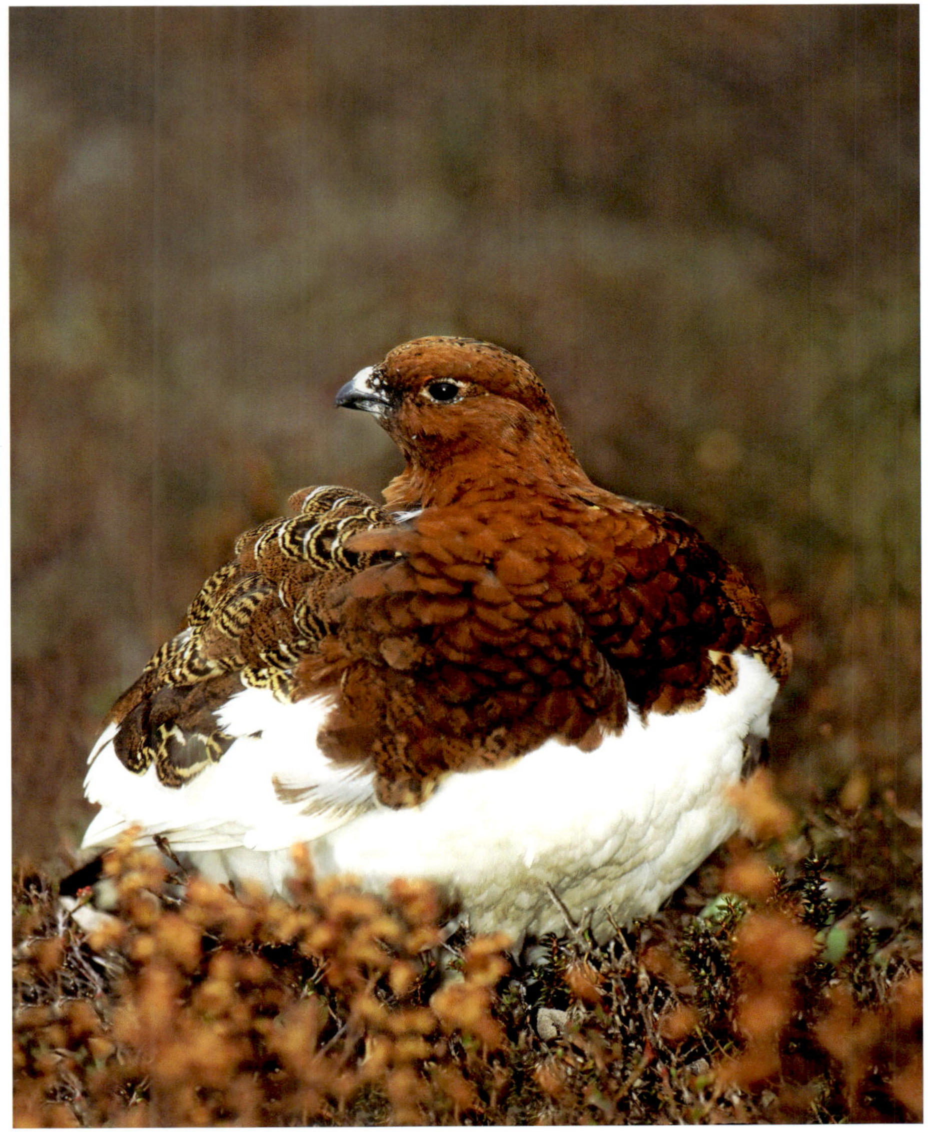

A male Willow Ptarmigan hugs the ground while it enjoys its favorite food of willow buds. It has a complete white plumage for all but the summer months, when it's warm, earth-tone feathers blend in perfectly with the ground cover. *Photo by Kevin T. Karlson*

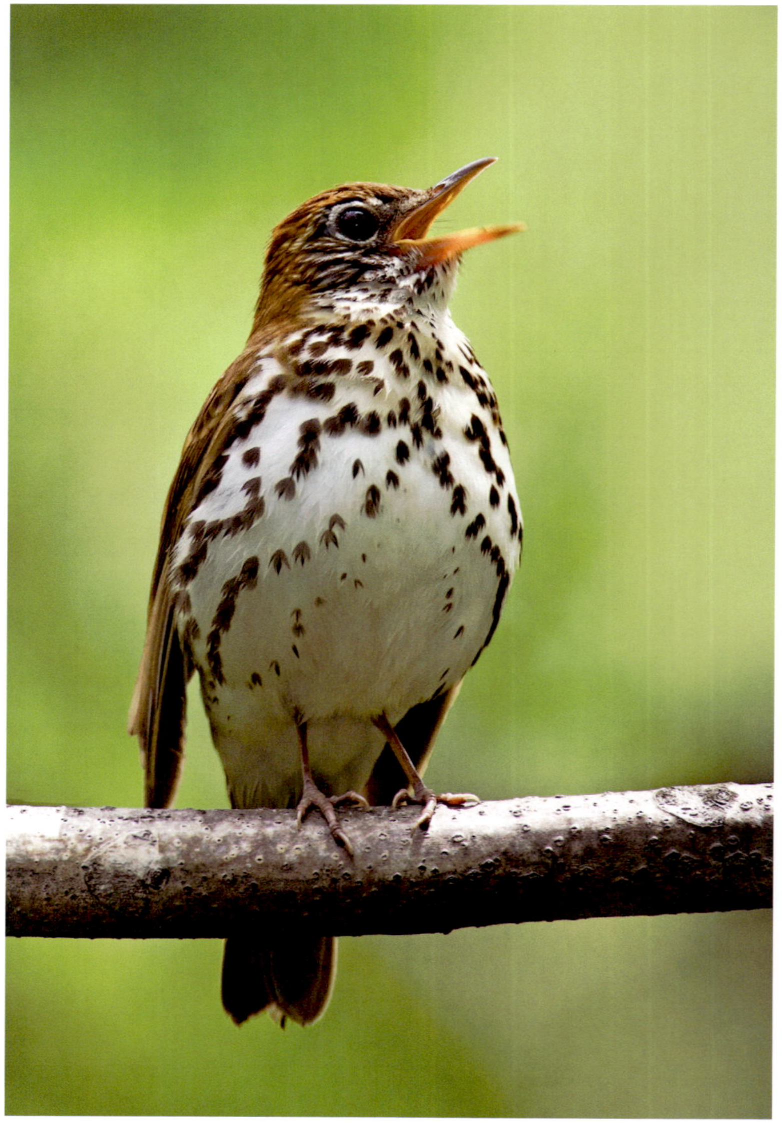

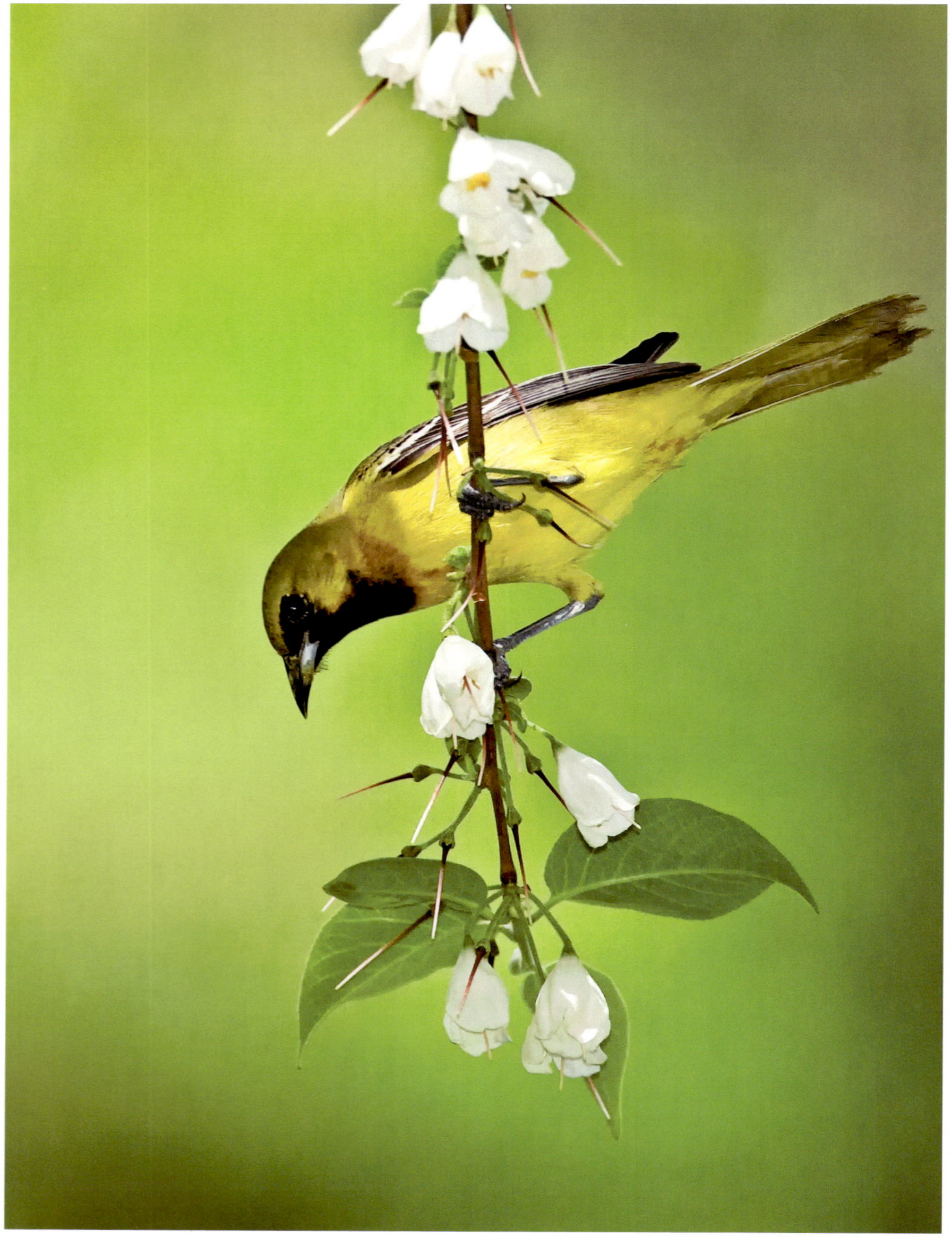

A Wood Thrush (left) and an immature male Orchard Oriole (above); these are common songbirds in the eastern United States. The Wood Thrush has a flute-like song that rivals any bird for its beautiful melodic quality, and the Orchard Oriole sings a song composed of sweet notes and chattering phrases. *Photos by Lloyd Spitalnik*

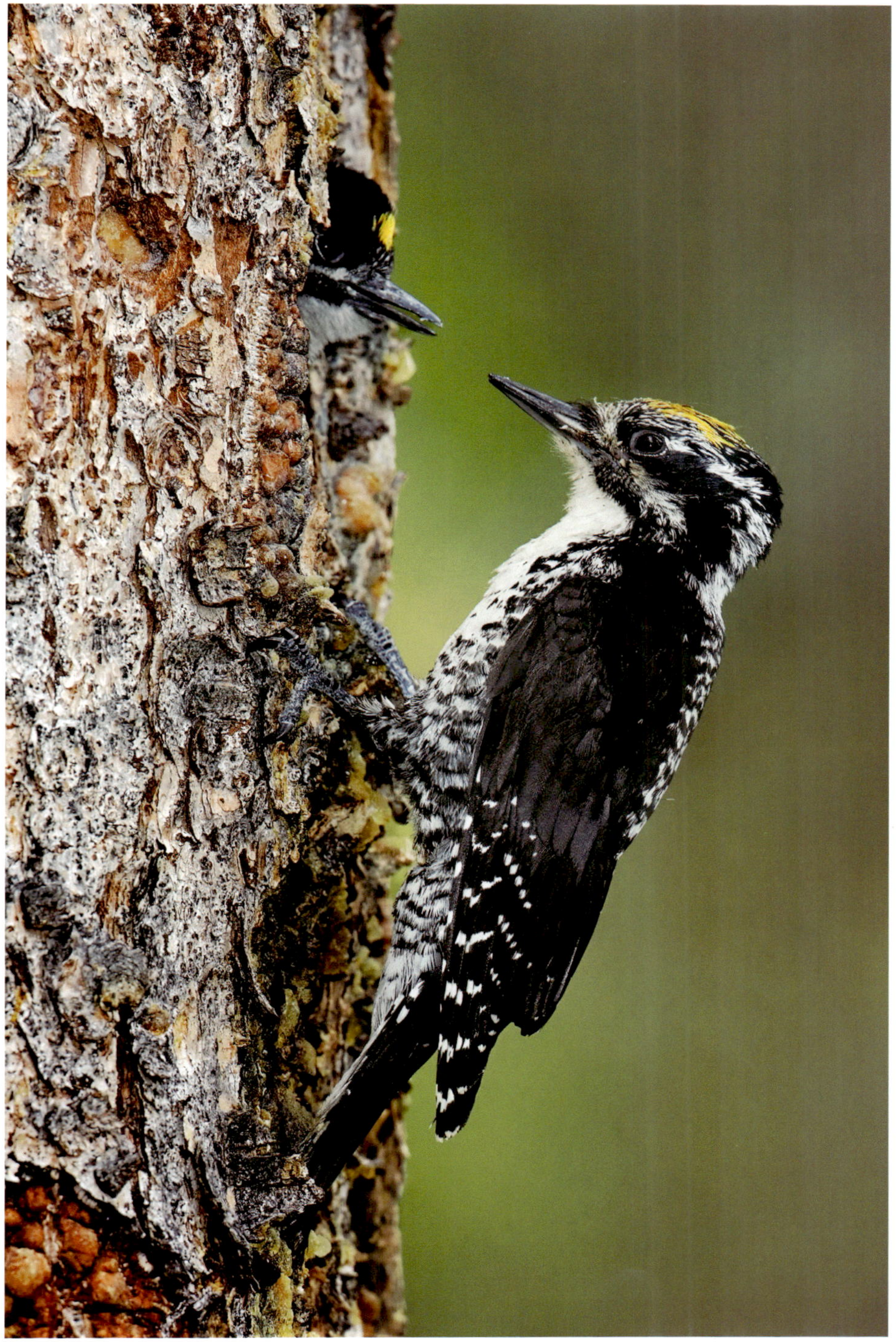

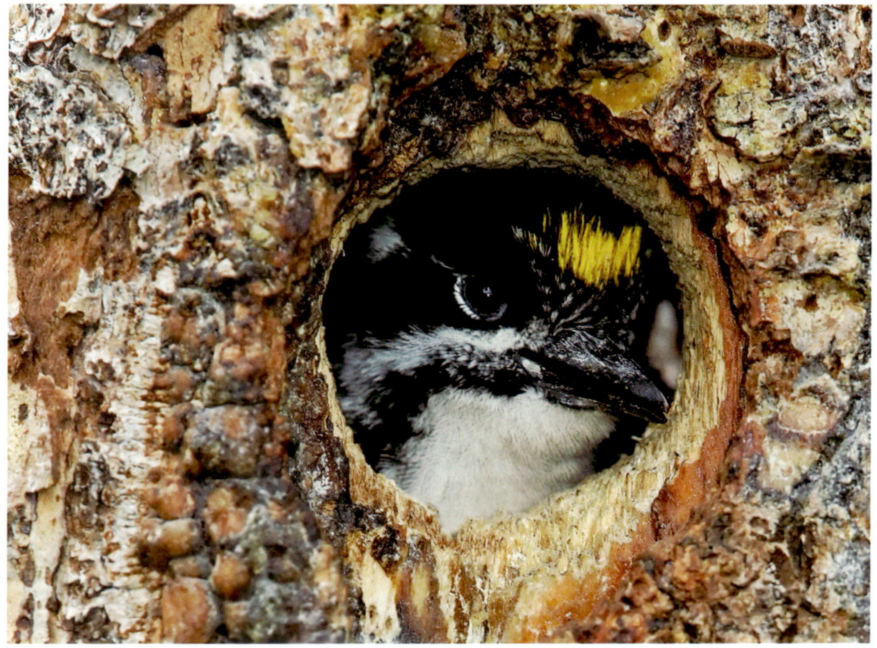

A juvenile Northern Three-toed Woodpecker is close to leaving its nest hole for the first and only time. Its curiosity about the big, wide world is evident in this photo.

Woodpeckers are specialized birds that occur in just about every forested region of North America. This uncommon Northern Three-toed Woodpecker lives on the west slope of the Rocky Mountains in British Columbia, and is typically found in coniferous forests.

Photos by Kevin T. Karlson

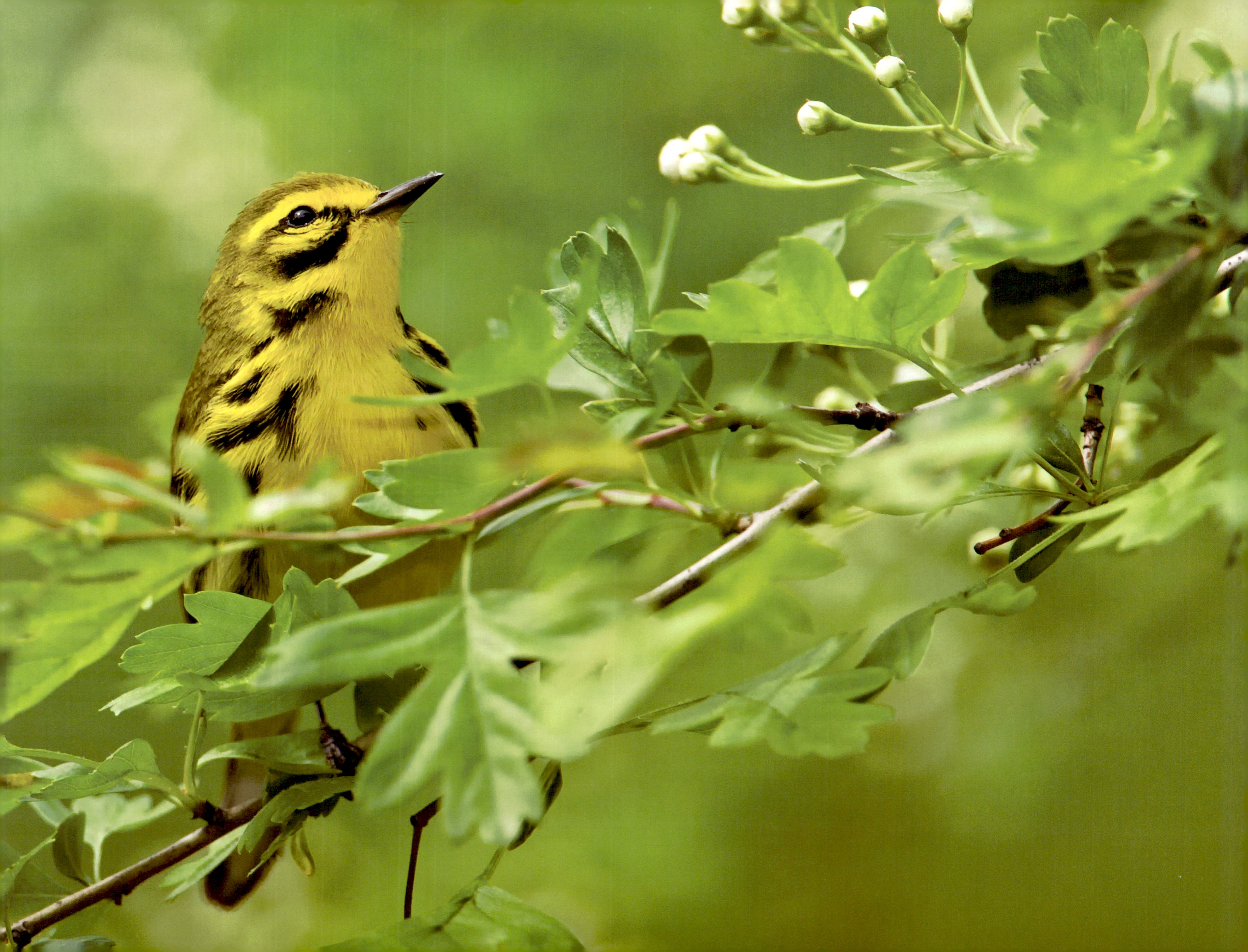

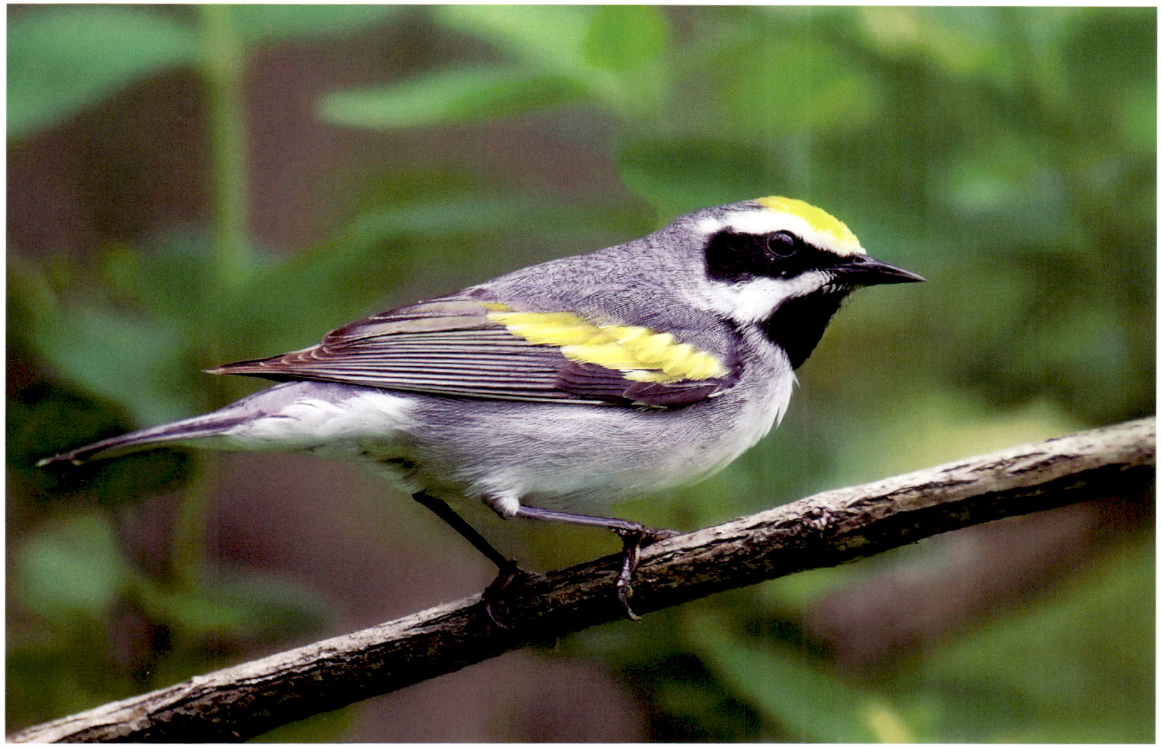

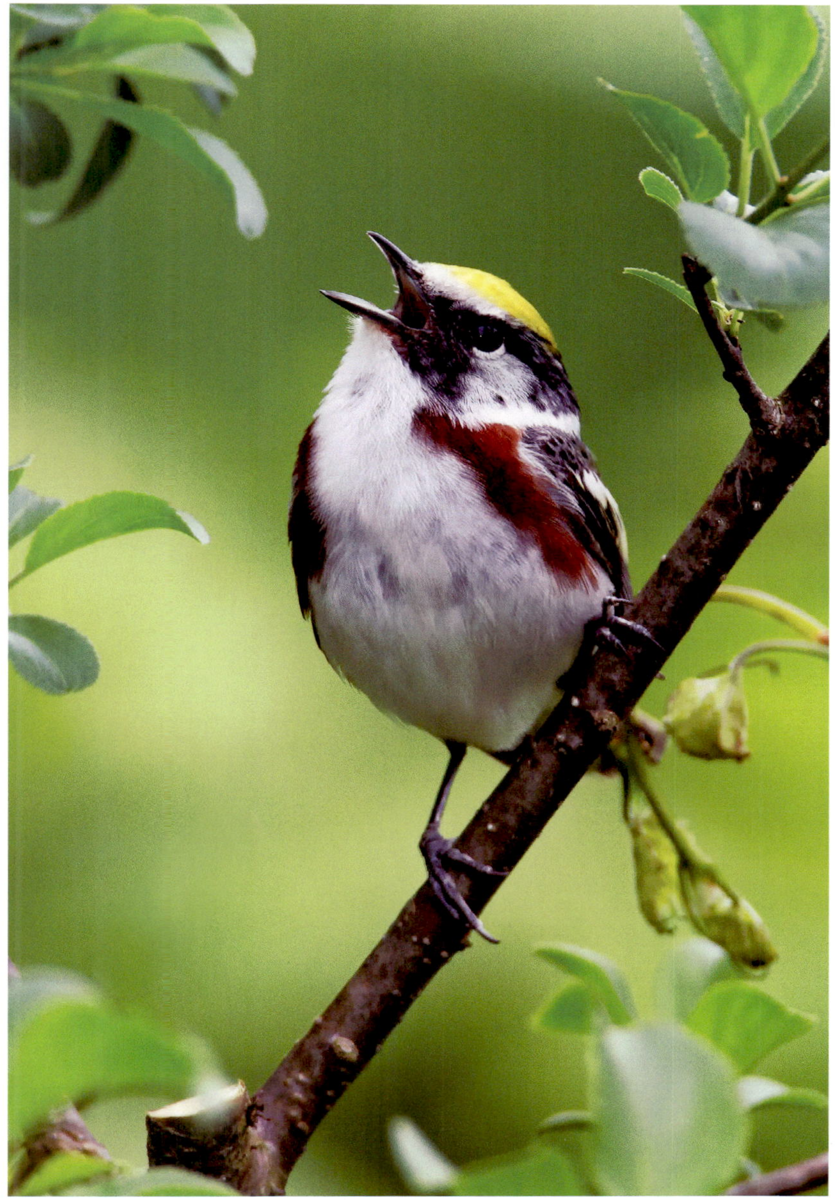

Warblers are jewels of the forest, and they fill the woods with sweet songs in spring and early summer. The male Golden-winged Warbler (above) has one of the most alluring mixes of color and patterns of all warblers, and is a special prize for birders.

A male Chestnut-sided Warbler (right) shows a striking yellow crown and bright chestnut flanks. This beautiful bird sings to attract a mate or define its territory.

Opposite: A Prairie Warbler peeks out from behind leaves as it searches for worms and bugs. *Photos by Lloyd Spitalnik*

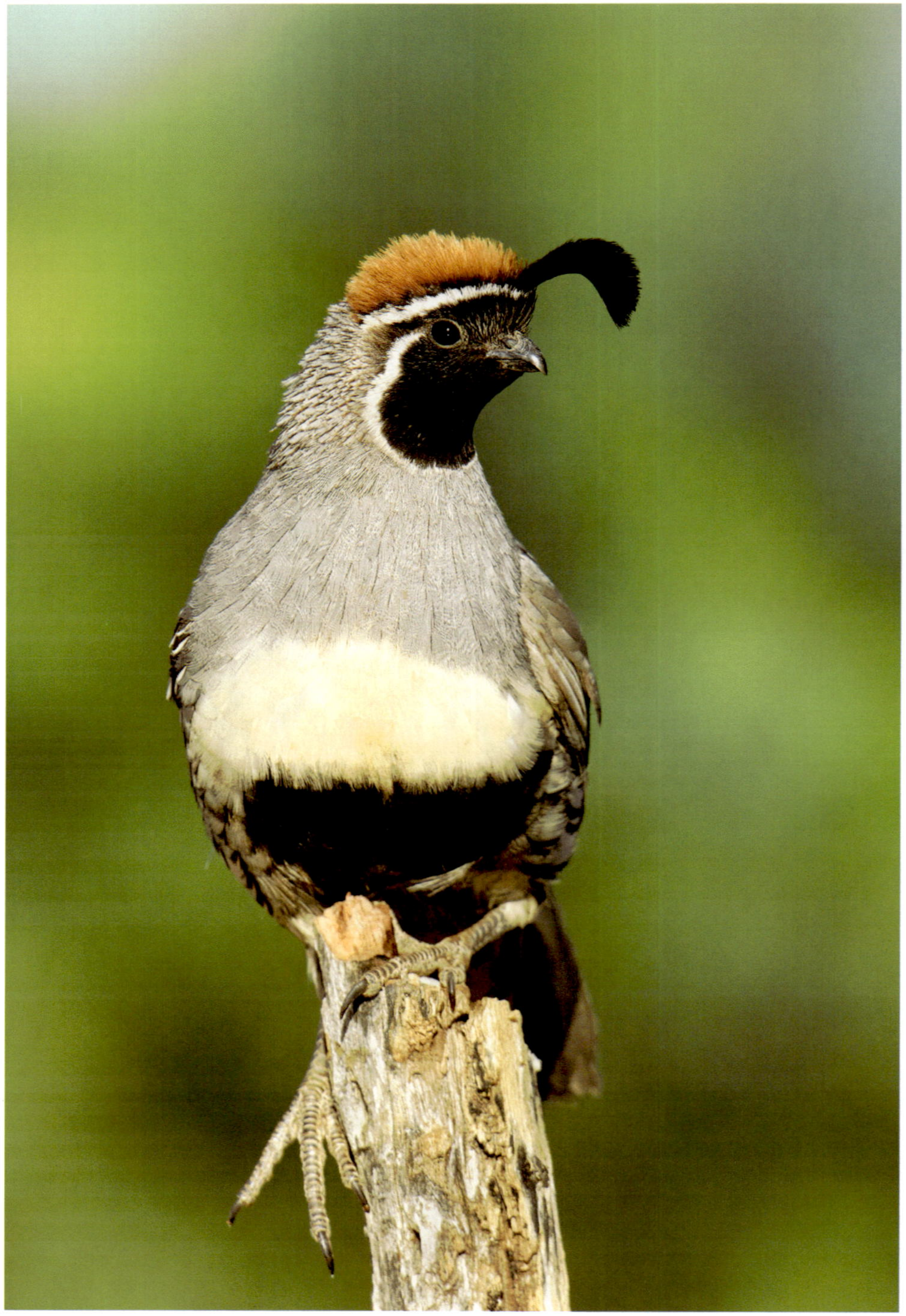

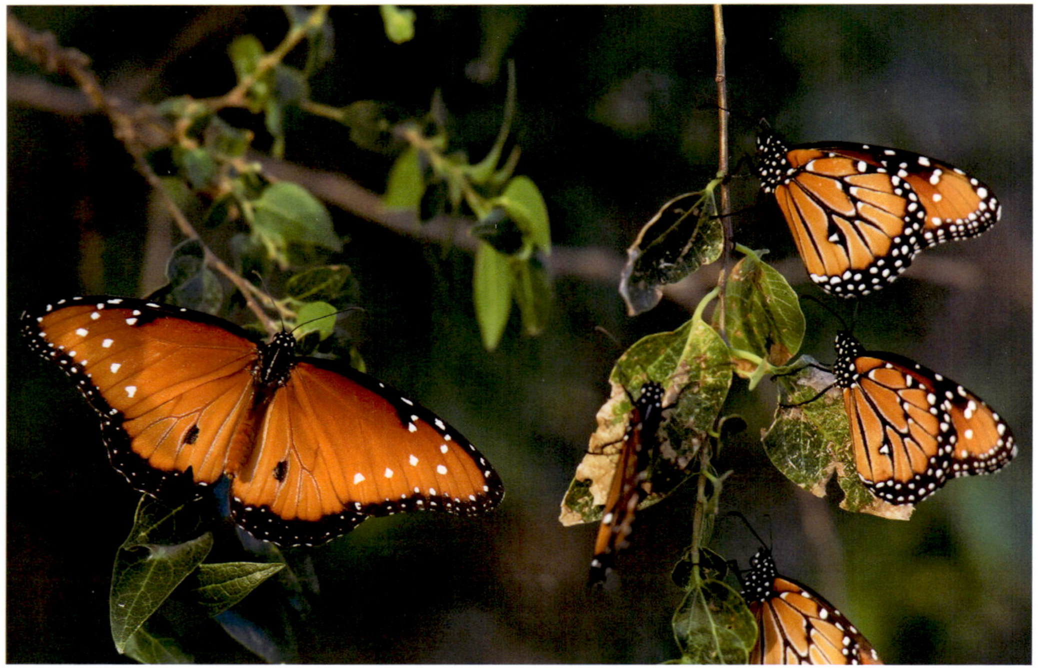

Rust is the earth tone that ties these two images together; both creatures live in southern locations of the United States. Queen butterflies are shown at a nighttime roost near Edinburg, Texas (above). *Photo by Kevin T. Karlson*

This handsome male Gambel's Quail (left) spends most of its life on the ground, but is perched here to better survey its desert surroundings. *Photo by Scott Elowitz*

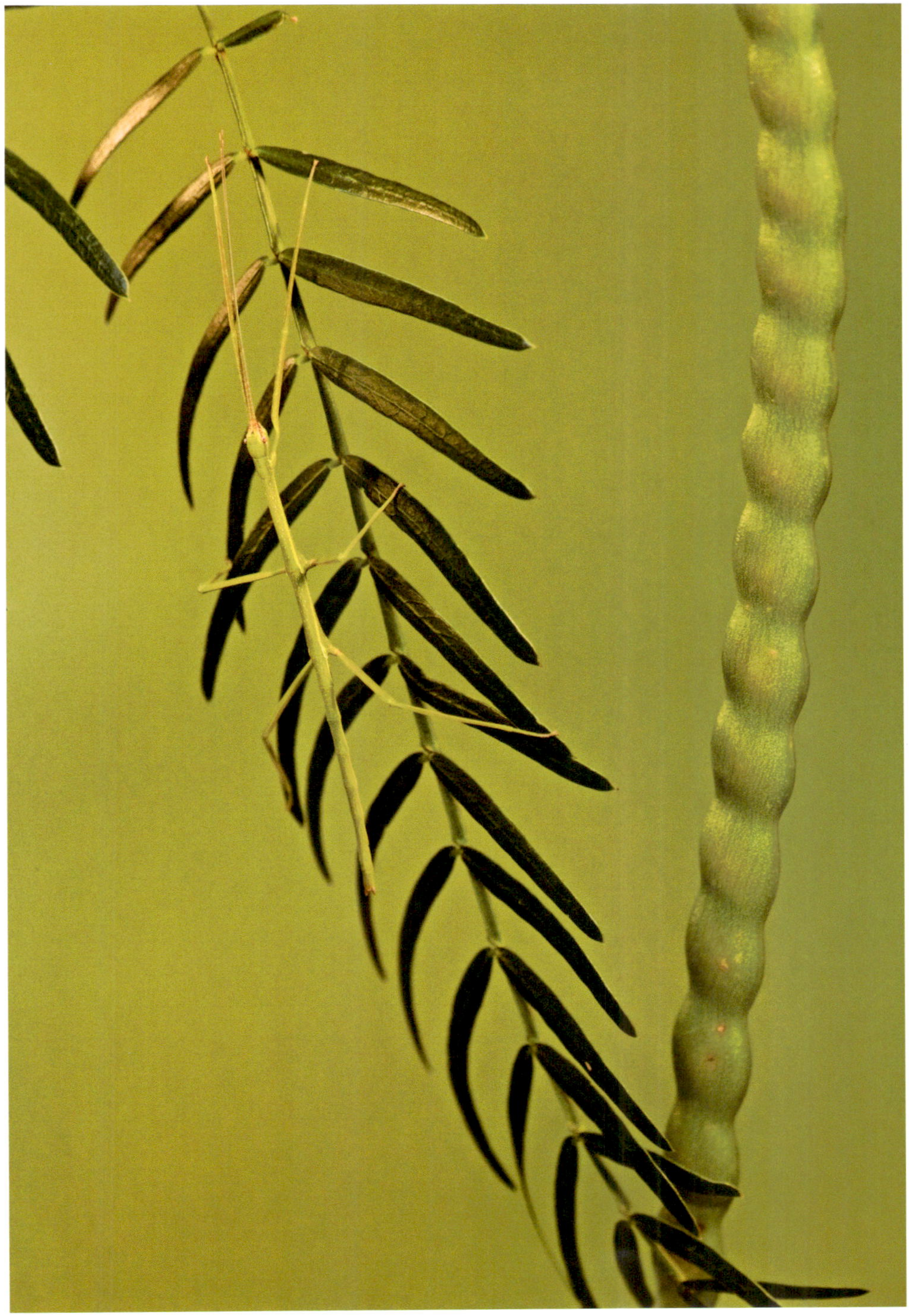

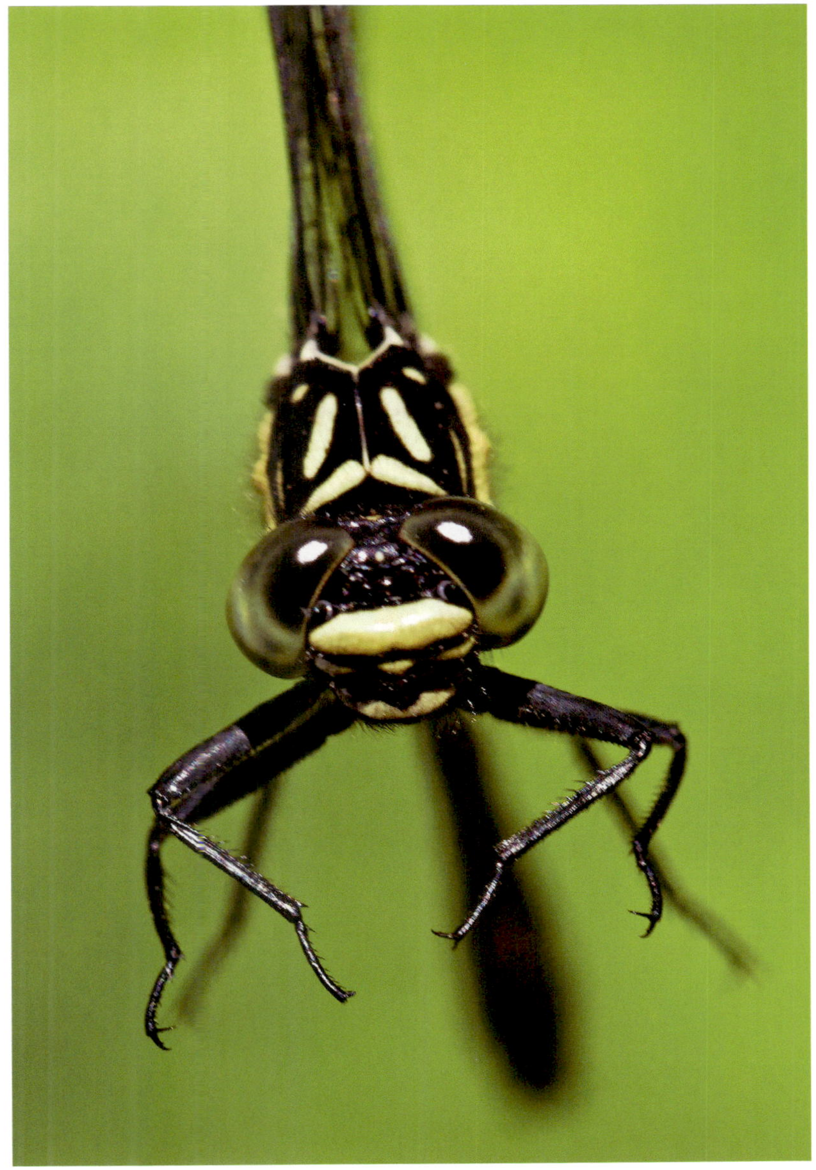

A close-up view highlights the amazing physical structure of a Southern Pygmy Clubtail dragonfly (above). *Photo by Lloyd Spitalnik*

A green walkingstick demonstrates how well this group of insects can hide in natural vegetation like this Honey Mesquite. *Photo by Mike Hannisian*

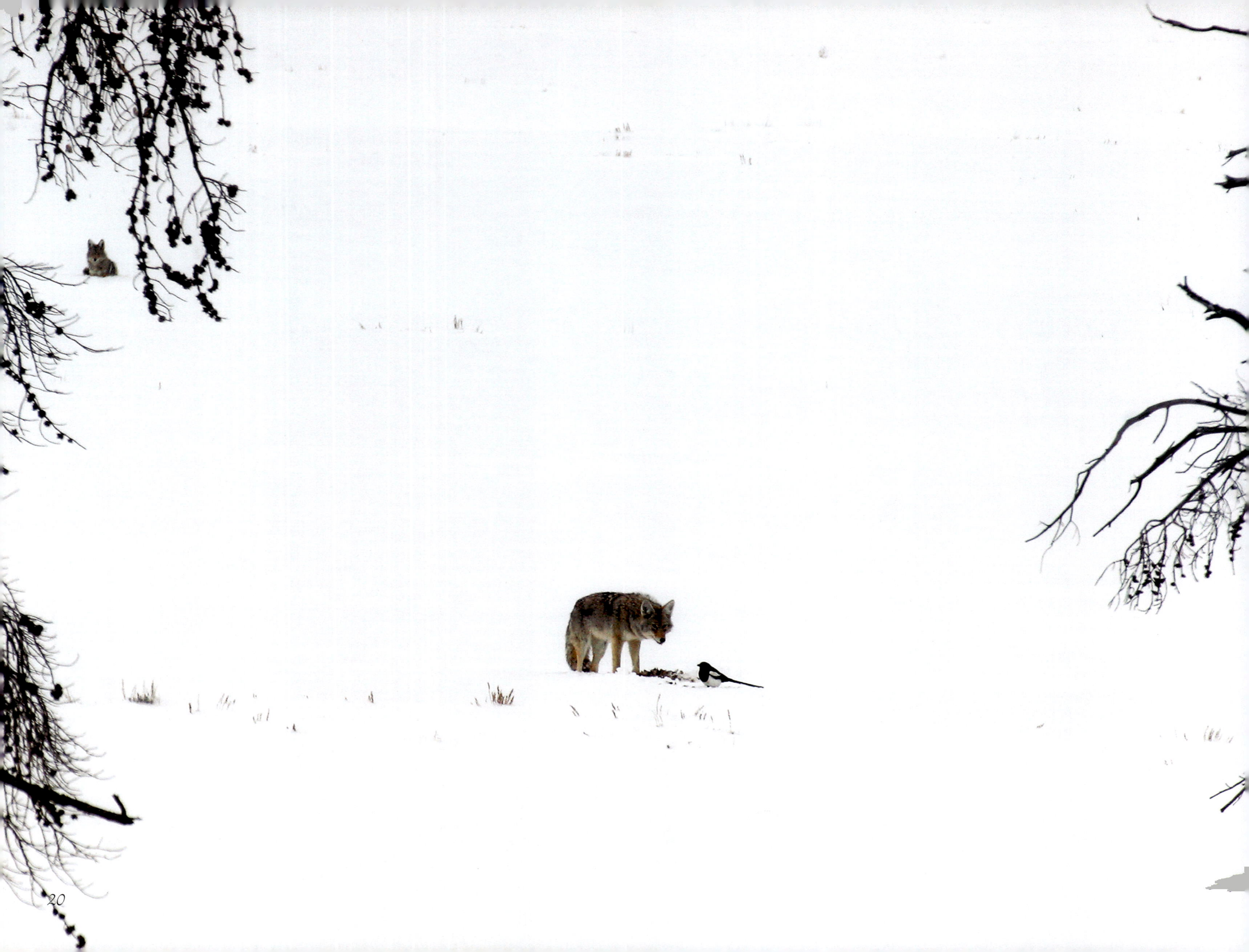

Opposite: While driving through Yellowstone National Park in February, Don Merwin and Tina Giaimo came across this scene. It looks like the Black-billed Magpie is hungry and trying to steal a scrap of food, but is unsure how close he can get without the wolf making a dinner of him. After watching this scene for a while, a second wolf was noticed waiting in the distance. *Photo by Don Merwin*

When we try to pick out anything by itself, we find it hitched to everything else in the universe.

— John Muir

Another resident of Yellowstone National Park is our largest owl, the Great Gray Owl (right). This large, fluffy bird with a massive head is a solitary creature that shows little fear of humans and usually allows a very close approach. *Photo by Scott Elowitz*

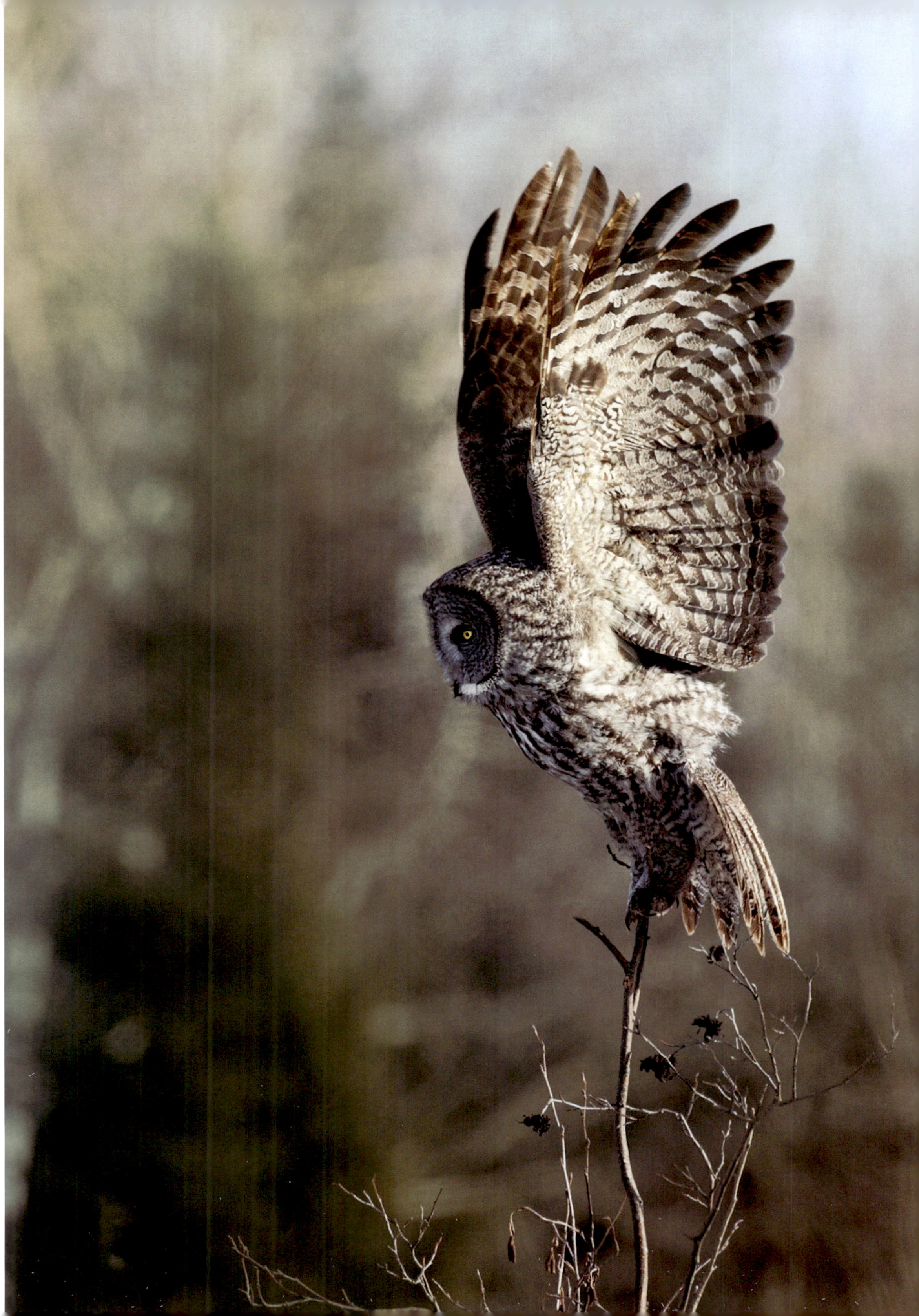

Time is nature's way to keep everything from happening at once.

— John Archibald Wheeler

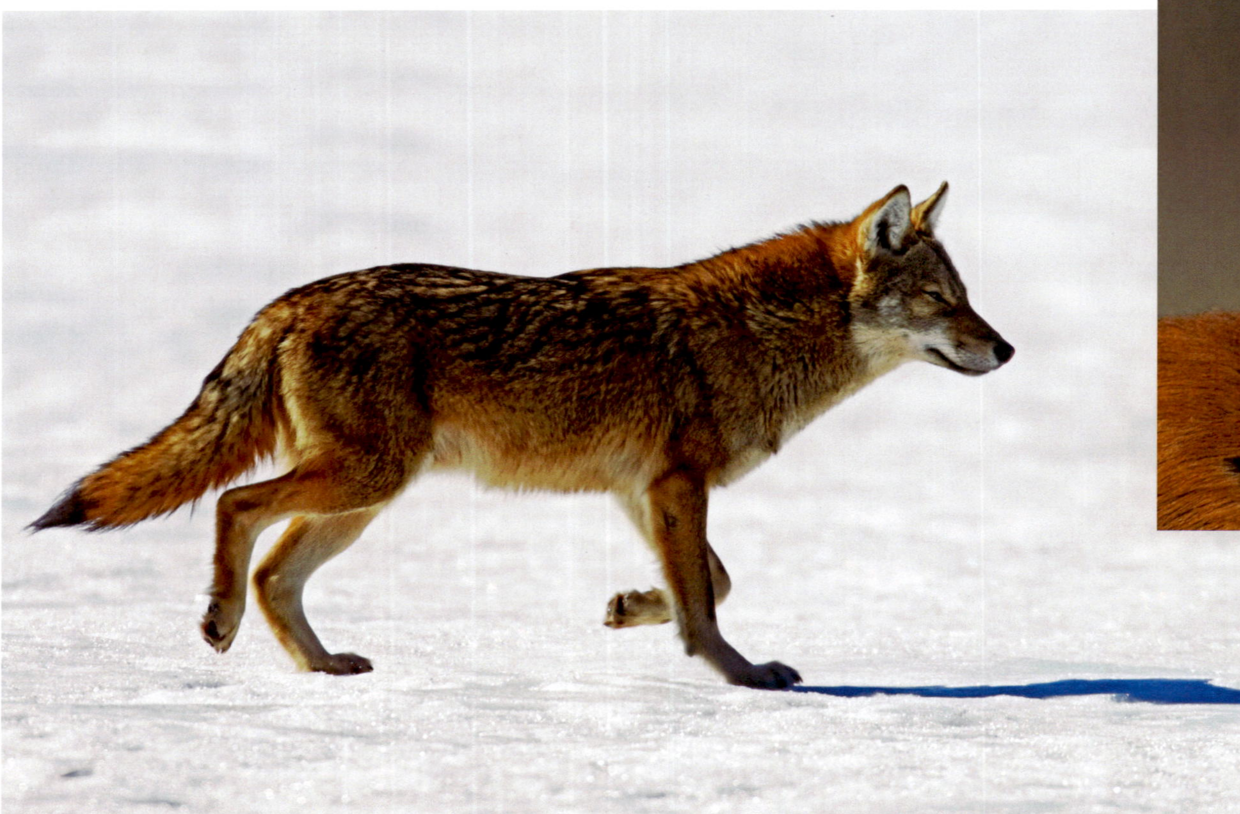

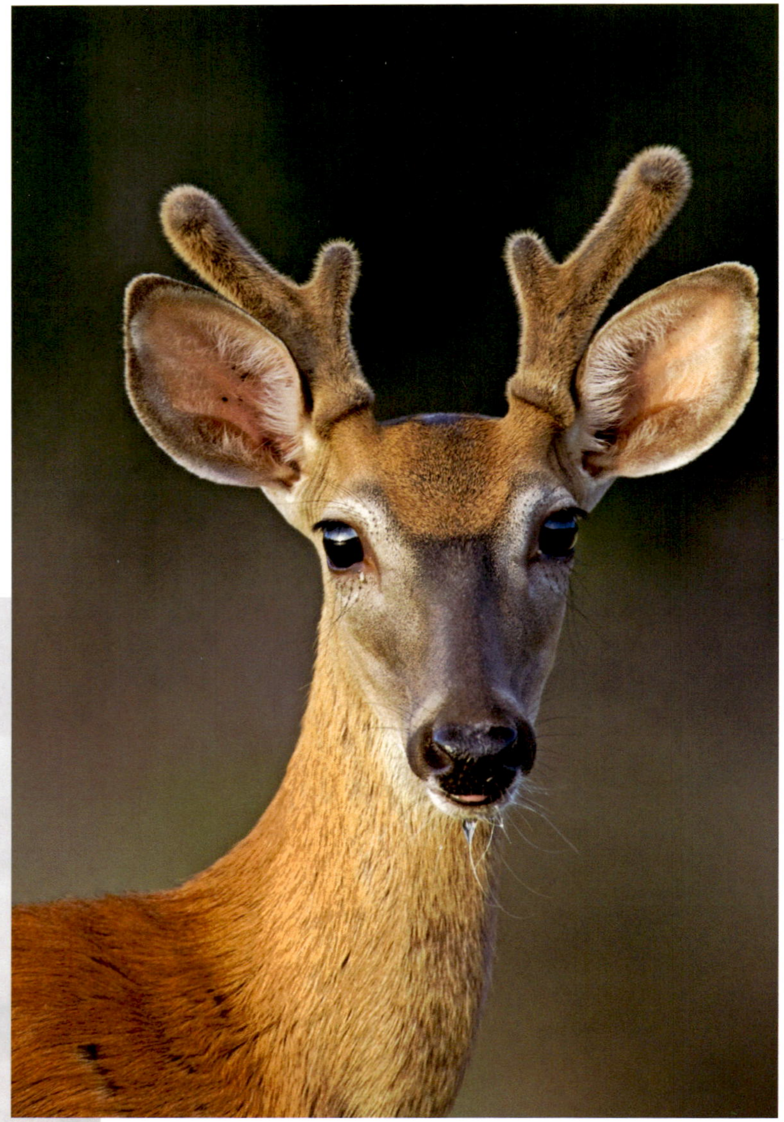

You don't often see these two attractive mammals together in nature, with coyote being an admirer of deer, but only as a meal and not for its soft beauty. *Photos by Nancy Watson (left) and Mike Hannisian (above)*

A juvenile Western Red-tailed Hawk (below) ponders the sign at the Klamath National Wildlife Refuge in Oregon and probably feels that pheasant would be a great choice for dinner.

On the other side of the country, a silvery-gray Florida Red-shouldered Hawk (right) relaxes on a post while scanning for a lizard or snake meal. *Photos by Kevin T. Karlson*

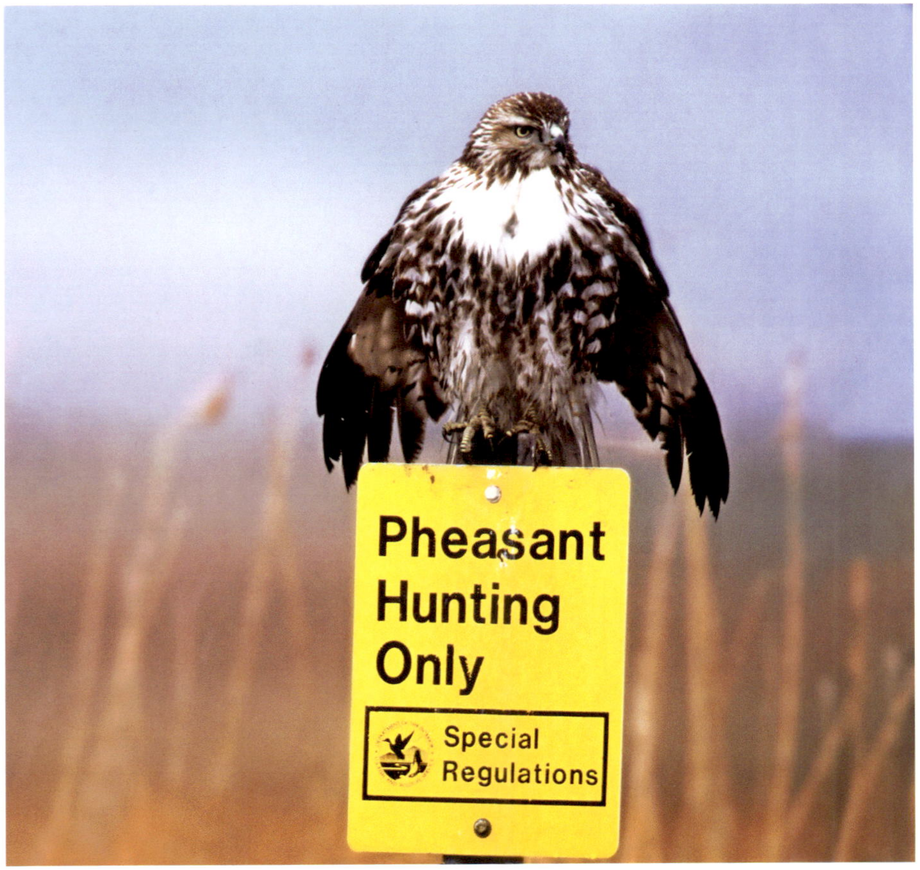

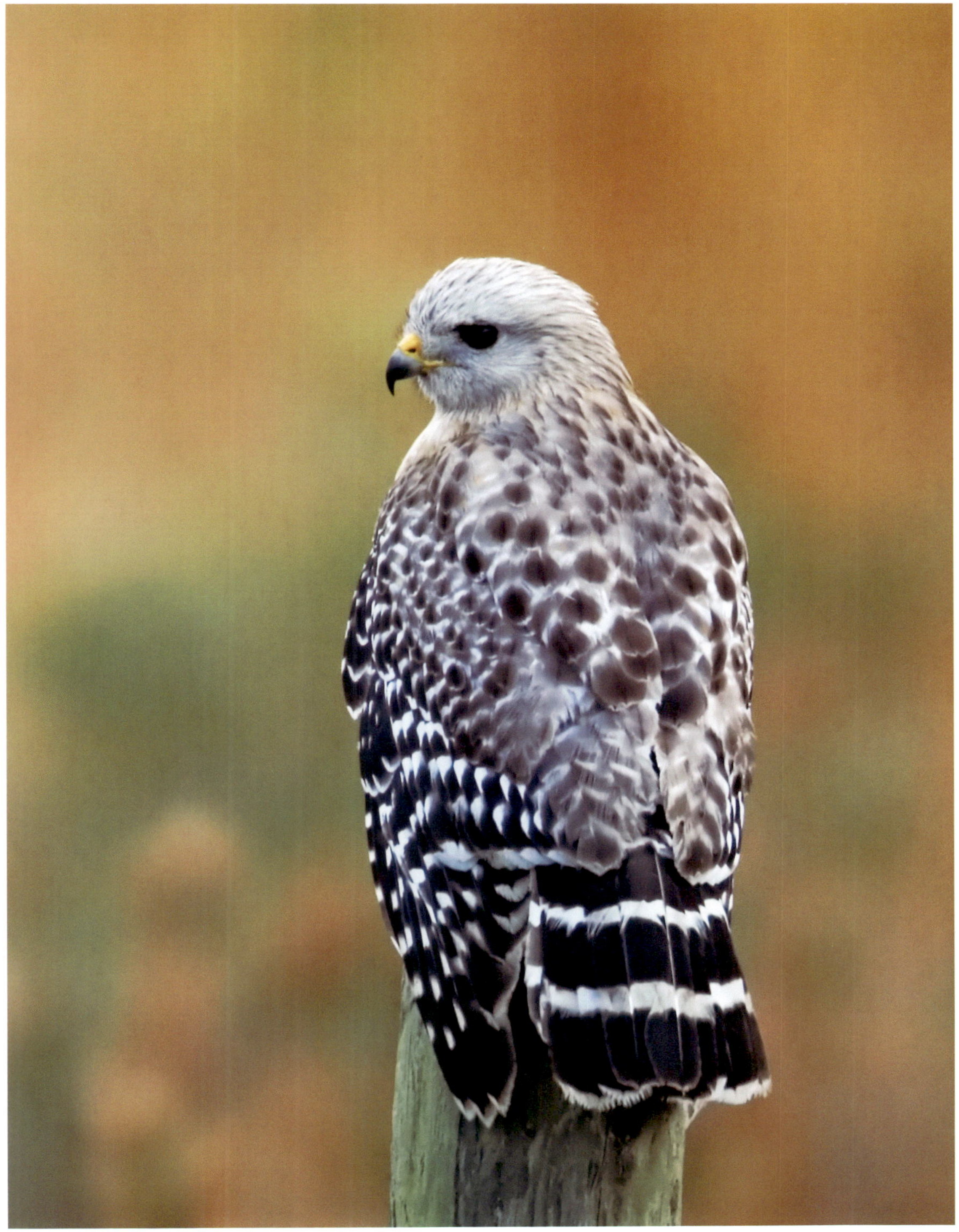

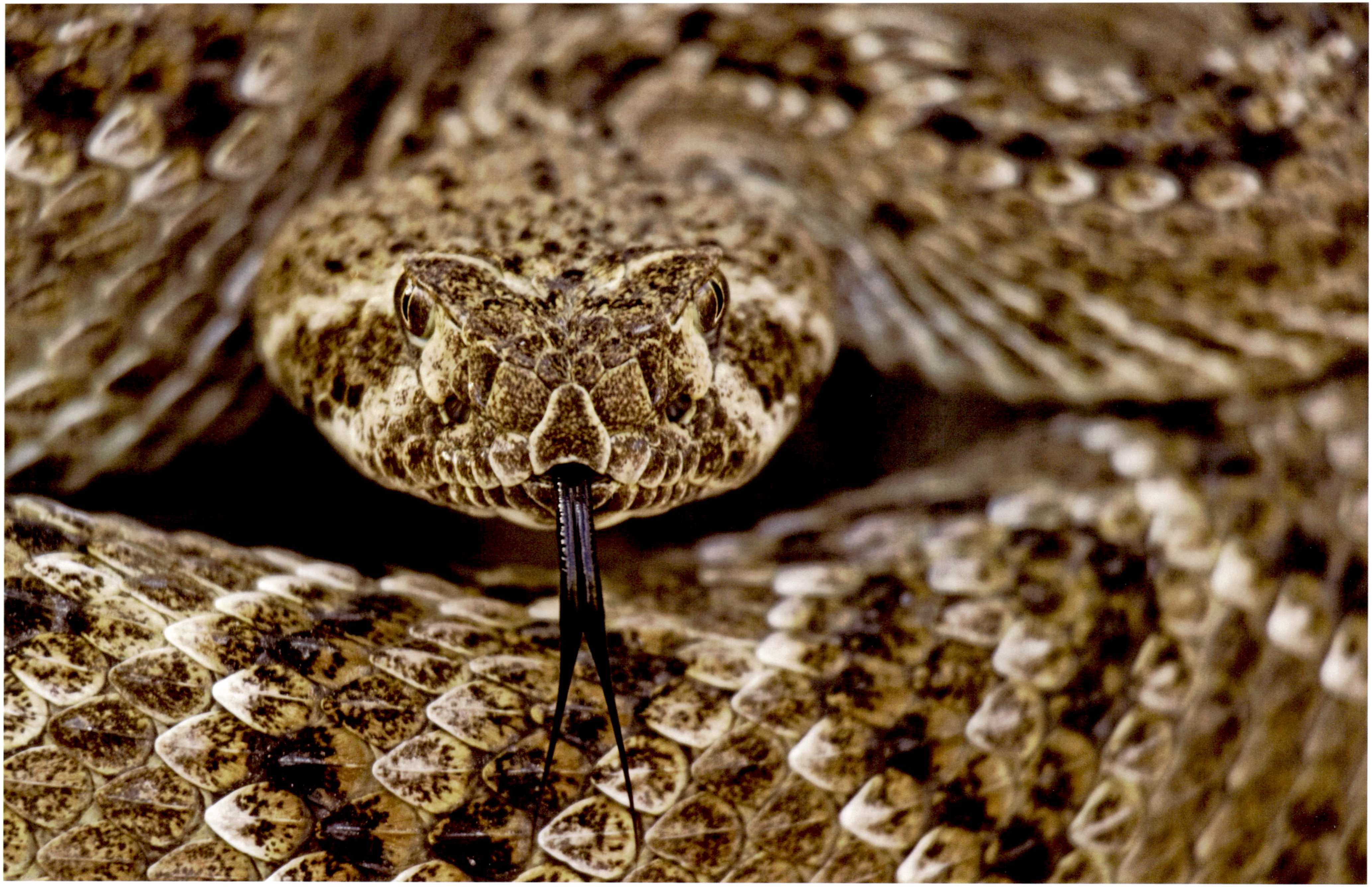

The primitive essence of a Western Diamondback Rattlesnakeis epitomized by armored scales and reptilian eyes. While searching for spiders to photograph, Nancy Watson discovered this large viper in Starr County, Texas. *Photo by Mike Hannisian*

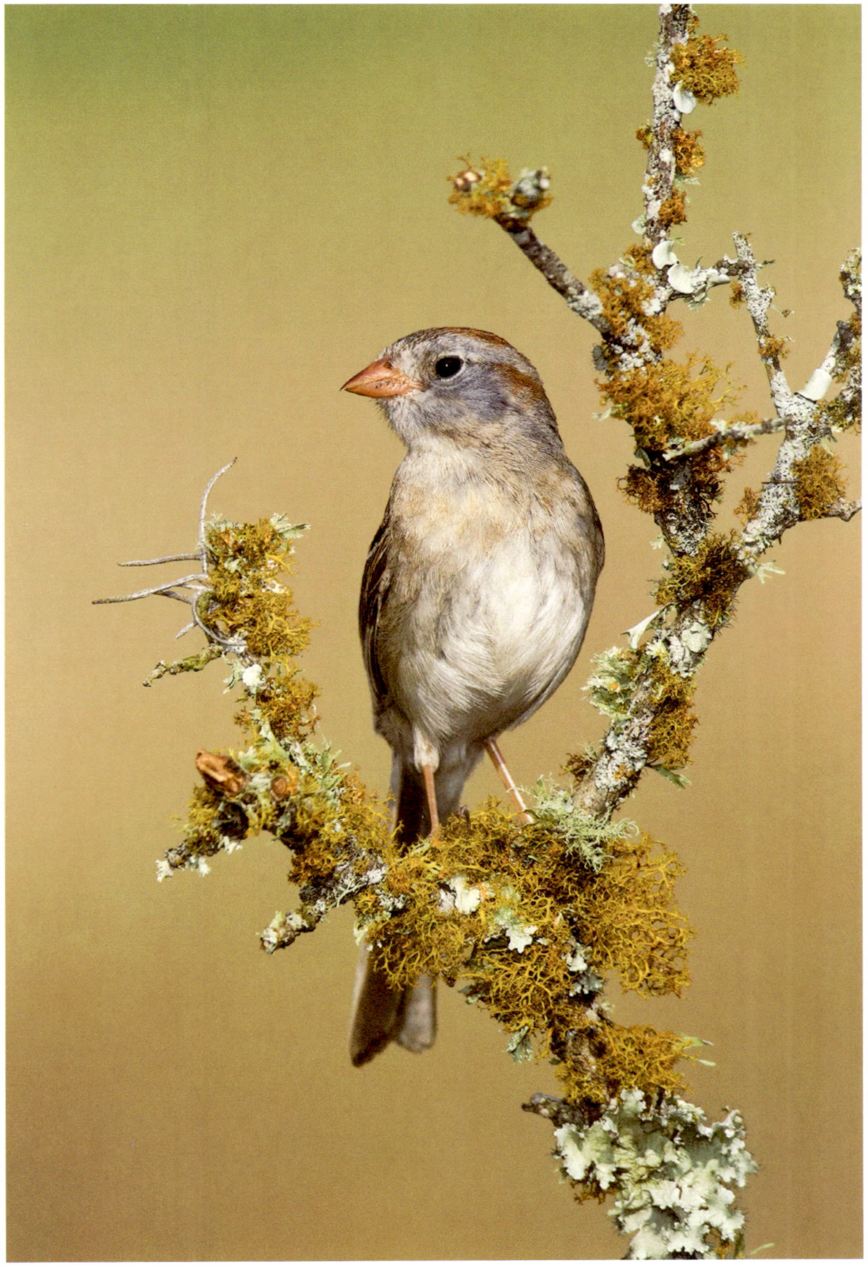

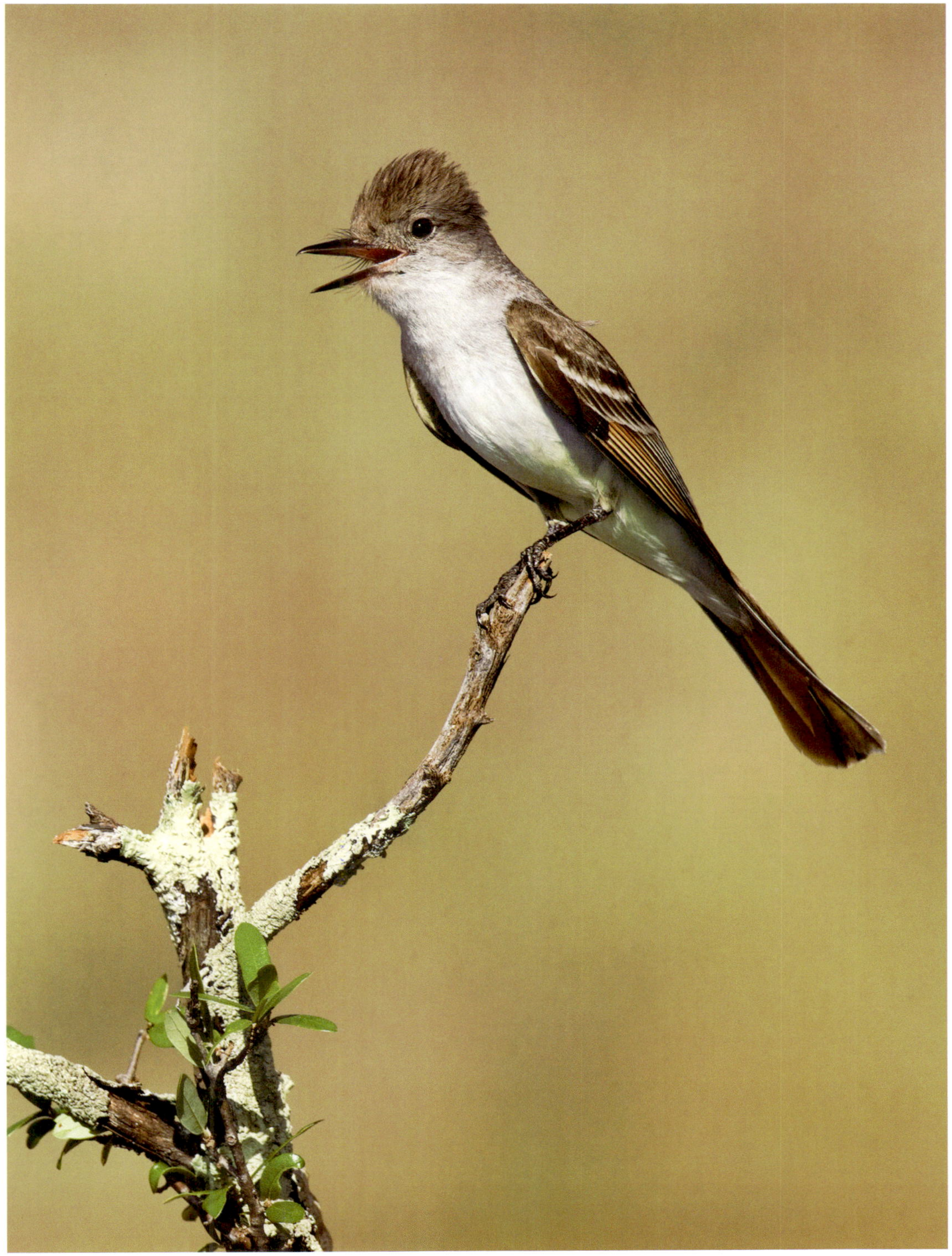

Muted earth tones are shared by two residents of the arid Southwest. A Field Sparrow (above) sits quietly on a lichen covered perch, while a feisty Ash-throated Flycatcher (right) vocalizes on his territory. *Photos by Scott Elowitz*

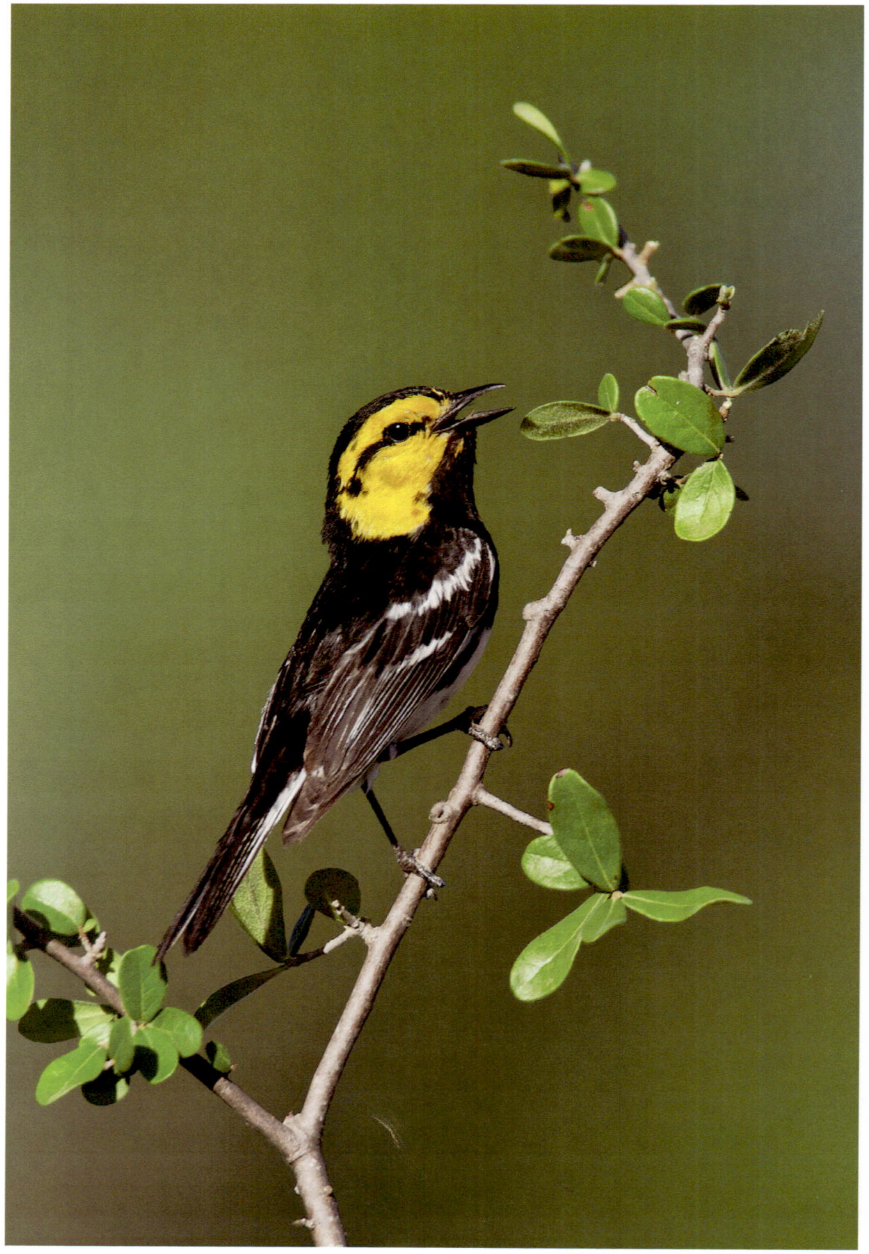

The dry hill country of Texas is home for these two stunning songbirds. The endangered Golden-cheeked Warbler (left) is found only in this location, and this male is singing on territory in spring.

Male Painted Buntings have the most striking mix of colors of all North American songbirds, and even border on the garish with a mix of lime green, yellow, cobalt blue and red. Male Painted Buntings have a hard time blending in with the earth's muted colors. *Photos by Scott Elowitz*

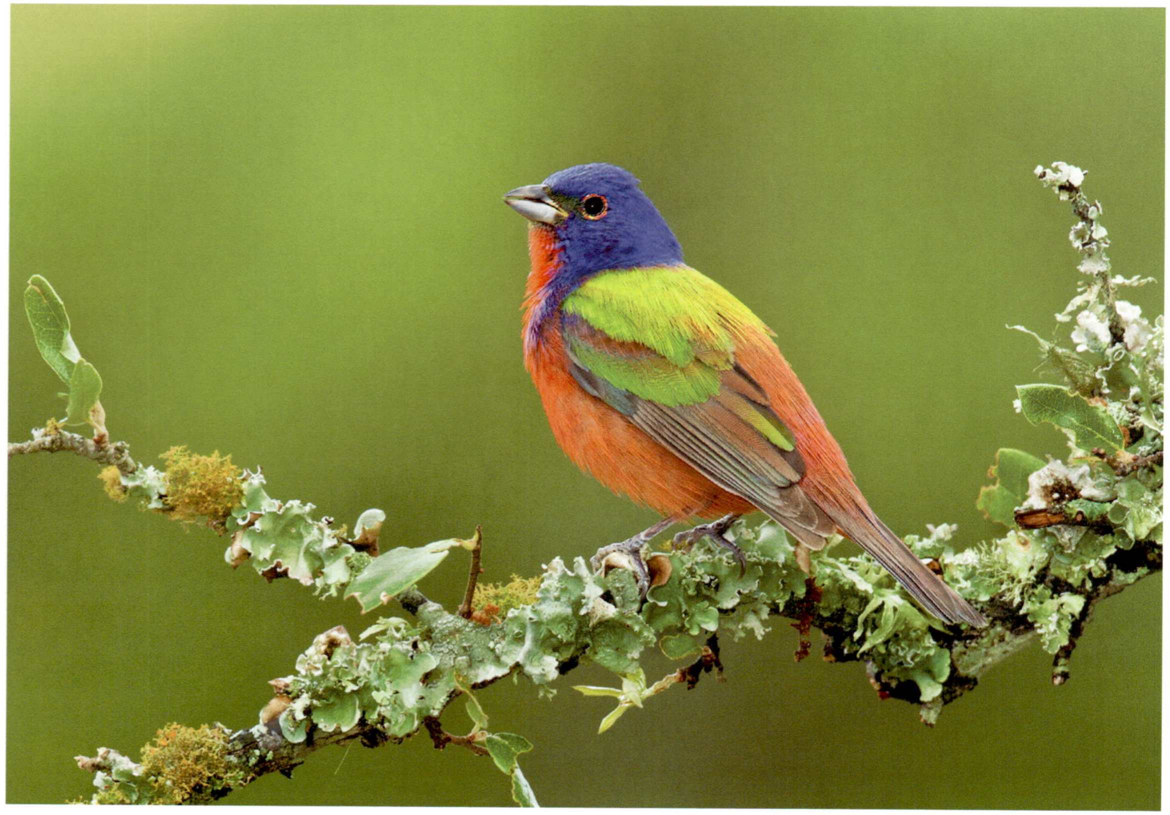

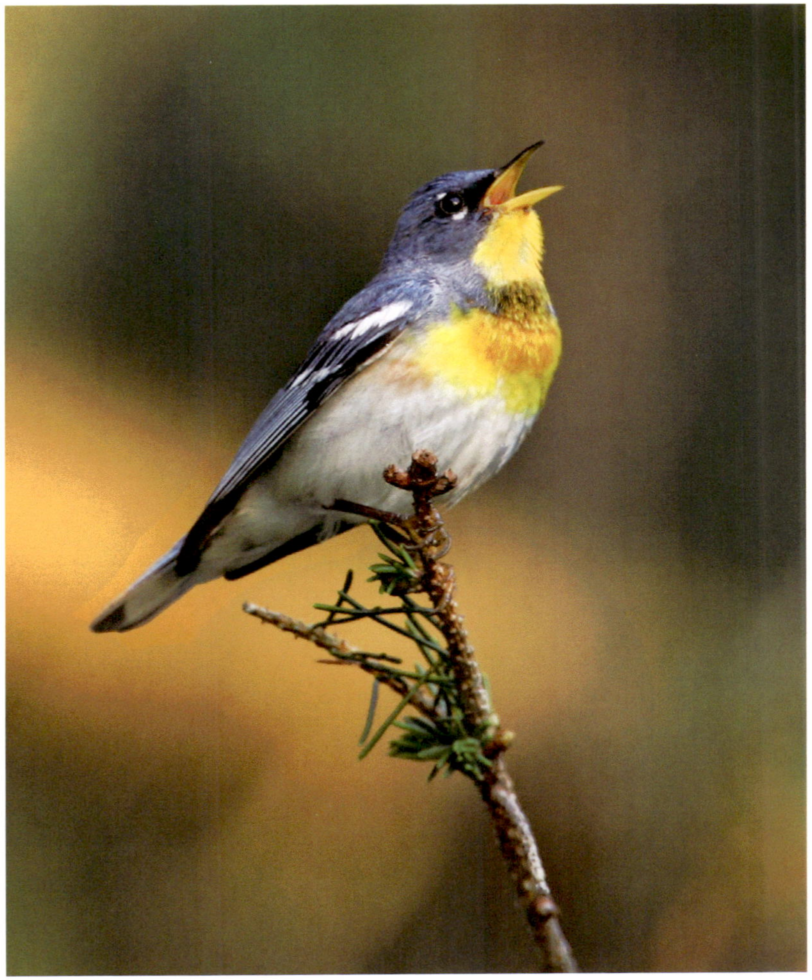

A bird is three things: Feathers, flight and song, And feathers are the least of these.

— Marjorie Allen Seiffert

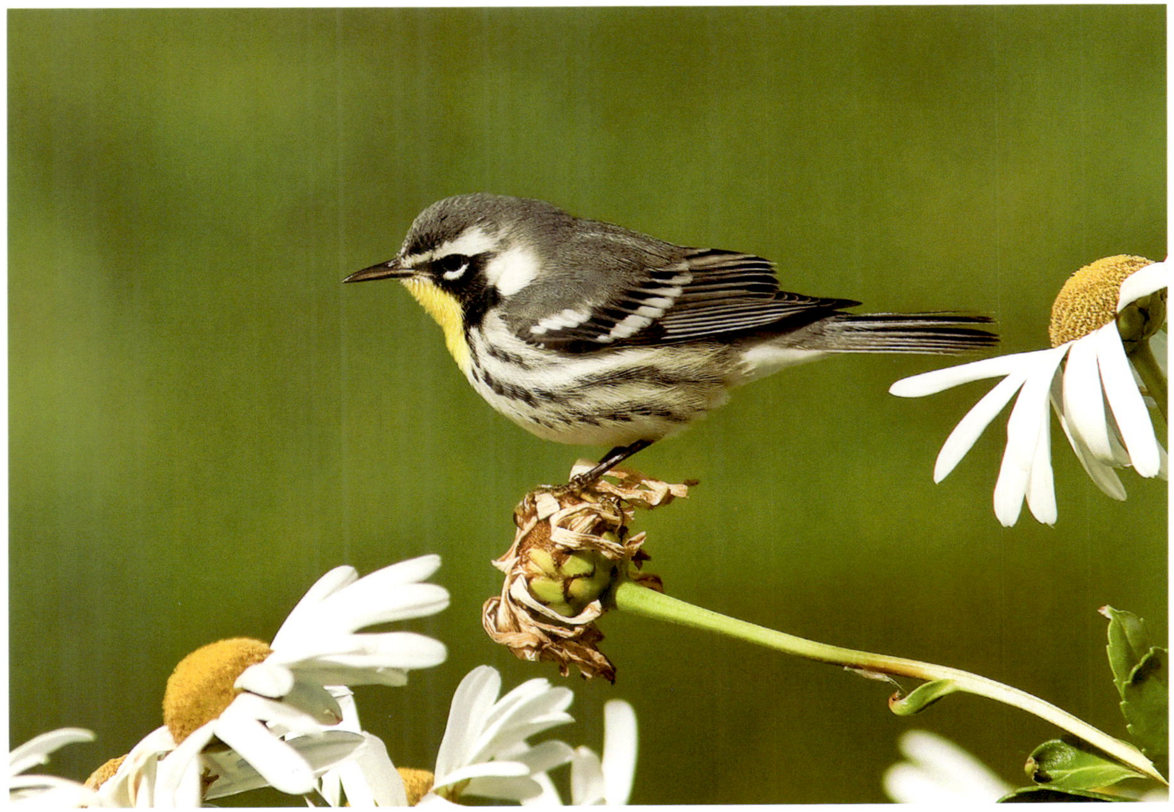

Two eastern warblers that possess beautiful colors and attractive plumage tones are Northern Parula (above) and Yellow-throated Warbler (right). *Photos by Scott Elowitz (above) and Lloyd Spitalnik (right)*

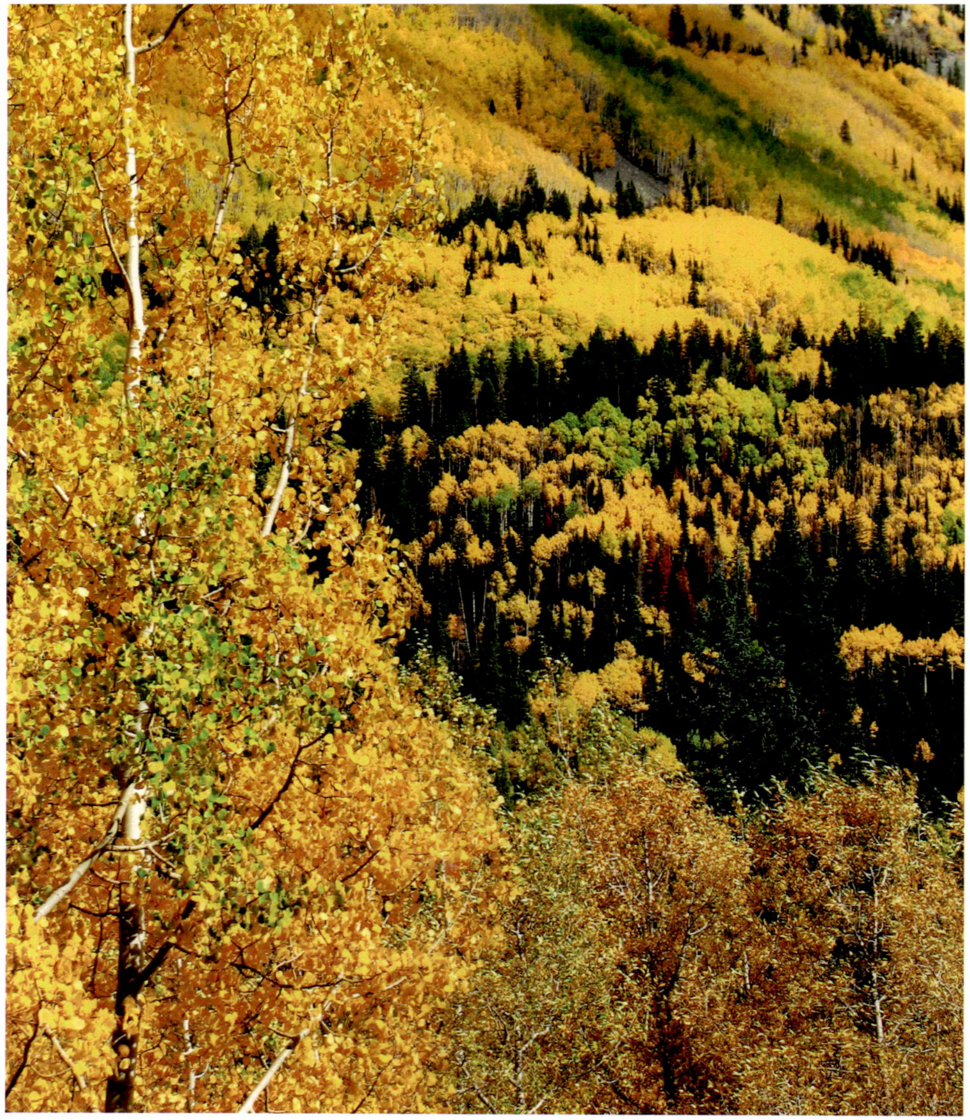

Climb the mountains and get their good tidings. Nature's peace will flow into you as sunshine flows into trees. The winds will blow their own freshness into you, and the storms their energy, while cares will drop off like autumn leaves.

— John Muir

As far as the eye can see, these Colorado mountains are ablaze in fall with yellow aspen leaves (above). Meanwhile a Yellow-rumped Warbler (right) shows a bright yellow rump as it prepares for a drink. *Photos by Dale Rosselet (above) and Scott Elowitz (right)*

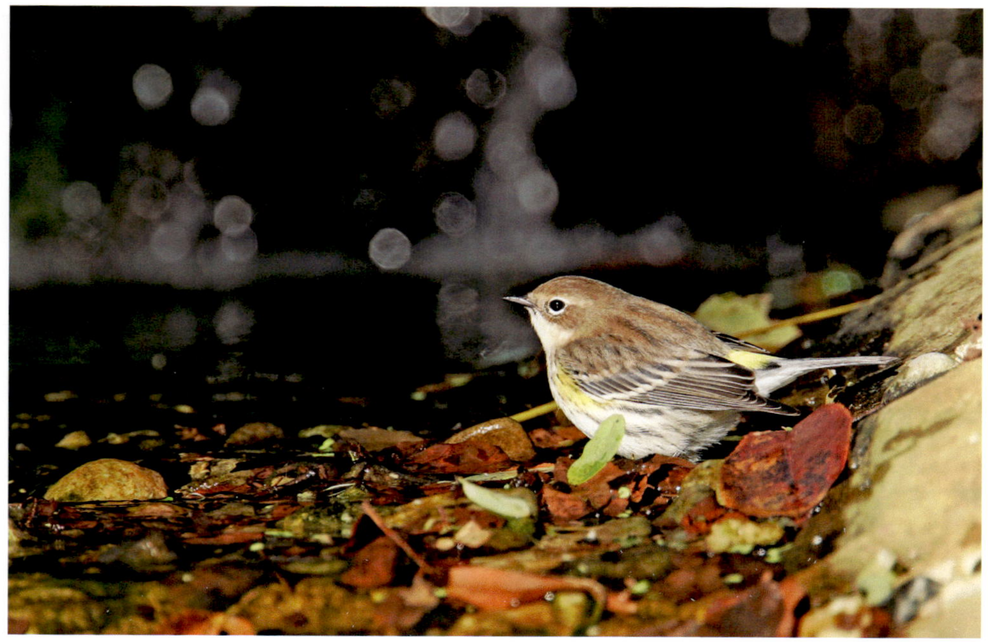

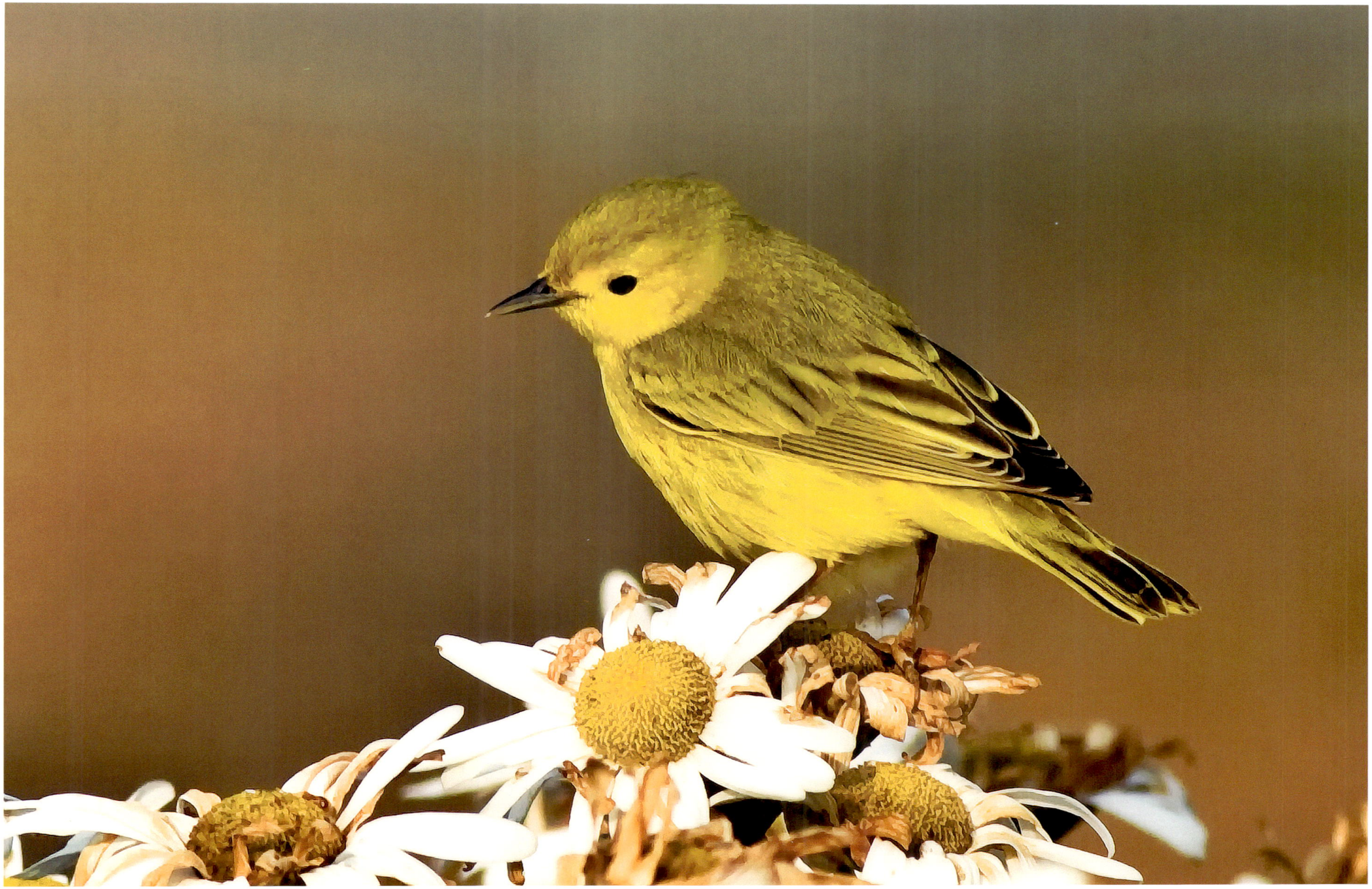

A female Yellow Warbler blends wonderfully with the bright yellow centers of nearby daisies. *Photo by Lloyd Spitalnik*

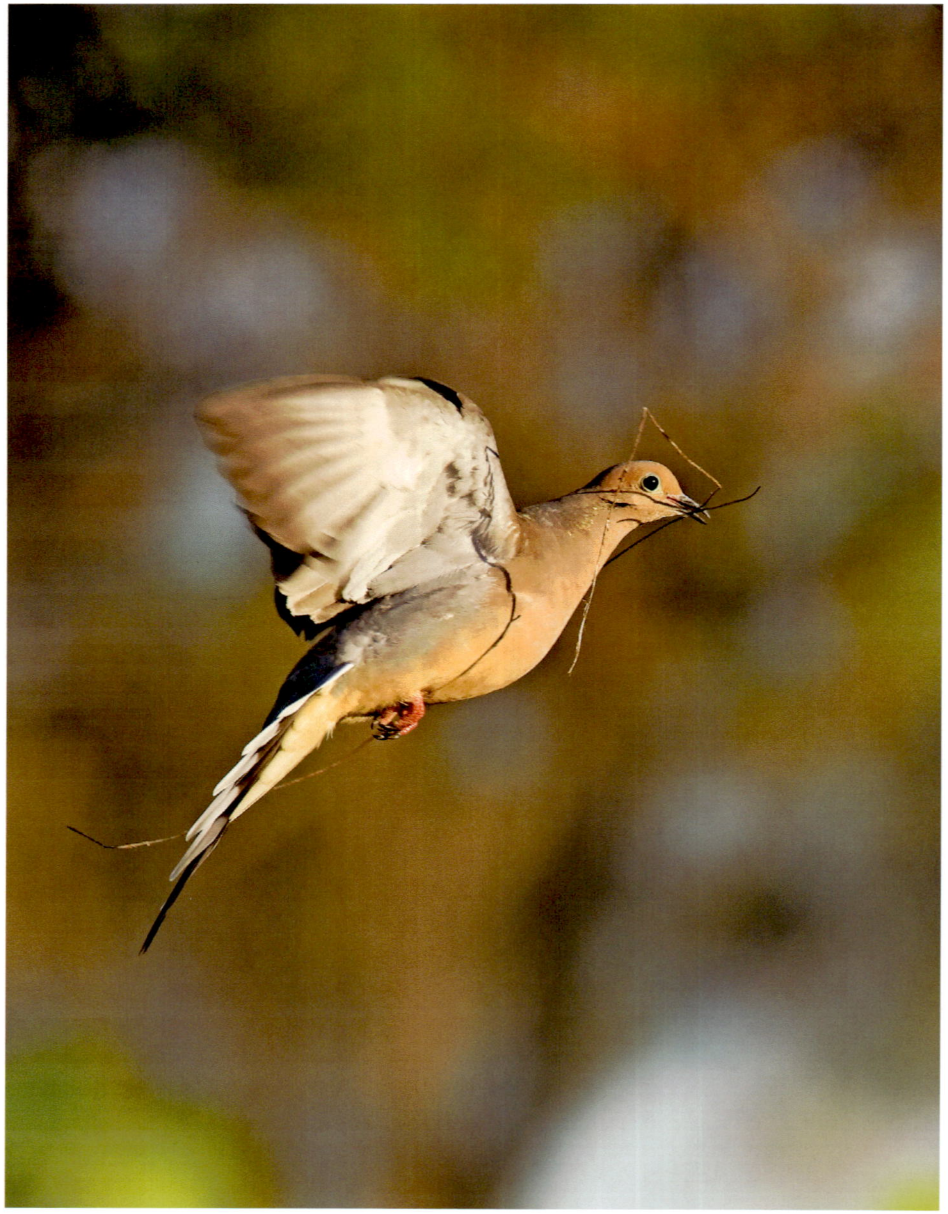

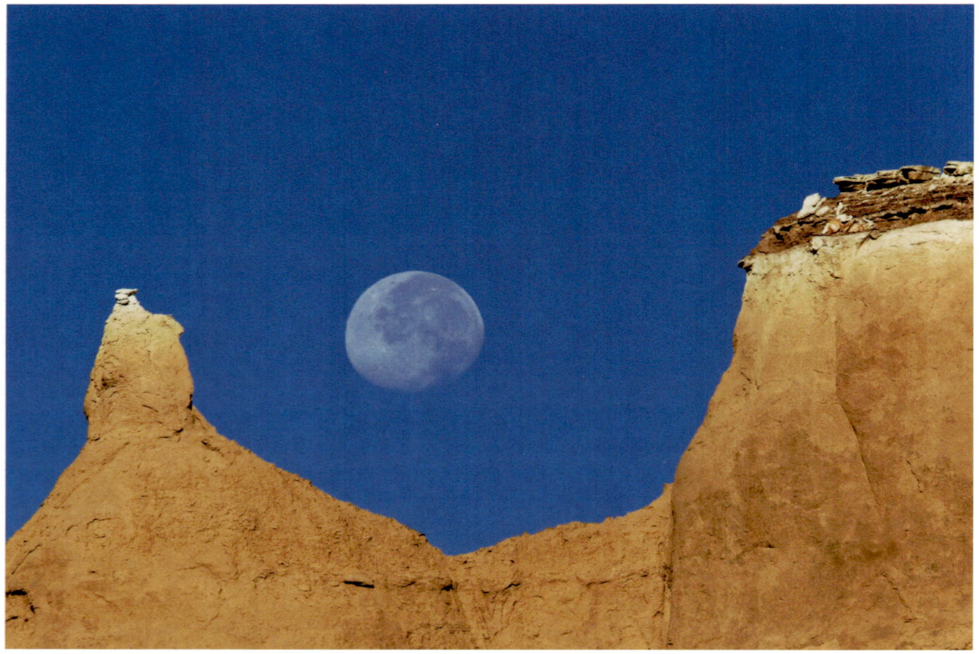

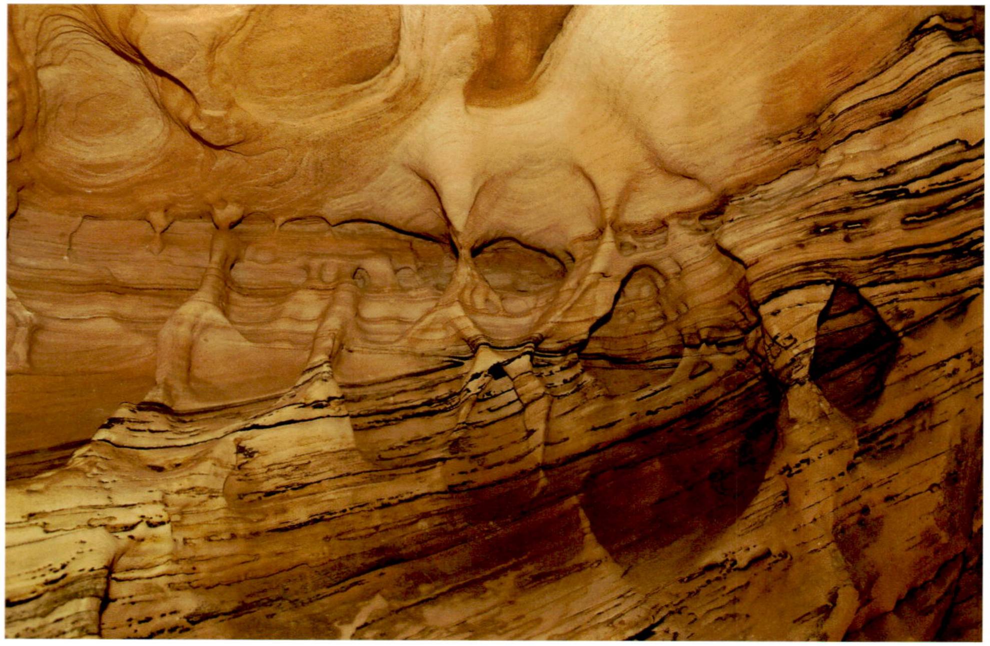

Earth-toned reddish brown rocks dominate the landscape in southwest Utah. A Mourning Dove carries nest material in this graceful flight image (above), while the moon sets next to a sandstone hoodoo (above right). Weathering from water and wind carved an unusual macro landscape in Kodachrome Canyon, Utah (lower right).

Photos by Scott Elowitz (above) and Kevin T. Karlson (upper and lower right)

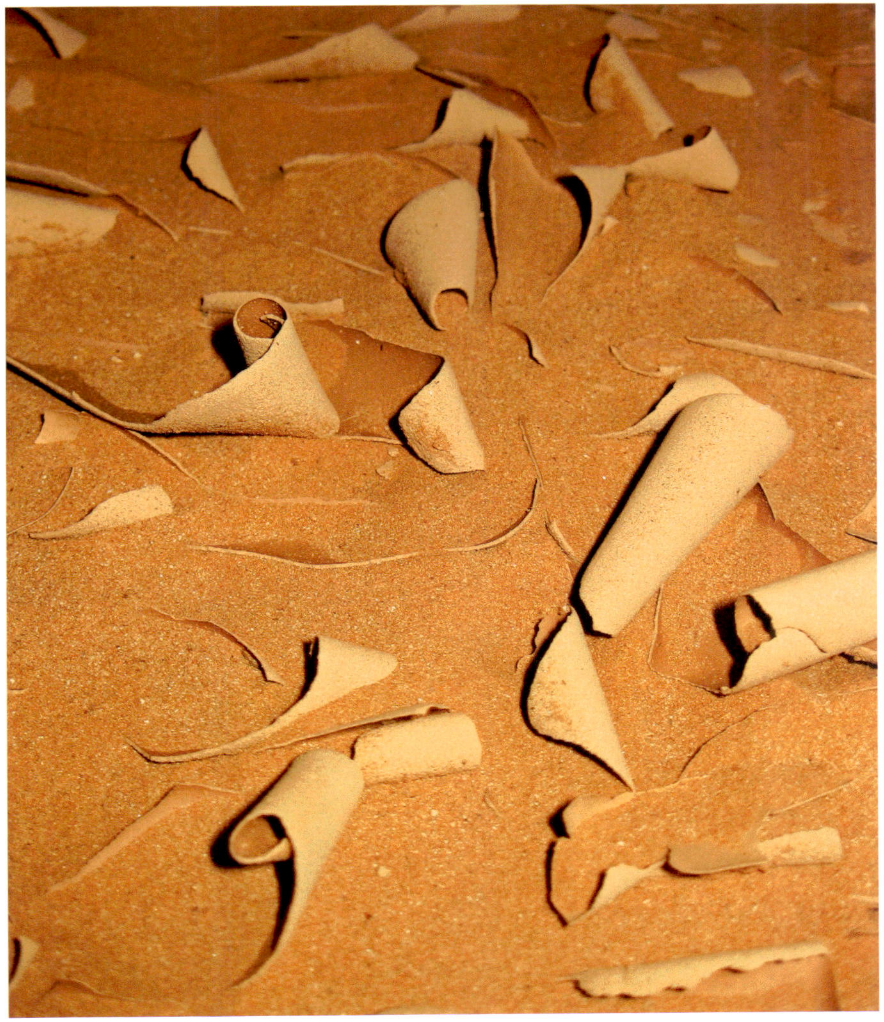

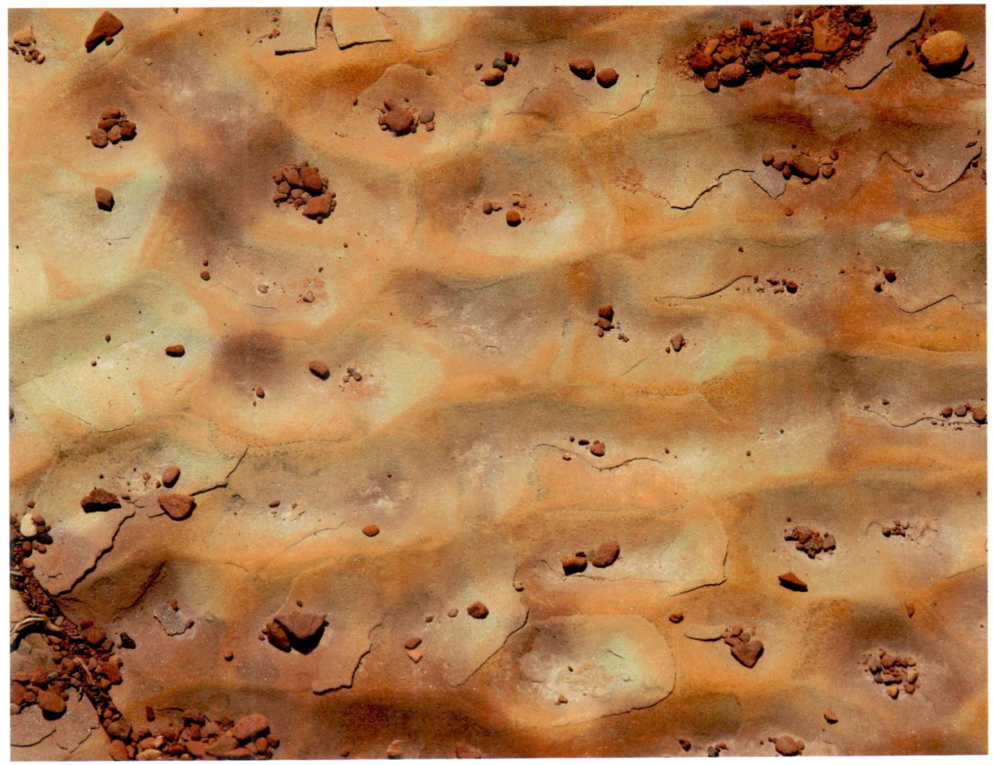

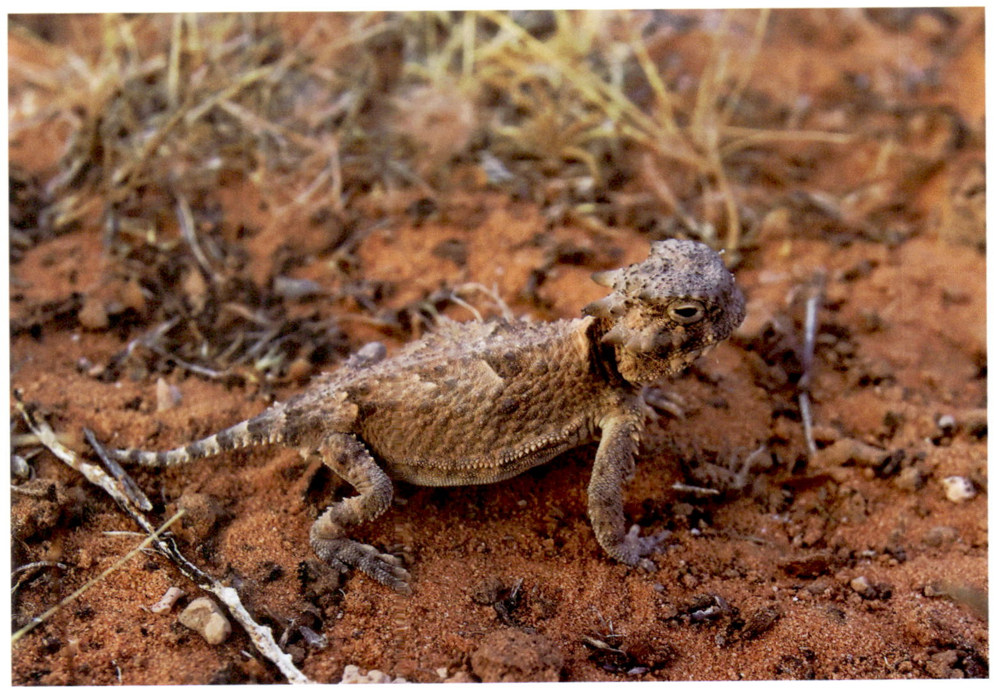

Dried mud creates paper-thin scrolls on the canyon floor (above), while water and pebbles carve small pockets in a red rock river bed near Capitol Reef National Park in Southern Utah (upper right). A Horned Lizard blends perfectly with its red sand habitat, and takes a quick break from hunting in the arid desert of northwest Nevada.

Photos by Dale Rosselet (above), Tina Giaimo (upper right) and Kevin T. Karlson (lower right)

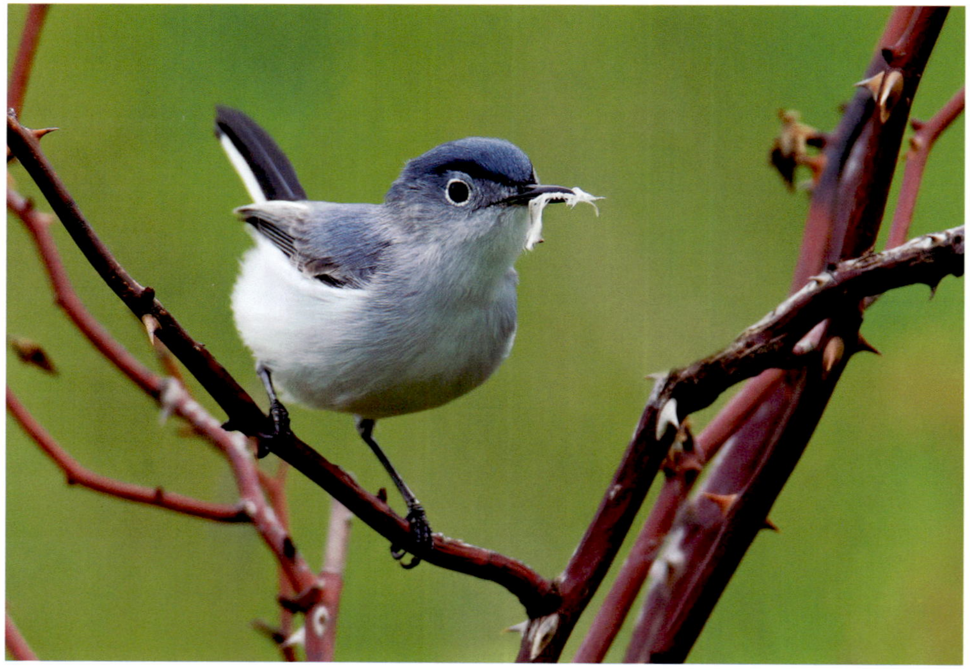

Opposite: An unusual perspective of a lush field of ferns was taken in spring from a chair lift near Williamstown, Massachusetts. *Photo by Tina Giaimo*

Go and walk with Nature; thou wilt find full many a gem in her enchanted cup.

— Isaac McLellan

Blue and green are important colors to the earth theme. A male Blue-gray Gnatcatcher (above) has an unidentified soft, white object in its bill that will probably be used to line his nest. The Cerulean Warbler (right) is one of a small number of warblers that exhibit rich blue tones in its plumage. This small forest warbler is highly sought after by birdwatchers.

Photos by Lloyd Spitalnik

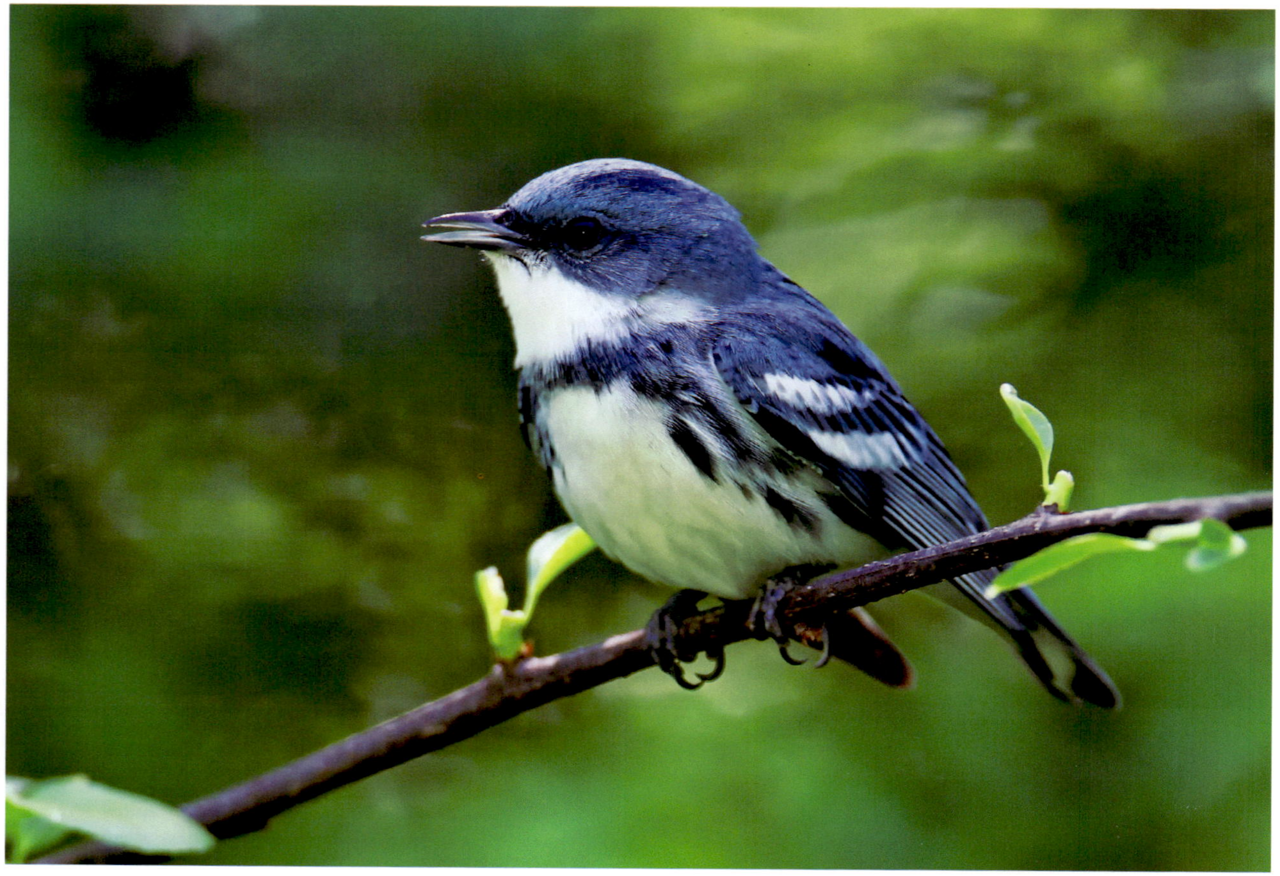

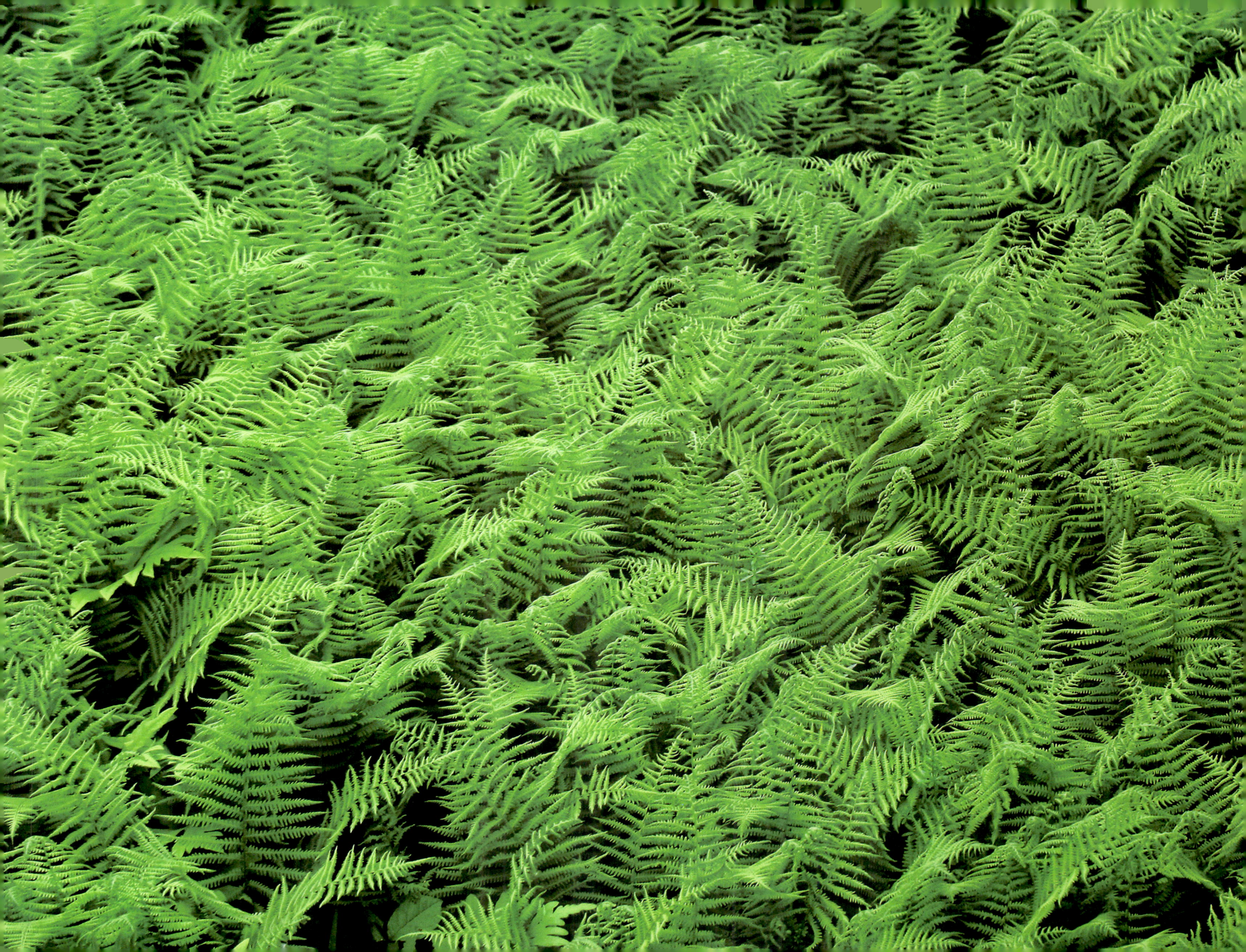

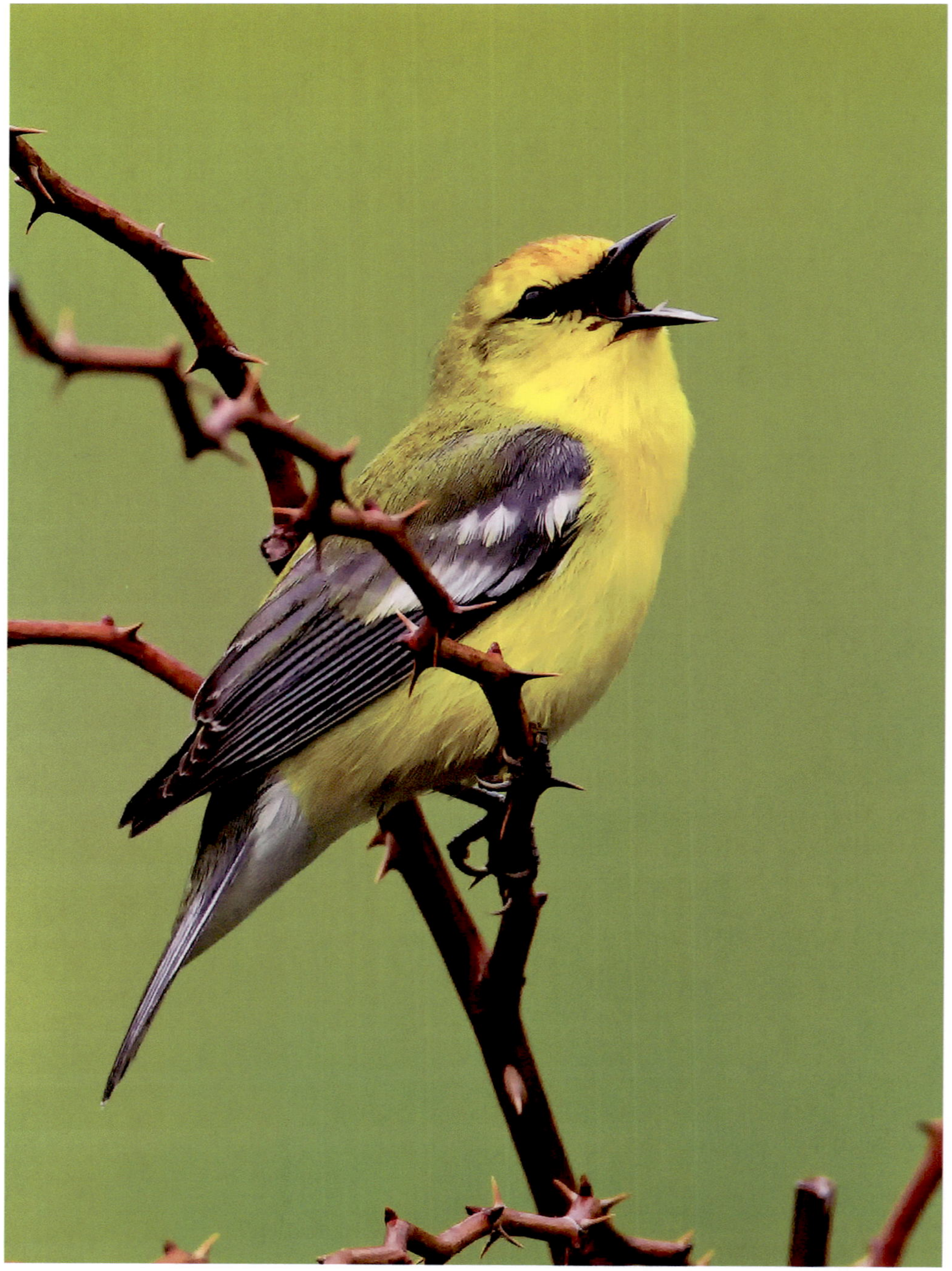

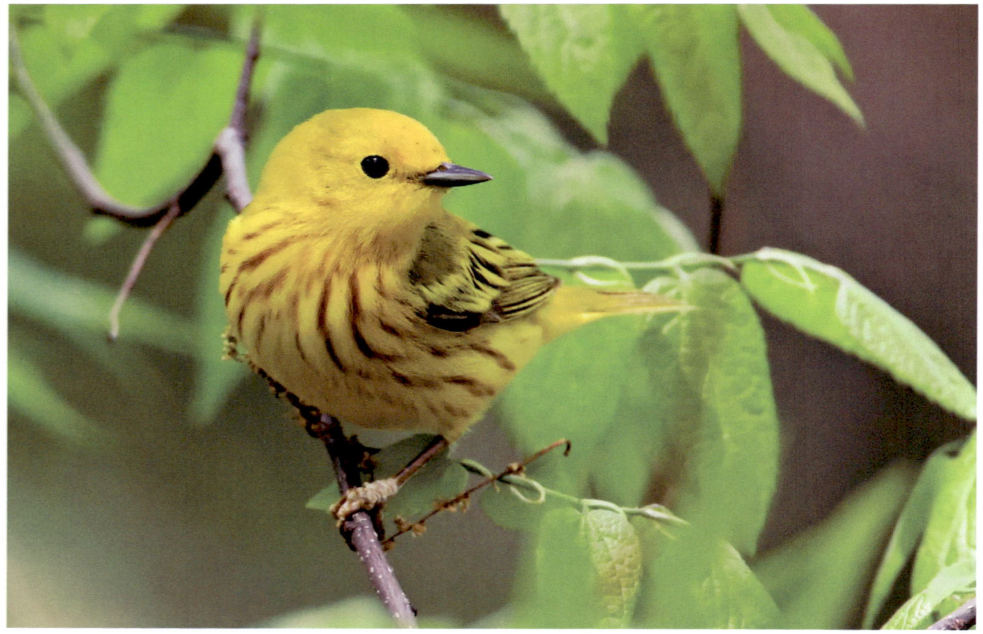

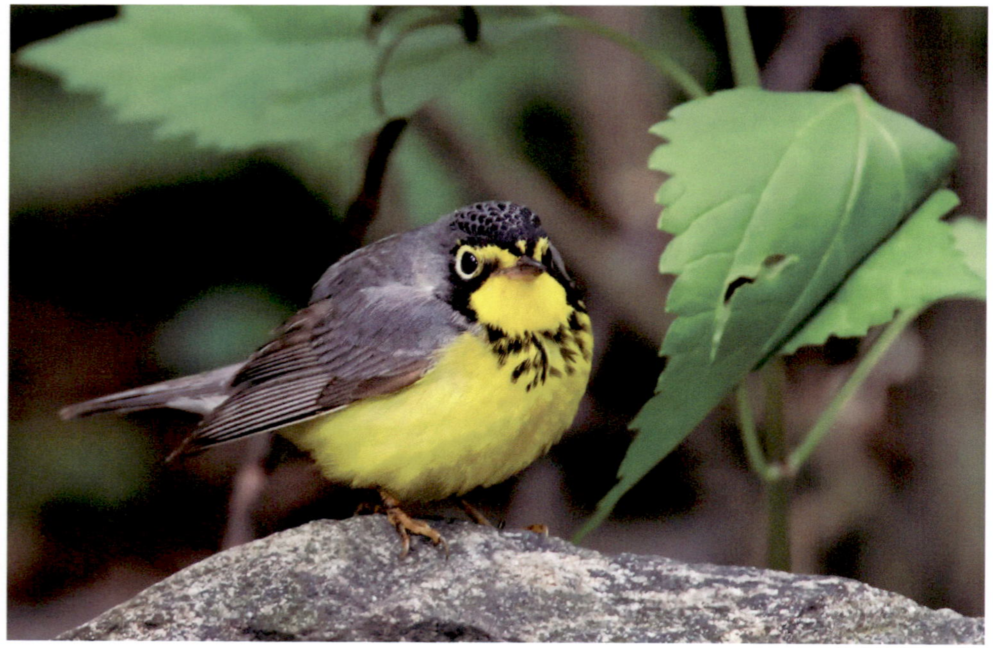

Yellow is well represented in the world of warblers.

Opposite: A Blue-winged Warbler belts out his buzzy song (far left), while a male Yellow Warbler (top right) and Canada Warbler (lower right) often take the breath away from excited birders. *Photos by Lloyd Spitalnik*

Male Prothonotary Warbler (below) sings on territory in Ohio, and a Nashville Warbler's red crest compliments pink apple blossoms in Michigan (right). *Photos by Kevin T. Karlson*

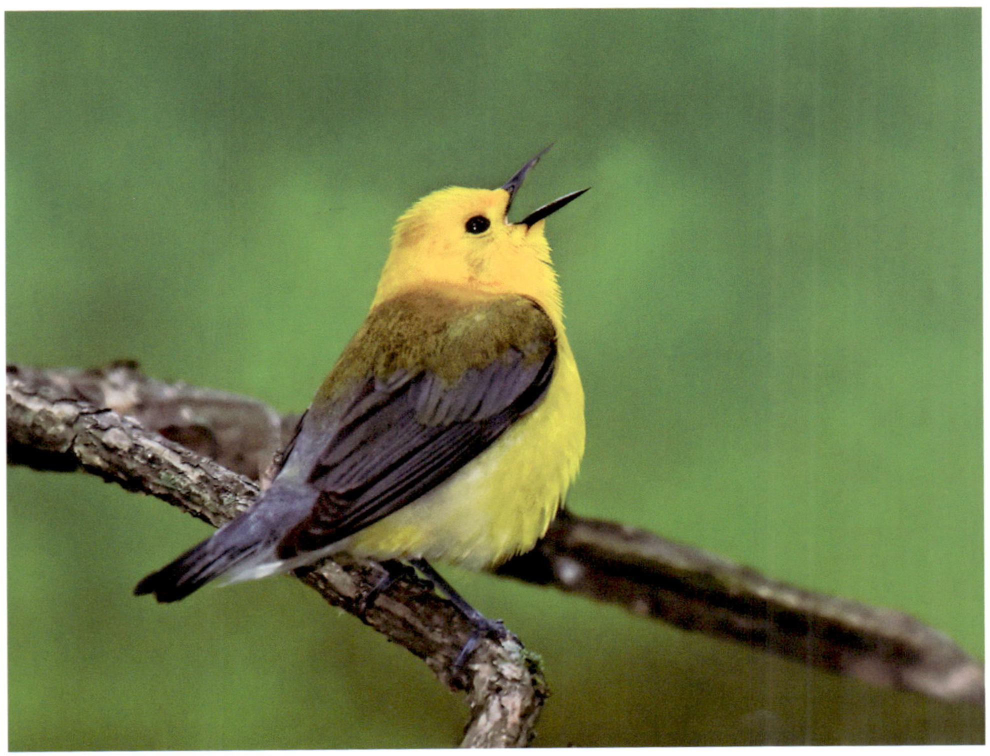

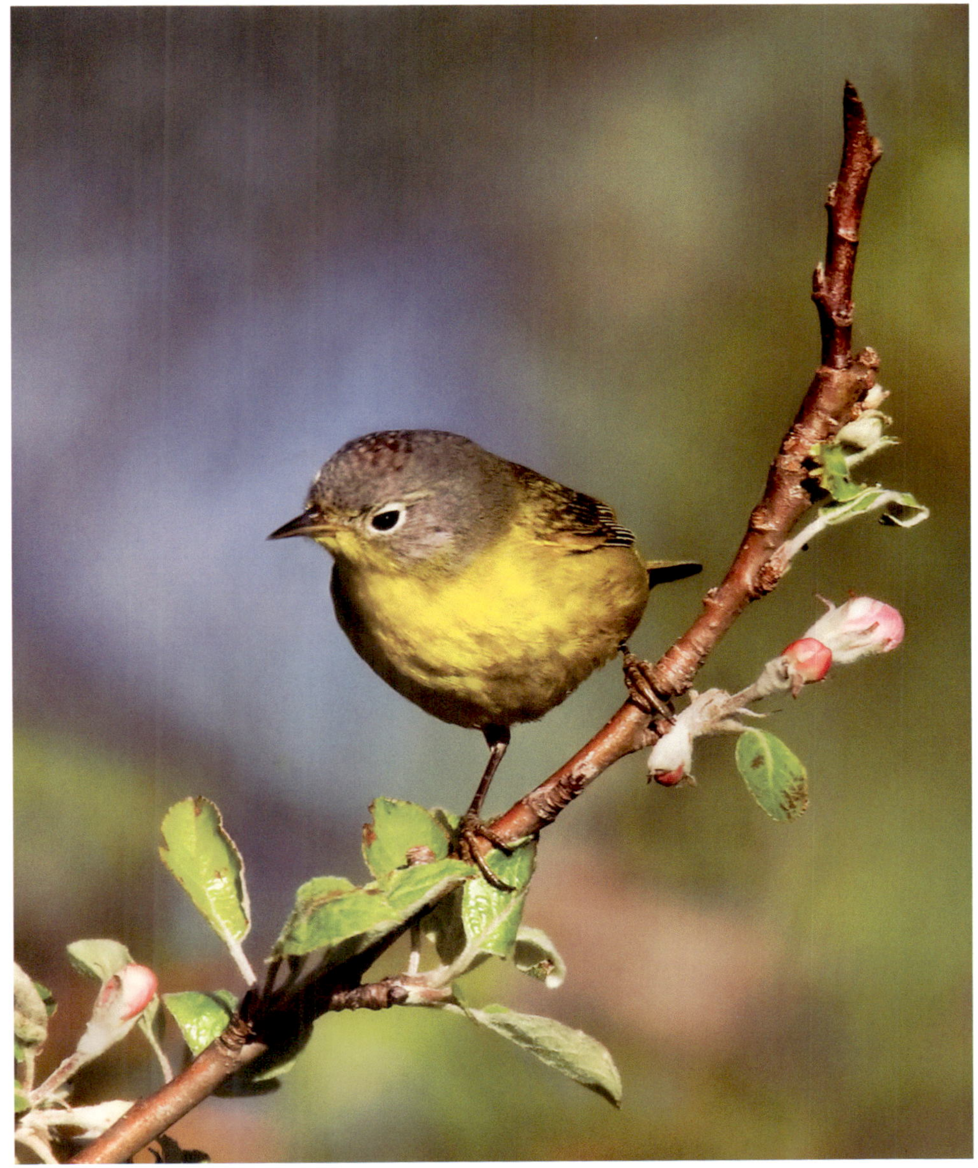

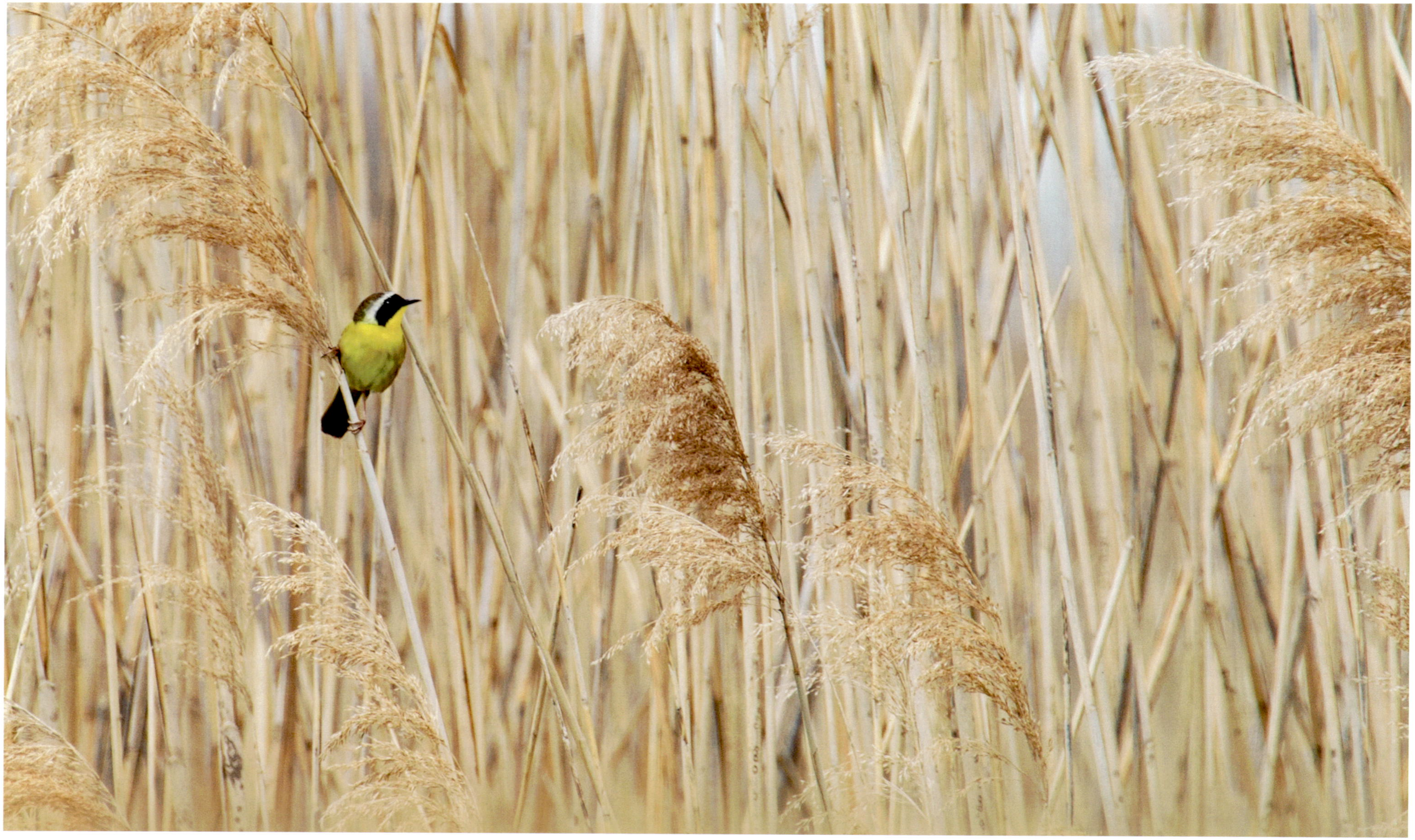

A male Common Yellowthroat sits in stark contrast to the Japanese-like patterns of *Phragmites* stalks.
Photo by Scott Elowitz

A backyard favorite, Black-capped Chickadee, perches on a hanging basket (below). A beautiful earth tone scene accompanies a rare South American vagrant, the Fork-tailed Flycatcher (right), in an early winter photo from Connecticut.
Photos by Lloyd Spitalnik

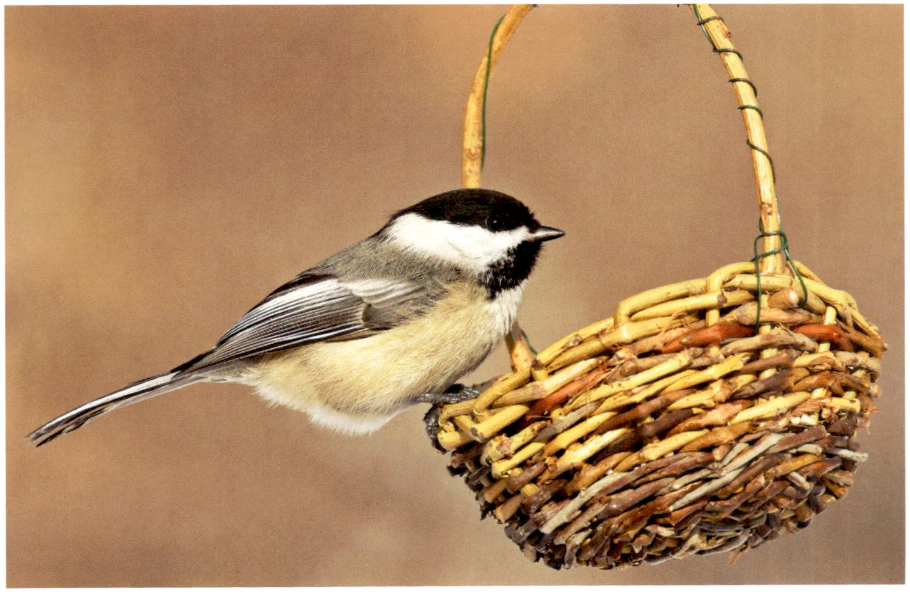

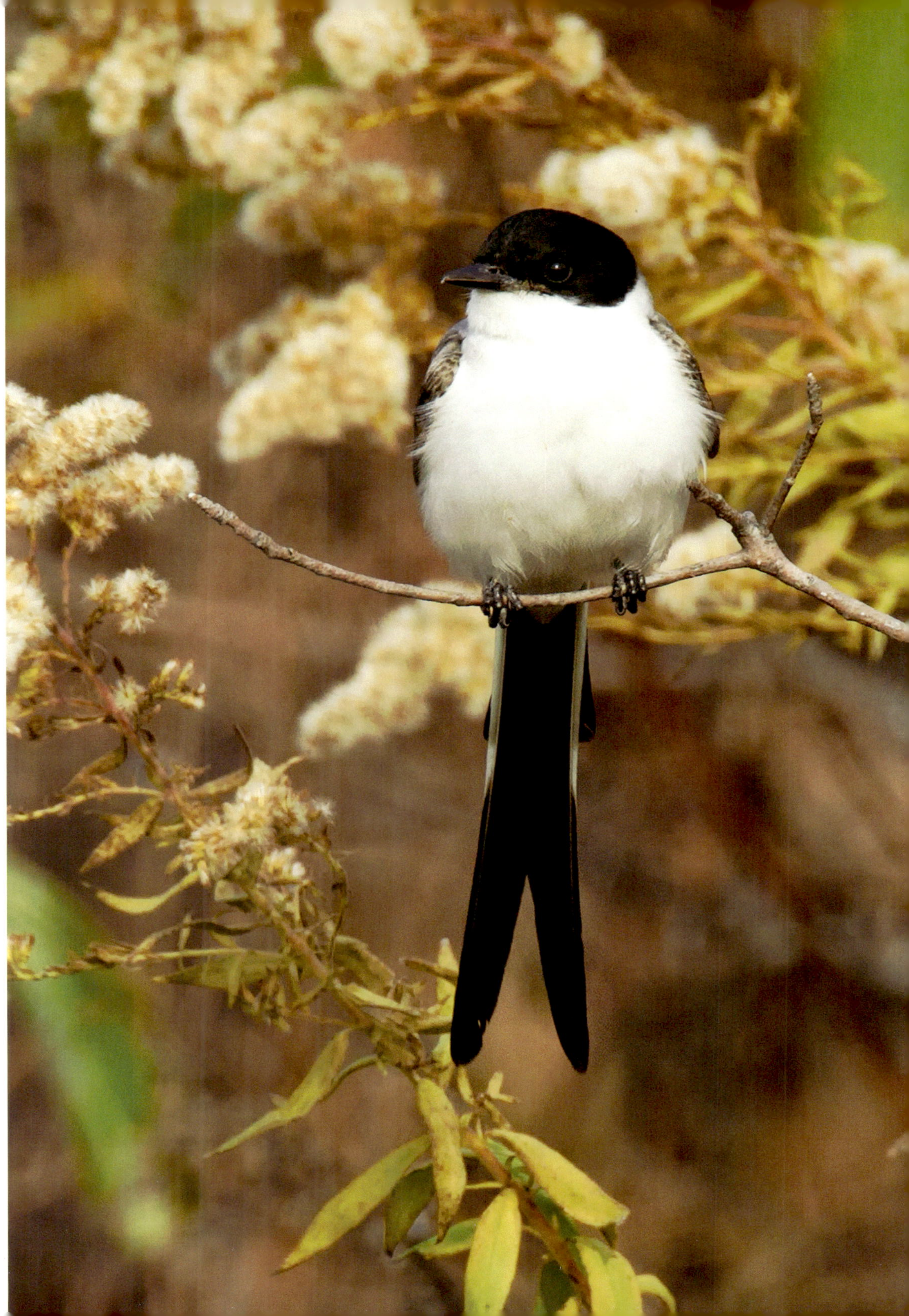

The heart has eyes which the brain knows nothing of.

— Charles H. Perkhurst

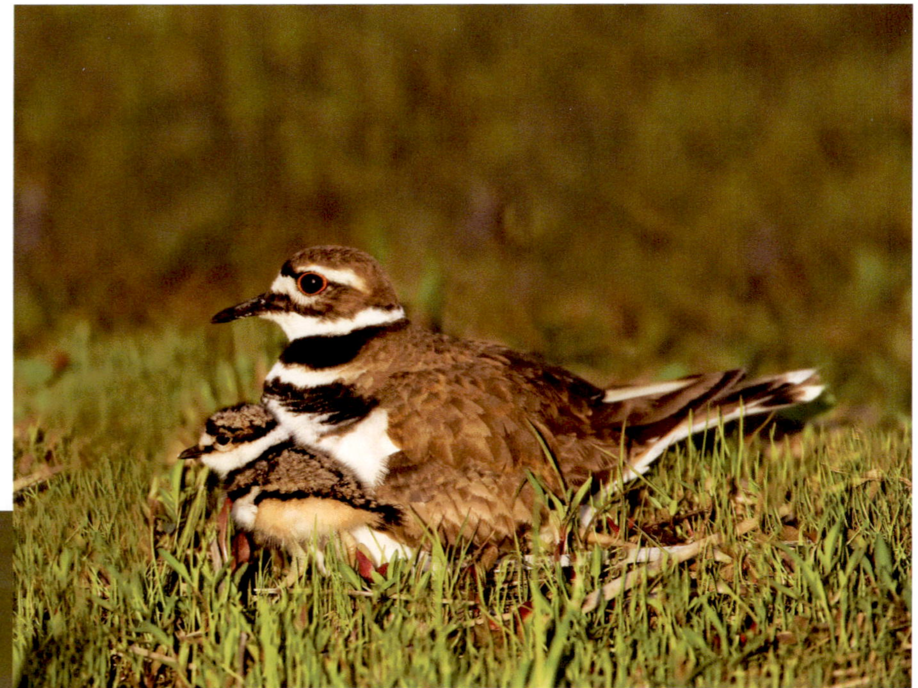

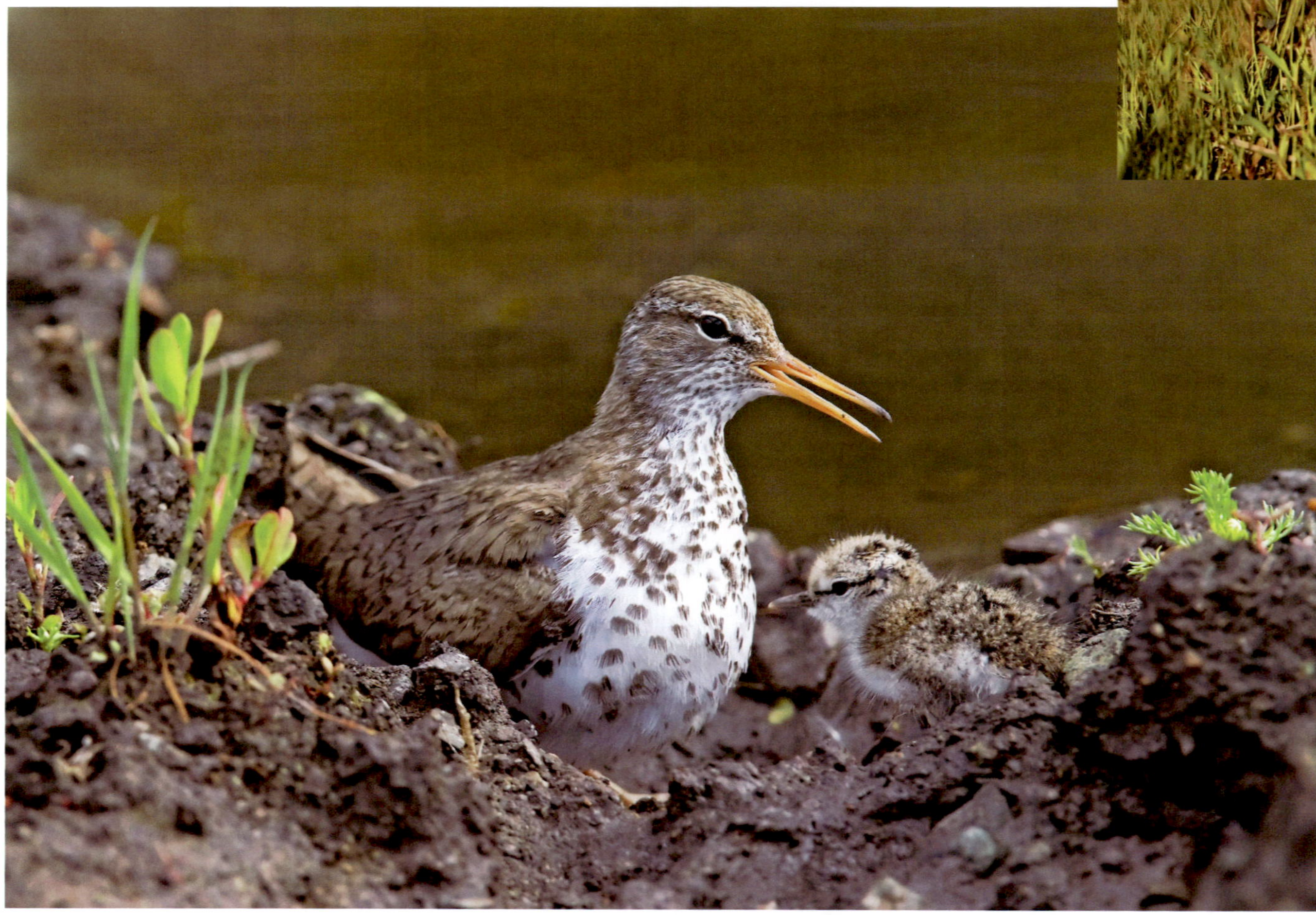

Two common North American shorebirds are shown caring for their chicks in early summer. A Killdeer (above) keeps an eye out for danger in southern New Jersey, while a Spotted Sandpiper calls to his chicks near a quiet pond in British Columbia. *Photos by Kevin T. Karlson*

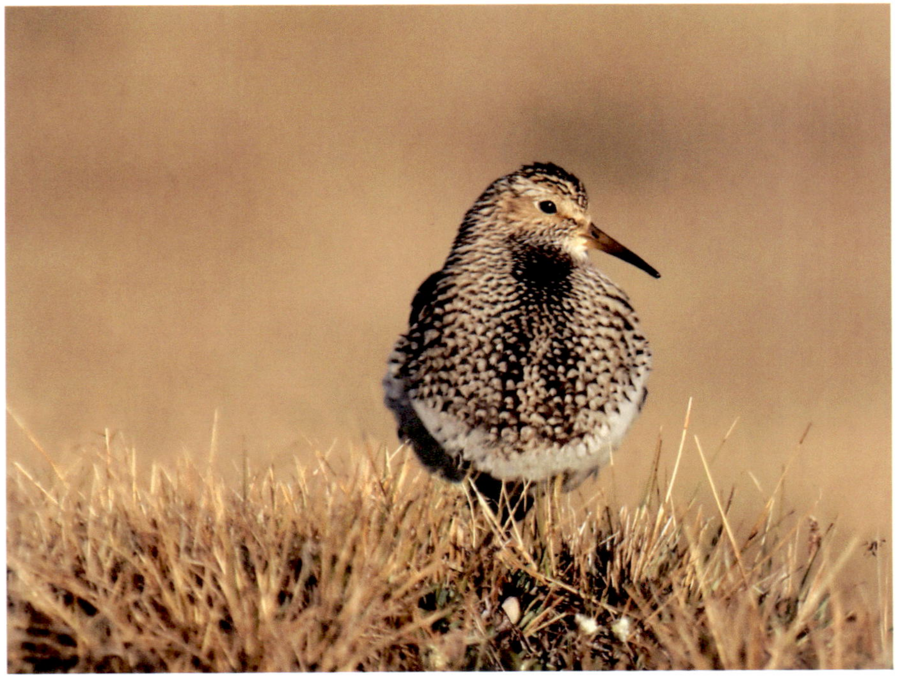

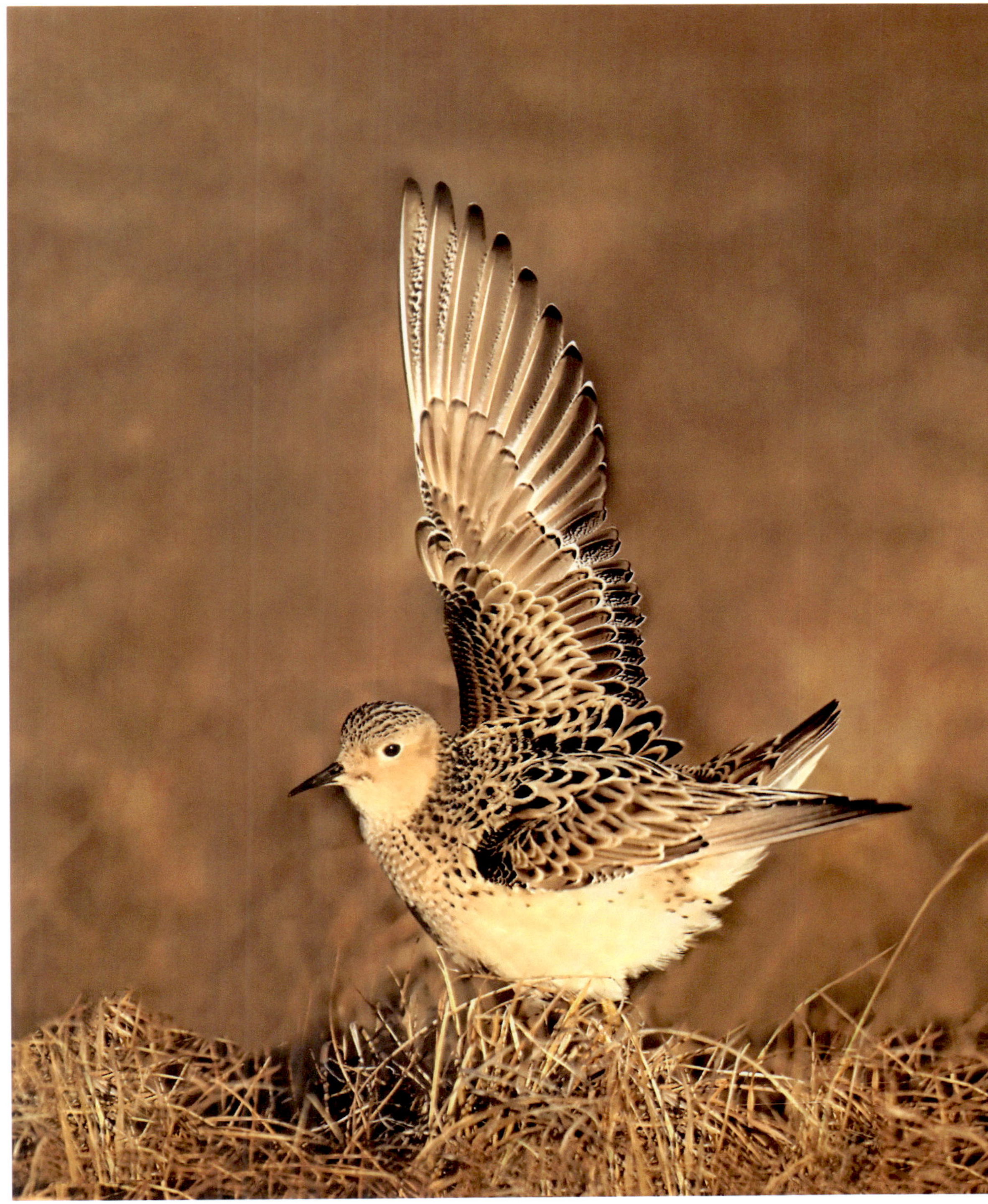

Alaska's Arctic tundra is the breeding area for these earth-toned shorebirds. A Pectoral Sandpiper (above) puffs out his chest to impress his harem of females. Nearby a Buff-breasted Sandpiper attempts to attract another female to his mating post. *Photos by Kevin T. Karlson*

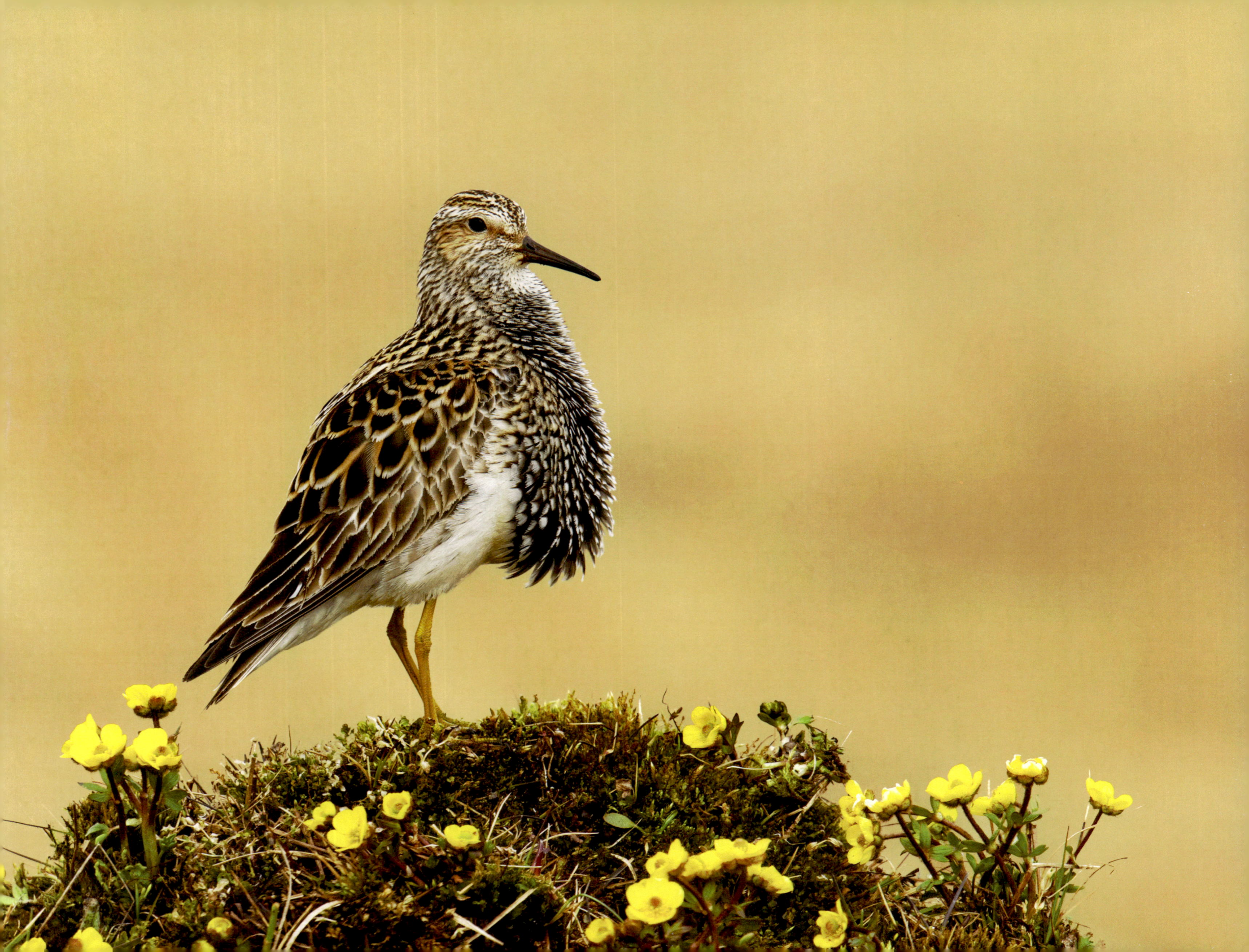

Opposite: A male Pectoral Sandpiper performs his unusual courtship display on the Arctic tundra, which involves inflating his pectoral sac and making deep hooting sounds. *Photo by Scott Elowitz*

Two residents of the arid desert regions of the Southwest. The Black-tailed Gnatcatcher (below) is a tiny, frenetic songbird that flits from bush to bush in search of insects. The Ash-throated Flycatcher (right) is a graceful bird that has just captured a butterfly, which might not make for a special meal due to its bitter taste. *Photos by Scott Elowitz*

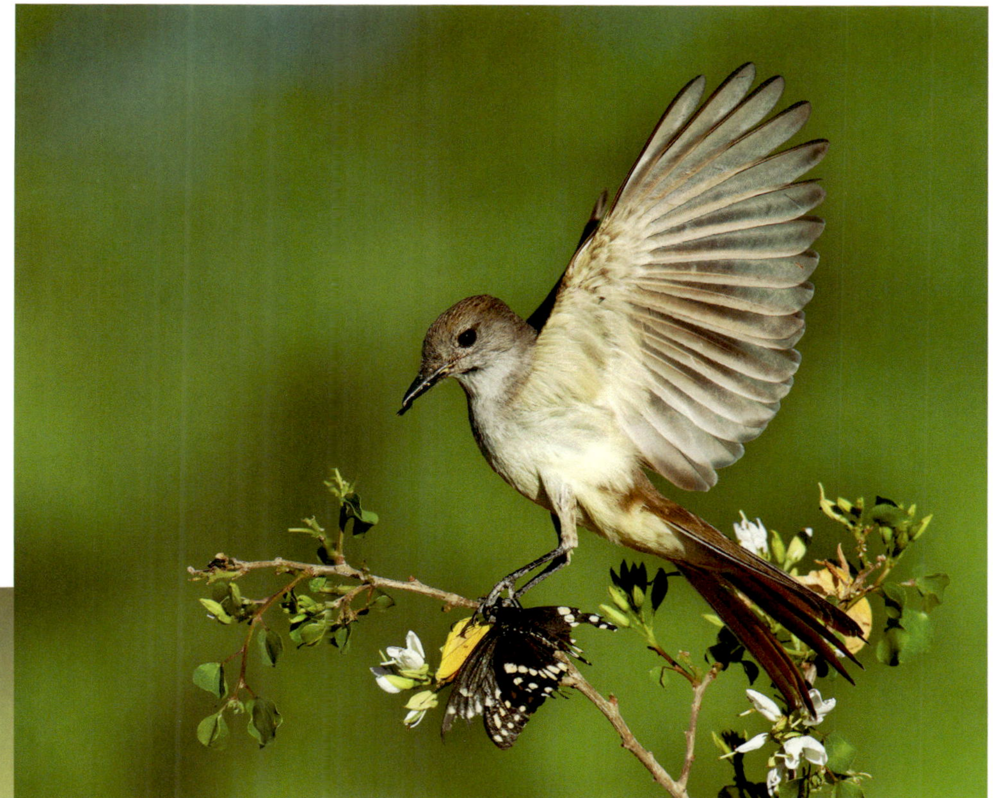

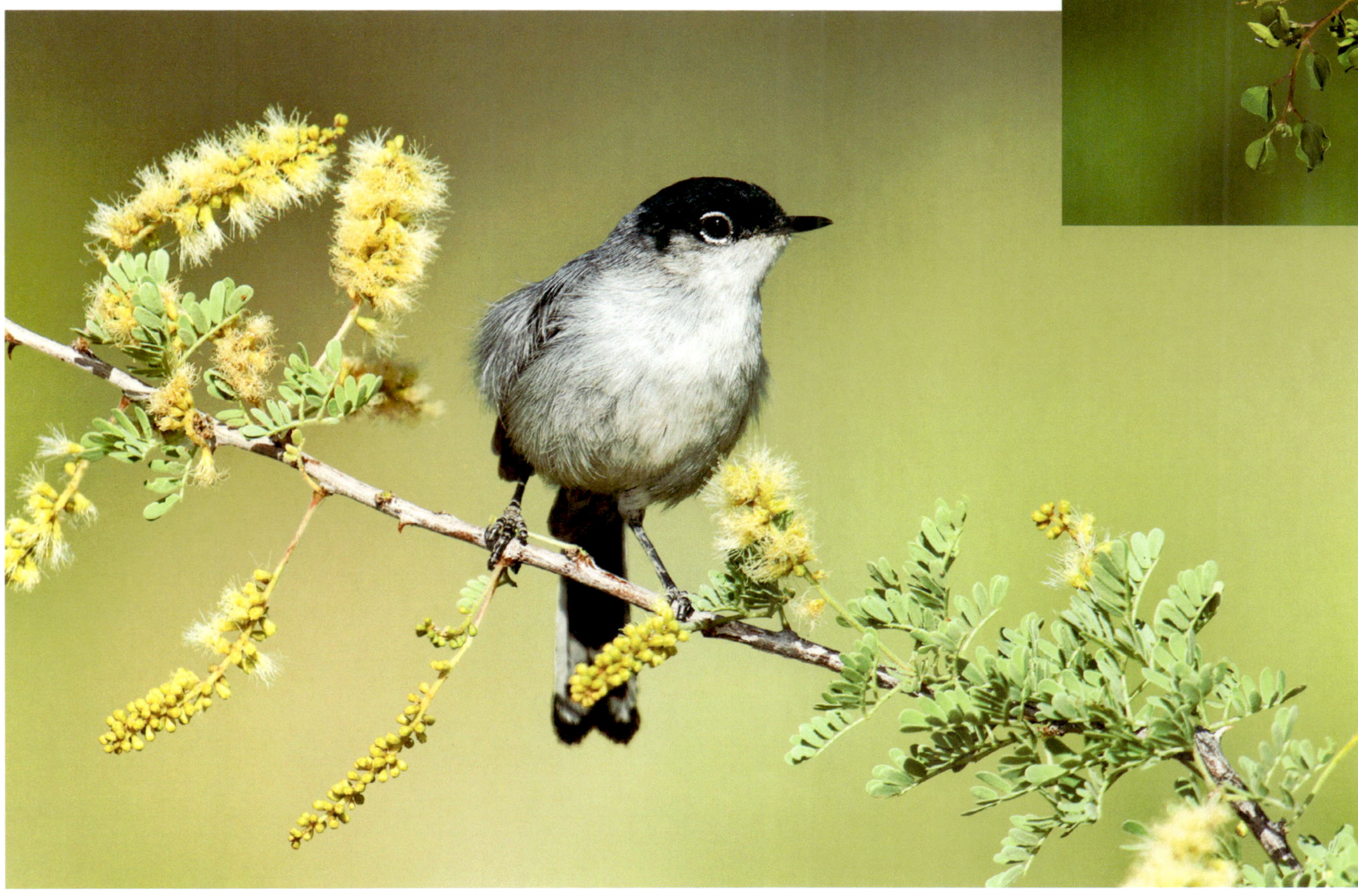

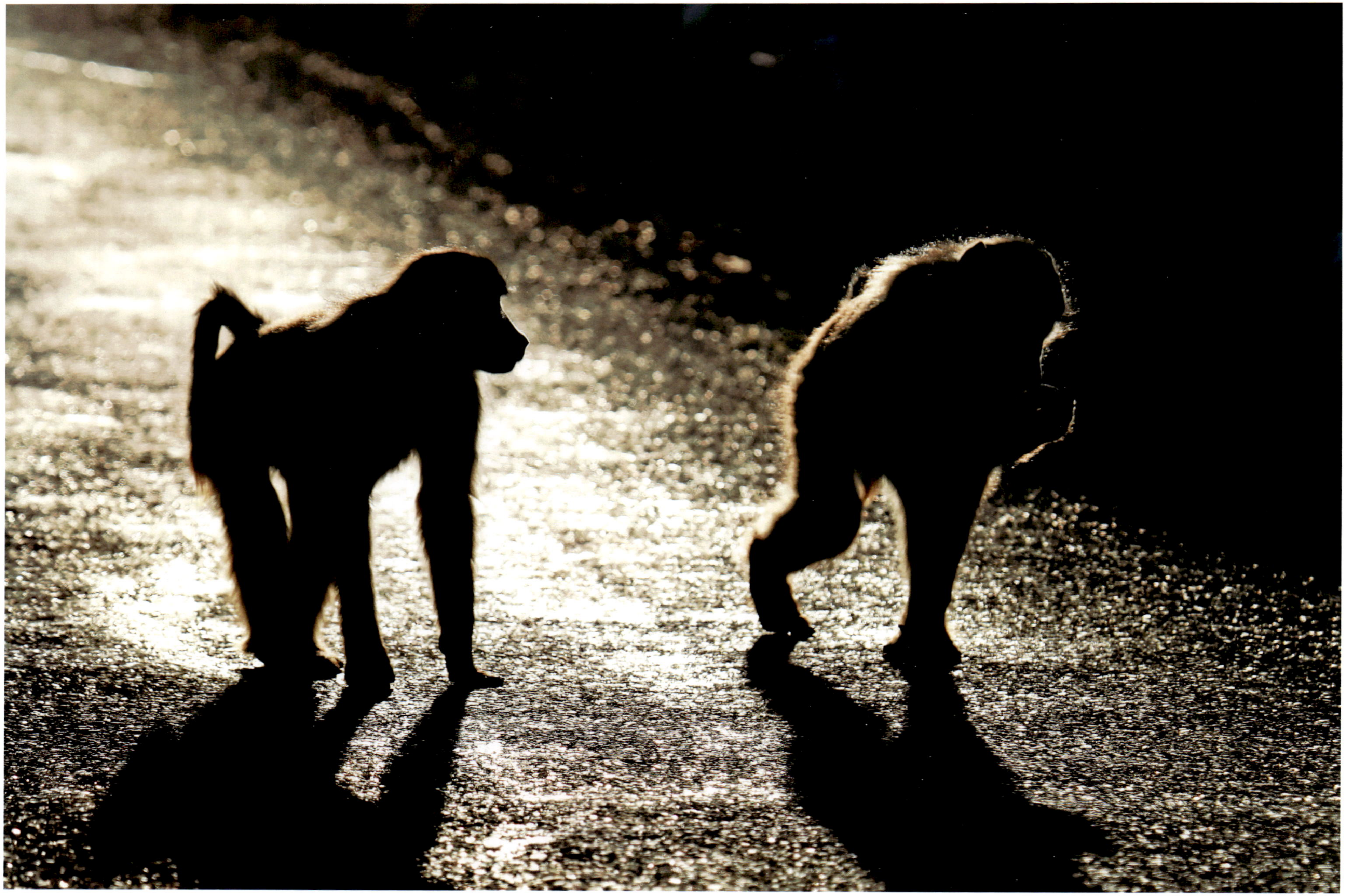

Chacma Baboons cadging scraps from passing motorists at the Cape of Good Hope, South Africa, are much-photographed, but shooting against the light makes the scene more interesting. Here, the slightly sinister light makes the thieving pair look like two of Fagin's boys from *Oliver Twist! Photo and caption by Mike Crewe*

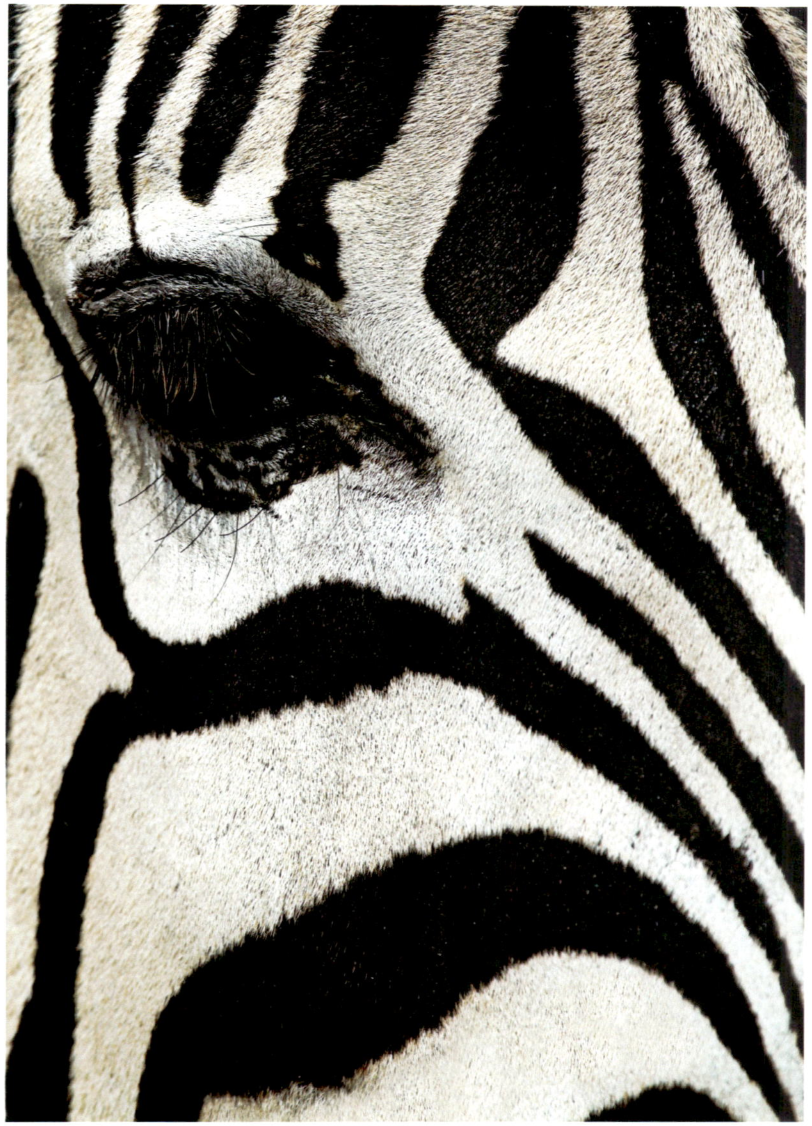

Nature is not a place to visit, it is home.

— Gary Snyder

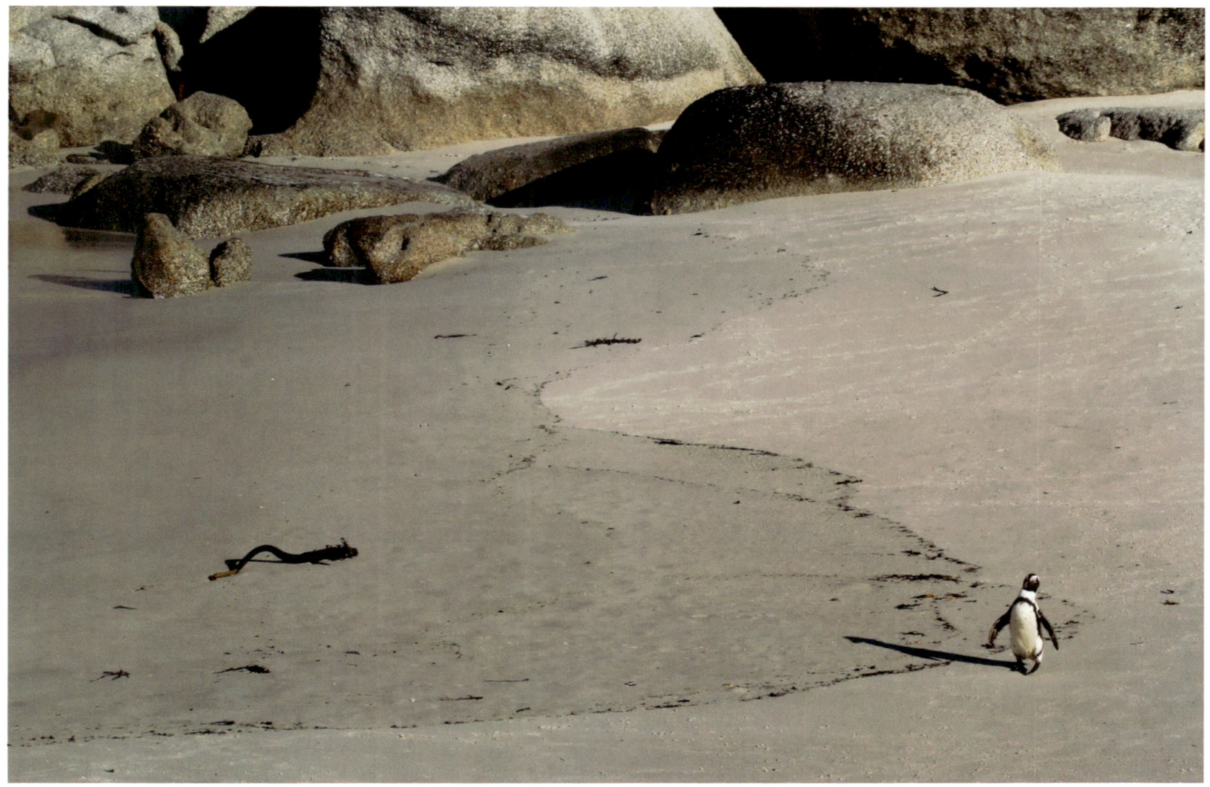

The Common Zebra, Etosha Pan, Namibia (above). "An enduring image from nature; a picture taken so many times and yet it still has instant appeal to our senses. Our eyes search the repetitive patterning until we notice the eye, then it all starts to make sense - but now it stops being abstract."

African Penguin**,** Boulders Beach, South Africa. "Sand, tideline, rocks; a typical beach scene, until you spot the penguin waddling along! We think of penguins as birds of icy places, so finding them on a beach in South Africa really comes as a surprise." *Photos and captions by Mike Crewe*

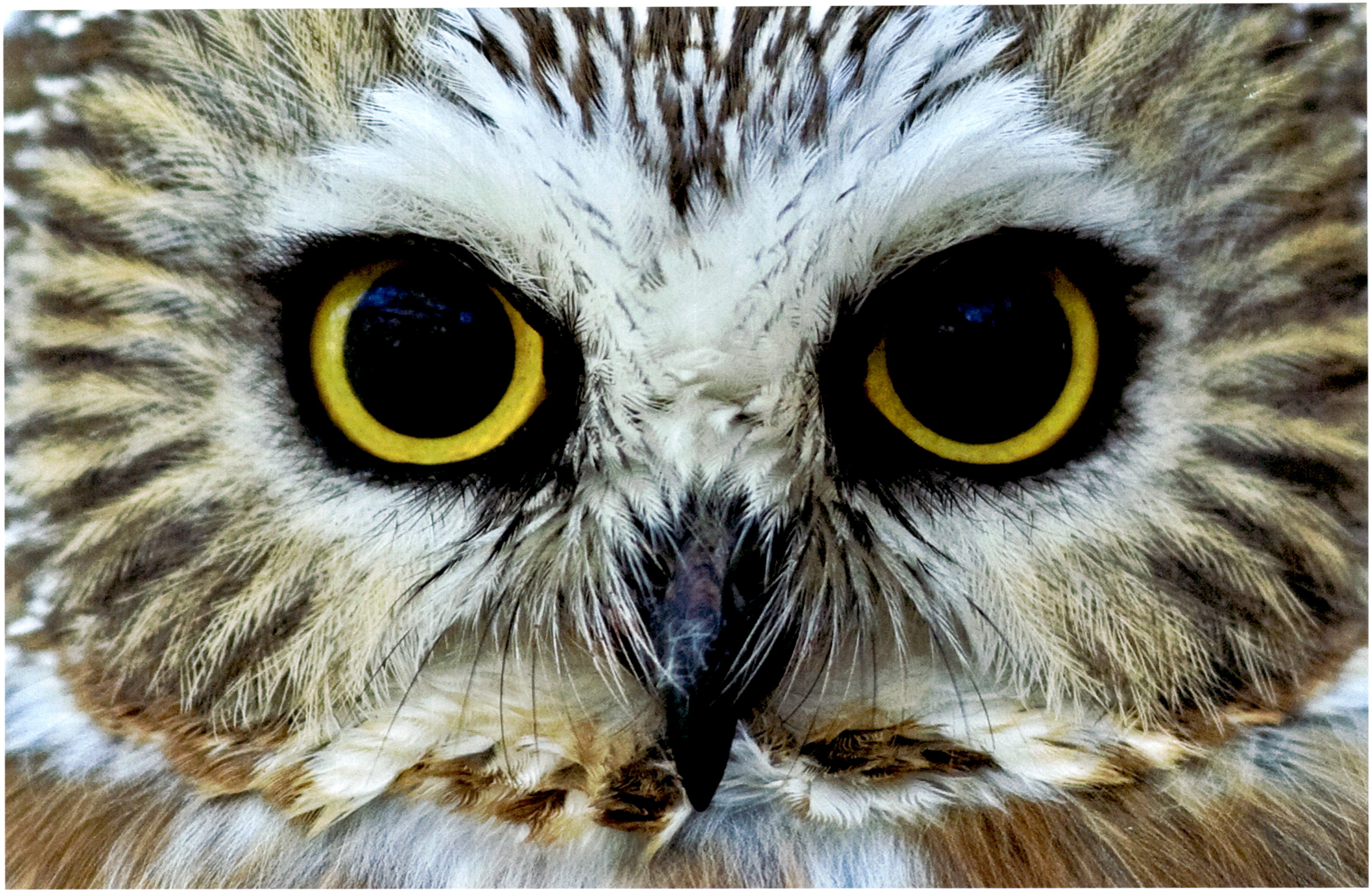

The penetrating eyes of a Saw-whet Owl reflect a winter's day in Central Park, New York City. *Photo by Lloyd Spitalnik*

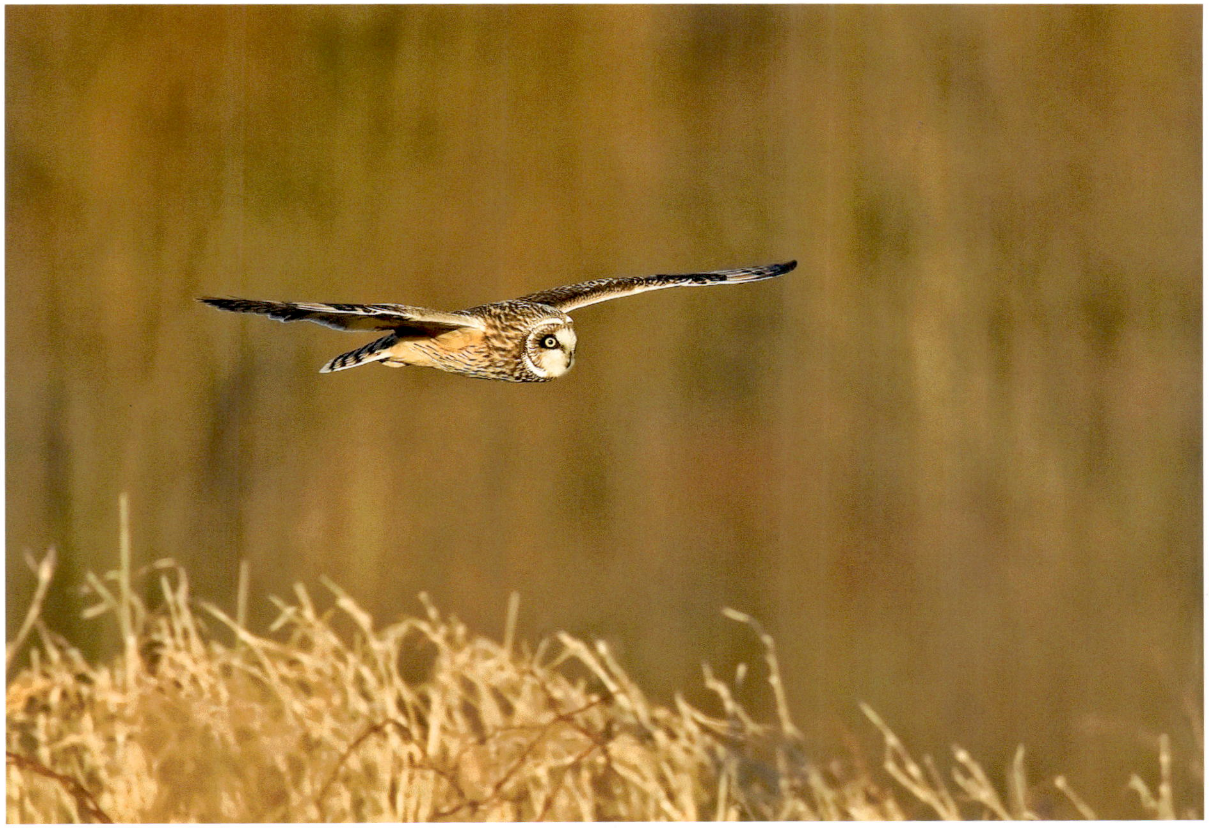

Warm, buff tones of late fall and winter are depicted in the two special birds shown here. A Short-eared Owl flies buoyantly above a grassy field in winter, while hunting for its favorite rodent prey (above).

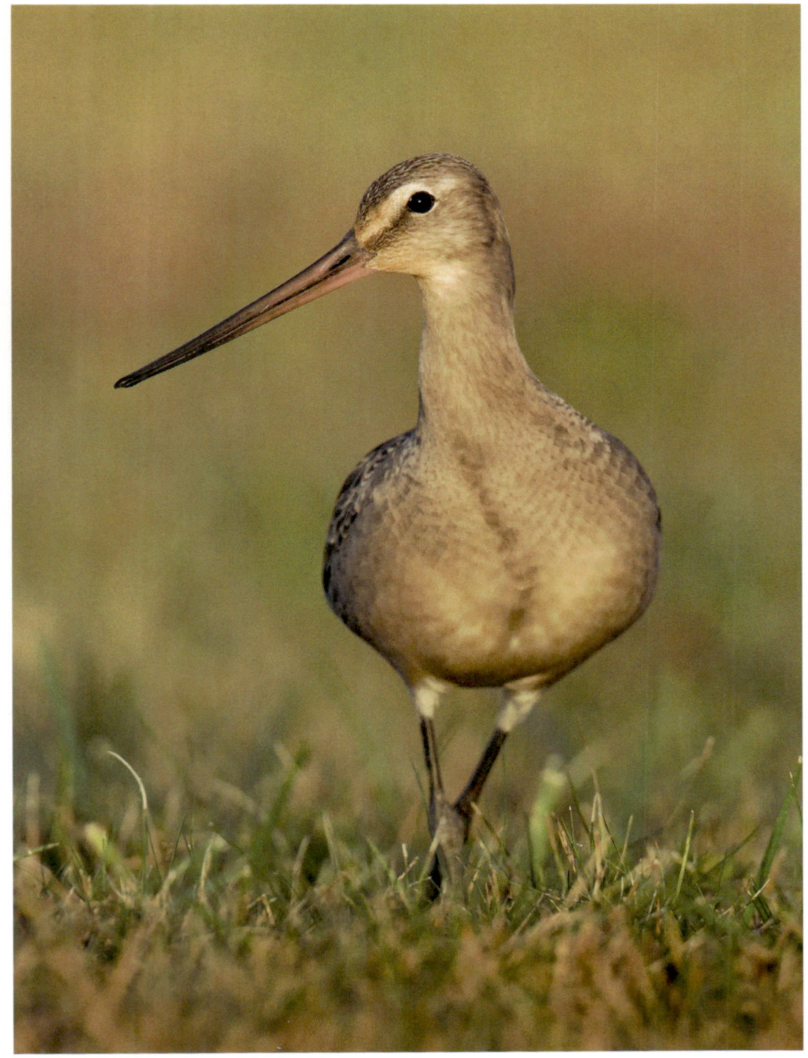

Hudsonian Godwit has one of the most beautiful juvenile plumages of all shorebirds, and it offers a soft, gentle feeling in this image full of earth tones. This photo was taken on the Connecticut coast during the bird's migration to southern South America. *Photos by Lloyd Spitalnik*

Open your eyes that you may see
The wonder that around you lies;
It will enrich your every day
And make you glad and kind and wise.

— Emma Boge Whisenand

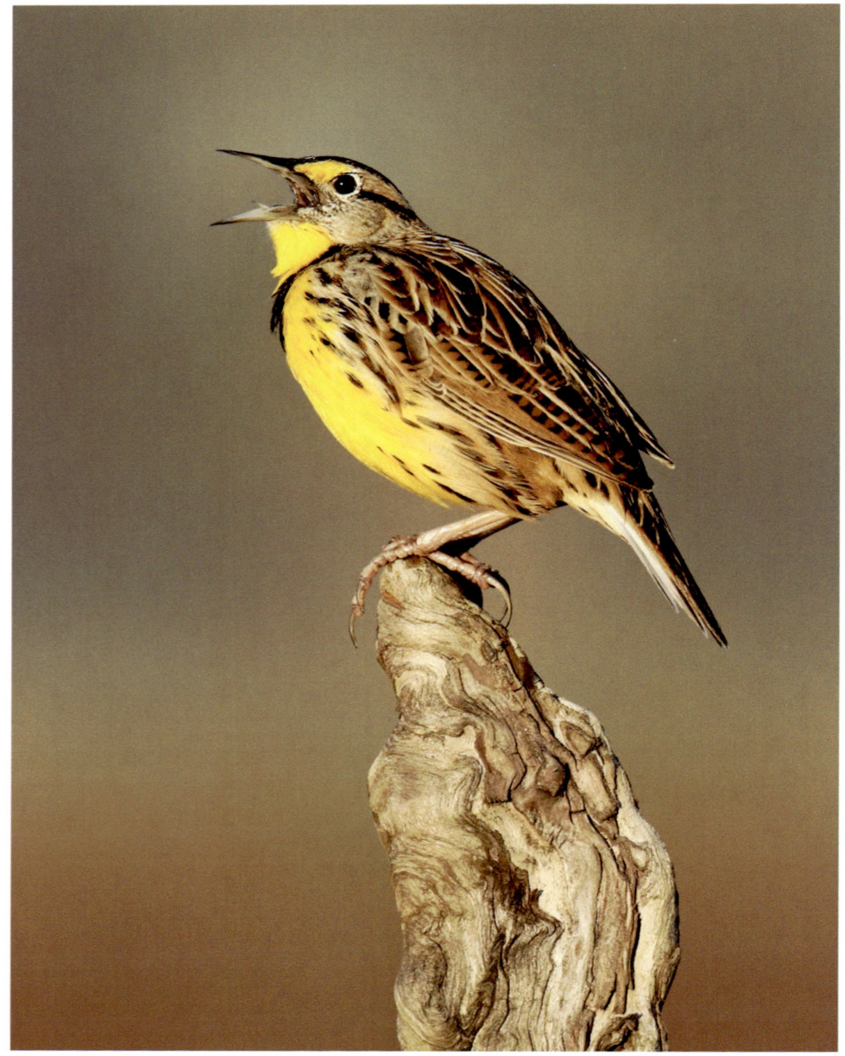

Eastern Meadowlarks sing their flute-like songs from exposed perches in grassland areas of North America (above). *Photo by Scott Elowitz*

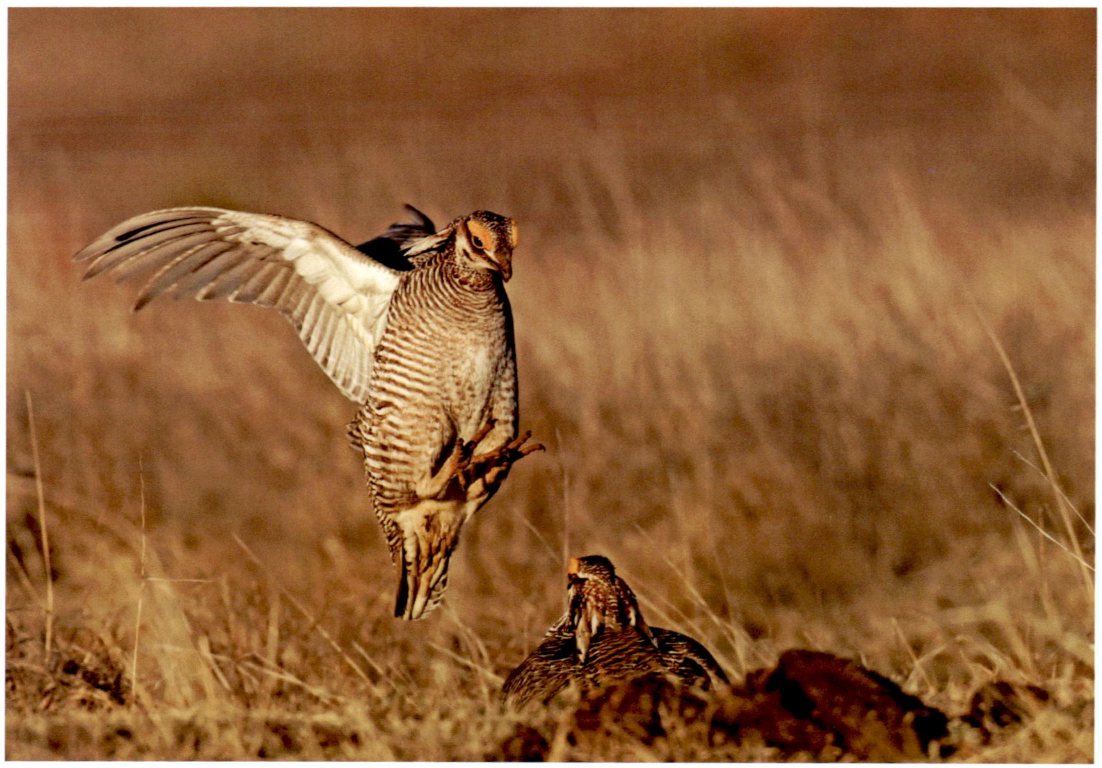

Every spring, for countless years, Lesser Prairie-Chicken males (left) have competed for the attention of females near the Kansas/Oklahoma border in animated lek displays. *Photo by Mike Hannisian*

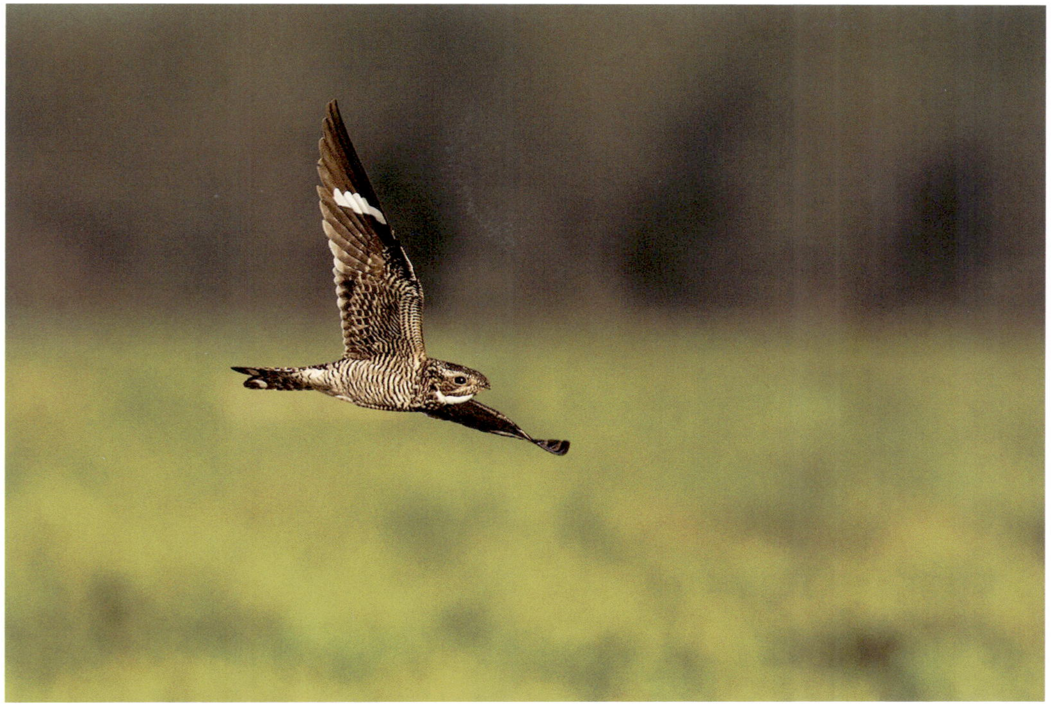

In the open spaces of the grasslands, birds rely on keen senses to spot danger before trouble occurs. The Common Nighthawk (above) nests on the ground and hunts insects while flying over grassy areas.

Burrowing Owl (right) nests underground and hunts its favorite food of lizards and frogs from exposed perches. *Photos by Scott Elowitz*

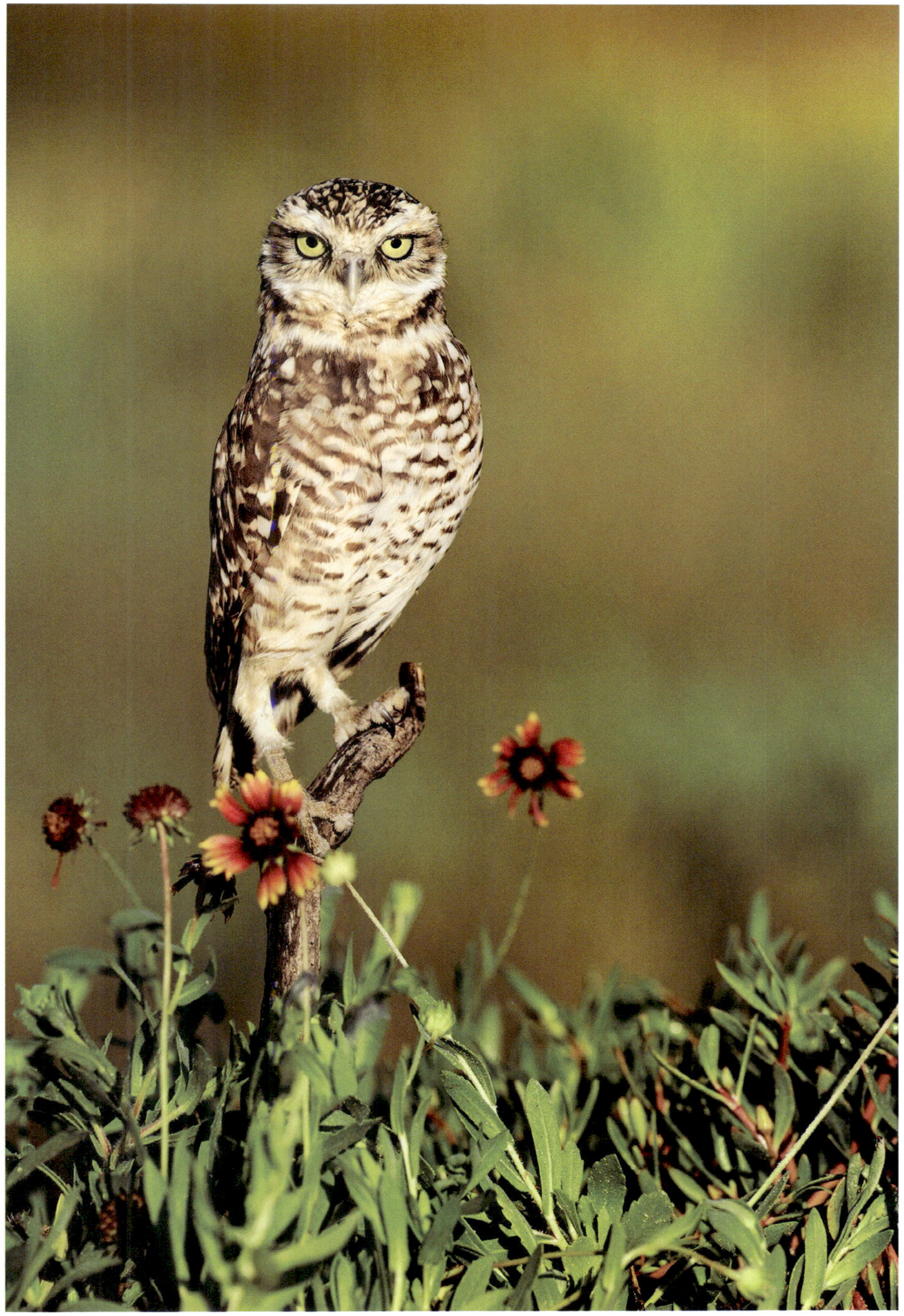

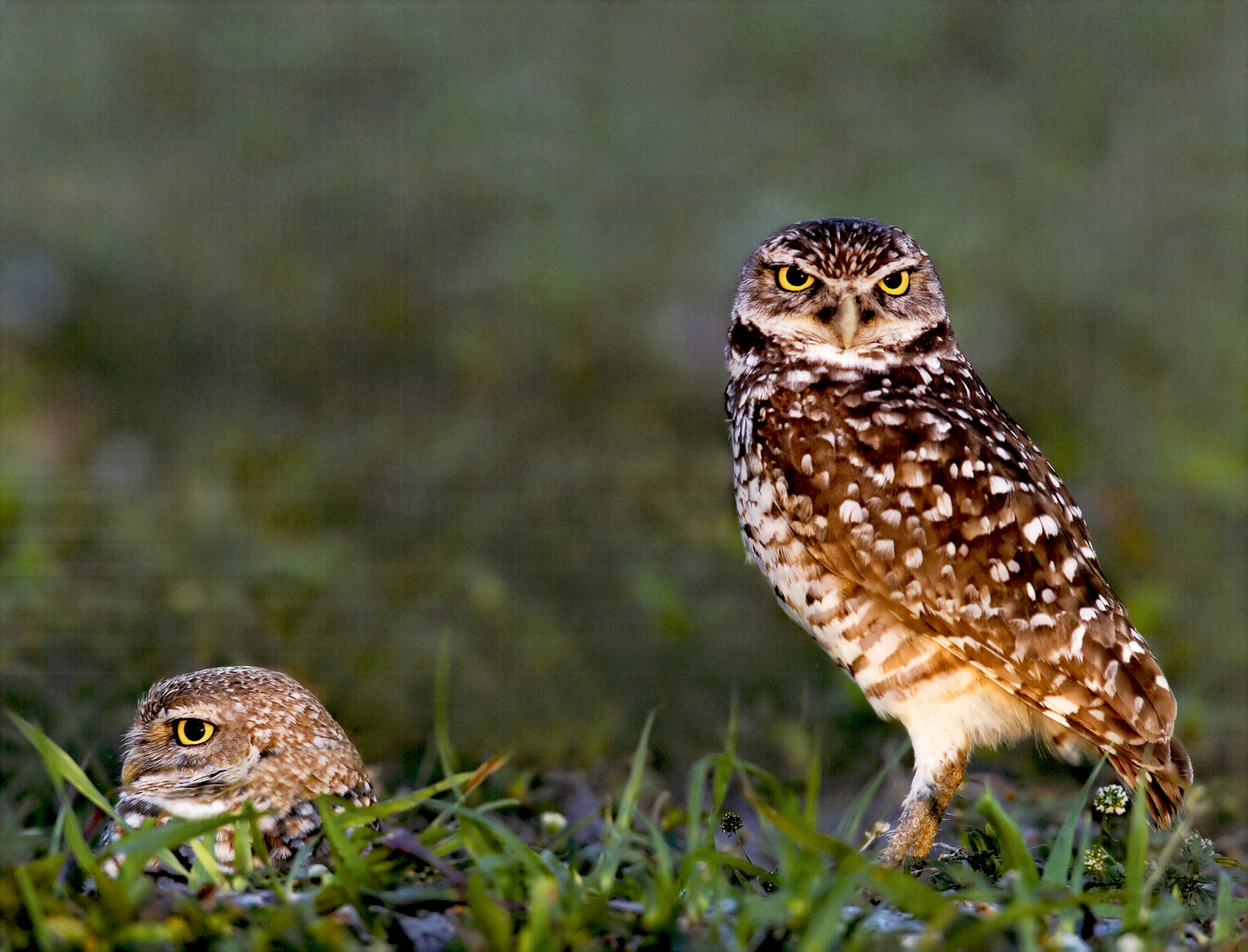

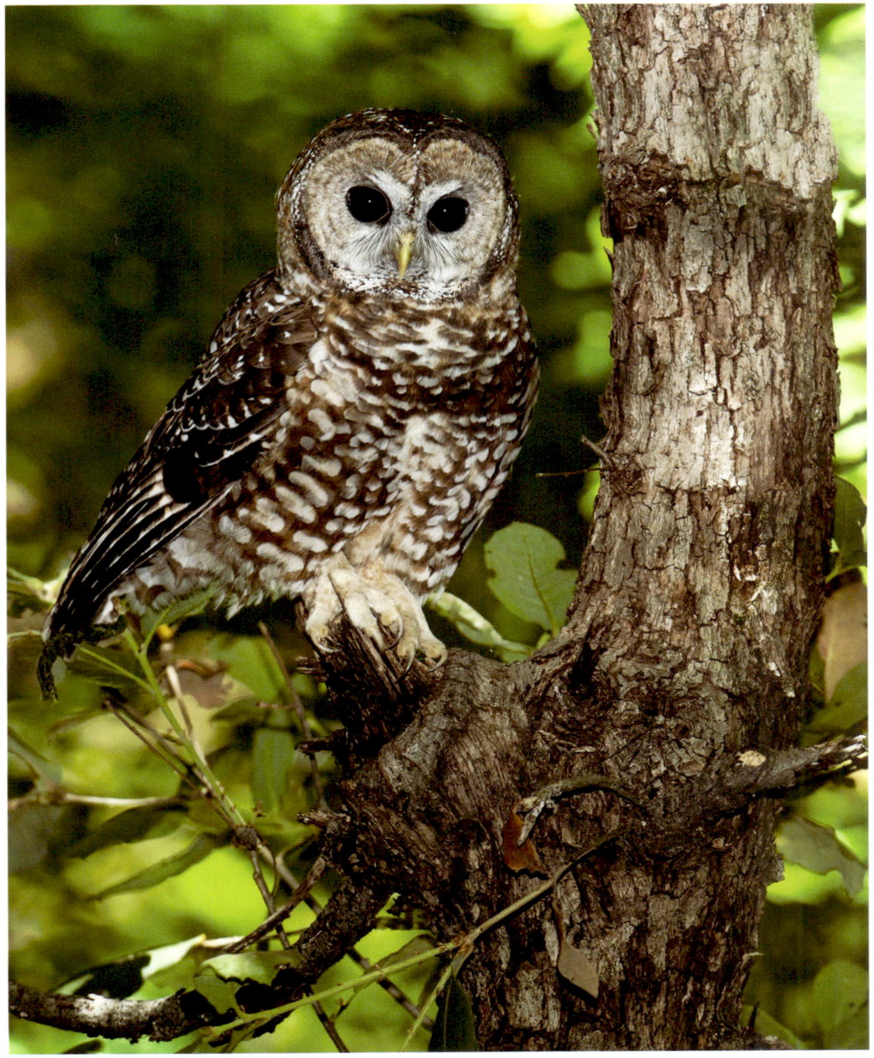

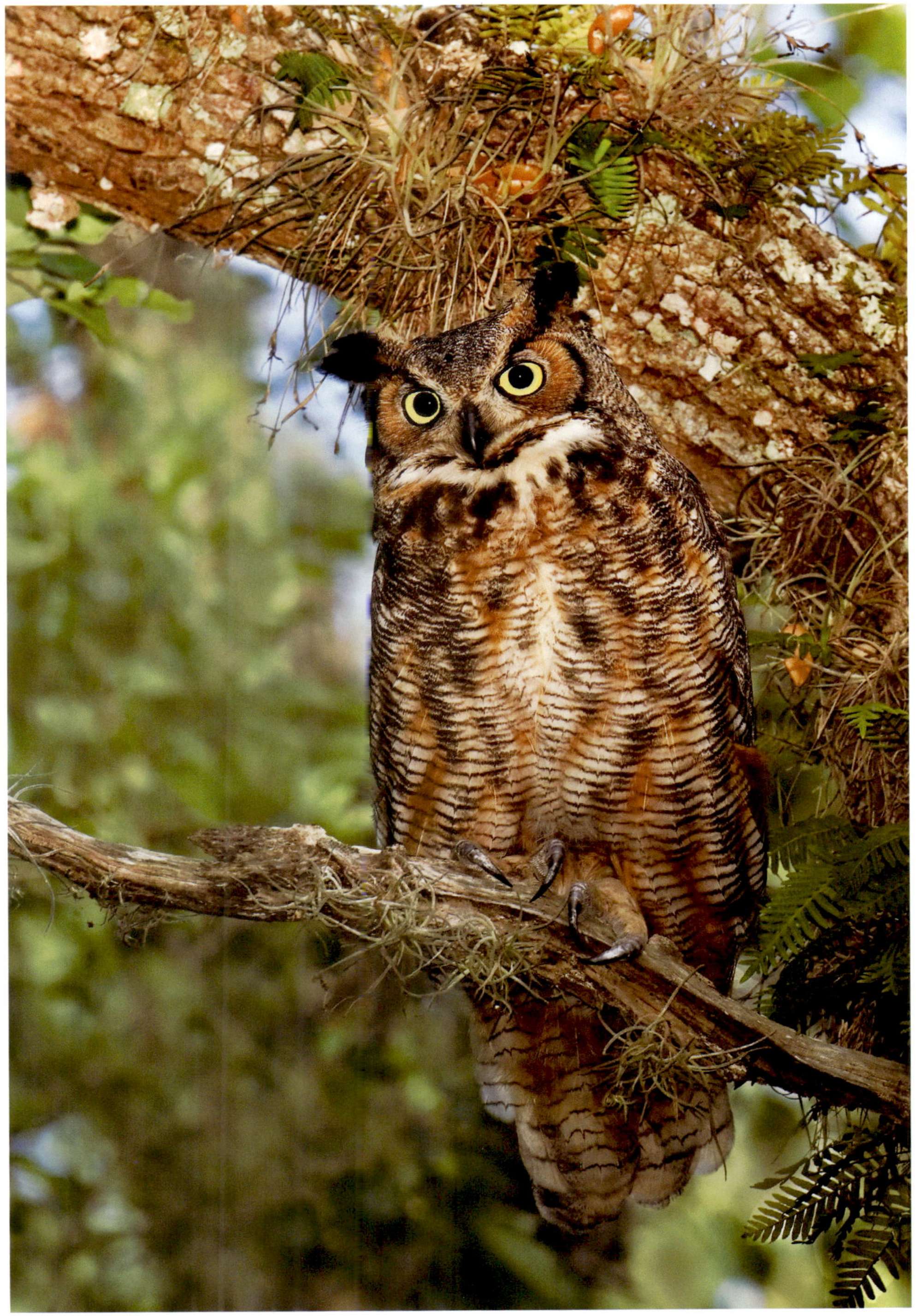

People are both fascinated and spooked by owls due to their solitary nature and secretive nocturnal habits. Ancient folklore suggests that owls are a link to the spirit world, which further enhances their mystery. Burrowing owls are small birds that live underground (opposite), while Spotted Owls (above) are larger and nest in tree cavities. Great Horned Owls (right) are very large and have no avian predators. *Photos by Scott Elowitz (upper left) and Kevin T. Karlson (opposite page and right)*

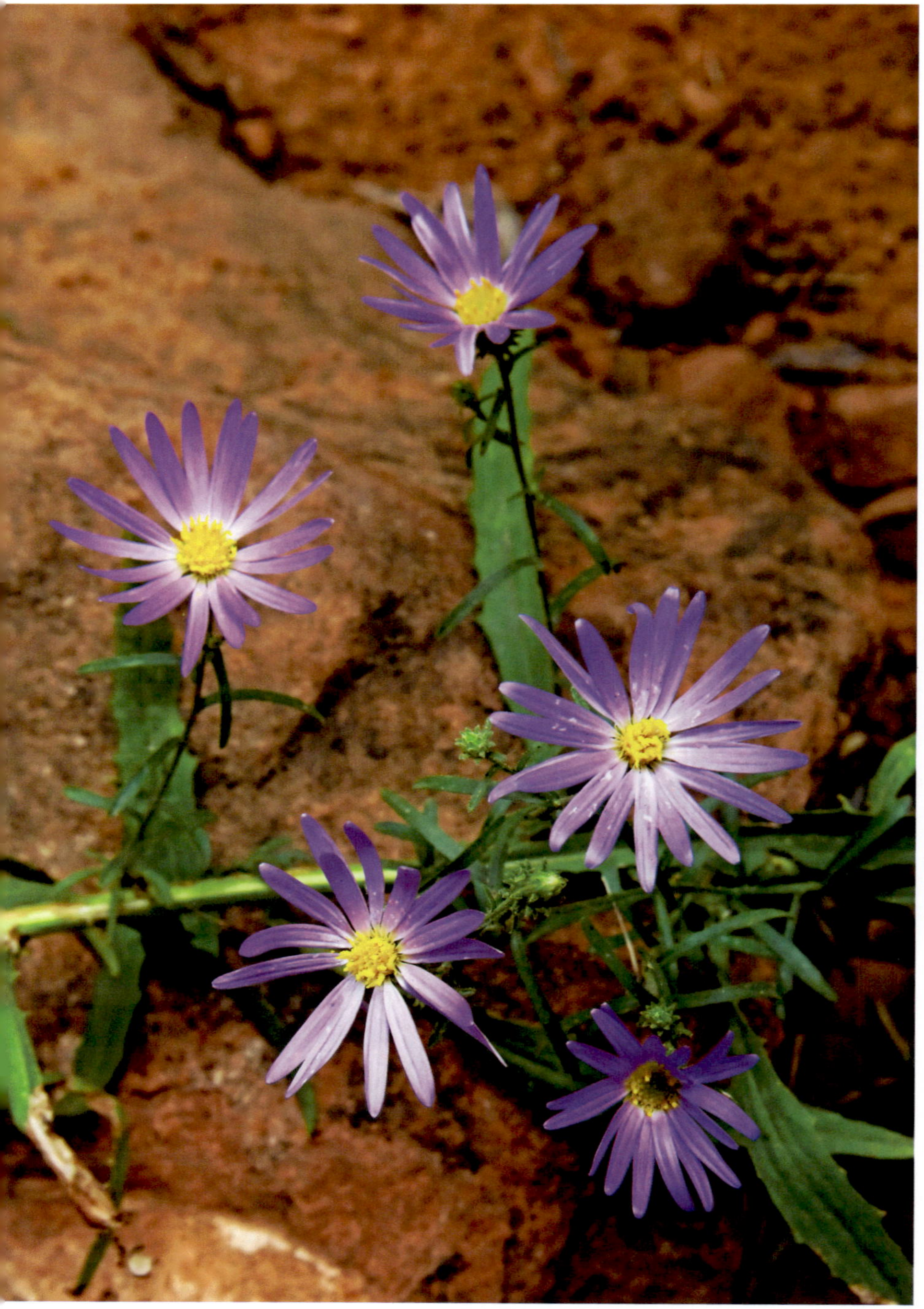

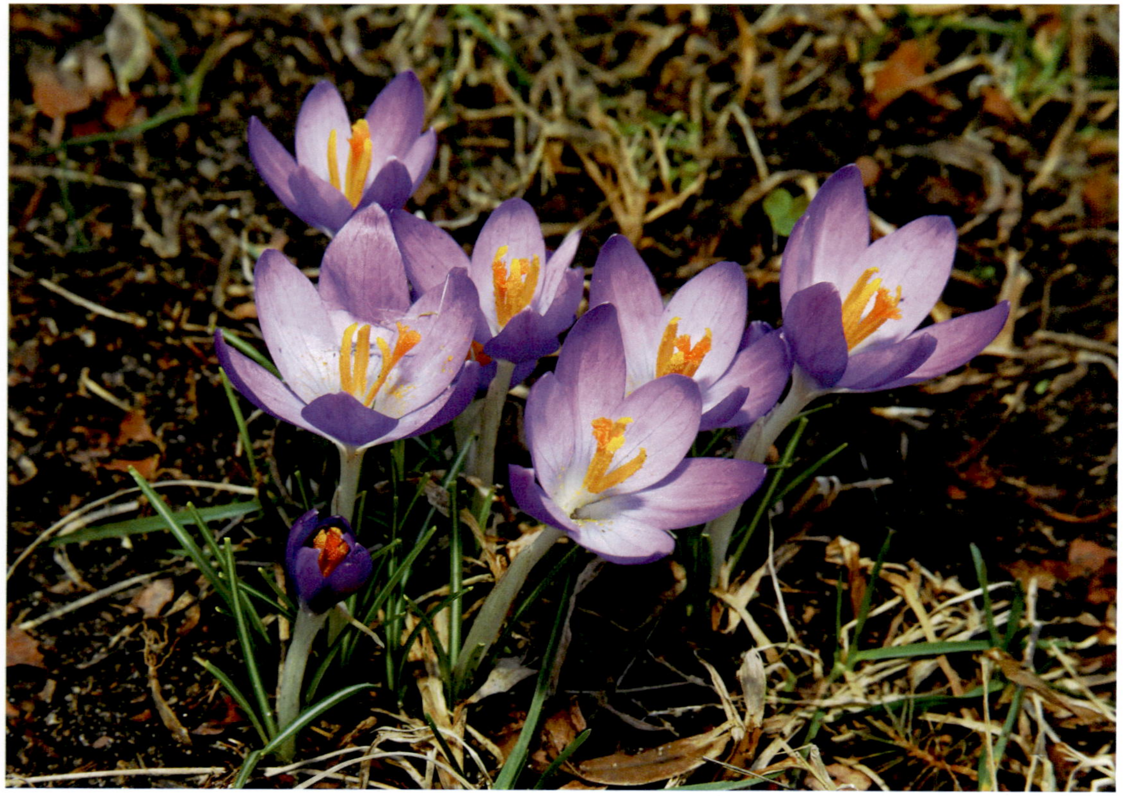

These special flowers share a soft, purple hue. Asters grow in harsh, rocky landscapes in the Western mountains (left), while Crocuses (above) emerge and splash the landscape with the first bright colors in early spring. *Photos by Kevin T. Karlson*

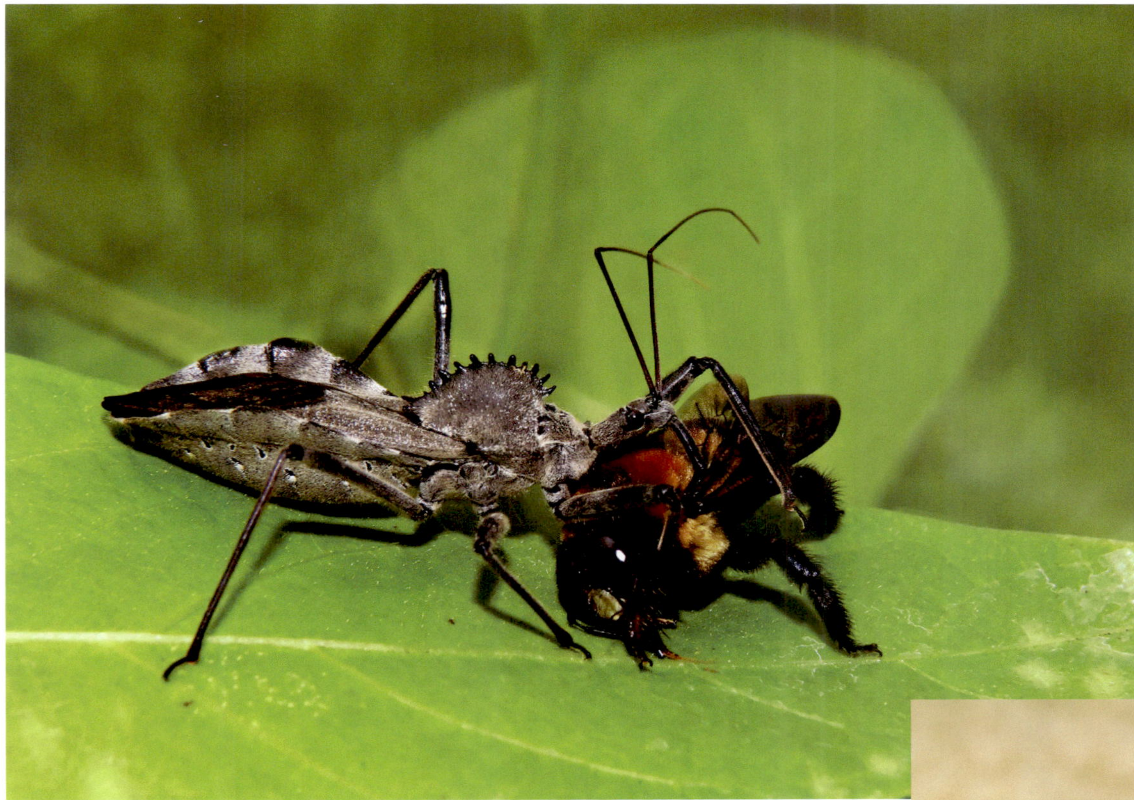

To see a world in a grain of sand,
And a heaven in a wild flower,
Hold infinity in the palm of your hand,
And eternity in an hour.

— William Blake

Nature isn't always sweet and idyllic. A life and death struggle takes place every day in the vast world that exists beneath our feet. An assassin bug (above) prepares to suck the fluid out of an unlucky bumblebee that it caught in the vegetable garden.

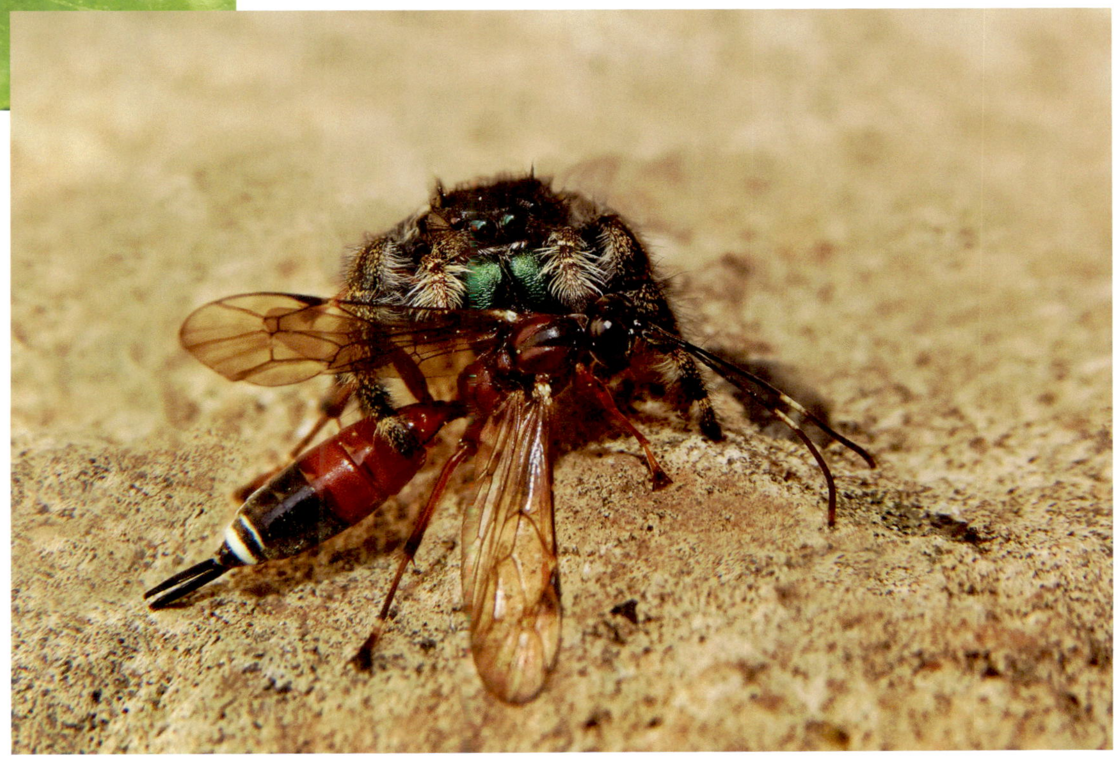

A large jumping spider has captured a parasitic wasp and is about to enjoy a meal. When you venture into the macro world of nature, some of the players seem to belong to a science fiction horror movie. *Photos by Kevin T. Karlson*

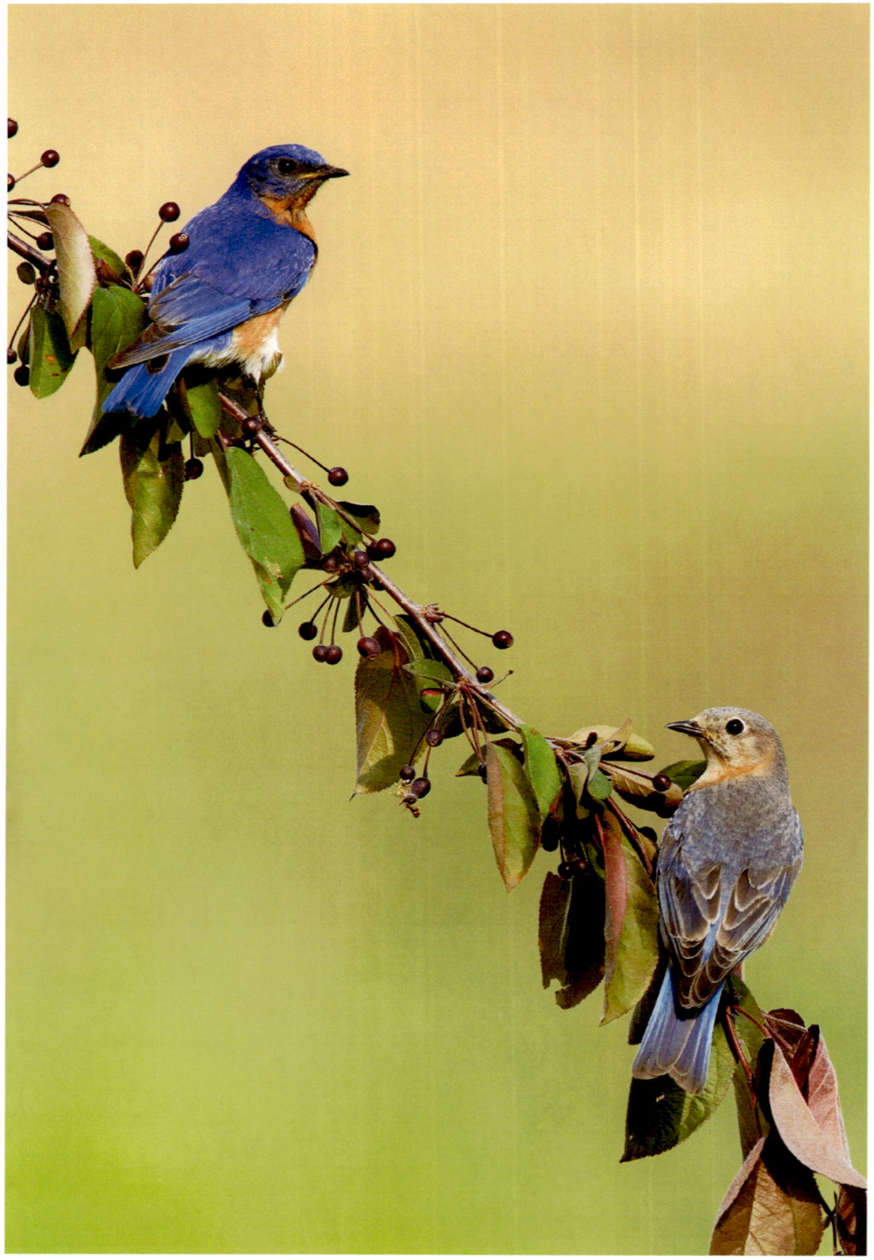

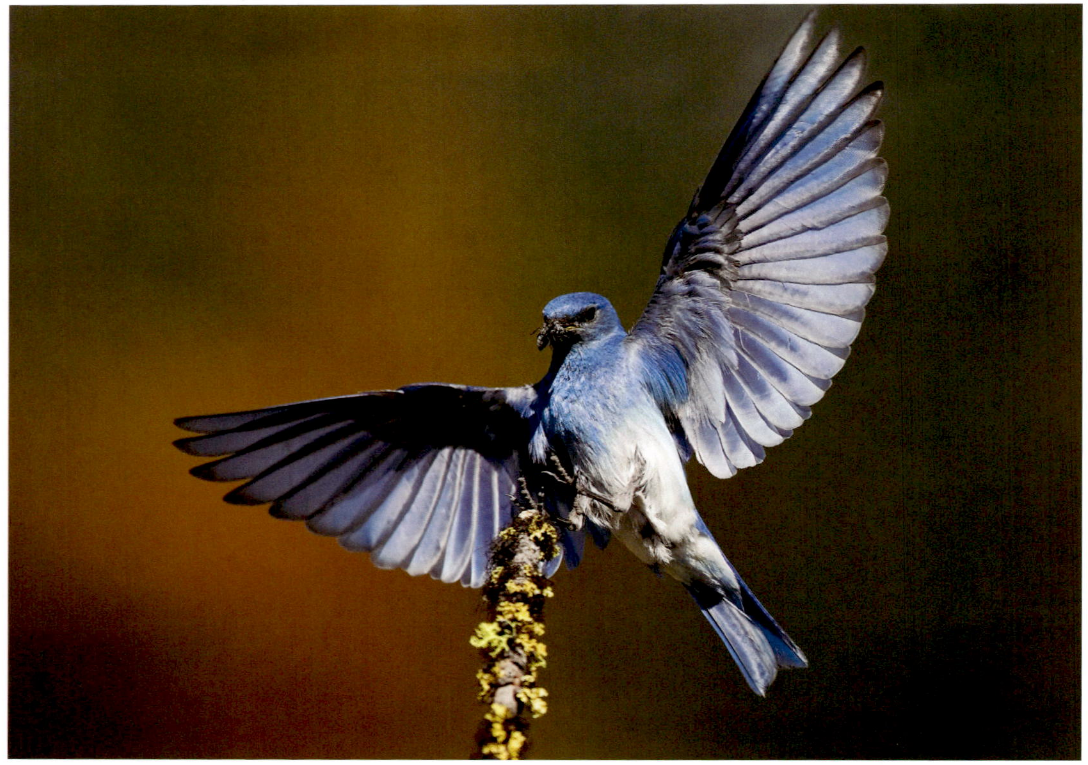

I have seen amazing sights in my many years but I would be hard pressed to name one that exceeds the wonder and magic of the first flight of a bluebird.

— Wendell Long

Eastern Bluebirds (left). Males have deeper blue upper parts than females. *Photo by Scott Elowitz*

A male Mountain Bluebird comes in for a landing before feeding his chicks with this juicy bug. *Photo by Kevin T. Karlson*

A Yellow-crowned Night-Heron flips the body of a crab into its throat. Shellfish are one of the favorite foods of this attractive heron. *Photo by Lloyd Spitalnik* (opposite page)

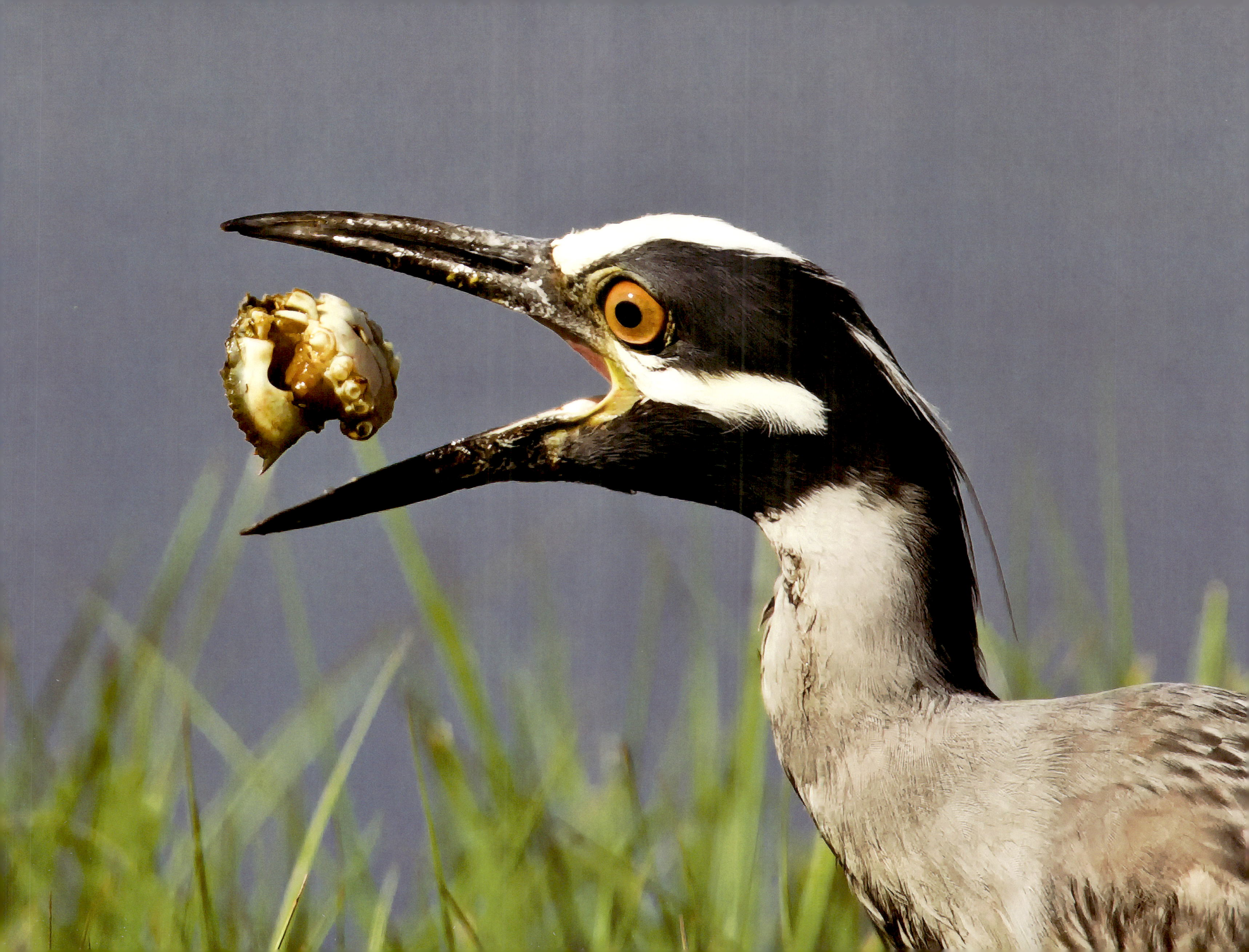

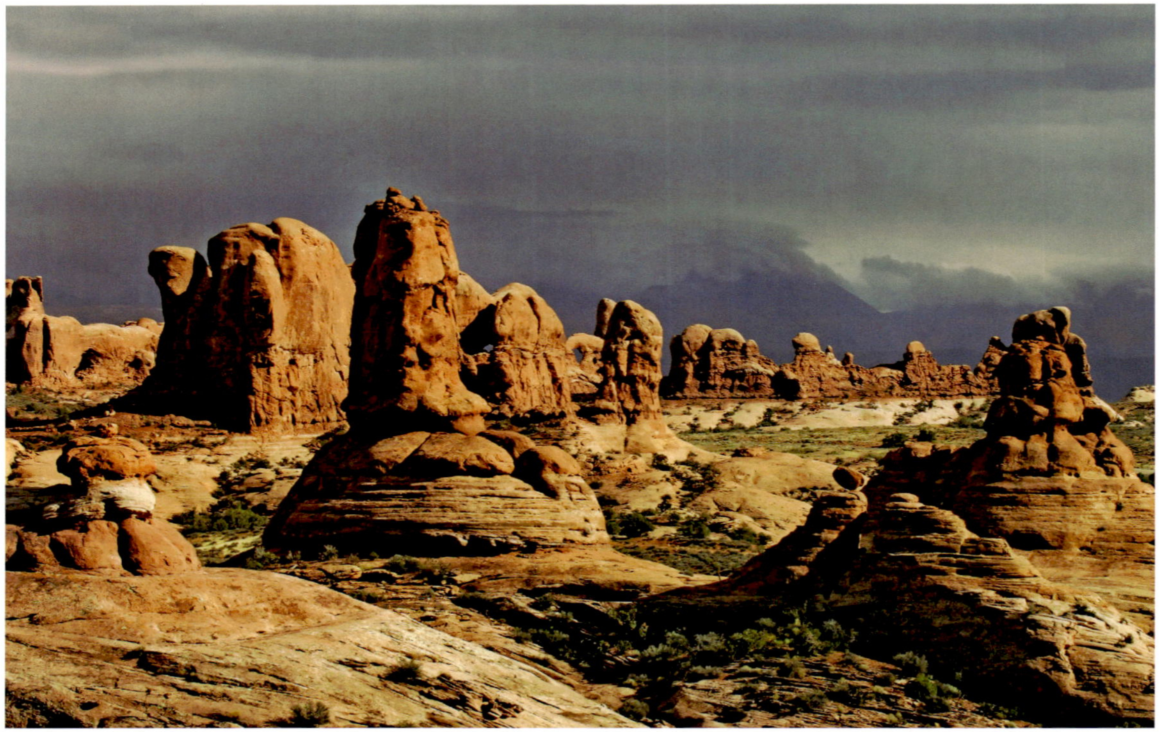

There are times when I cannot believe I am separate from this earth, when I could swear the wind blows through me as it does the woven needles of the pine tree by the creek, when I feel my feet planted deep in the earth with the roots of trees and wildflowers, drawing essence.

— Cathy Johnson

Rugged, rocky landscapes characterize Arches National Park in Utah. A stormy sky creates a dramatic scene (above) in a sculptured valley; with a little imagination, you might envision a few dinosaurs coming around the corner.

This unique rock formation (right) from Arches is called "The Dark Angel." It is located at the end of a 5-mile hike, and its large size and imposing essence make it an unforgettable and rewarding destination. *Photos by Kevin T. Karlson*

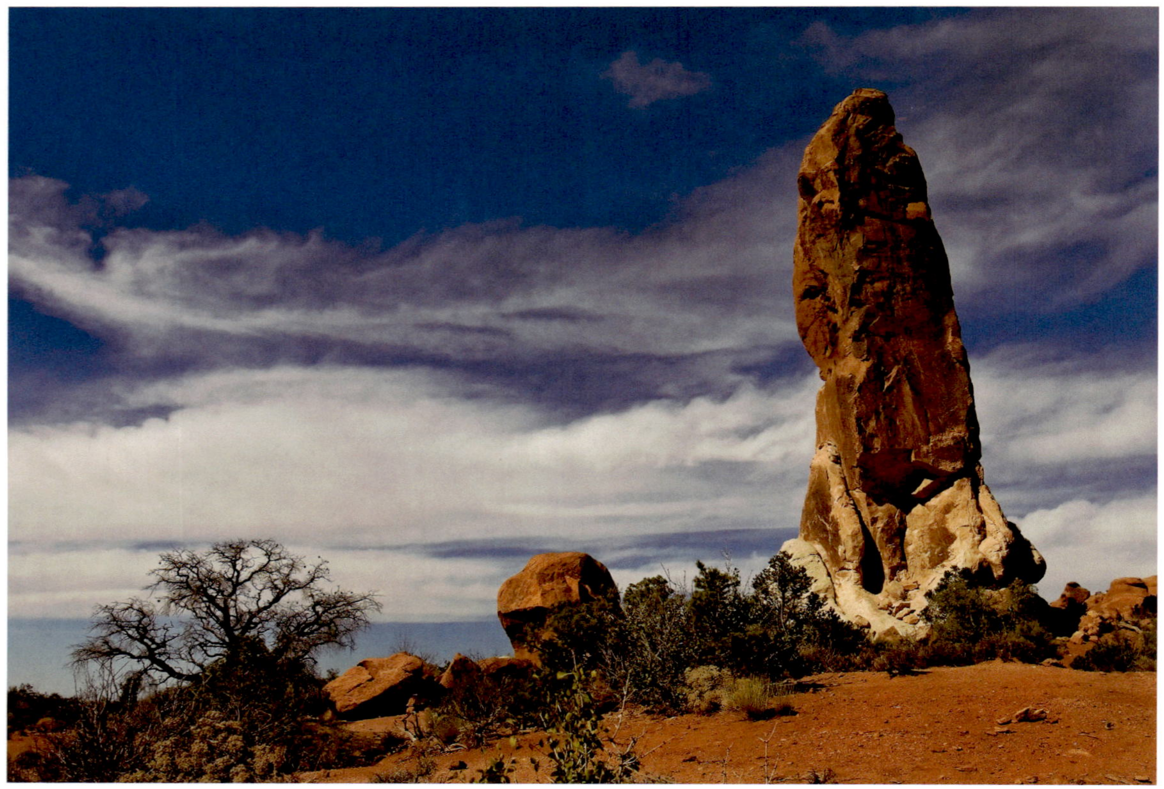

Two striking woodpeckers from the mountains of western North America are shown here. A male Williamson's Sapsucker prepares to feed its young a mouthful of ants (below), while a male Red-naped Sapsucker (right) exits its nest hole below a knot in the tree after feeding his young. *Photos by Kevin T. Karlson*

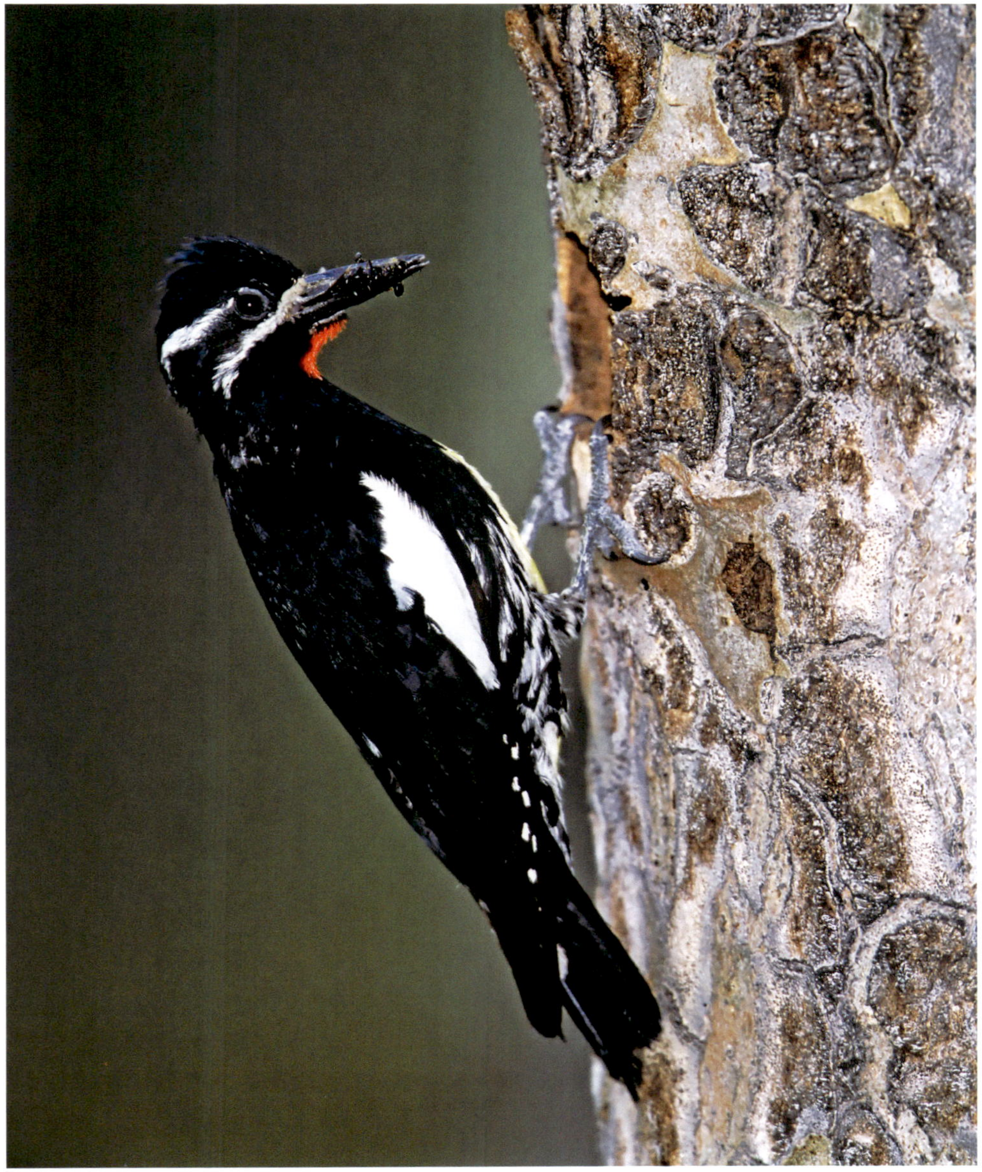

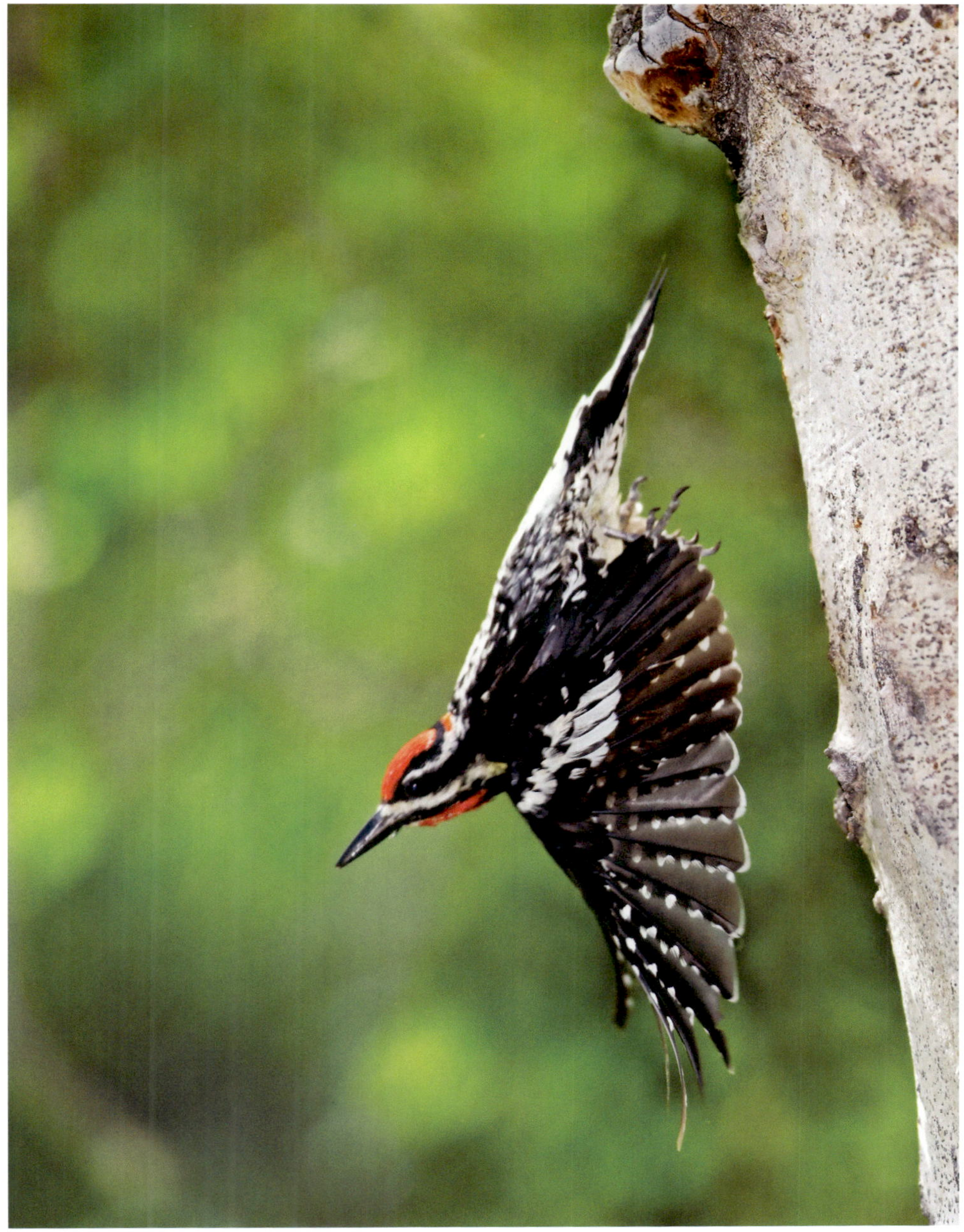

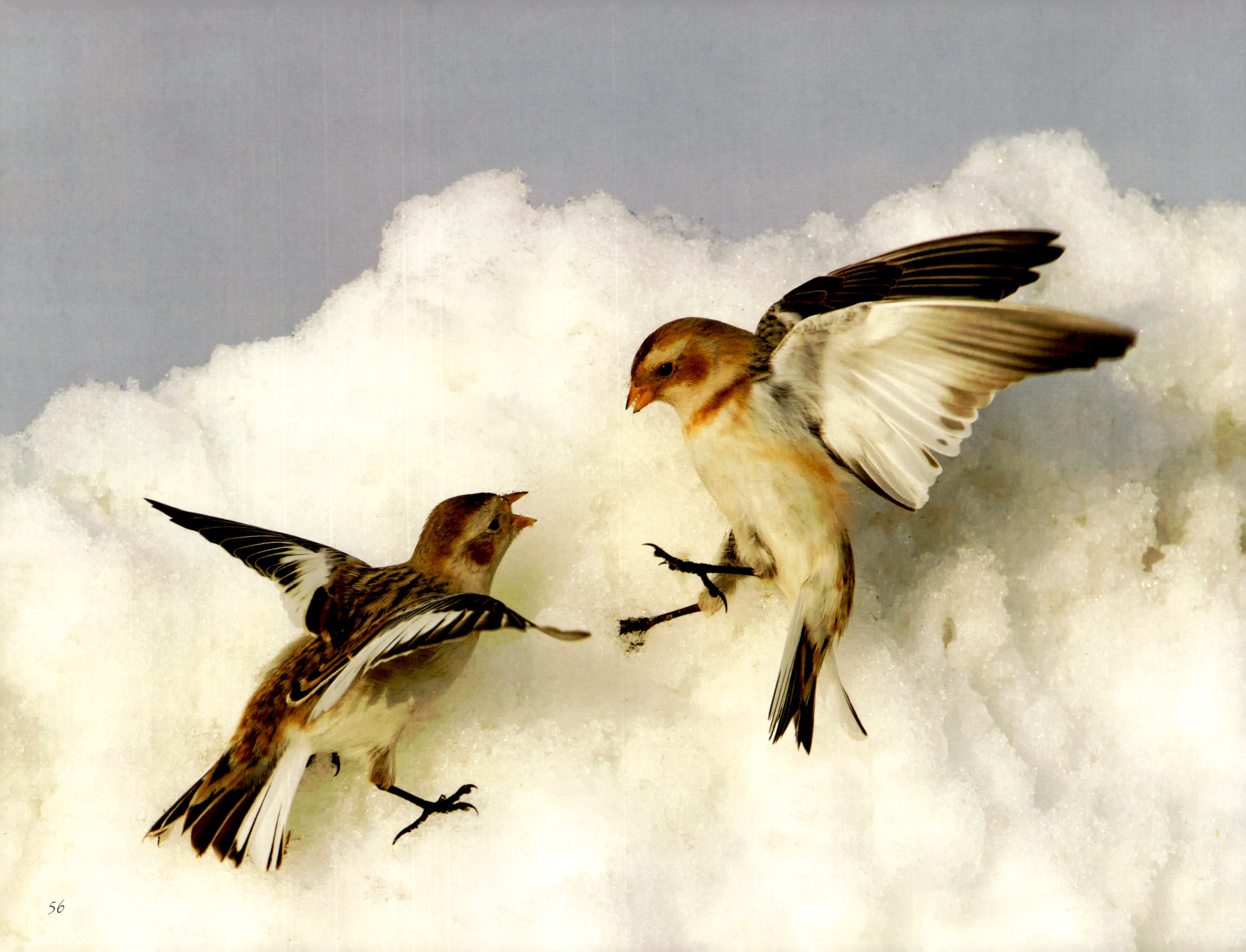

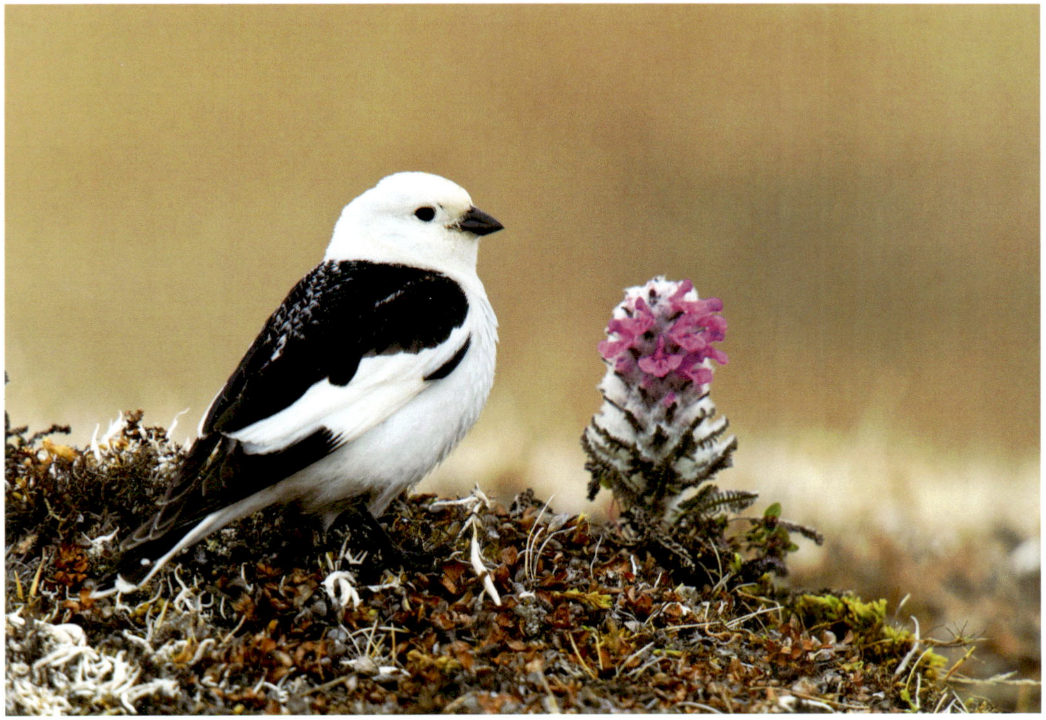

A breeding male Snow Bunting (left) has a pied, black and white plumage, and his sweet song is one of few musical sounds in the Arctic during warm summer months. *Photo by Scott Elowitz*

A very rare, breeding Ross's Gull (below) has a muted gray and white plumage, but a crisp, artistic head marking and bright red legs give this bird a distinctive appearance. Ross's Gulls spend most of their lives in cold, Arctic habitats. *Photo by Kevin T. Karlson*

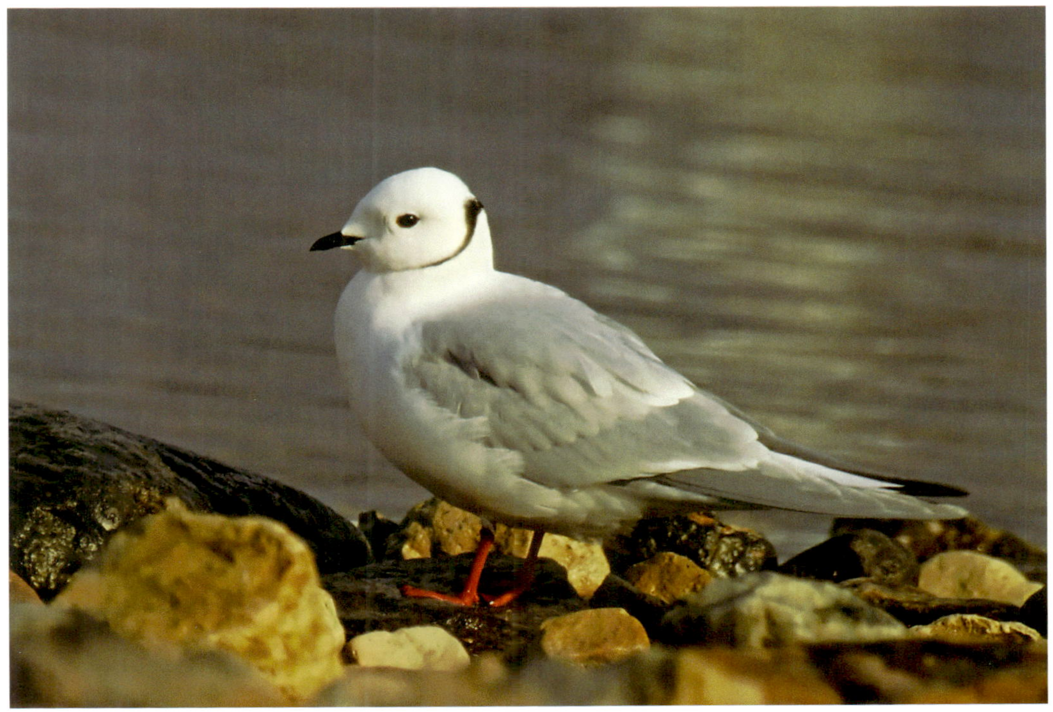

Opposite: Non-breeding Snow Buntings have a different plumage than the breeding male shown above. These two birds are having a difference of opinion on a snow mound. *Photo by Lloyd Spitalnik*

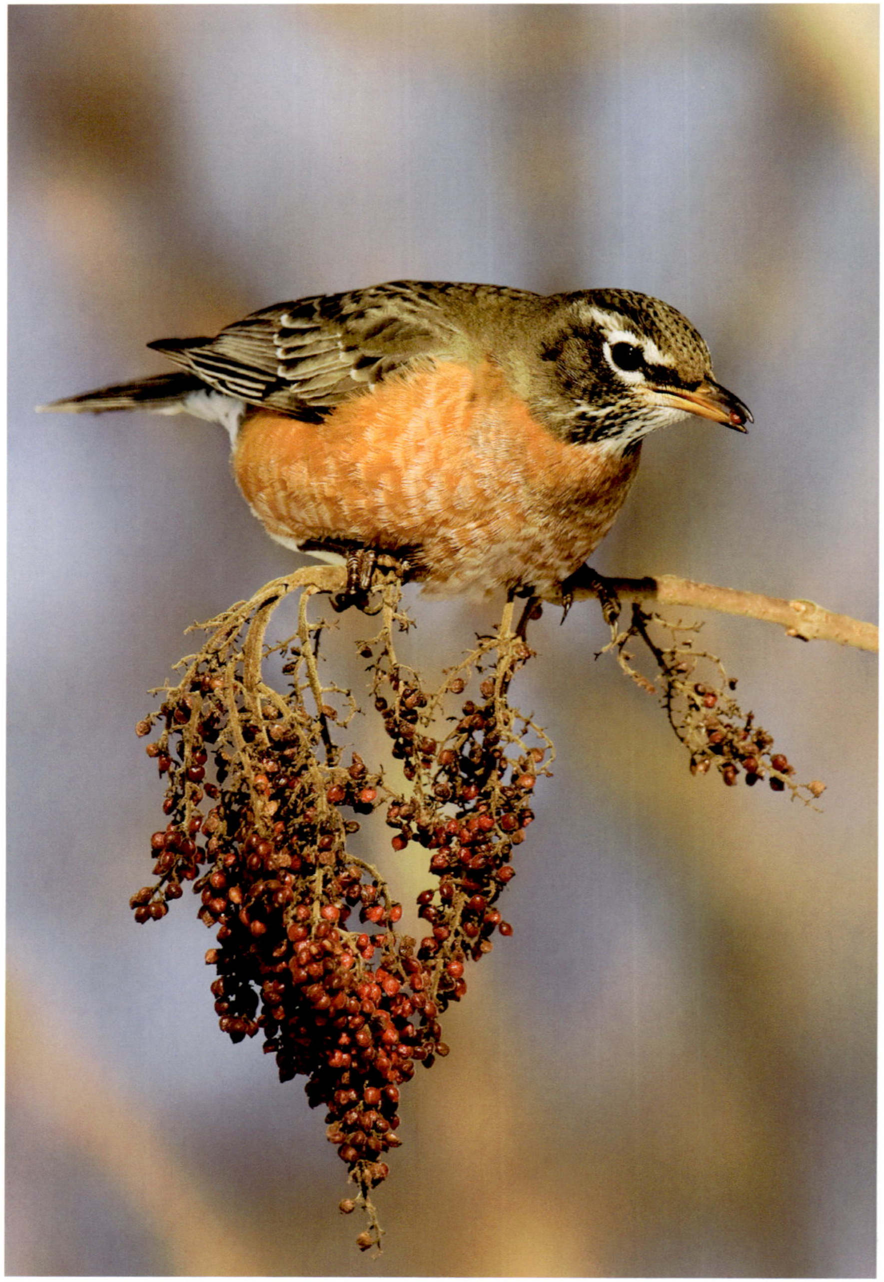

An American Robin is shown eating Sumac berries, which is an important food source for wintering birds. *Photo by Scott Elowitz*

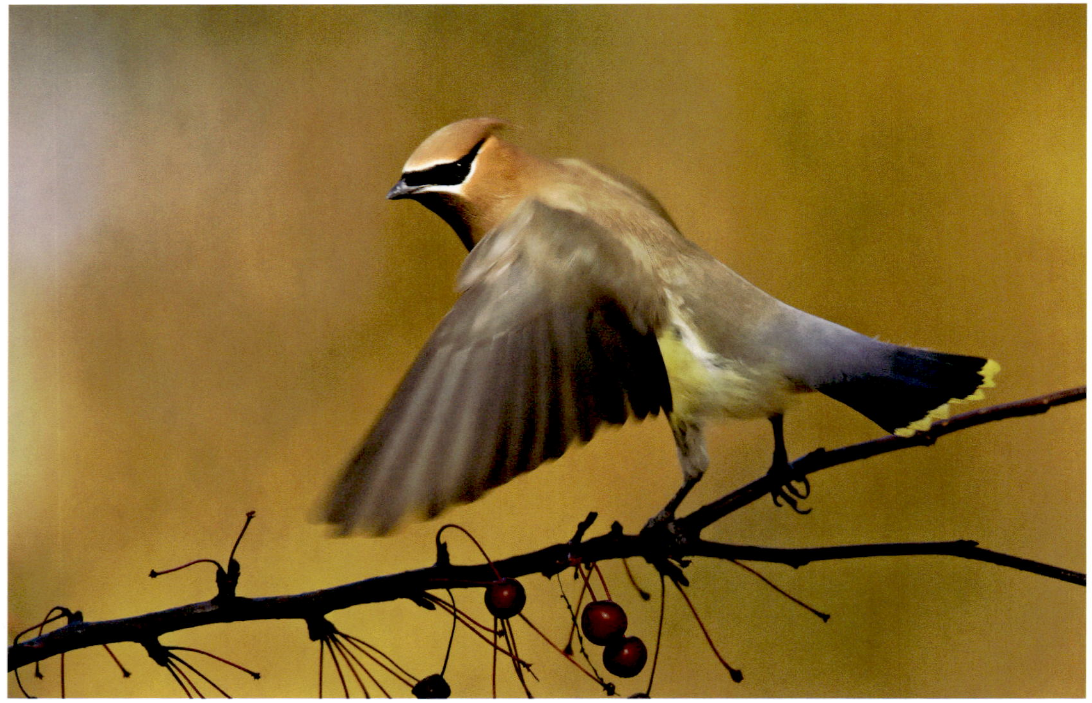

A Cedar Waxwing lifts off a branch as it takes flight. *Photo by Lloyd Spitalnik*

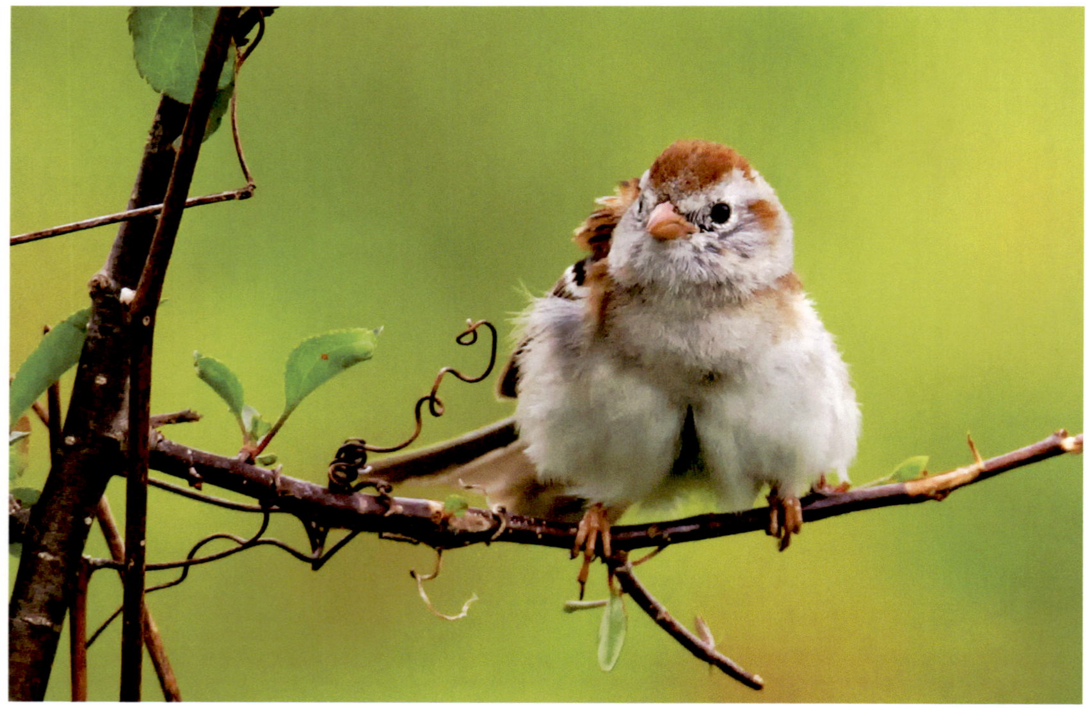

This Field Sparrow shows a different appearance with its fluffed feathers. *Photo by Lloyd Spitalnik*

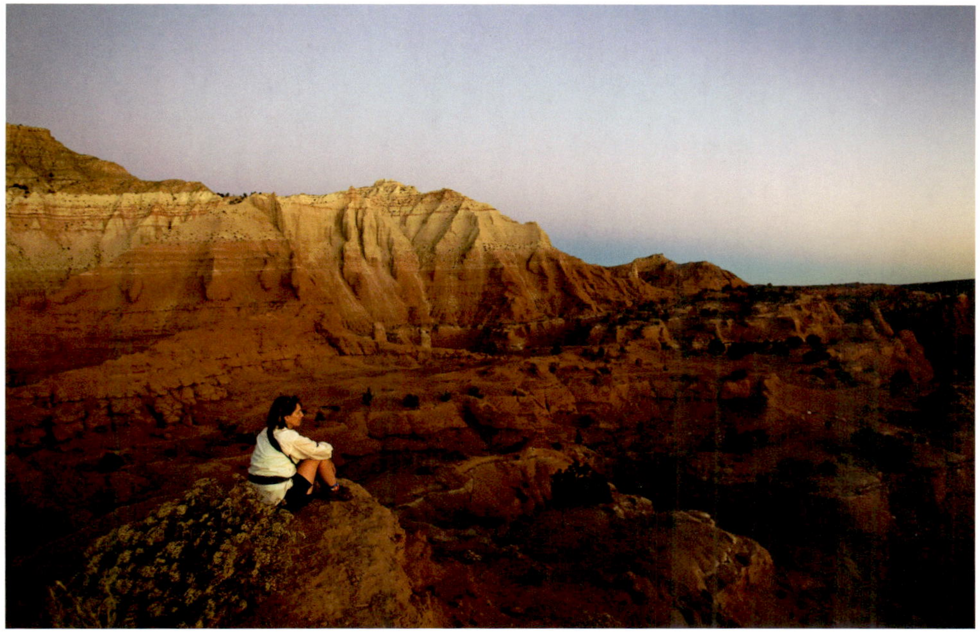

Touch the earth, love the earth, honor the earth, her plains, her valleys, her hills, and her seas; rest your spirit in her solitary places.

— Henry Beston

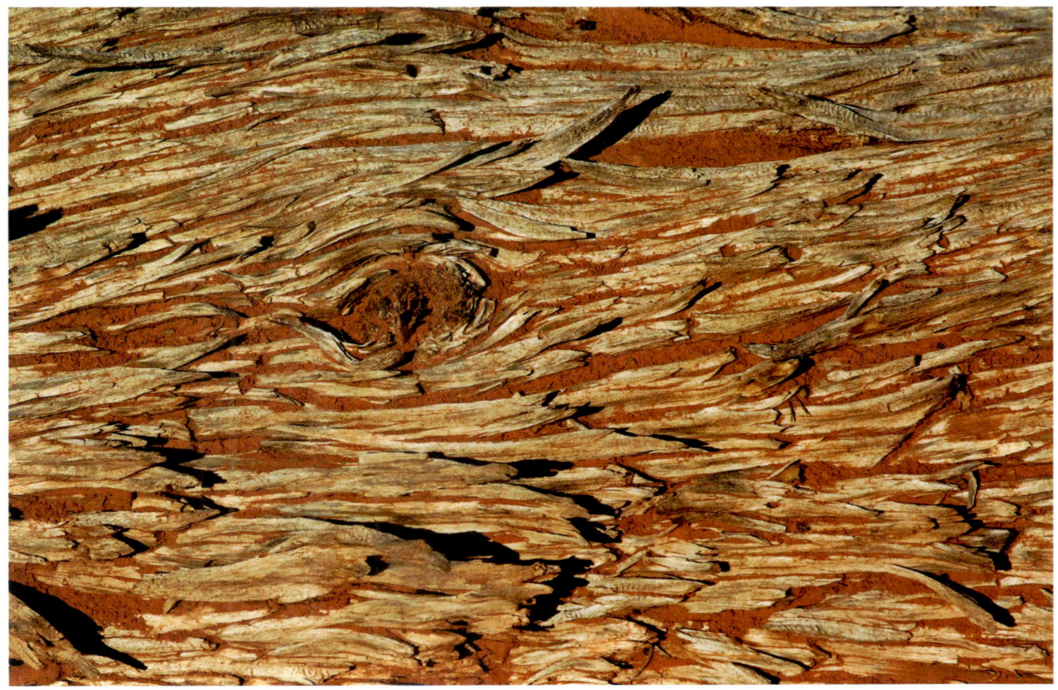

Kevin's wife Dale gazes upon a rugged earth scene at Kodachrome State Park in Utah, which is as picturesque as its name suggests.

A decaying juniper in the Utah desert catches airborne sand in its bark.
Photos by Kevin T. Karlson

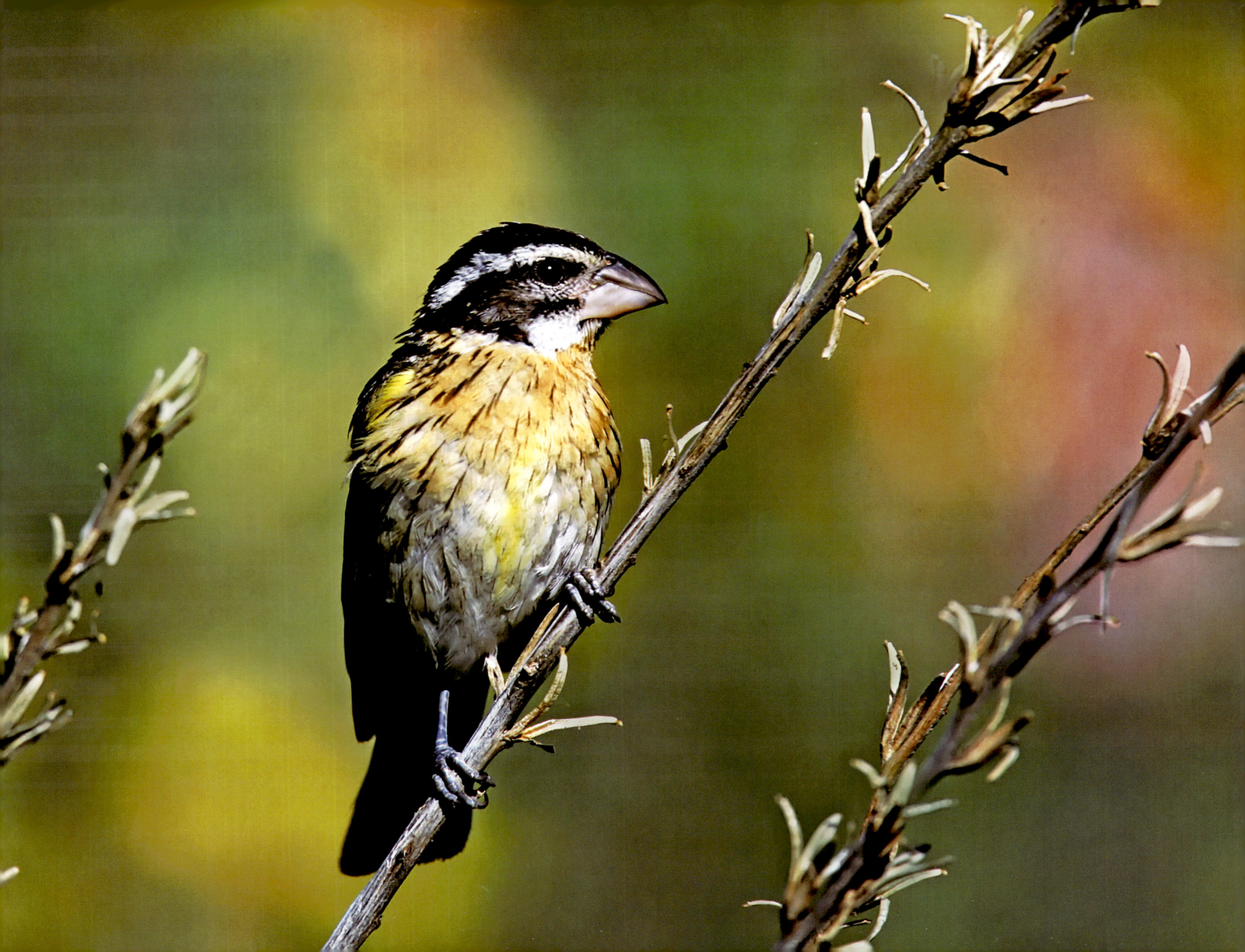

Opposite: This photo of a female Black-headed Grosbeak has always been one of Kevin's favorites because of the blurred colorful flowers in the background and the symmetrical nature of the branches. *Photo by Kevin T. Karlson*

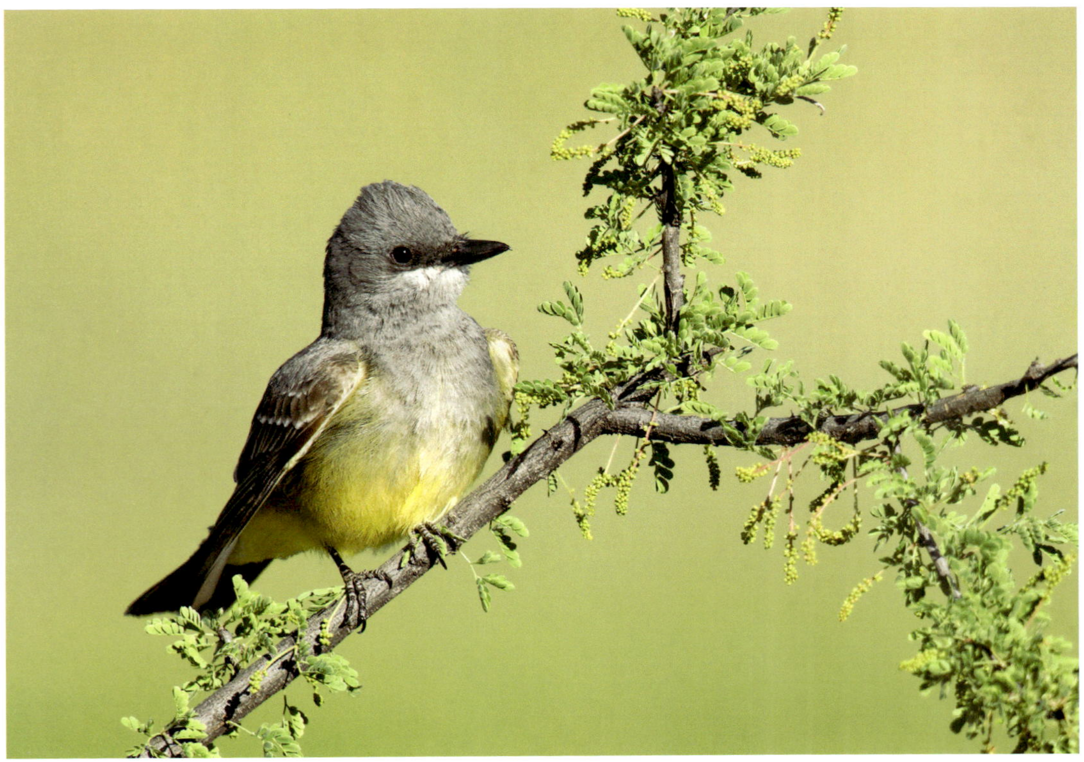

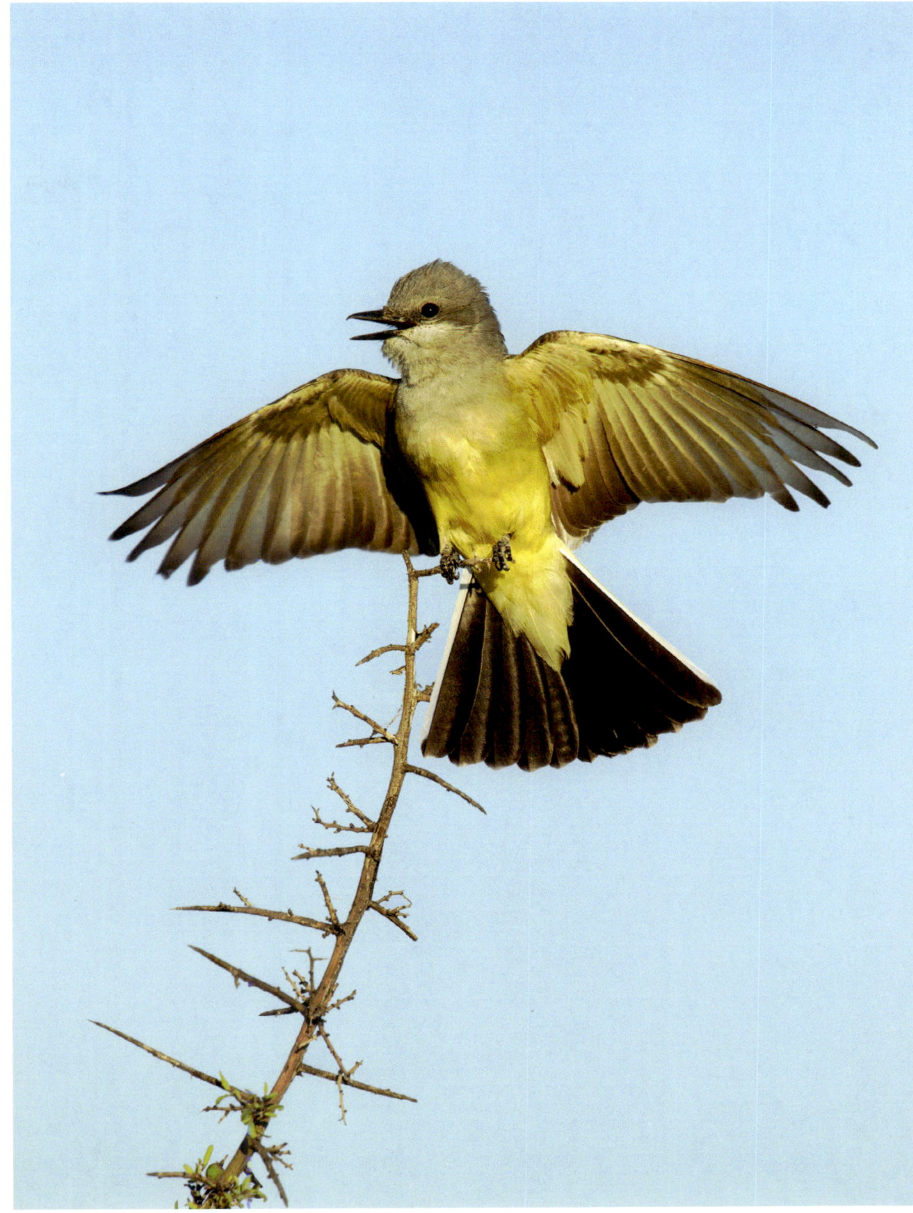

Cassin's Kingbird (left) is a feisty flycatcher that lords over his territory with vim and vigor. Western Kingbird (above) is similar to Cassin's in attitude and plumage, but has white outer tail feather edges and a paler gray chest. *Photos by Scott Elowitz*

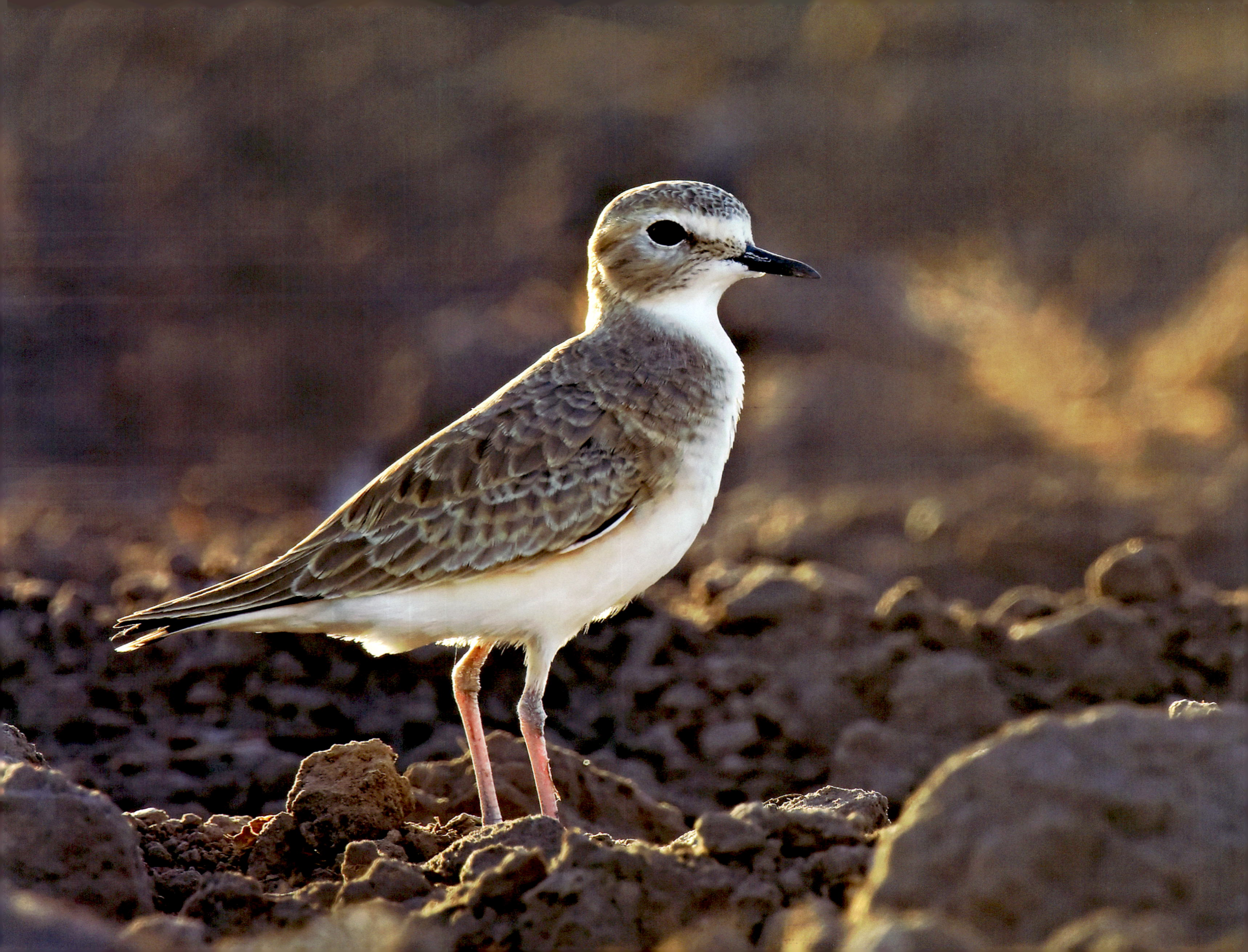

Opposite: The Mountain Plover is fondly referred to as the "ghost of the prairies" due to its pale earth-tone plumage and uncanny ability to vanish right before your eyes on the prairies. This juvenile bird was a long-awaited prize in Sebastian, Texas, in November 2010. *Photo by Kevin T. Karlson*

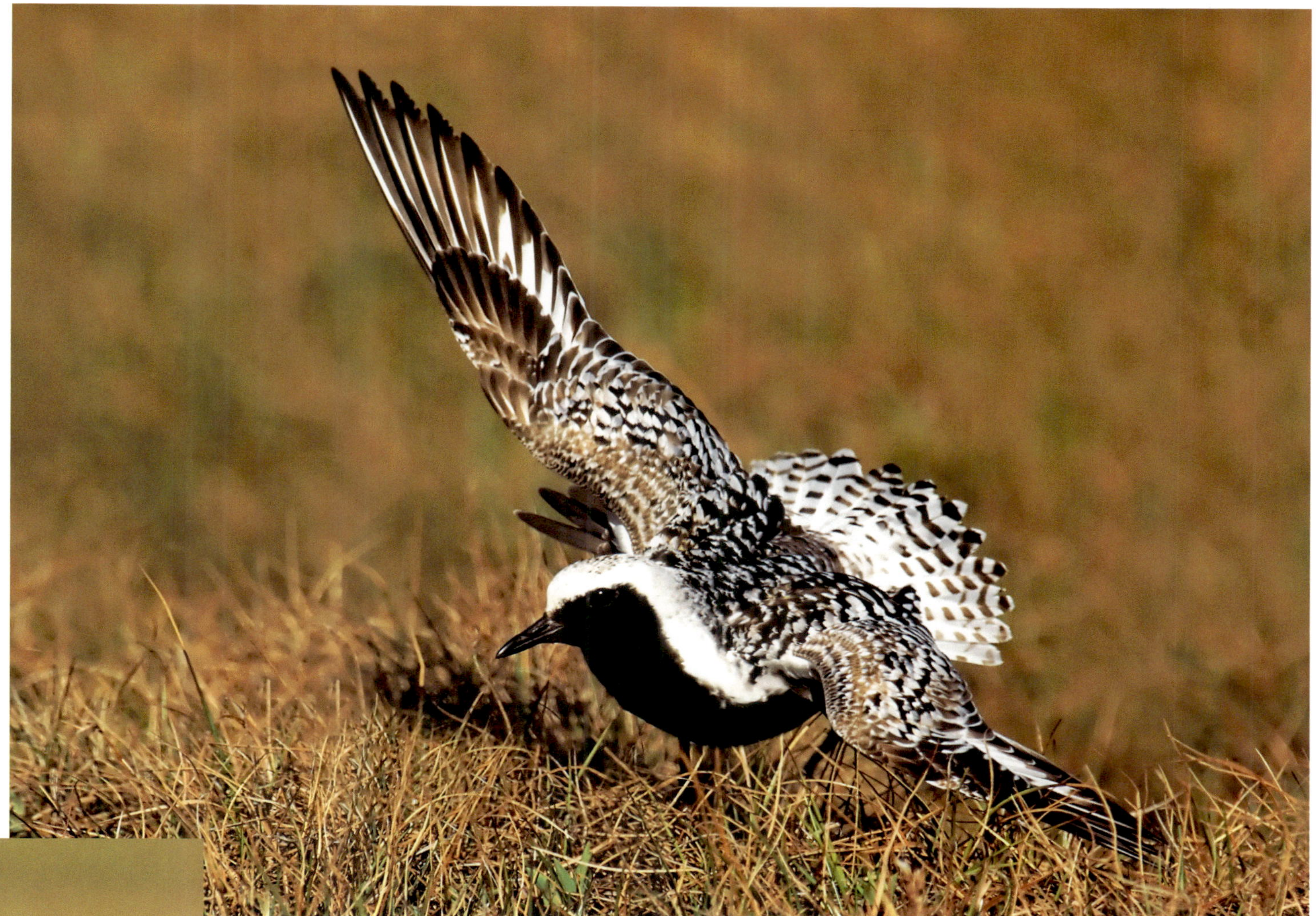

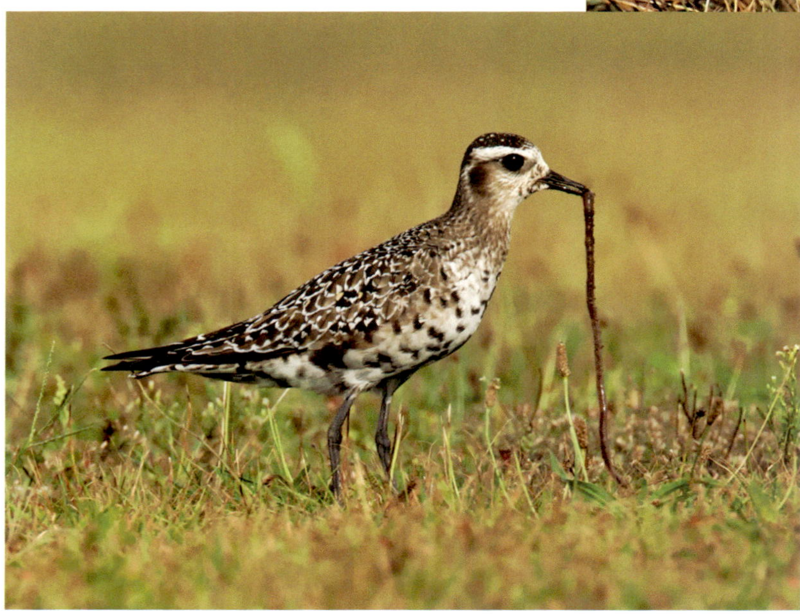

A breeding male Black-bellied Plover (above) is shown performing a distraction display near his nest on the Arctic tundra. A molting American Golden Plover (left) is about to enjoy a protein-rich worm meal. *Photos by Kevin T. Karlson (upper) and Lloyd Spitalnik (left)*

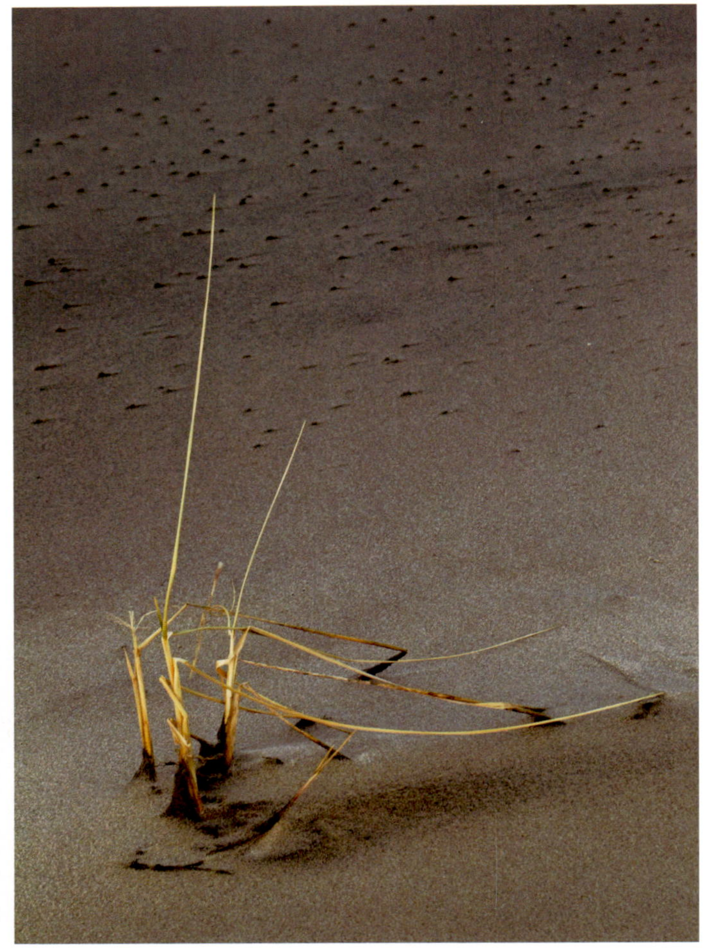

Earth is often represented by subtle tones of gray that blend to black. Wind, waves and beach grass are responsible for the Zen-like mood depicted in these photos. *Photos by Kevin T. Karlson*

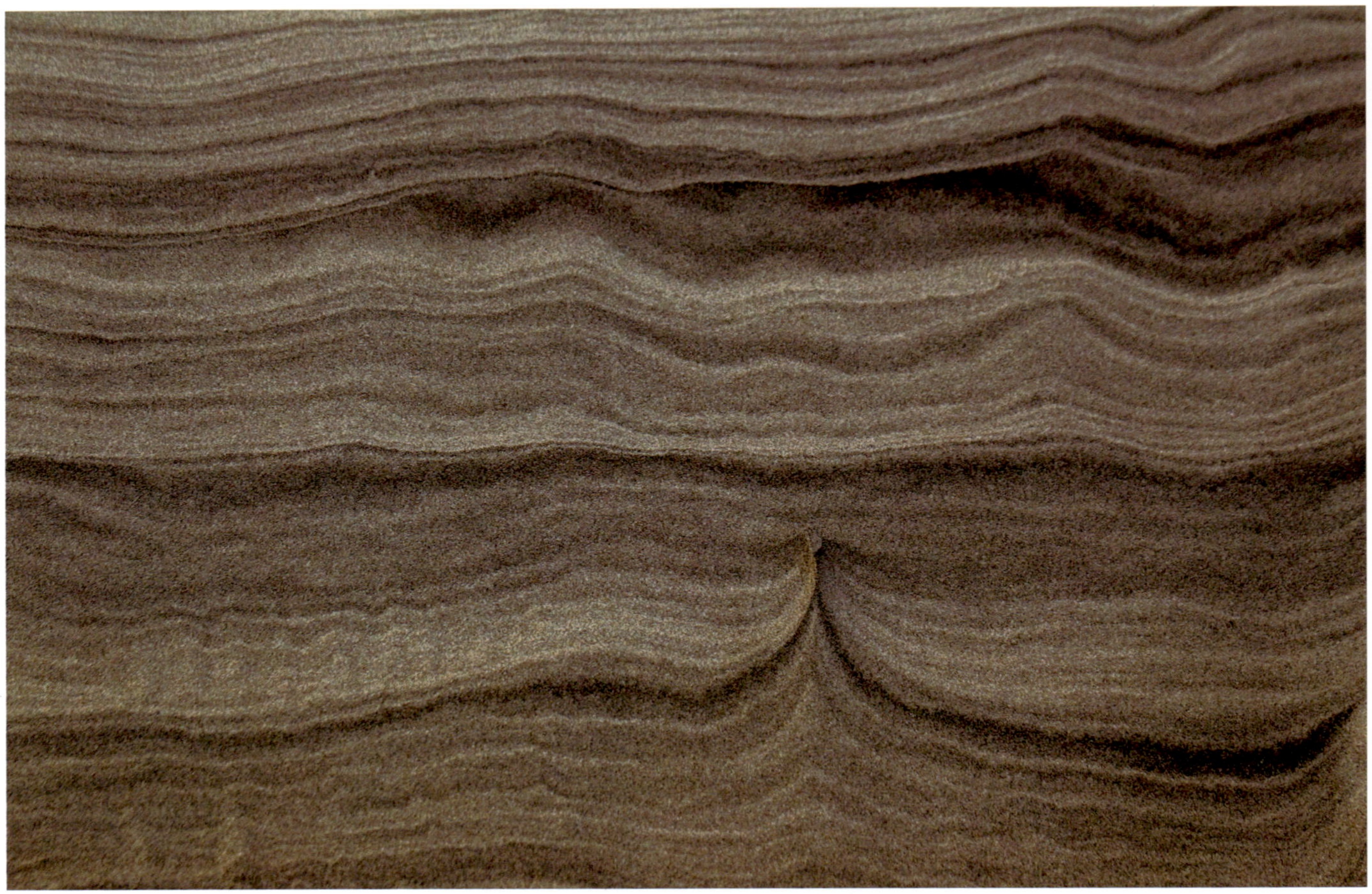

Opposite: Differential weathering of the earth's bedrock creates animated rock formations called "hoodoos." These two hoodoos were purposefully underexposed at midday, which resulted in the silhouette impression of two people walking along the ridge. With some imagination, you might see a woman carrying a baby on her shoulder. *Photo by Kevin T. Karlson*

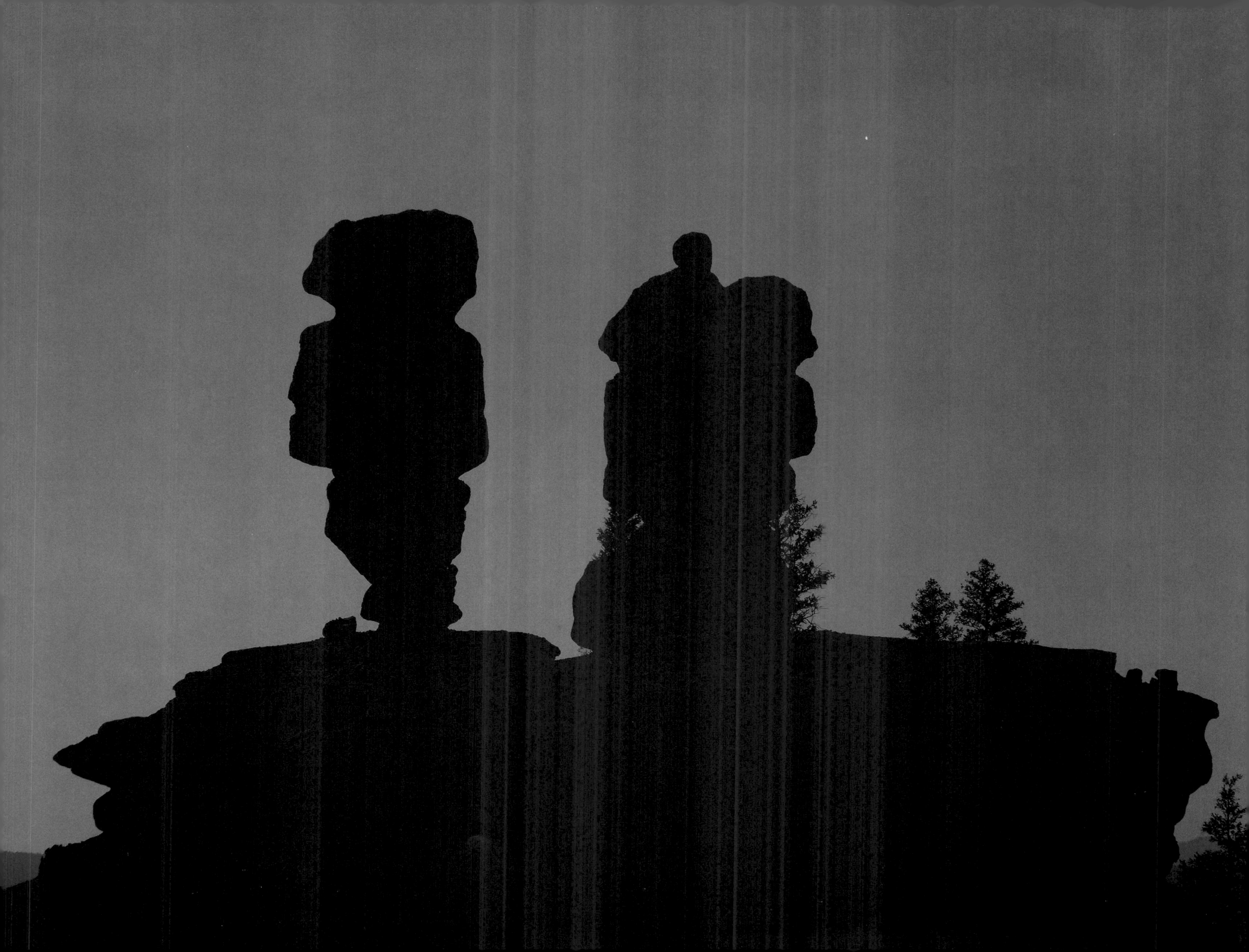

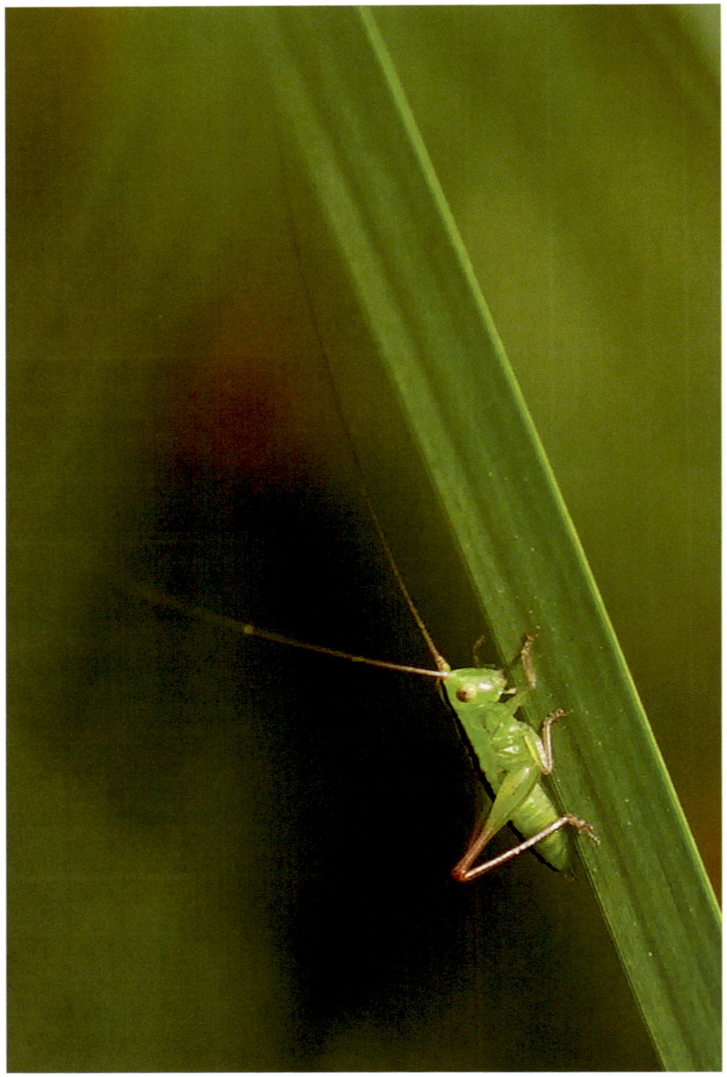

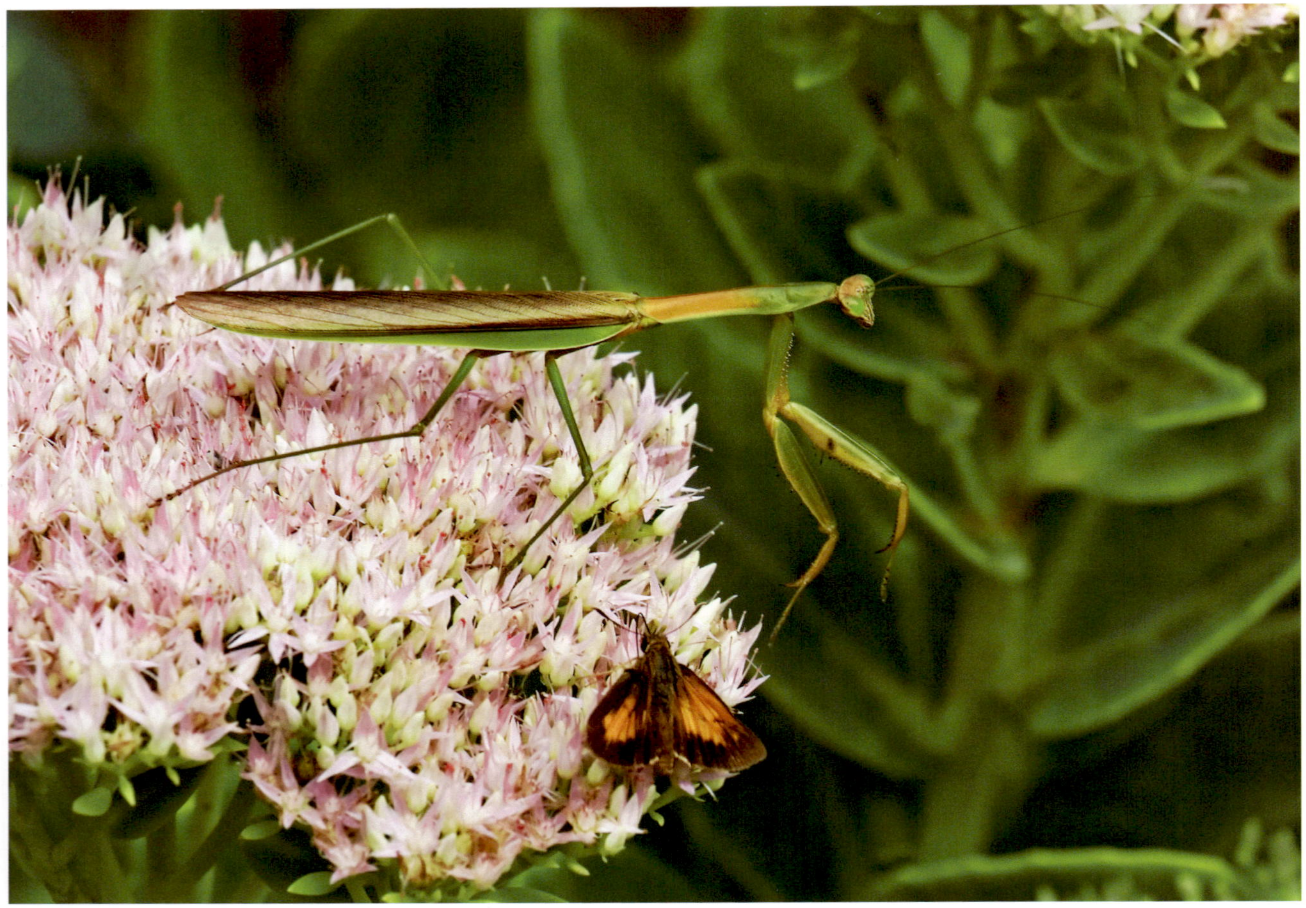

Lesser Meadow Katydid nymph (left) is a tiny insect whose size is well depicted by its direct comparison to a blade of grass. *Photo by Lloyd Spitalnik*

A skipper butterfly (above) takes a big chance by nectaring on a flowering sedum while a predatory Praying Mantis looms nearby. The mantis disregarded the butterfly — this time! *Photo by Kevin T. Karlson*

Opposite: A Cedar Waxwing plucks a ripe Fiddlewood berry on South Padre Island, Texas. *Photo by Mike Hannisian*

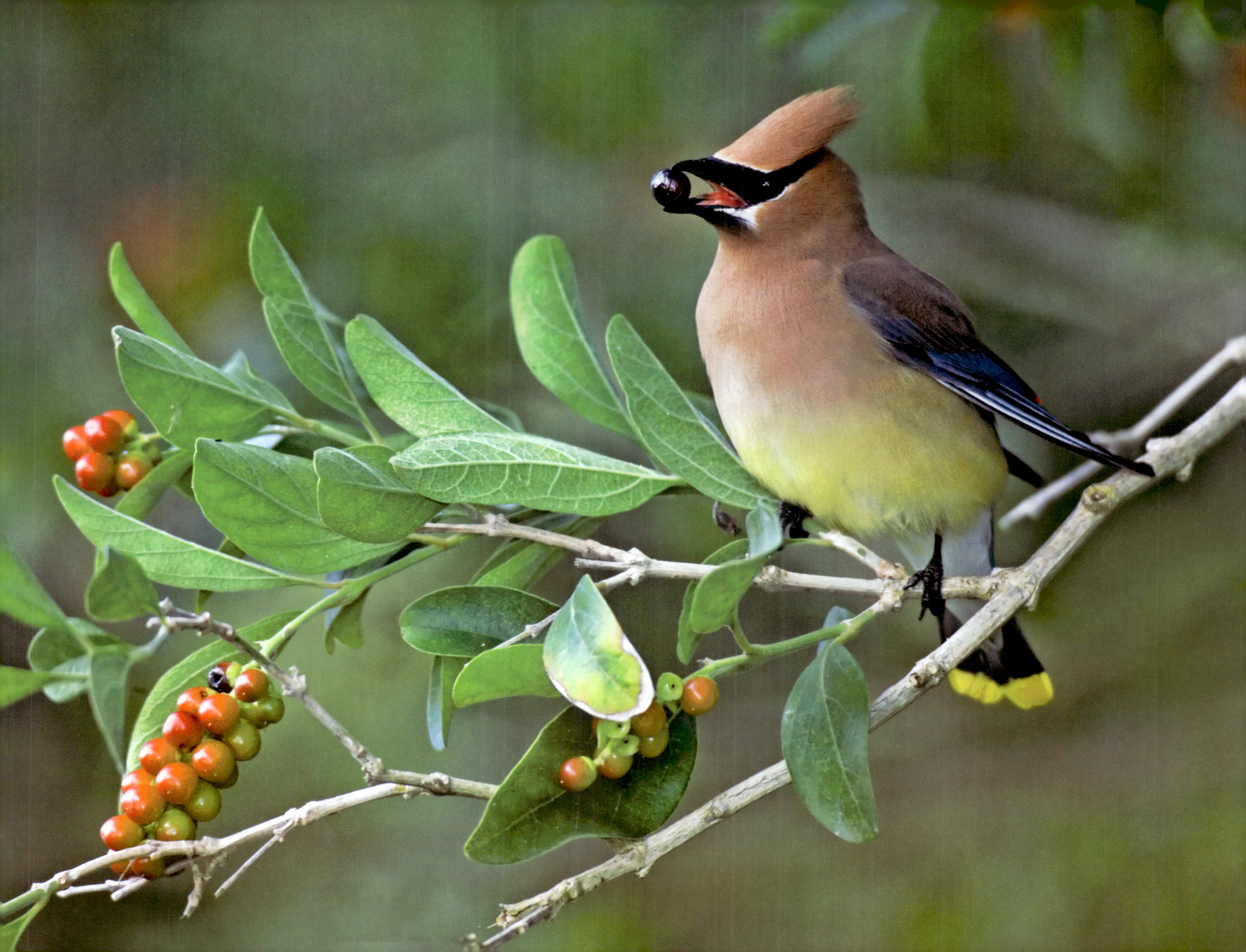

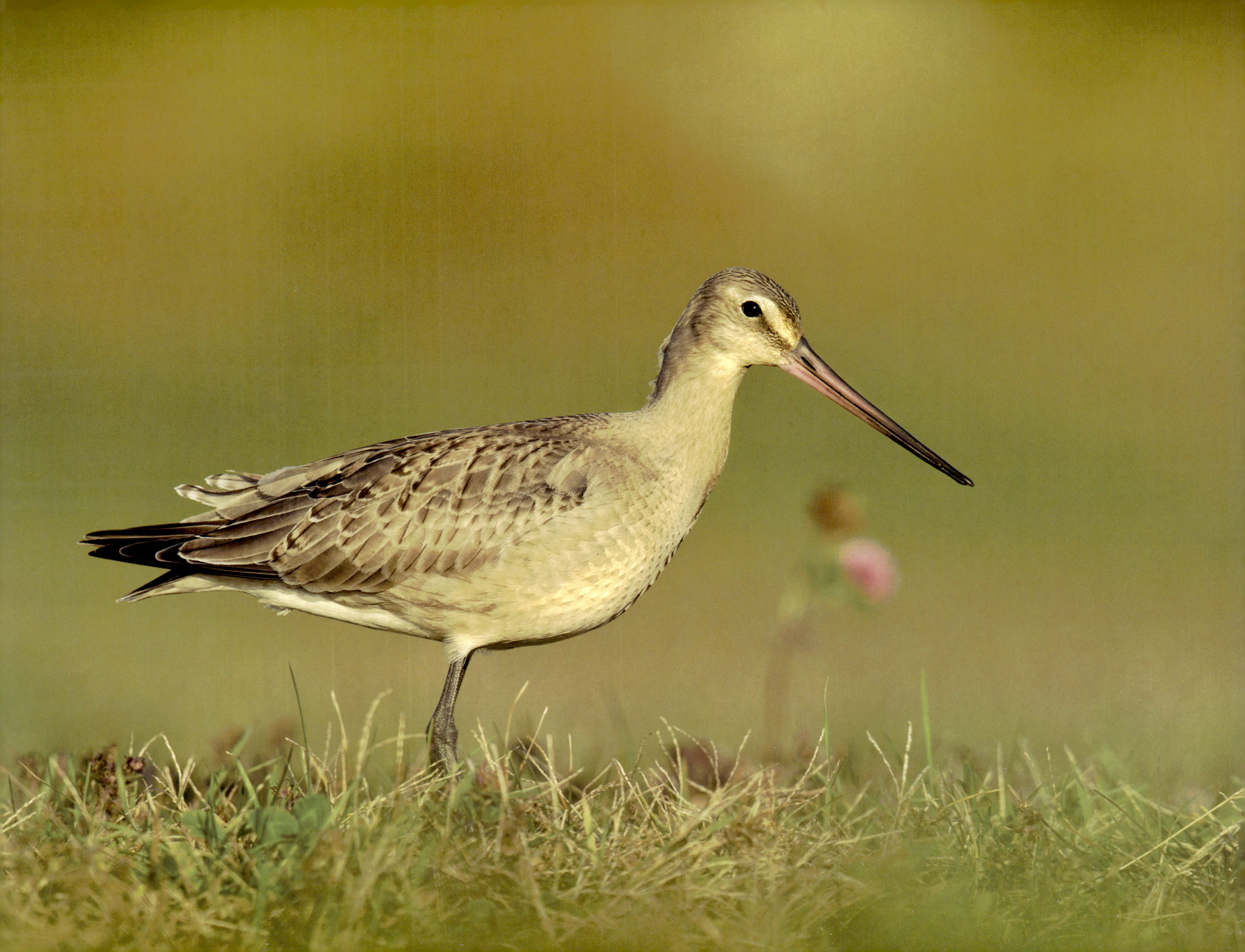

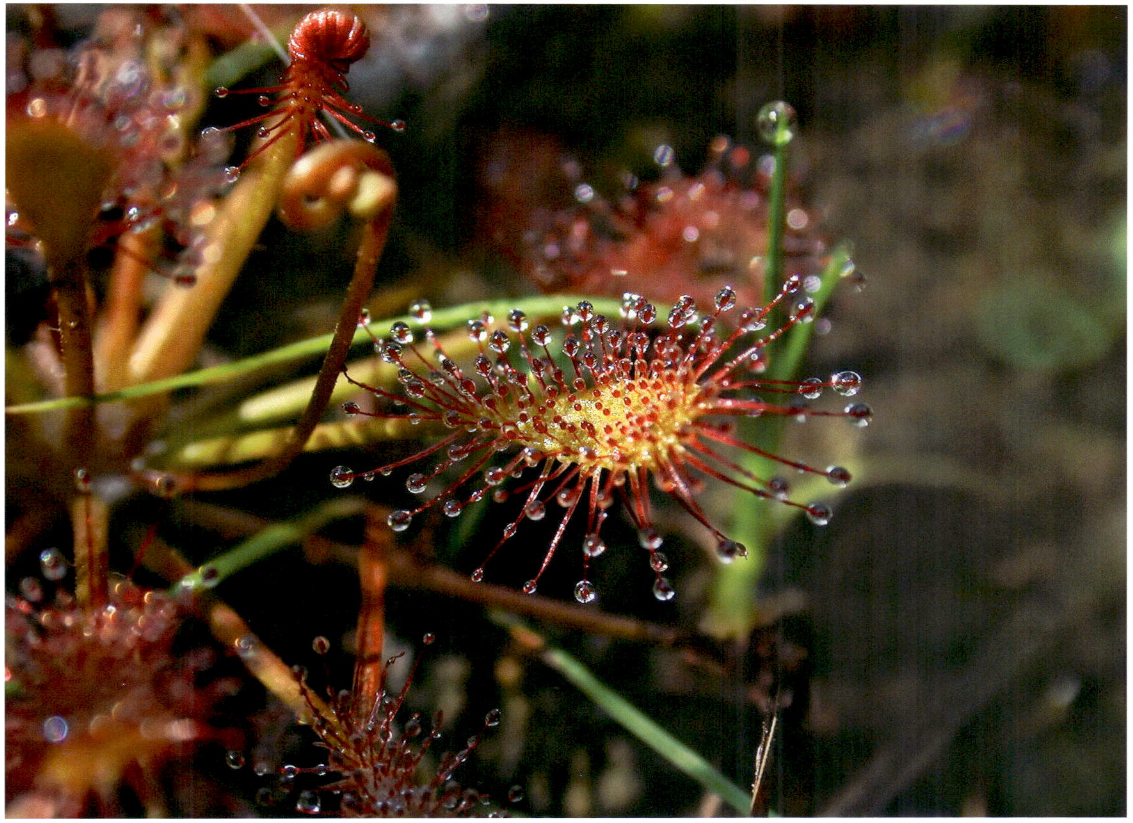

Never lose an opportunity of seeing anything that is beautiful, for beauty is God's handwriting — a wayside sacrament. Welcome it in every fair face, in every fair sky, in every flower, and thank God for it as a cup of blessing.

— Ralph Waldo Emerson

Honey traps work well when danger is disguised by beauty. The glistening globules on these Spoon-leaved Sundew leaves look wonderful, but are there to attract insects. Unfortunates who venture too close end their lives as food for the plant, allowing Sundews to grow in otherwise nutrient-poor areas such as sphagnum bogs. *Photo and caption by Mike Crewe*

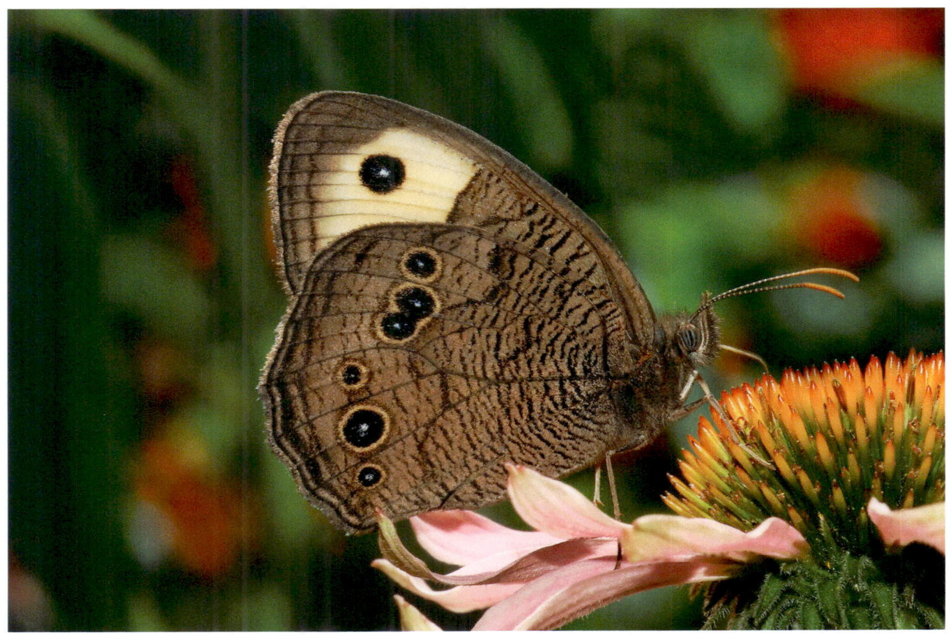

A Common Wood-Nymph (right) is so wonderfully camouflaged that it seemingly disappears from view when perched on a tree trunk. This one was lured to a Purple Coneflower in the photographer's wildlife garden in Goshen, New Jersey. *Photo by Pat Sutton*

Opposite: Although a bird of wet habitats, the Hudsonian Godwit occasionally forages in grassy areas. This smart-looking juvenile was photographed feeding on a grass border near the Connecticut shoreline in fall during its southern migration. *Photo by Scott Elowitz*

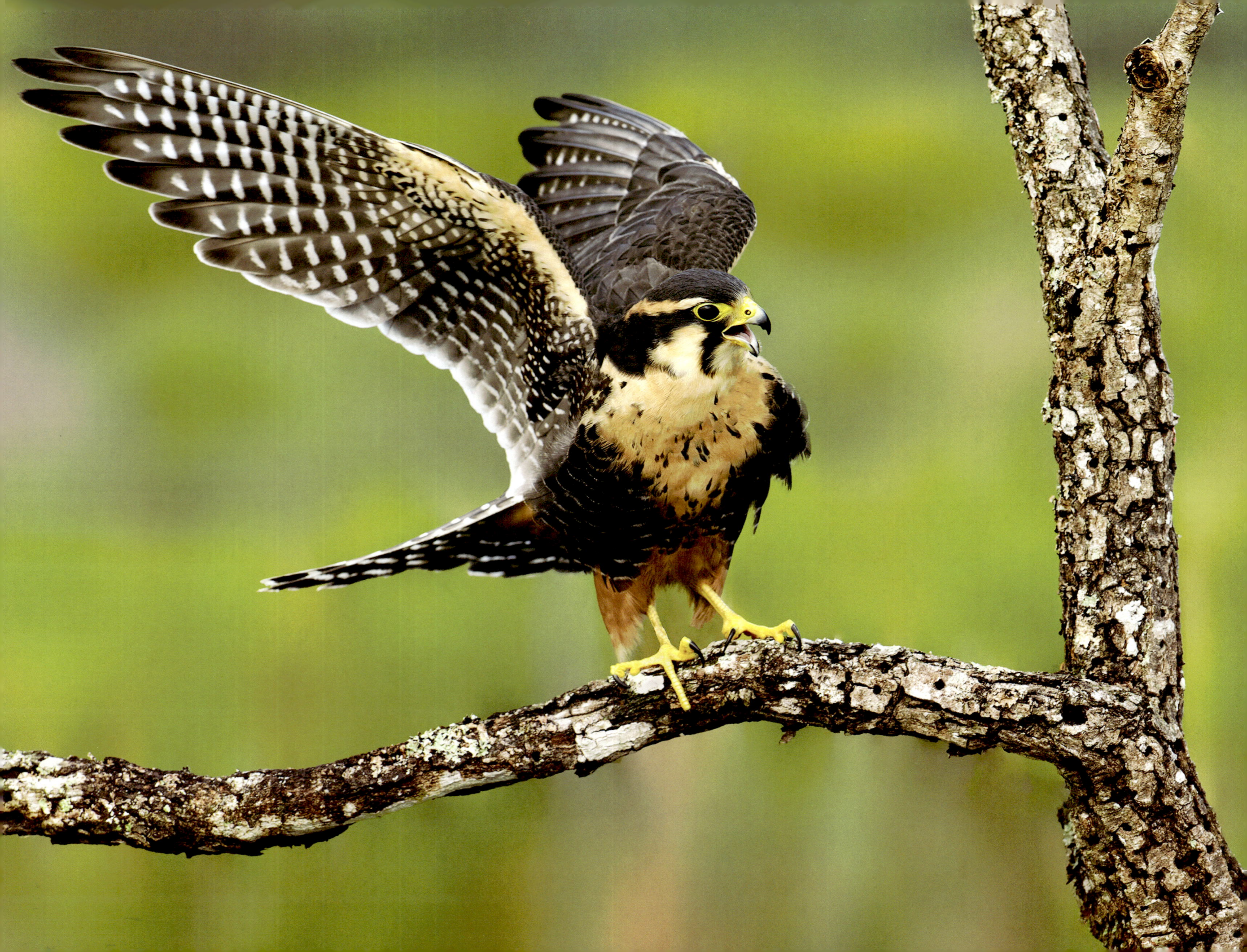

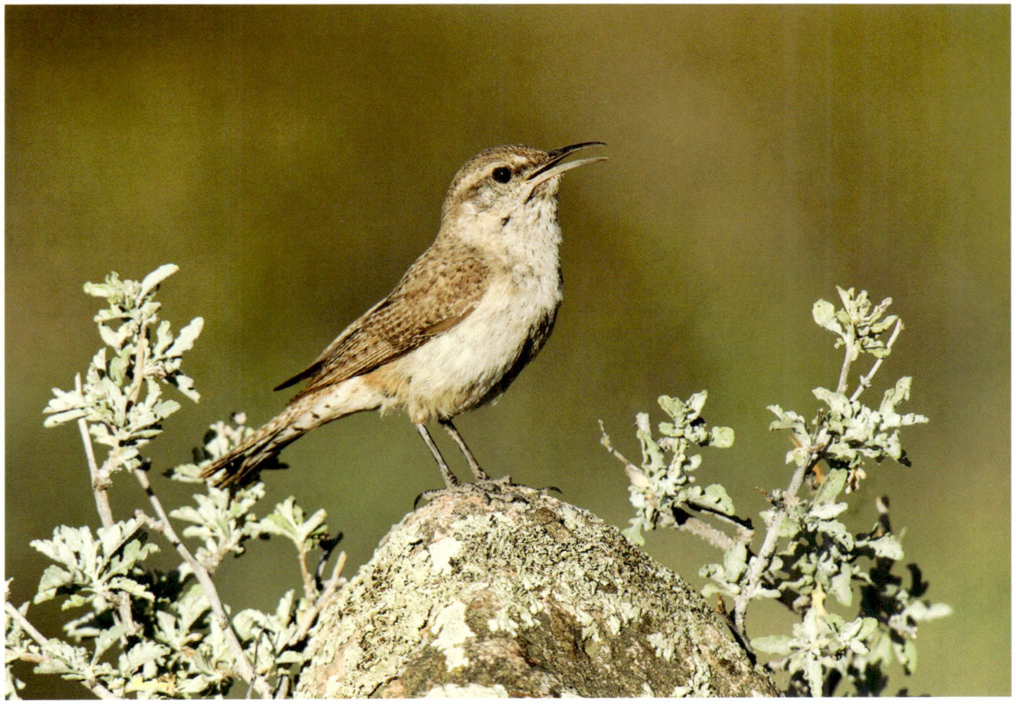

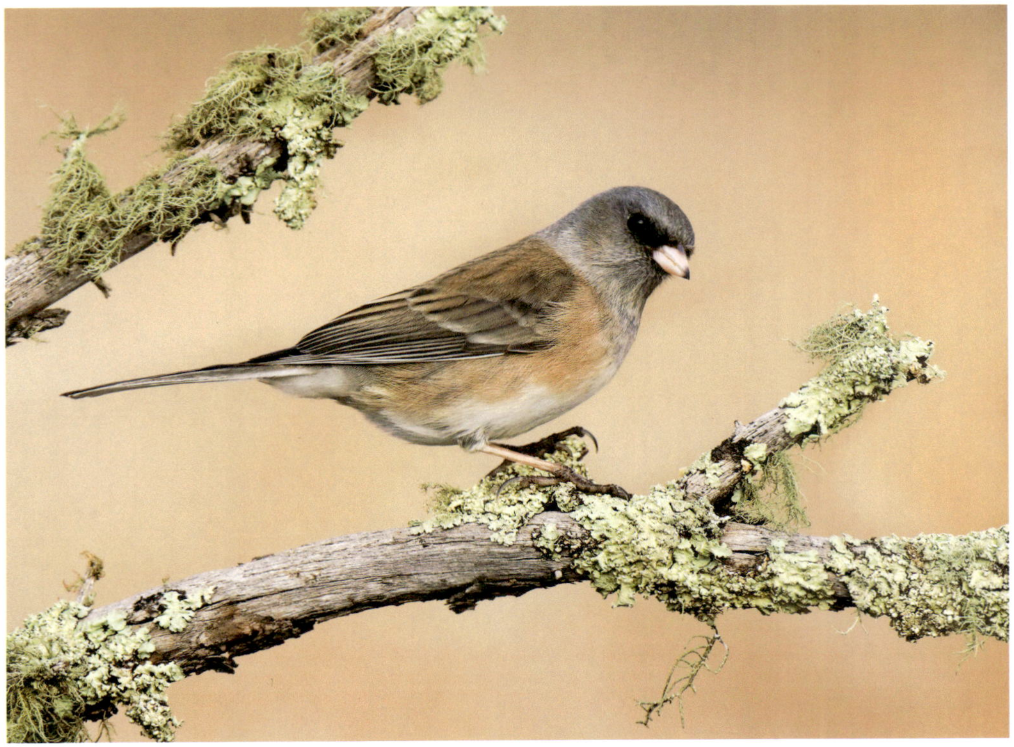

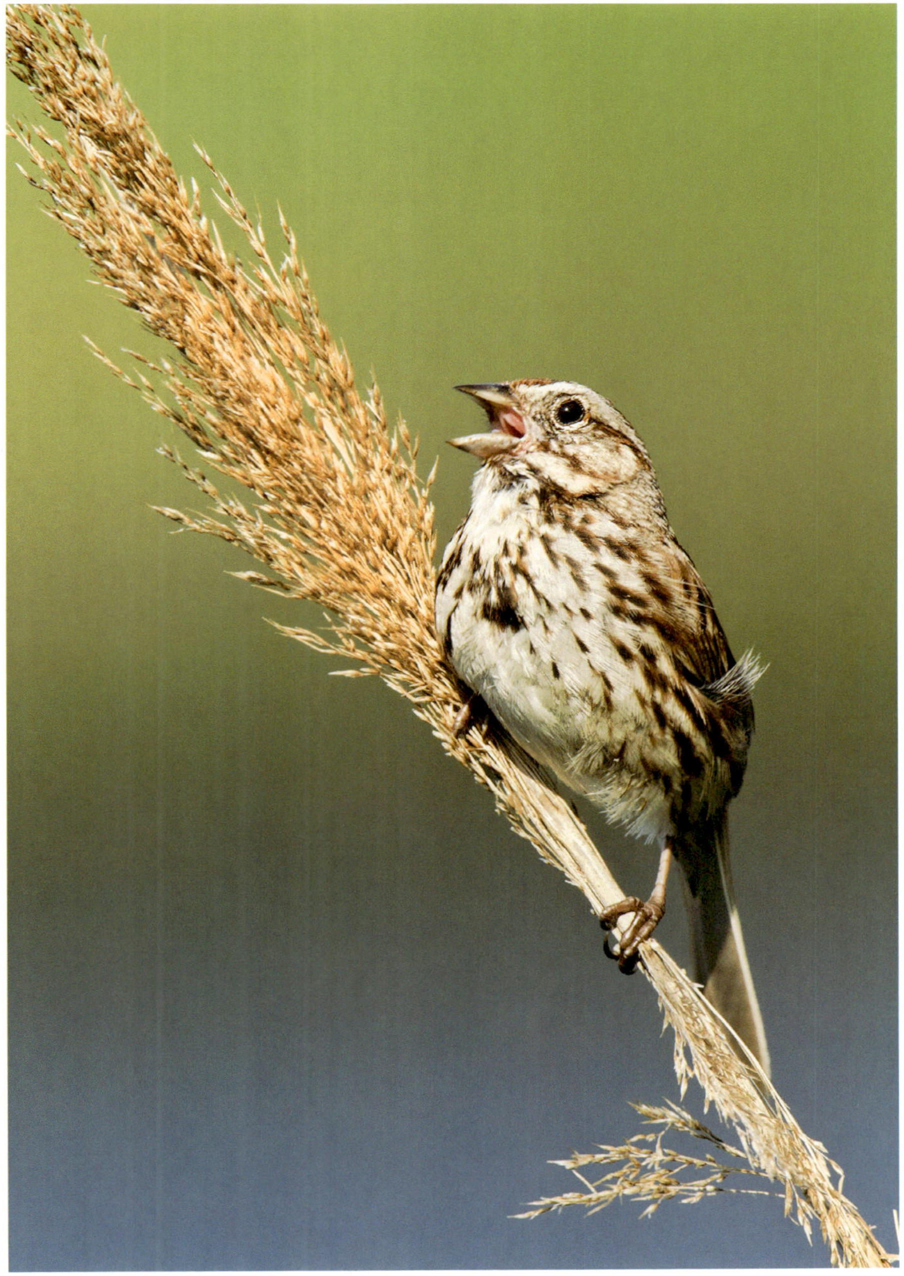

A Rock Wren (upper left) sings a warbling song in a desert landscape. Two images of Pink-sided Junco (left) and a singing Song Sparrow (above) are rich with warm earth tones. *Photos by Scott Elowitz*

Opposite: An Aplomado Falcon flashes its wings as it lands on a branch. *Photo by Scott Elowitz*

Fire

Fire is the most volatile of all the earth's elements. Its unbridled fury can either rejuvenate or destroy. In our minds, the sun often suggests fire, since it is the ultimate ball of fire in the sky and has the ability to transform the cool blue tones of a late day sky into a fiery inferno, like the sunset shown on this page. Ever since humans learned to control fire, it has provided us with a force of nature that has the ability to transform our lives. When fire gets out of control, such as recent wildfires in the western U.S., it can cause destruction beyond belief.

Many scenes in nature approximate the mood of fire because of their red, yellow, or orange colors. Sunsets are the most obvious representation of fire, but so are other parts of nature that stimulate our imagination to envision fire. These include autumn leaves, flowers, butterflies, insects, plants, bird's plumages, and red soil or bedrock. Some images in this section may only have a small red splotch of color, but it is enough to awaken the mood of fire in our minds.

Sunsets are so beautiful that they almost seem as if we were looking through the gates of heaven.

— John Lubbock

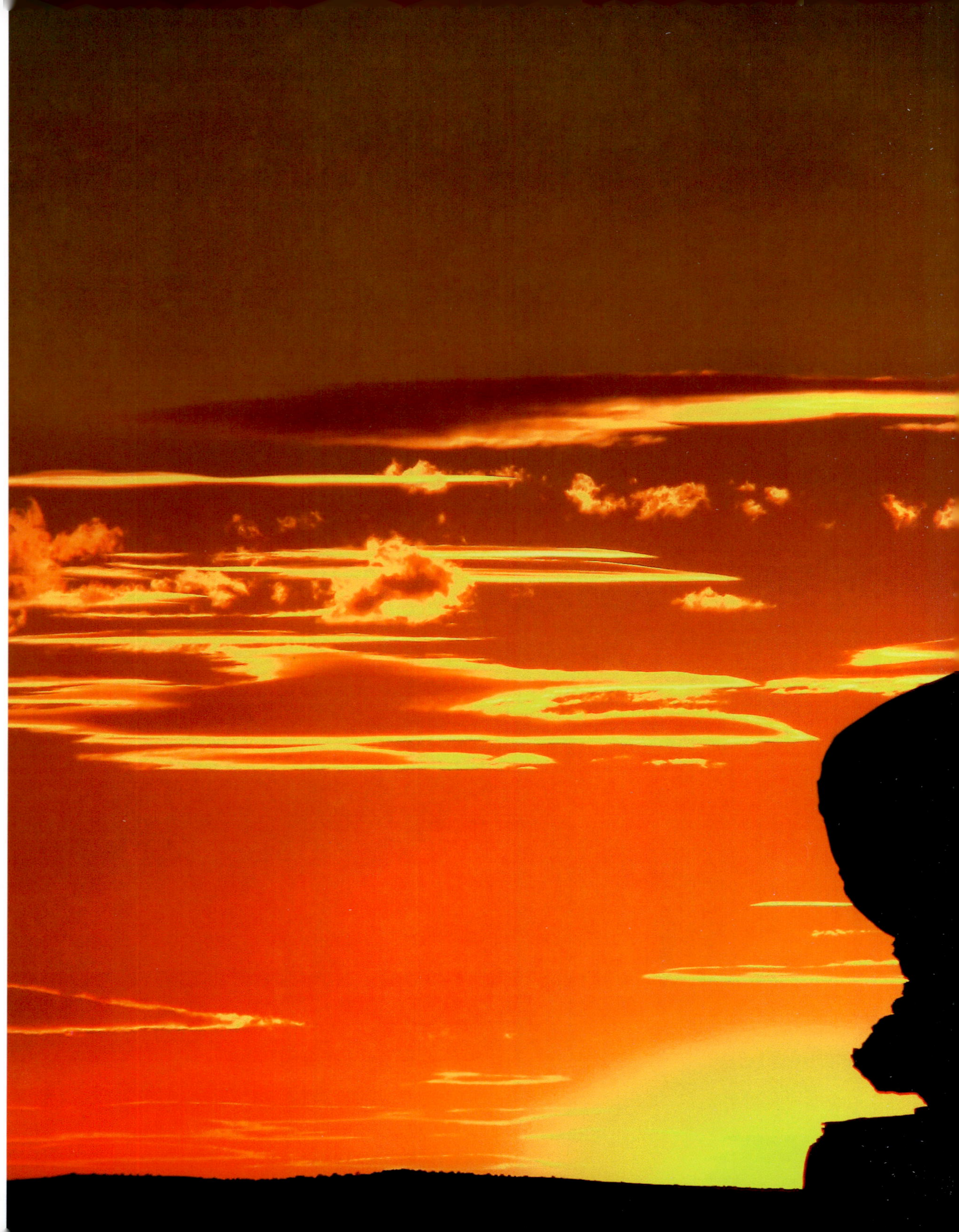

The sky is ablaze in this amazing sunset framed by a cliff face in Canyonlands National Monument in Utah. *Photo by Dale Rosselet*

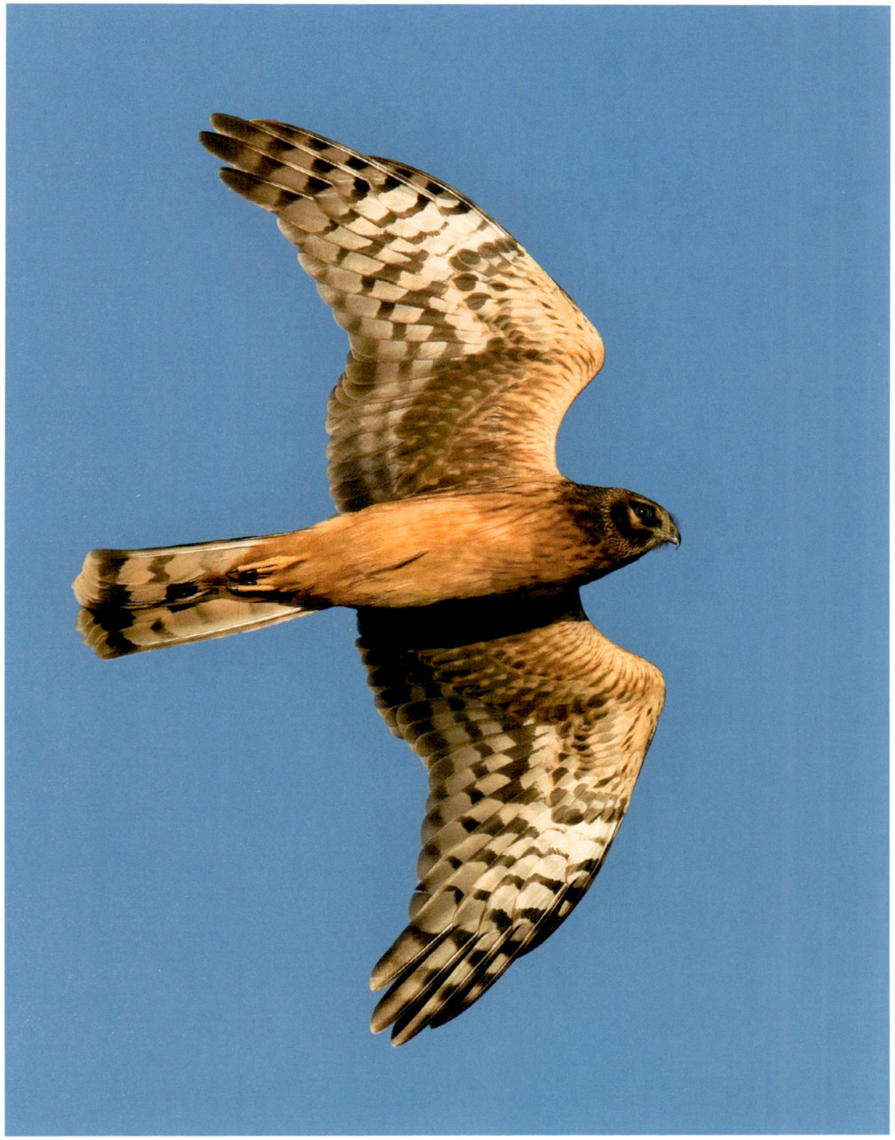

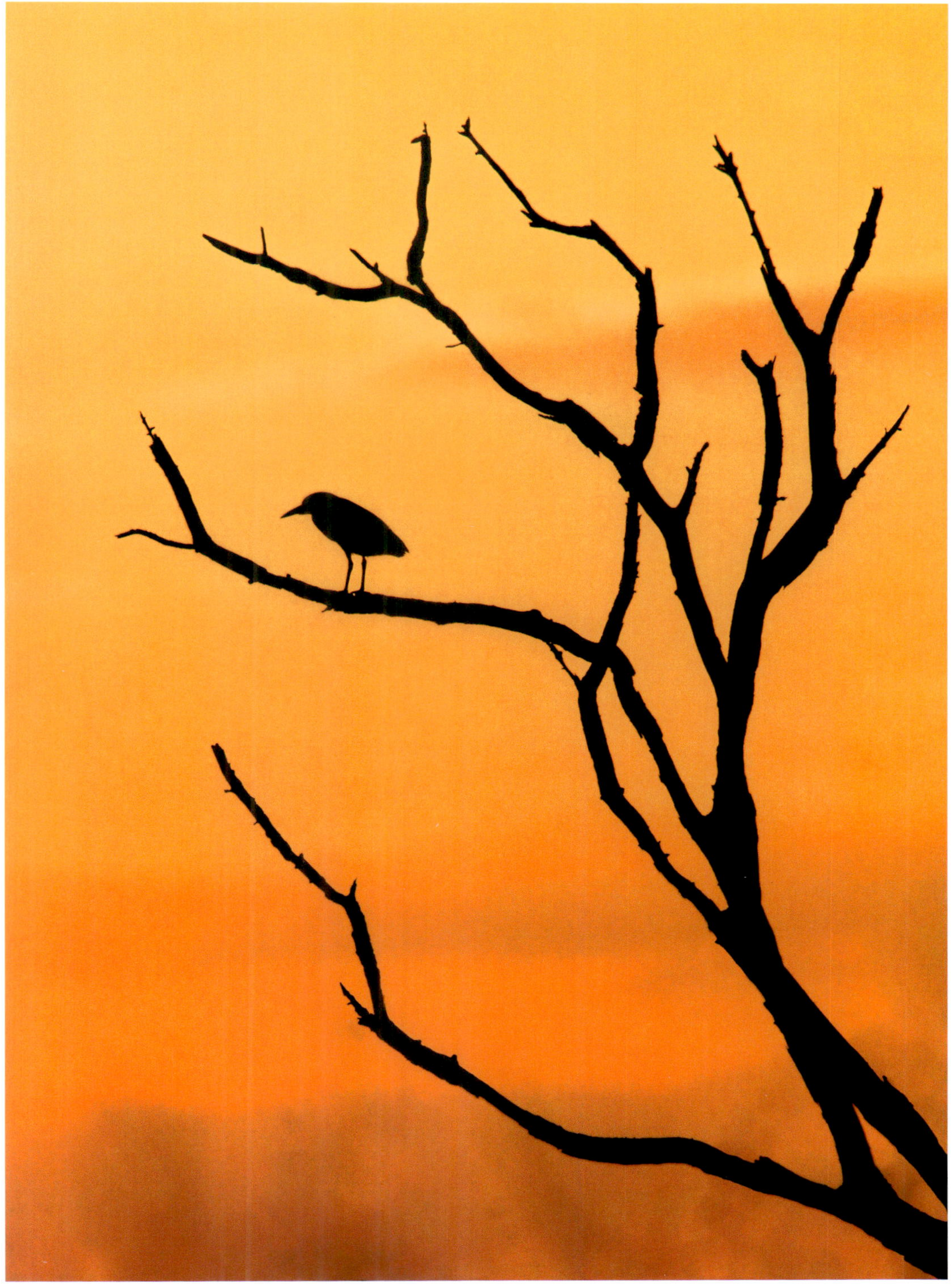

Late day light warms the breast feathers of this juvenile Northern Harrier (above), while a lone Black-crowned Night-Heron is silhouetted against the setting sun in a stark tree. *Photos by Scott Elowitz*

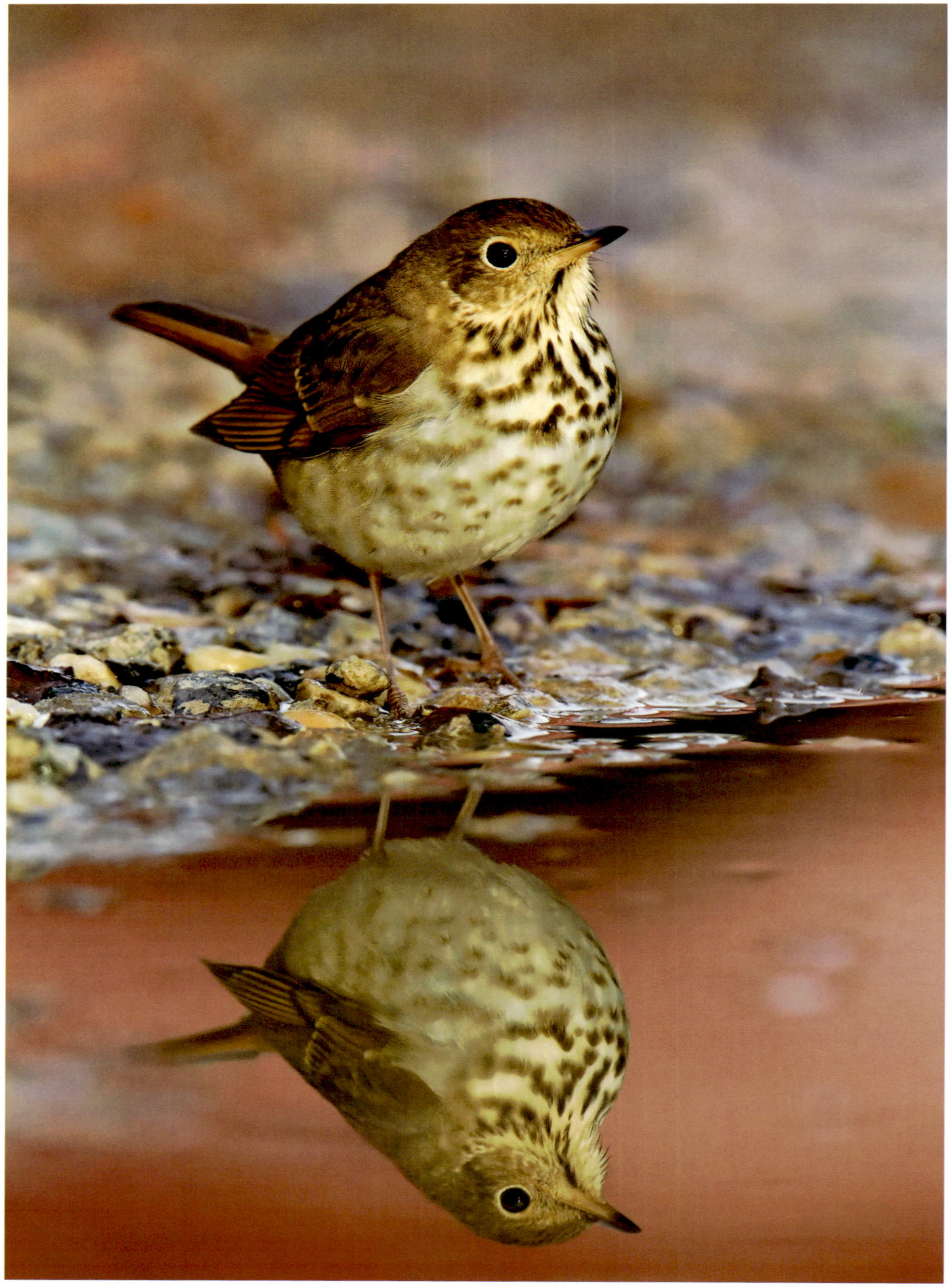

A Hermit Thrush in late fall is mirrored in a water pool, which reflects the fiery colors of autumn and the red van parked nearby. *Photo by Kevin T. Karlson*

The deep red bark of a prostrate Manzanita at the top of Angel's Landing in Zion National Park imparts a subtle fiery. *Photo by Kevin T. Karlson*

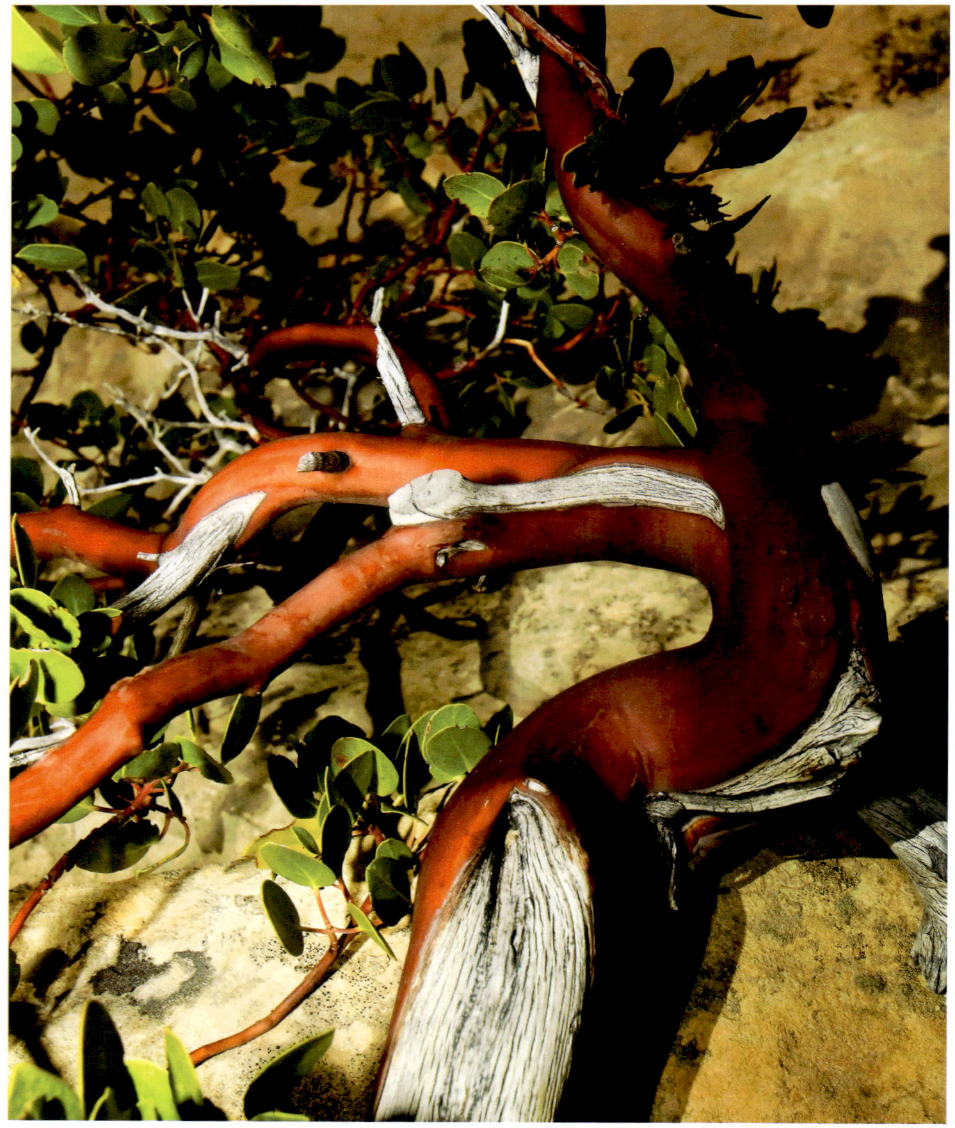

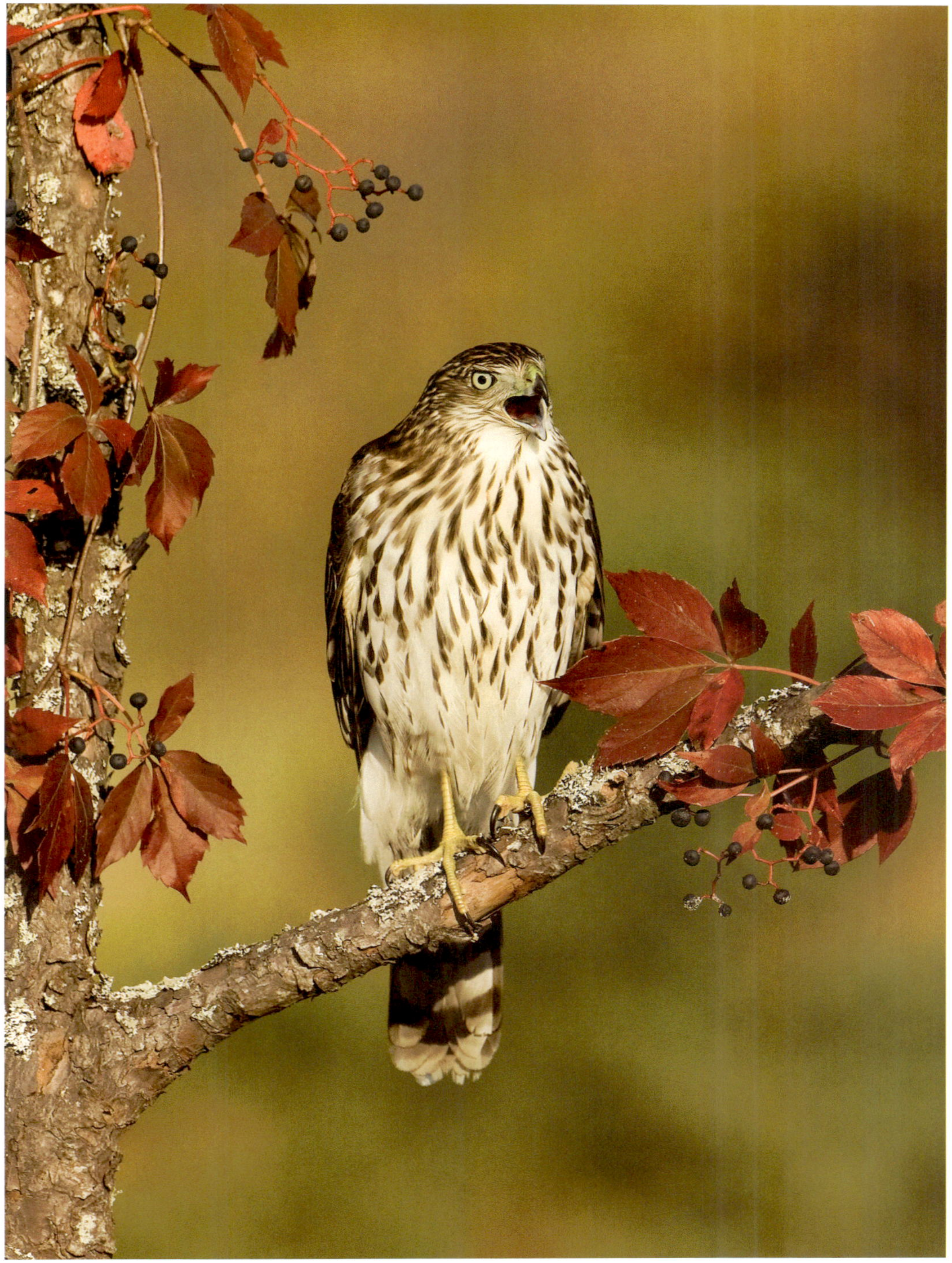

An immature Cooper's Hawk calls from a branch adorned with Virginia Creeper leaves and berries. *Photo by Scott Elowitz*

Virginia Creeper vines turn crimson red in early autumn. *Photo by Kevin T. Karlson*

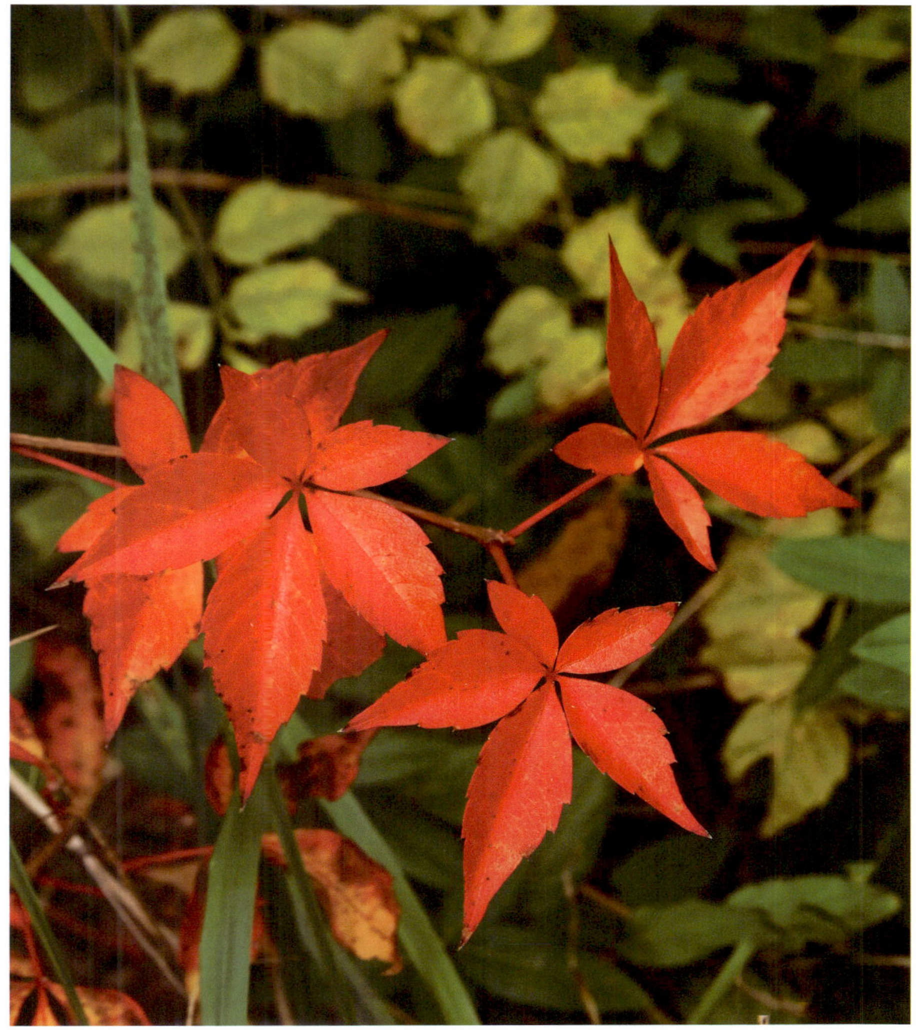

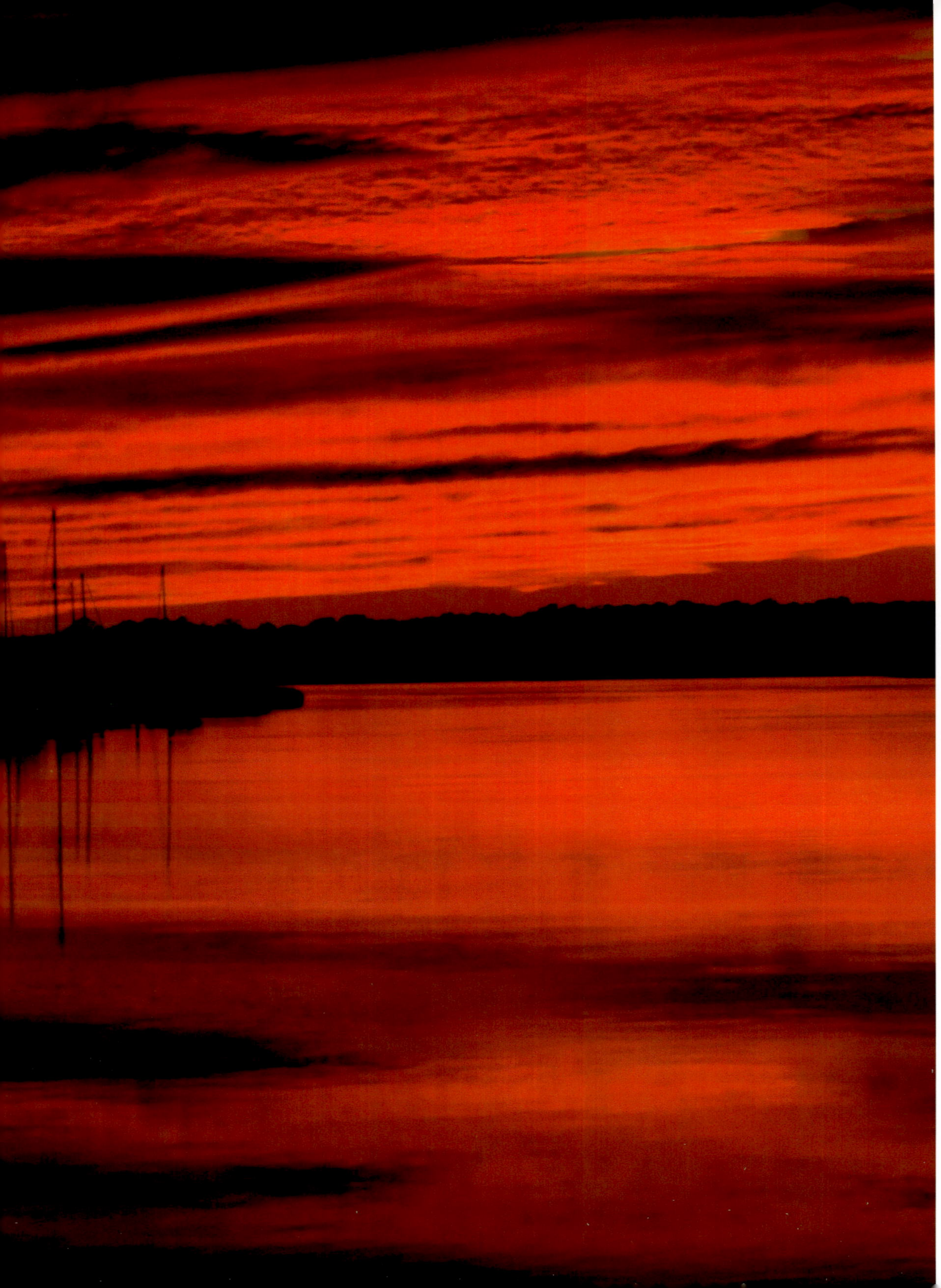

The sky broke like an egg into full sunset and the water caught fire.

— Pamela Hansford Johnson

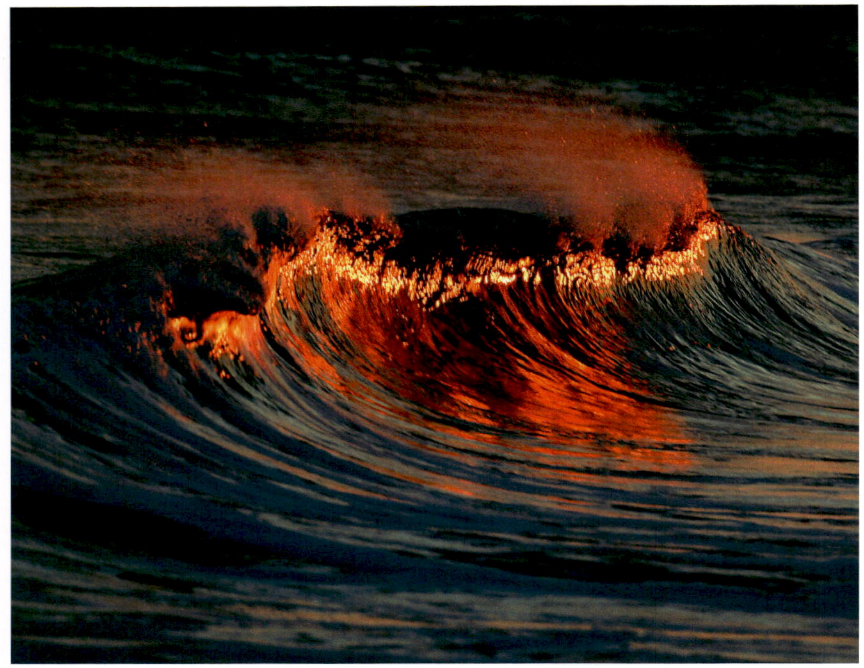

A fiery sunset stretches the levels of our imagination on the scenic Maurice River in Leesburg, New Jersey. No filters or Photoshop enhancements were used in this photo. *Photo by Pat Sutton*

Because of its low light angle in January, a bright red setting sun was beautifully reflected in the face of the wave at Poverty Beach in Cape May, New Jersey. *Photo by Don Merwin*

Vermillion is one of the richest shades of the color red, and the two images on this page carry its essence like a flaming sword. The Vermillion Flycatcher (right) is one of the most breathtaking birds in North America, while a Cardinal Flower (below) demands attention and appreciation every time you walk by. *Photos by Scott Elowitz (right) and Kevin T. Karlson (below)*

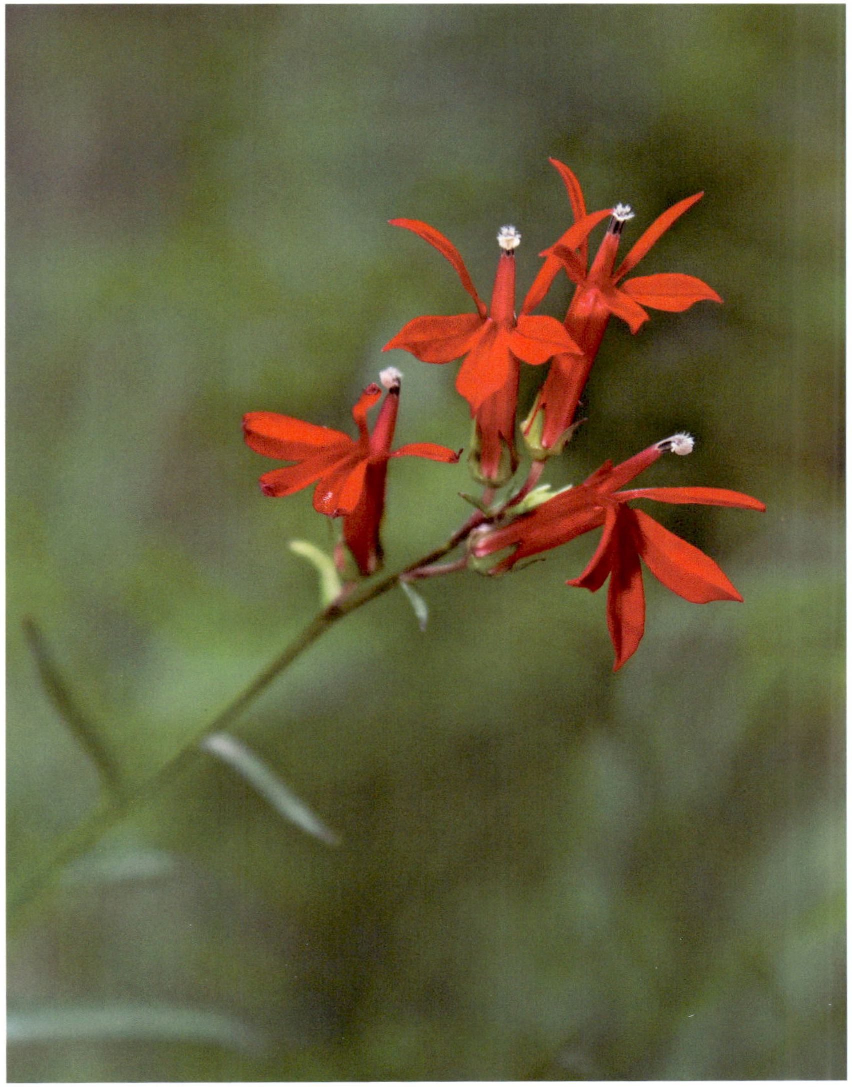

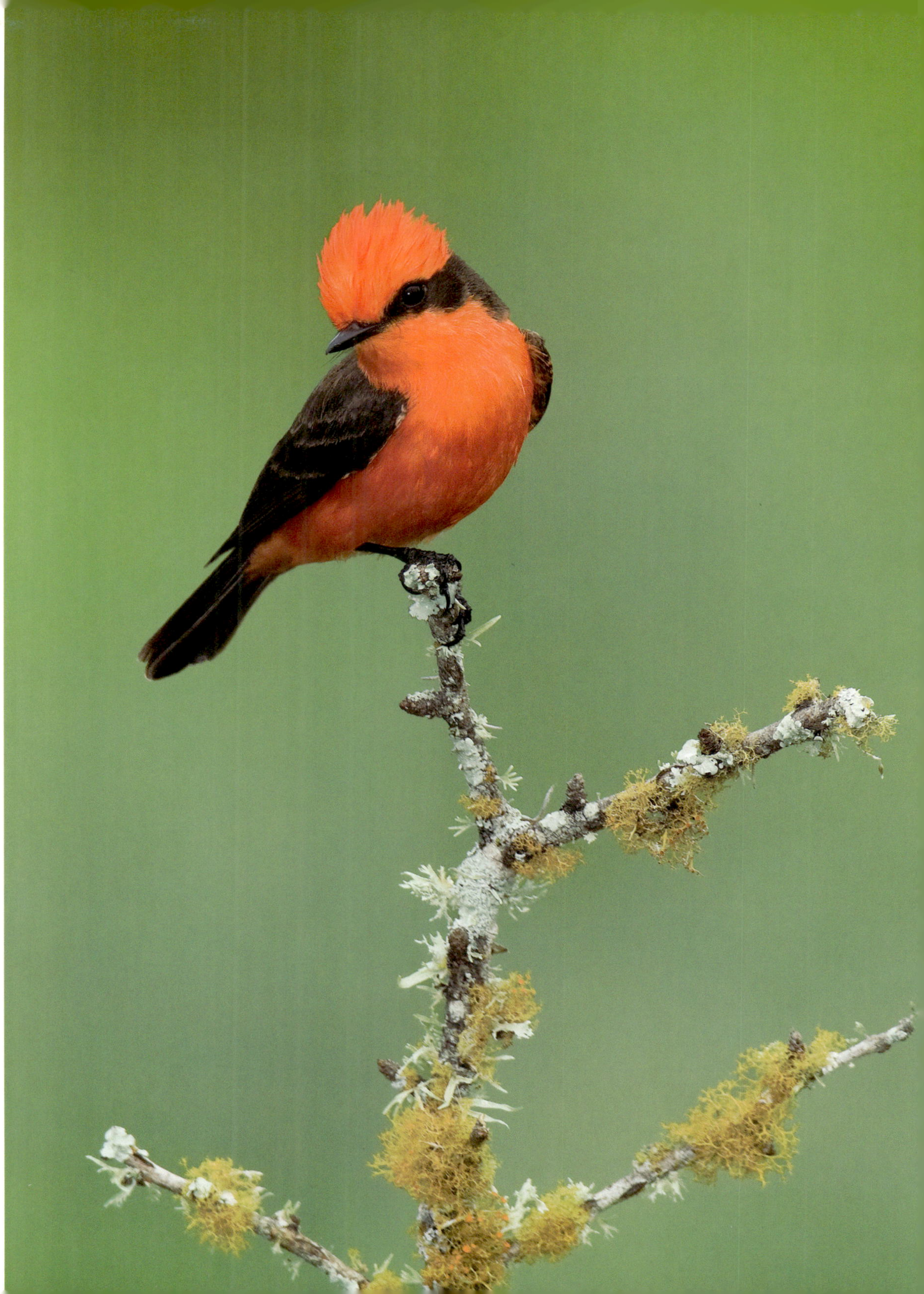

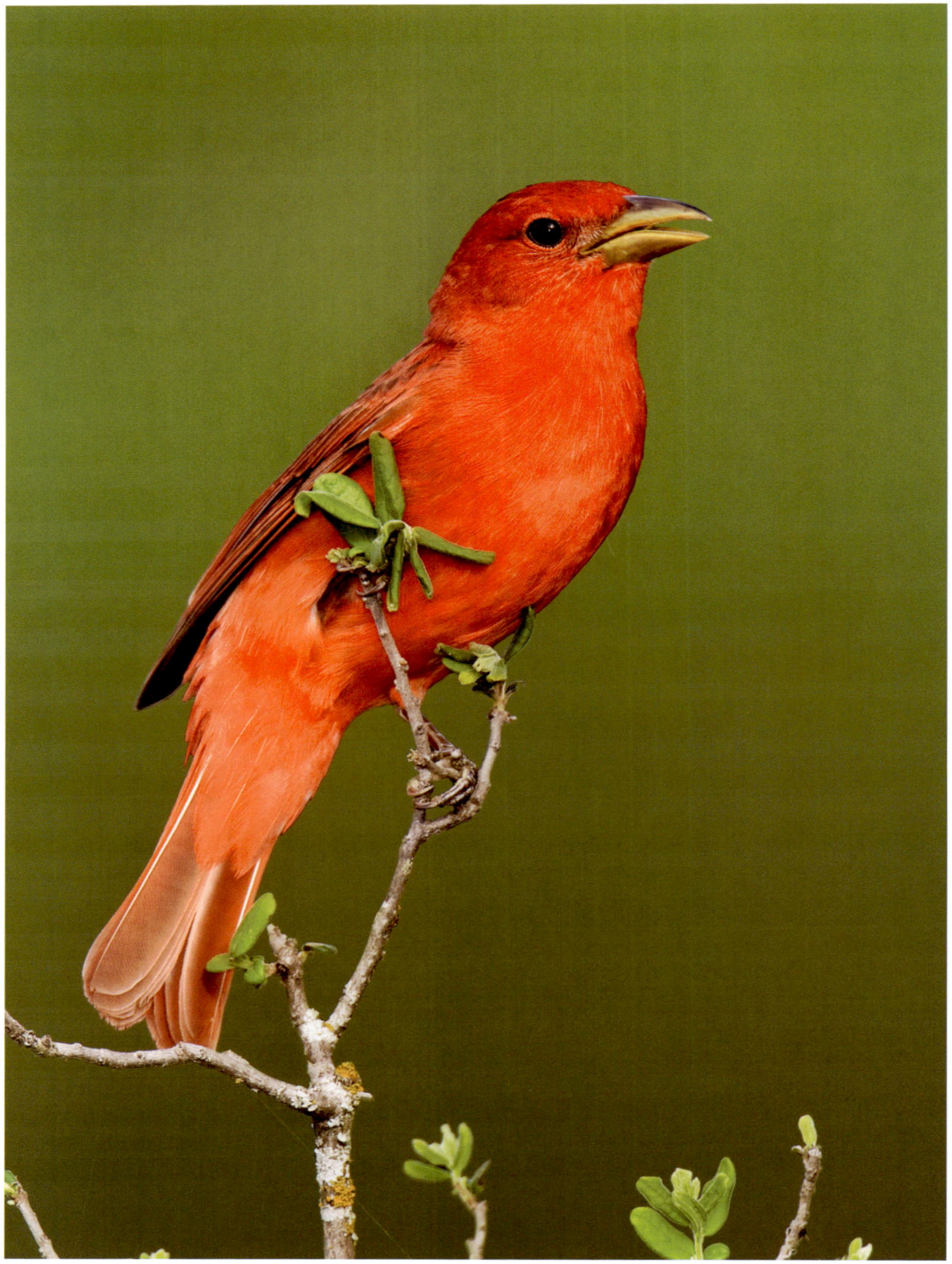

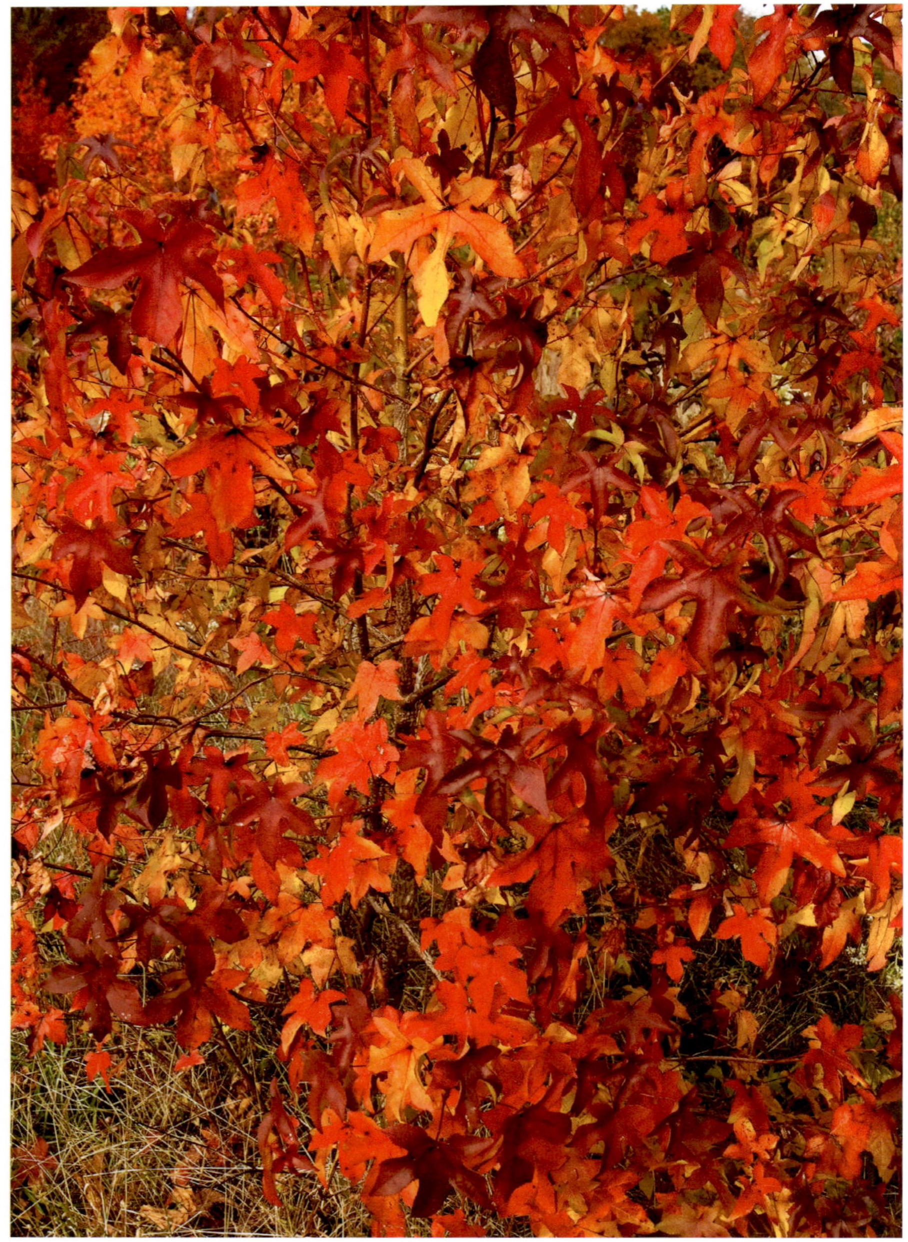

The rich, red color of a male Summer Tanager (left) matches some of the red leaves of a late fall Sweet Gum tree in southern New Jersey. *Photos by Lloyd Spitalnik (left) and Kevin T. Karlson (above)*

Opposite: The male Wood Duck arguably has the most dramatic mix of colors and plumage patterns of all North American birds. The eye and its ring possess a bold, fiery color. *Photo by Scott Elowitz*

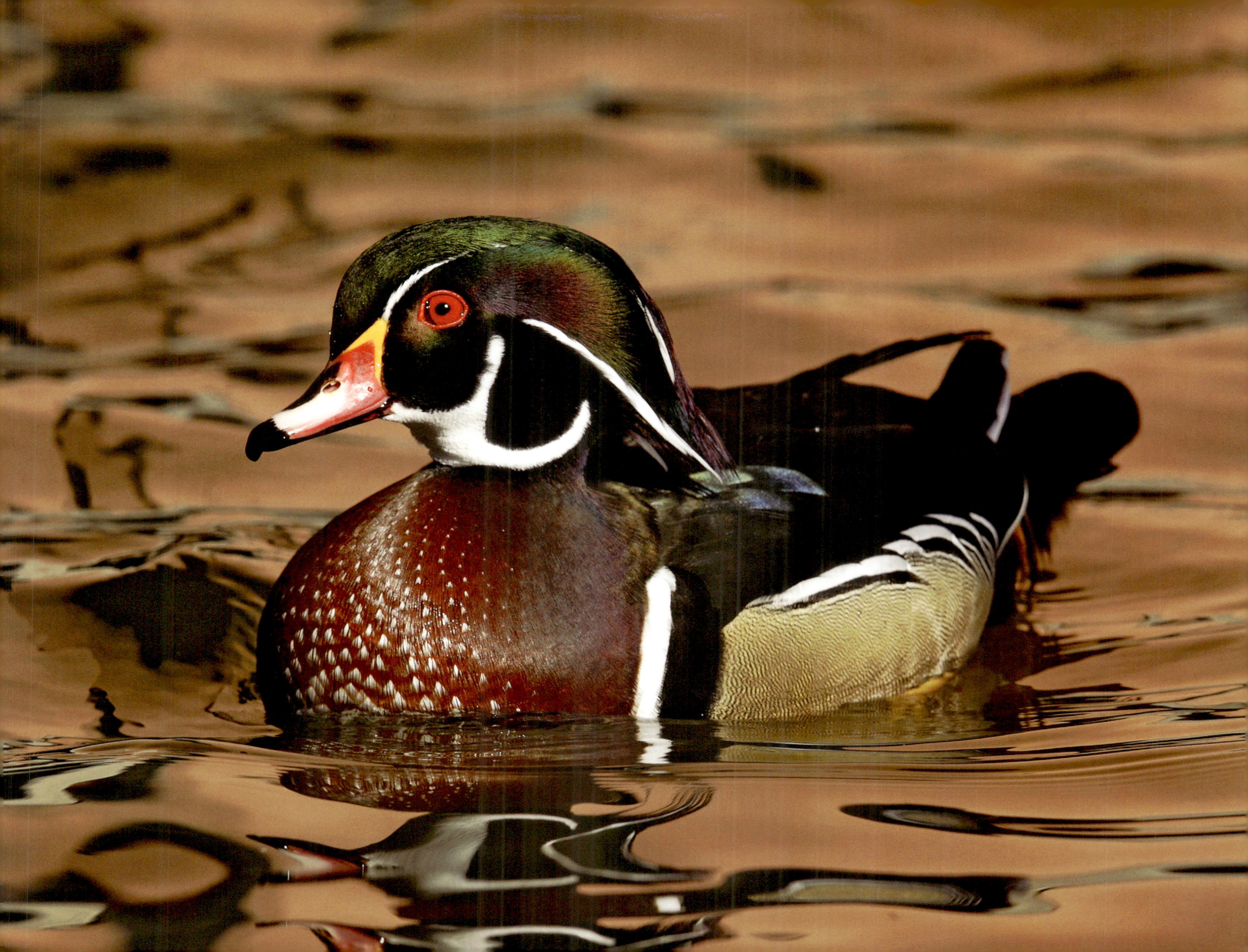

In order to see birds it is necessary to become part of the silence.

— Robert Lynd

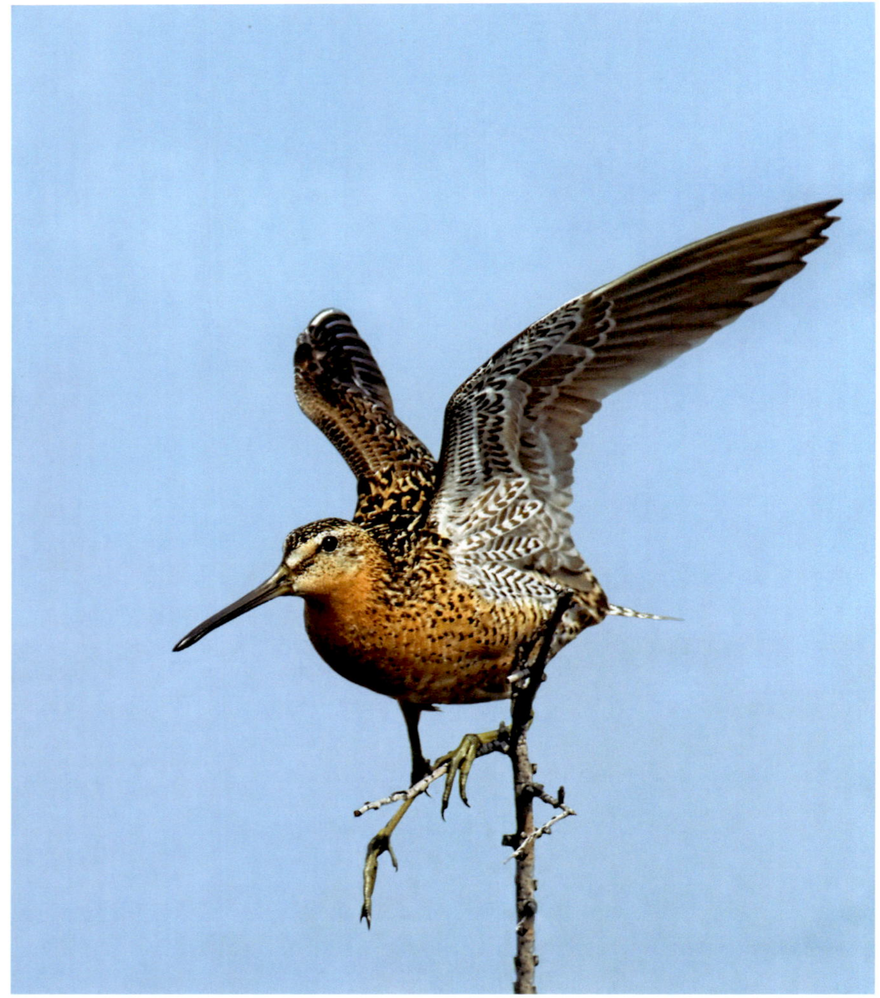

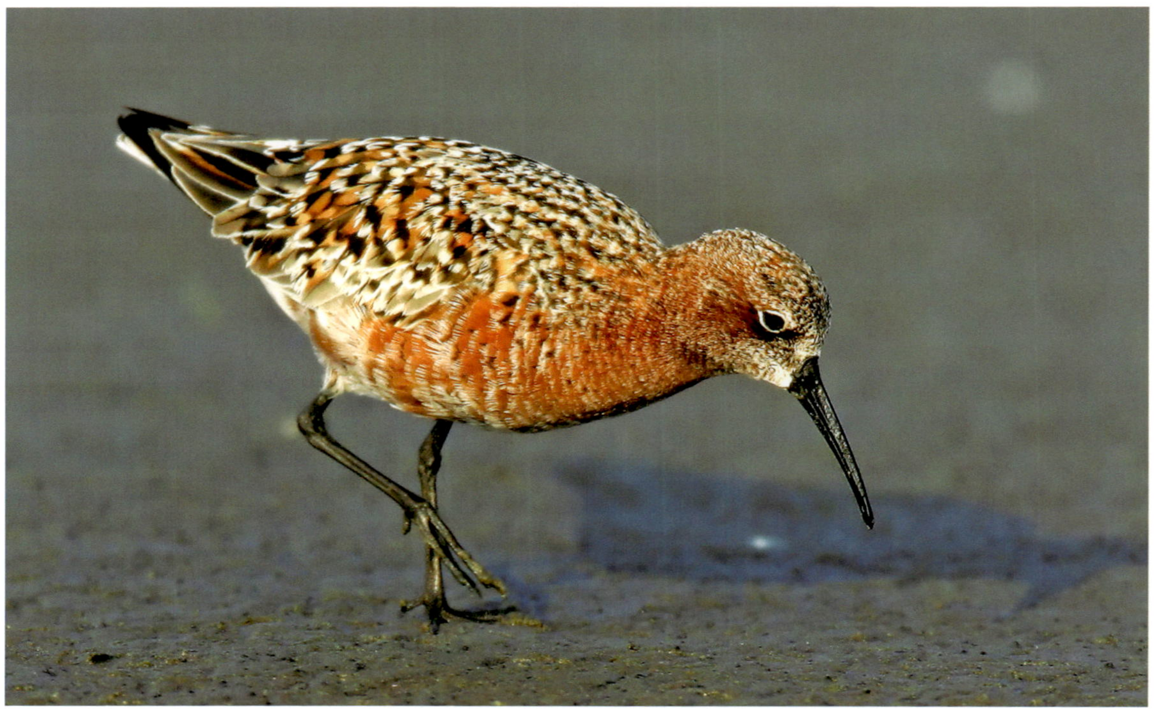

These two Arctic-breeding shorebirds have a fiery summer plumage. A Short-billed Dowitcher (above) balancing on a small tree branch shows the orange of a warm fire on its breast, while a Curlew Sandpiper (left) has the brick red color of glowing embers. *Photos by Kevin T. Karlson*

Merritt Island National Wildlife Refuge is the setting for these images that convey the mood of fire in a waning sunset. A Reddish Egret (right) is silhouetted against the sun's glow, while a lone mangrove bush balances a serene setting in the stillness of dusk (below). *Photos by Kevin T. Karlson*

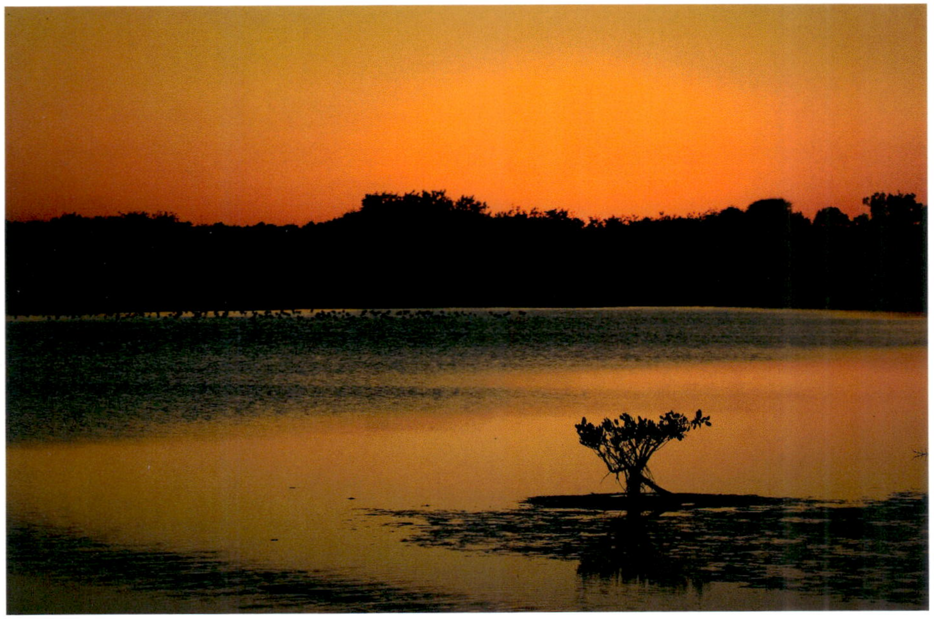

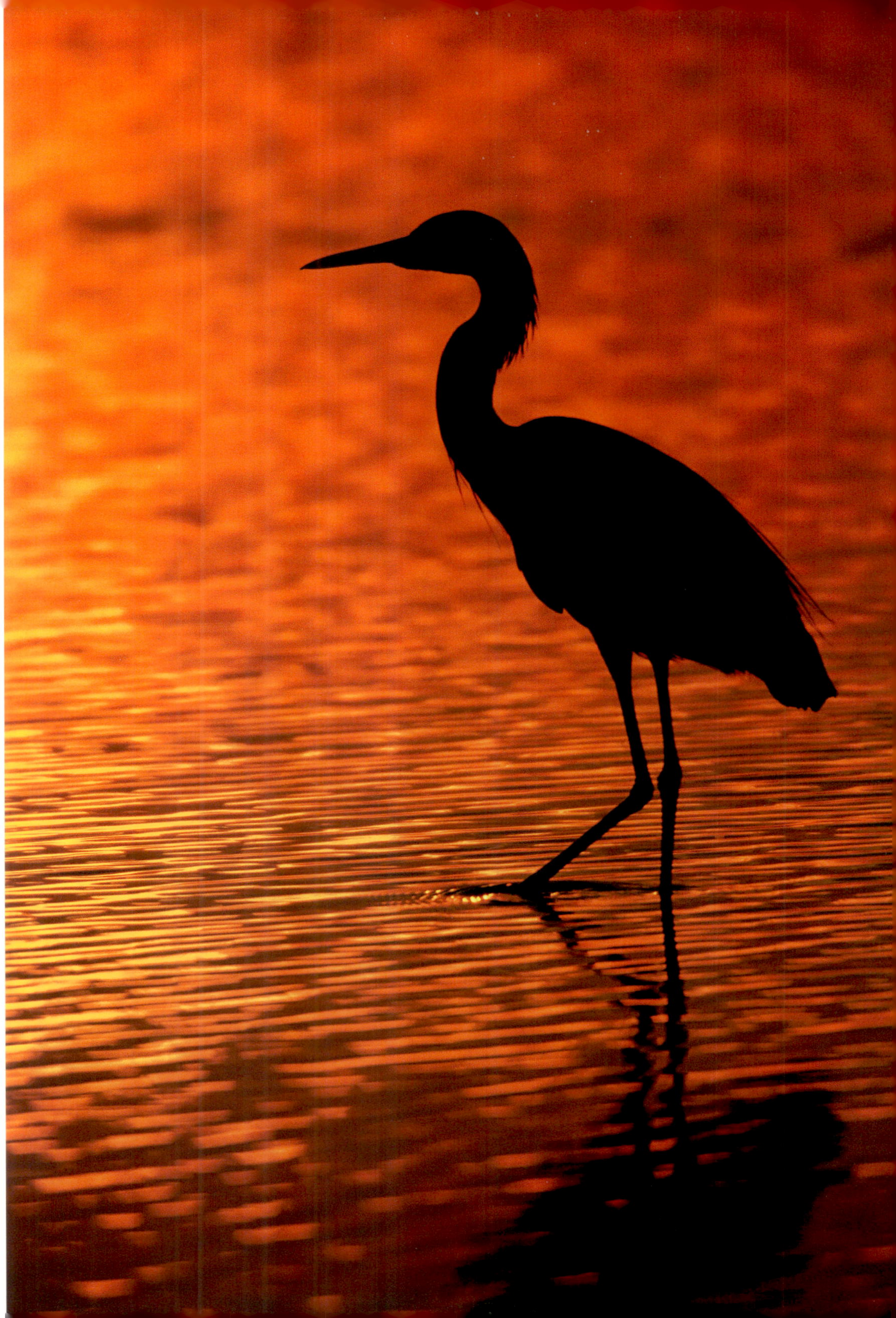

Although each has its own distinct mood, fire is the theme of these three photos. The setting sun gives a gnarled tree in Costa Rica new life, while a hoodoo and red rock formation in Utah reflects new warmth from the late day sun (upper right). The Cape May New Jersey lighthouse is silhouetted against a deep orange sky. *Photos by Tina Giaimo (below) and Kevin T. Karlson (upper and lower right)*

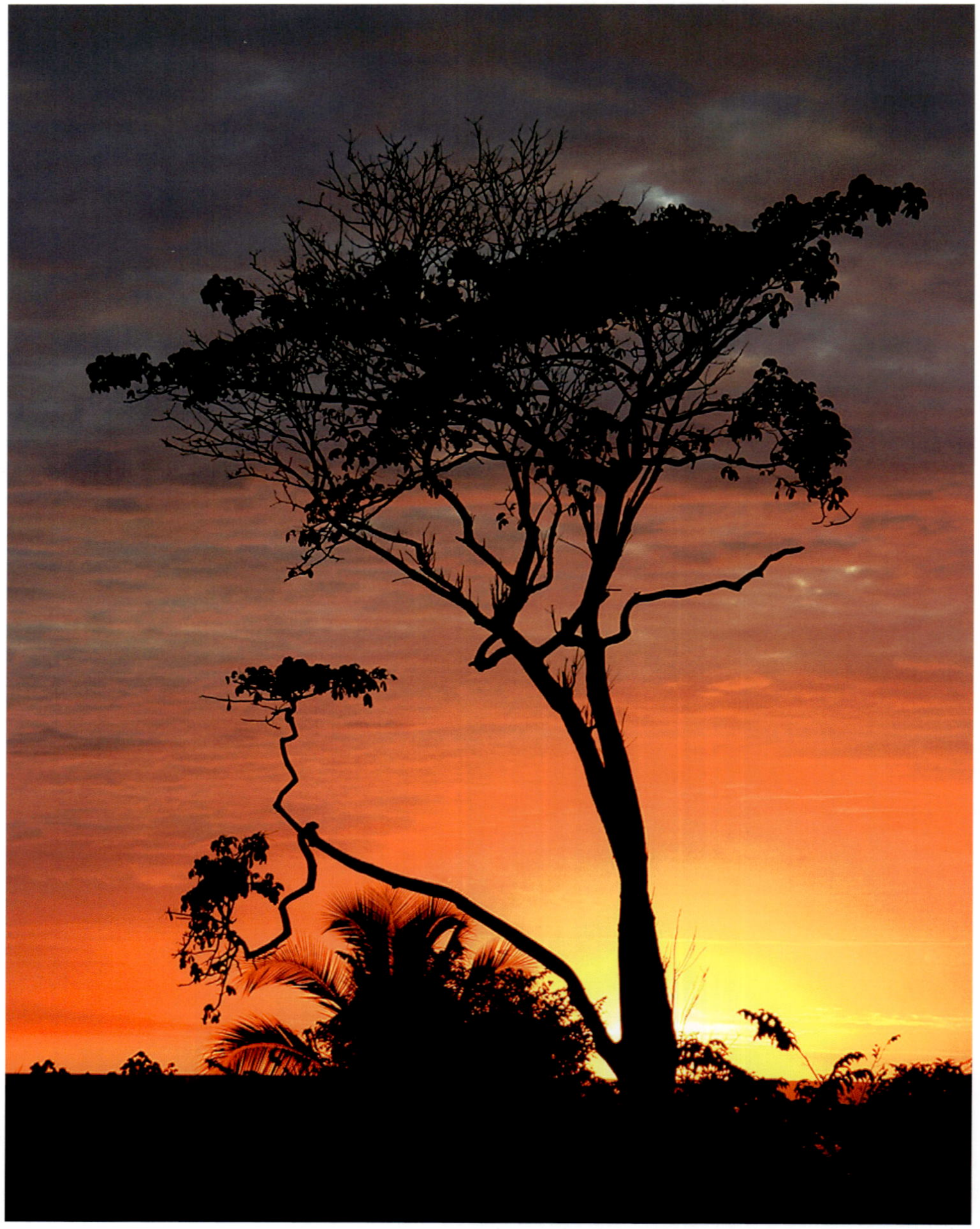

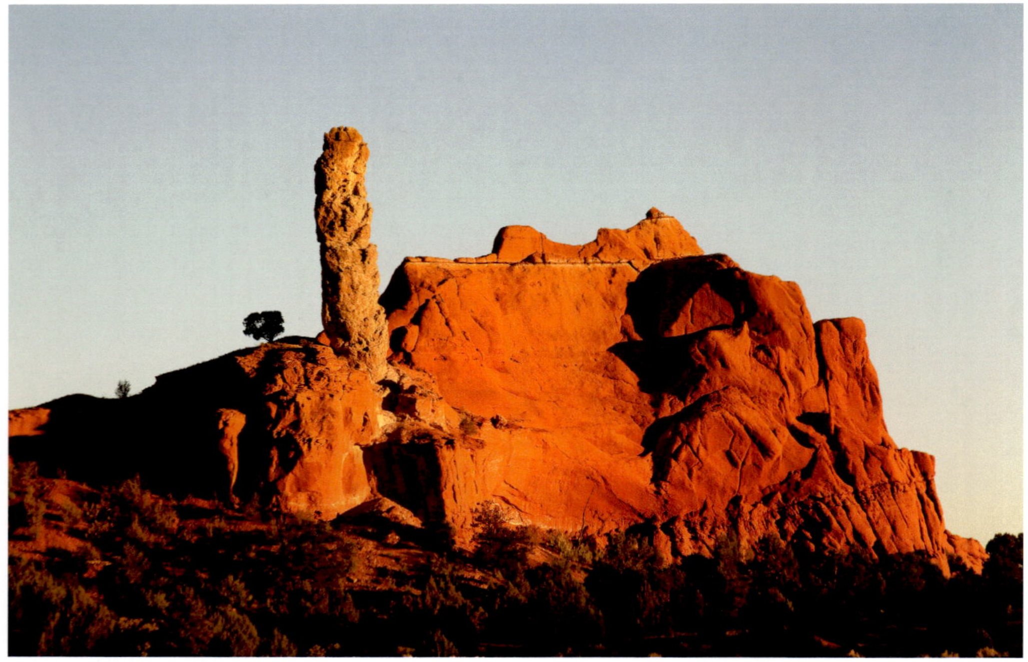

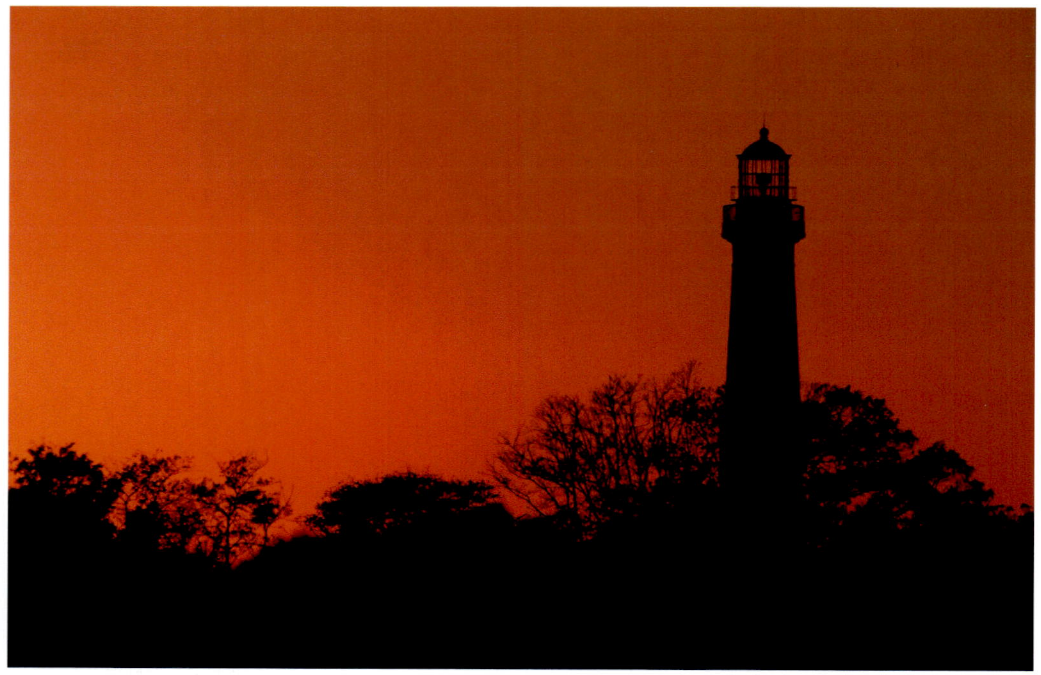

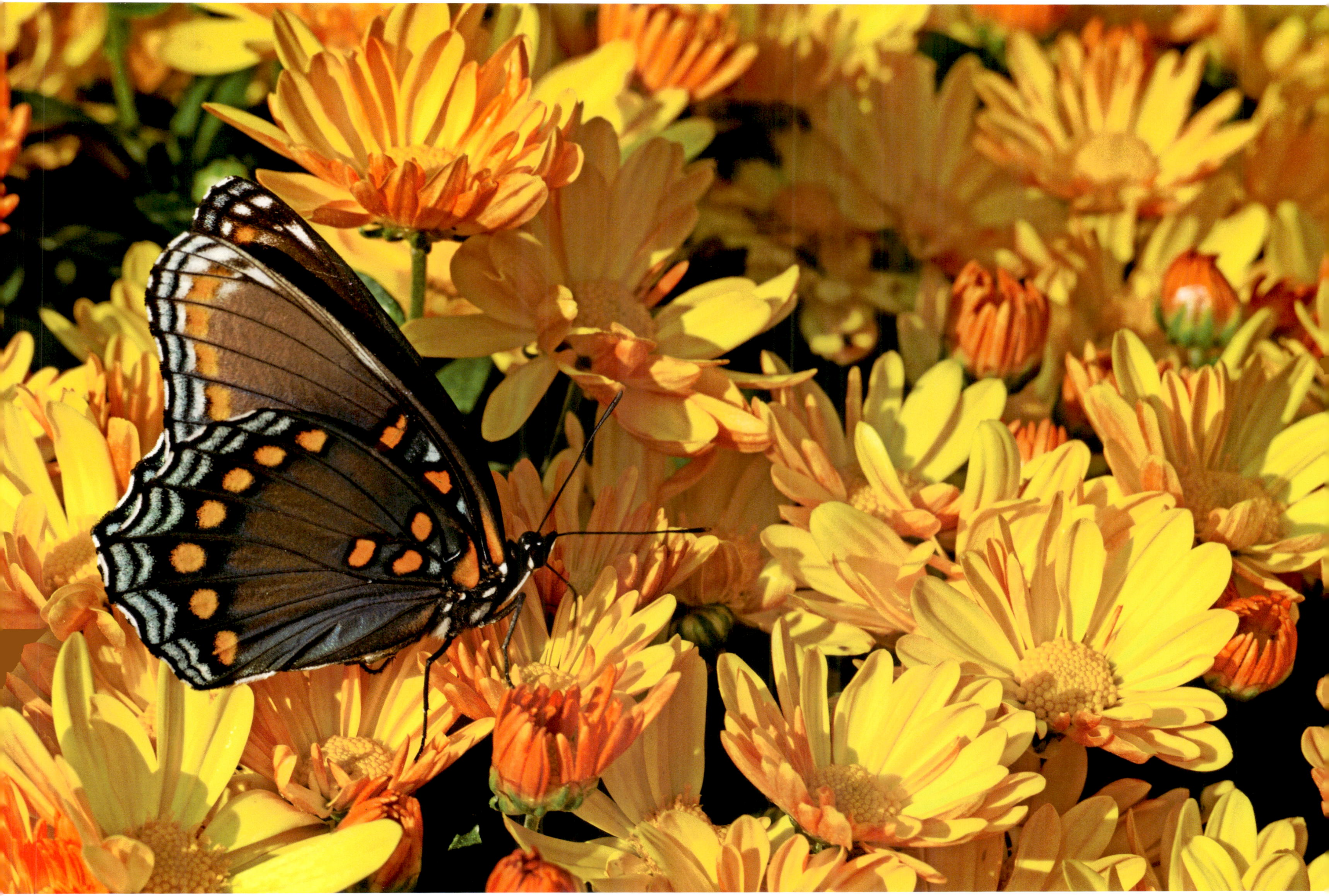

A Red-spotted Purple butterfly adds to the blaze of yellow and red colors of a Chrysanthemum flower field in this image that inflames the visual senses. *Photo by Mike Hannisian*

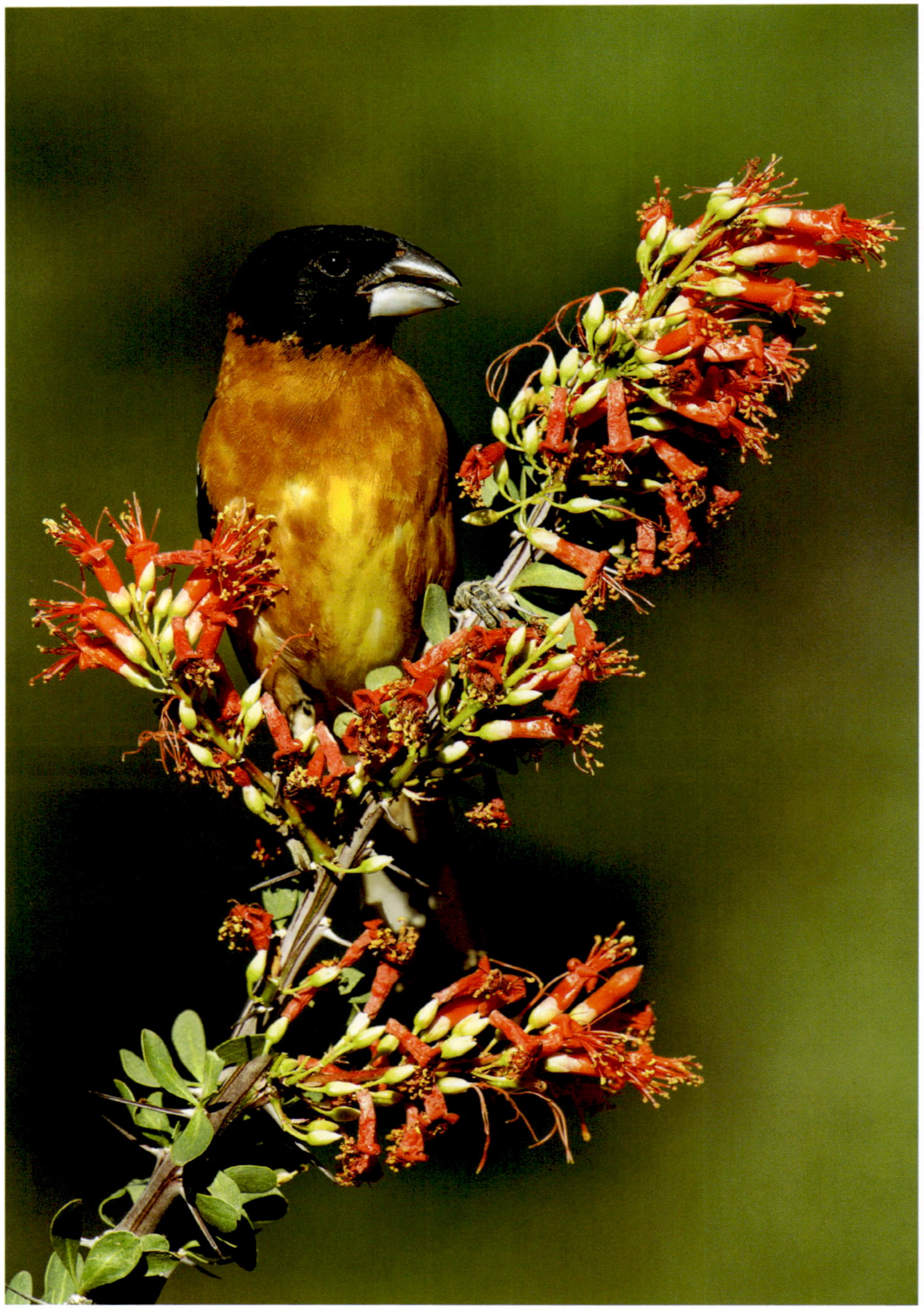

Burnt orange and yellow on the breast of a Black-headed Grosbeak convey the feeling of a waning fire, but the bright red color of the flowers adds a fiery mood to this image. *Photo by Scott Elowitz*

Male Scarlet Tanager exemplifies the color red in the avian world of North America, and the electric red of this bird combines with rich, black wings and tail to create a visual impression of fire. *Photo by Lloyd Spitalnik*

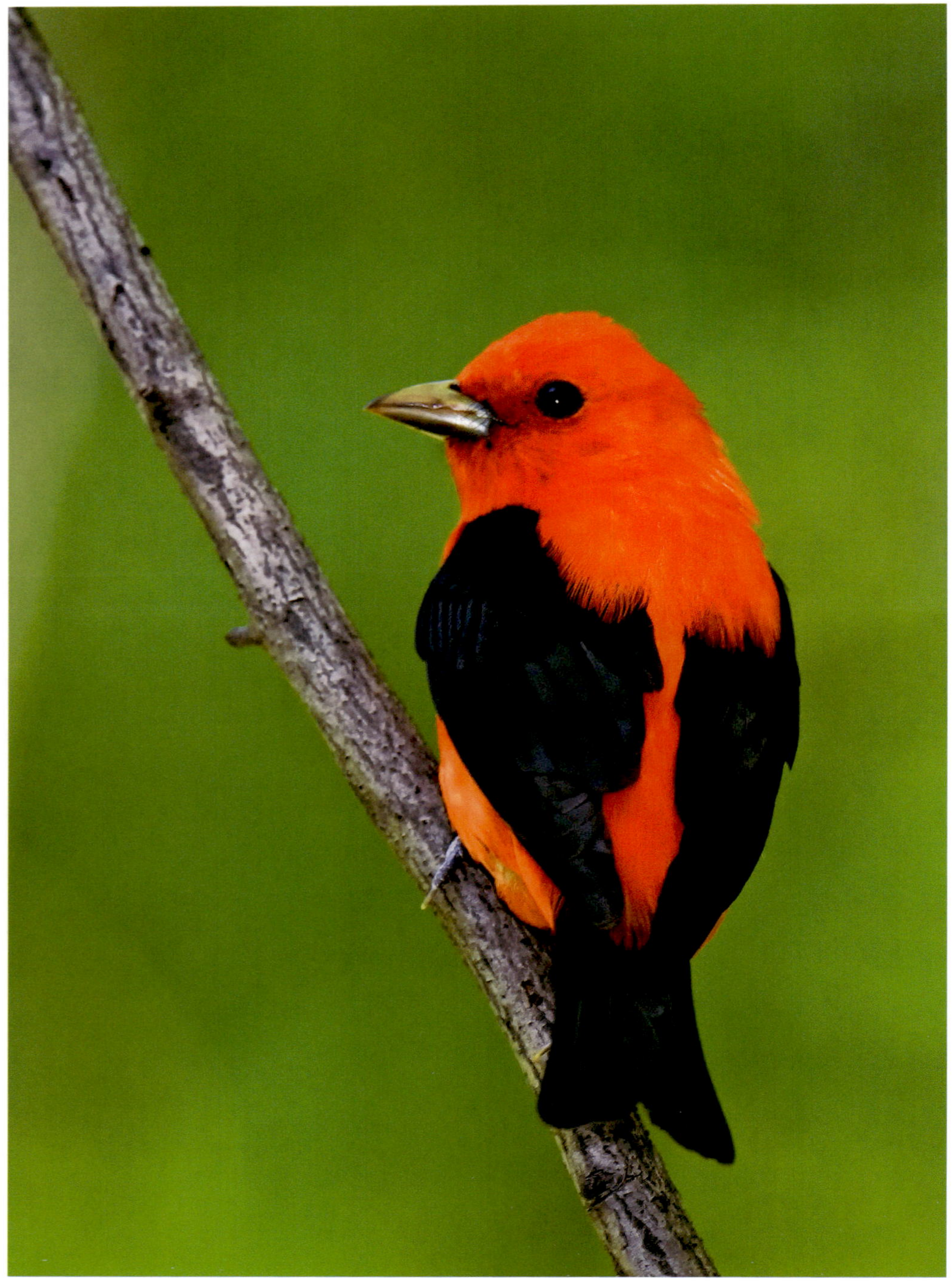

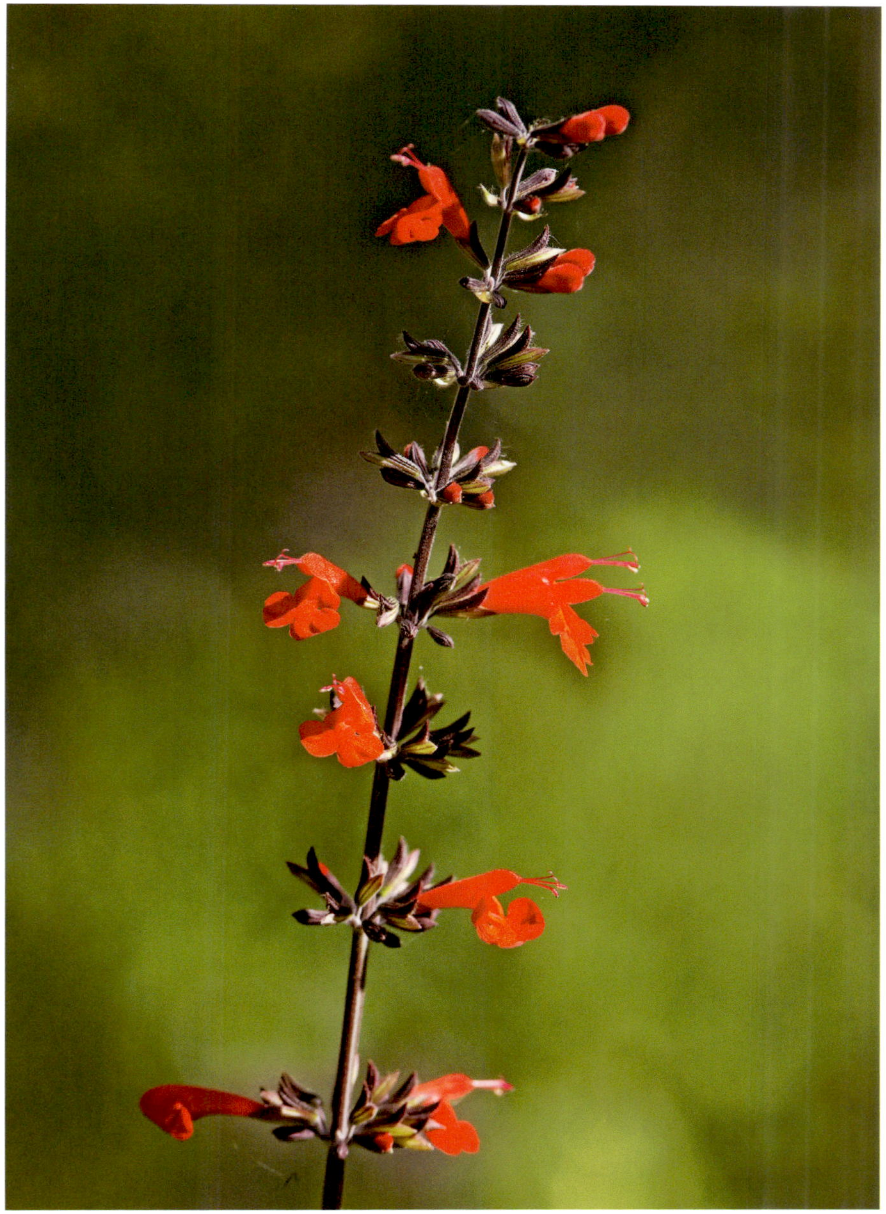

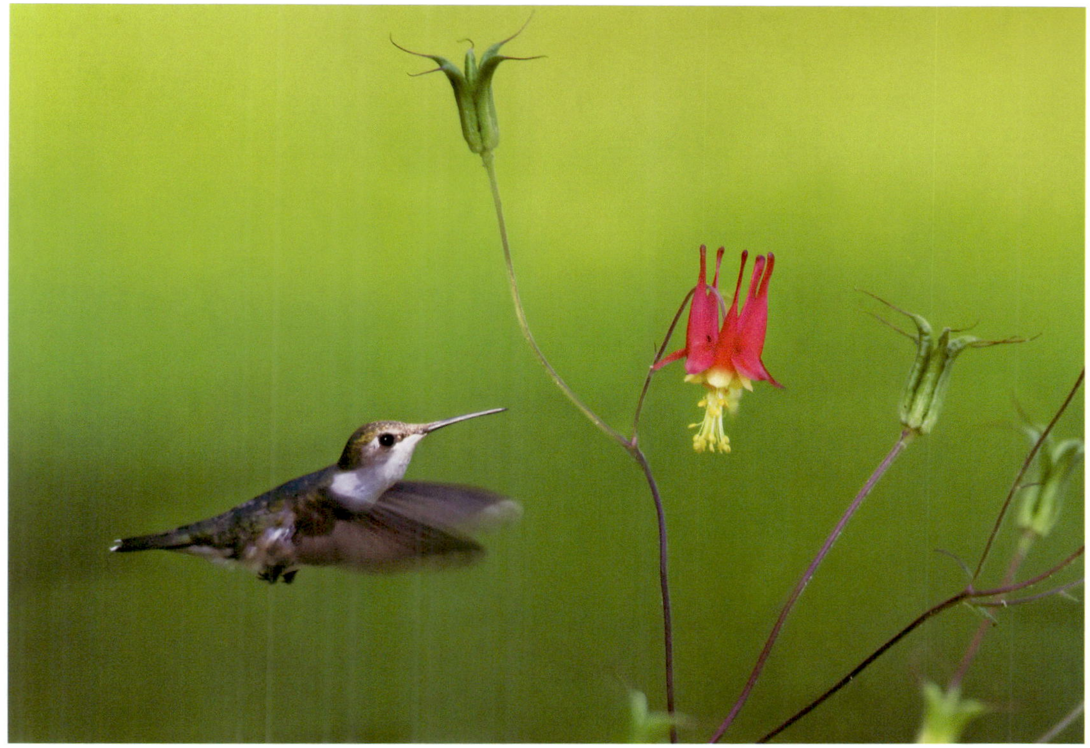

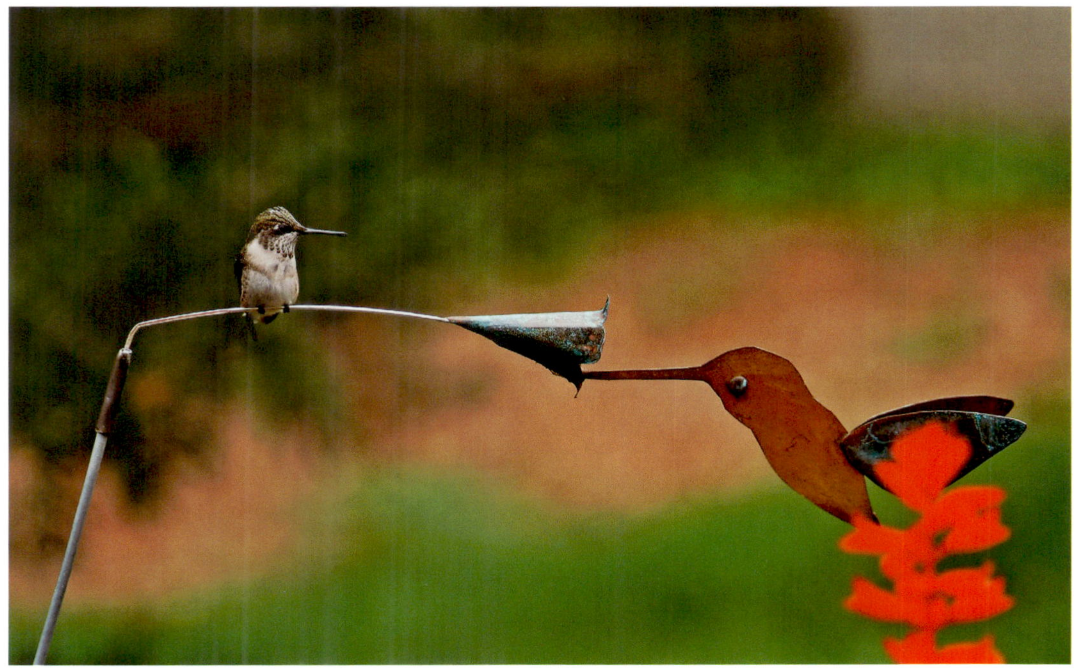

Hummingbirds are attracted to the color red, since it usually means there is sweet nectar awaiting. A female Ruby-throated Hummingbird gets ready to nectar on a coral pink Columbine (upper right), while a young male Ruby-throat seems puzzled by the competition in Pat Sutton's wildlife garden in Goshen, New Jersey (right). A fiery wildflower from East Texas has the bright red color that attracts hummingbirds. *Photos by Pat Sutton (lower right) and Kevin T. Karlson (above and upper right)*

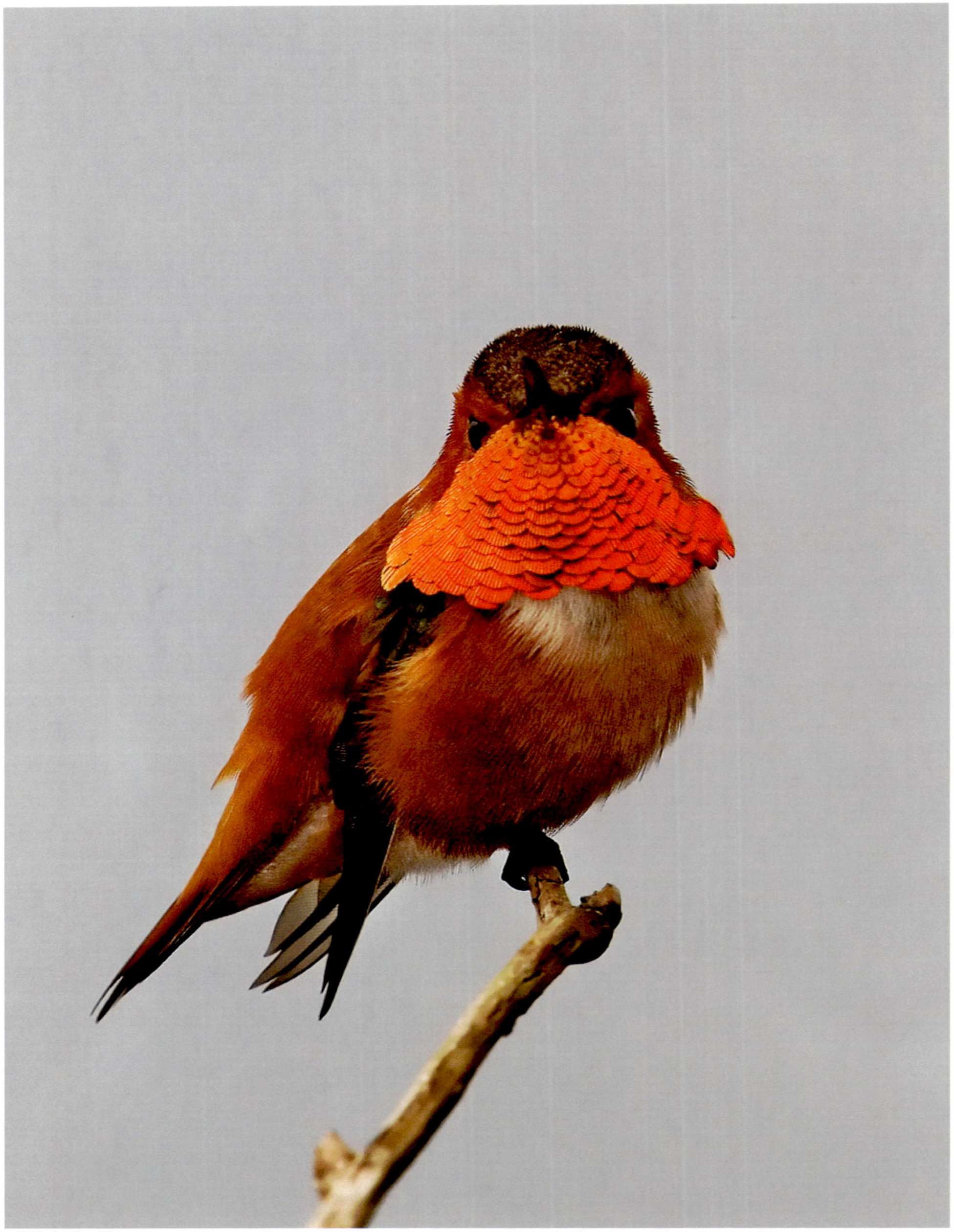

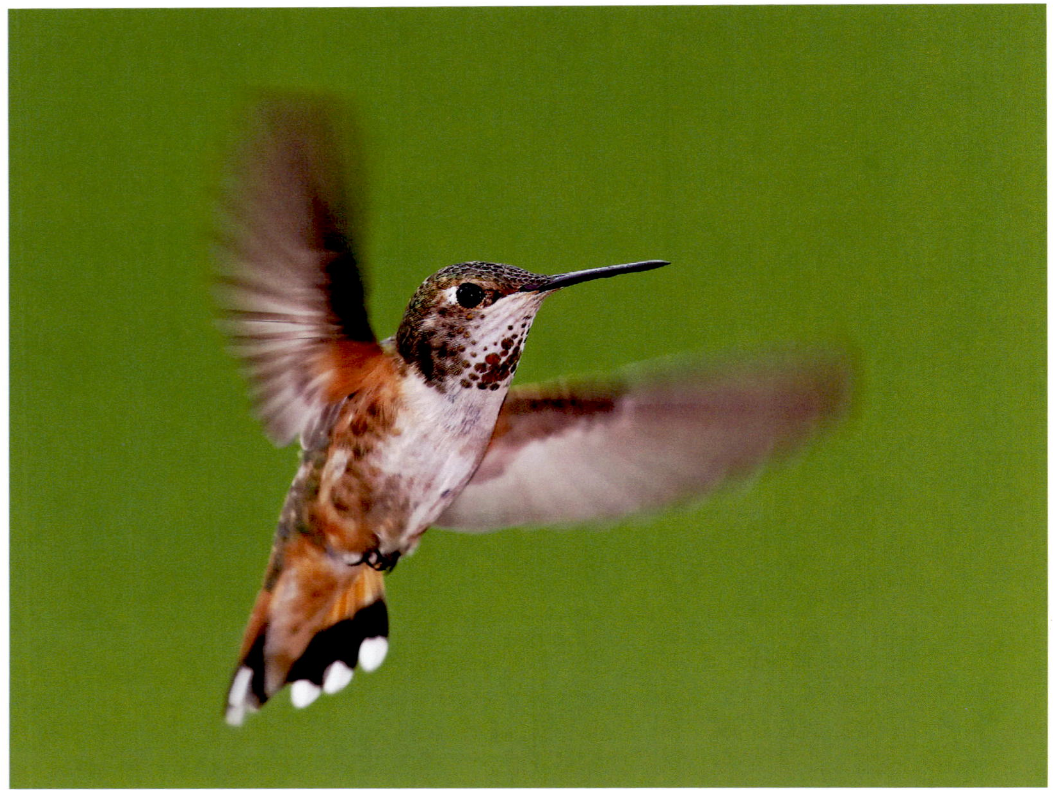

The bright throat of a male Rufous Hummingbird (left) bursts into a fiery metallic pattern when it reflects the light in Milo Burcham's back yard in Cordova, Alaska. *Photo by Kevin T. Karlson*

Rufous Hummingbird is appropriately named, since the male has a rich, rufous coloration to his chest and back. Females (above) have less red, but still show splotches of color on their bodies. *Photo by Kevin T. Karlson*

Opposite: Red-breasted Nuthatch is a tiny bird that forages for seeds and insects in coniferous trees. This male shows a rich, reddish-orange breast that approximates the warmth of a winter fire. *Photo by Scott Elowitz*

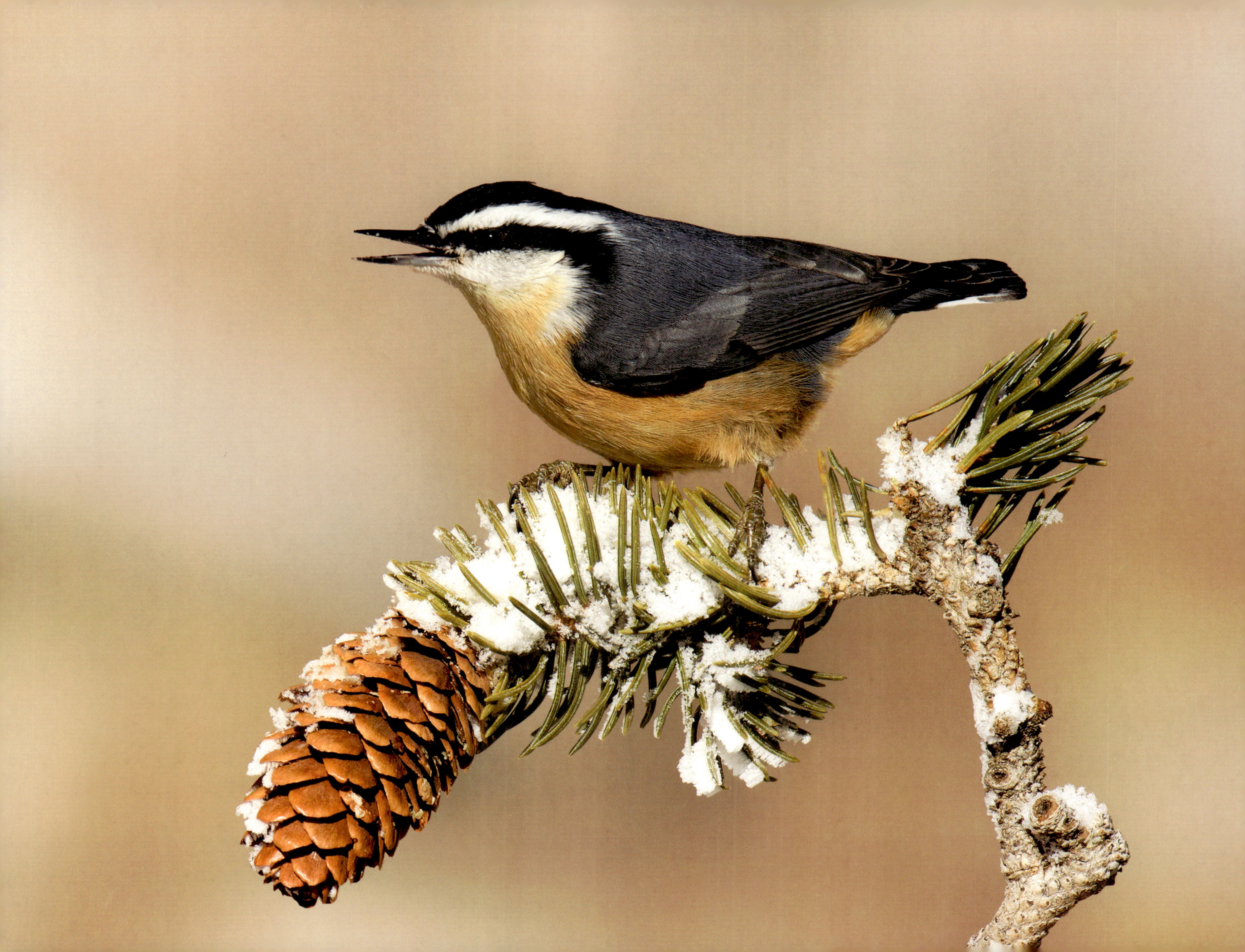

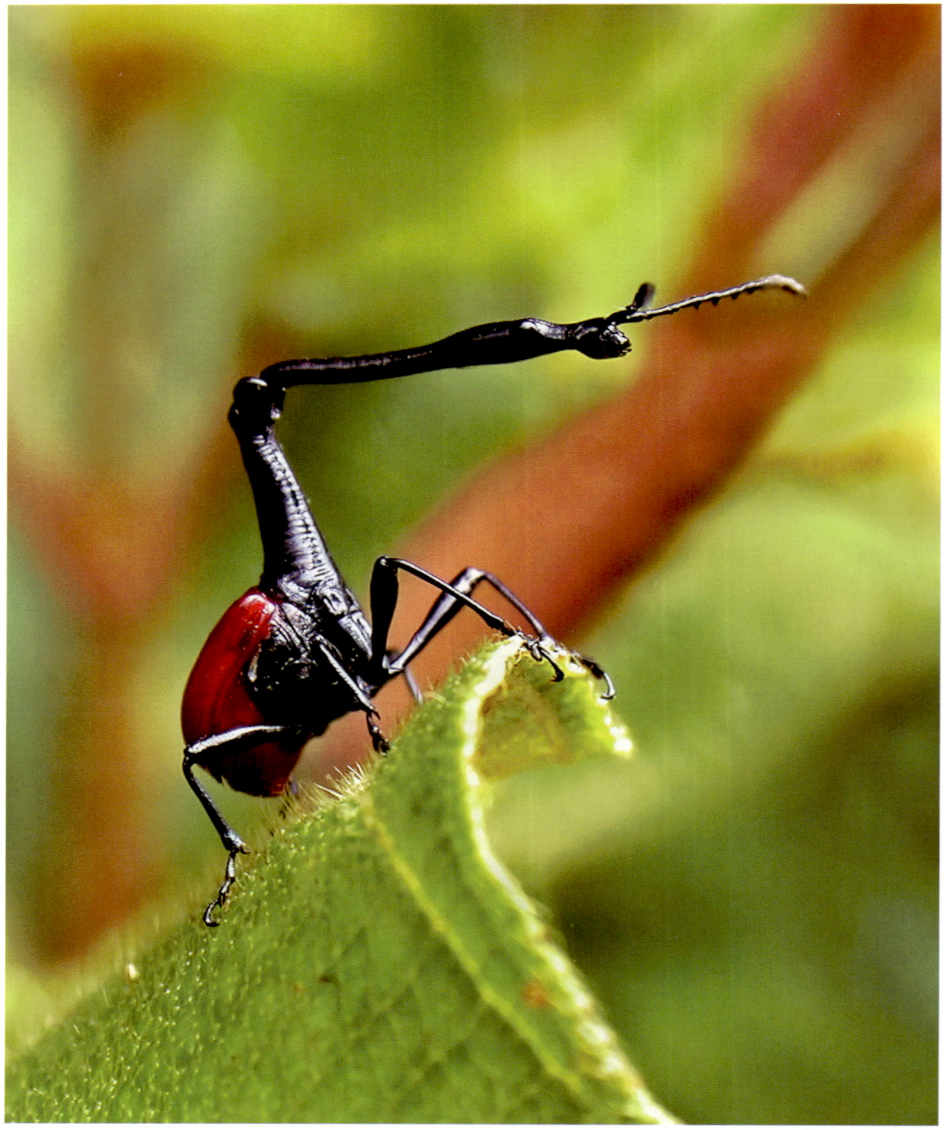

Giraffe-necked Weevil, Andasibe-Mantadia National Park. As humans with inquiring minds, we may look for rhyme or reason in everything that we encounter, yet sometimes nature produces the seemingly bizarre just for the heck of it! This peculiar beetle is endemic to Madagascar and is generally found on a particular family of plants. *Photo and caption by Mike Crewe*

Morpho butterfly caterpillars, Itatiaia National Park, Brazil. "Repetition of design in nature provides something of interest for us. Perhaps it's a sense of order developing in what may otherwise feel like chaos. Somehow this reminds me of train wagons, linked up in short chains in a railway marshalling yard." *Photo and caption by Mike Crewe*

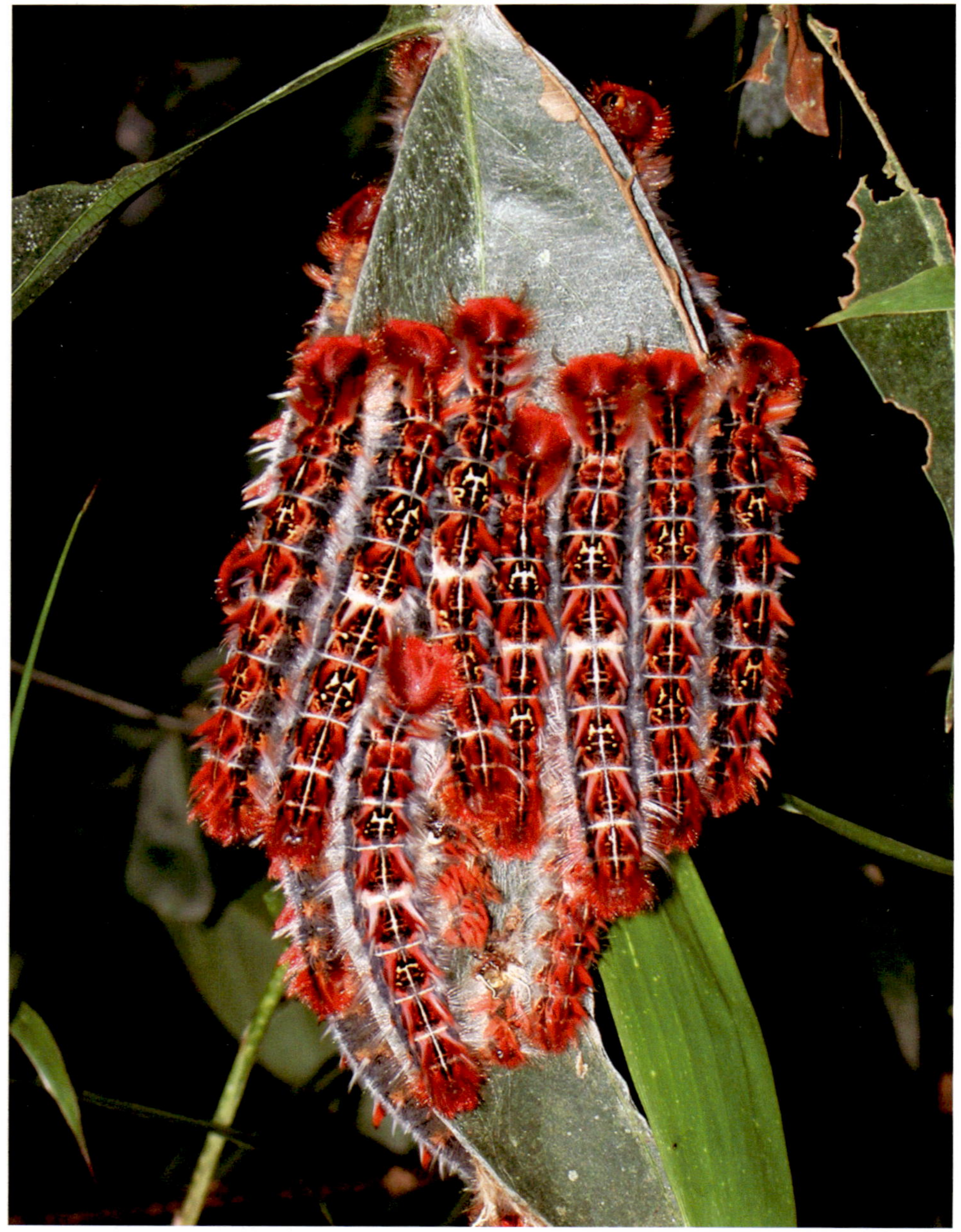

If I can put one touch of rosy sunset into the life of any man or woman, I shall feel that I have worked with God.

— G.K. Chesterton

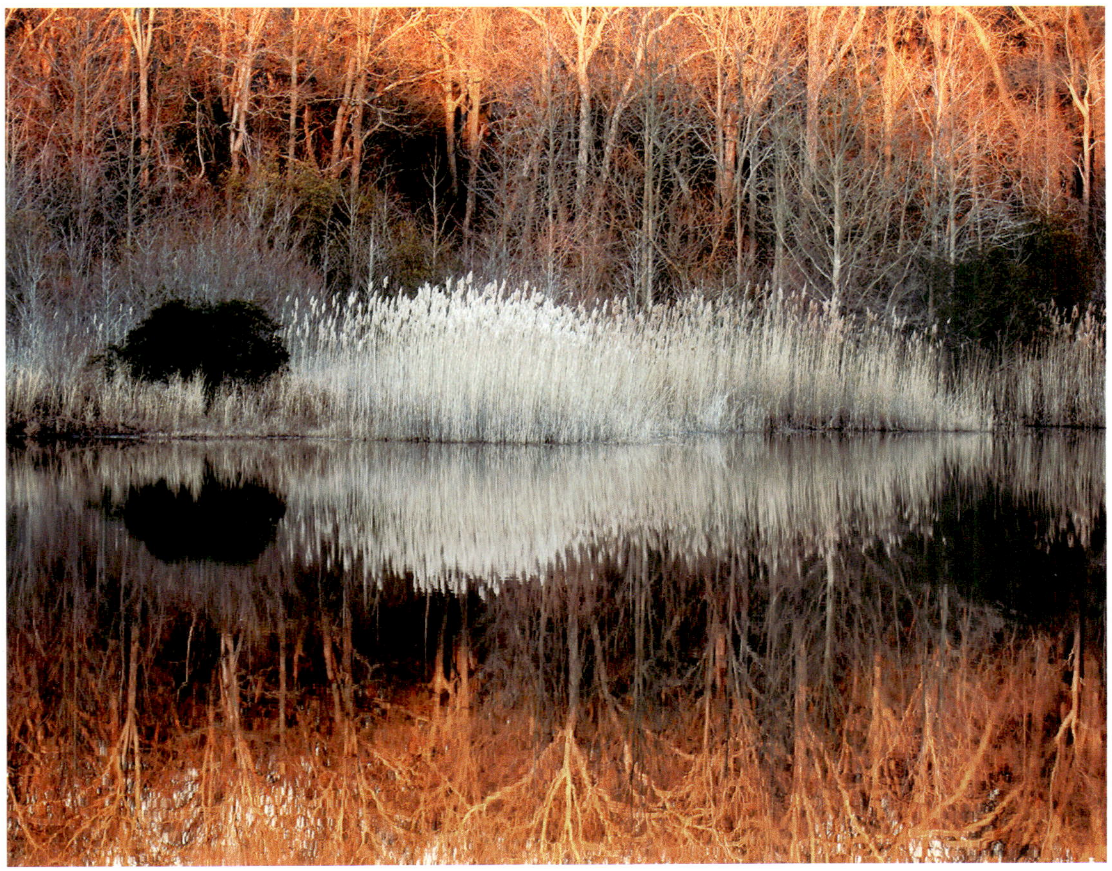

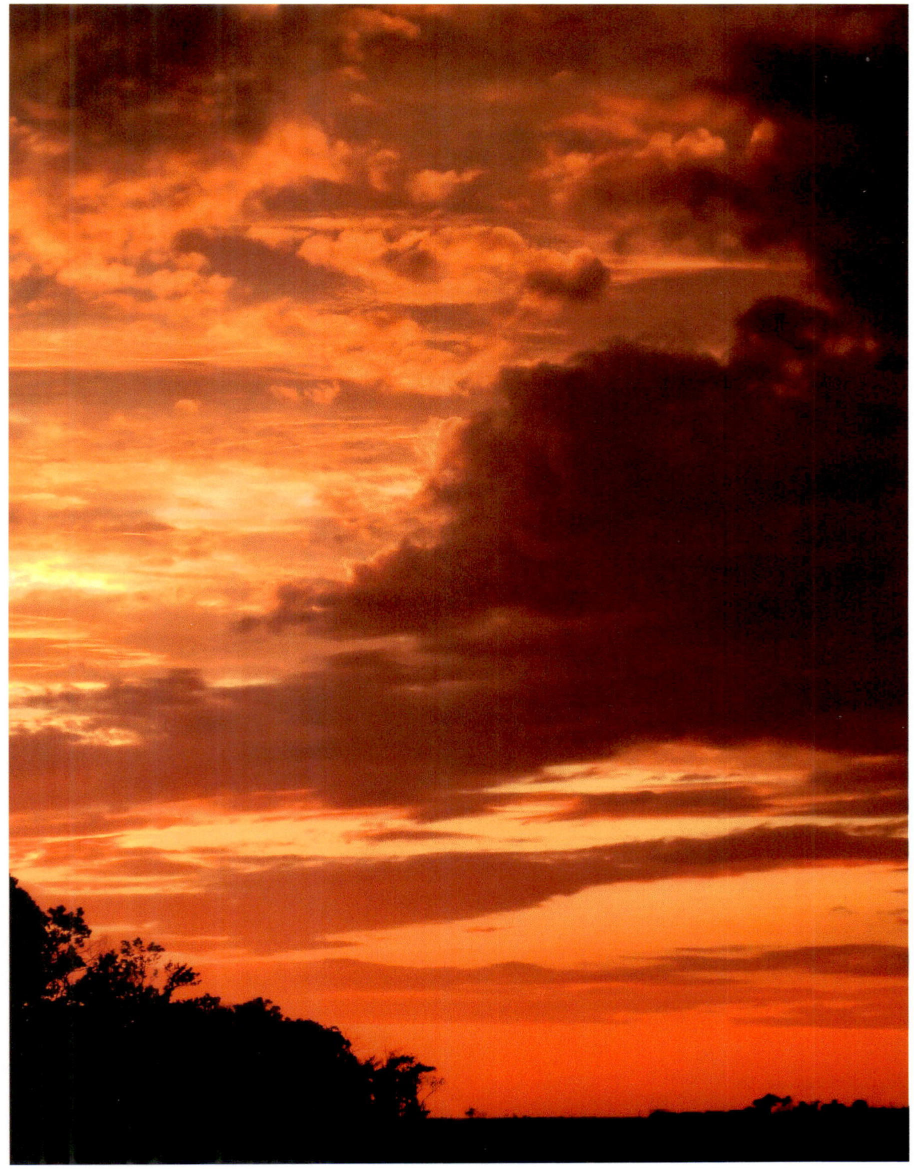

The captivating photo at the left shows the reflection of trees and grasses in a still pond near Cape May, New Jersey. The warmth of the setting sun turned these bare autumn trees a rich, orange color. *Photo by Don Merwin*

A sky full of assorted cloud shapes came to life when the sun brought a warm glow to the scene. *Photo by Dale Rosselet*

Brant at sunset, Cley-next-the-sea, Norfolk, UK. "For me, nothing man-made comes close to the spiritual effect that a sunrise or sunset has on the inner self. I have no idea why we carry these vestiges of our past into the modern age, but I am glad that we do. Add the extra element of skeins of Brant coming to roost and you have a moment to be captured – and cherished for life." *Photo and caption by Mike Crewe*

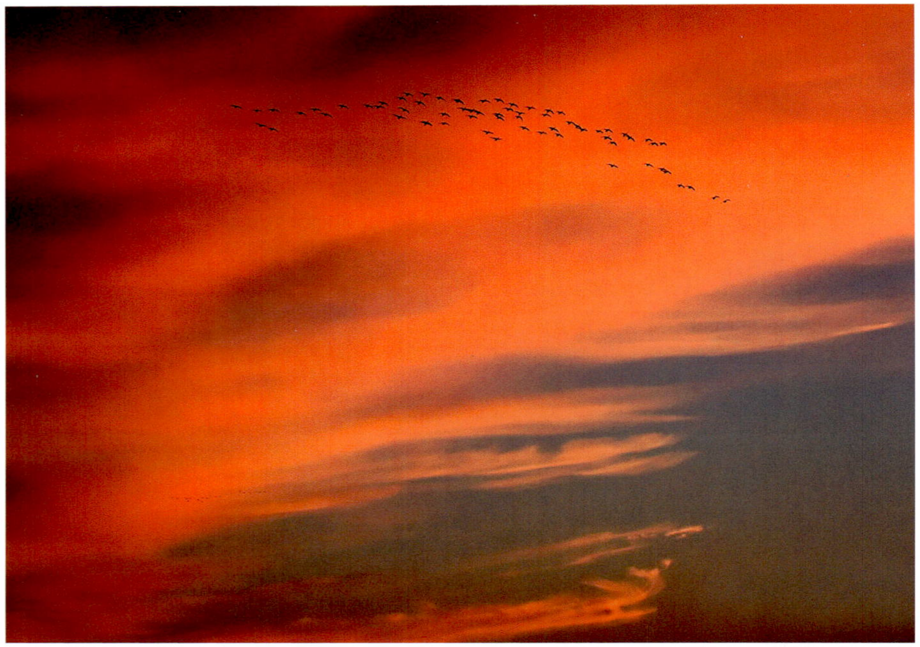

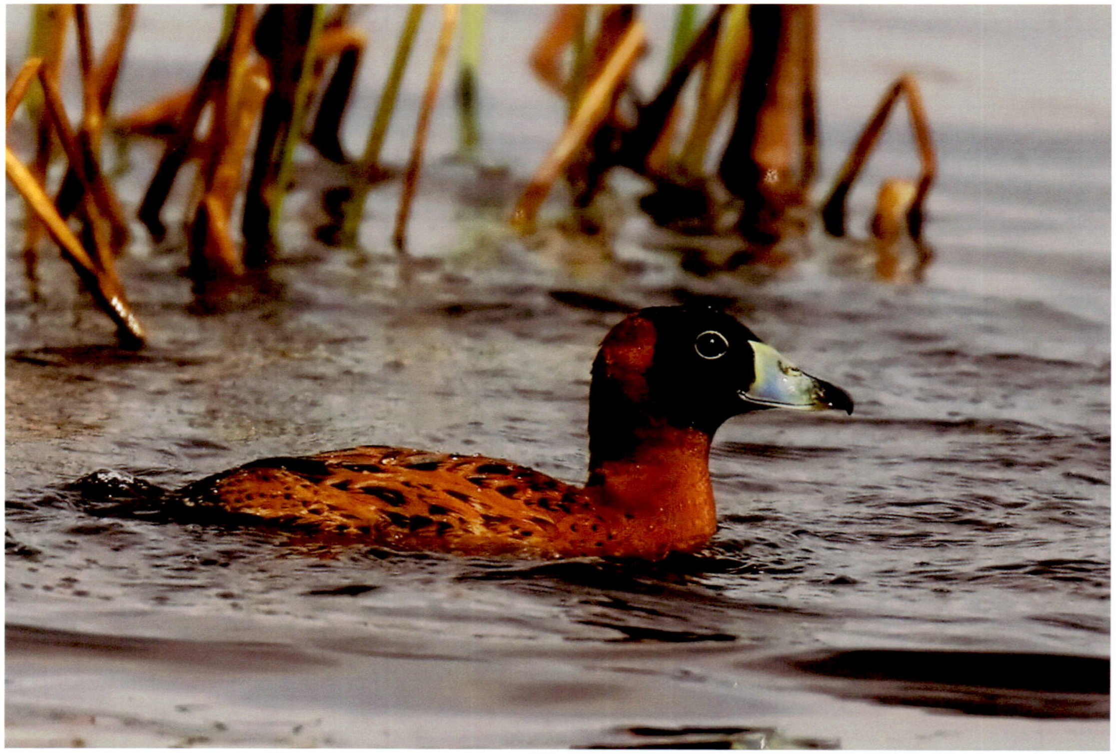

A rare male Masked Duck made a showing at the Viera Wetlands near Melbourne, Florida, in the winter of 2010. The rich red plumage is similar to the sunset above, and brings the feeling of fire to the imaginative mind. *Photo by Kevin T. Karlson*

Two Cosmos flowers show vibrant, coral-red colors, adding a splash of excitement to a hot summer day. *Photo by Kevin T. Karlson*

Reflections in rippled water creates an impressionistic mood with a splotch of red in the center. These water reflections (below) at the Ramapo Reservoir in Mahwah, New Jersey, are fondly called "Monet's Autumn Reflections" by the photographer. *Photo by Don Merwin*

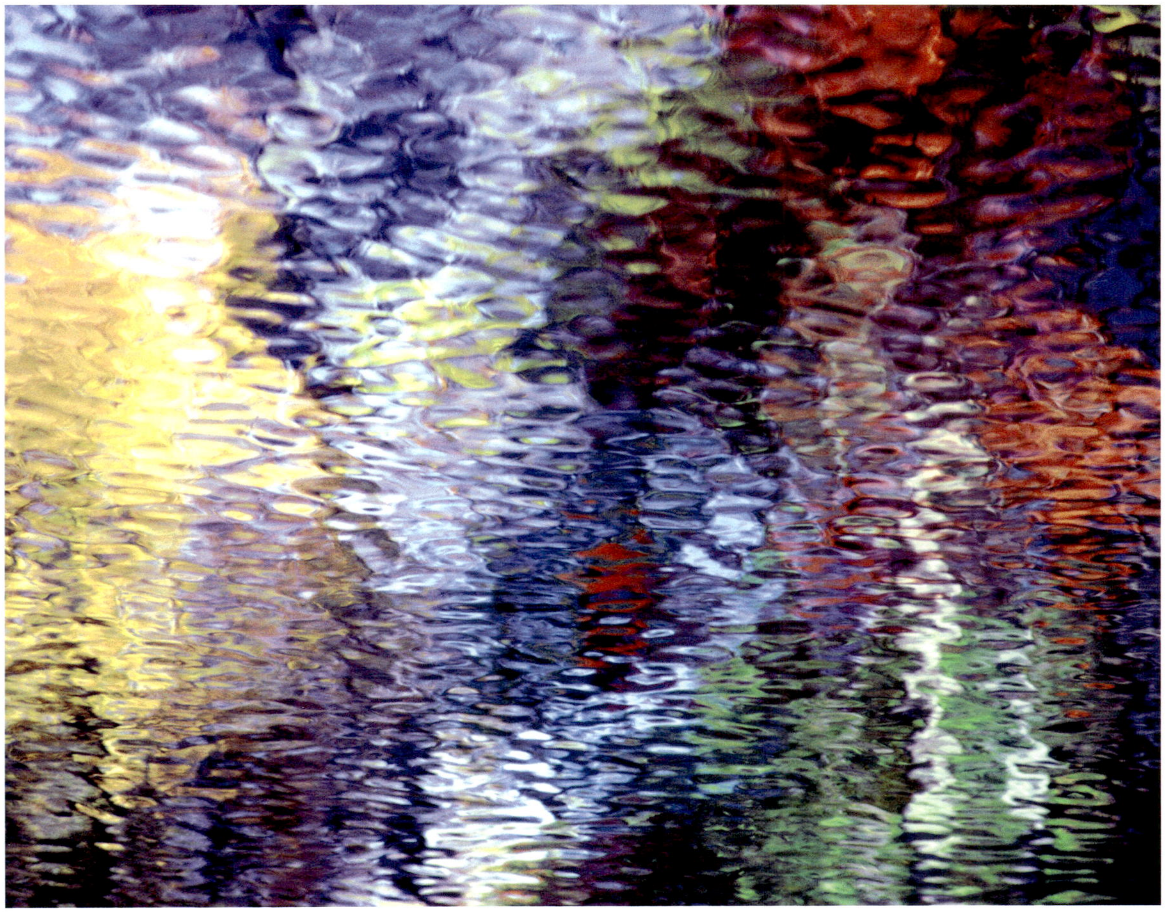

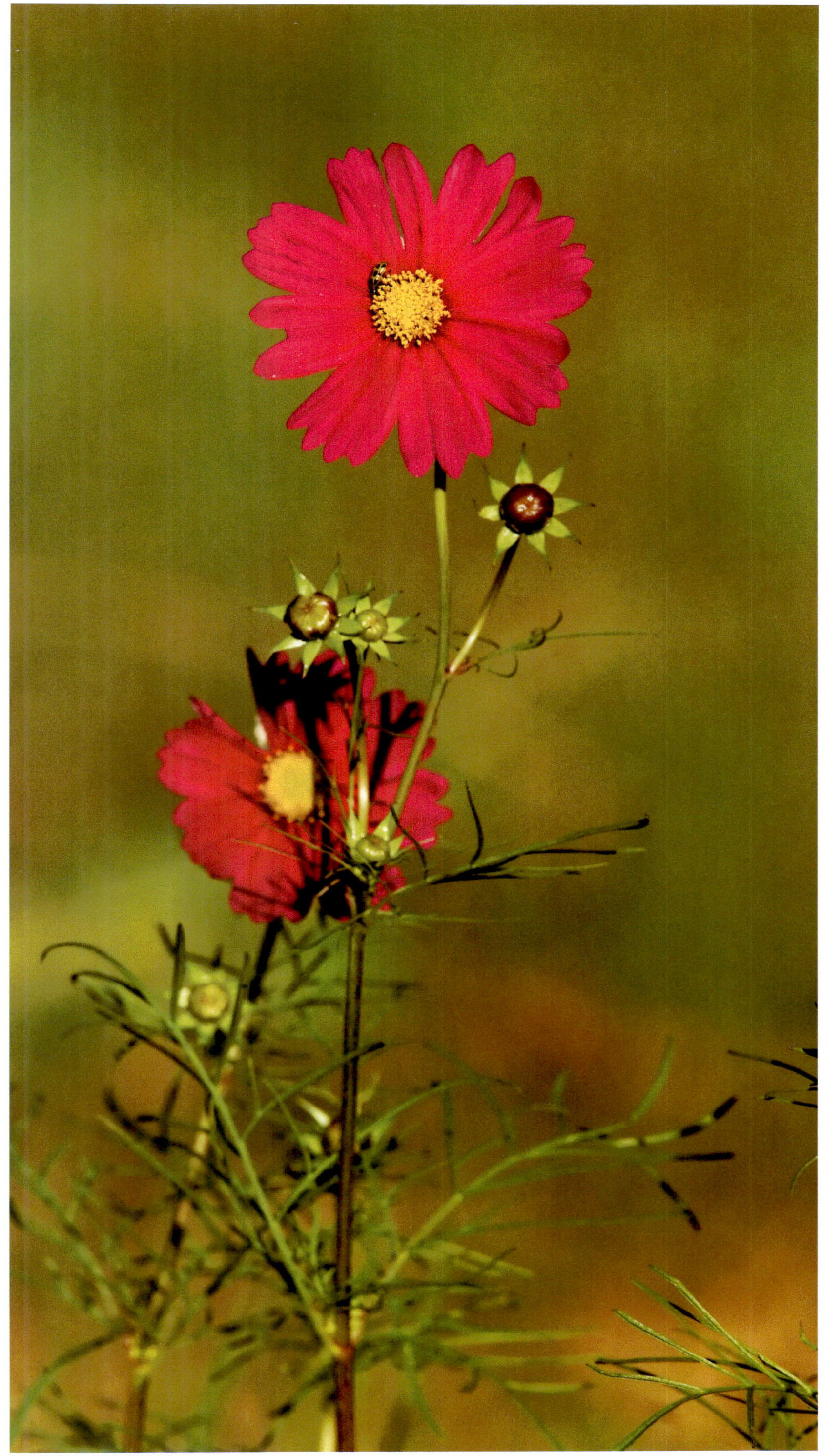

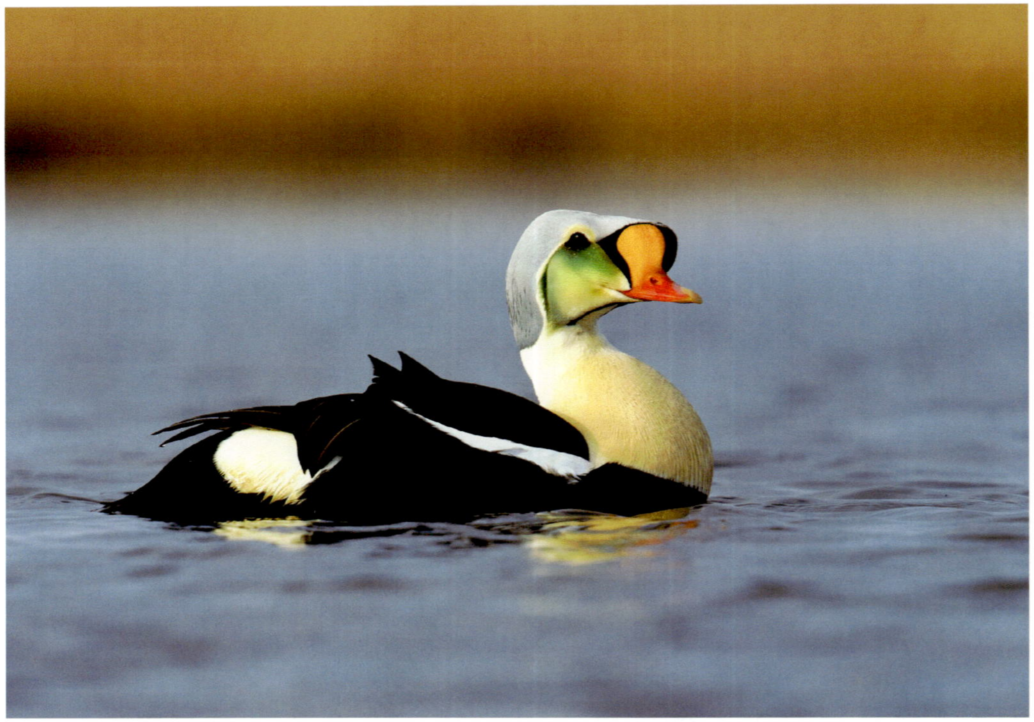

King Eiders combine beauty with the bizarre in their breeding plumage on the Arctic tundra. A fiery red bill combines with a swollen, orange breeding knob to create a bold contrast with the soft beauty of the King Eider's plumage. *Photos by Scott Elowitz (left) and Kevin T. Karlson (below)*

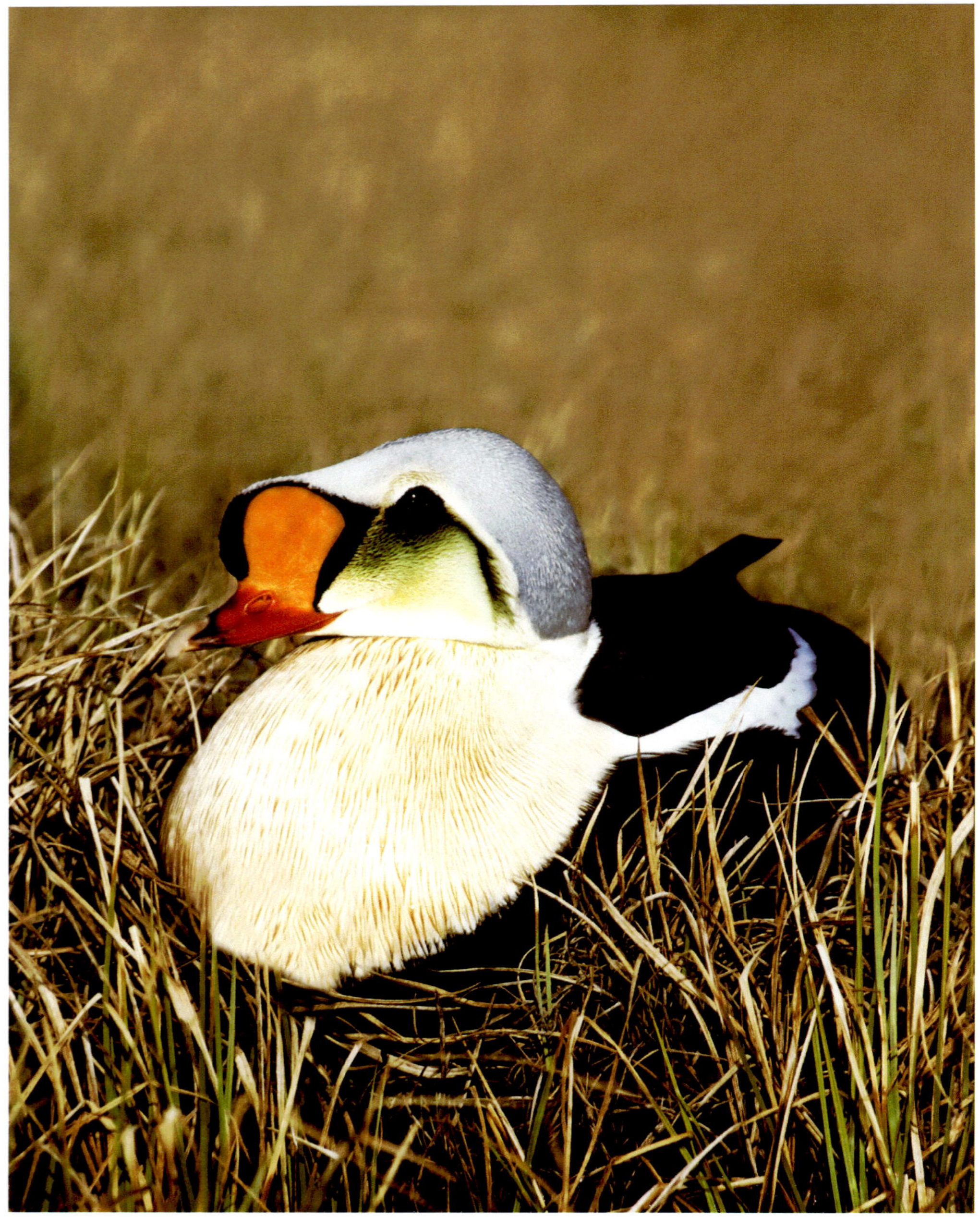

Hope is the thing with feathers
that perches in the soul.

— Emily Dickinson

Two other Arctic-breeding birds with fiery plumage tones are the Red-throated Loon (below) and the Hudsonian Godwit (right). Both lose the reddish coloration after breeding season. *Photos by Kevin T. Karlson*

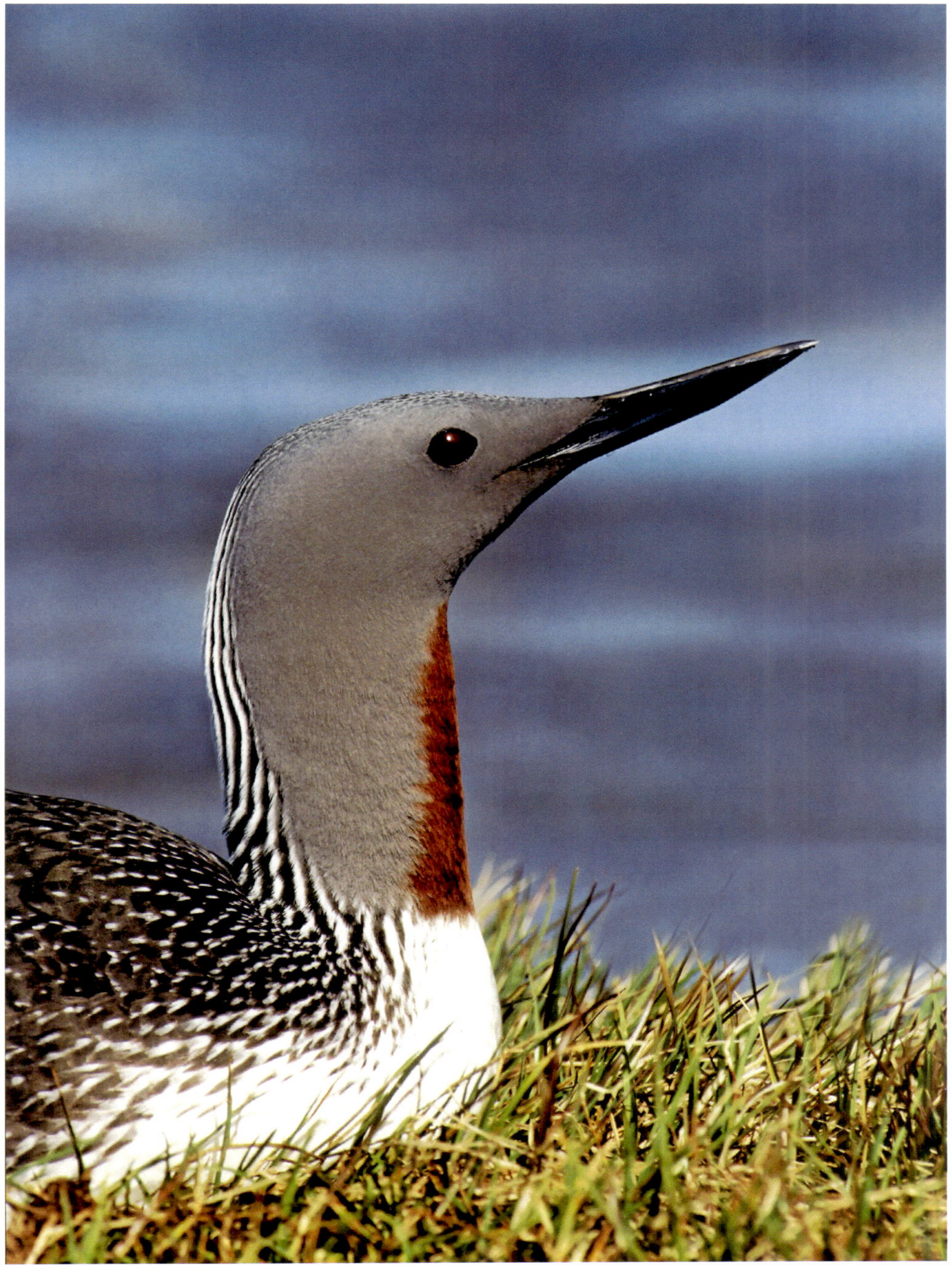

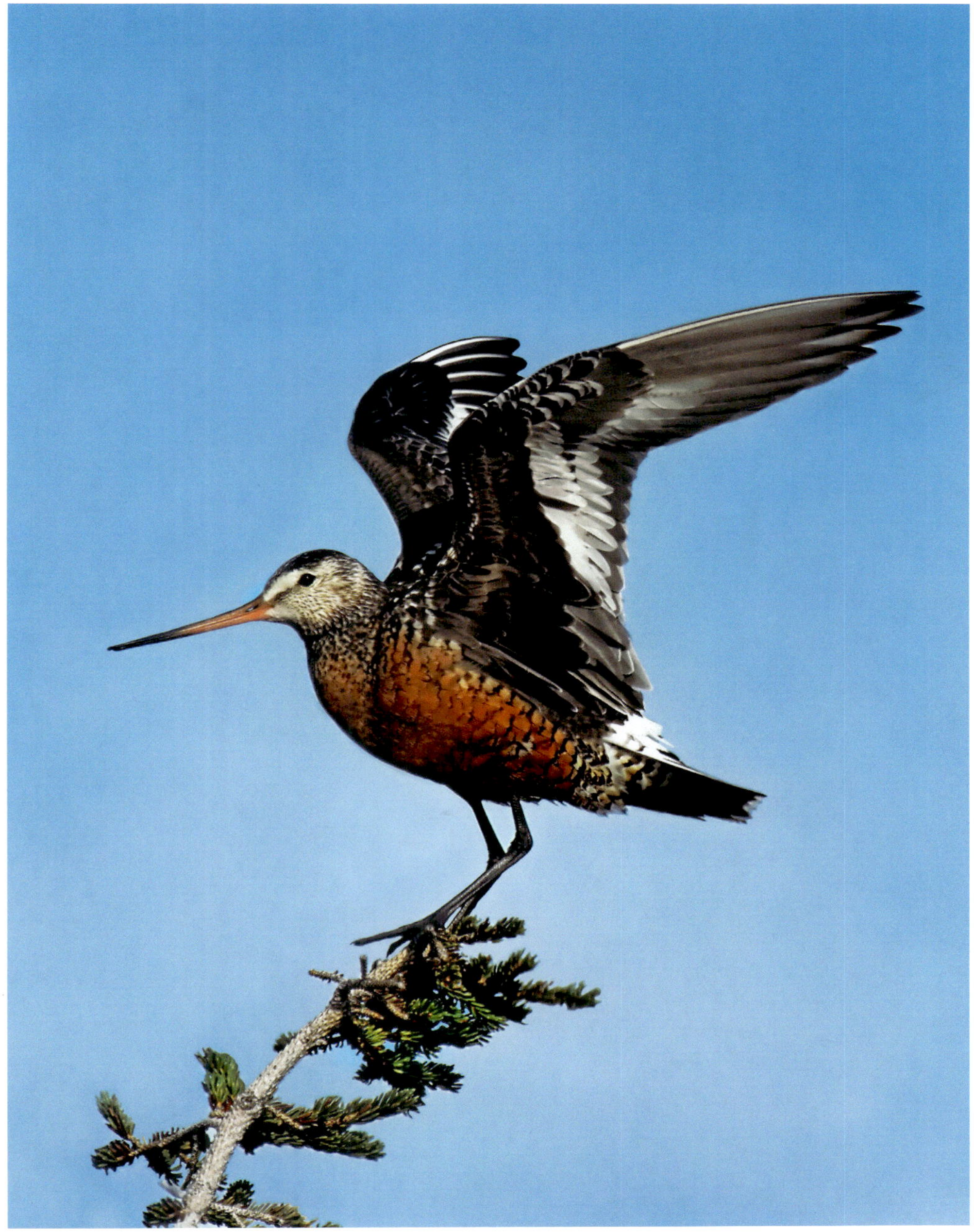

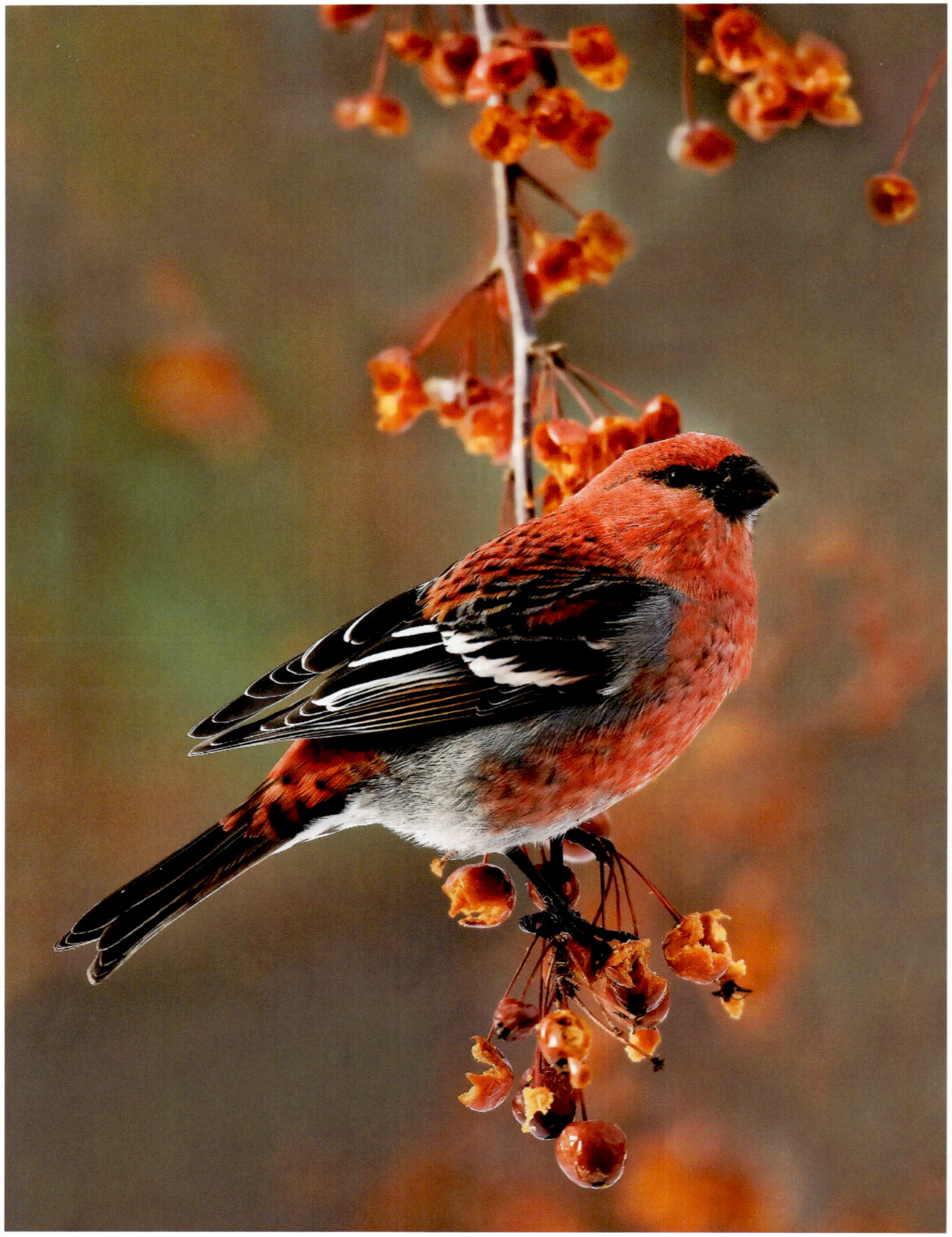

Pine Grosbeaks are hearty finches and true “snowbirds.” They don’t migrate south to warmer climates in winter, but stay in frigid northern locations. Despite the cold winter temperatures, their rich, red raspberry color imparts a fiery feeling, especially when you see them against the snow. *Photos by Kevin T. Karlson (left) and Lloyd Spitalnik (below)*

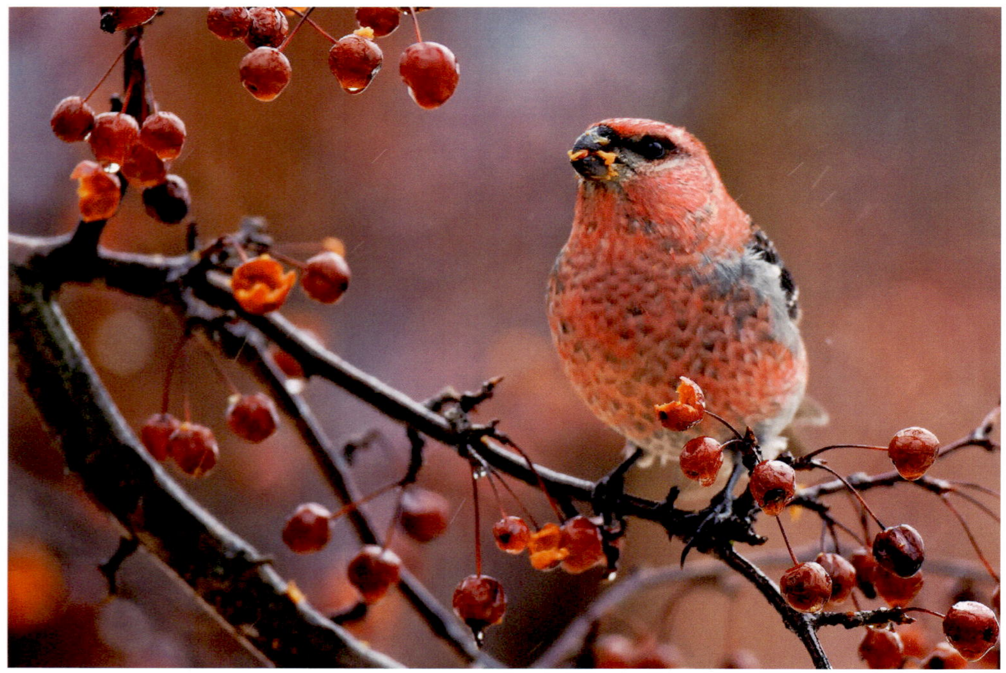

This photo of Red-legged Thrush from the island of Andros has always been one of Kevin's favorites, in part because of the rich, golden leaves around the tree and the bird's fiery-colored eye ring. *Photo by Kevin T. Karlson*

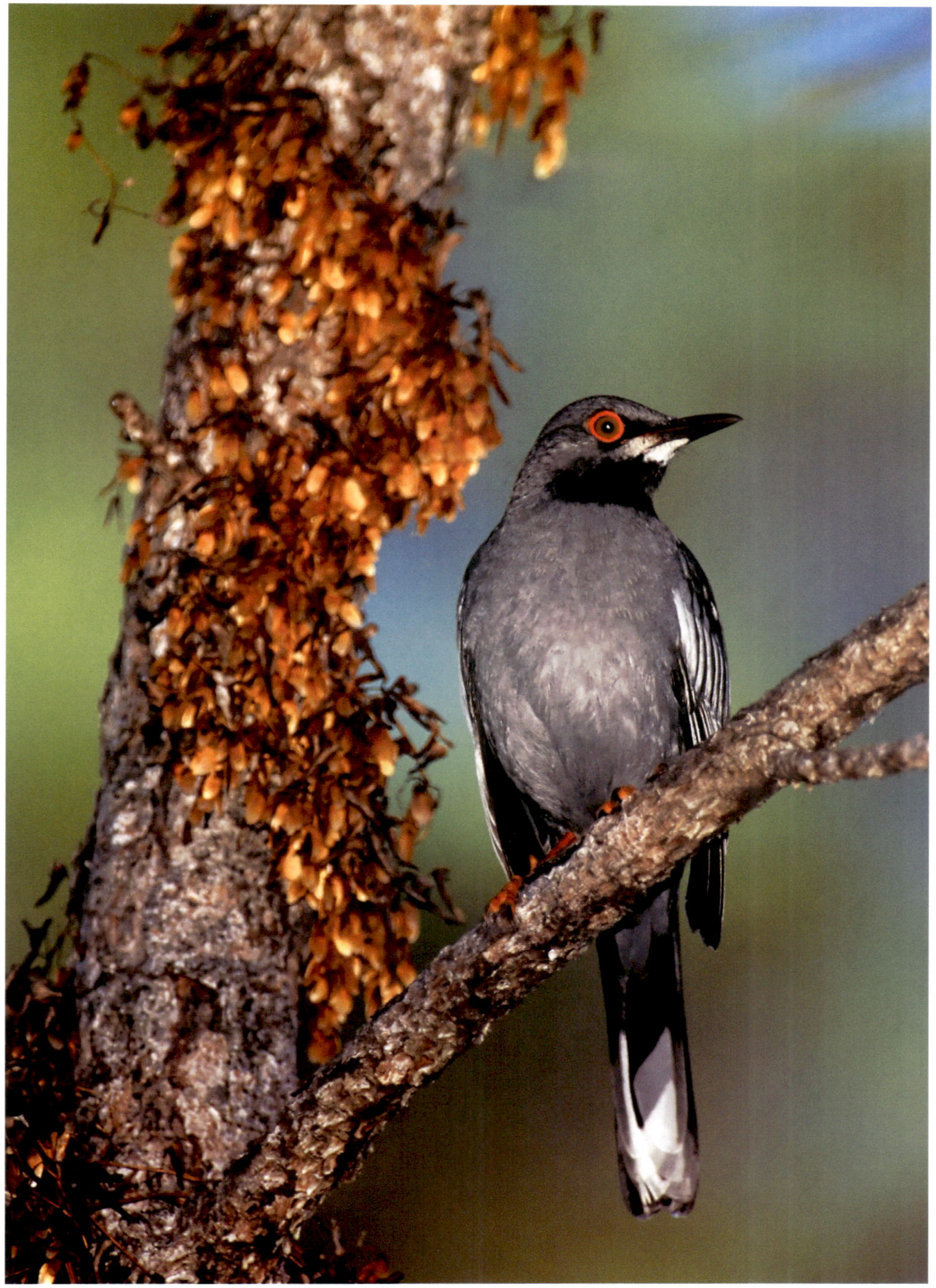

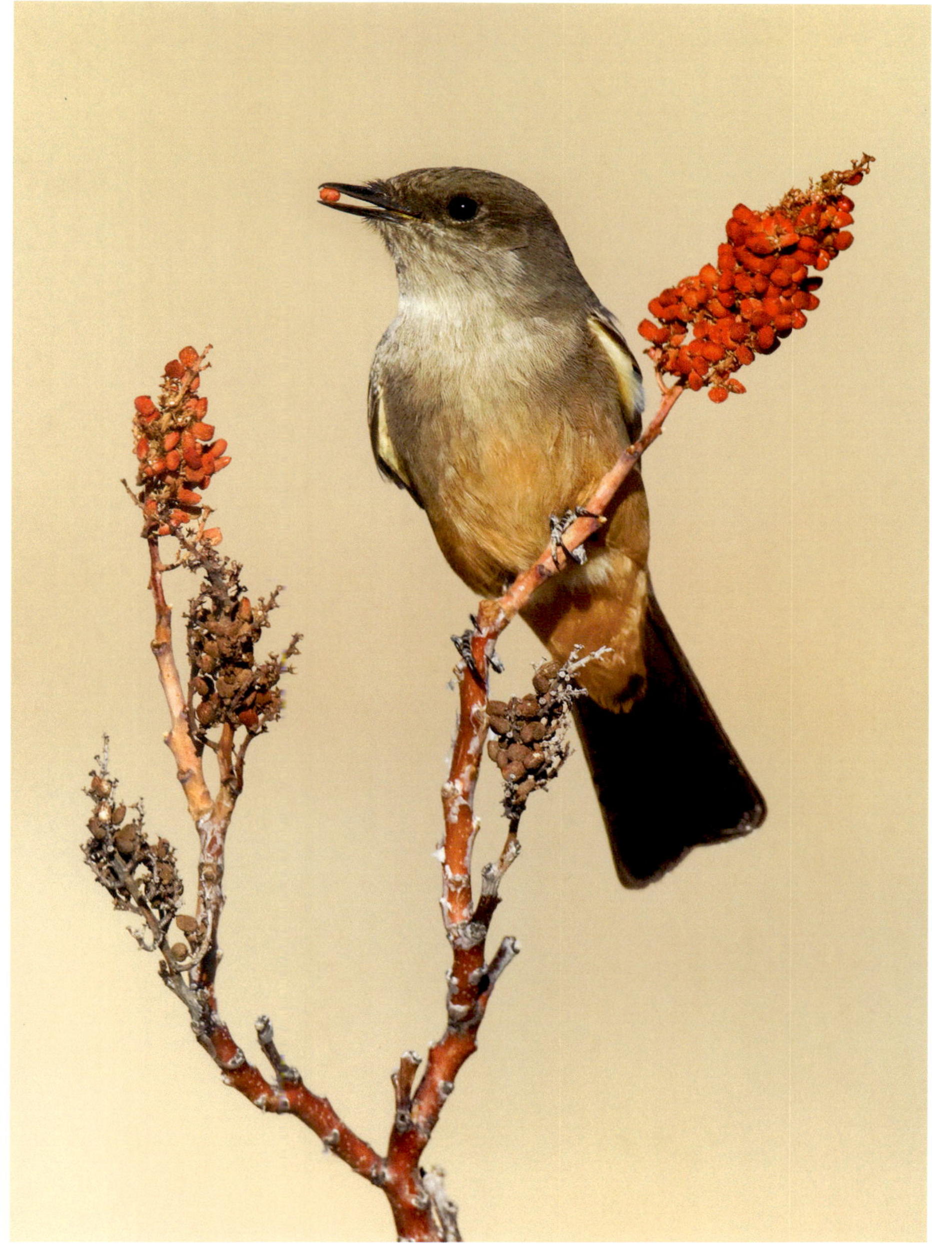

While the breast of this Say's Phoebe has the warm feeling of glowing embers, the sumac berries add a flame-like mood to the image. *Photo by Scott Elowitz*

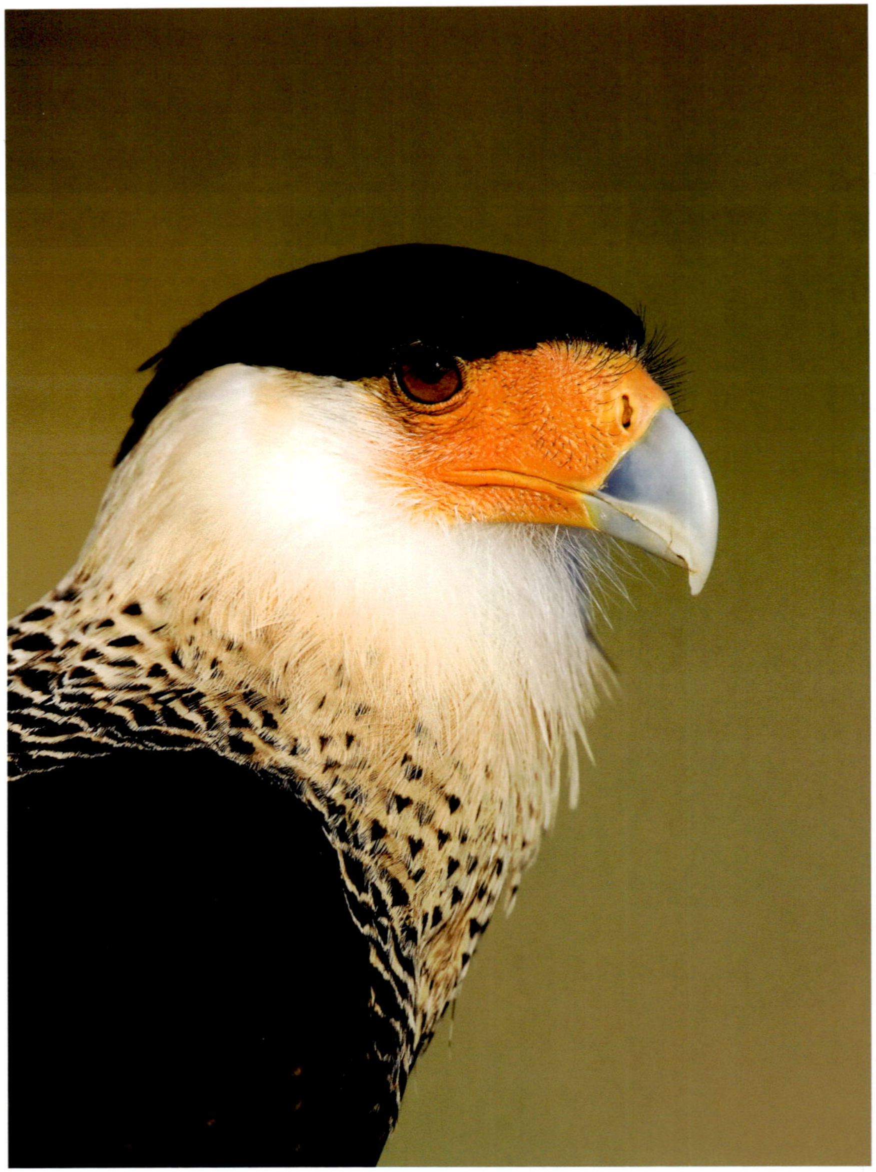

He who can no longer pause to wonder and stand rapt in awe is as good as dead; his eyes are closed.

— Albert Einstein

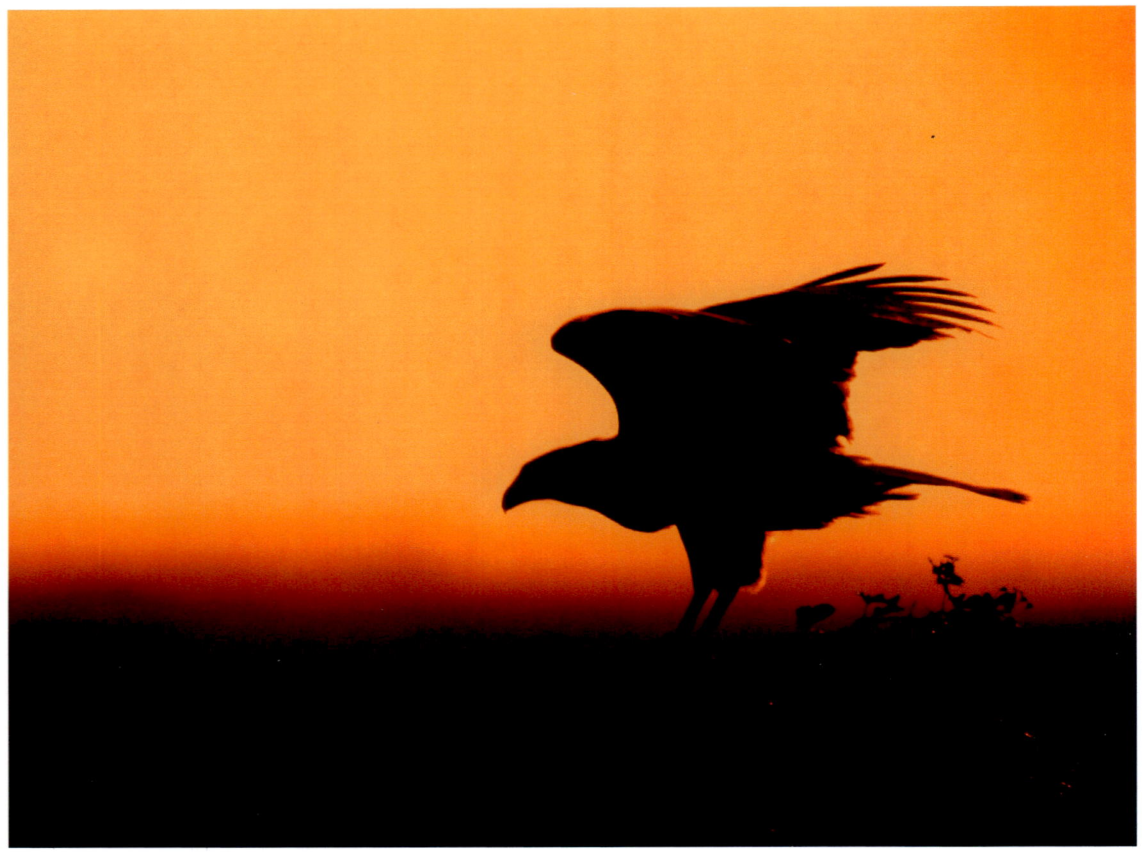

Crested Caracaras are fondly called the "Mexican Eagles" by residents of south Texas and Mexico. This large raptor has an imposing bill highlighted by rich orange facial skin. Silhouetted against a fiery Texas sunset, the Caracara surveys his domain. *Photos by Kevin T. Karlson*

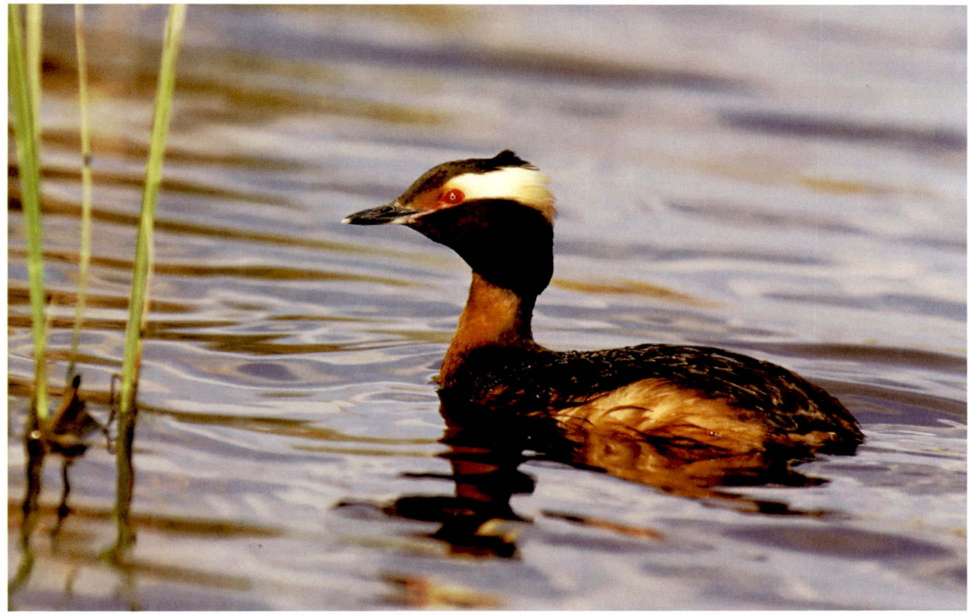

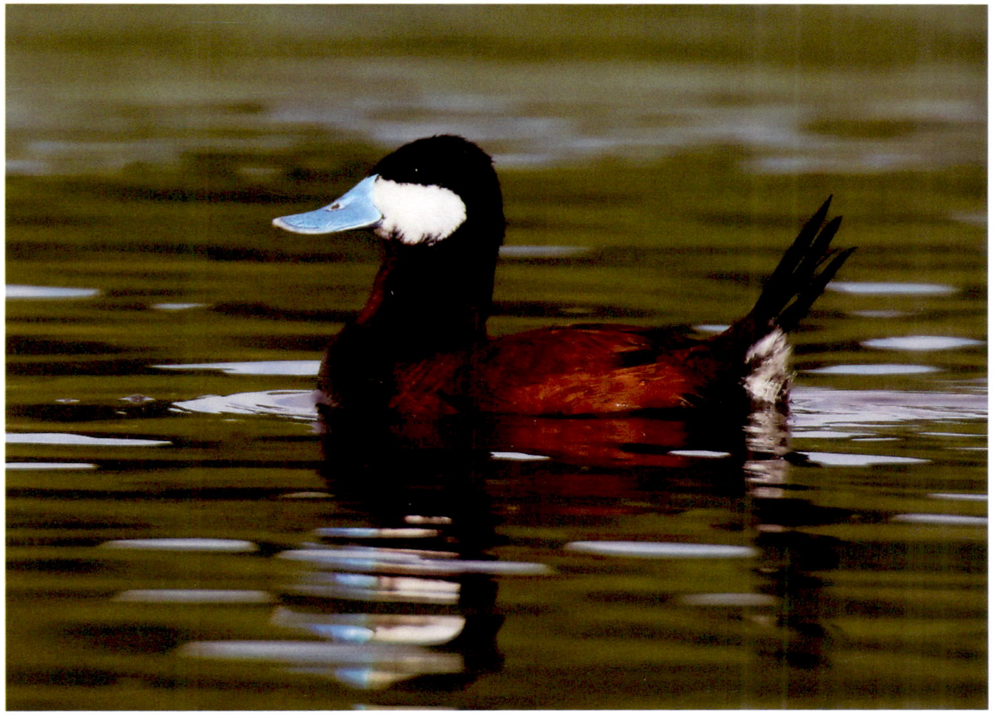

Breeding male Ruddy Ducks (above) have a rich, reddish plumage that matches the flank feathers of a breeding Eared Grebe (lower right). The electric red eye of the Eared Grebe is hypnotic in its intensity, and almost matched by the bright red eye of the Horned Grebe (upper right). *Photos by Kevin T. Karlson*

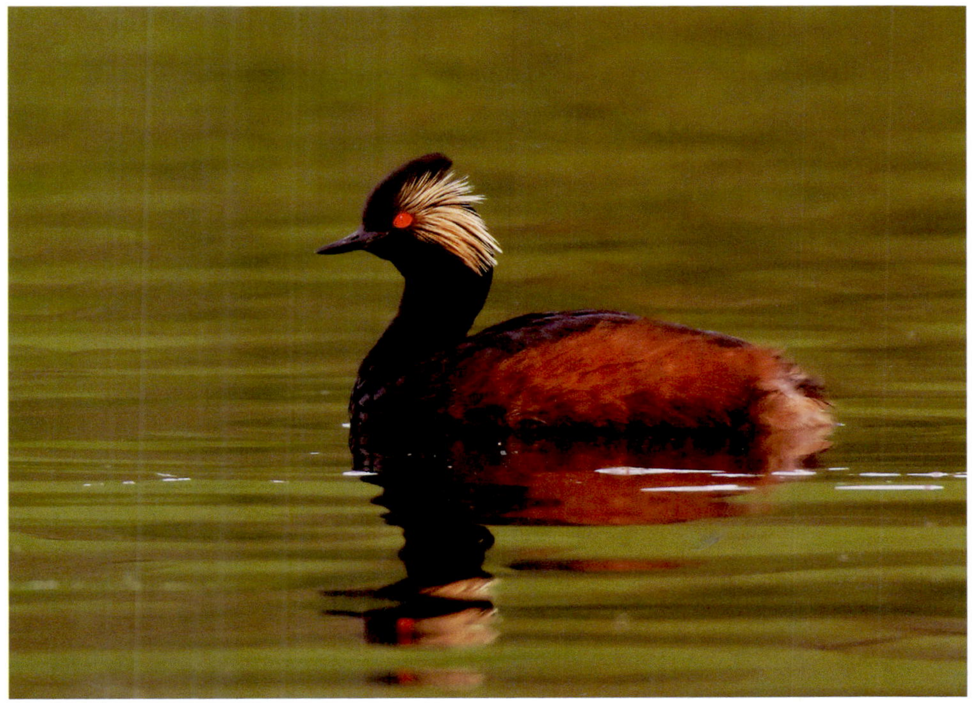

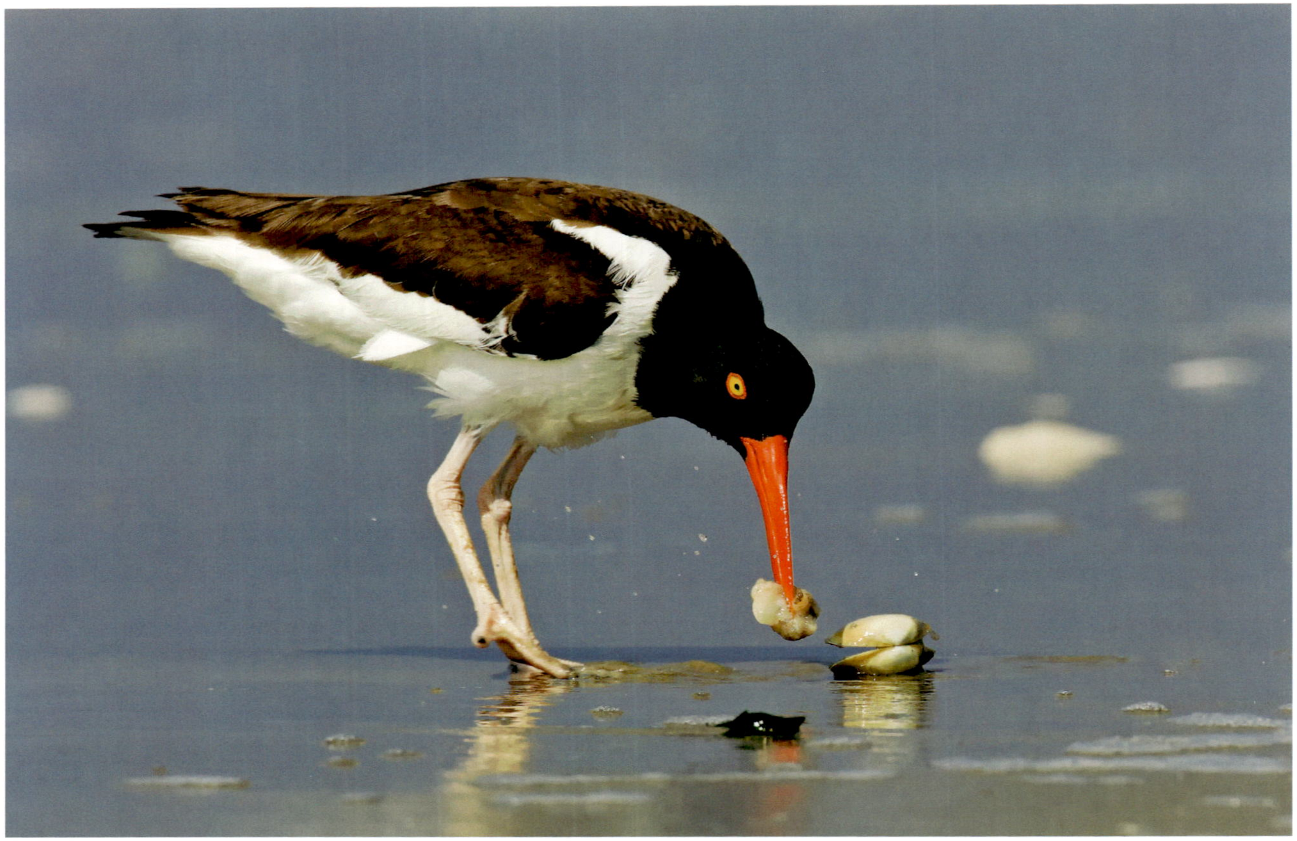

American Oystercatchers' long, carrot-like bills and orange eyes outlined in red makes them good candidates for the fire section. This photo array shows American Oystercatchers feeding (upper left), displaying (lower left) and crouching over a nest (lower right). *Photos by Lloyd Spitalnik (upper and lower left) and Kevin T. Karlson (lower right)*

Opposite: Black Skimmers have unusual red and black bills that are used to trap fish while they fly just above the water's surface. This close-up image shows a very young chick under the watchful eye of its parent. *Photo by Lloyd Spitalnik*

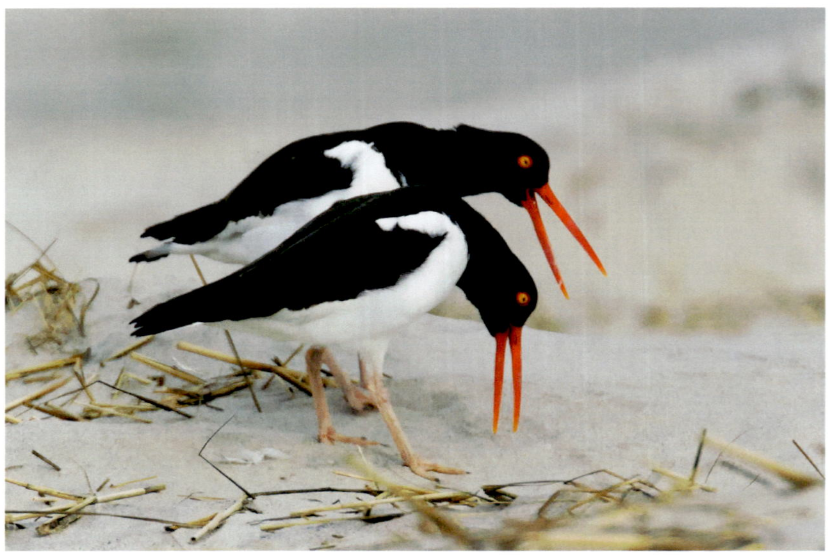

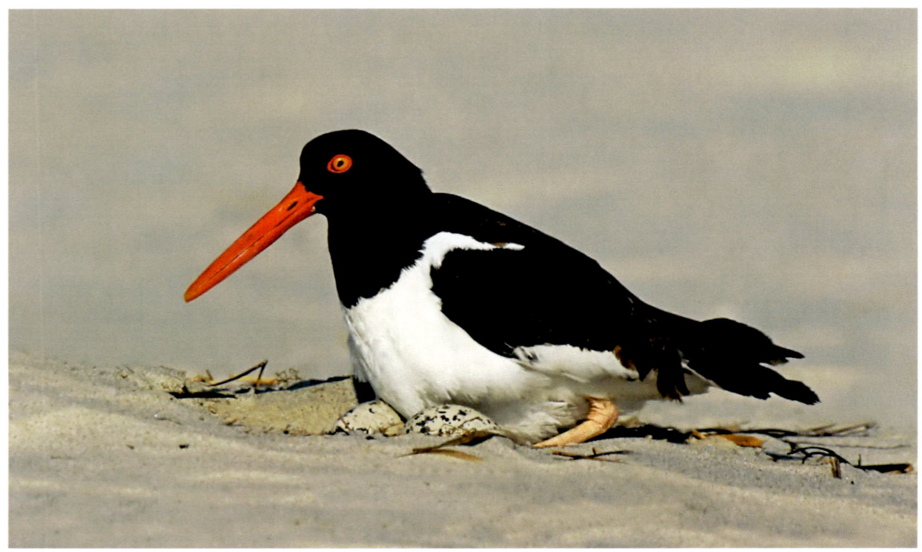

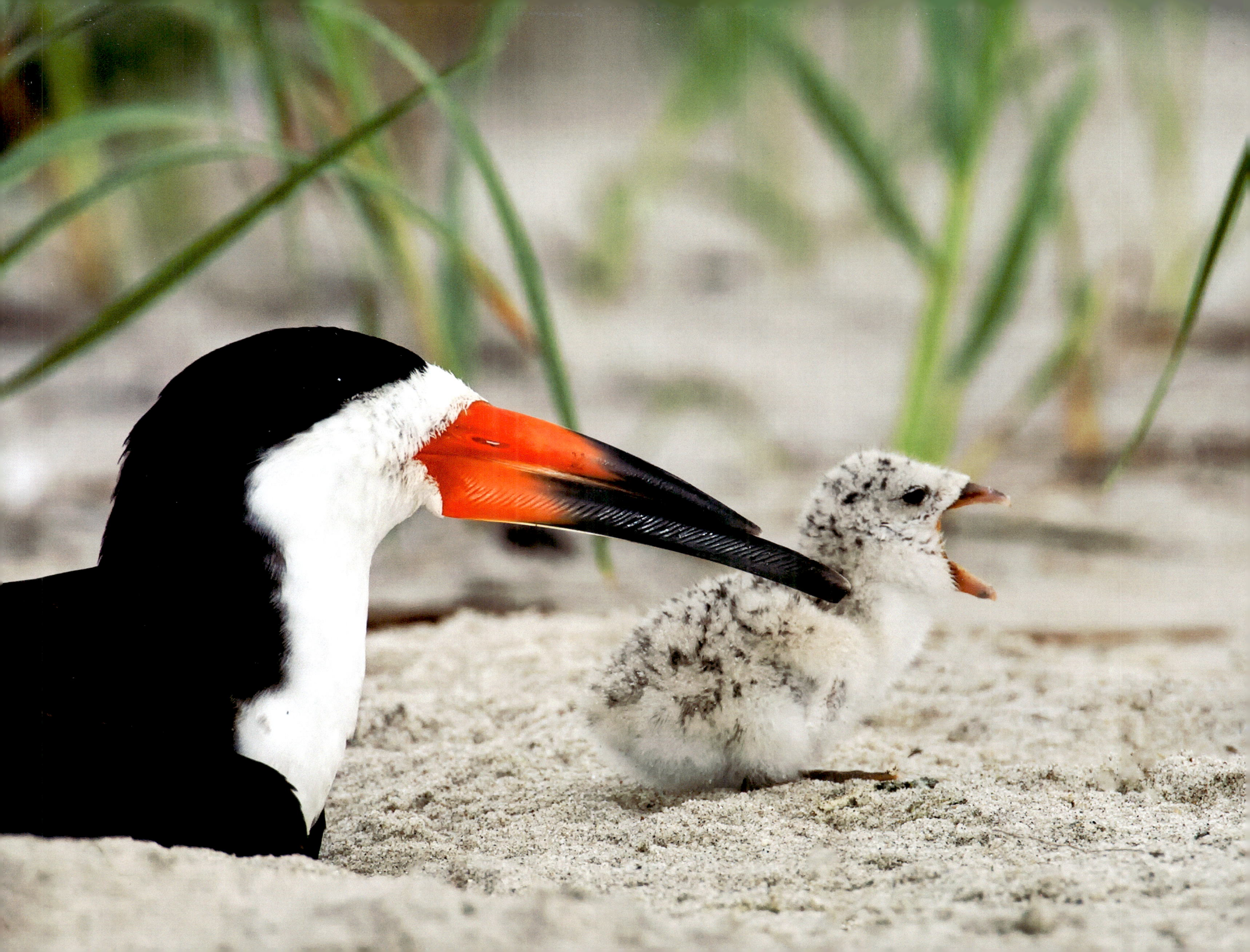

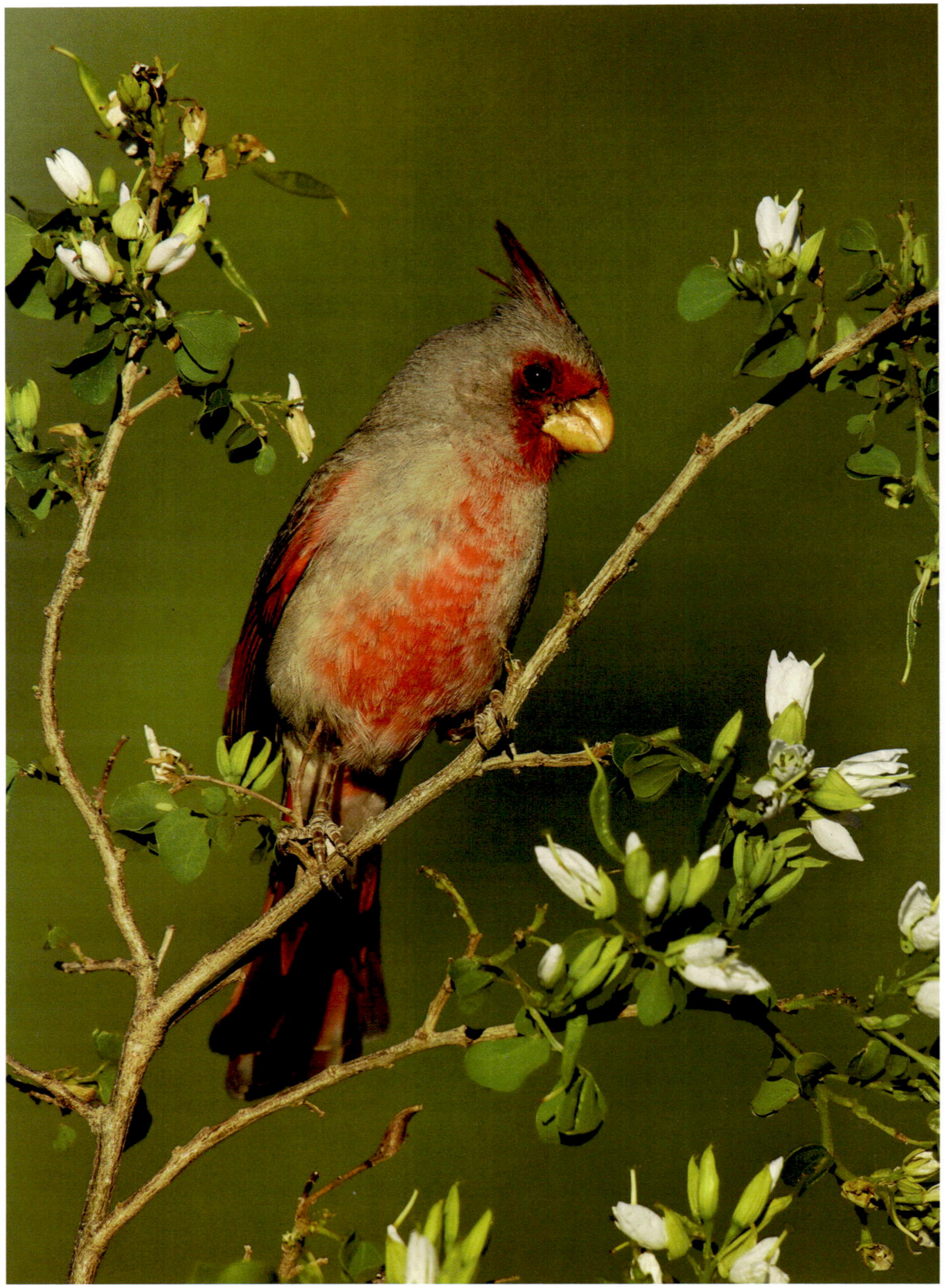

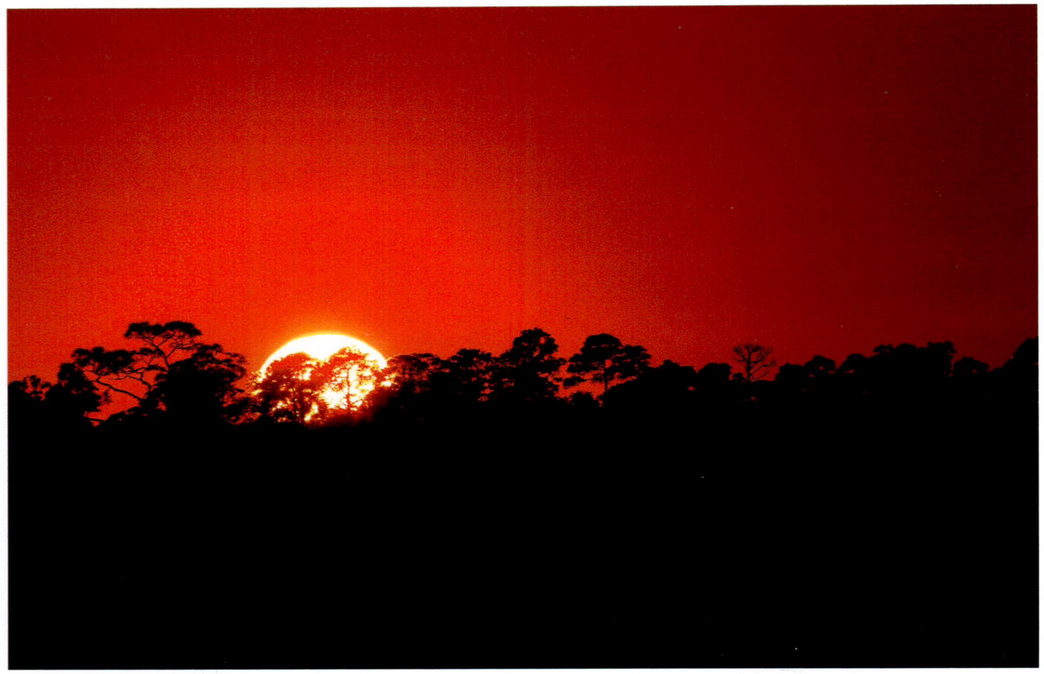

Rich plumage colors on this male Pyrrhuloxia complement the red tones of the sunset (above). *Photo by Scott Elowitz*

A fiery sunset was captured in Florida in September at the Viera Wetlands. No filters were used on this image, and the color saturation was not enhanced. *Photo by Kevin T. Karlson*

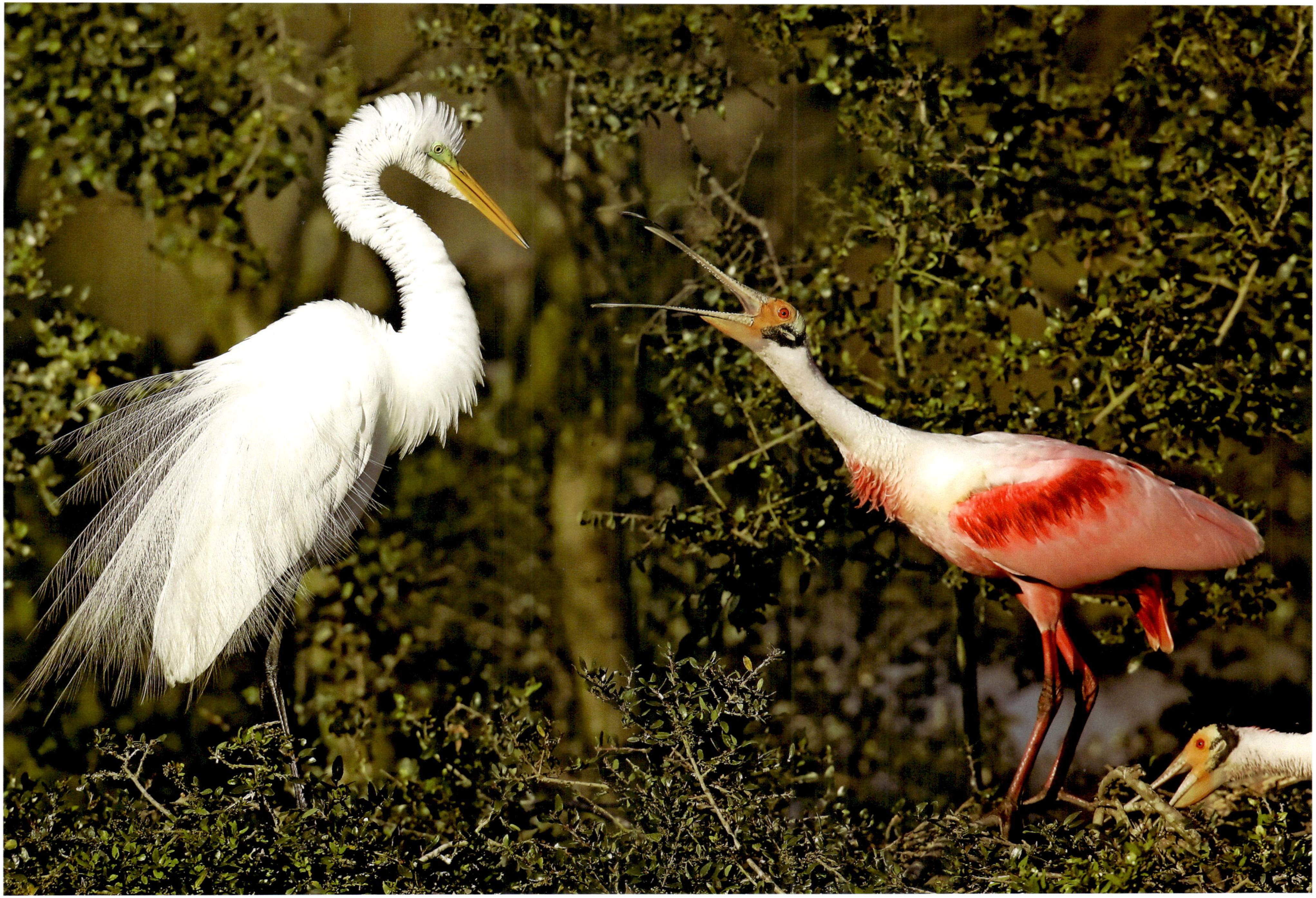

A nesting male Roseate Spoonbill is fending off an intruding Great Egret who has eyes on the nest site, while the female Spoonbill nervously arranges the nest.
Photo by Kevin T. Karlson

And pluck till time and times are done
the silver apples of the moon
the golden apples of the sun.

—William B. Yeats

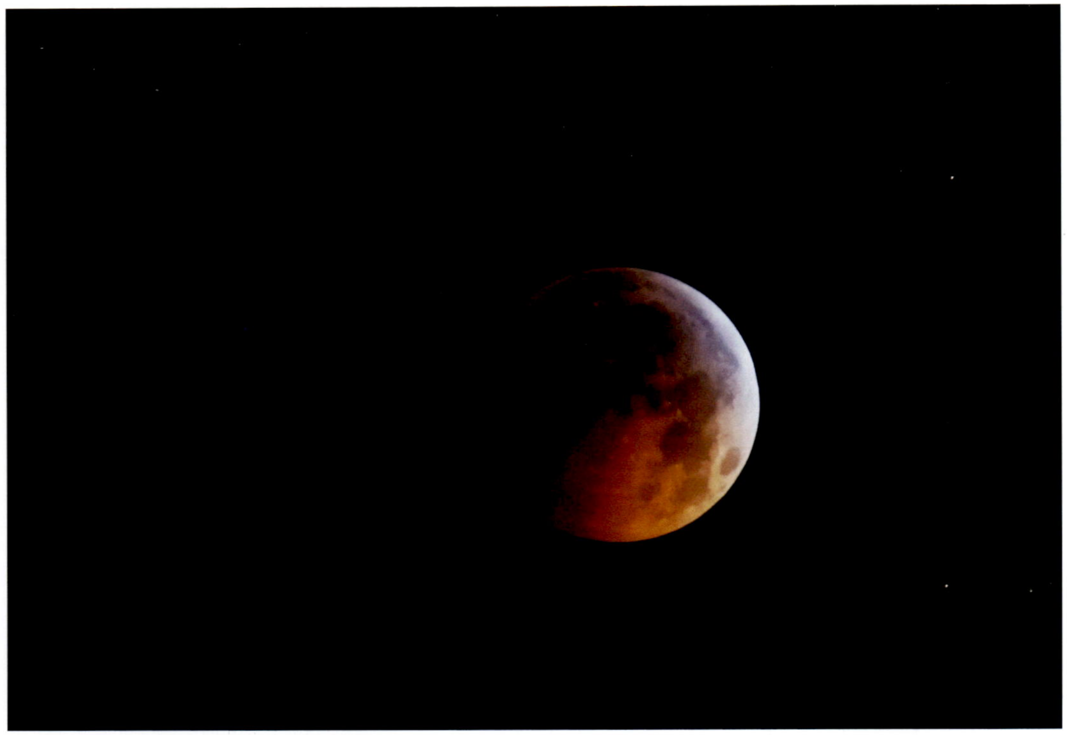

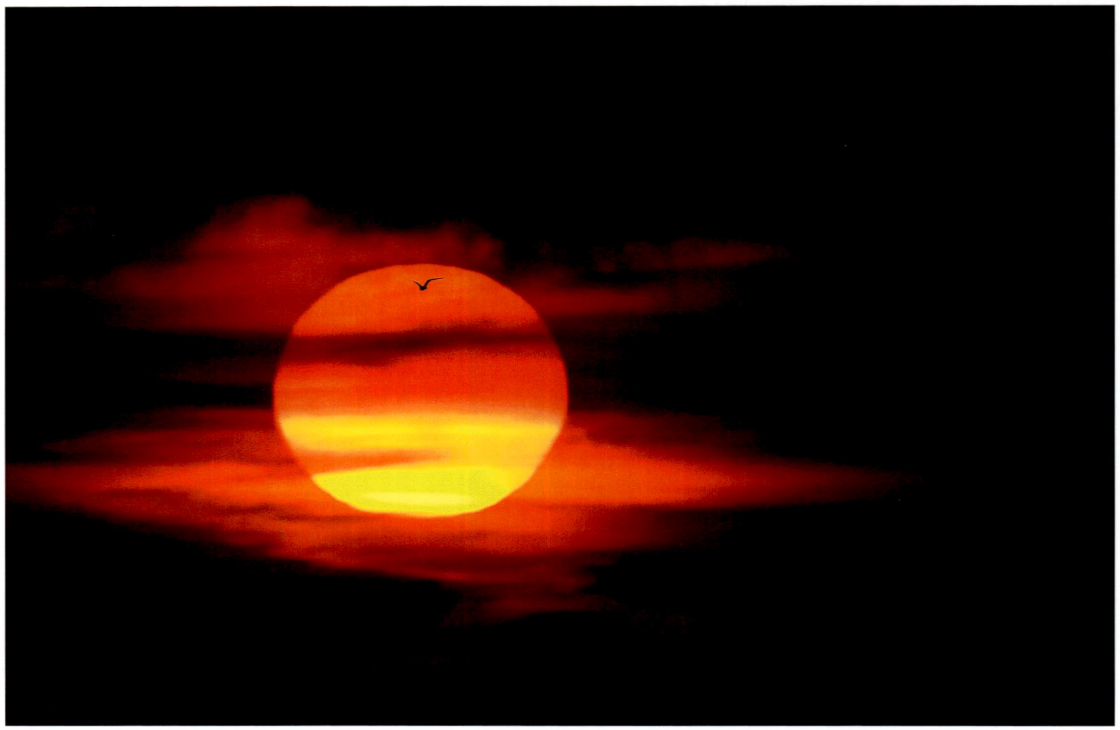

The lunar eclipse (above) on December 21, 2010, gave the moon a warm, reddish glow instead of the usual white hot appearance. You never see stars around a full moon, but the several bright ones in this image gave the scene a surreal mood.

A warm sunset in St. Augustine Florida is enhanced by the single bird flying against the sun. Clouds give the image a moody feeling. *Photos by Kevin T. Karlson*

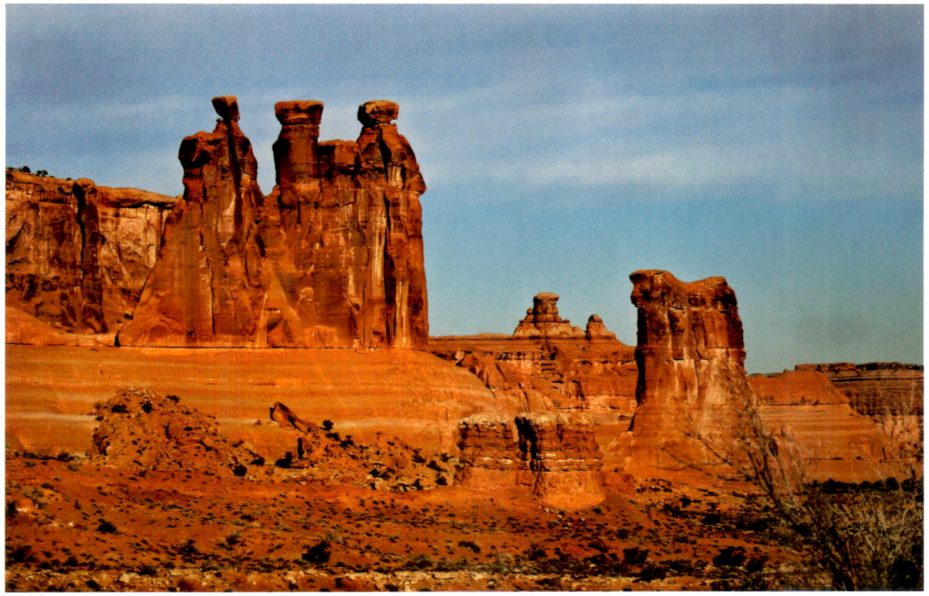

Arches National Park in Utah is the setting for these red rock images, including the famous Delicate Arch (right). Three Sisters is the name given to the upper photo, but a bit of imagination might allow you to see the three wise men from biblical literature. The impressive arch below was the longest freestanding rock arch in the world until it collapsed in 2006. *Photos by Kevin T. Karlson*

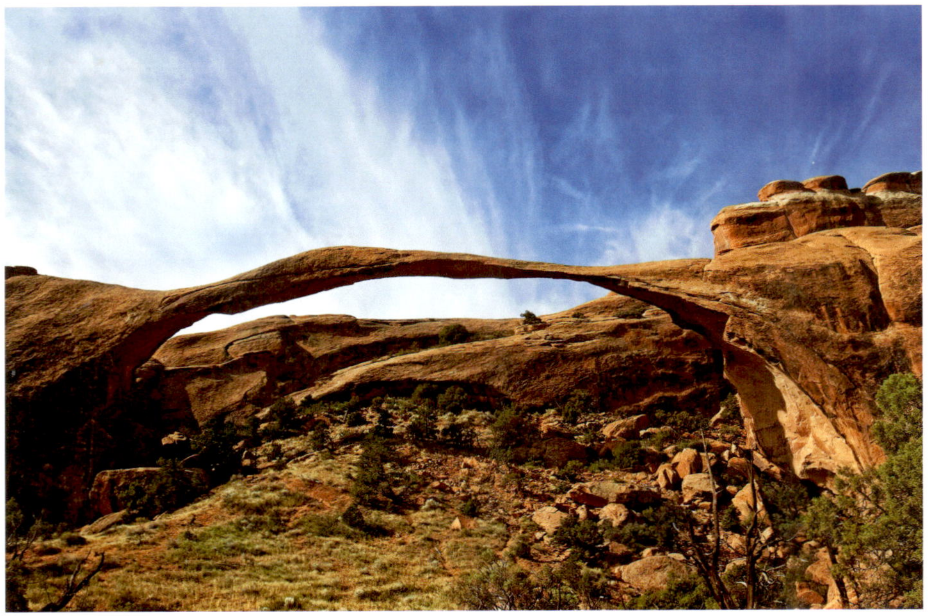

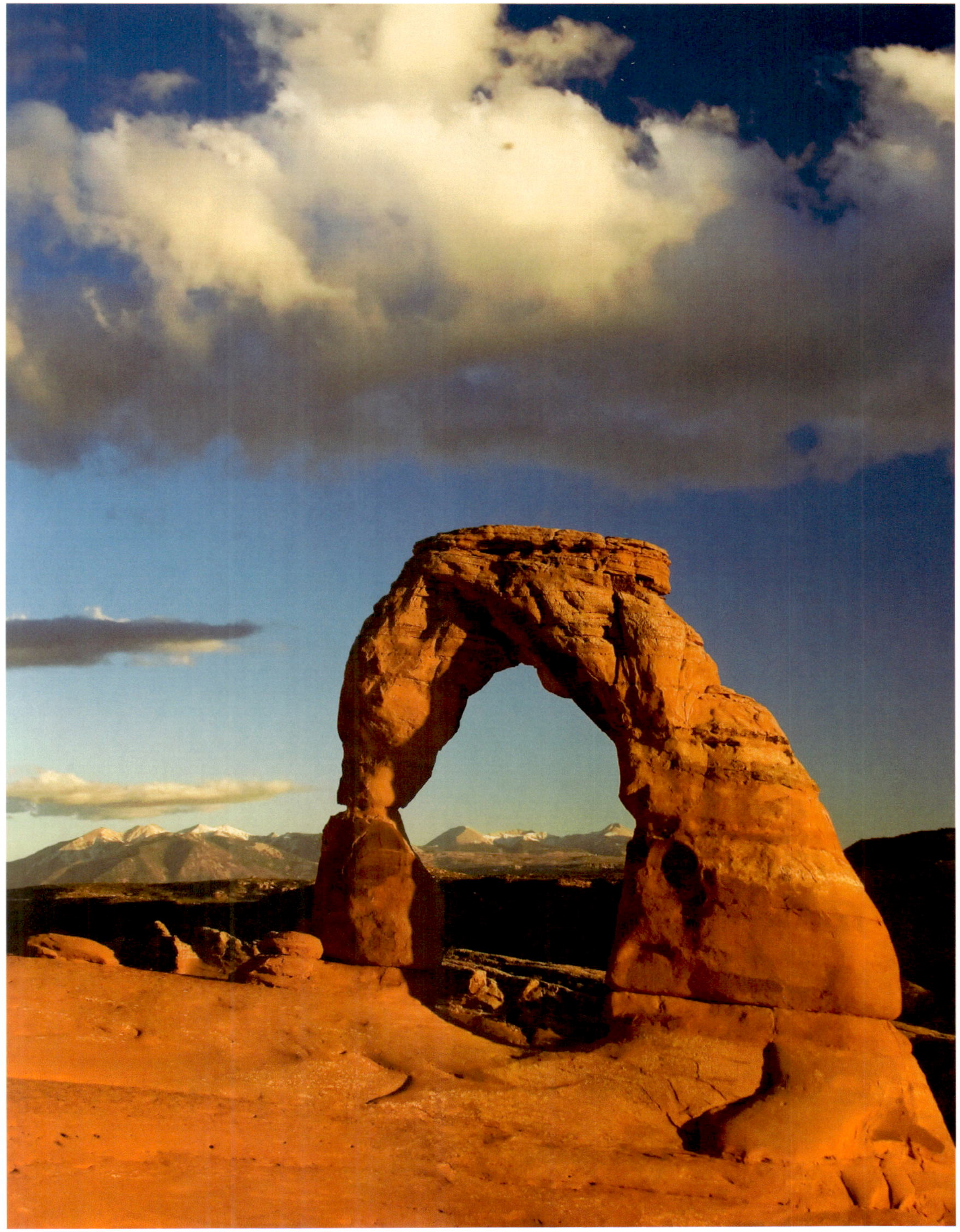

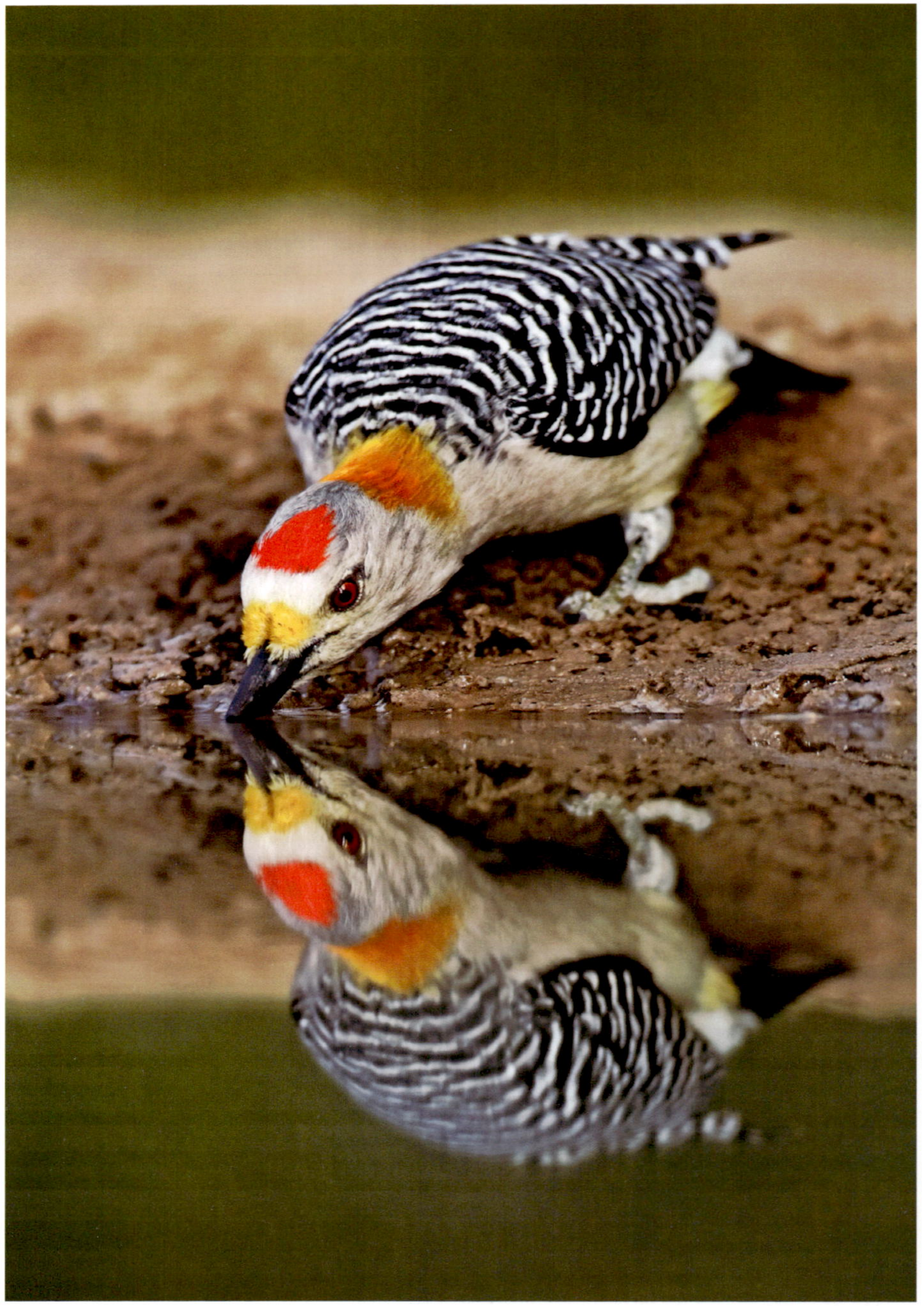

A Golden-fronted Woodpecker carries the fire theme in its orange and red head markings and deep red eye. *Photo by Mike Hannisian*

A displaying tom Wild Turkey exposes a bold, red throat pouch while fanning its impressive tail and raising most of the body feathers. This male is behaving in an animated fashion because two slender female Turkeys were standing nearby. *Photo by Kevin T. Karlson*

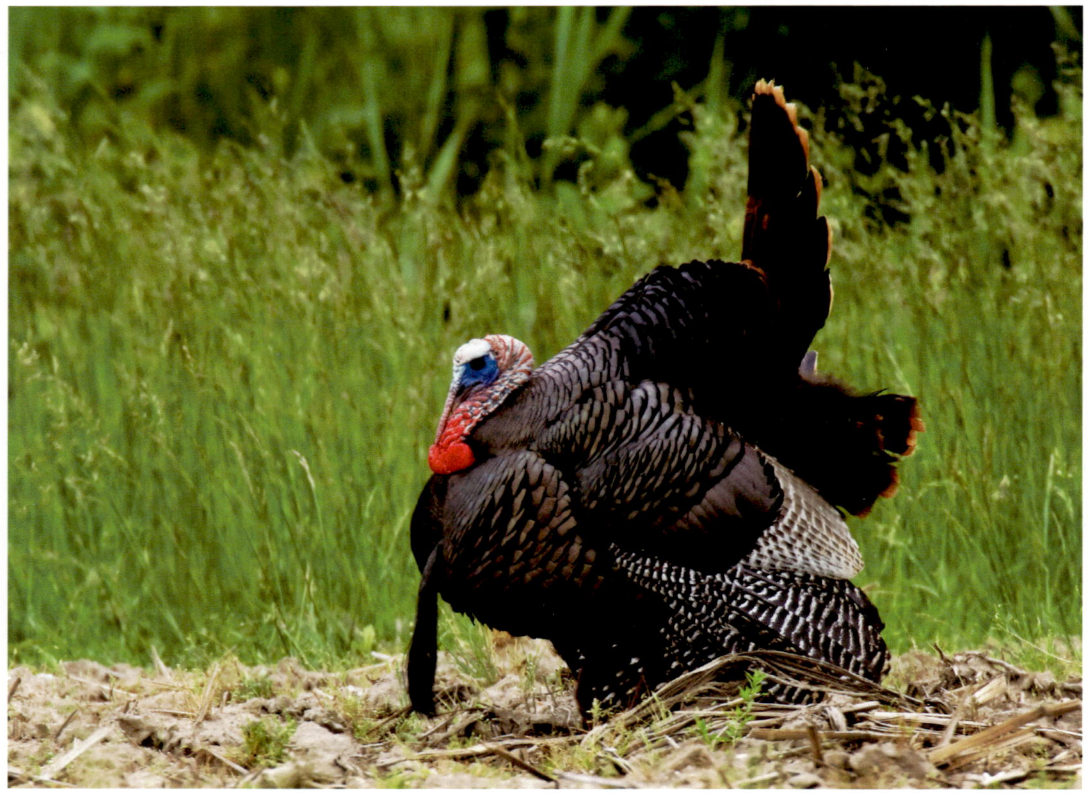

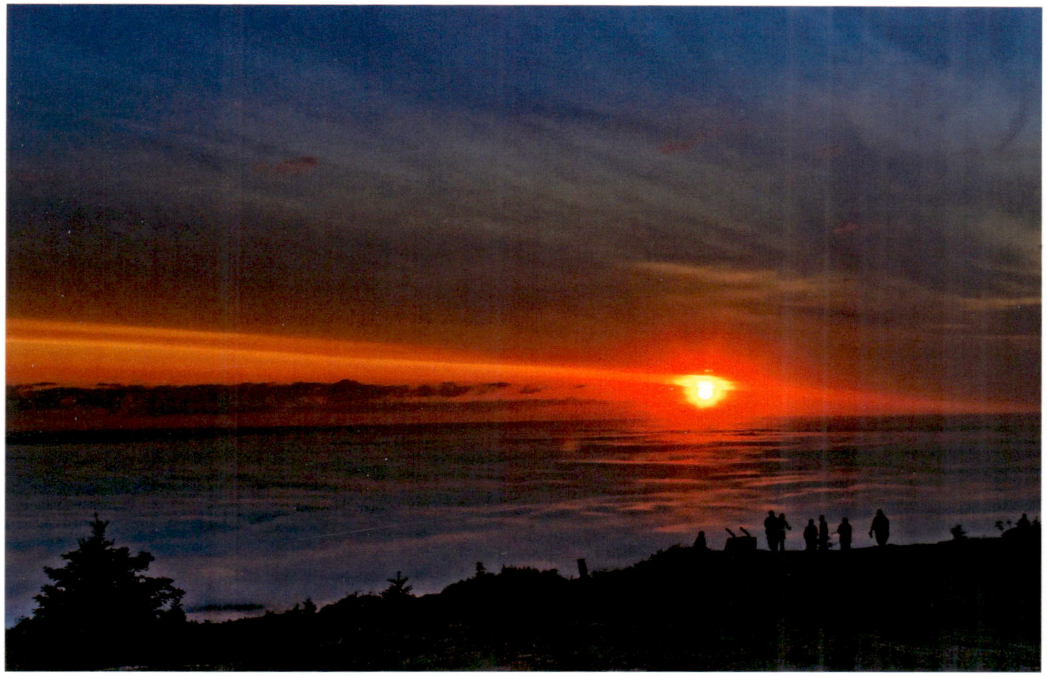

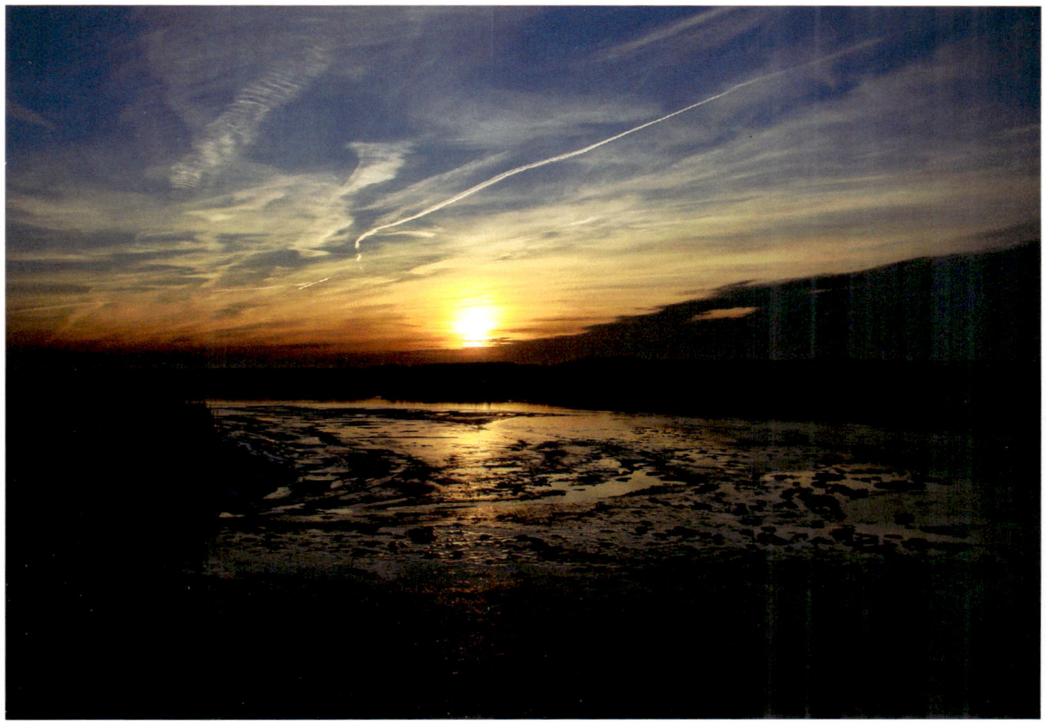

Moods of the sun start with a fiery sunrise on Cadillac Mountain in Maine (upper left), and end with a cooler mood in this icy water sunset image in southern New Jersey (lower left) A sunset afterglow is depicted in the Arizona scene (below), complete with Saguaro Cactus. *Photos by Mike Hannisian (upper left), Pat Sutton (lower left) and Dale Rosselet (below)*

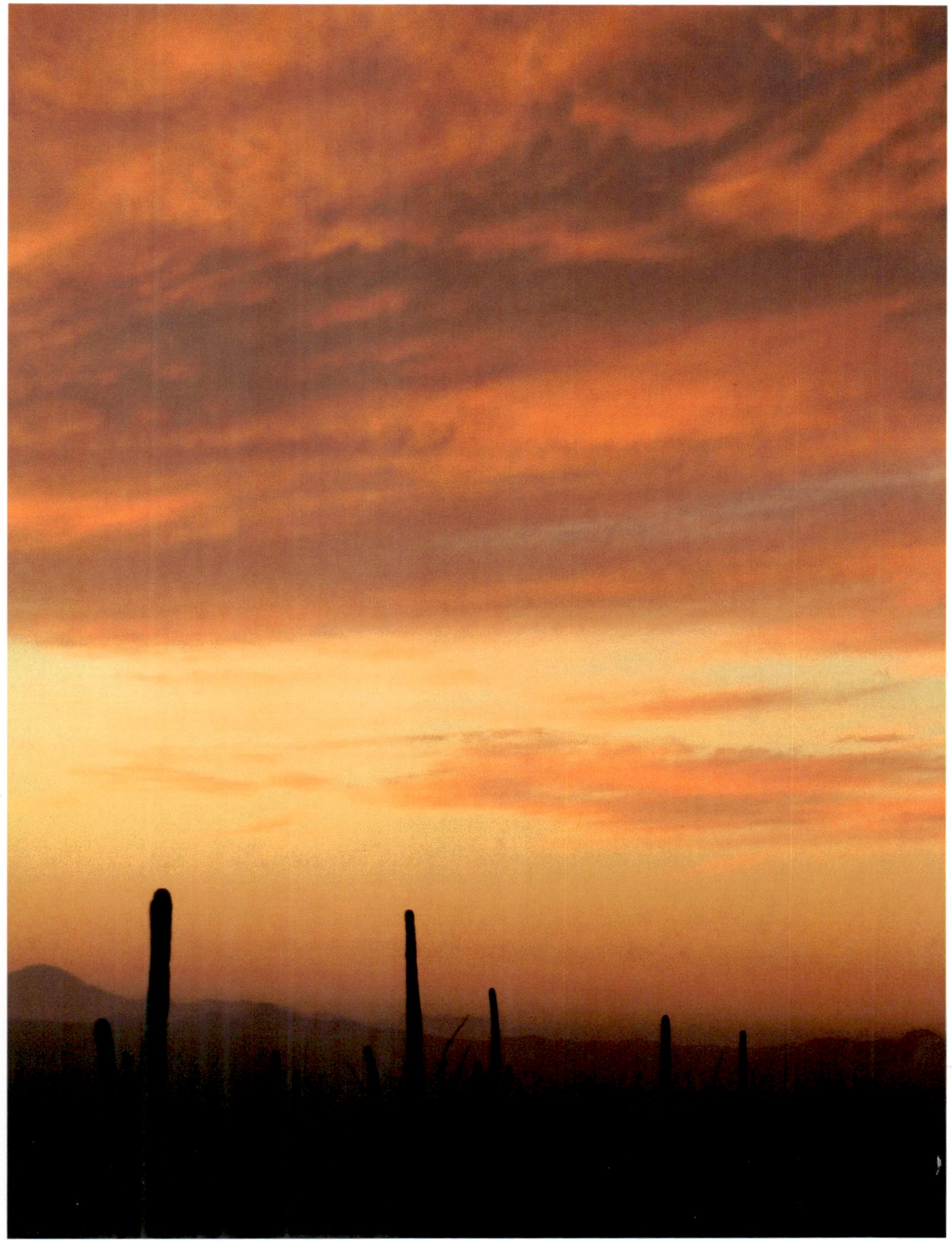

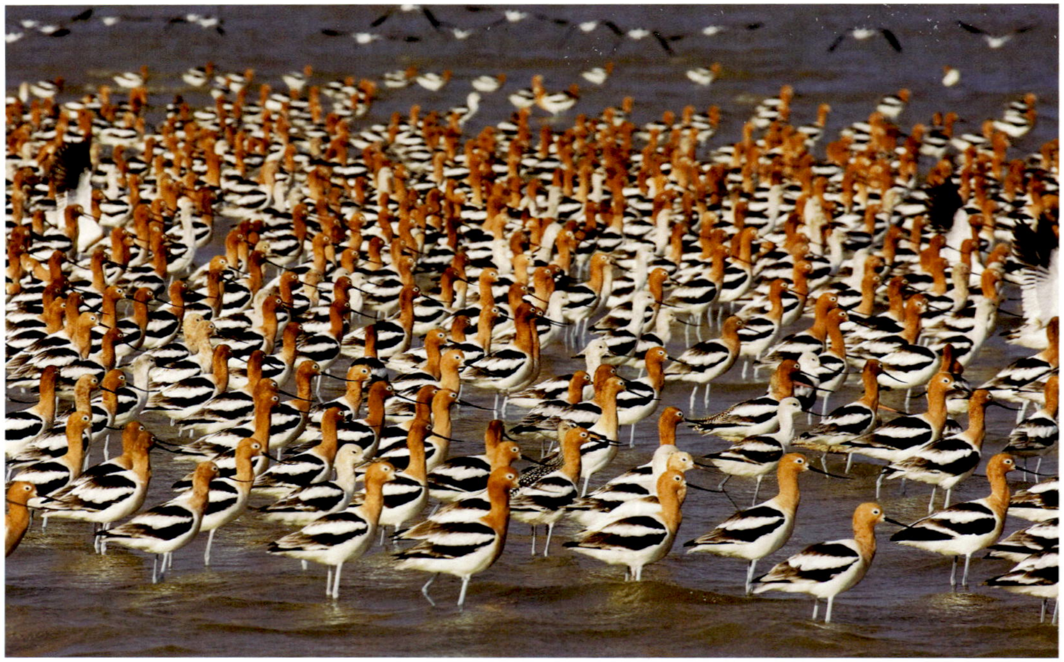

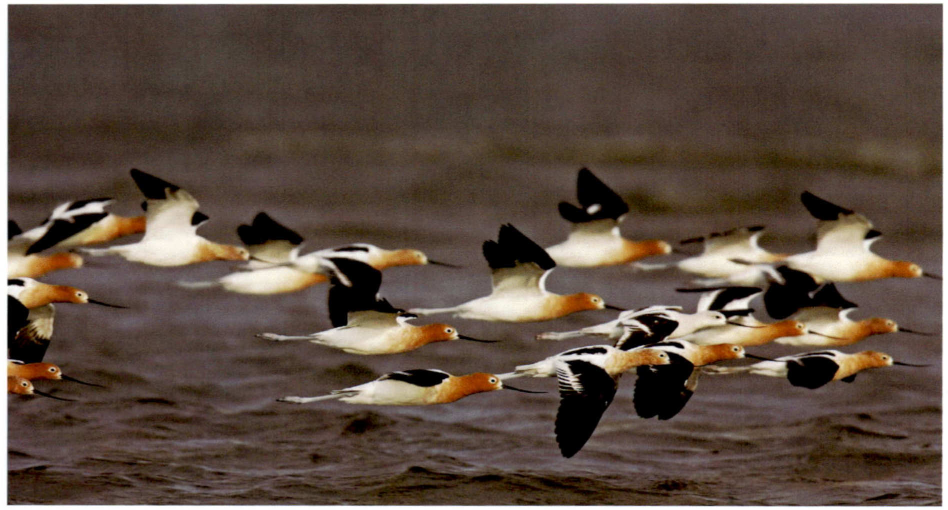

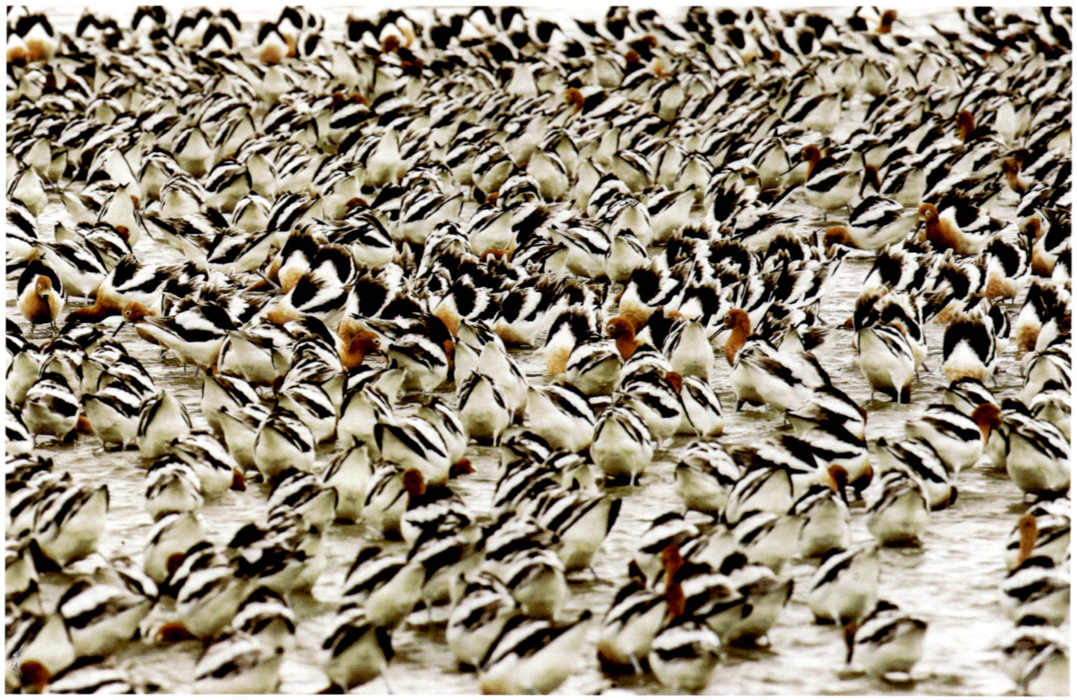

American Avocets are black and white birds, but breeding plumage adds a rich buff-orange tone to their heads and necks, suggesting the color of smoldering embers. A large flock of Avocets feeding in synchronous style (lower left), with some birds going one way while others move in other directions. This image is reminiscent of an M.C. Escher illustration with its hypnotic and repetitive patterns. *Photos by Kevin T. Karlson*

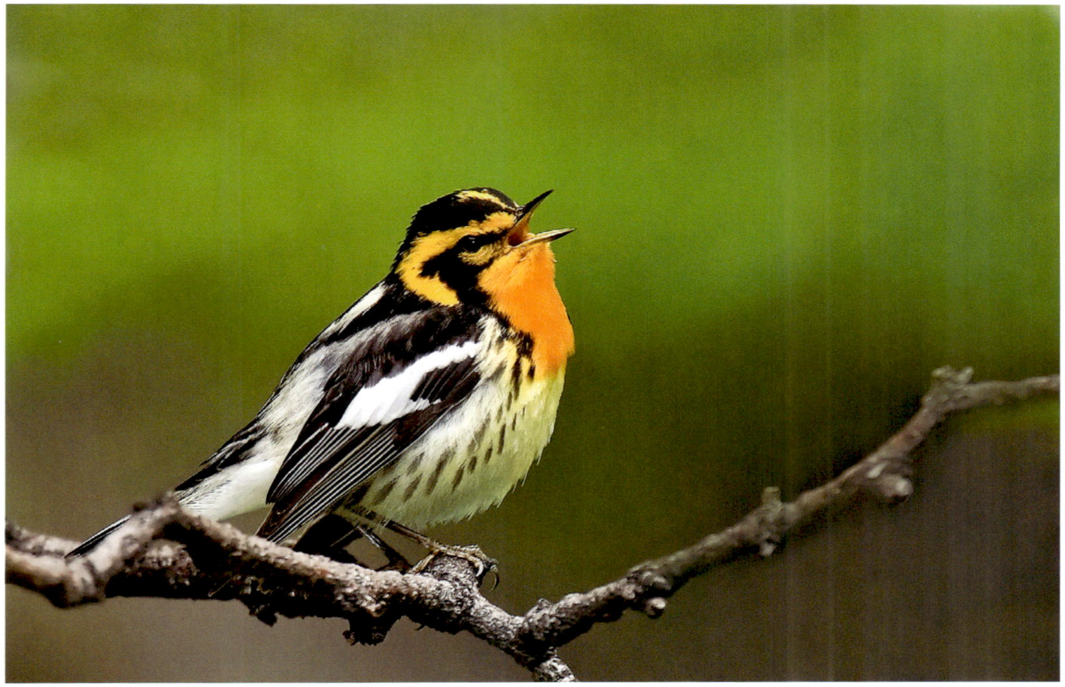

Two of the most fiery orange birds in North America are the male Blackburnian Warbler (above), with its flaming orange throat and face, and the male Baltimore Oriole, which shows a similar orange color to its underparts, and a deeper reddish cast to the upper breast. *Photos by Lloyd Spitalnik*

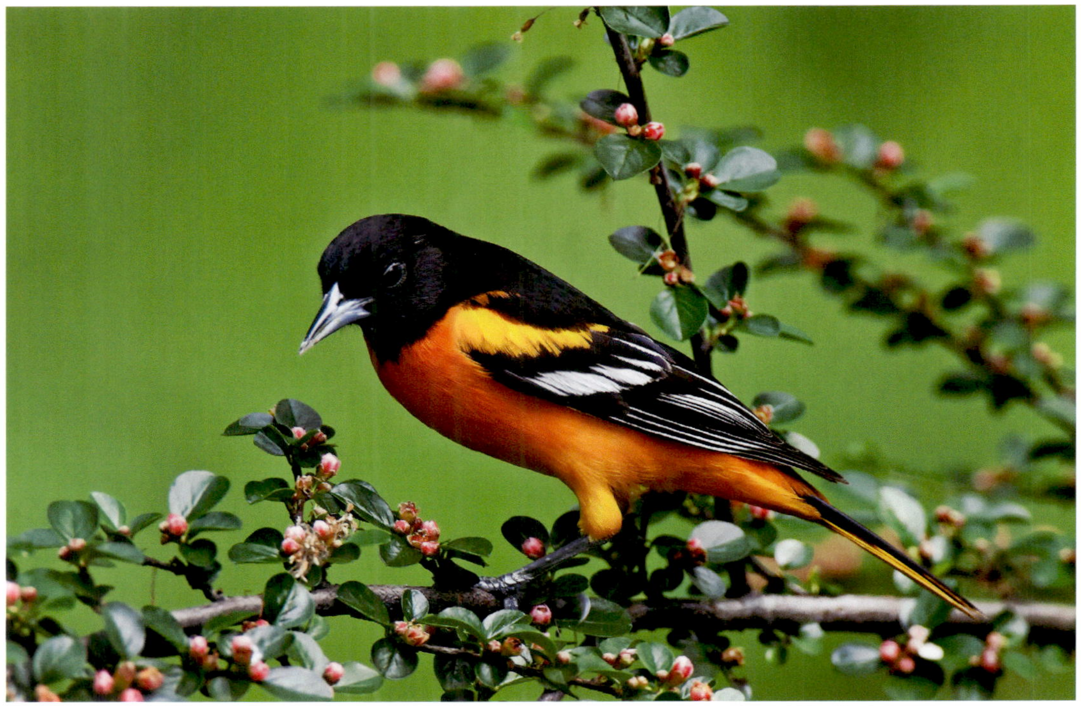

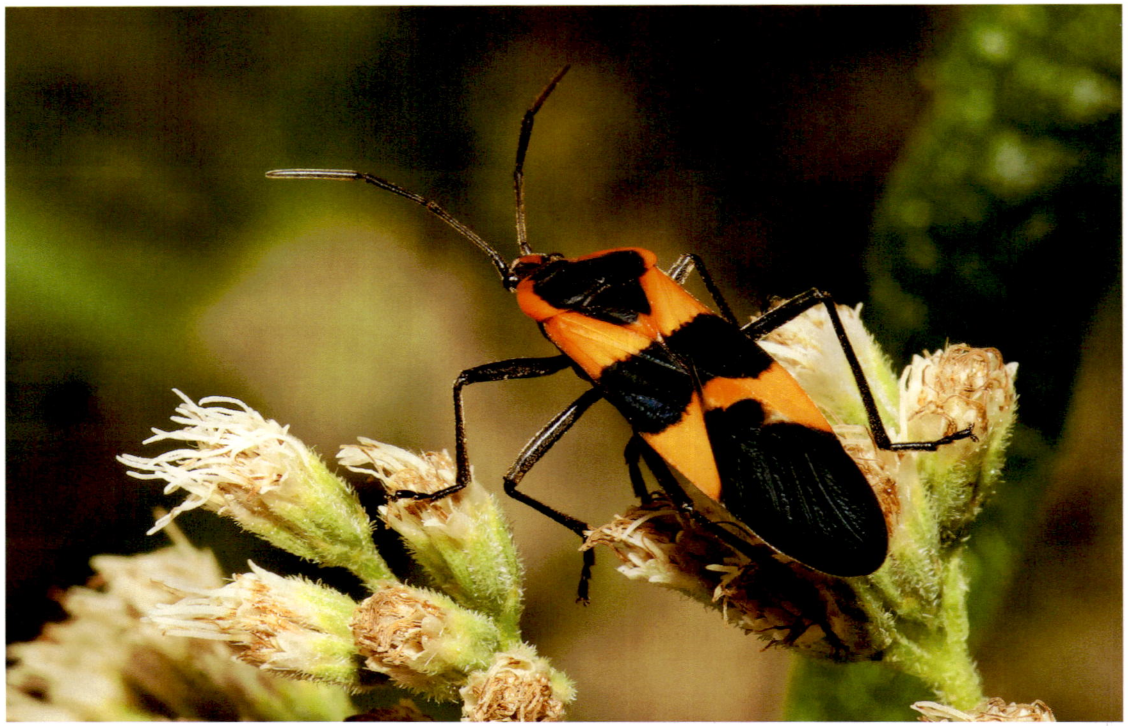

Bugs are not going to inherit the earth. They own it now. So we might as well make peace with the landlord.

— T. Eisner

Many insects carry the color of fire on their backs, and usually it is a warning to predators that they taste bitter and will not make a tasty meal. An orange and black Milkweed bug paints an impressive picture with its striking color patterns (above), while a pair of deep red and black Milkweed beetles makes sure that there are other beetles to take their place when their time is up. *Photos by Lloyd Spitalnik*

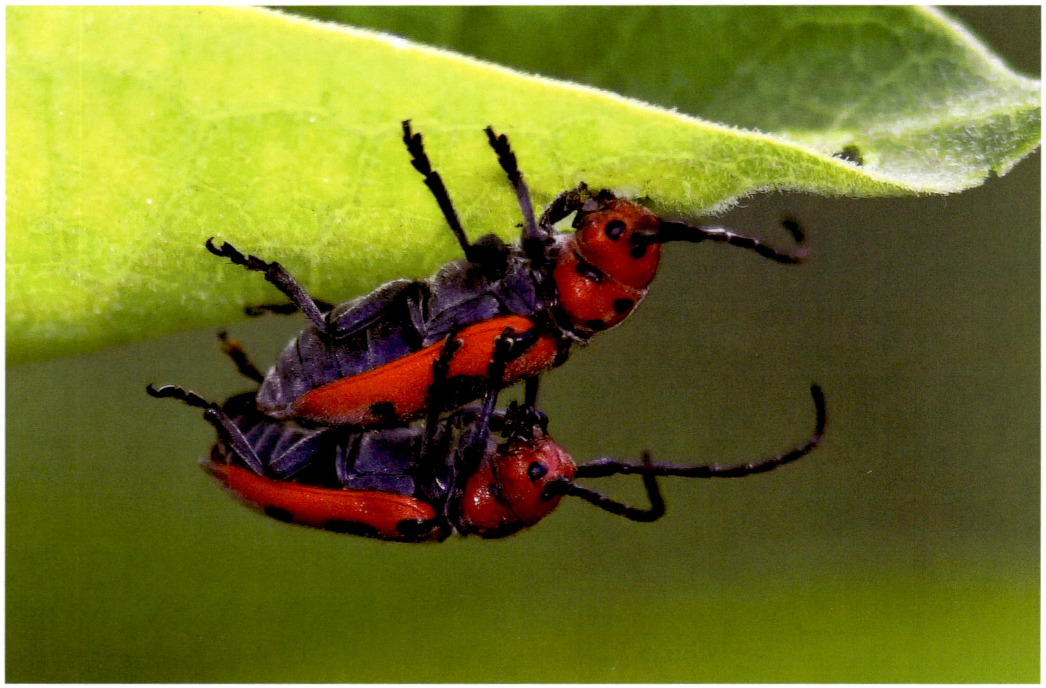

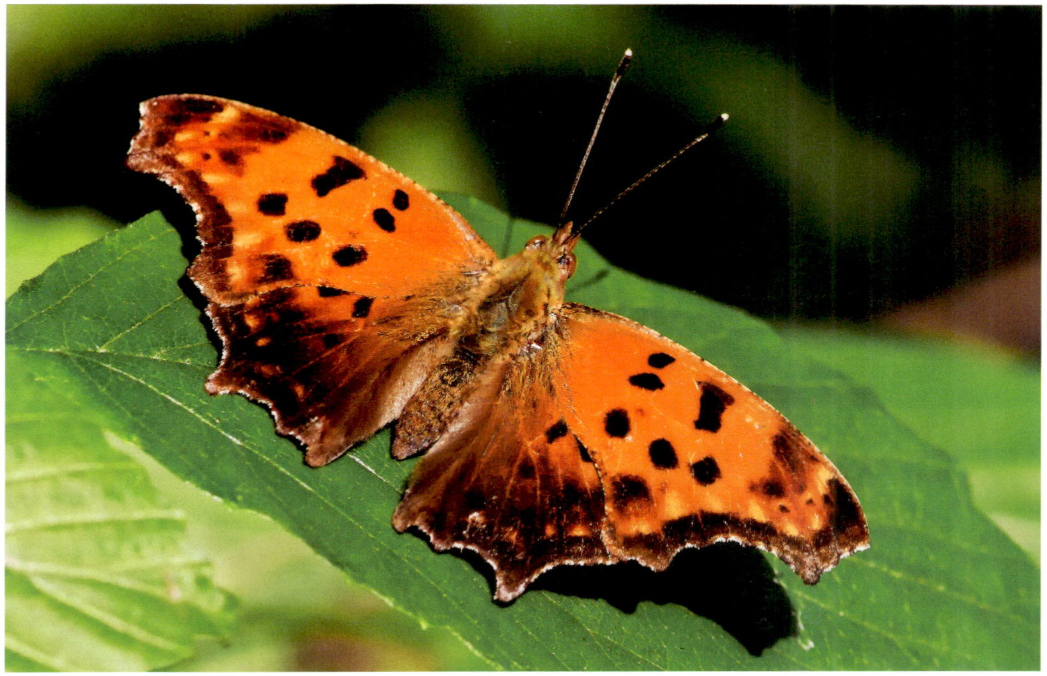

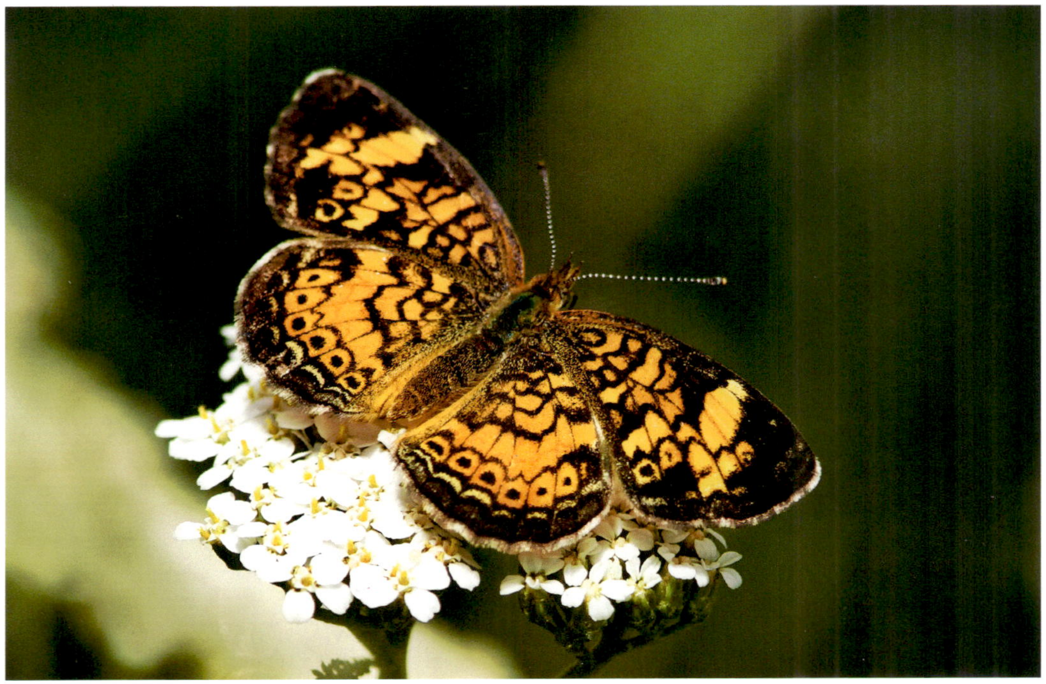

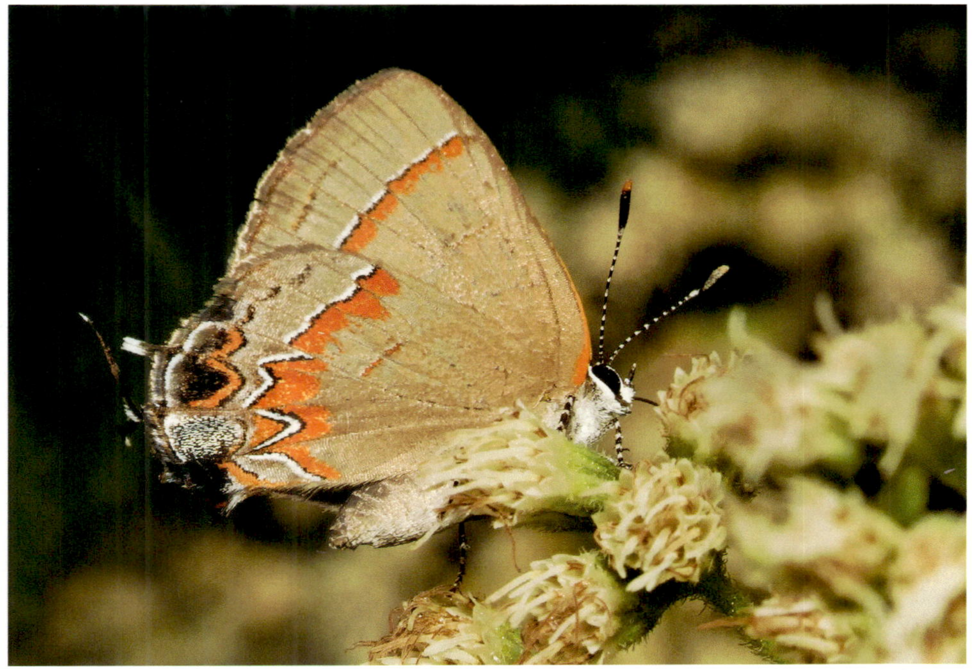

An Eastern Comma (upper left) has a rich mix of deep orange and brown colors, while a Pearl Crescent (lower left) shows a more complex pattern of orange and brown on its wings. A tiny Red-banded Hairstreak (above) only shows this bold orange pattern on its underwing. *Photos by Lloyd Spitalnik*

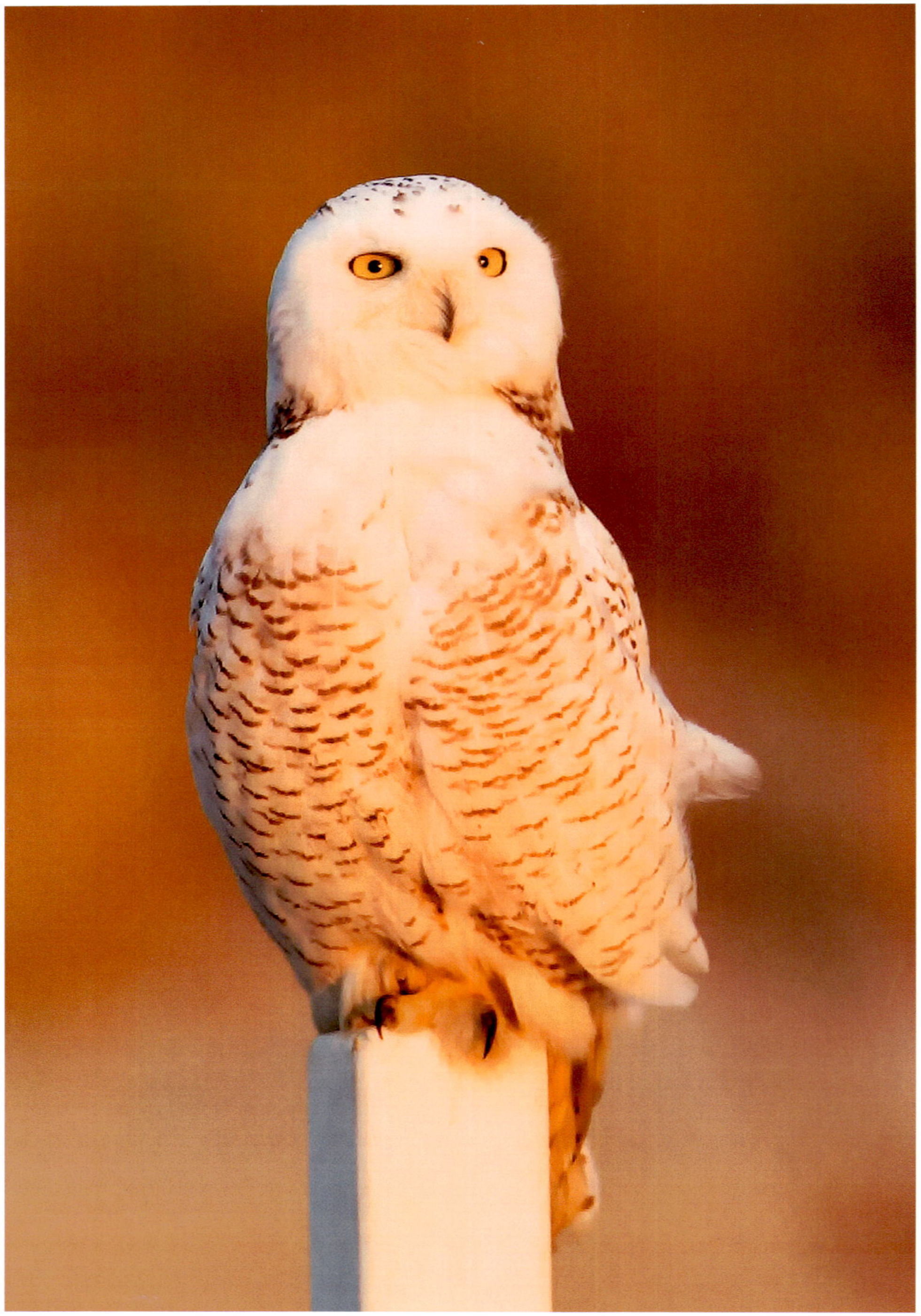

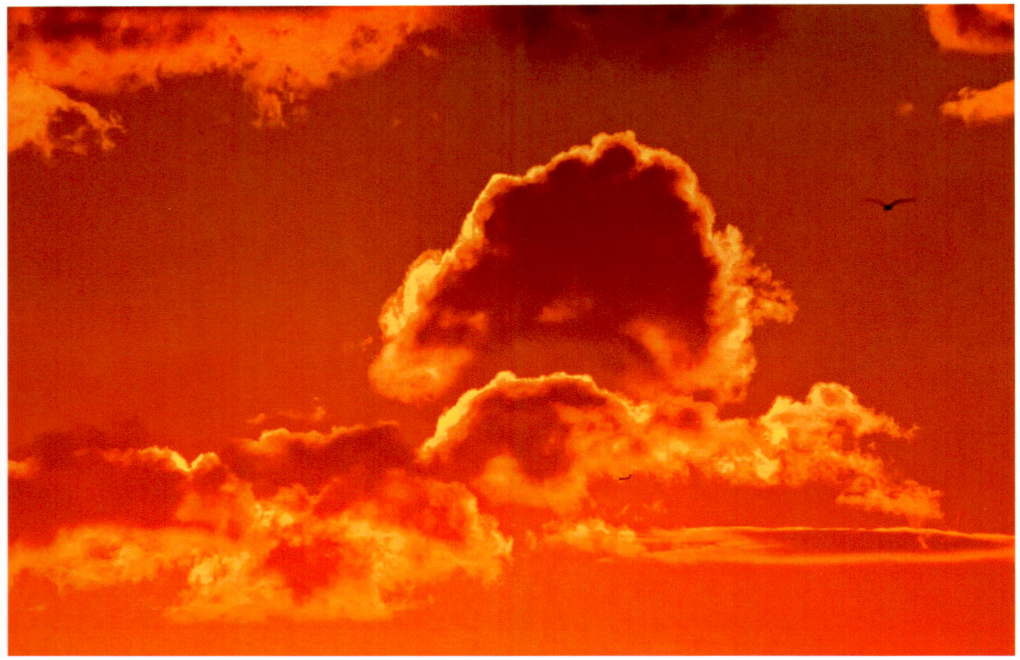

A Snowy Owl takes on a warm, pink glow in the late day sunlight, while a colorful sunset shows a range of warm reddish to yellow-orange tones. *Photos by Lloyd Spitalnik*

Opposite: A flock of Common Terns flying against a warm orange sky at dusk conveys a feeling of soft fire in this photo taken near Rockaway Beach, New York.
Photo by Lloyd Spitalnik

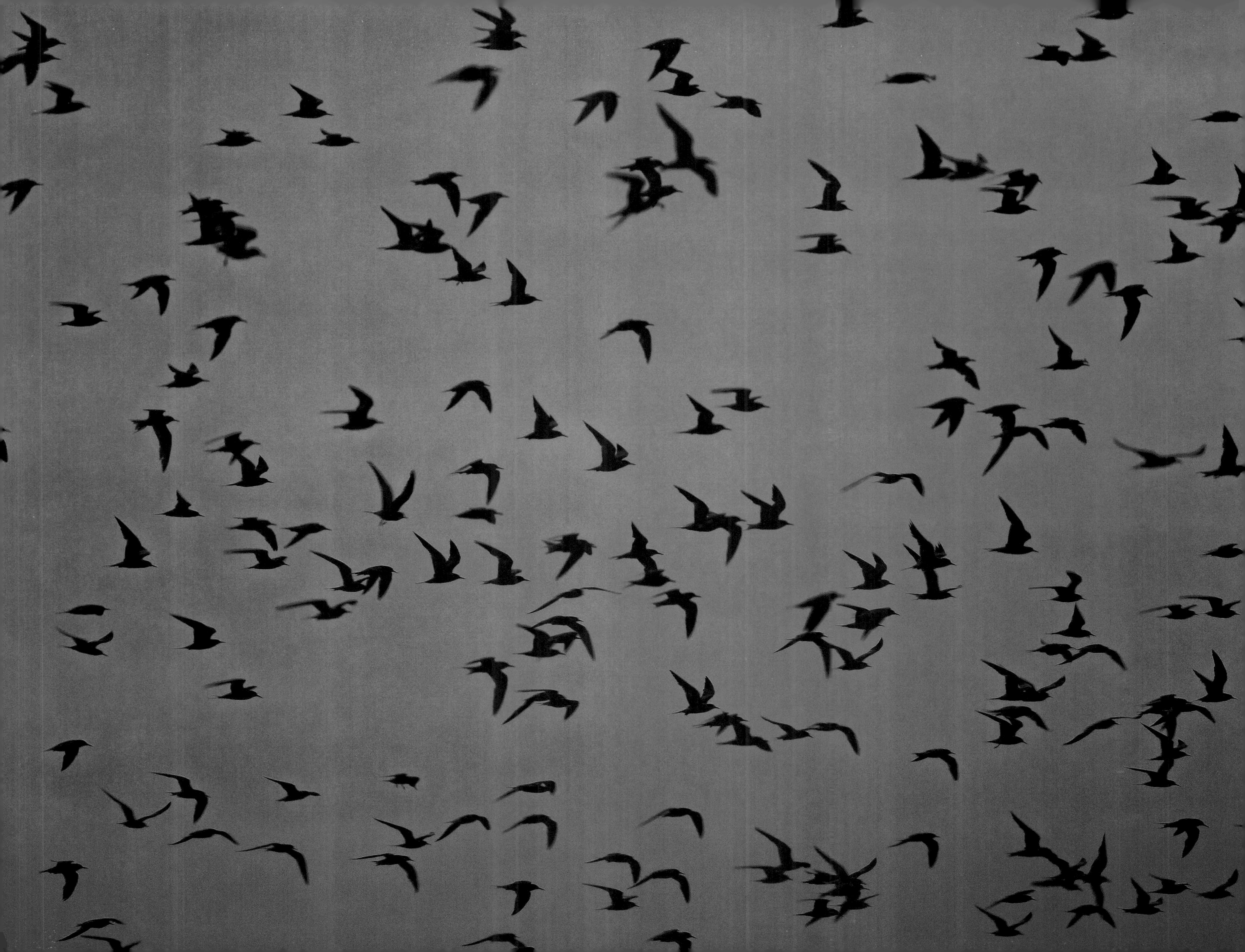

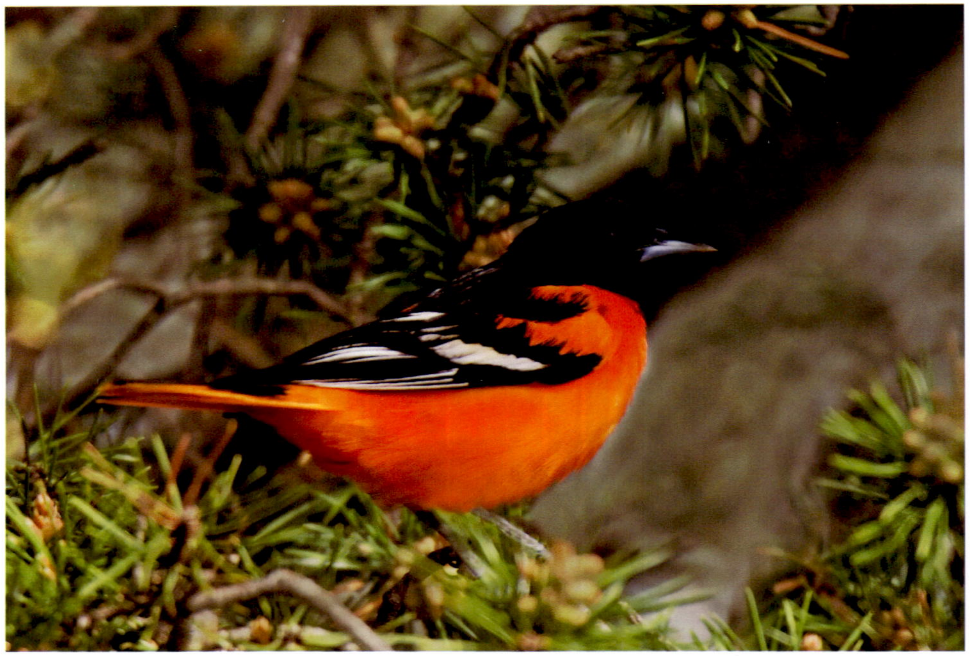

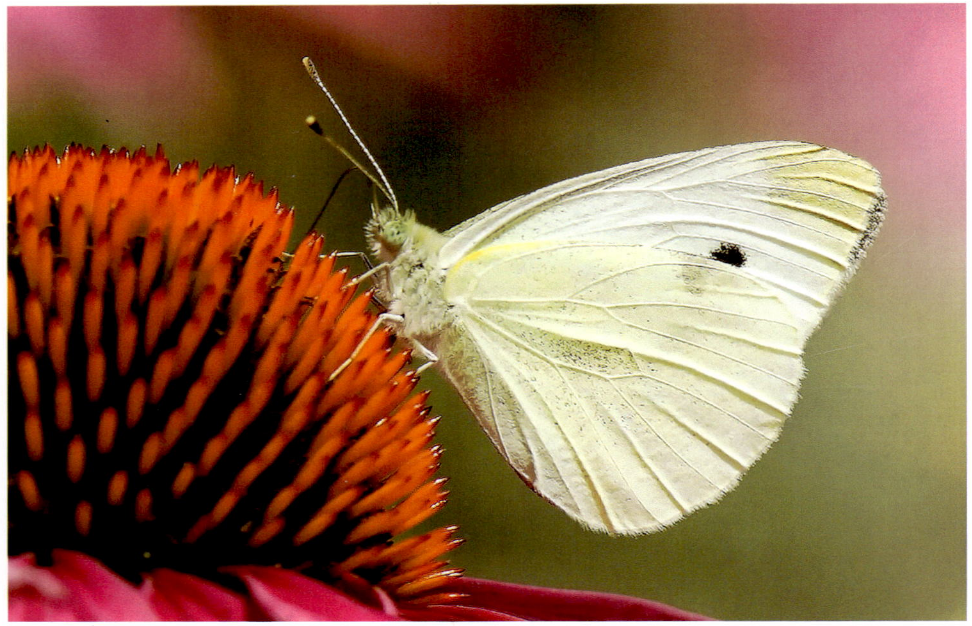

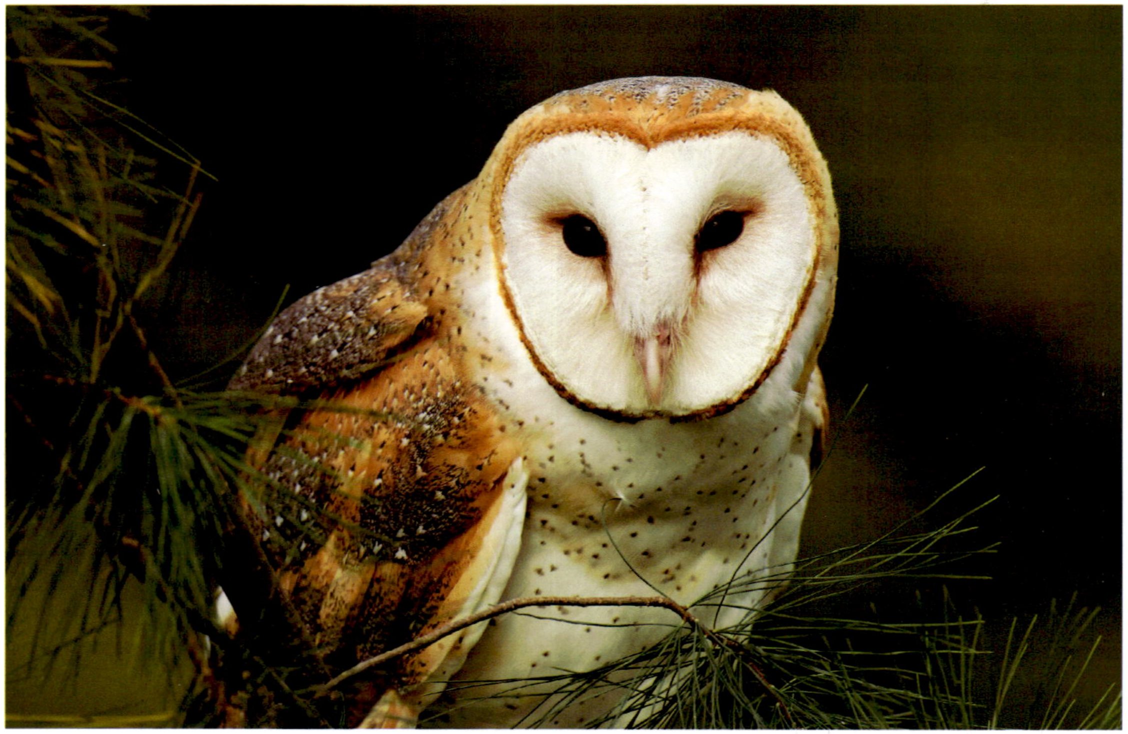

Colors on this page range from the bold orange-red color on the breast and tail of a breeding male Baltimore Oriole (upper left) to a rich orange coneflower providing nectar to a Cabbage White butterfly (above). A close-up shot of a Barn Owl shows the soft, warm buff colors that add to this ghostly owl's plumage. *Photos by Kevin T. Karlson (upper left) and Lloyd Spitalnik*

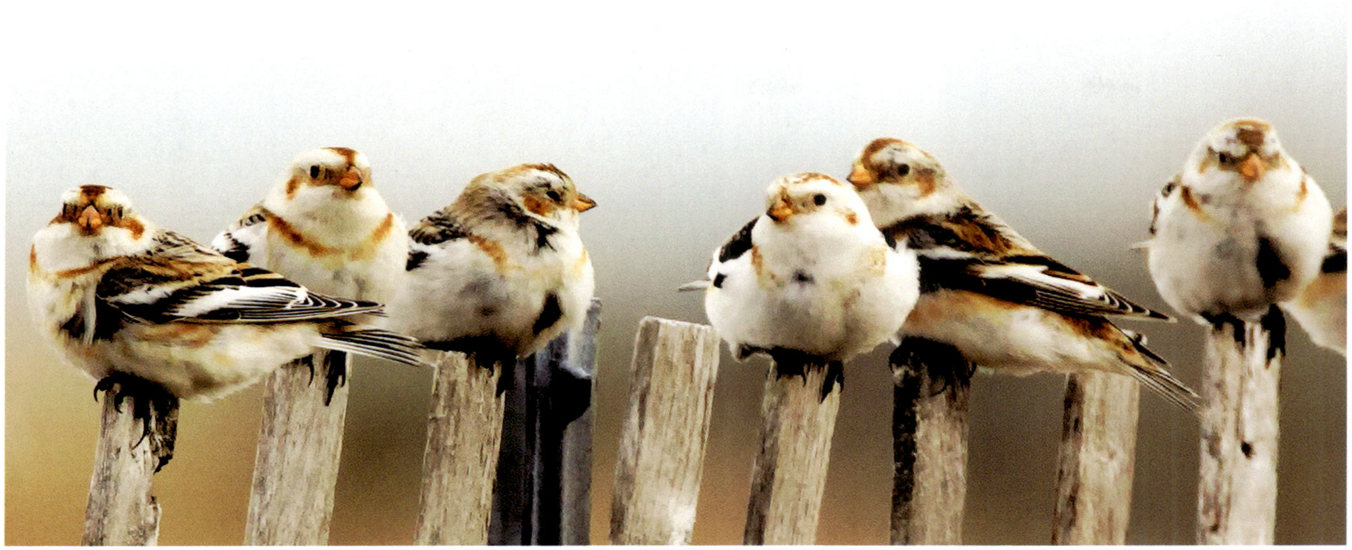

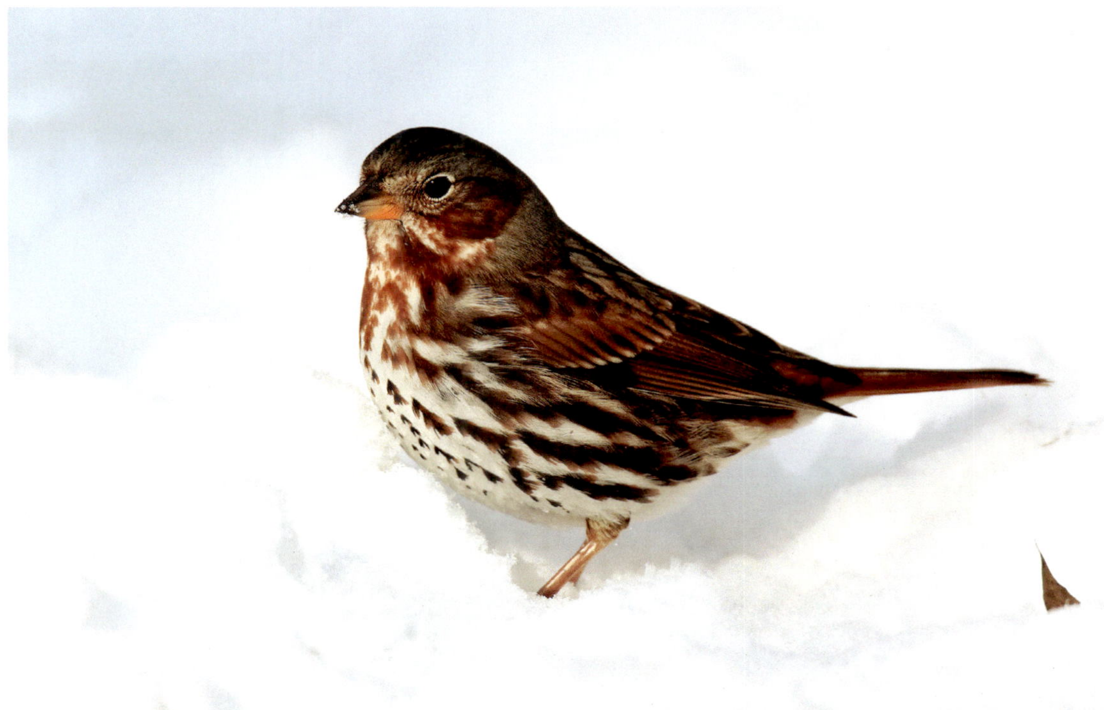

Even in winter, a gang of Snow Buntings roosting on a snow fence show a few warm, orange markings to their plumage, but a Fox Sparrow exhibits a truly fiery appearance with its rich, red coloration. *Photos by Lloyd Spitalnik*

Softly the evening came. The sun from the western horizon
Like a magician extended his golden wand o'er the landscape;
Twinkling vapors arose; and sky and water and forest
Seemed all on fire at the touch, and melted and mingled together.

— Henry Wadsworth Longfellow

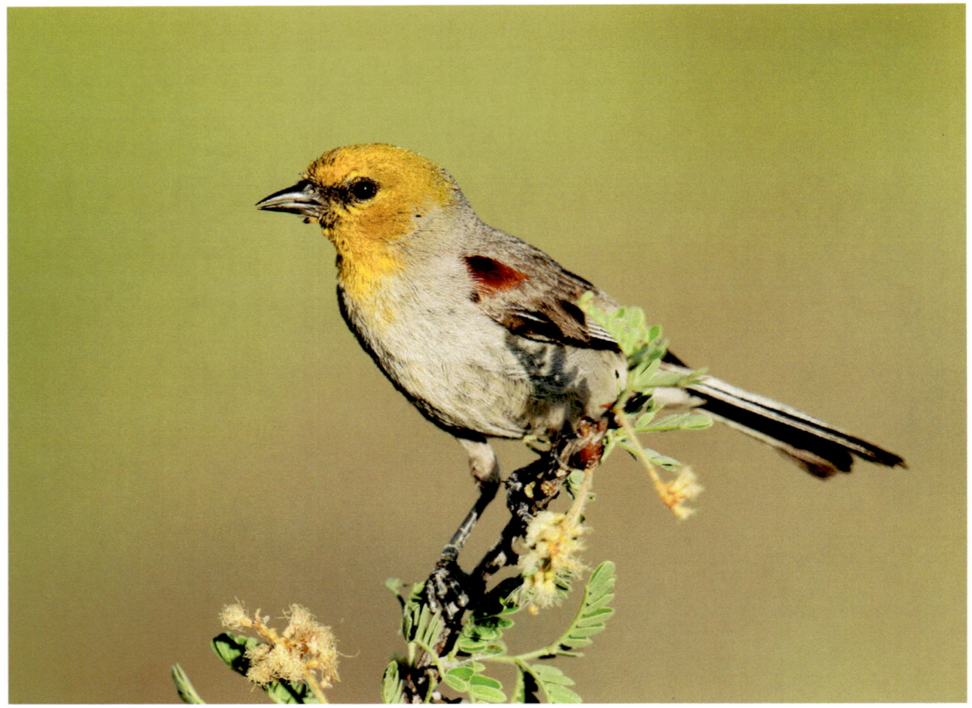

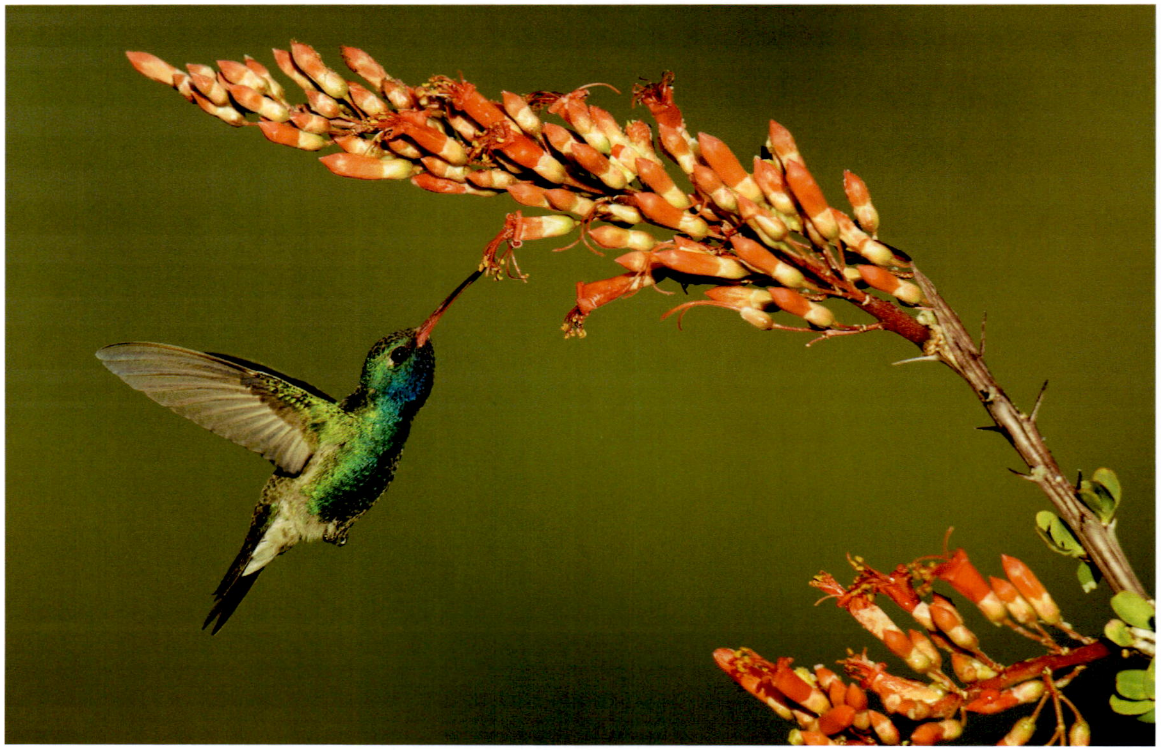

Two birds that live in the desert Southwest carry the fire theme in different ways. A male Verdin (above) shows a rich, chestnut-red patch on his wing, while a Broad-billed Hummingbird (left) has a fiery red bill that matches the firecracker-like flowers he is nectaring on. *Photos by Scott Elowitz*

Opposite: This sunset tested the limits of our visual senses as we rode to a fireworks display near Logan Lake, British Columbia. The colors in this photo were not enhanced! *Photo by Kevin T. Karlson*

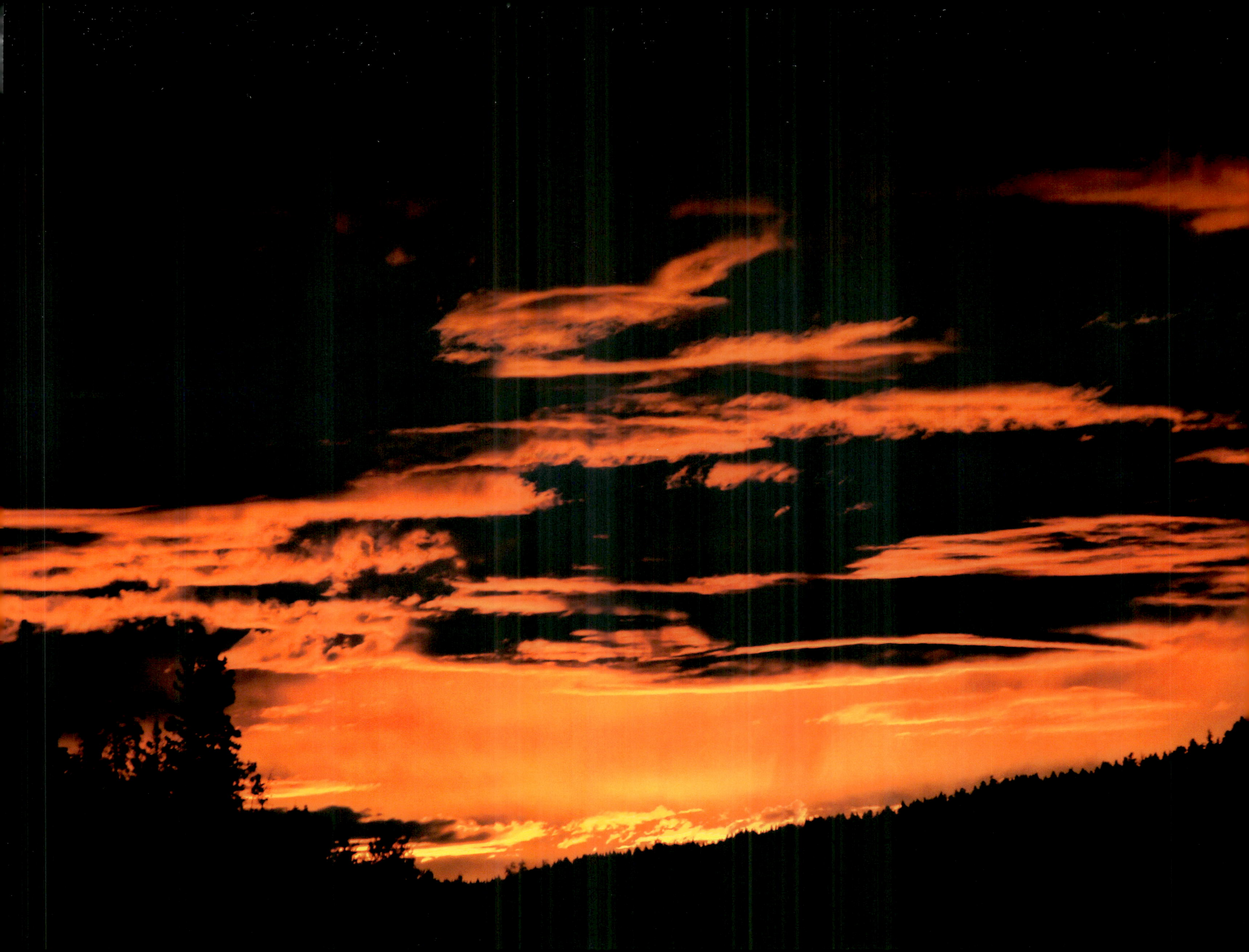

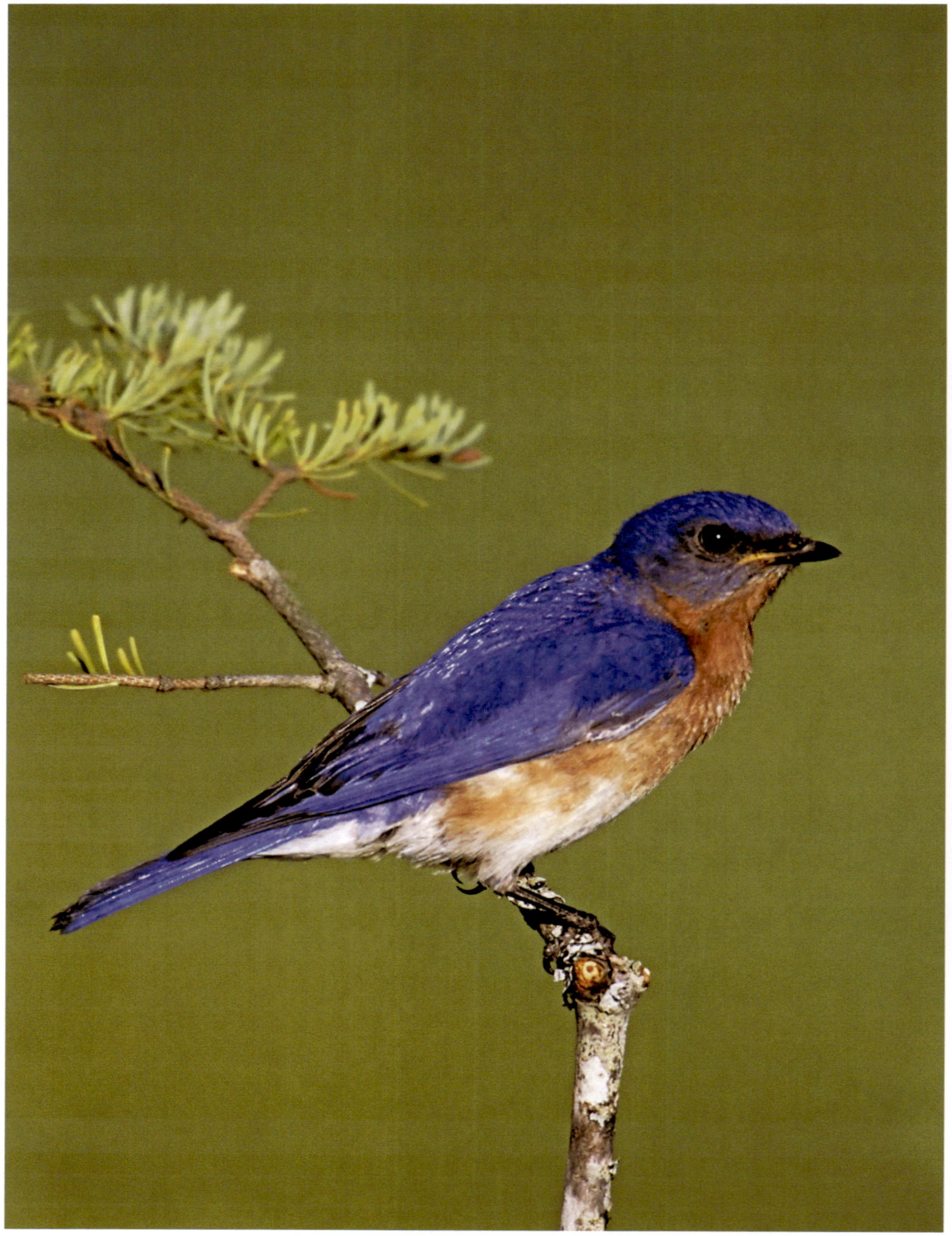

Eastern Bluebird first impresses you with iridescent blue color, but the rust shading on the breast is reminiscent of smoldering embers. *Photo by Kevin T. Karlson*

Artistic vision is having the clarity to fall in love with what you see.

— Chogyam Trungpa

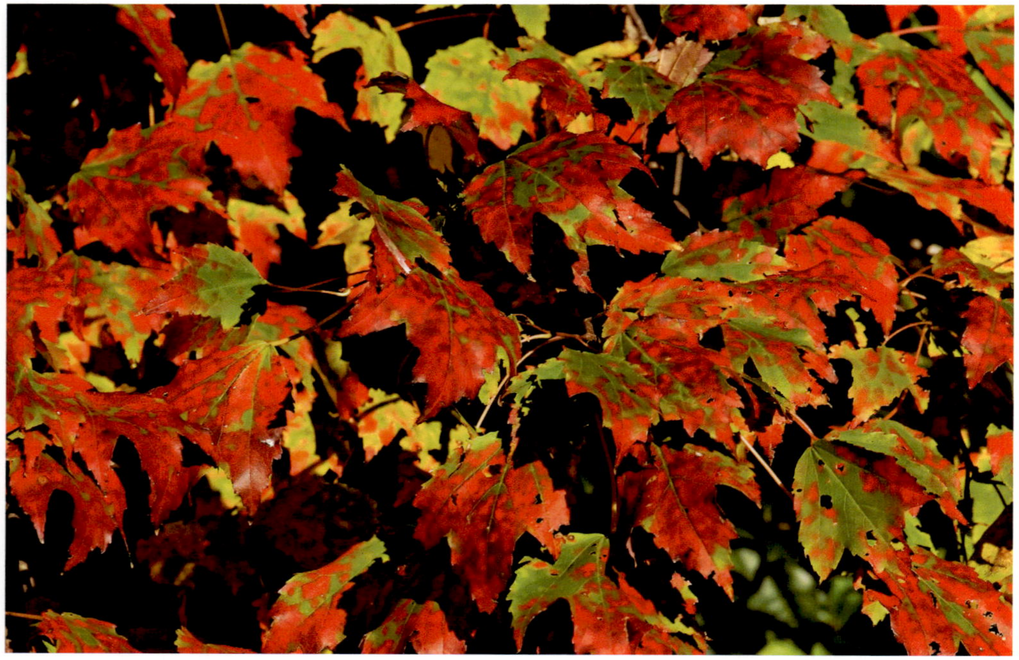

Red Maple leaves change to a fiery red color in the fall, and often mix with leftover summer green tones to create a beautiful splash of autumn. *Photo by Kevin T. Karlson*

Opposite. Male Northern Cardinal is perhaps the most recognized songbird in North America, and its bright red plumage is a fine example of the fire element theme in nature. *Photo by Scott Elowitz*

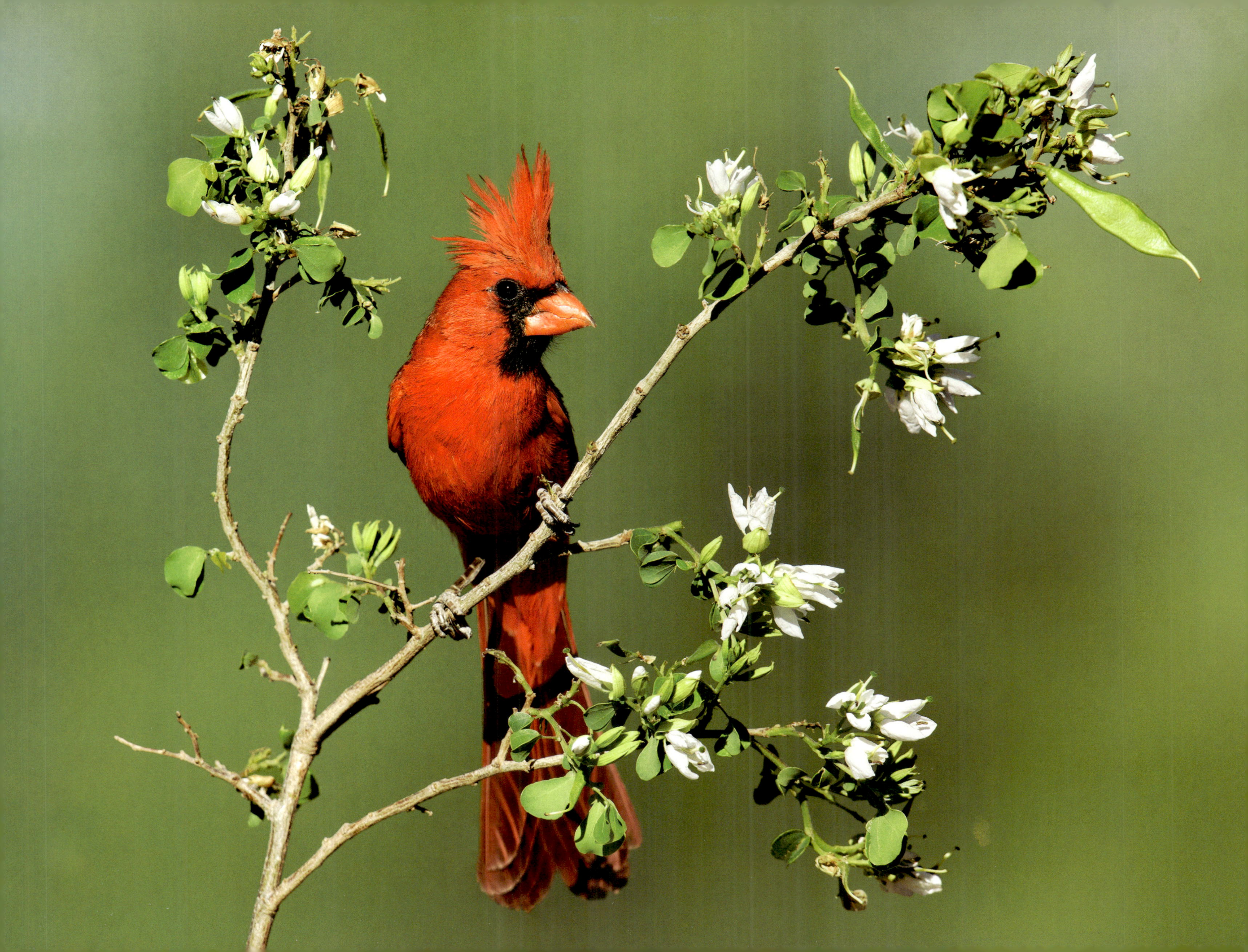

Air

Air is the ethereal element of the planet. We cannot see it, taste it, or touch it, but its presence is revealed to us when the wind blows. As humans, grounded to the earth, we can only imagine the joy of flying with little gravitational restraint to weigh us down. Many of earth's creatures enjoy the gift of flight, and thus bridge the gap between two distinct worlds: the earth and the sky.

This section contains images of many creatures that make the air and sky their home, at least for part of their lives. The joy and freedom of flight is captured in many of these pictures, and the grace of these creatures is reminiscent of an aerial ballet. Other images show celestial bodies that ride in the heavens, with the sun and moon playing a major part in the human psyche. Clouds also have an important role in the interaction between air and water, and the resulting artistic patterns often resemble familiar shapes from everyday life. Fog is a by-product of air and water mixing, and nothing is more dramatic than a landscape engulfed in a mysterious fog bank.

The sky and the strong wind have moved the spirit inside me till I am carried away trembling with joy.

— Uvavnuk

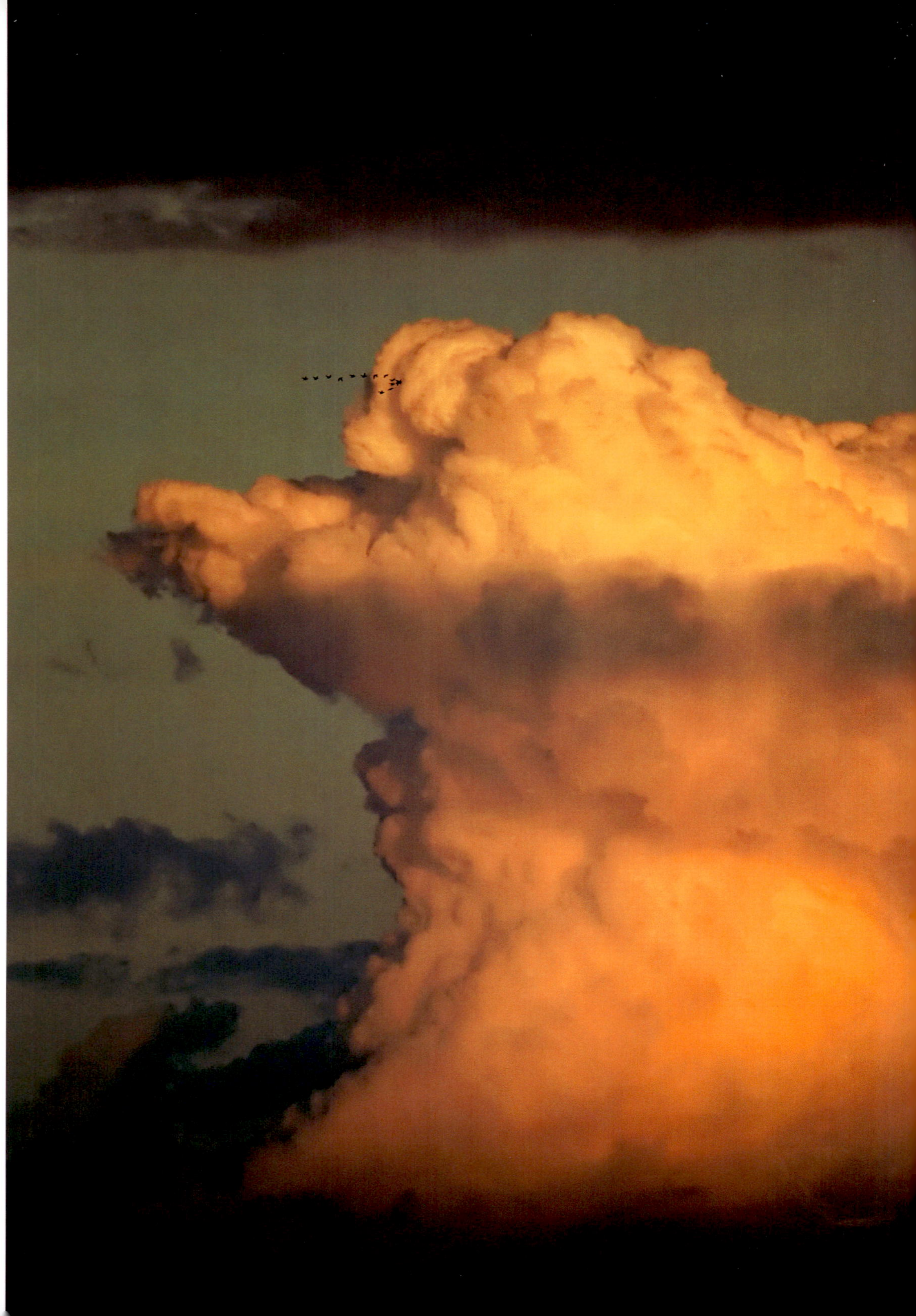

A moody cloud bank prompted Kevin to take this photo, which reminded him of a poodle. After seeing the picture, he noticed a flock of birds migrating high in the sky near the poodle's forehead. *Photo by Kevin T. Karlson*

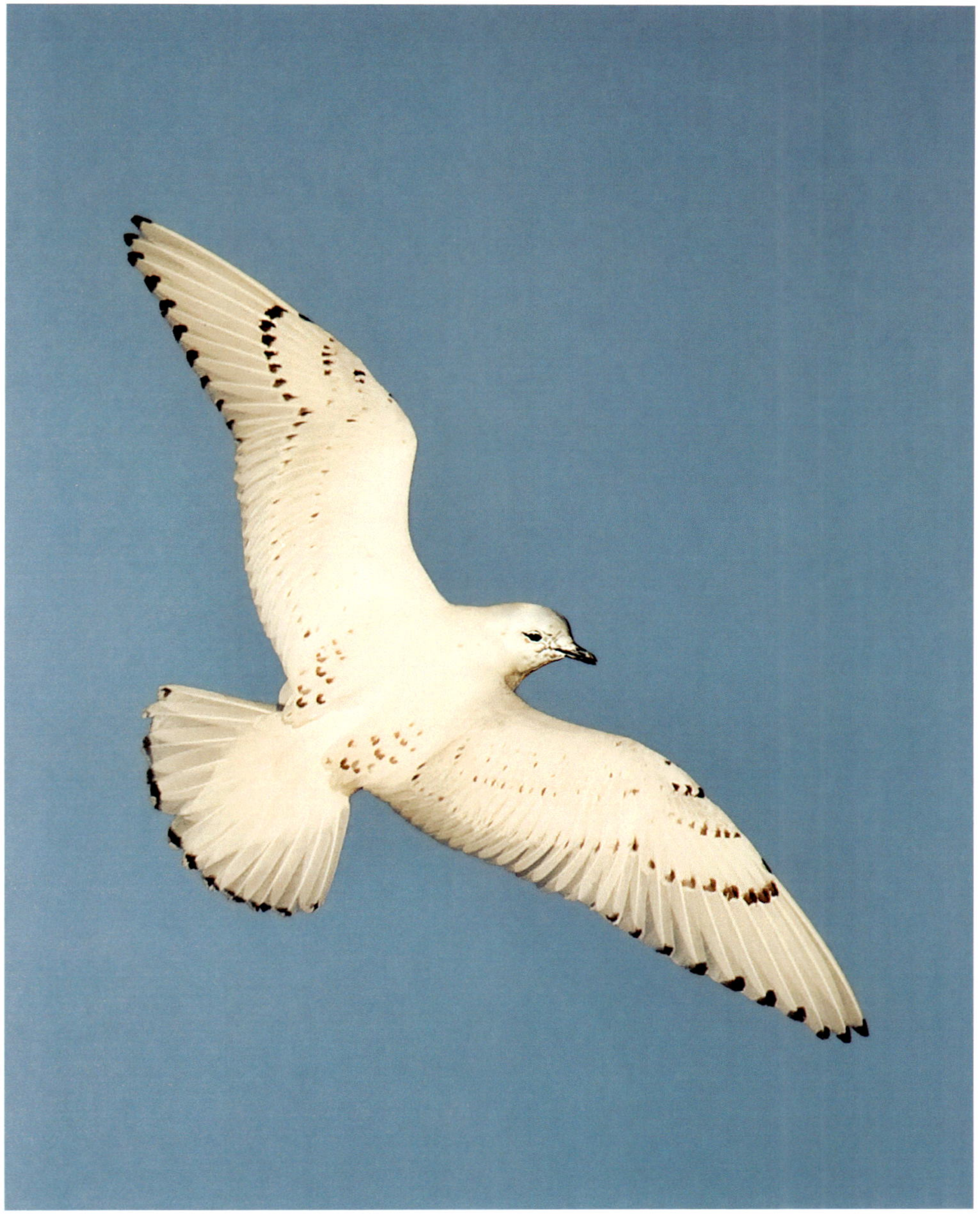

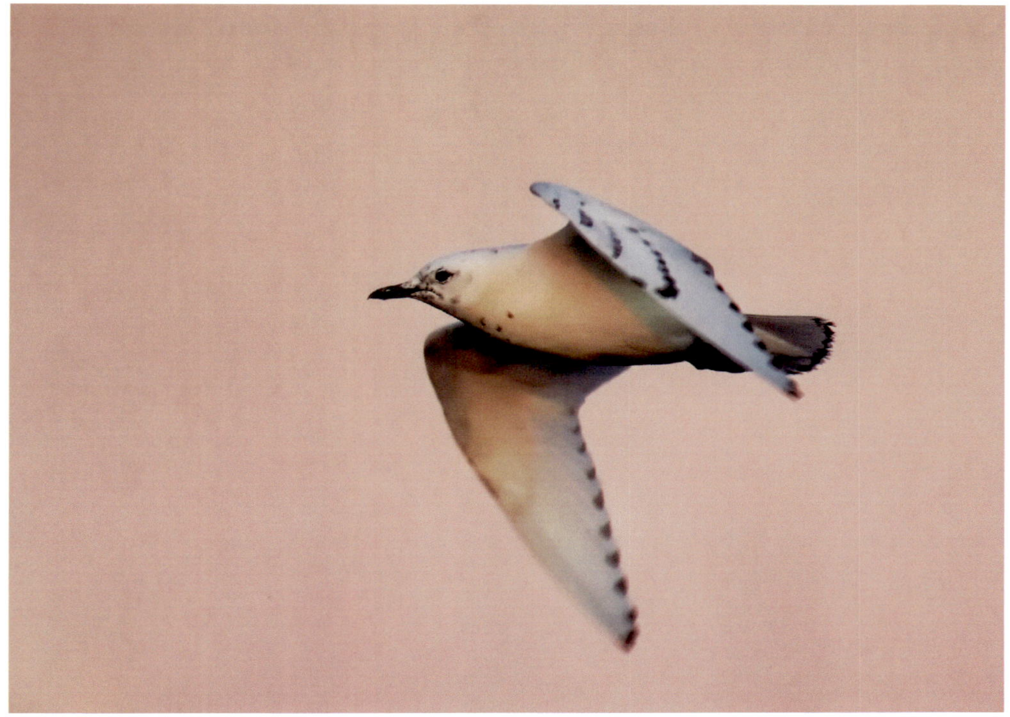

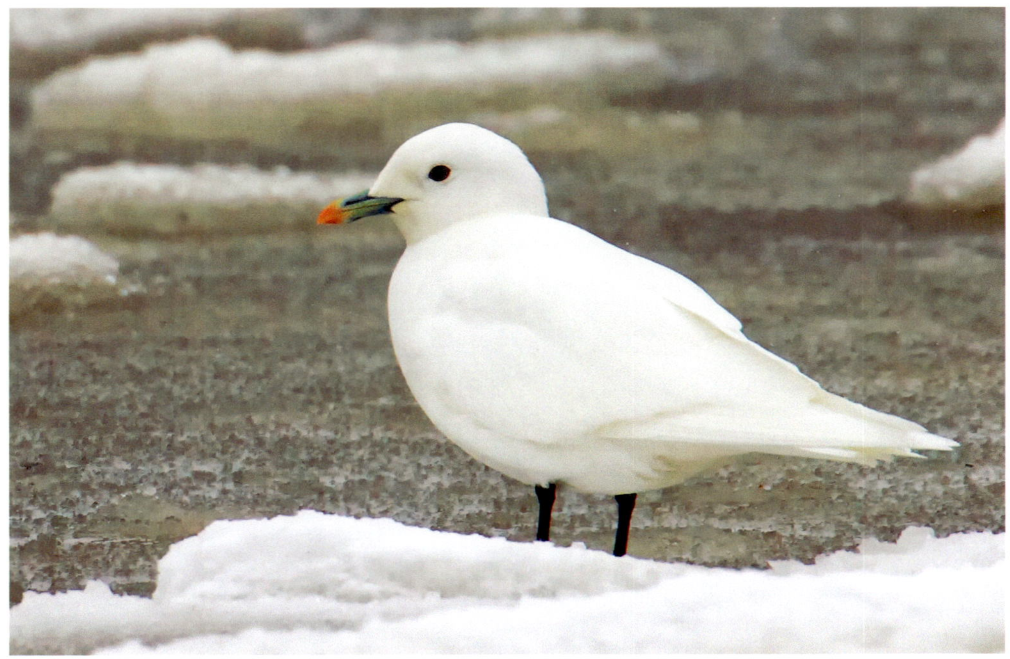

Ivory Gulls are one of the hardest birds in the world to see, since they live their entire lives around ice floes in high Arctic regions. Adults have pure white plumage (lower right), while immatures are variably mottled with black flecks. The mostly white plumage and delicate features of this small gull are reminiscent of angels, if you are lucky enough to see one. *Photos by Scott Elowitz (above), Kevin T. Karlson (upper right) and Lloyd Spitalnik (lower right)*

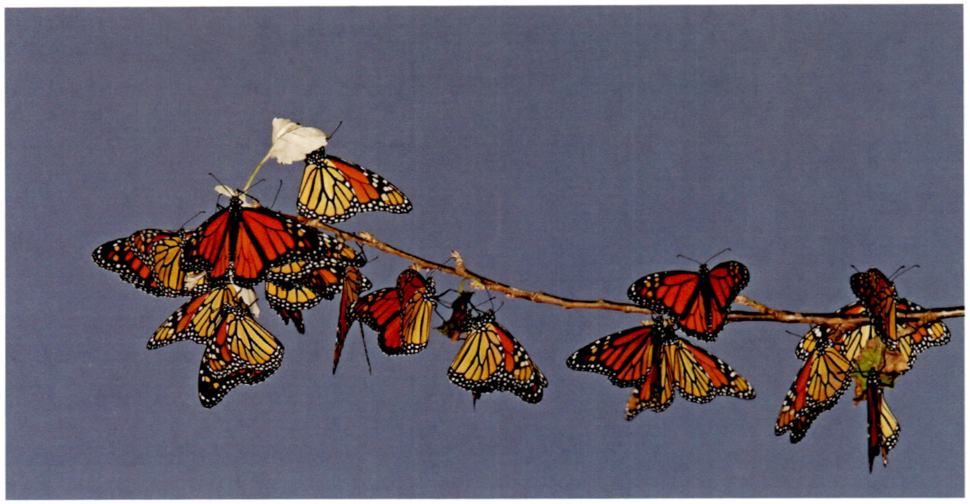

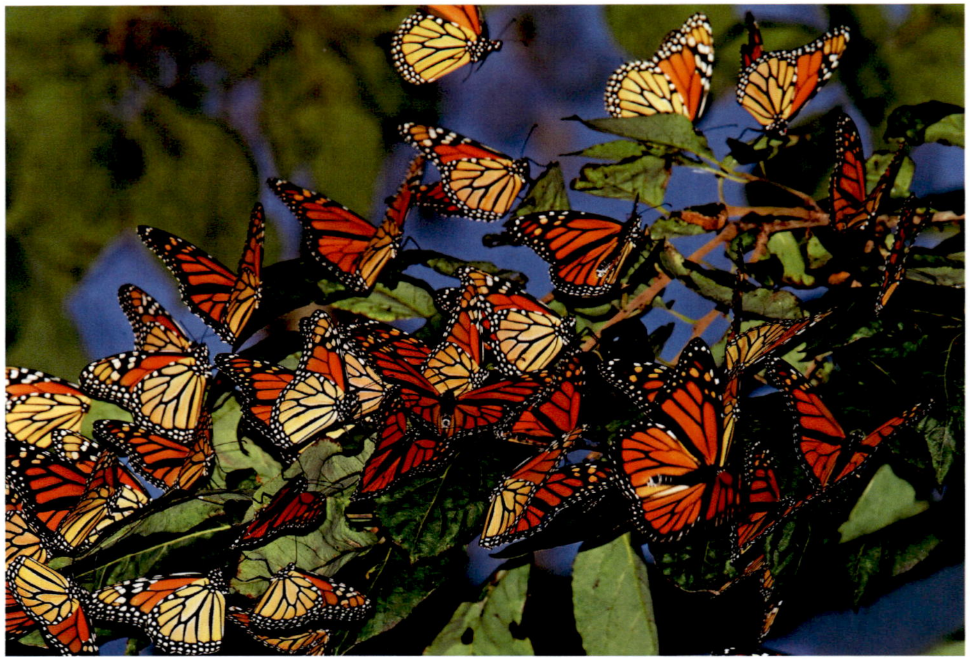

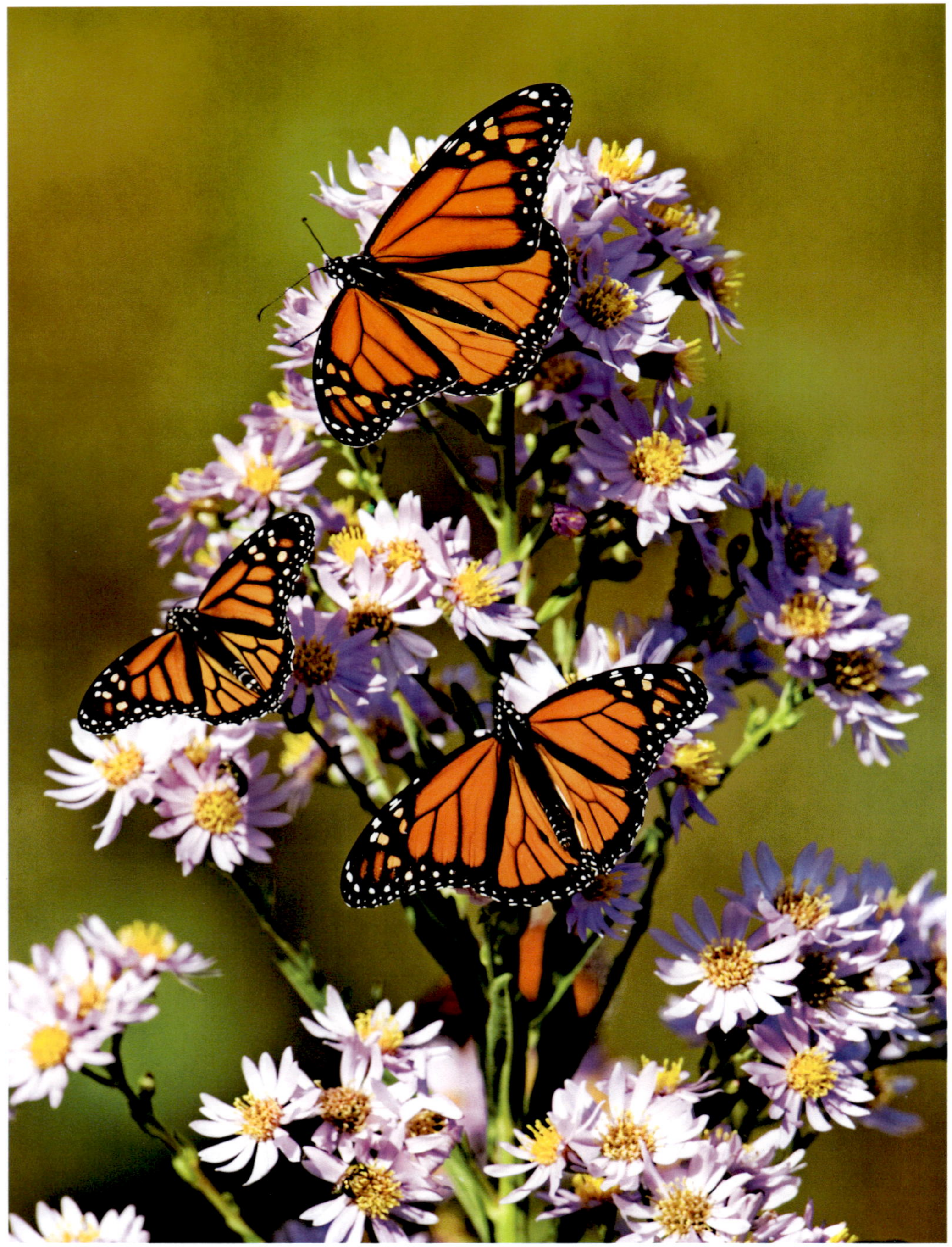

Monarchs have the longest annual migration of all butterflies, with some flying thousands of miles to their wintering area in Mexico. The two photos of roosting butterflies were taken in Cape May, New Jersey, in September 2010, when over a million Monarchs were seen in one day. *Photos by Kevin T. Karlson*

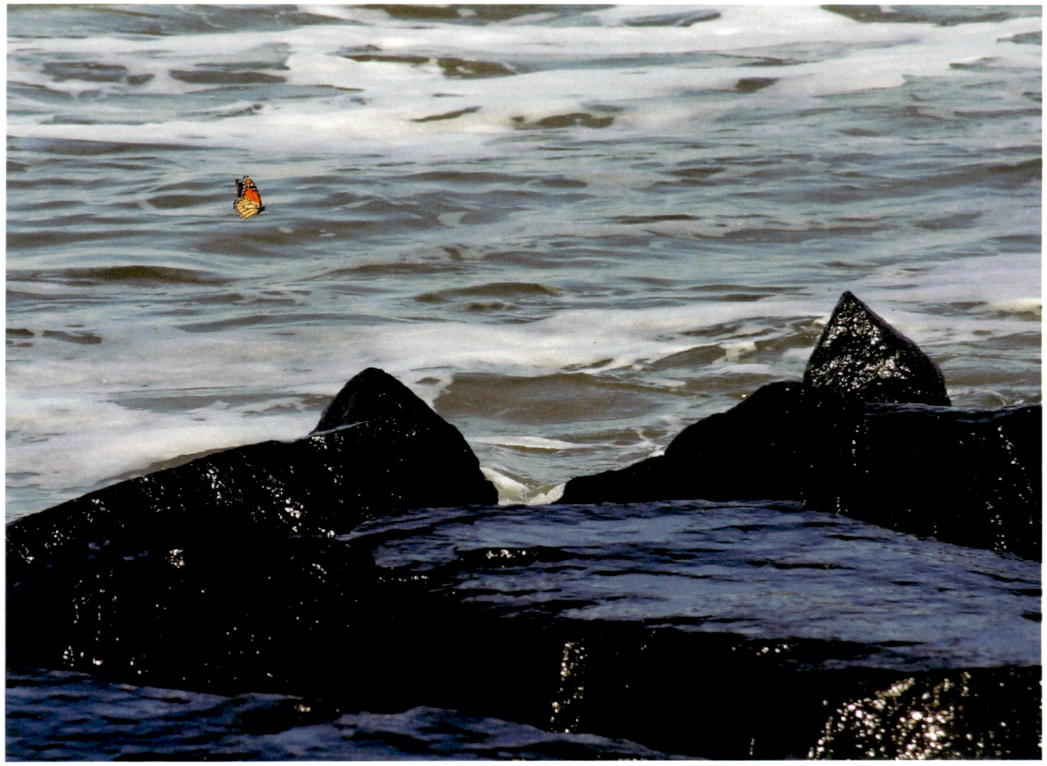

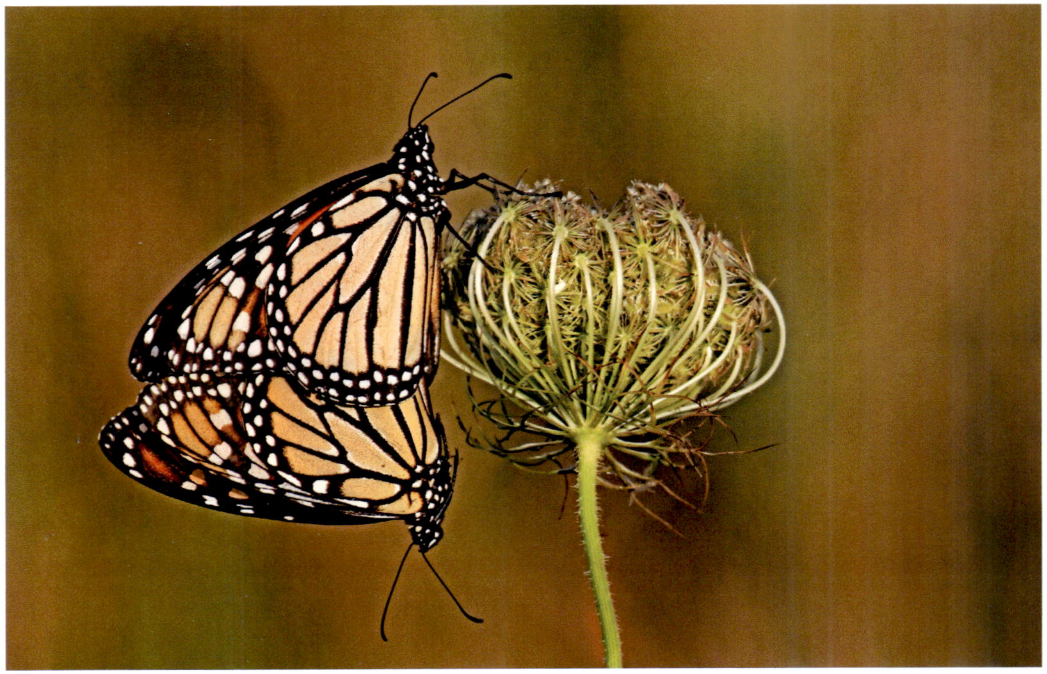

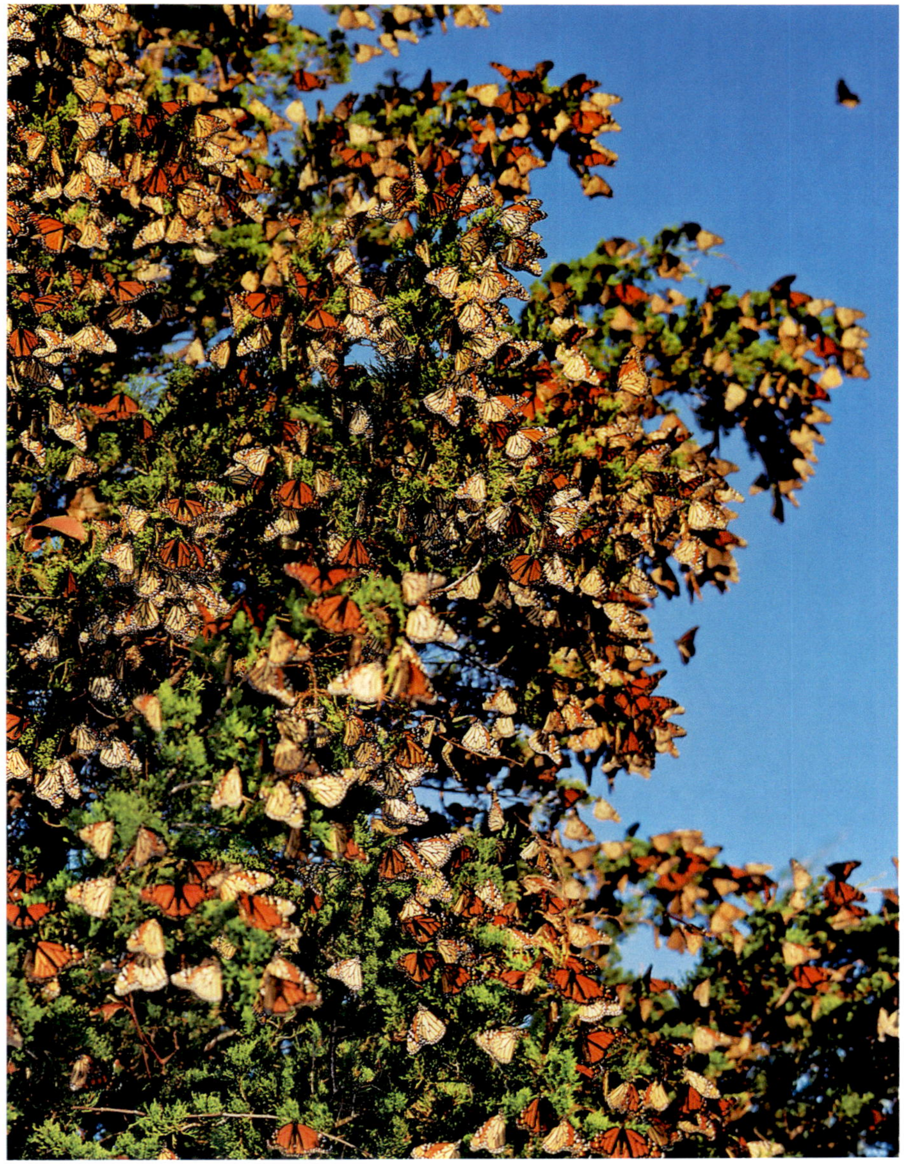

The butterfly counts not months but moments, and has time enough.

— Rabindranath Tagore

Monarchs photos: upper left: "Monarch Migrating," *by Tina Giaimo;* lower left: "Monarchs Mating" *by Nancy Watson*; above: "Monarch Roost in Cape May, New Jersey" *by Pat Sutton*

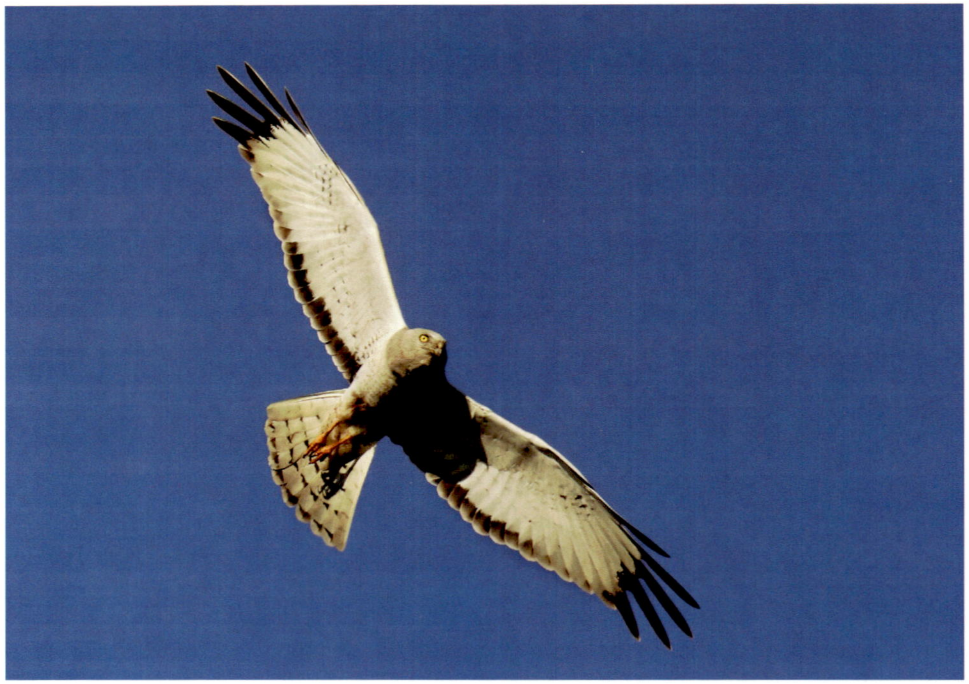

Northern Harriers, elegant raptors and favorites of birders everywhere. Adult males (upper and lower left) are fondly known as "Gray Ghosts" in part because of their pale gray plumage and ghost-like presence. Immature birds (below) have buff-colored underparts. *Photos by Kevin T. Karlson*

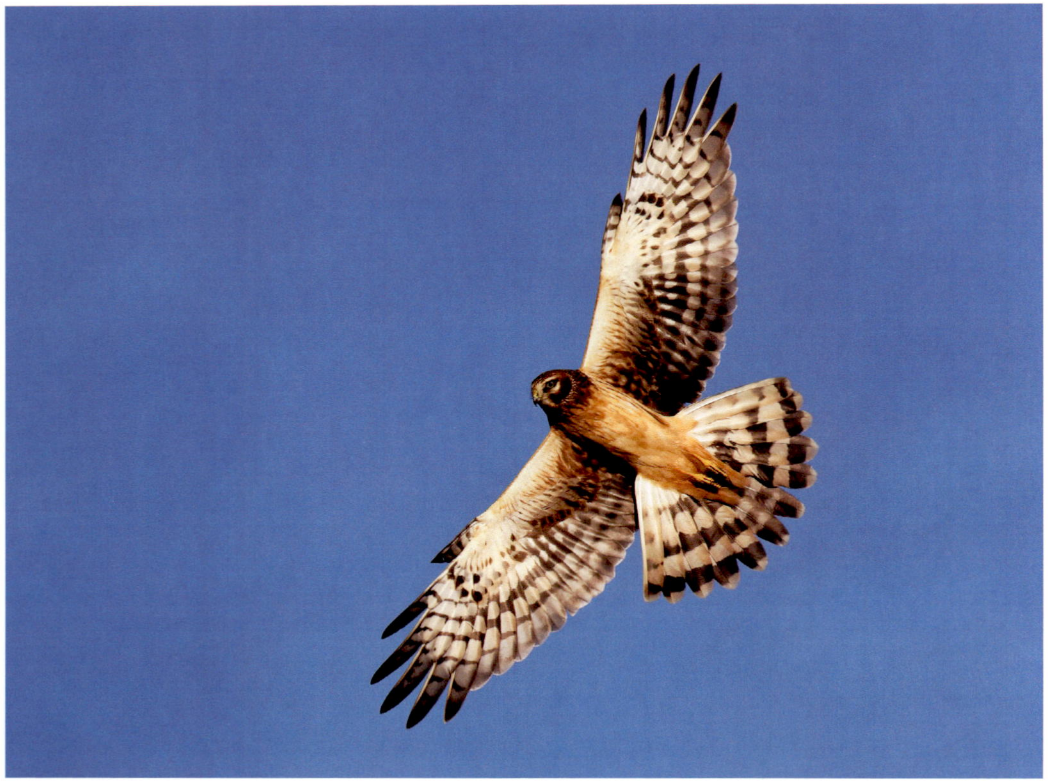

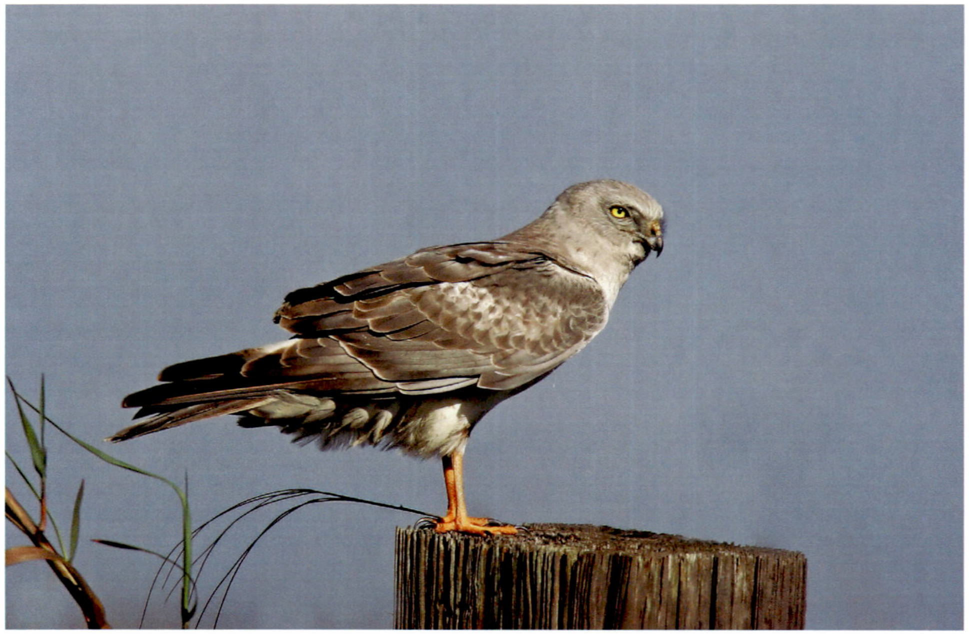

The reason birds can fly and we can't is simply that they have perfect faith, for to have faith is to have wings.

—J.M. Barrie

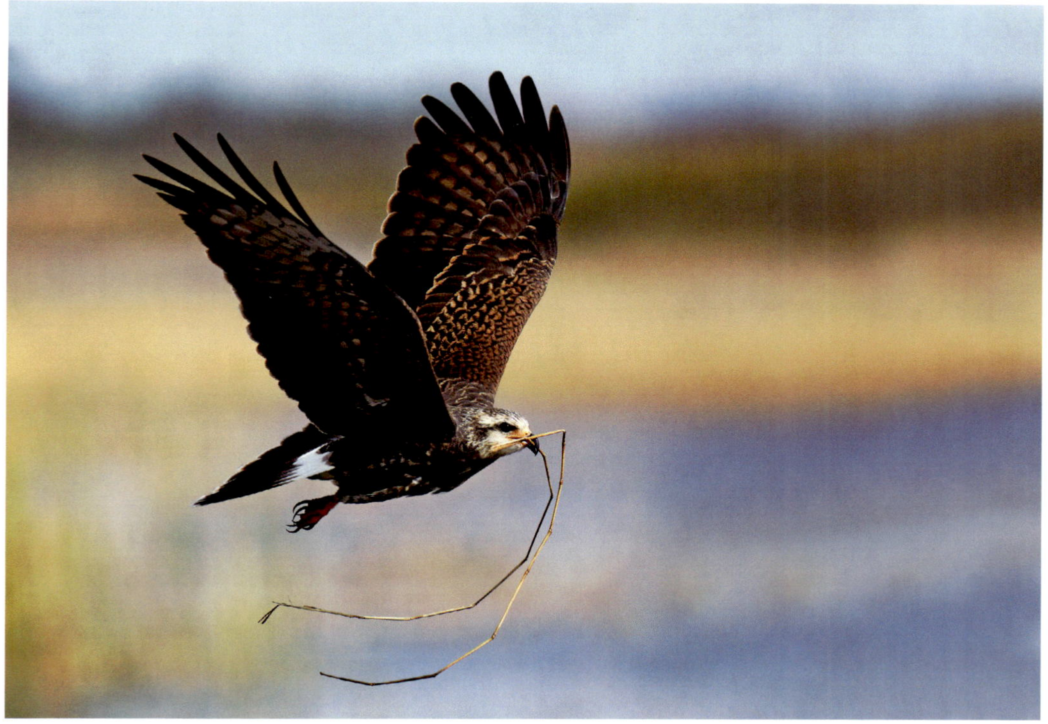

Snail Kites spend most of their lives around freshwater habitats and their diet consists mainly of large snails. Adult males (below) are charcoal gray, while females (lower left) and immatures have a mottled plumage. *Photos by Kevin T. Karlson*

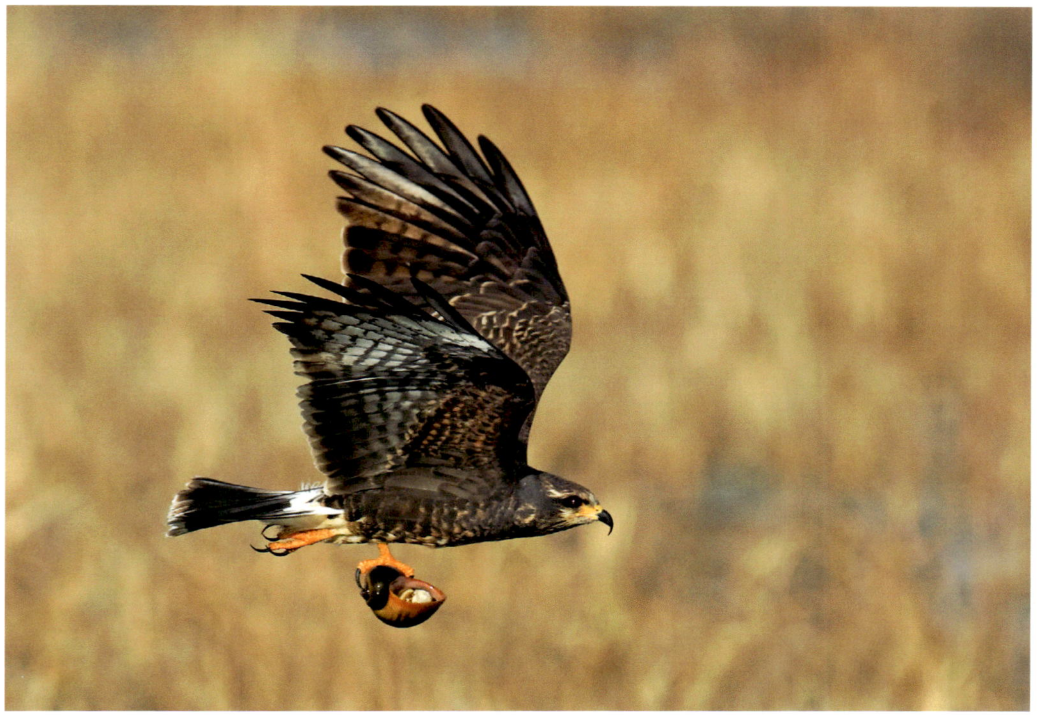

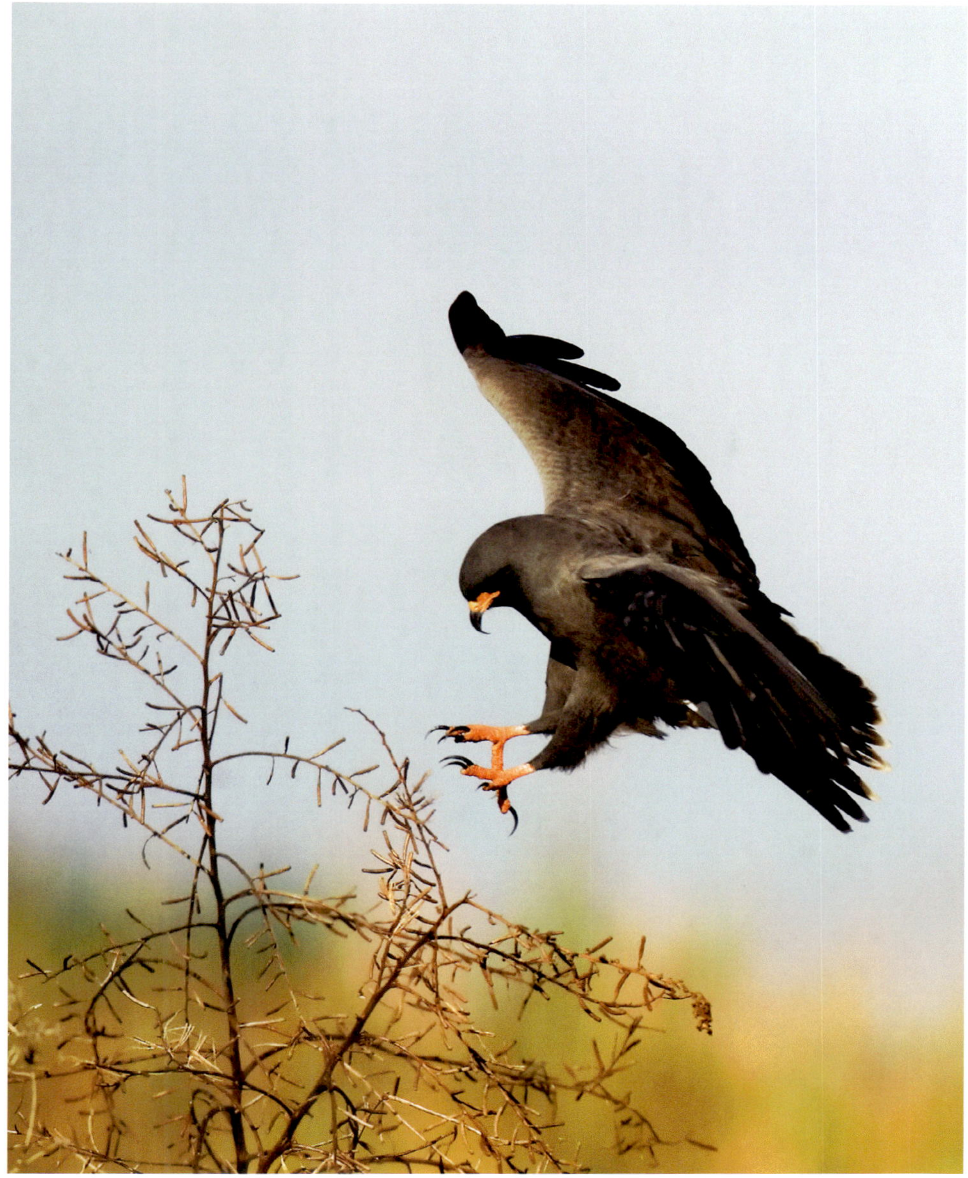

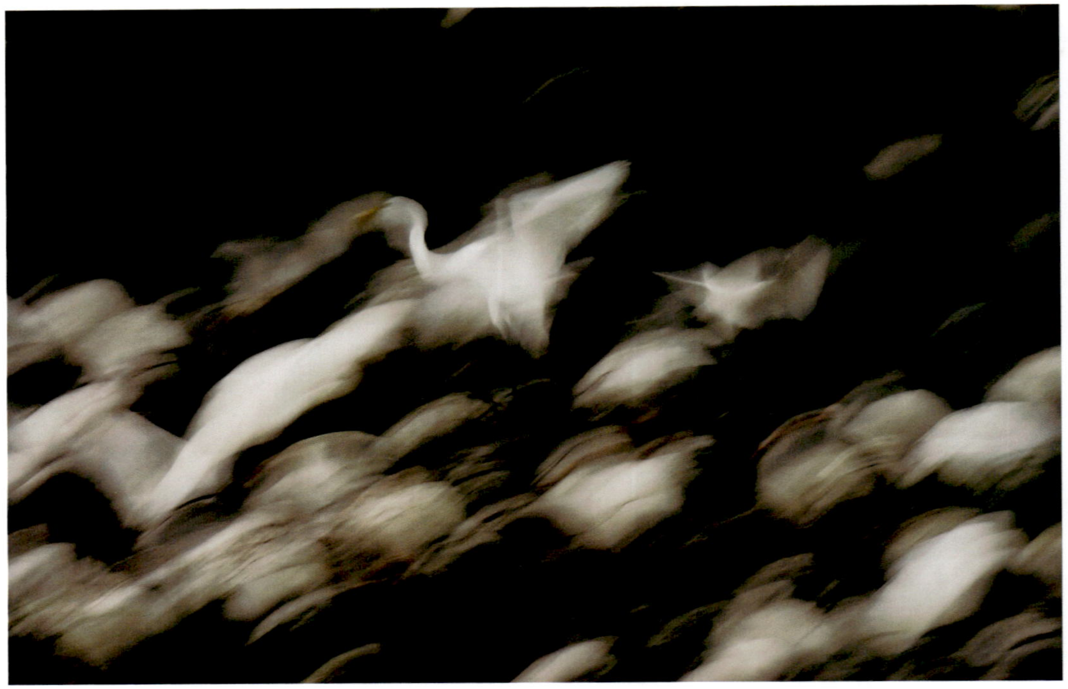

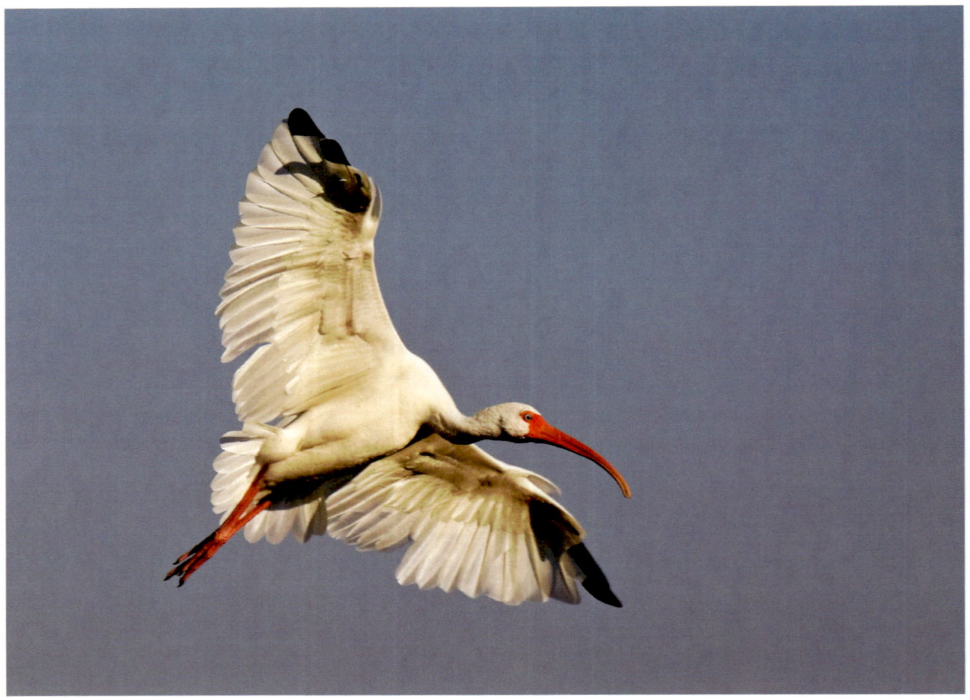

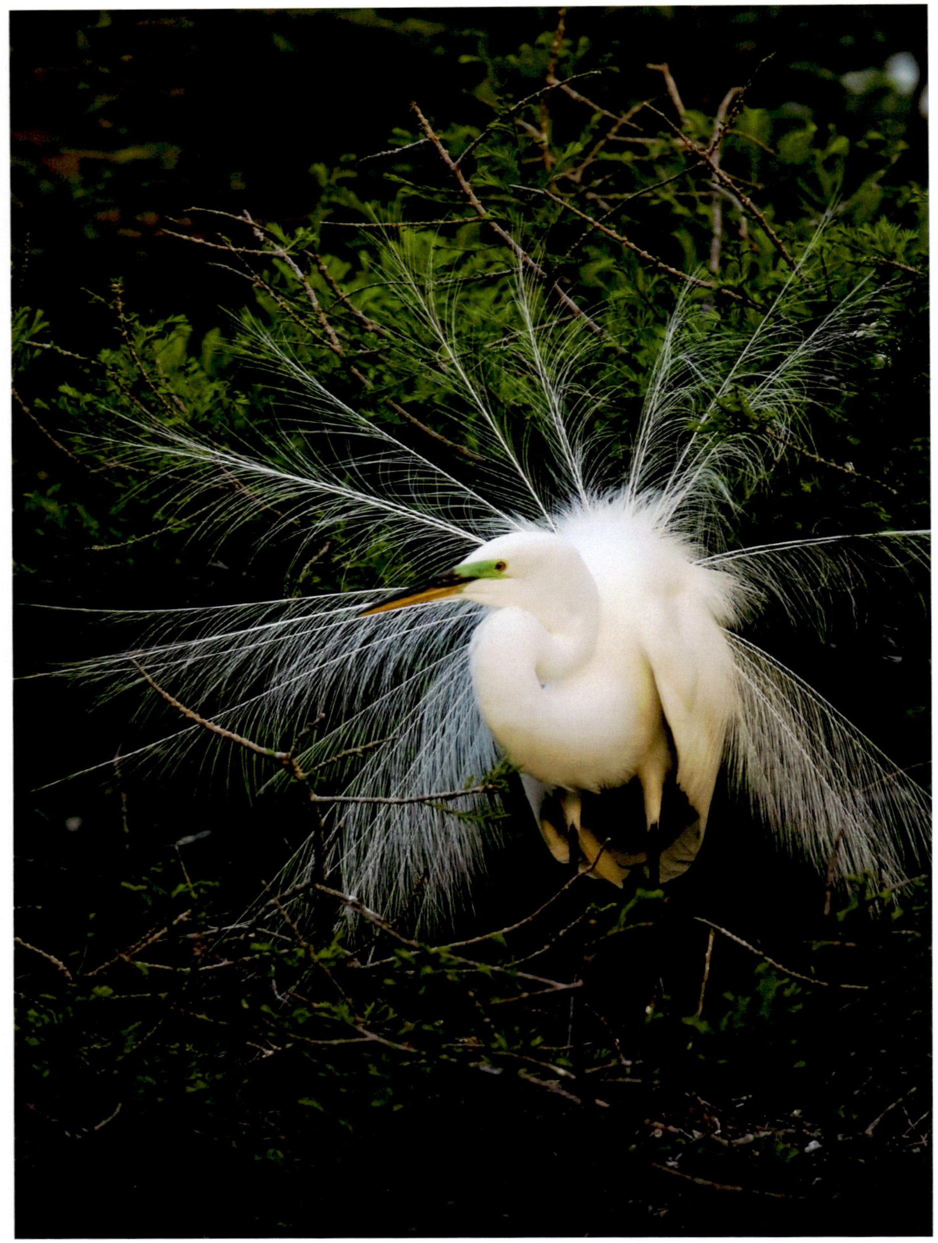

Wading birds are a special attraction in Florida, where large concentrations gather in night time roosts (upper left). Included in this blur photo are White Ibises (lower left) and Great Egrets. A Great Egret (above) is shown raising its showy plumes in a nest display. *Photos by Kevin T. Karlson*

Opposite: A Great Blue Heron approaches its nest with more building material. *Photo by Kevin T. Karlson*

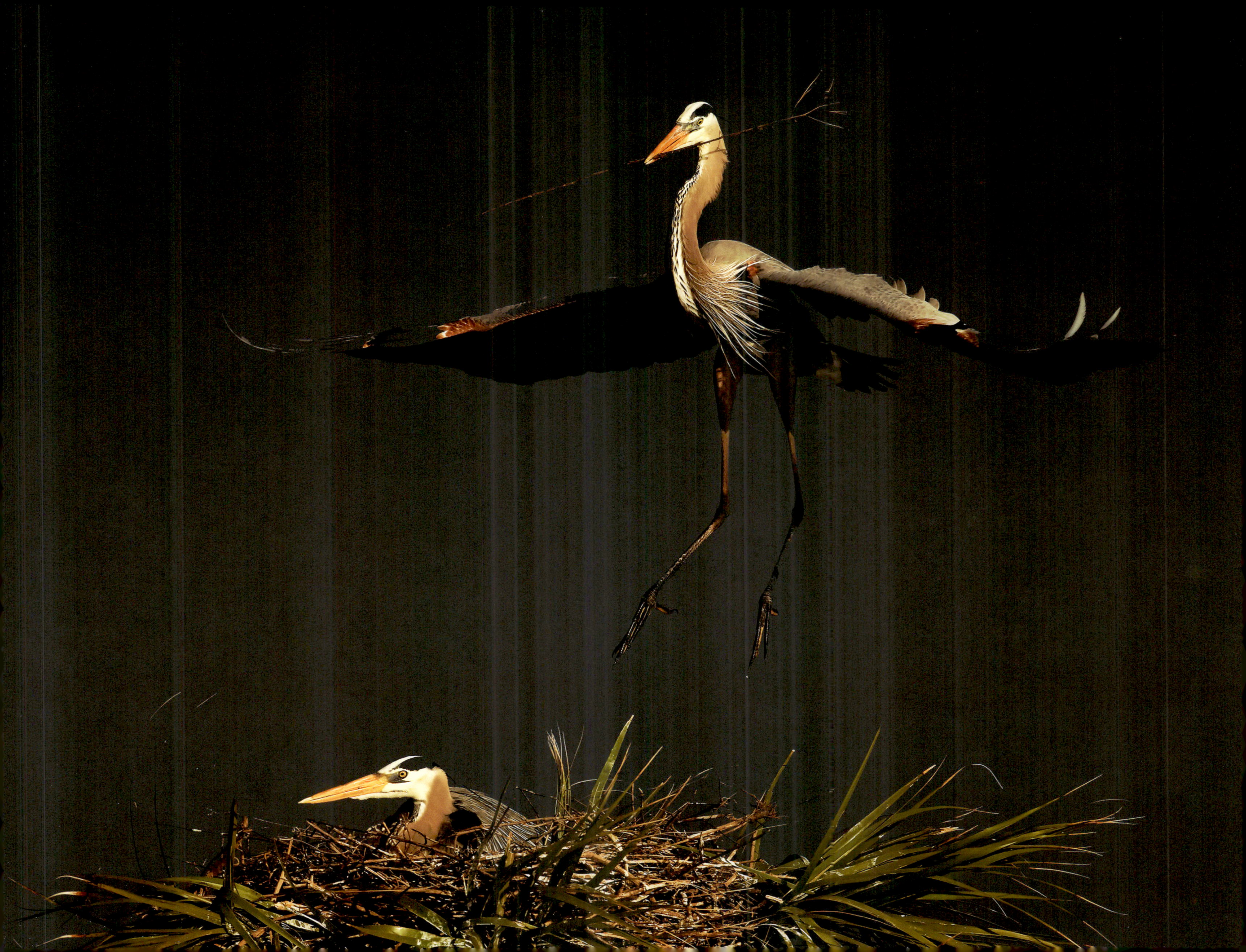

There are no limits to either time or distance, except as man himself may make them. I have but to touch the wind to know these things.

— Hal Borland

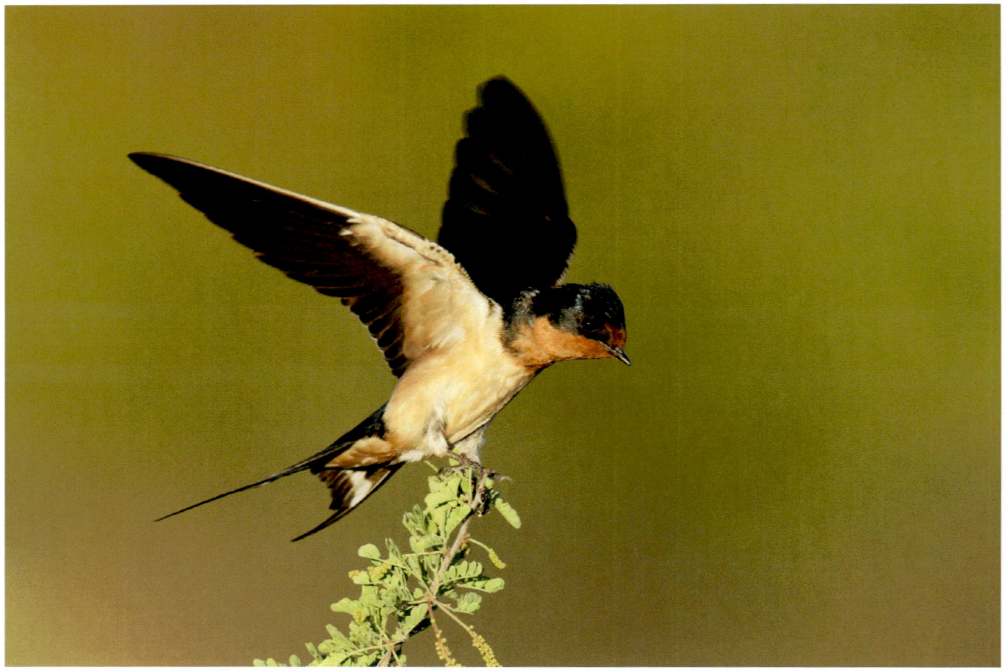

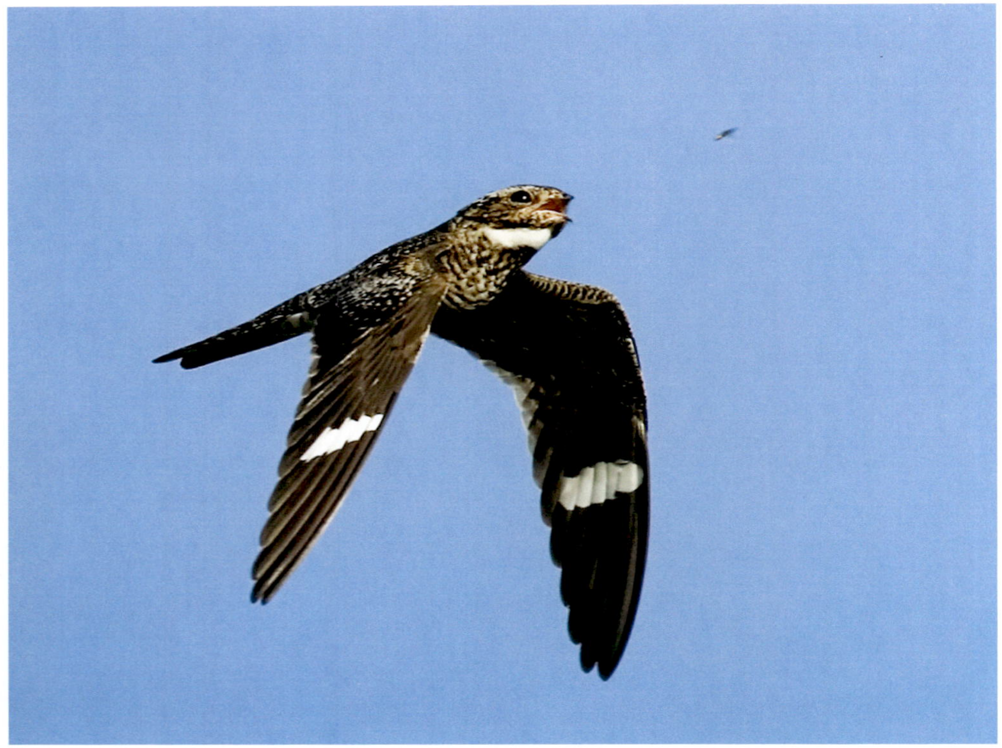

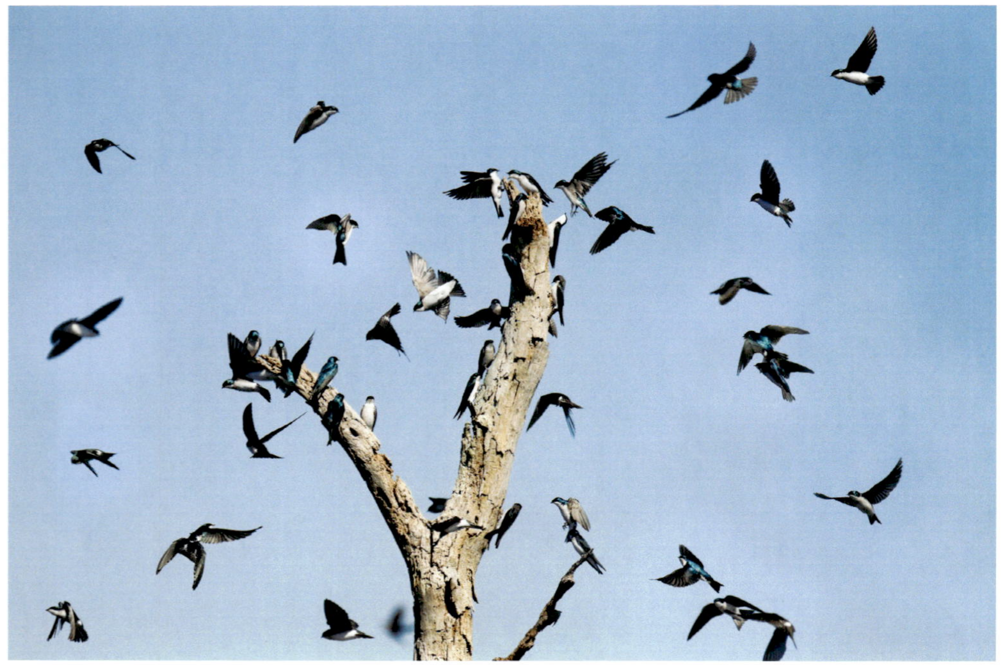

All the birds on this page feed on insects while flying. The Barn Swallow (above) is a beautiful mix of blue, buff, and rust colors, and has a long, forked tail. A Common Nighthawk (upper right) is shown just before it grabs a flying insect. Tree Swallows (lower right) form very large flocks in migration and winter. *Photos by Scott Elowitz (above) and Kevin T. Karlson (upper and lower right)*

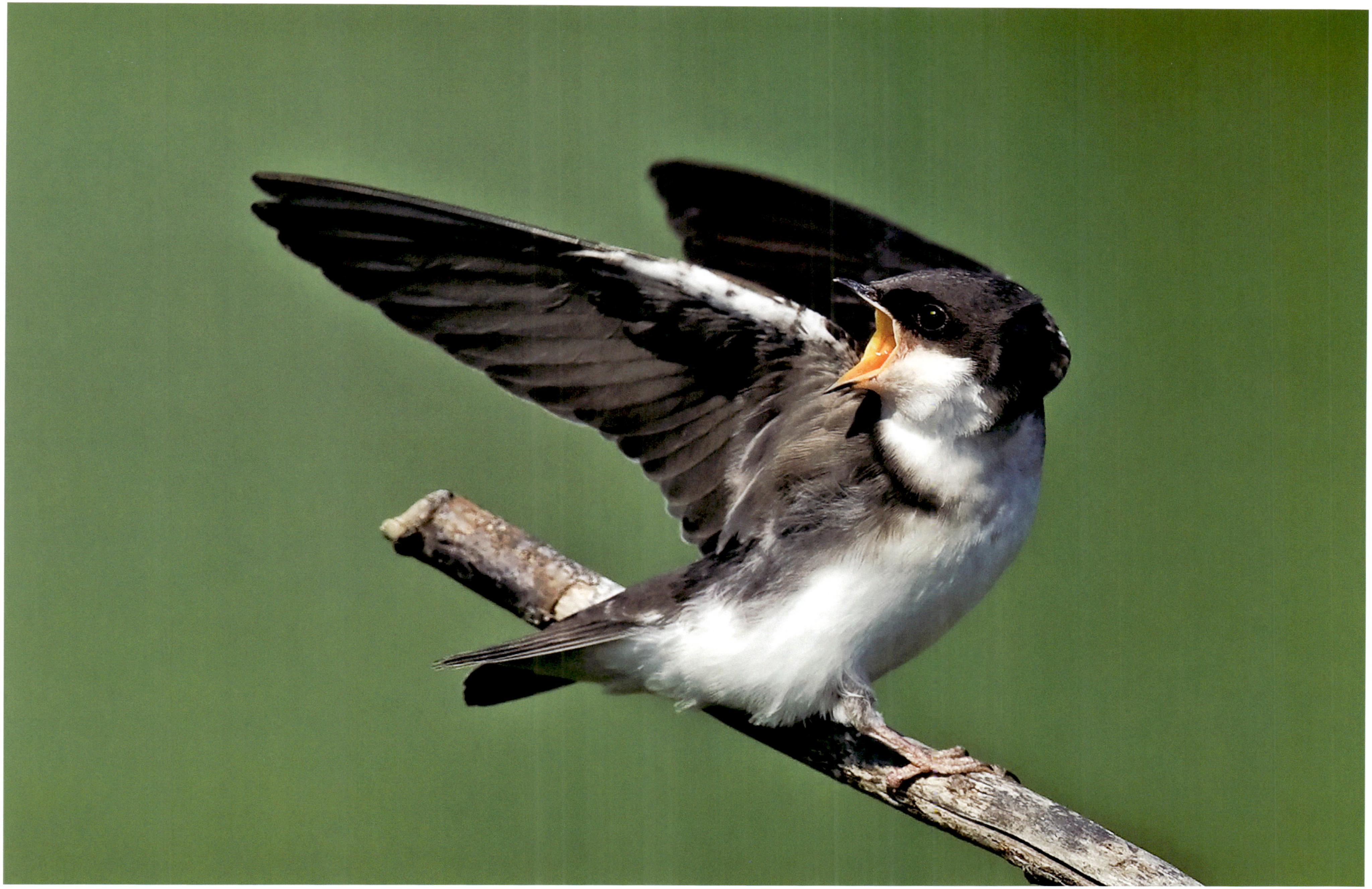

A juvenile Tree Swallow begging for food is shown just before its parent arrives with dinner. *Photo by Lloyd Spitalnik*

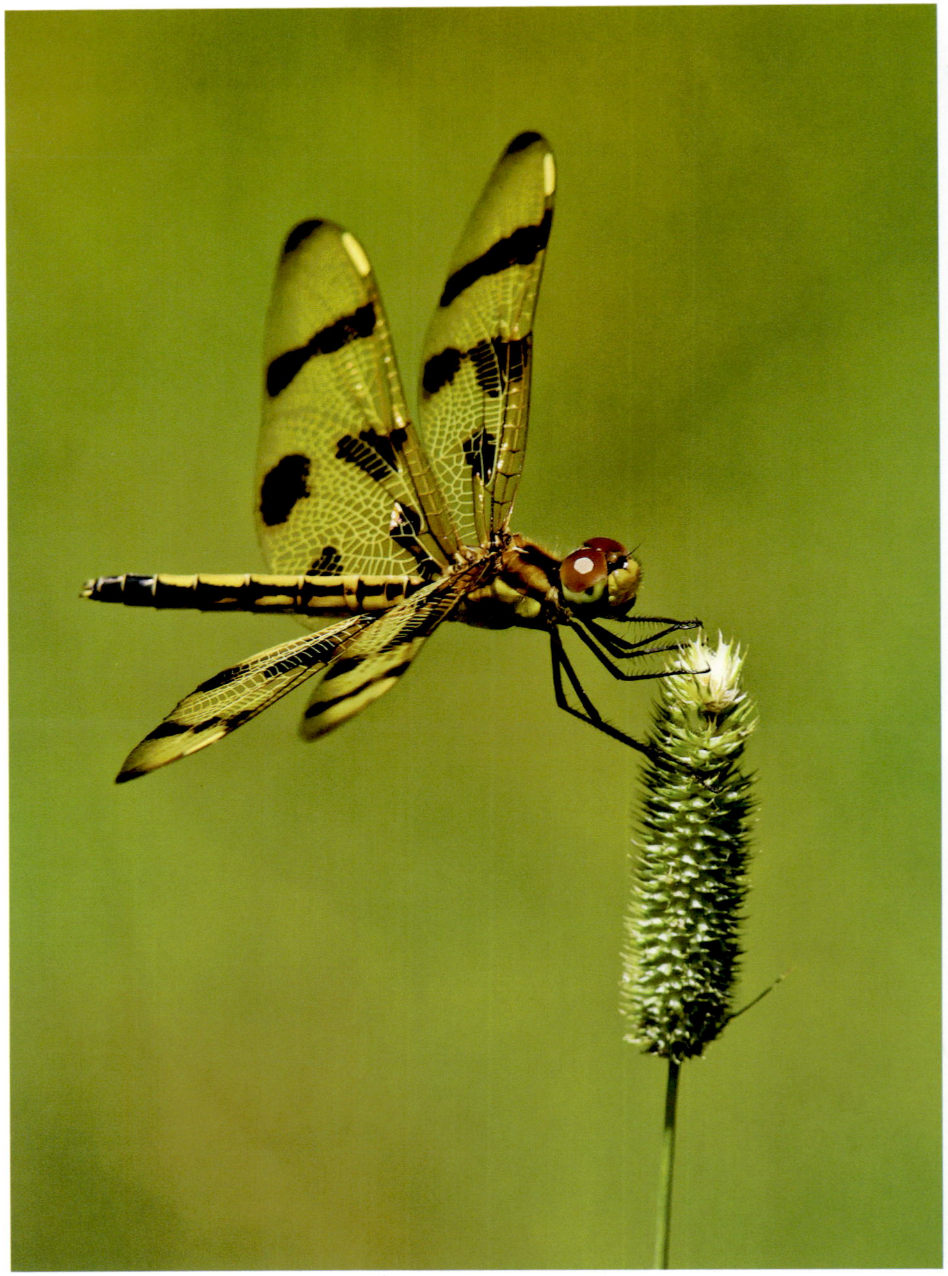

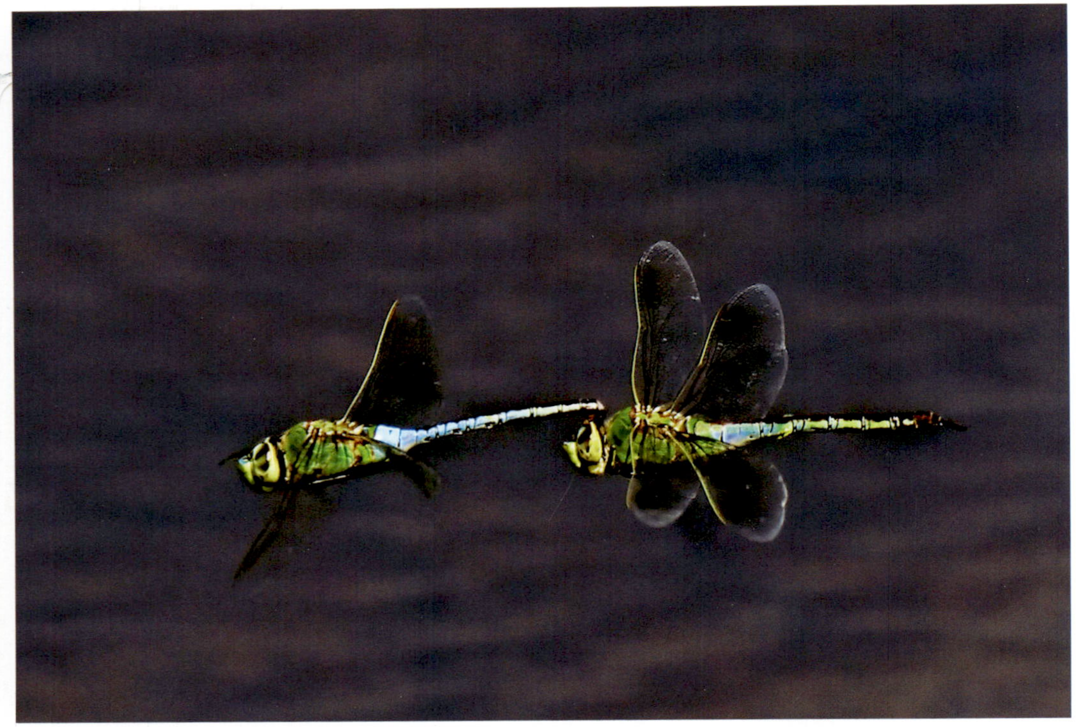

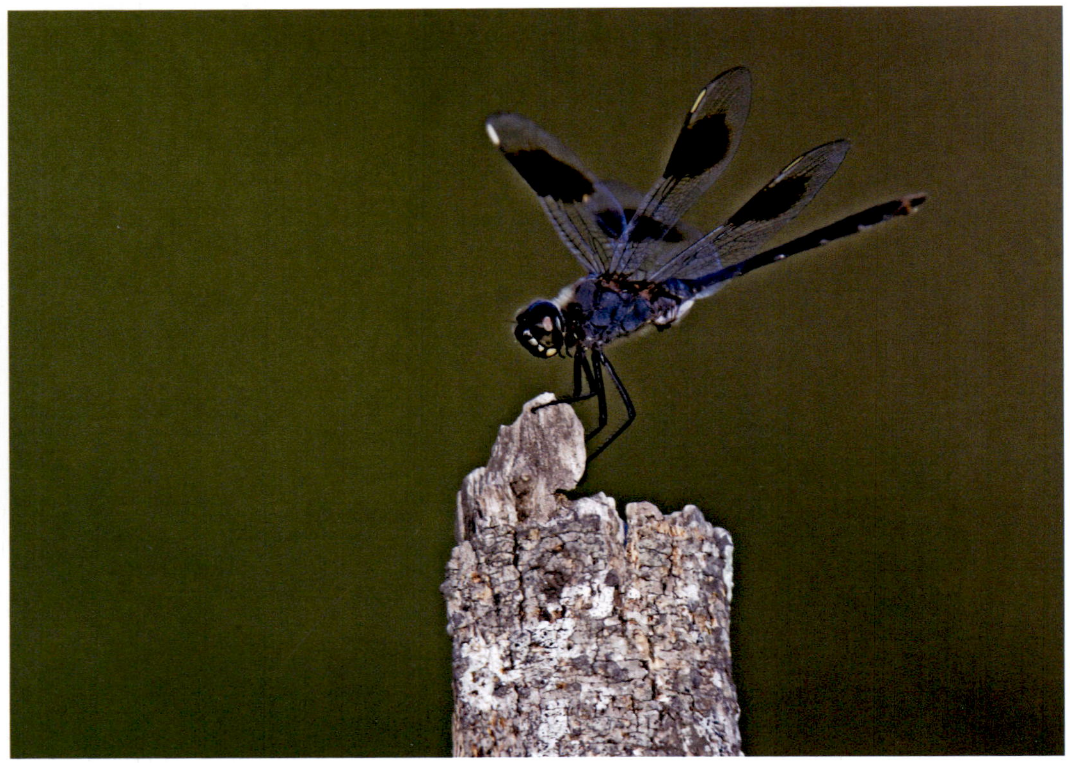

When the heat of the summer made drowsy the land,
A dragon-fly came and sat on my hand.

— Eleanor Farjeon

Opposite: Dragonflies are some of the most amazing and misunderstood creatures. They eat a tremendous number of flying insects, including many pests, and possess a gentle spirit that you only have to commune with to understand. Halloween Pennant (left) *by Lloyd Spitalnik;* Green Darners (upper right) *by Kevin T. Karlson;* and Four-spotted Pennant, (lower right) *by Mike Hannisian*

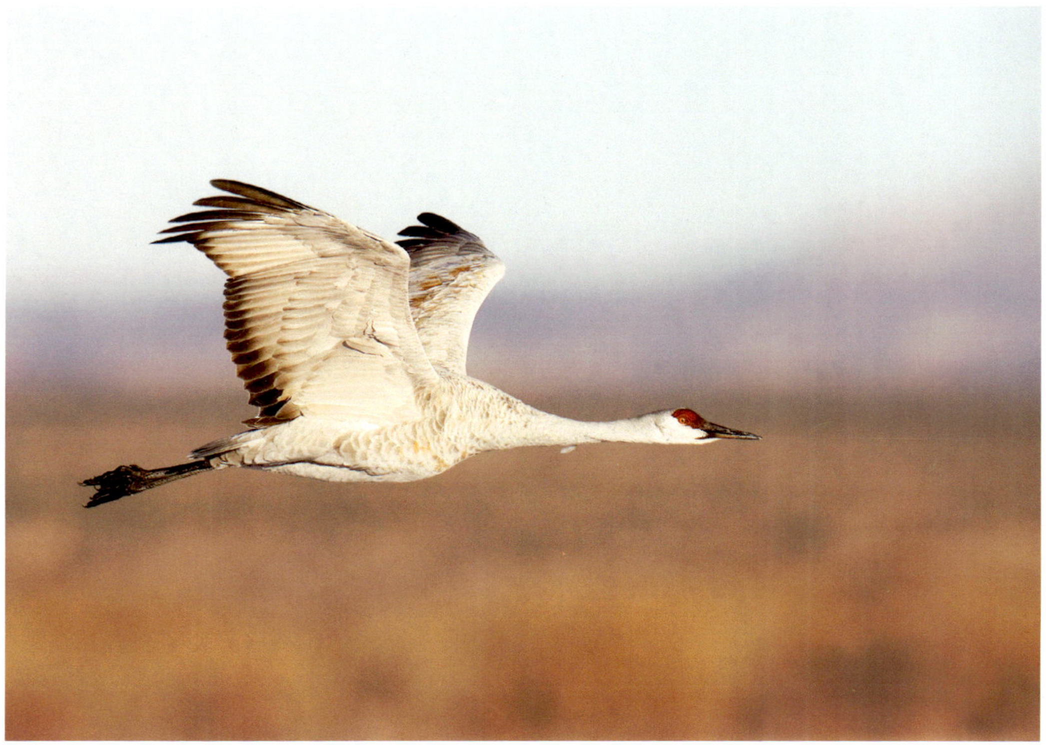

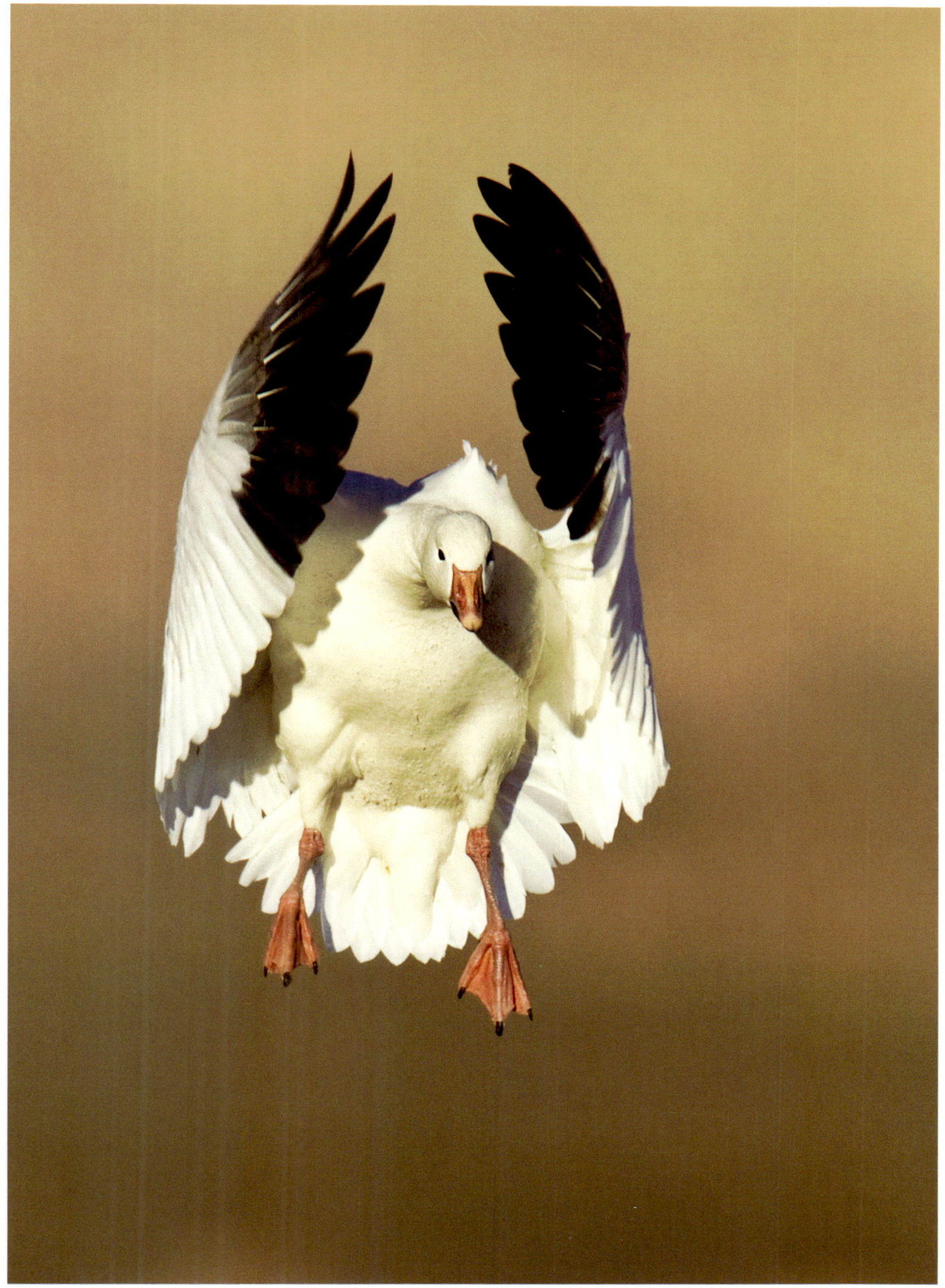

Bosque del Apache, New Mexico, is the location for these two airy images. A Sandhill Crane (left) flies leisurely above the desert landscape, while a Snow Goose (above) comes in for a landing. *Photos by Scott Elowitz*

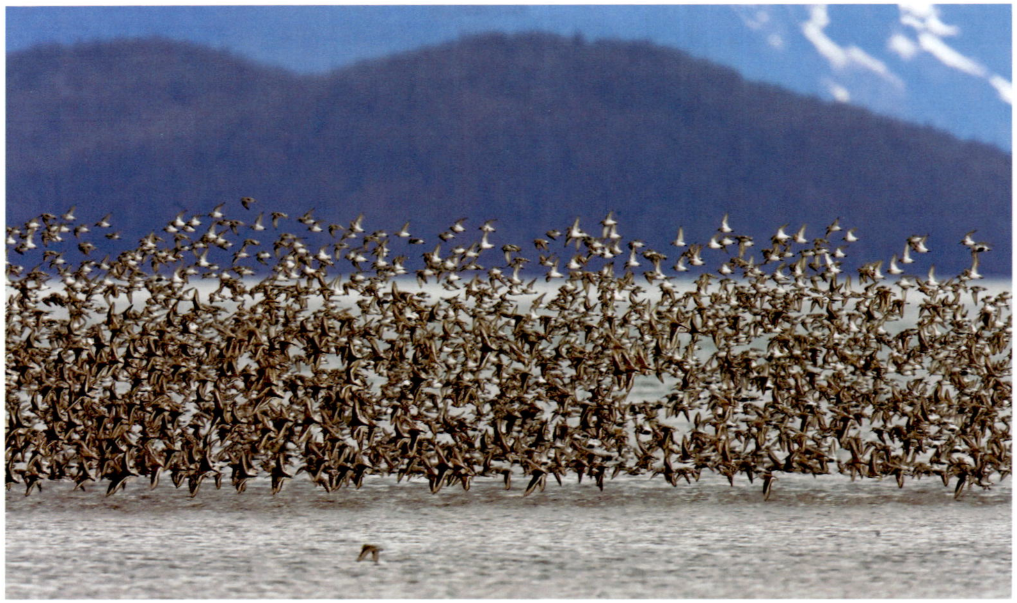

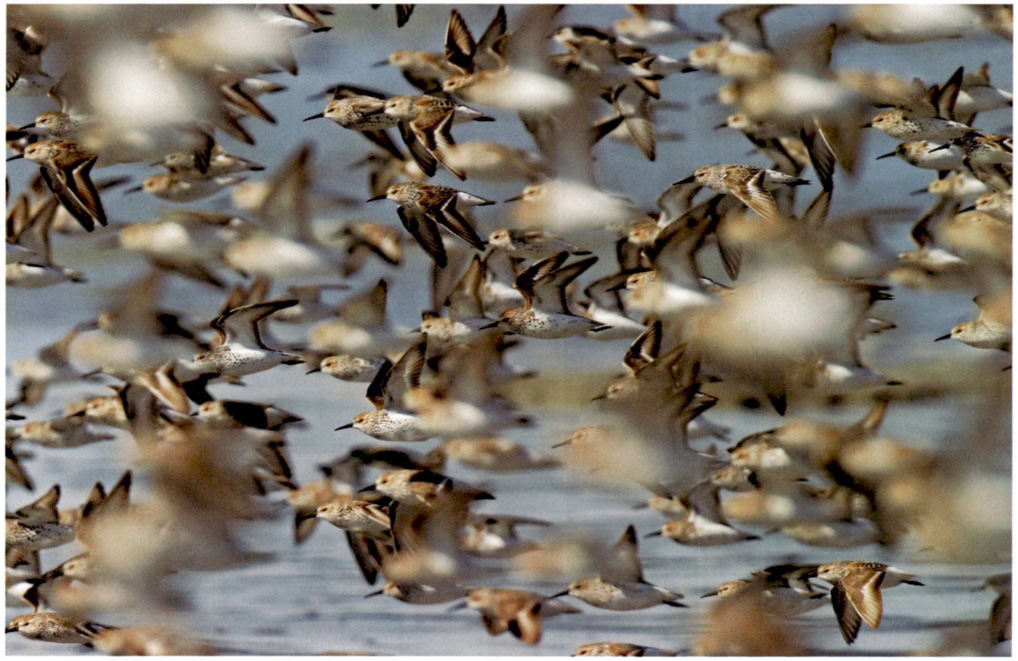

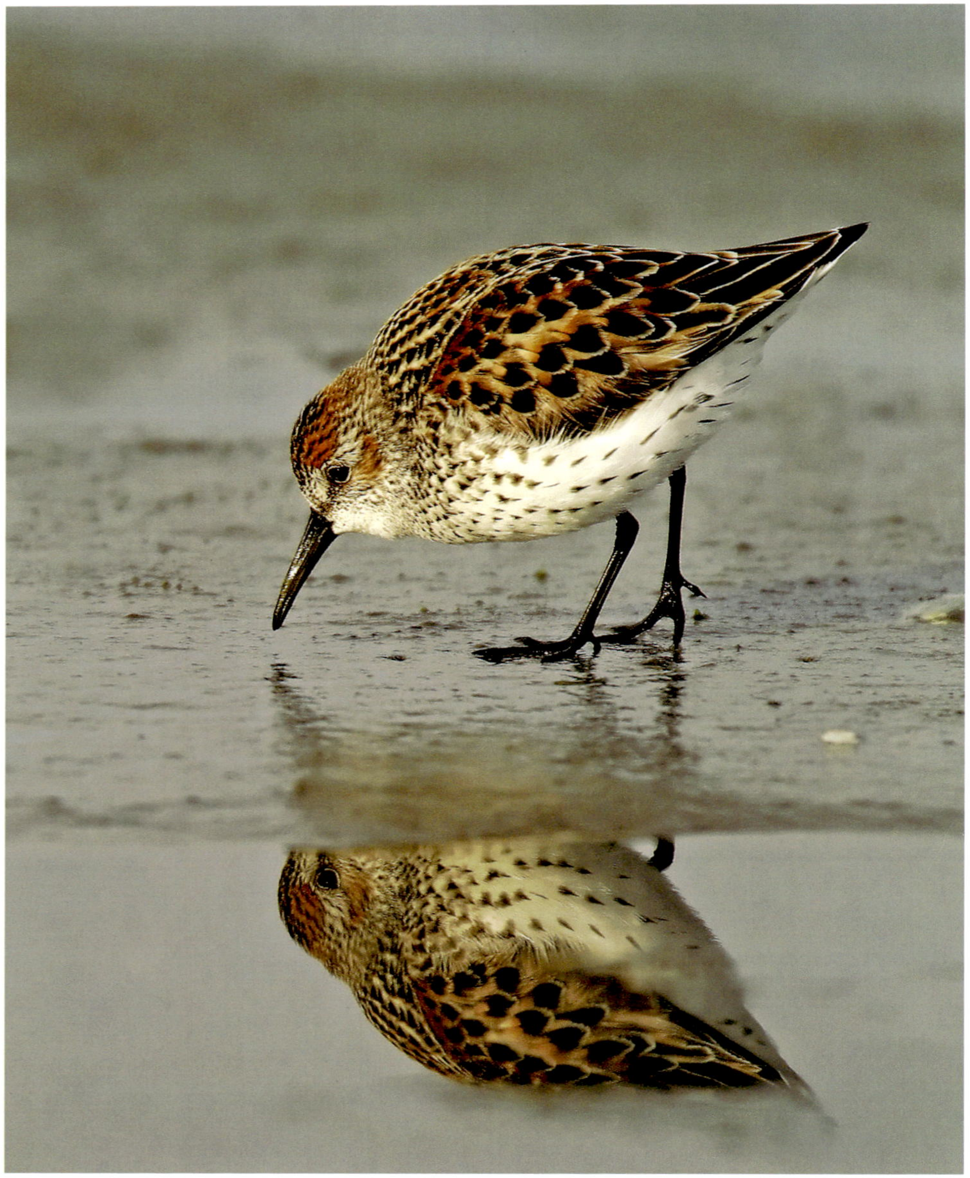

Western Sandpipers are small shorebirds that breed in Arctic regions of Alaska. Their breeding plumage (above) is a rich mix of rust, black, and white. Up to four million Westerns (left) stop to feed near Cordova, Alaska, in May, before continuing to Arctic breeding sites. *Photos by Kevin T. Karlson*

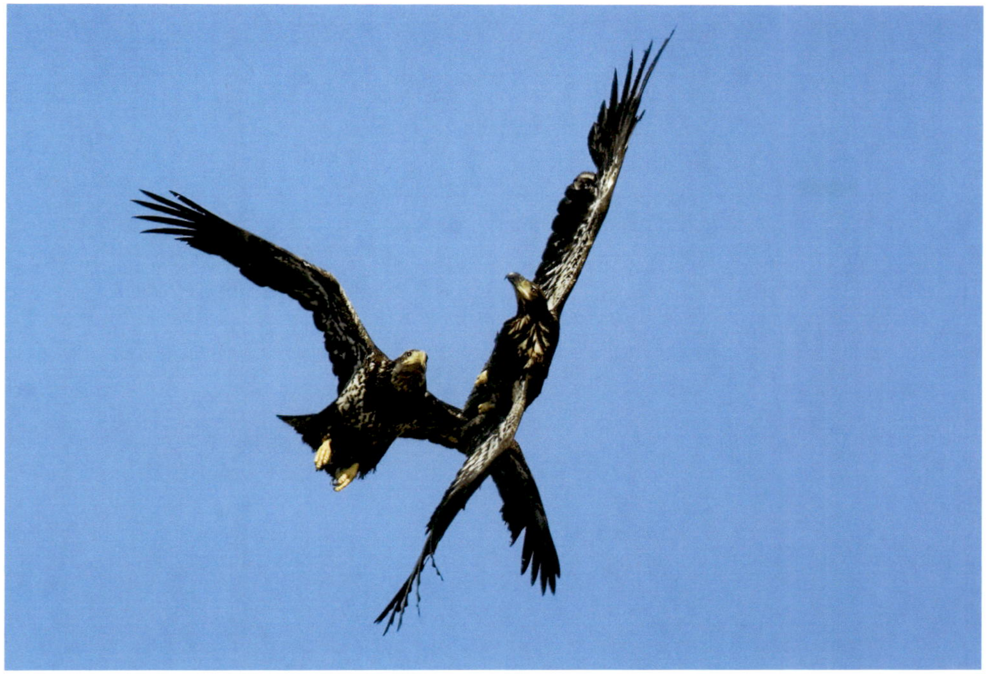

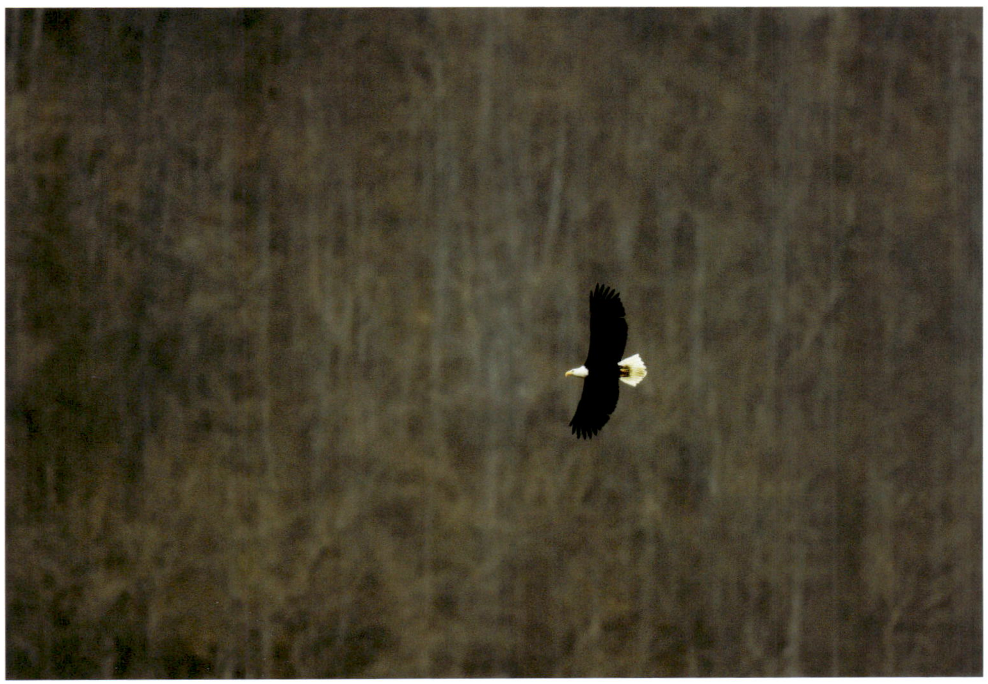

The elegant and powerful Bald Eagle always captivates those who are fortunate to see one. These photos were taken in Alaska, where sightings are common occurrences. The two young eagles (left) are practicing their aerial maneuvers by jousting with each other. *Photos by Kevin T. Karlson*

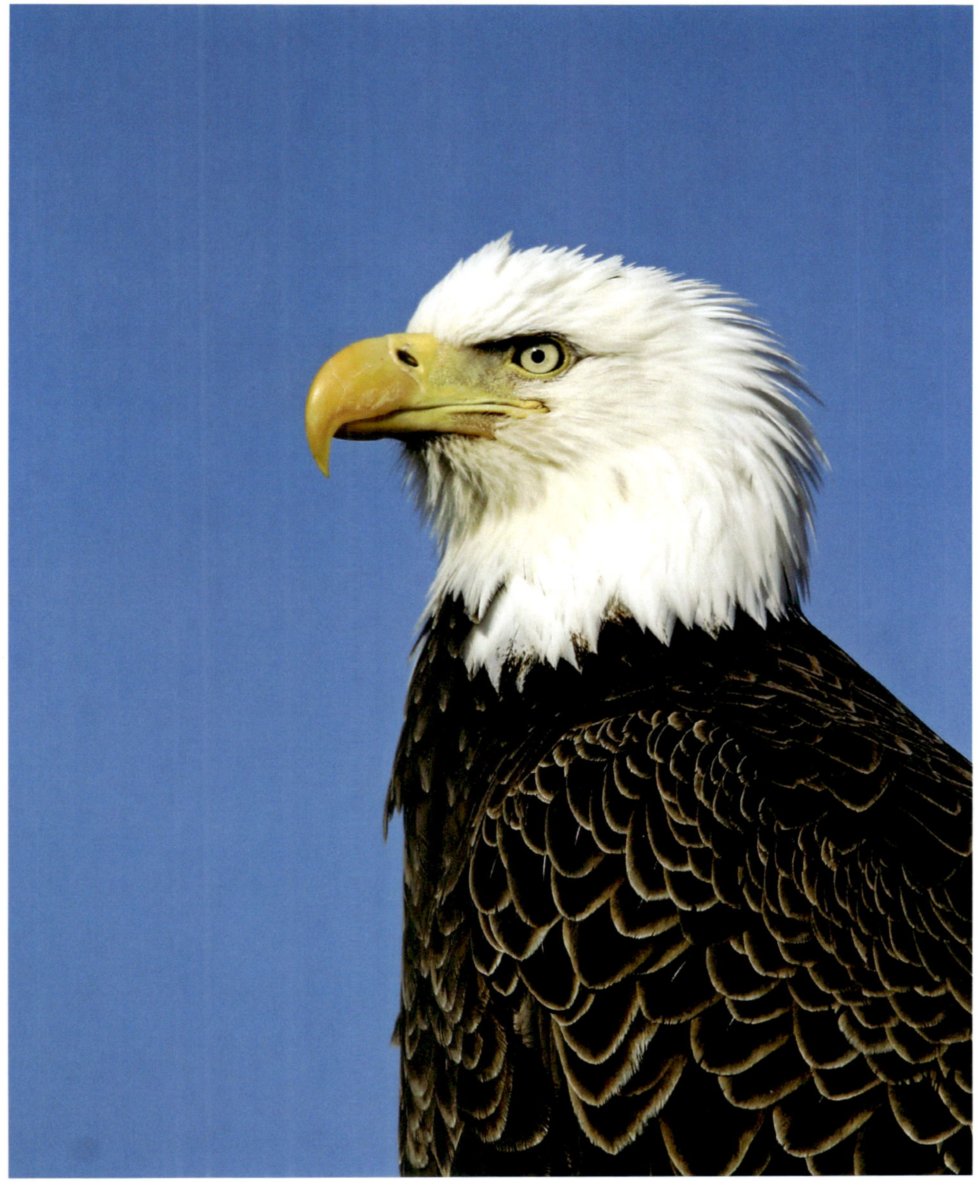

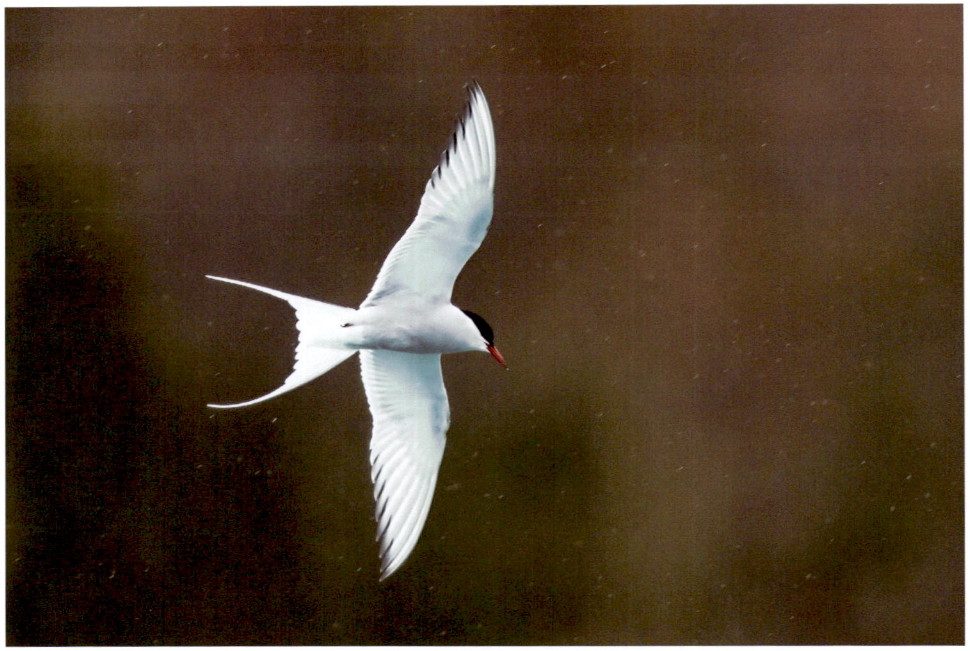

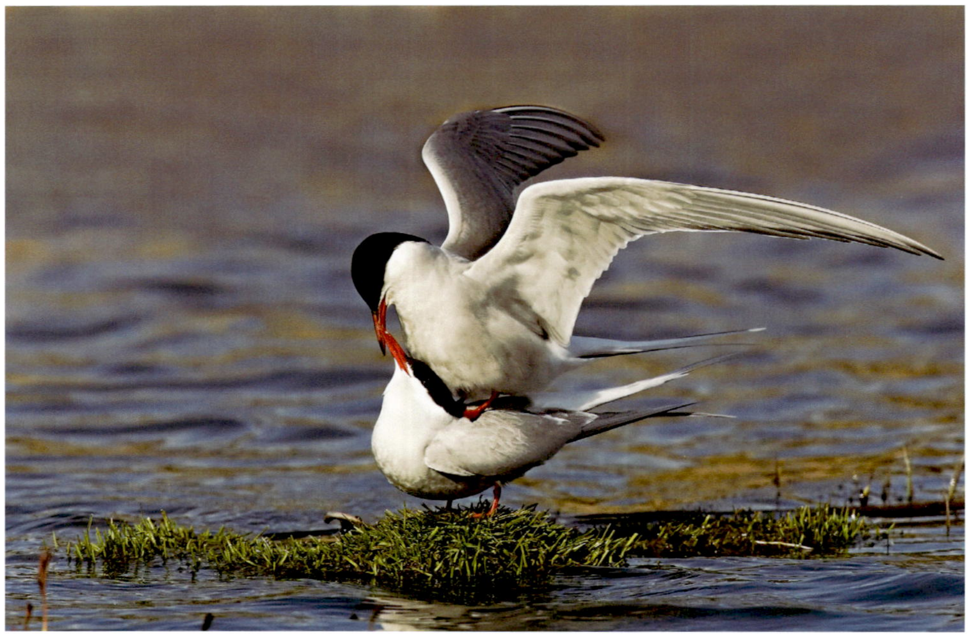

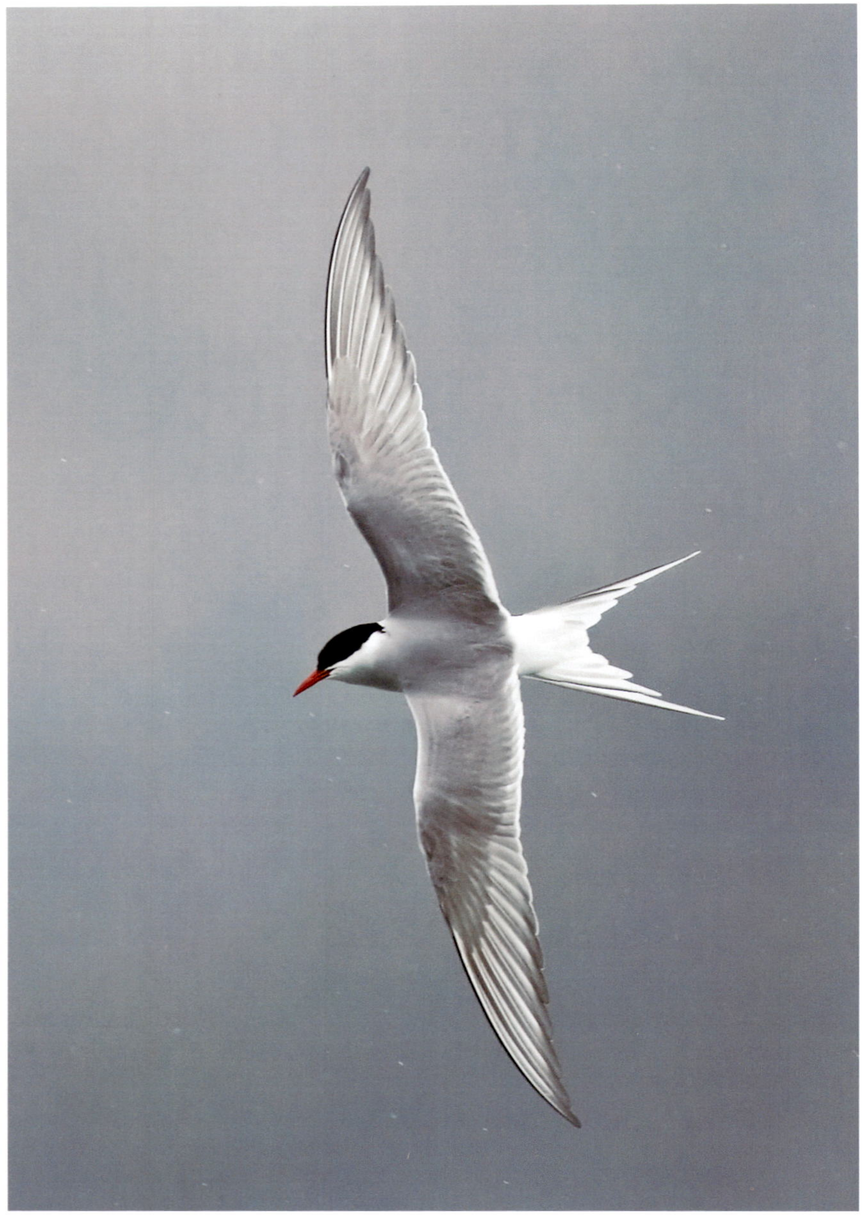

Arctic Terns have a round trip migration each year that encompasses almost 20,000 miles from the Arctic to the Antarctic. The two flight images were taken in cloudy, rainy conditions, which truly capture the subtle shades of gray without overexposing the whites. *Photos by Kevin T. Karlson*

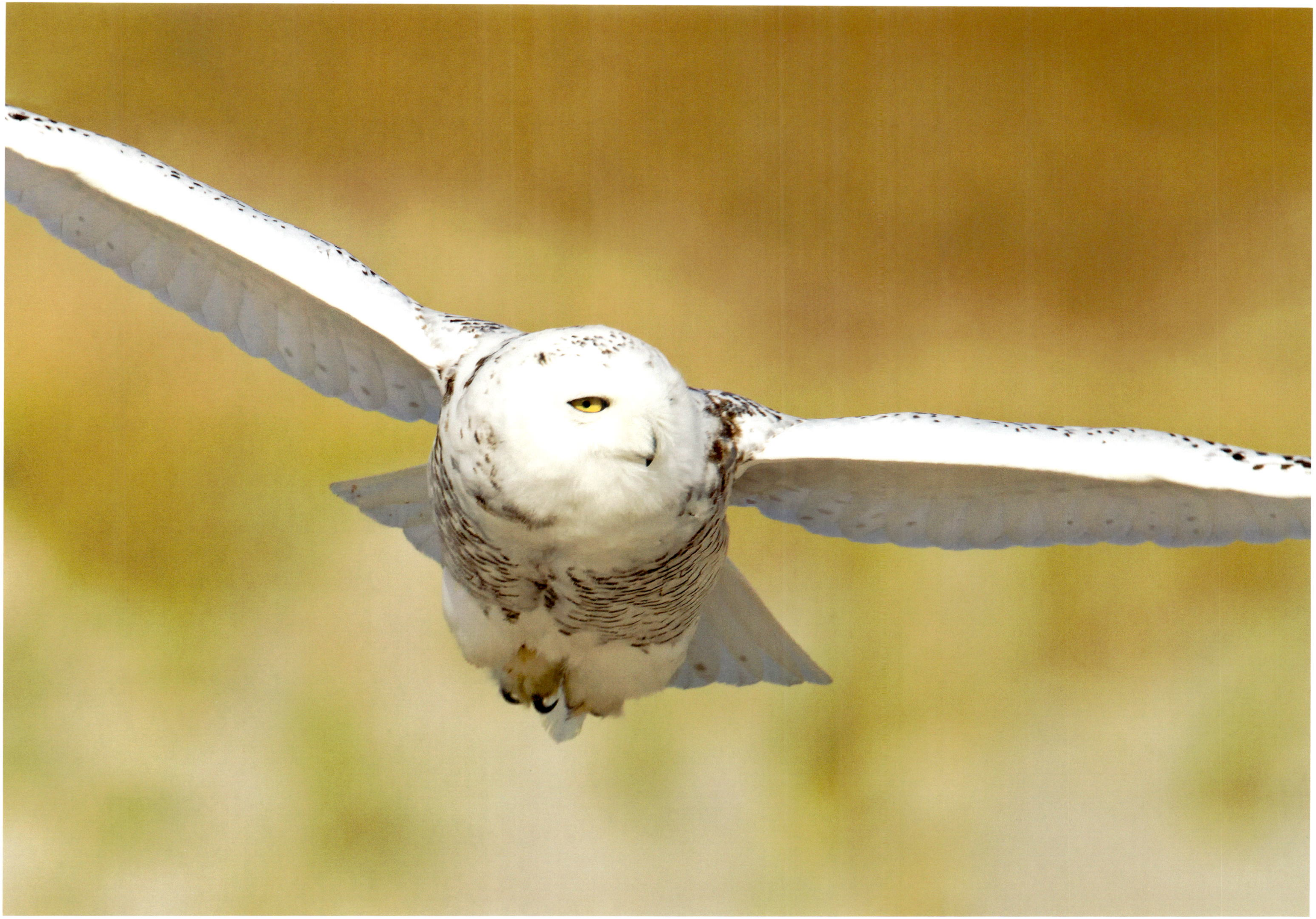

This striking Snowy Owl shares Arctic habitats with the Arctic Tern from the opposite page. Its large size and fierce nature result in it having no predators in the avian world, and its ground nesting habits create a bridge between the air and the earth. *Photo by Lloyd Spitalnik*

Rainbows apologize for angry skies.

— Sylvia Voirol

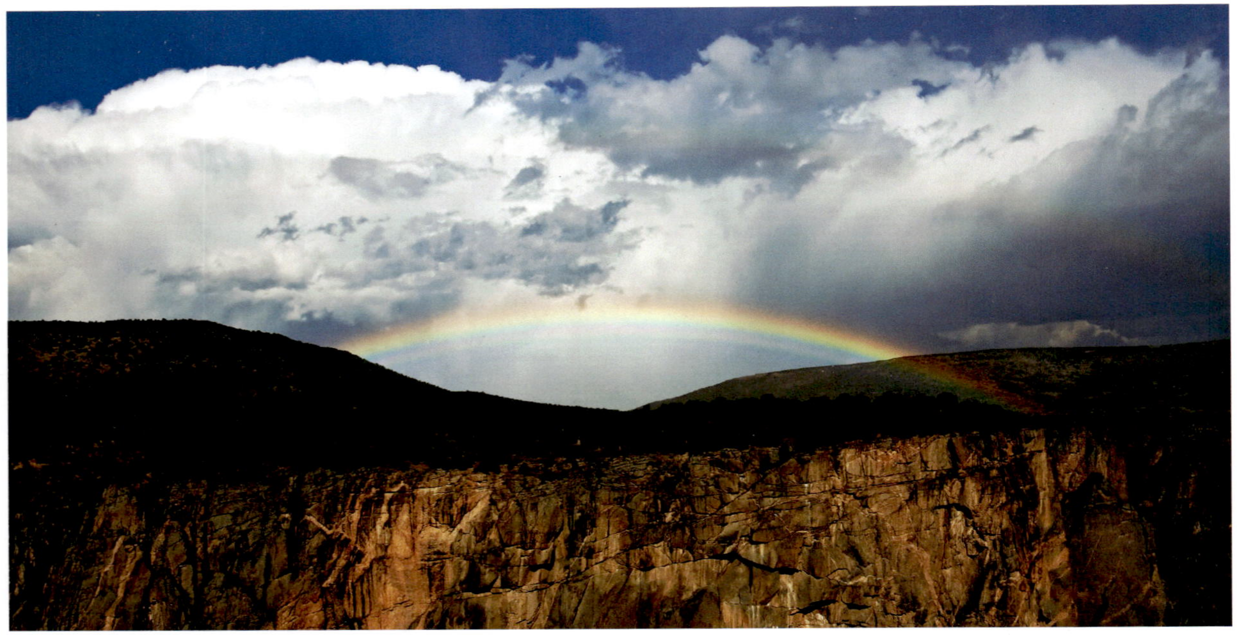

A complete rainbow stretches across a wide ravine in Gunnison, Colorado, allowing us to see where it joined the earth at both ends. Unfortunately, the ravine kept us from harvesting the pots of gold at the end of the rainbow. *Photo by Kevin T. Karlson*

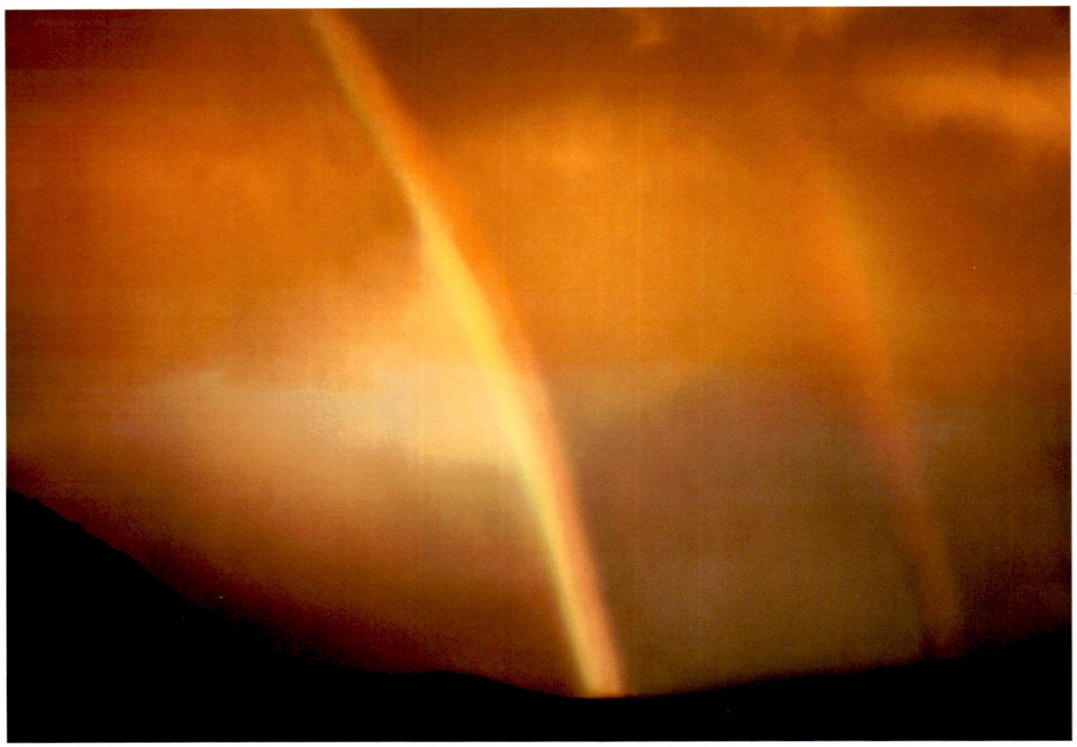

A double rainbow appeared after a violent thunderstorm in Colorado at dusk. *Photo by Kevin T. Karlson*

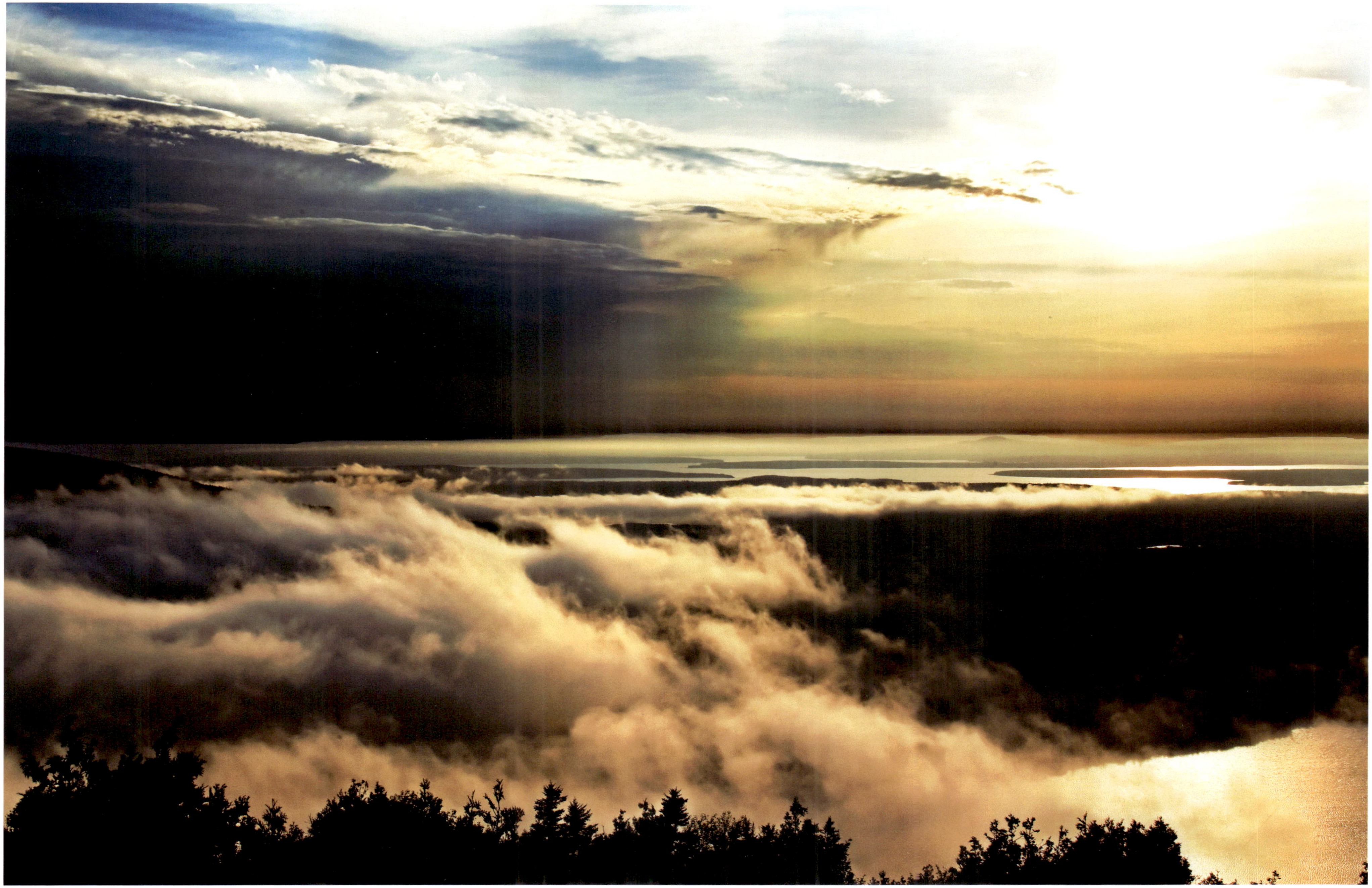

Sunset on Cadillac Mountain, Acadia National Park. The fog began to rise as the sun was setting over the lake-dotted landscape near the coast of Maine. The warmth of the sun's reflection in the water gives way to the cool blue tones of dusk as the sun moves towards the horizon. *Photo by Kevin T. Karlson*

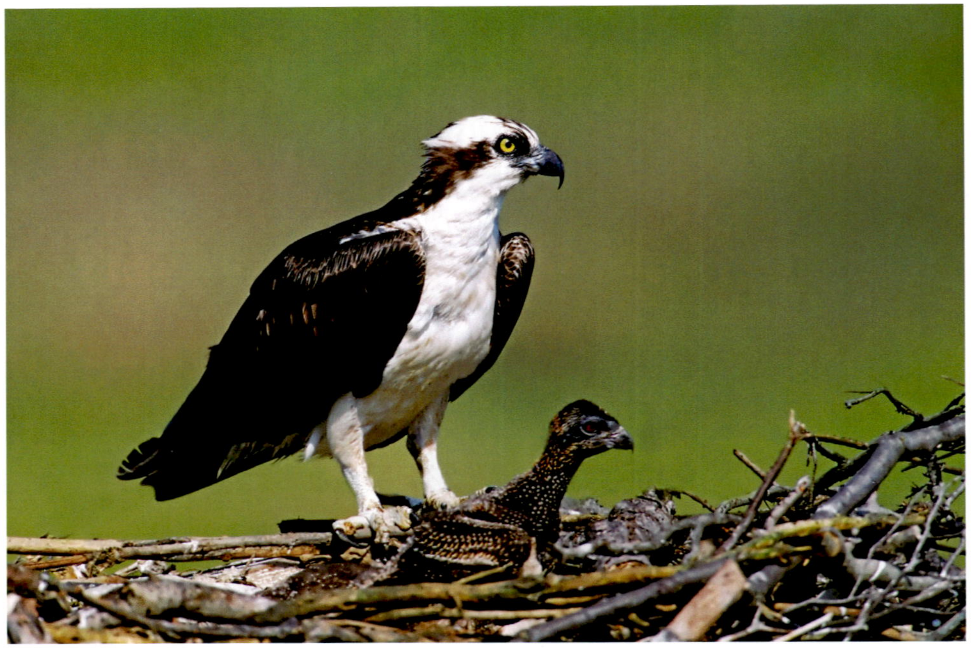

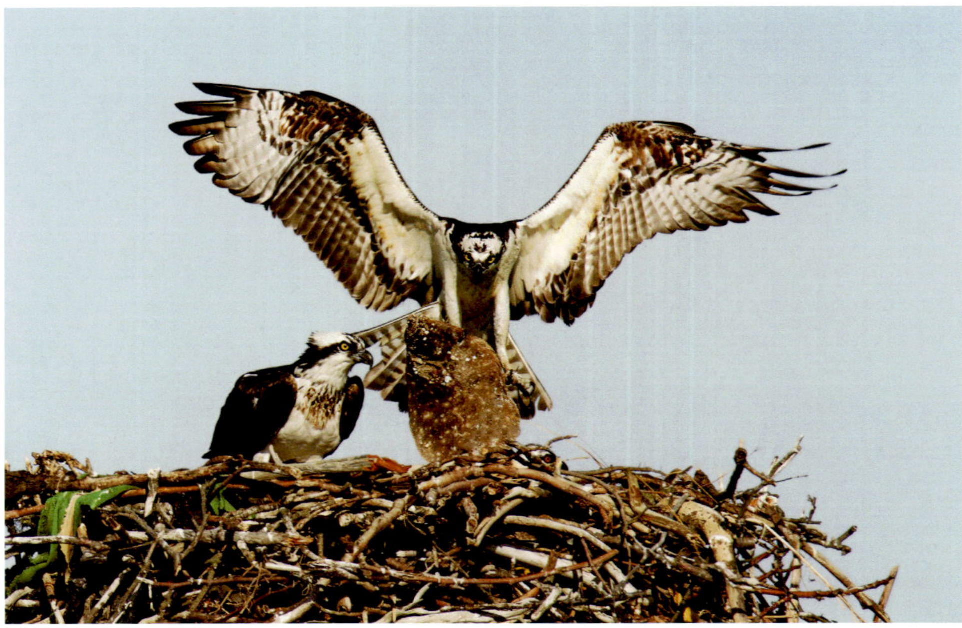

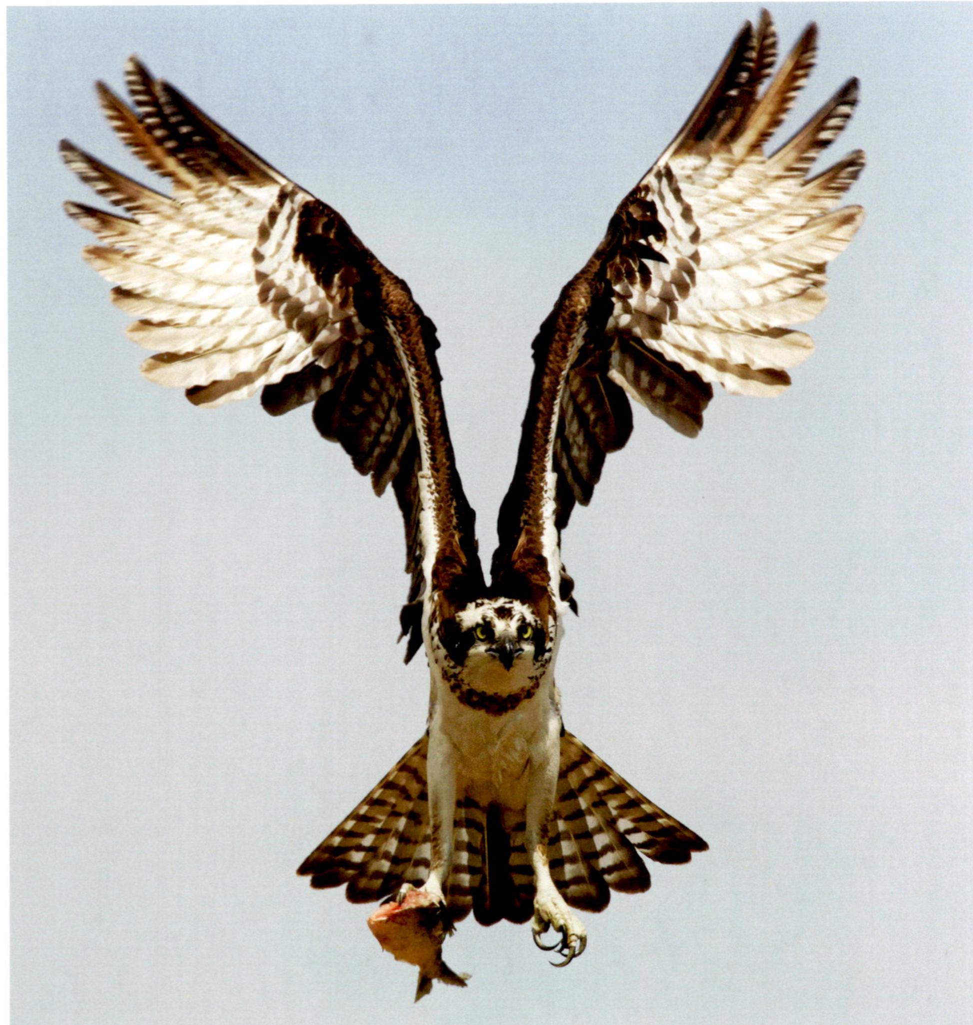

Ospreys are specialists in the raptor family since they feed exclusively on fish, which they catch by plunging into the water feet first. Males (upper left with chick) are smaller than females (above), and lack the spotted necklace. Ospreys build large stick nests on raised structures, and typically raise two young each year. A male Osprey is shown bringing a huge flounder-type fish to his admiring mate in the lower left photo. *Photos by Lloyd Spitalnik (above), Kevin T. Karlson (upper left) and Scott Elowitz (lower left).*

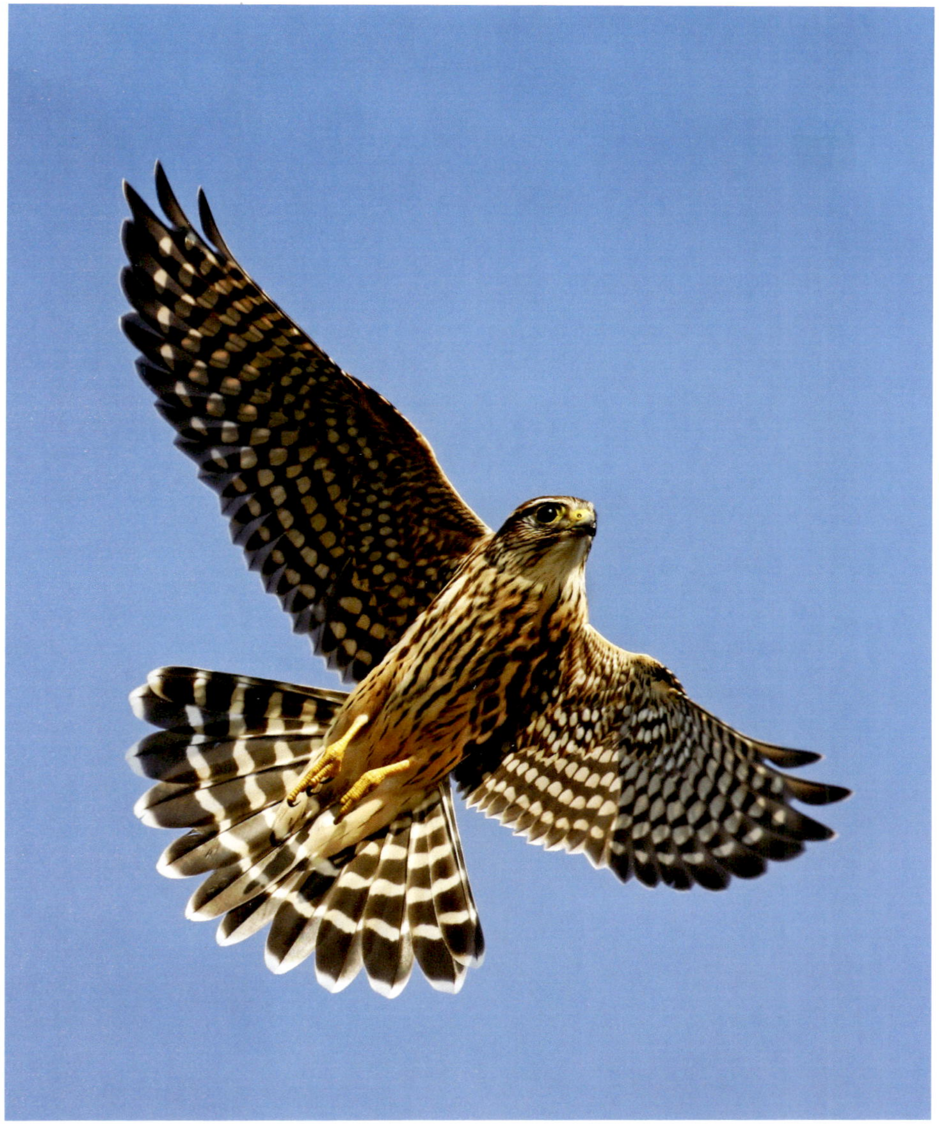

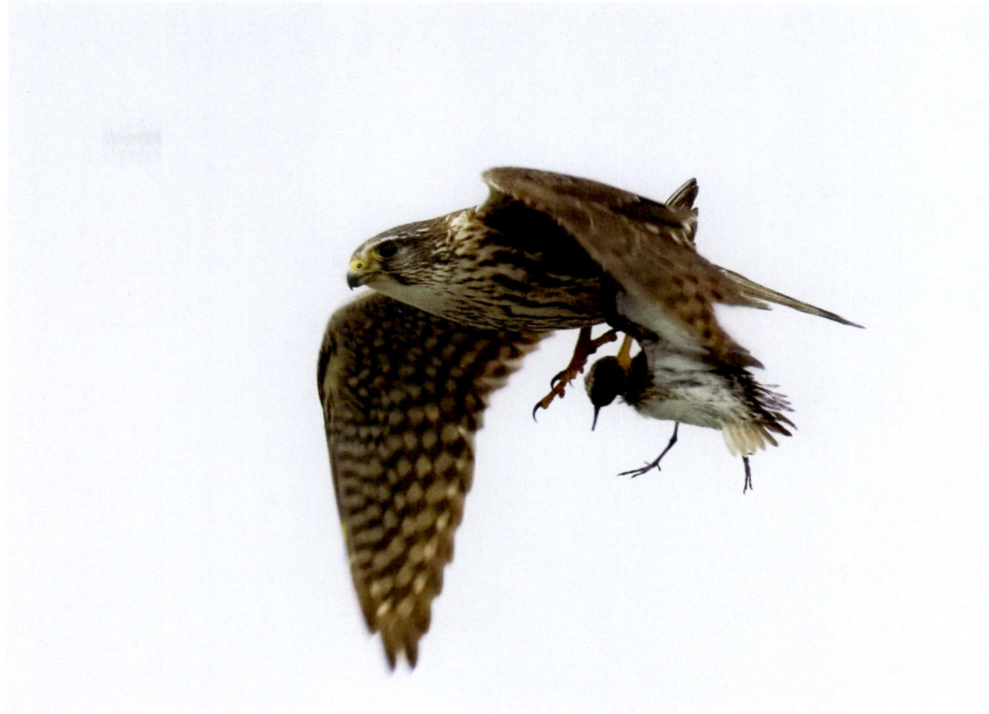

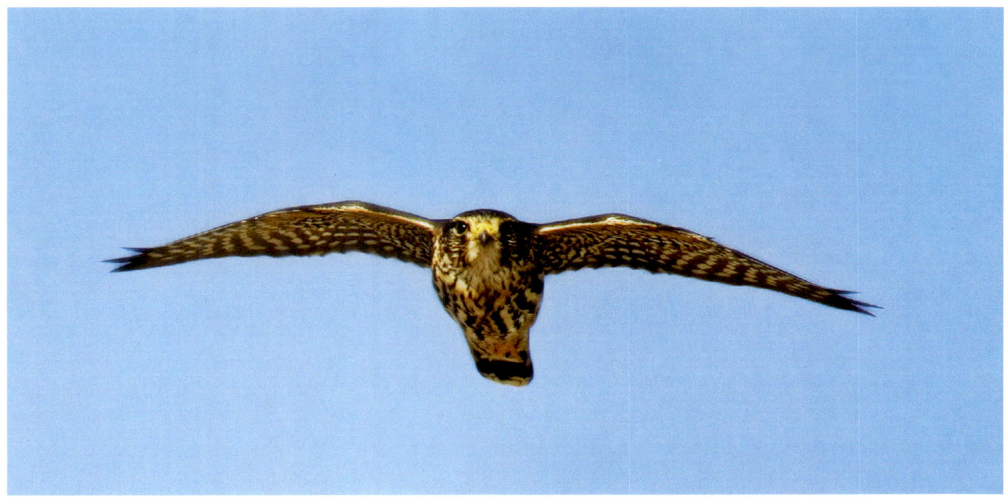

Merlins are one of the feistiest of all raptors and will attack much larger birds of prey just for fun. This medium-sized falcon is an efficient hunter of birds, as a Western Sandpiper in the talons of an adult female found out (upper right). *Photos by Kevin T. Karlson*

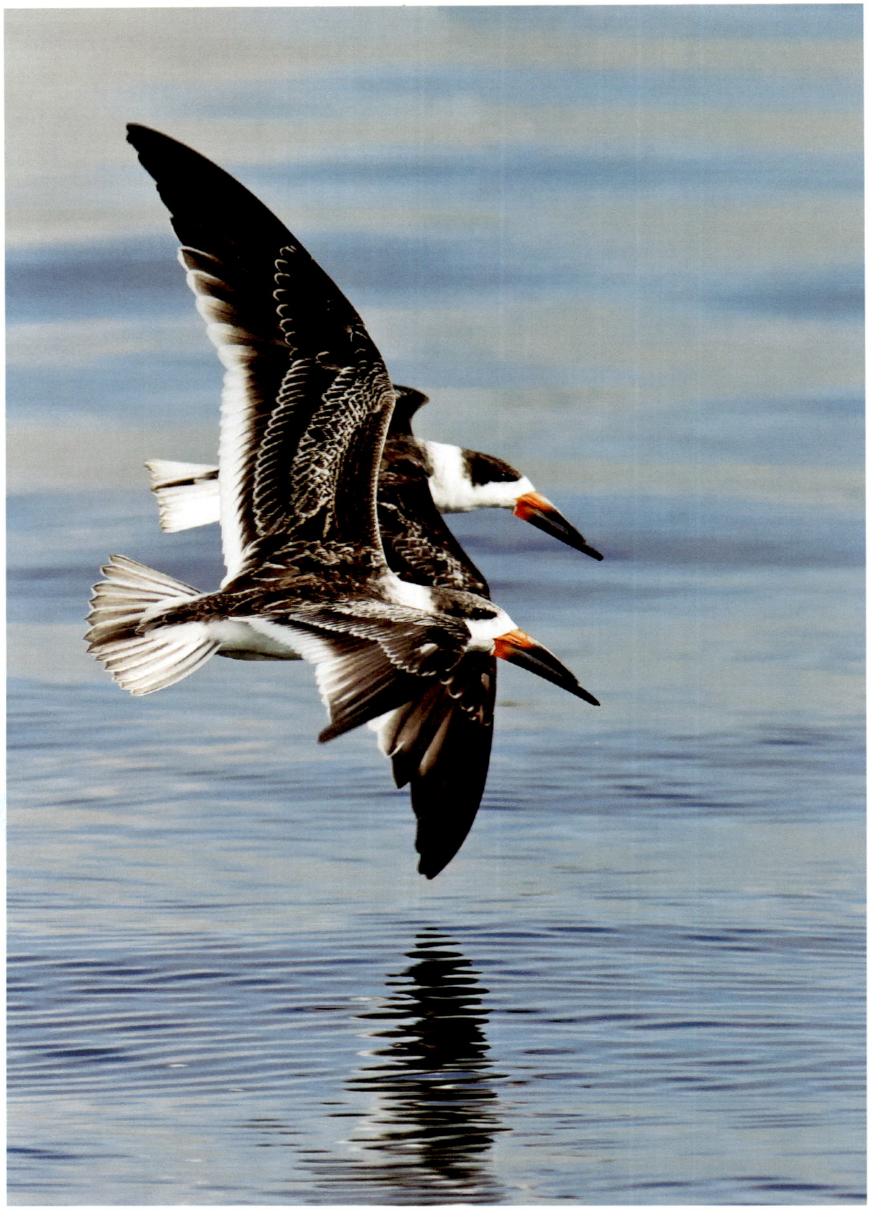

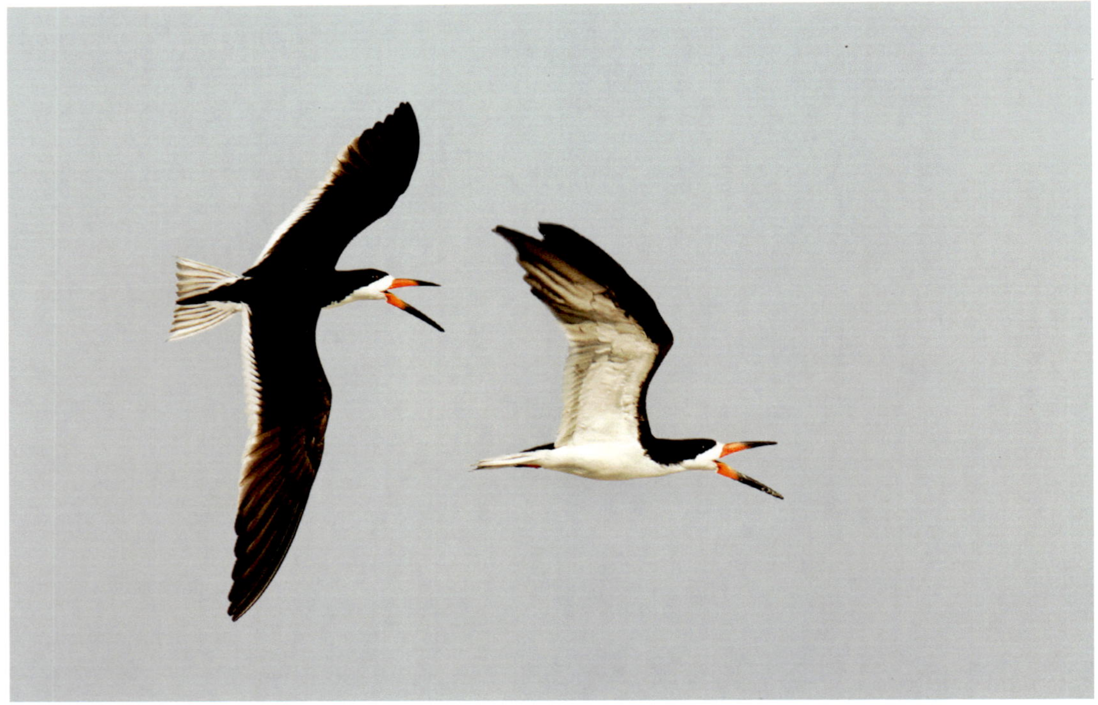

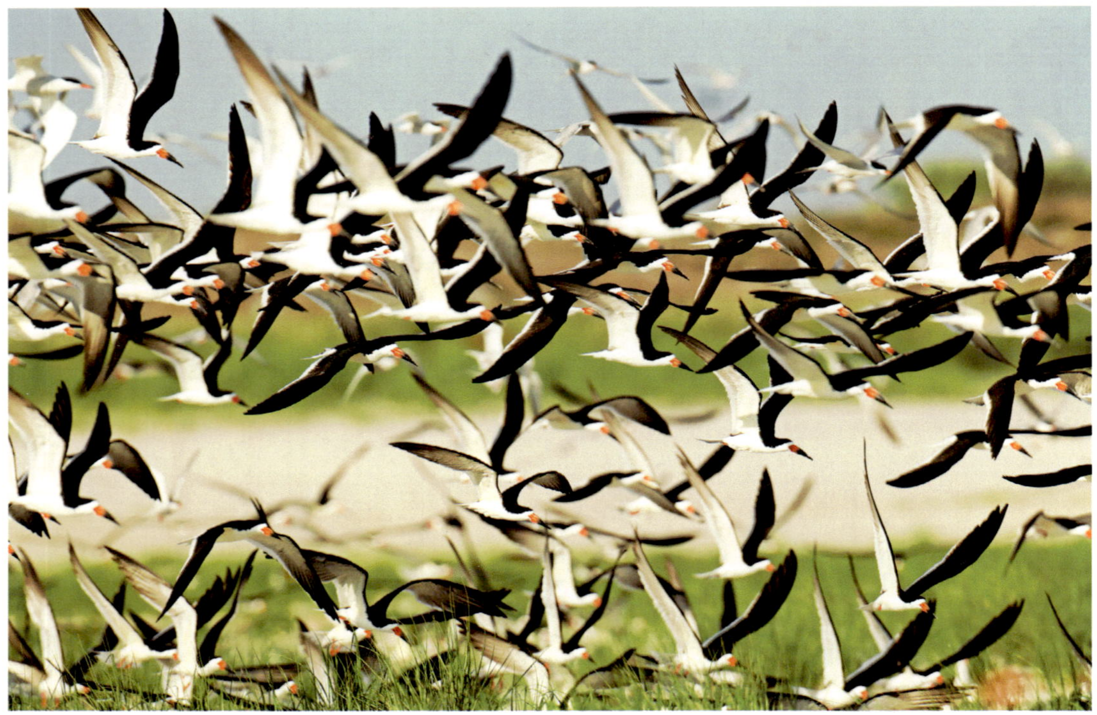

Black Skimmers are aerial acrobats as they skim along the water's surface trolling for fish with their long, lower bill inserted into the water. When a fish strikes the bill, it snaps shut with a seafood prize. *Photos by Lloyd Spitalnik (above and lower right) and Scott Elowitz (upper right)*

These graceful angels seem to defy gravity as they hover in the sky, unencumbered by earthly restraints.

— Kevin T. Karlson

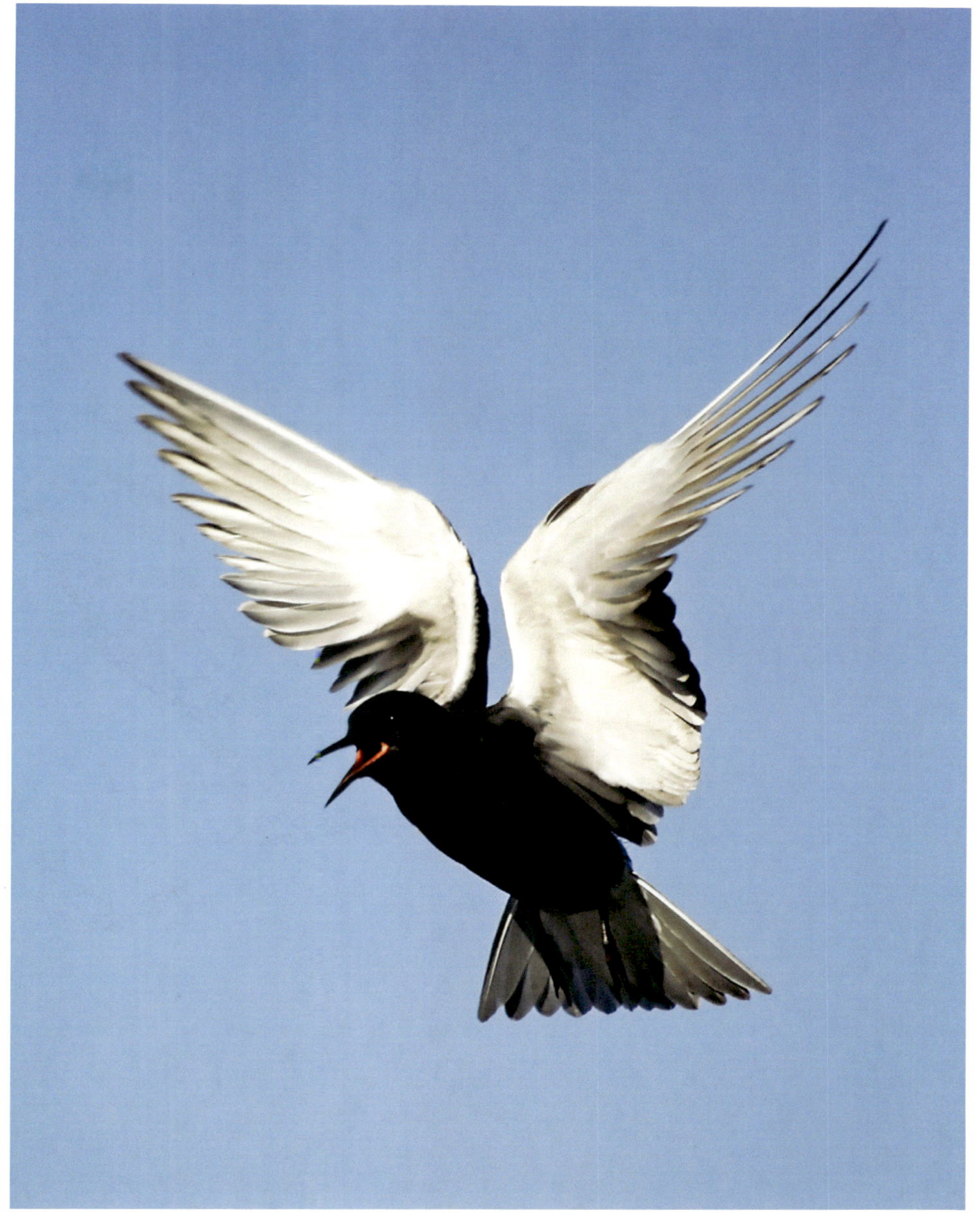

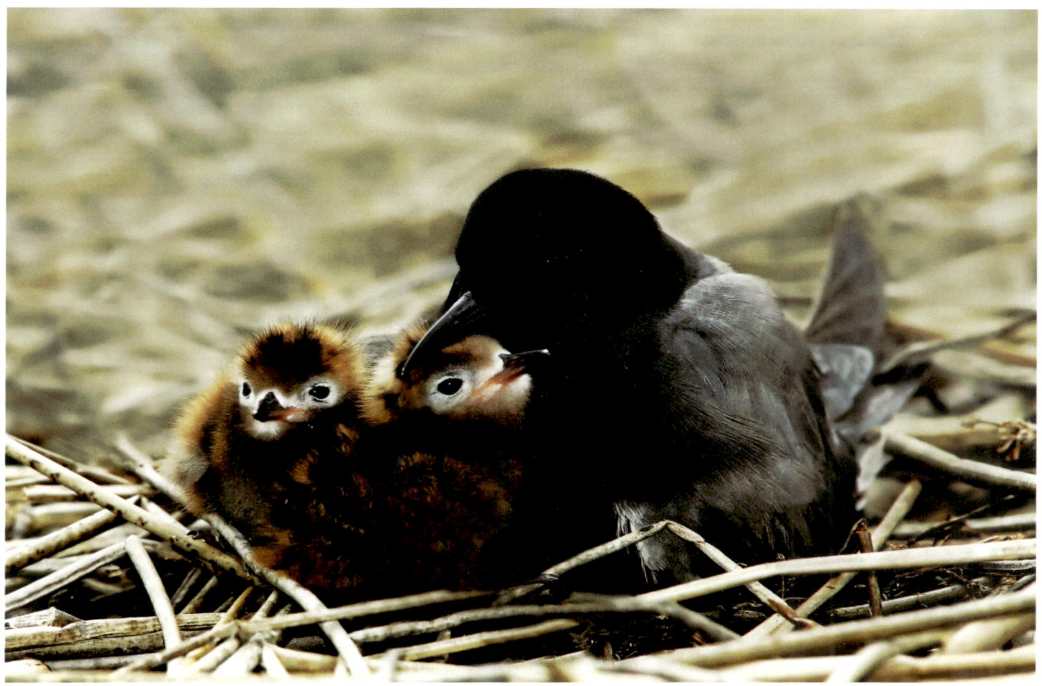

Black Terns' breeding plumage is a striking mix of black, gray, and white. Their chicks are some of the cutest of all birds' offspring, with a soft mix of rust and black feathers and pale blue color around the eye. *Photos by Kevin T. Karlson*

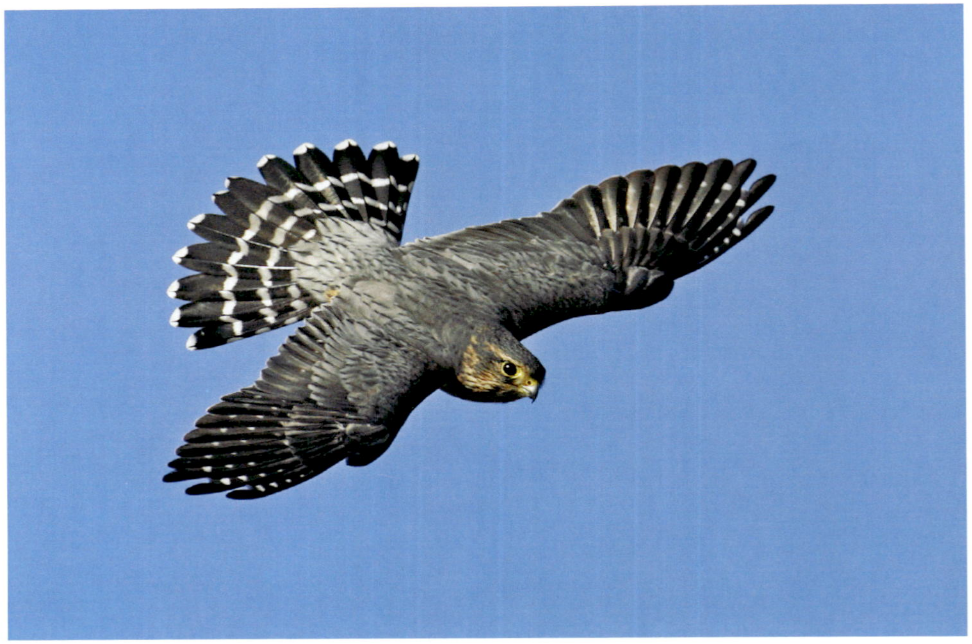

Adult male Merlins (left) are fondly called "Blue Jack" by hawk enthusiasts and are a mixture of speed and power as they pursue their avian prey. Harris's Hawks (below) are graceful residents of arid southern habitats and often hunt cooperatively with other members of their clan. *Photos by Scott Elowitz*

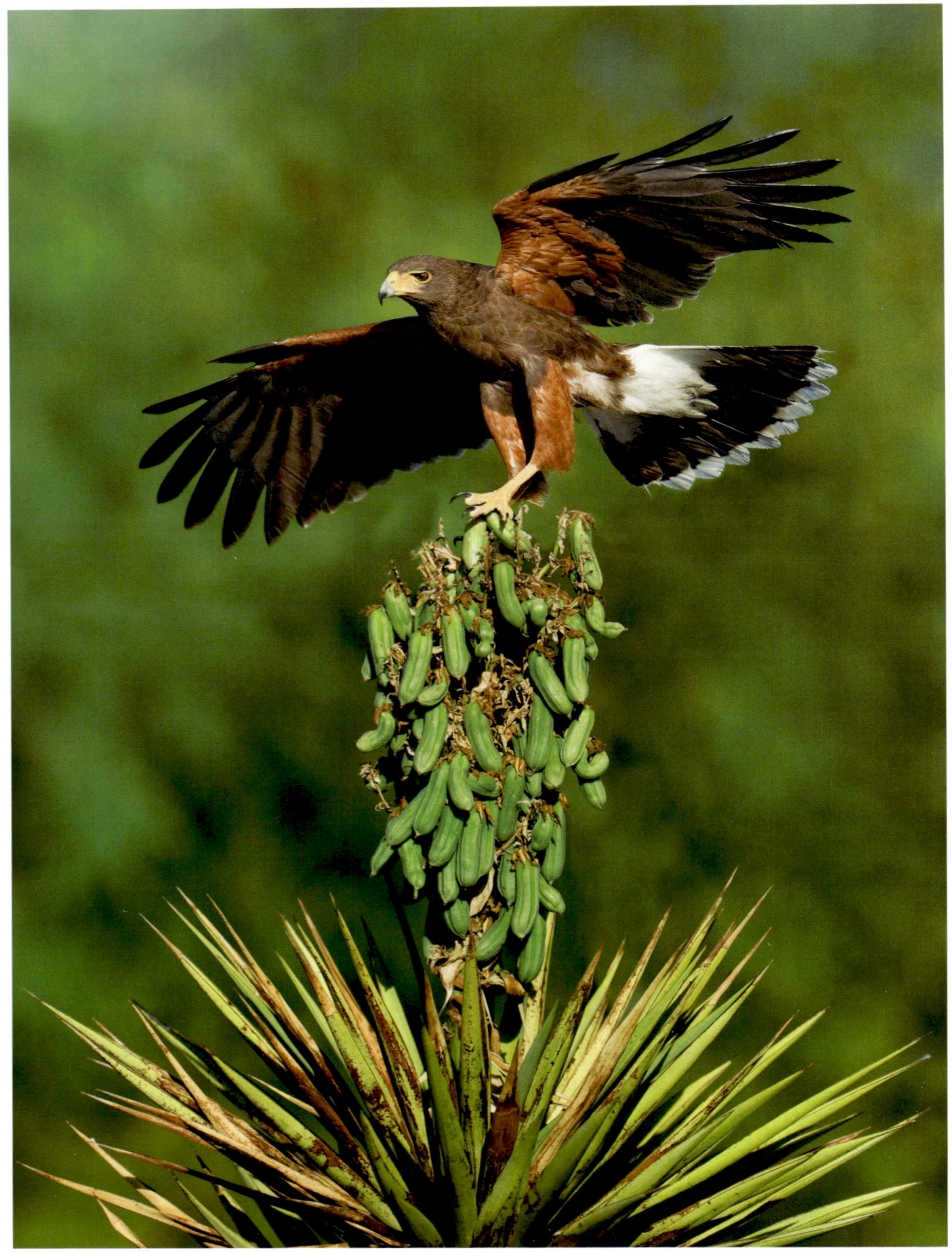

When once you have tasted flight, you will forever walk the earth with your eyes turned skyward, for there you have been, and there you will always long to return.

— Leonardo Da Vinci

American Kestrels are the smallest of five falcons that inhabit in North America. Males shown in both photos have a striking mix of blue, rust, and black patterns. This special bird of prey has declined about sixty percent in the eastern U.S. over the last 20 years, for reasons unknown. *Photos by Scott Elowitz (below) and Kevin T. Karlson (right)*

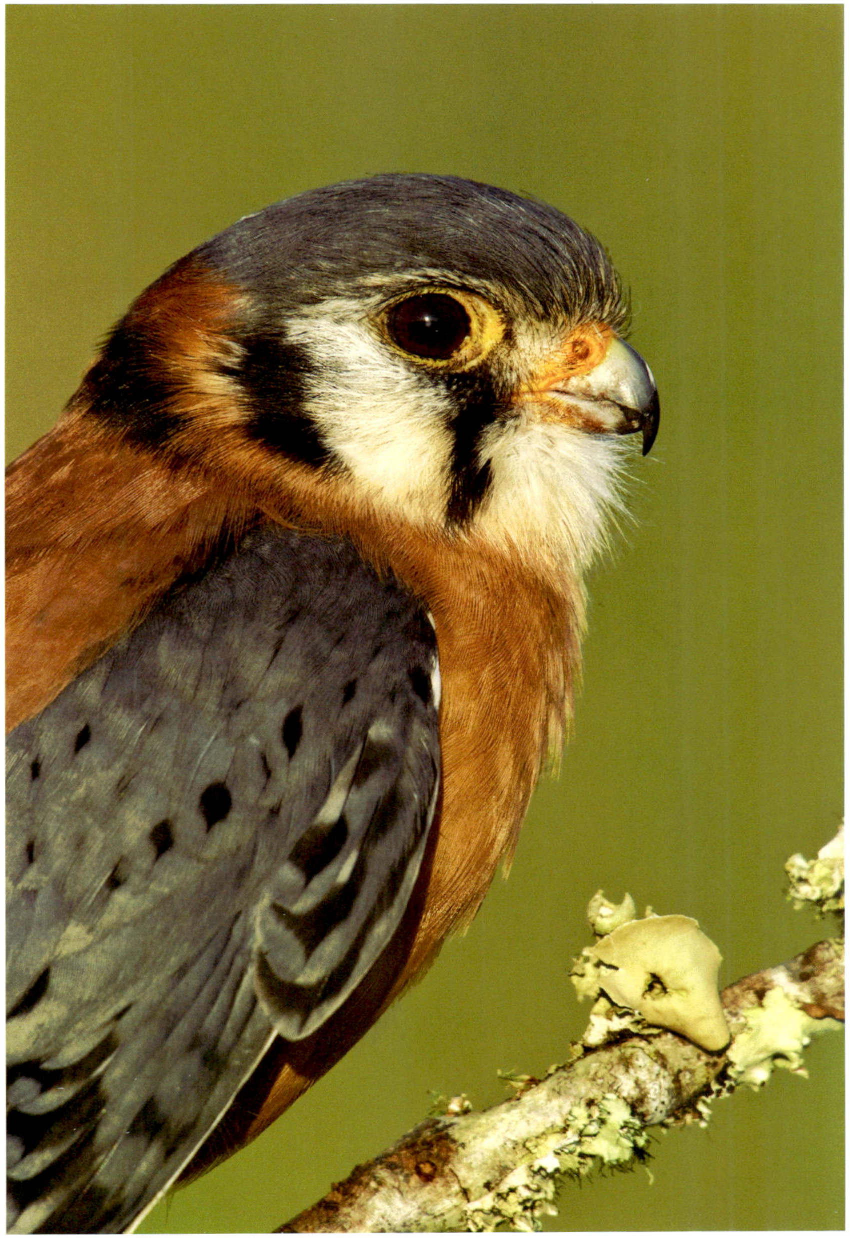

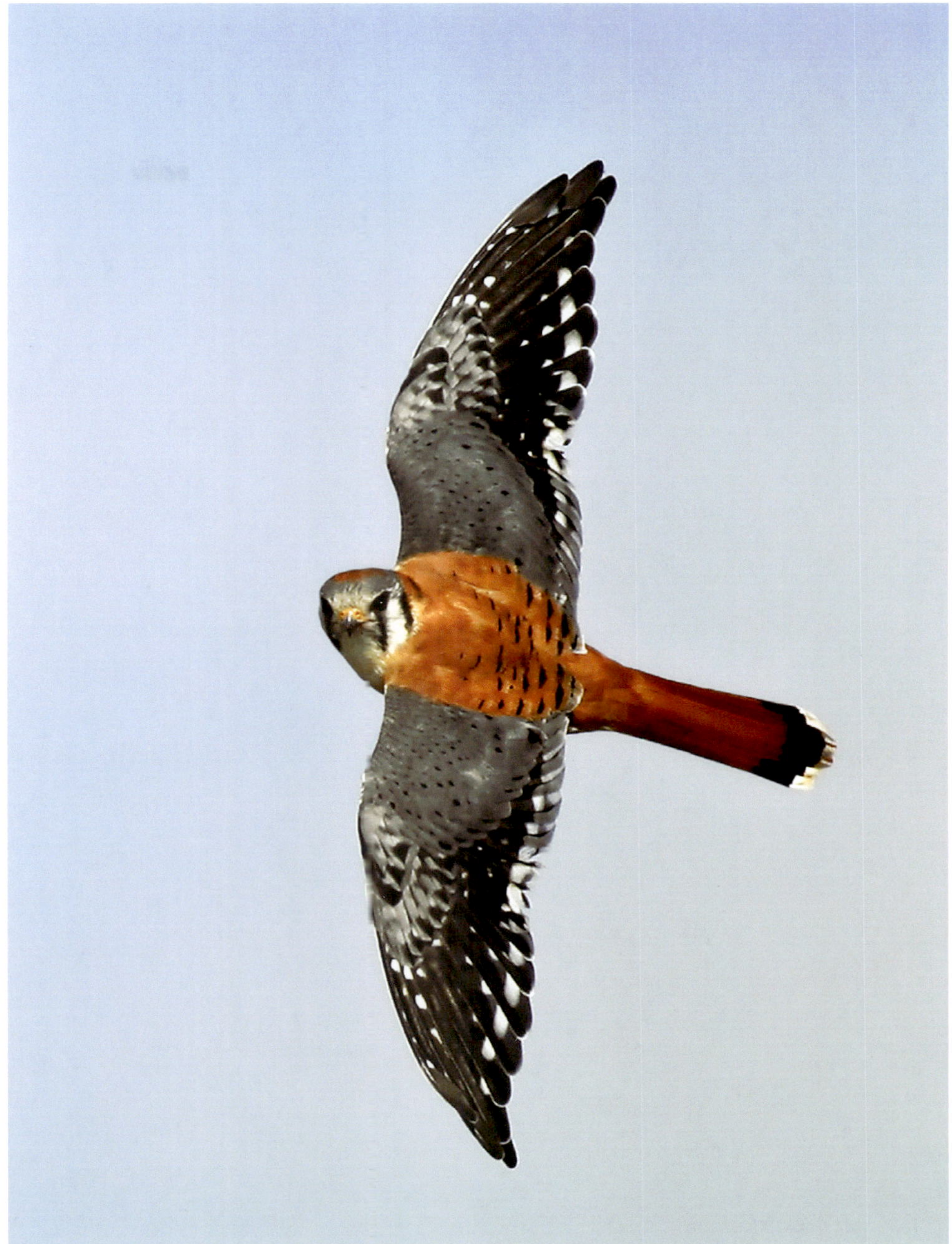

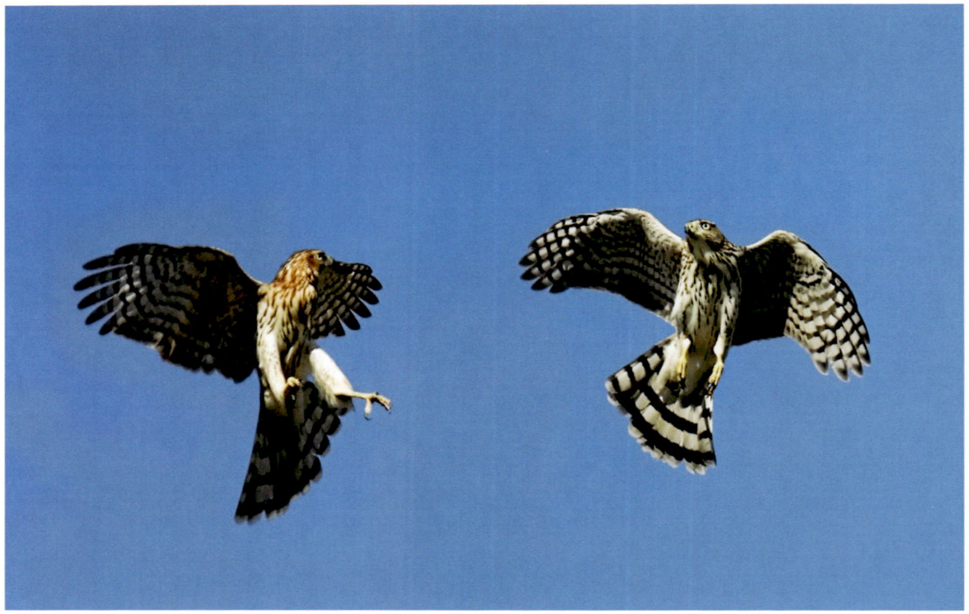

No issue is more compelling than the air we breathe, be it hot or cold, be it hawk or human.

— Jack Nicholson

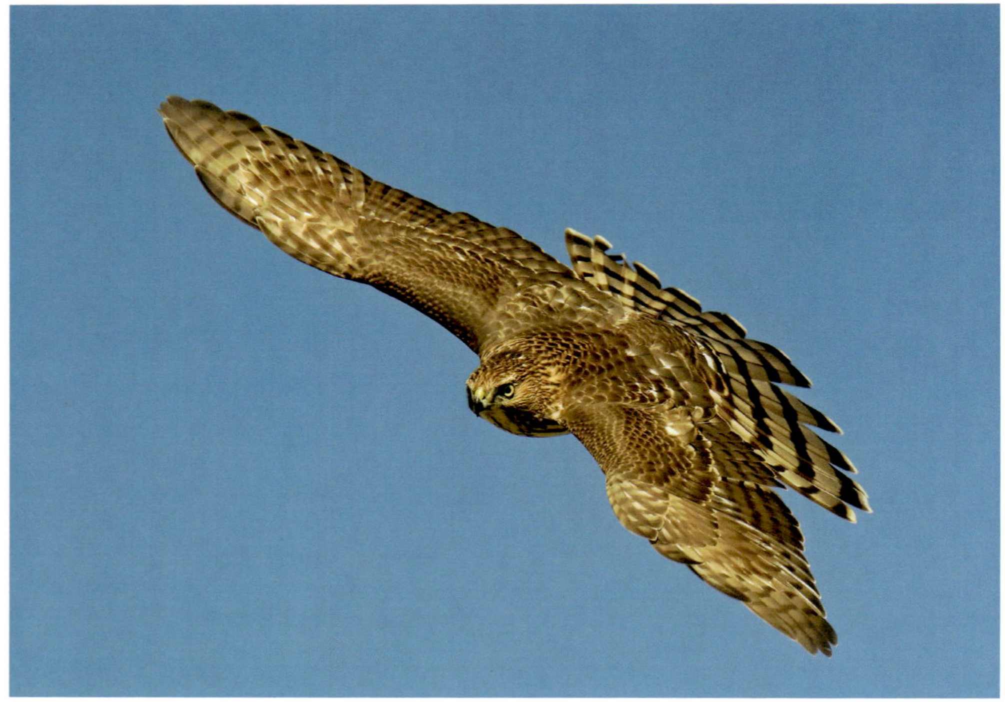

Cooper's Hawks (above) are common birds of prey throughout North America in forested areas. All the birds shown here are immatures. The two birds in the upper left photo are jousting in a disagreement over airspace rights. A kettle of raptors and vultures soar against a half moon in Cape May, New Jersey, in late October (left). *Photos by Kevin T. Karlson*

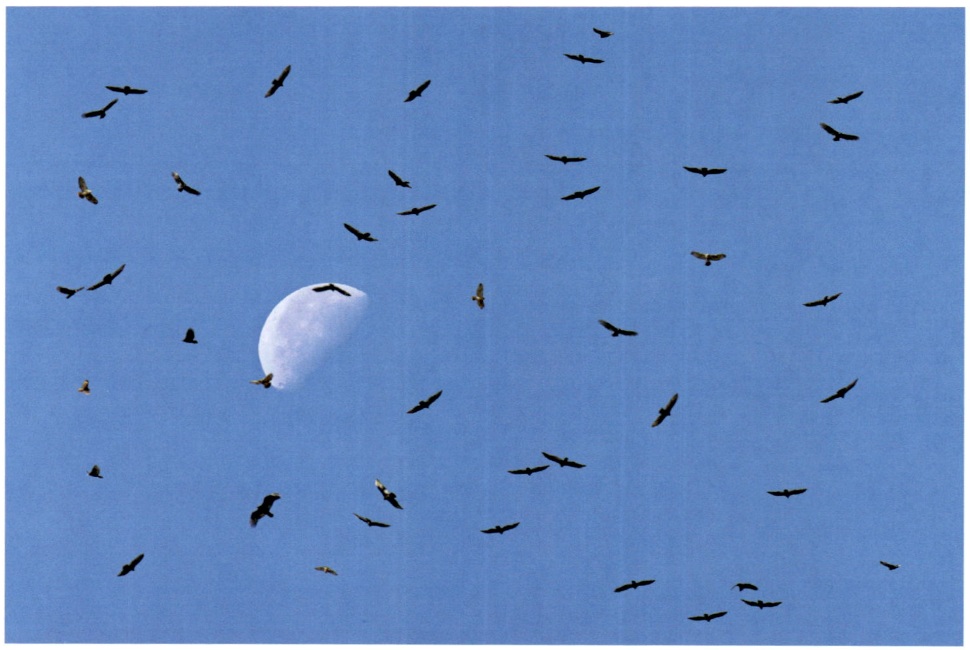

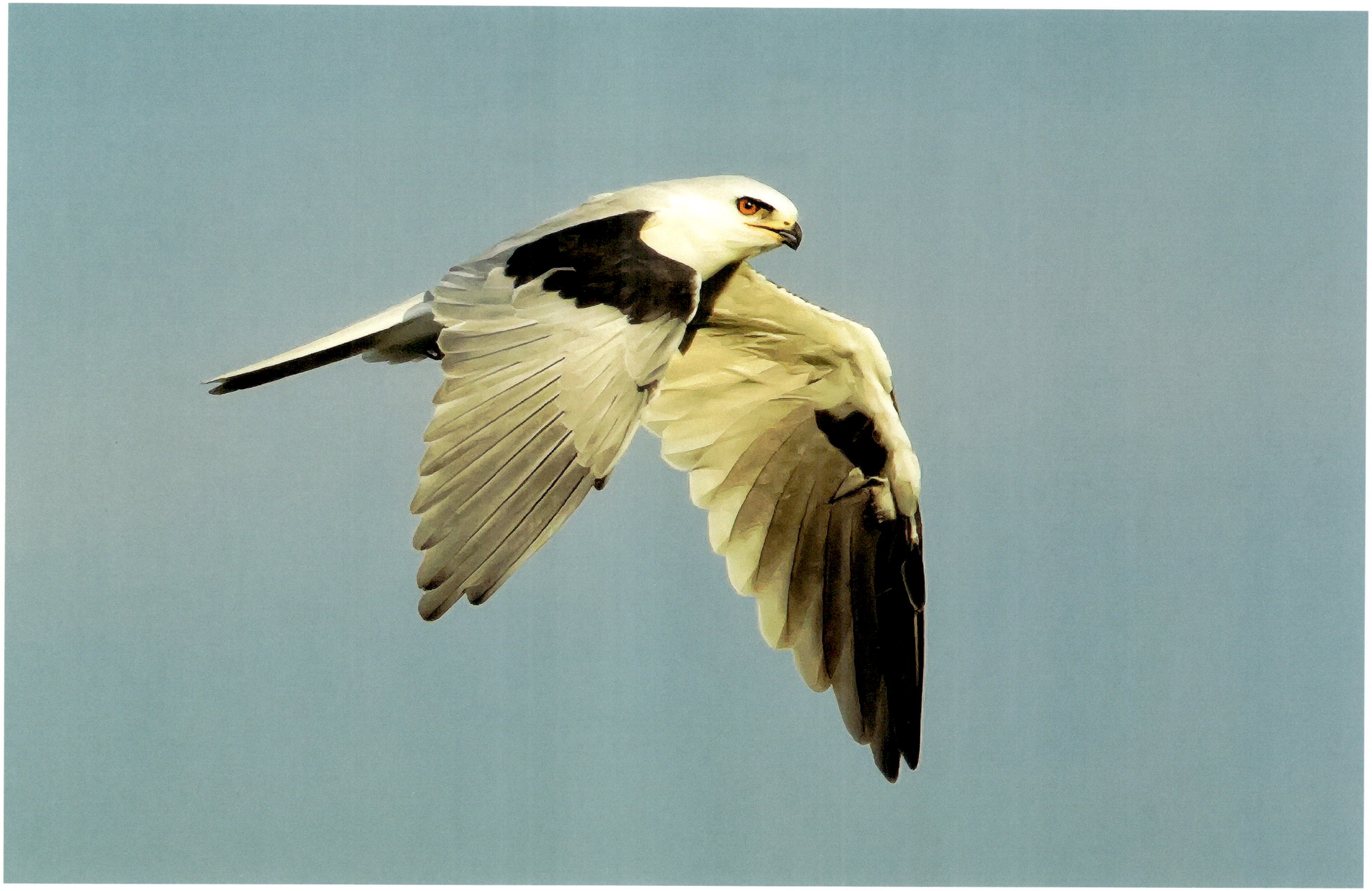

This stunningly attractive adult White-tailed Kite was photographed well outside its range in Connecticut in the summer of 2010. In the eastern United States, this aerial master is a resident of extreme South Florida and the east Texas Coast. *Photo by Lloyd Spitalnik*

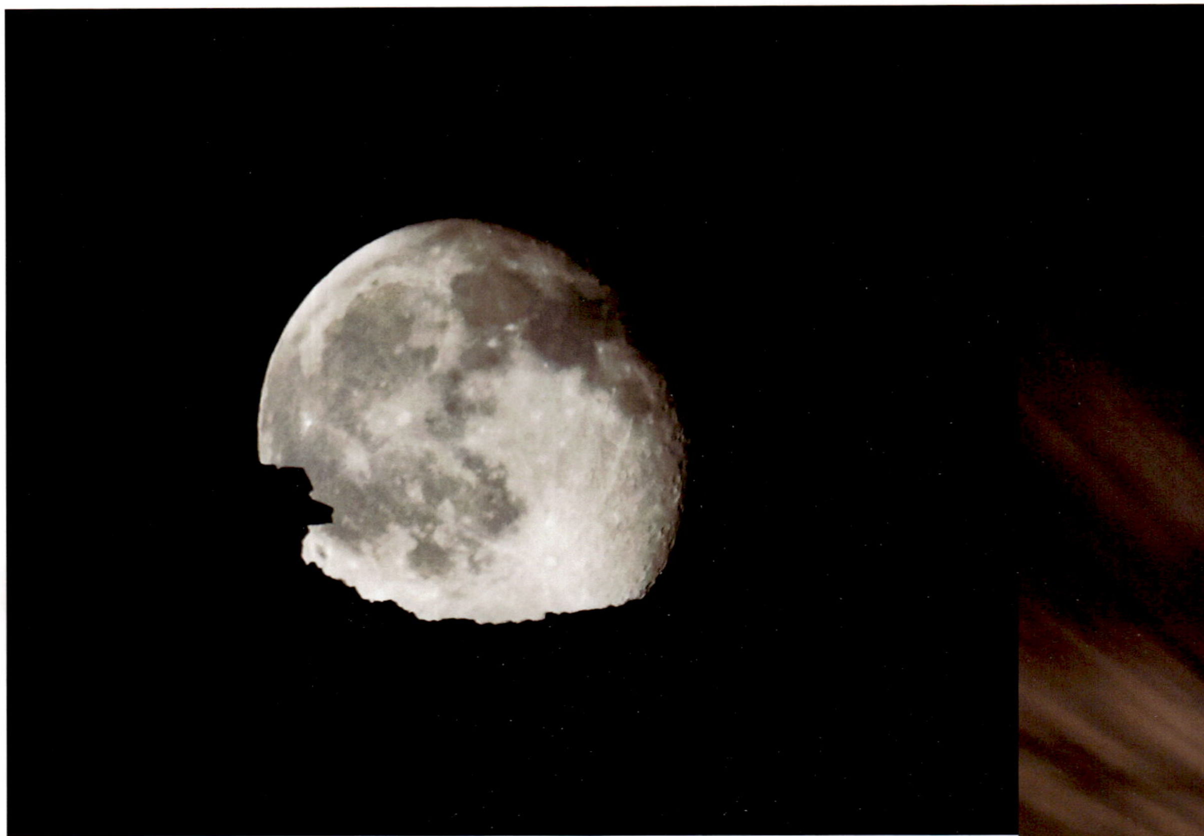

Moon rising in Utah. *Photo by Kevin T. Karlson*

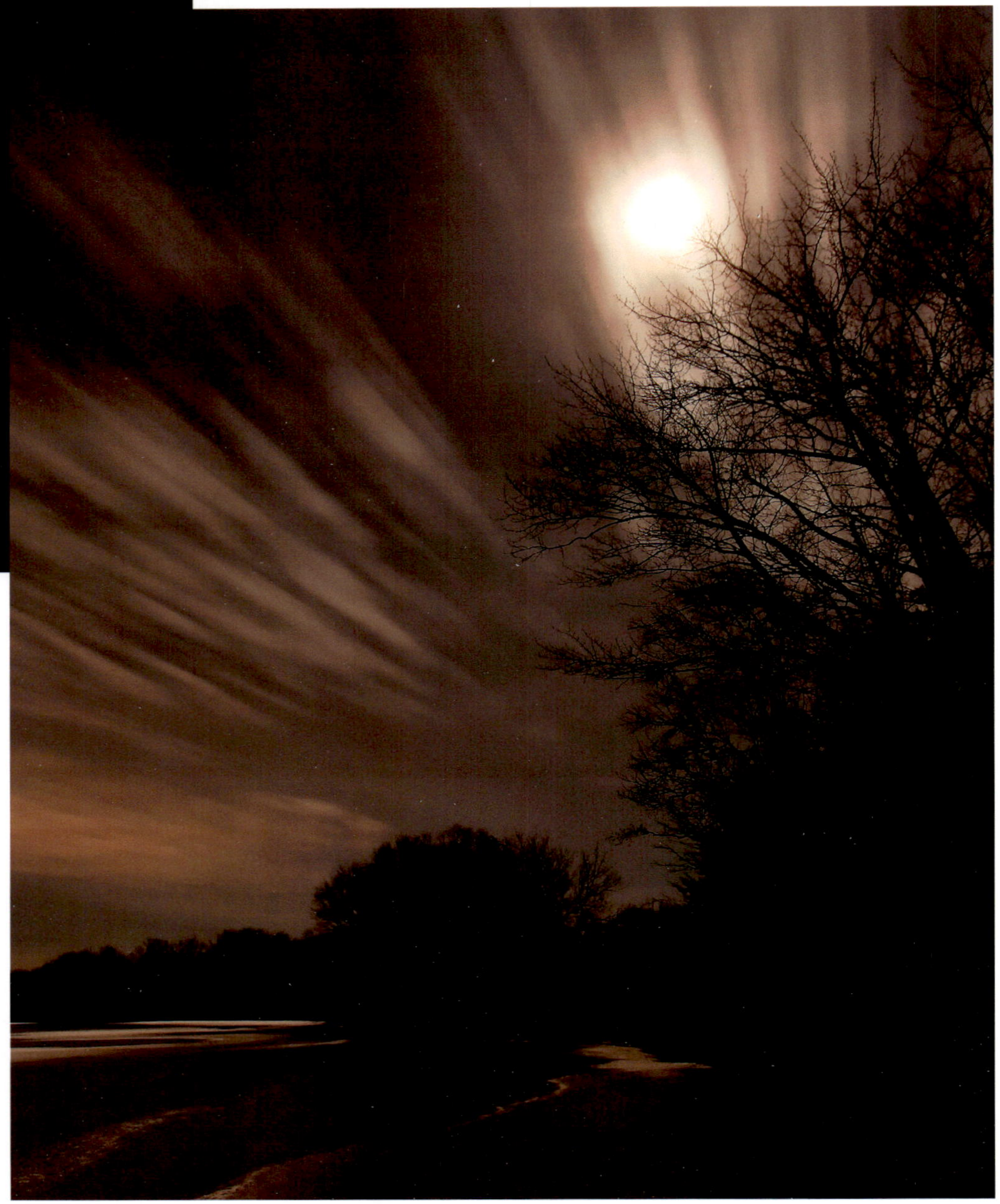

A winter solstice full moon, combined with ethereal moon streaks, casts an eerie glow over the Pickle Factory Pond in Eldora, New Jersey. *Photo by Don Merwin*

The night walked down the sky
with the moon in her hand.

— Frederic Lawrence Knowles

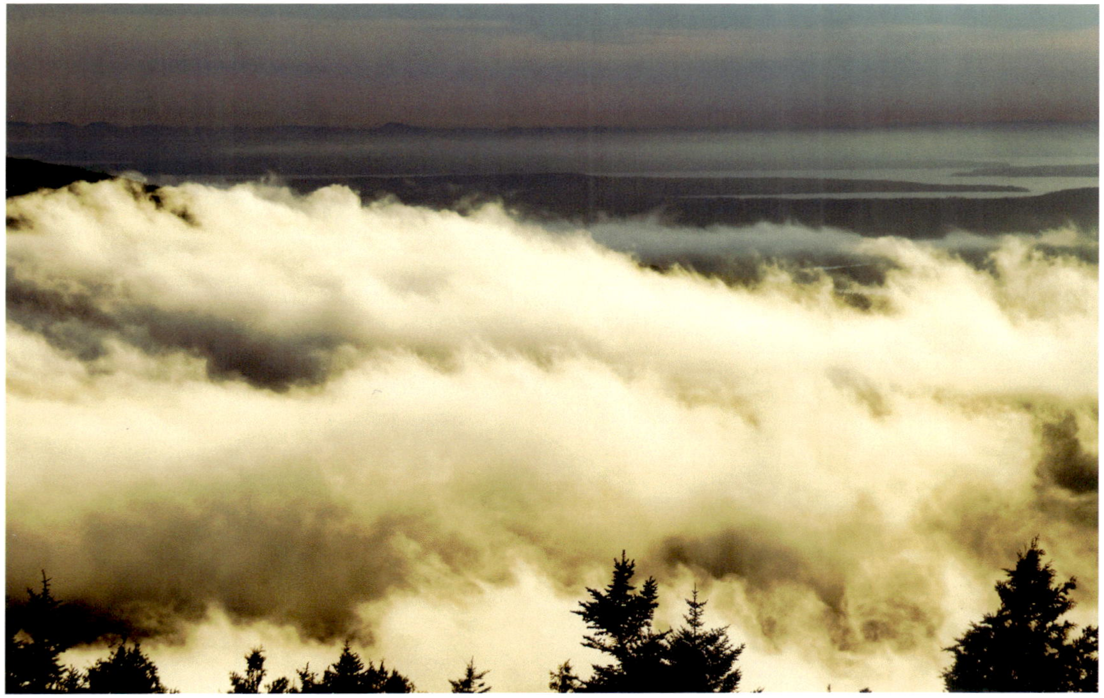

The fog is rising.

— Emily Dickinson's last words

At sunset, fog rises up from the valley below Cadillac Mountain, Acadia National Park. *Photo by Kevin T. Karlson*

Coastal fog rises near the Olympic National Forest in Washington. *Photo by Tina Giaimo*

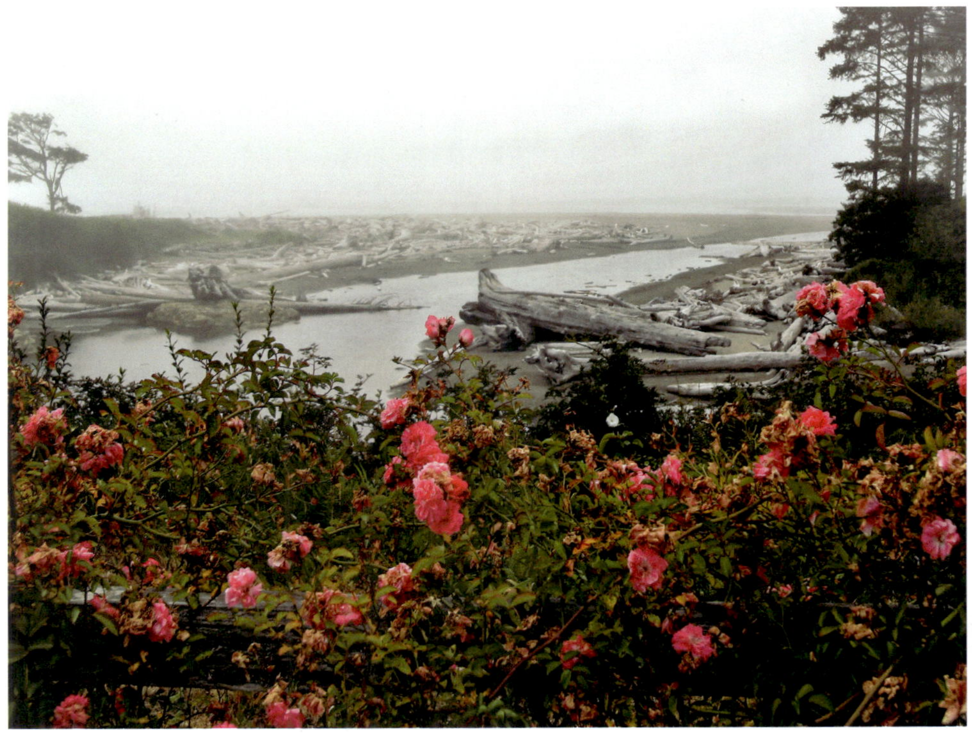

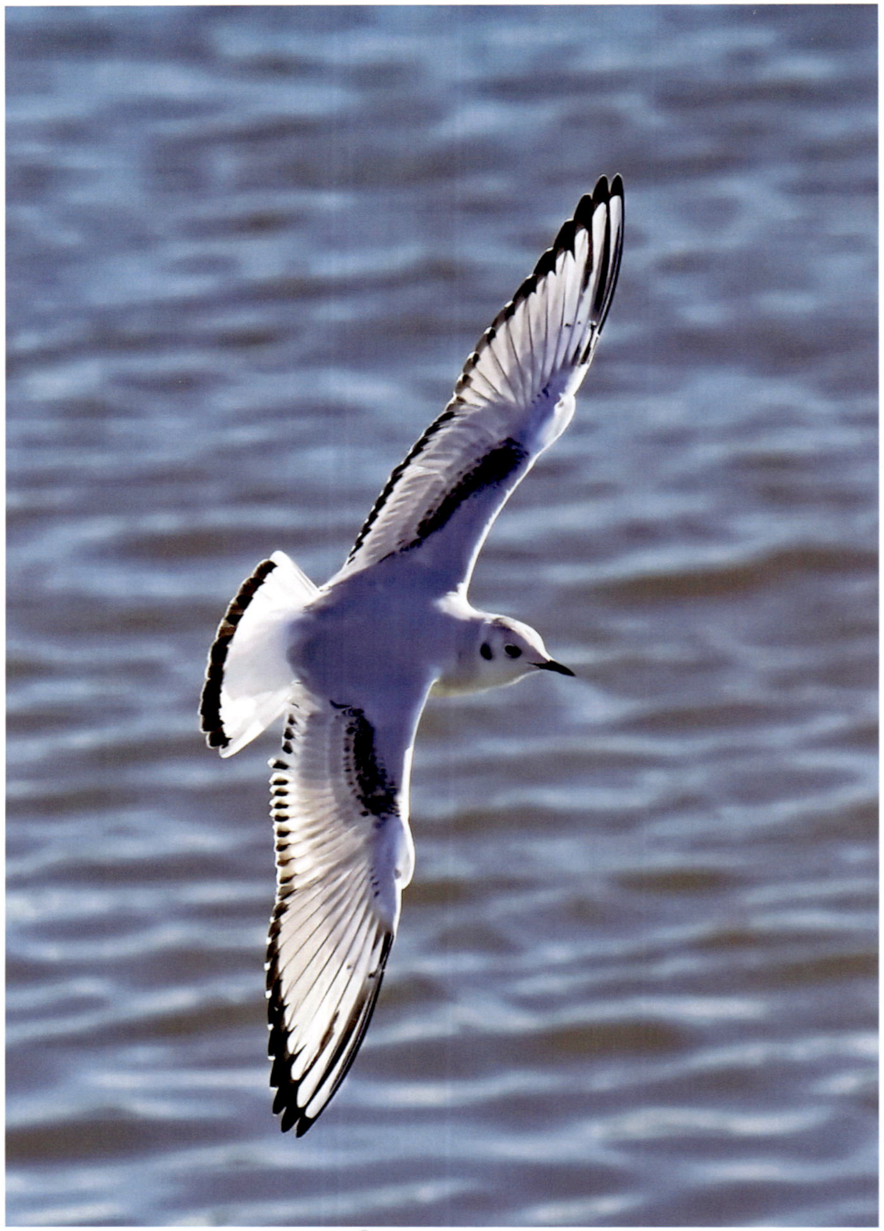

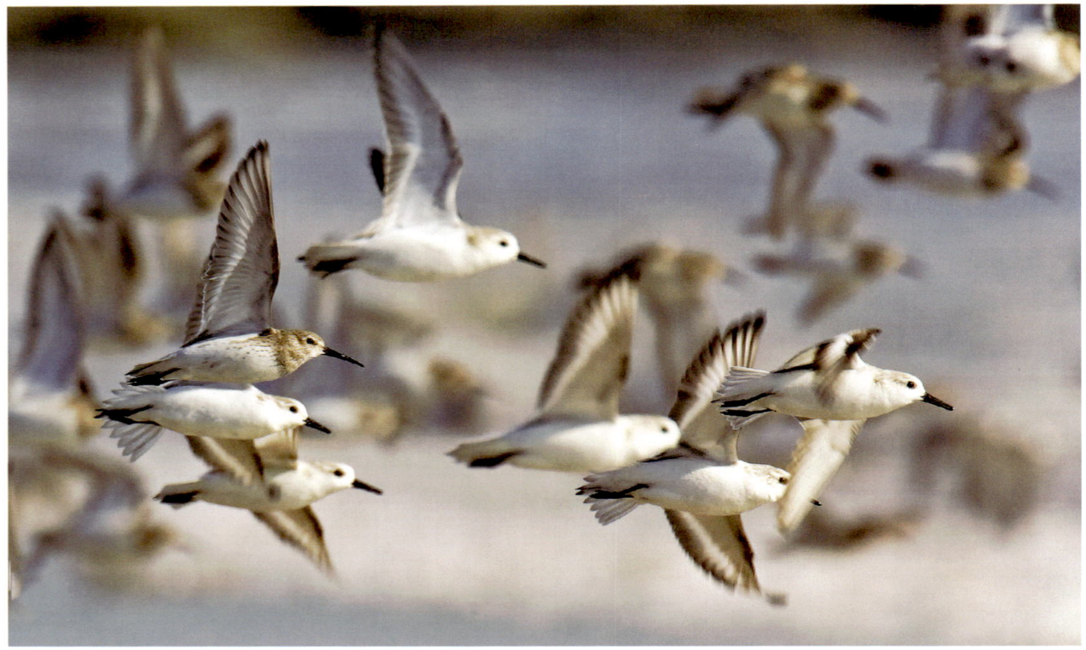

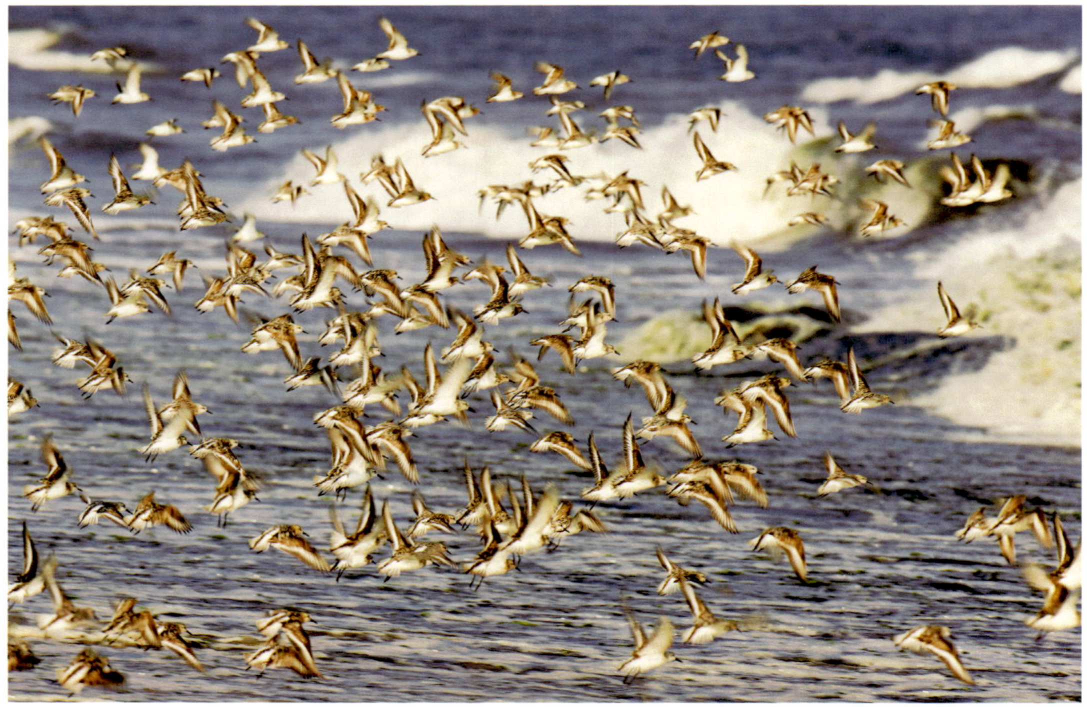

Shorebirds frequent Atlantic coastal areas, with Dunlin and Sanderling being two common species. A first winter plumage Bonaparte's Gull appears ghostly with back lighting (above). *Photos by Kevin T. Karlson (above) and Lloyd Spitalnik (upper and lower right)*

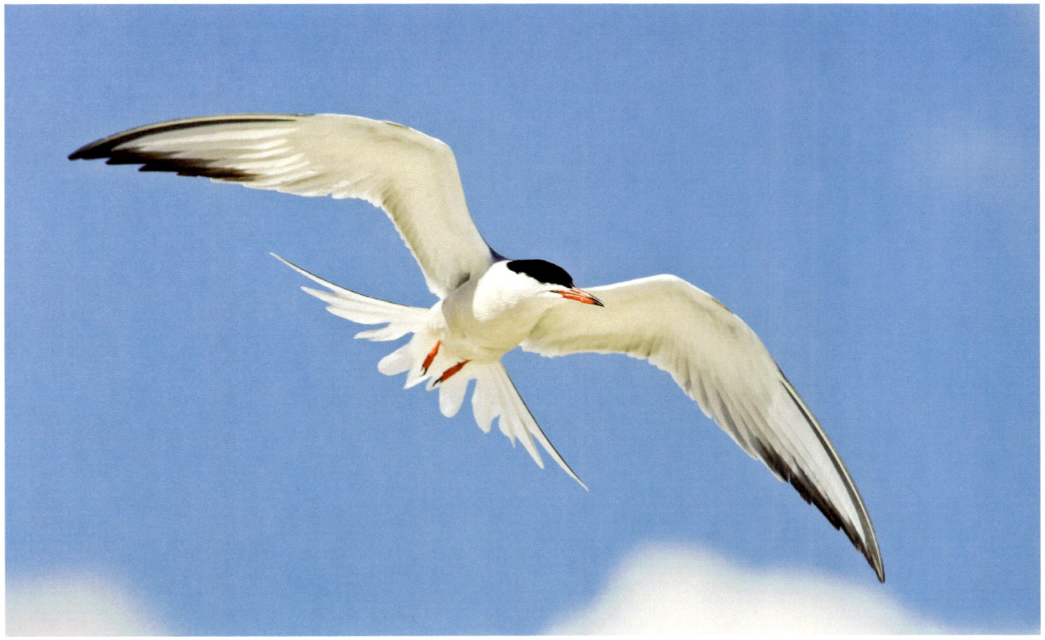

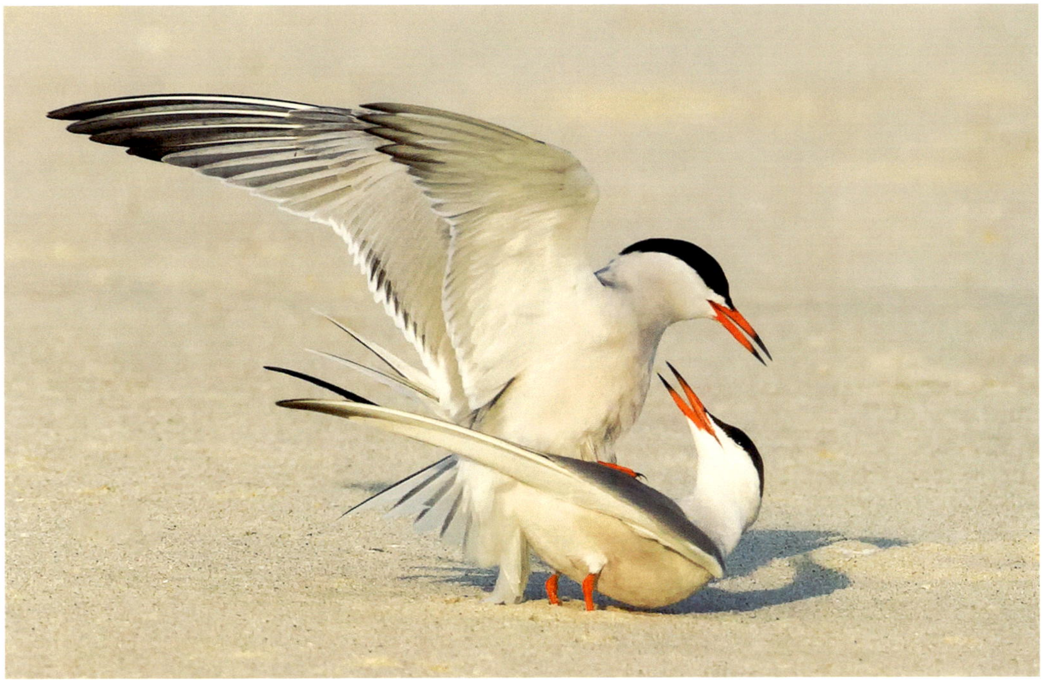

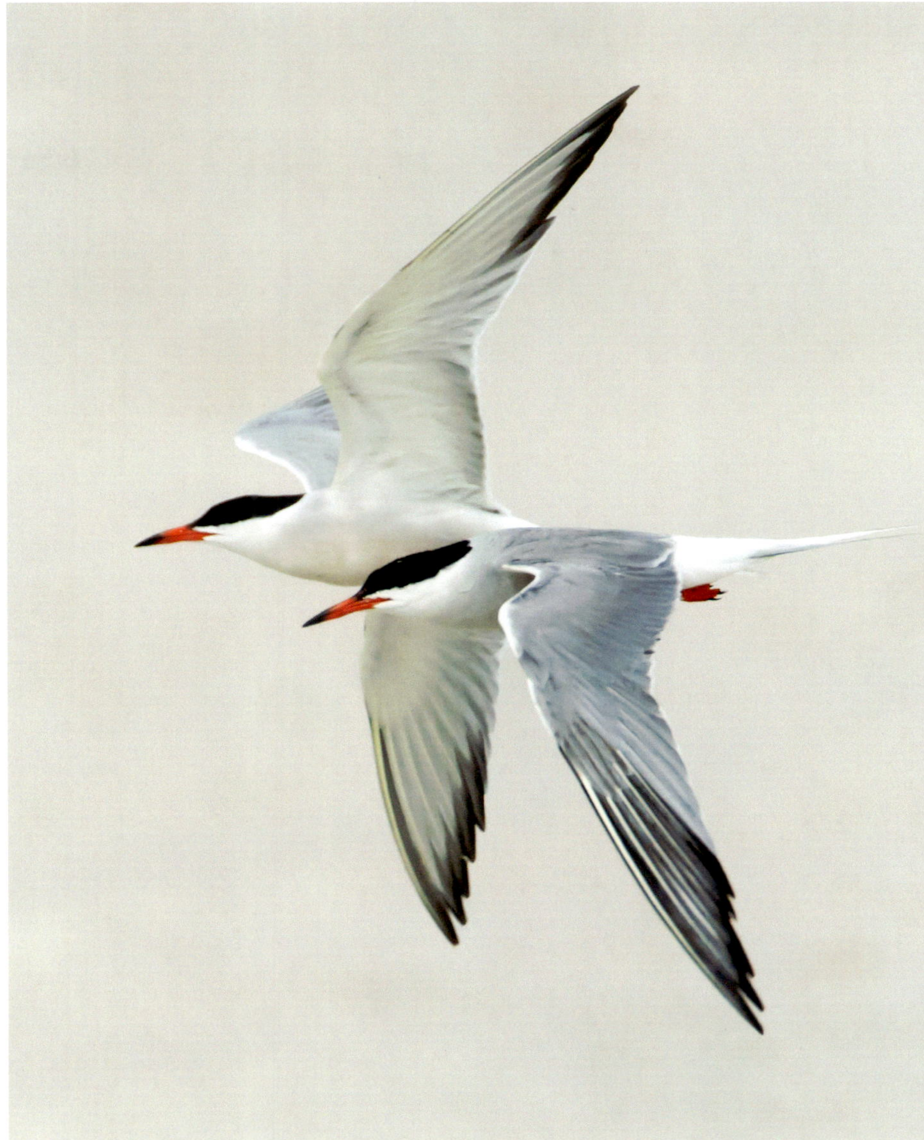

Buoyant and graceful Common Terns nest colonially along beach fronts and fiercely defend their nests against potential predators with speed dives and stabs of their pointed bills. In winter, they migrate to South America. *Photos by Lloyd Spitalnik*

We are the birds of fire, we fly over the sky.
Our light is a voice, we make a road
for the spirit to pass over.

— Algonquin Song of the Stars

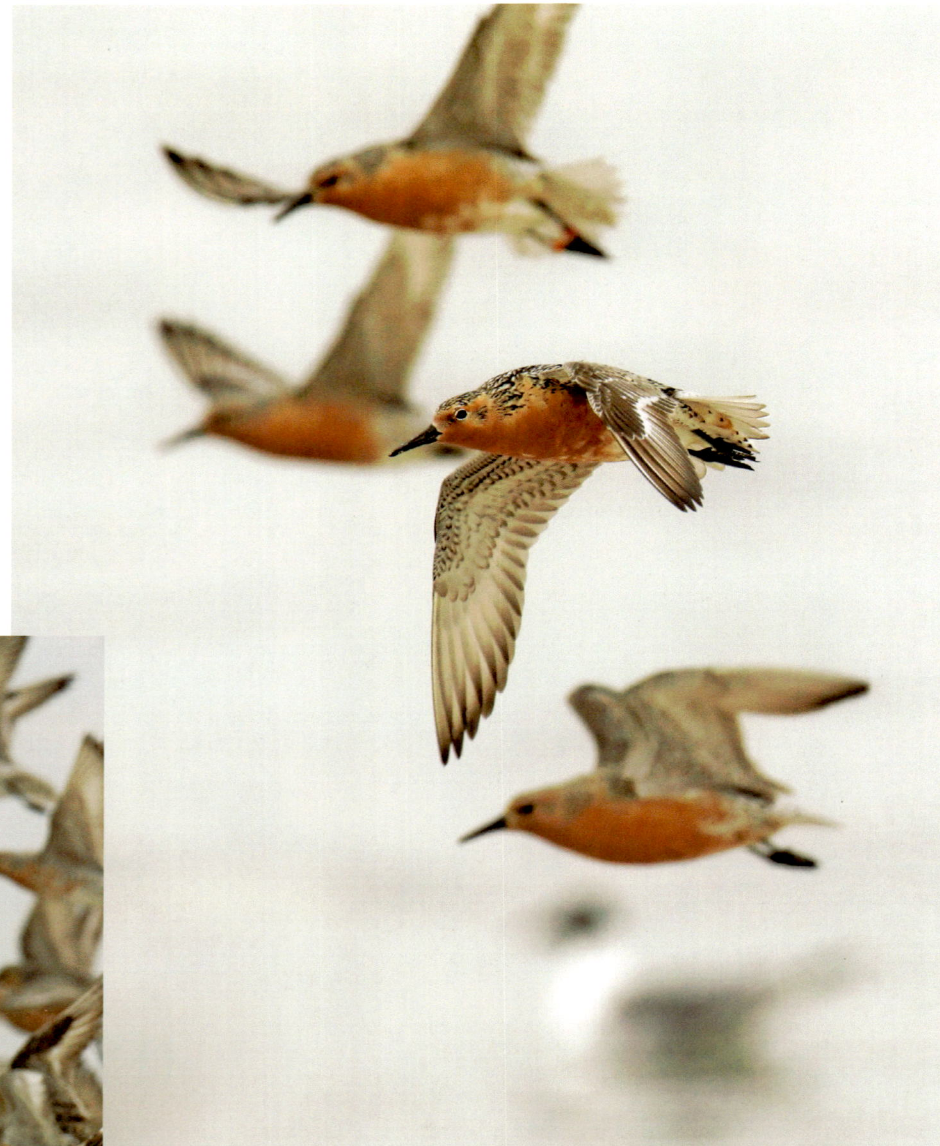

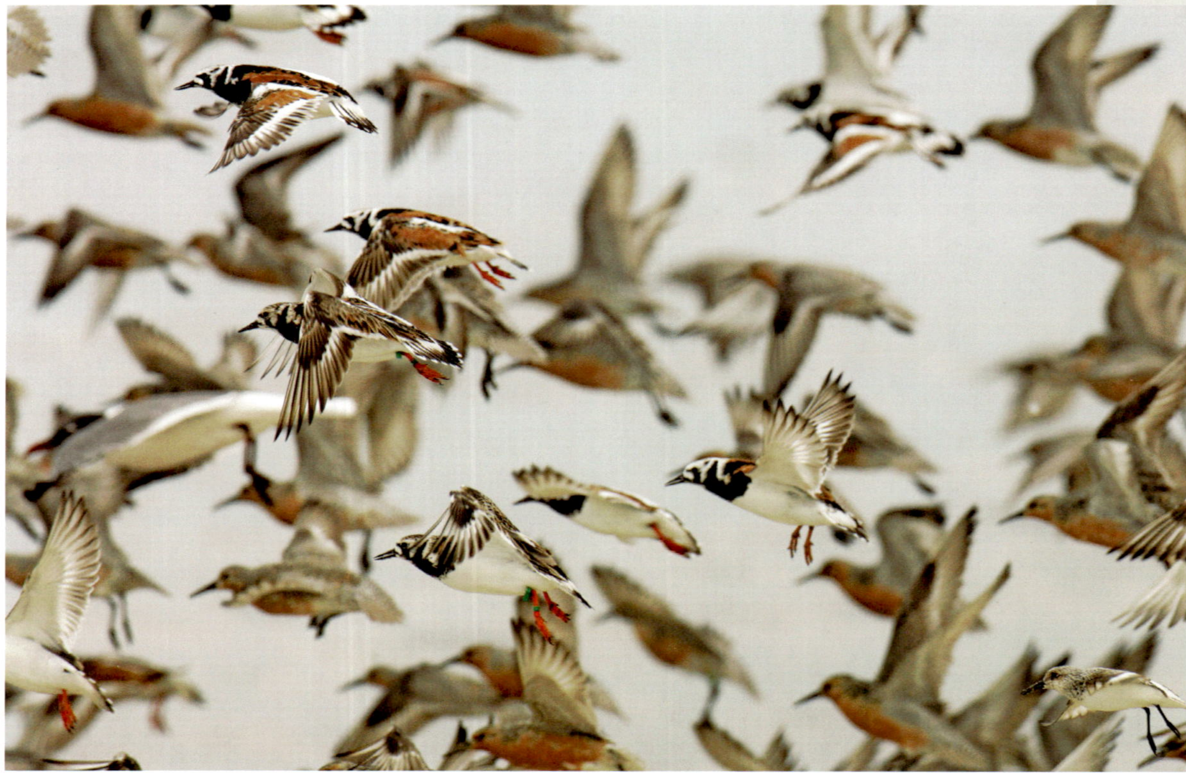

Red Knots (above) and Ruddy Turnstones are two major players in the amazing migration spectacle on the Delaware Bayshore of New Jersey and Delaware in May. After fattening up on Horseshoe Crab eggs, these birds fly several thousand miles nonstop to their Arctic breeding grounds. *Photos by Scott Elowitz*

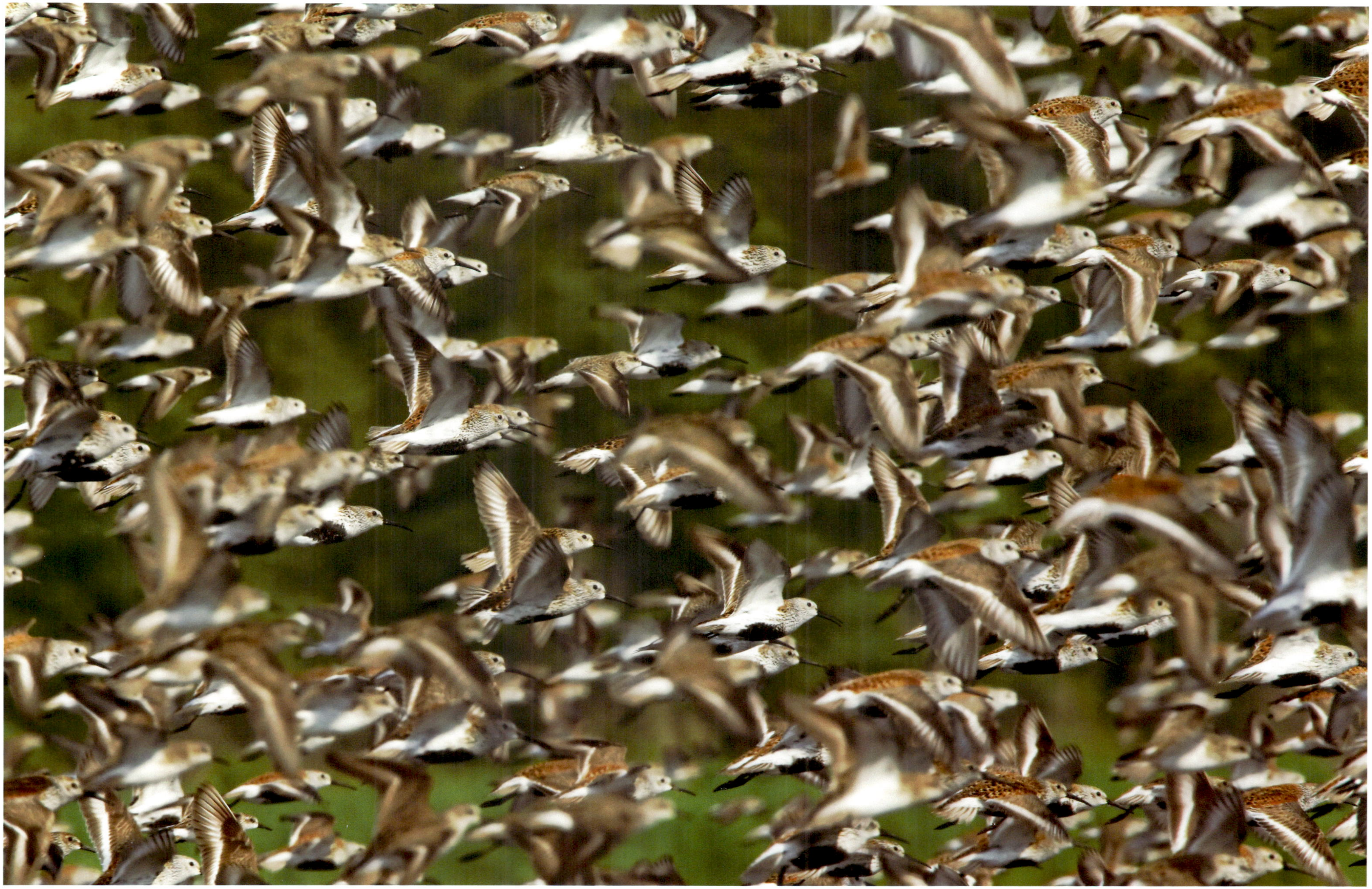

Over 5,000 colorful Dunlins took flight simultaneously when a Peregrine Falcon flew over a pond in Heislerville, New Jersey. Good depth of field was achieved by shooting this image with an aperture opening of F-16. *Photo by Kevin T. Karlson*

Have you ever observed a hummingbird moving about in an aerial dance among the flowers – a living prismatic gem that changes its color with every change of position.

— W.H. Hudson

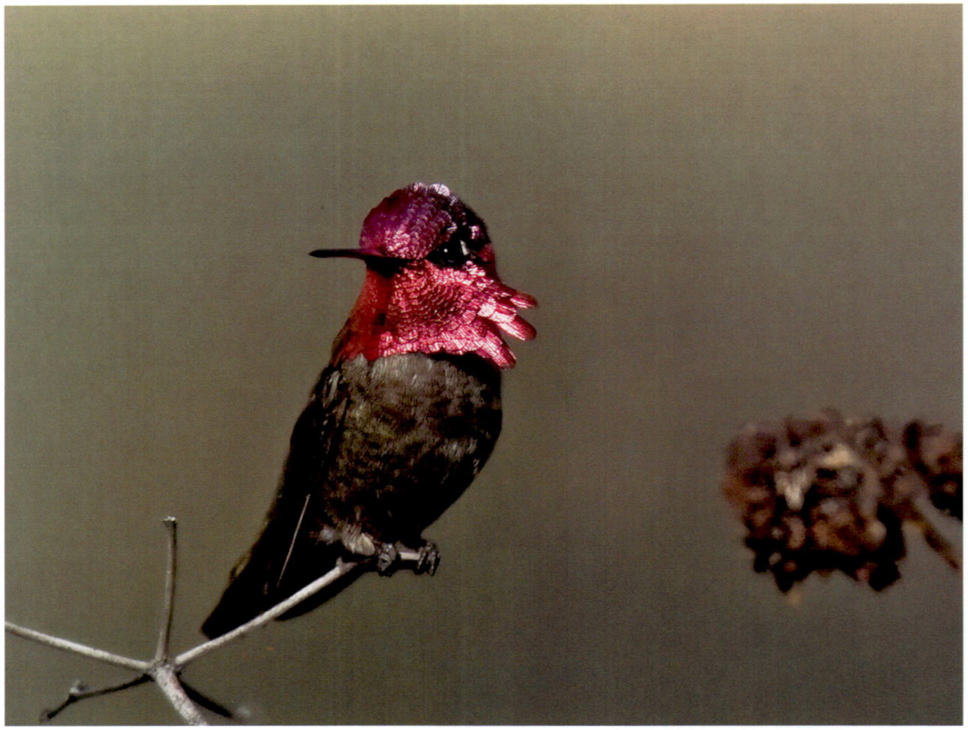

Hummingbirds are true masters of flight and represent the only bird that can fly backwards. These male hummingbirds show colorful head and throat feathers, which light up when the sun reflects off them at just the right angle. Shown are Anna's (above), Costa's (upper right), and Calliope Hummingbirds (lower right). *Photos by Kevin T. Karlson*

Opposite: A Roseate Spoonbill comes in for a landing at Smith Oaks Woods, Texas. *Photo by Kevin T. Karlson*

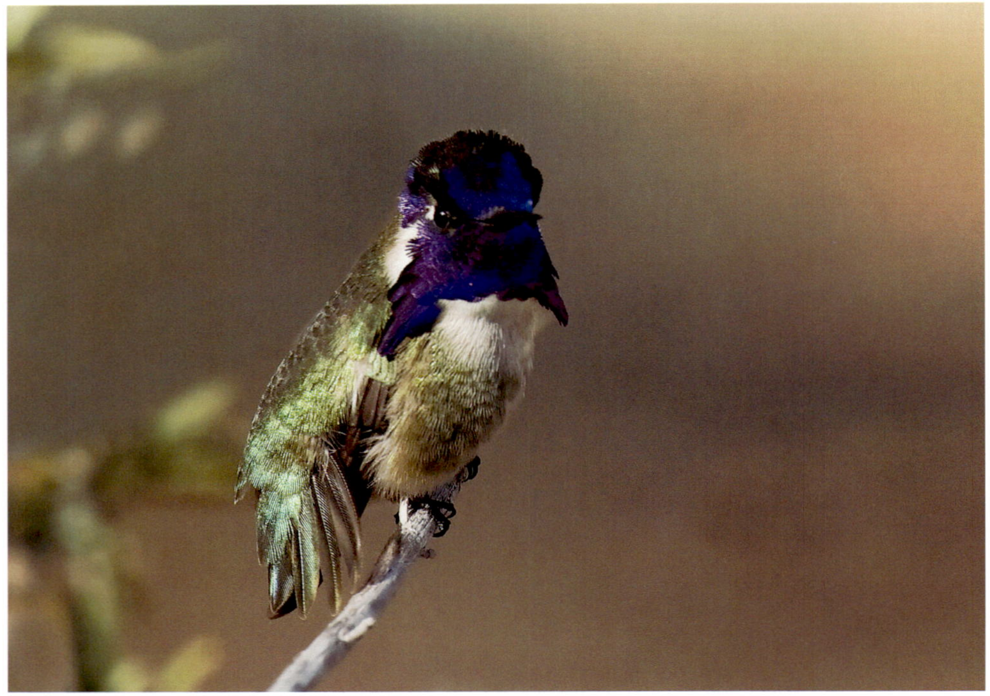

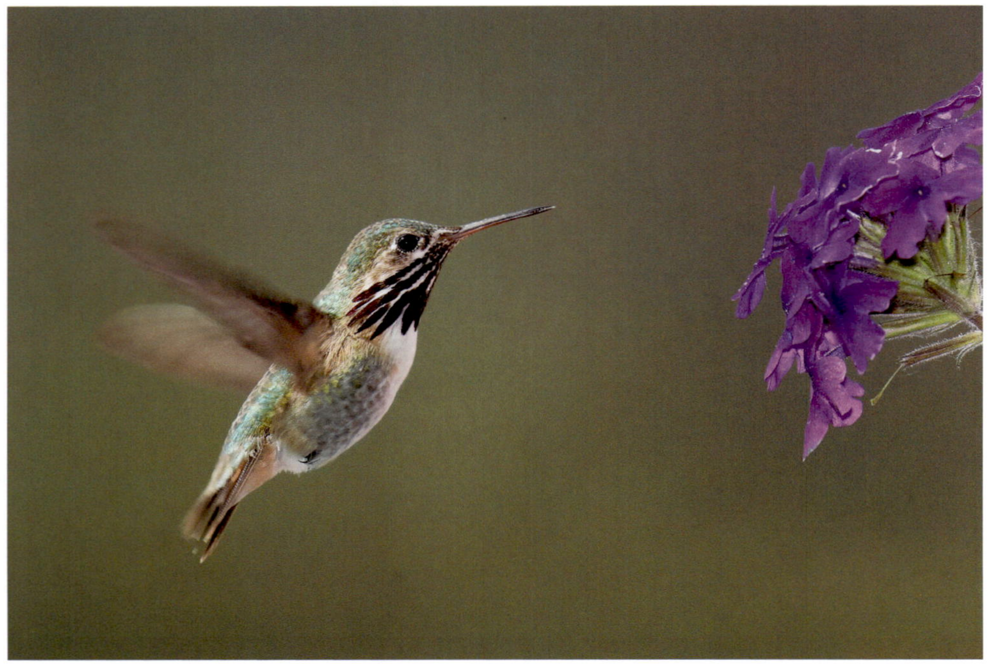

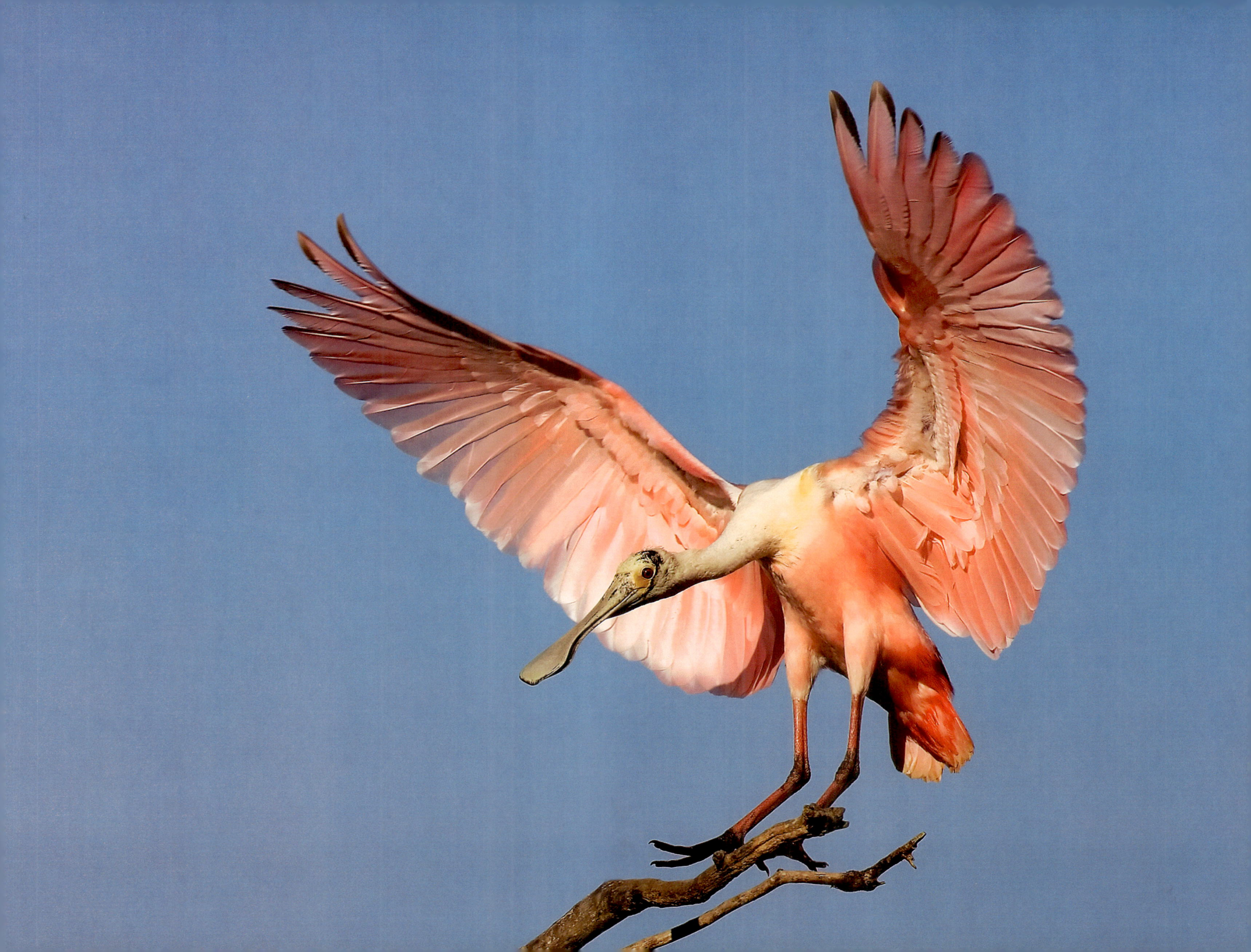

"Pale Male," the famous Red-tailed Hawk of Central Park, New York relaxes after eating a squirrel, with blood still on his feet (below). An immature female Cooper's Hawk comes in feet first in pursuit of its prey (right). Note the sharp talons that are used to puncture its prey of small mammals or birds. *Photos by Lloyd Spitalnik*

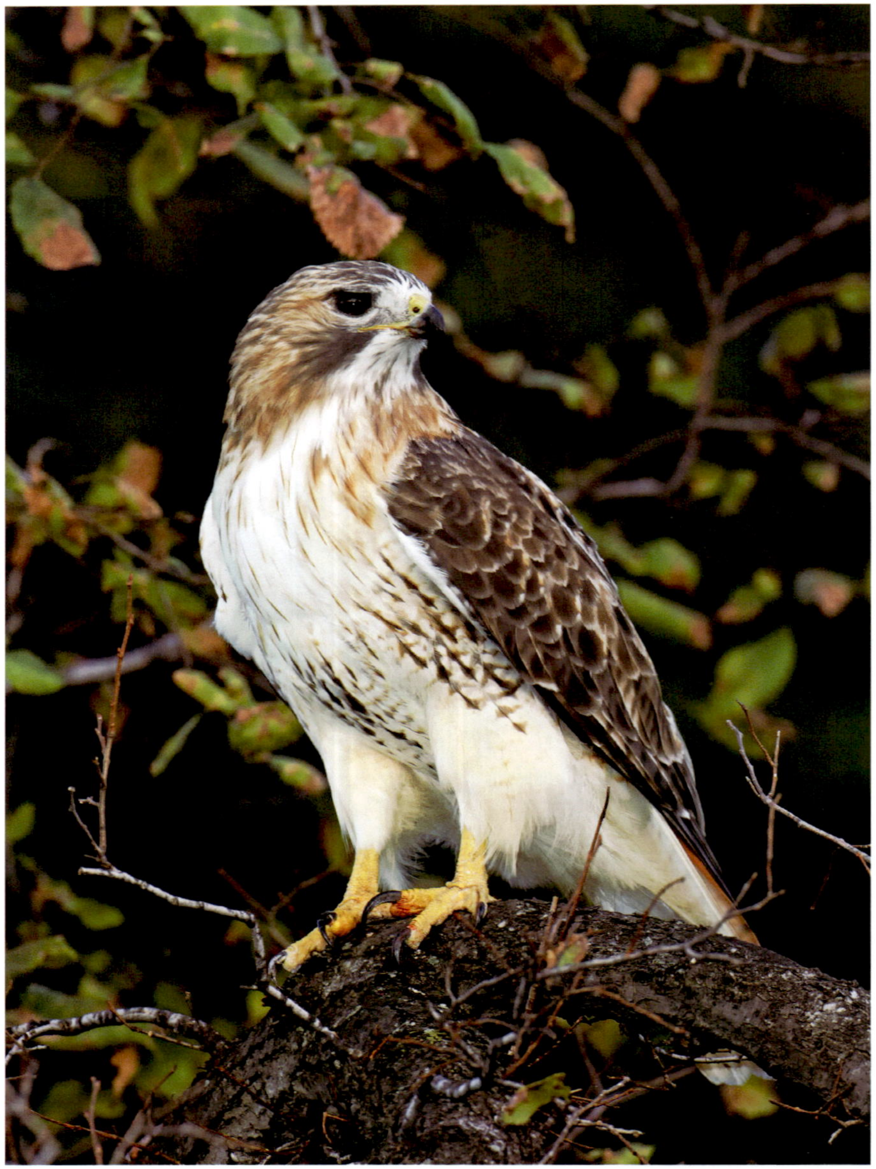

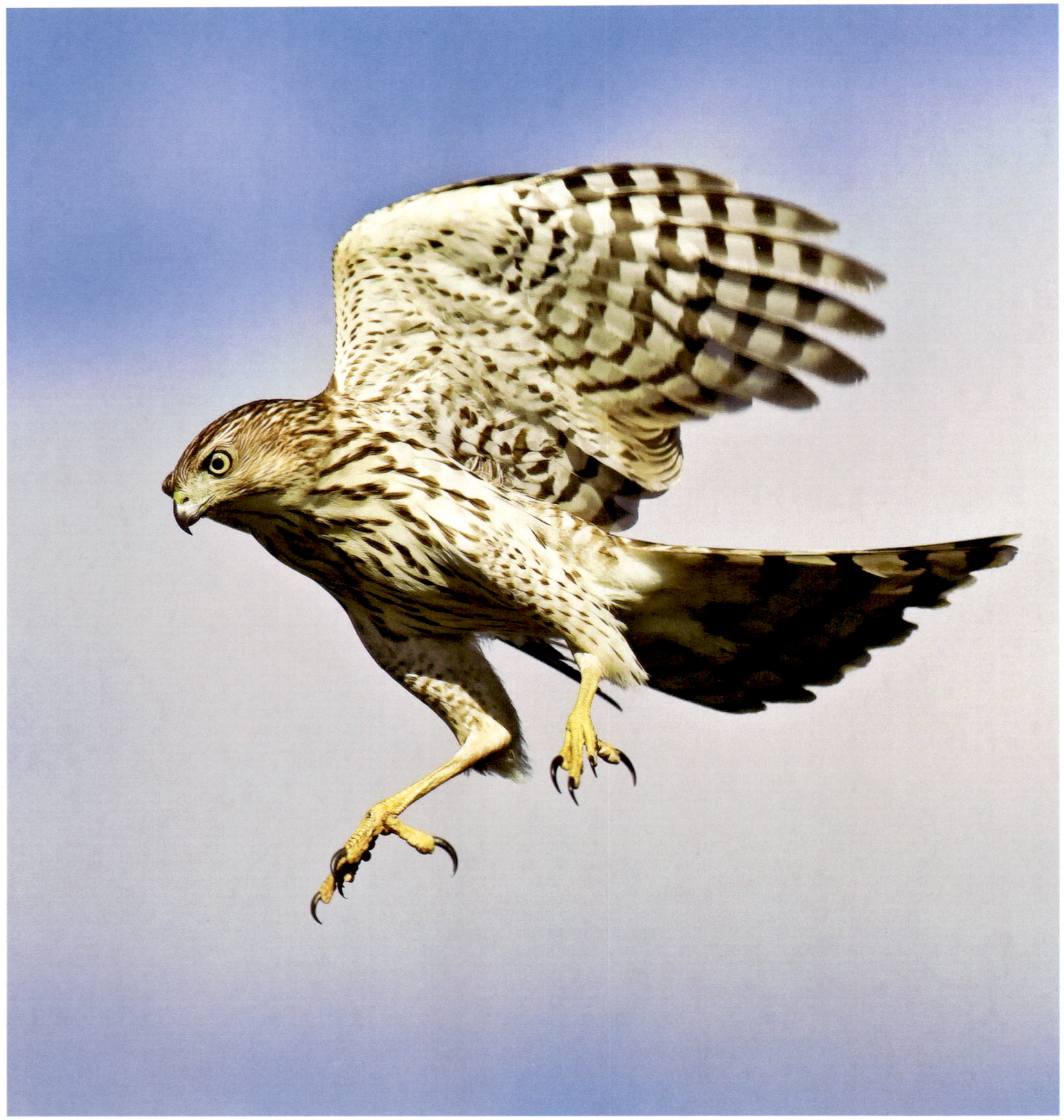

The wild hawk stood with the down on his beak, and stared with his foot on the prey.

— Lord Alfred Tennyson

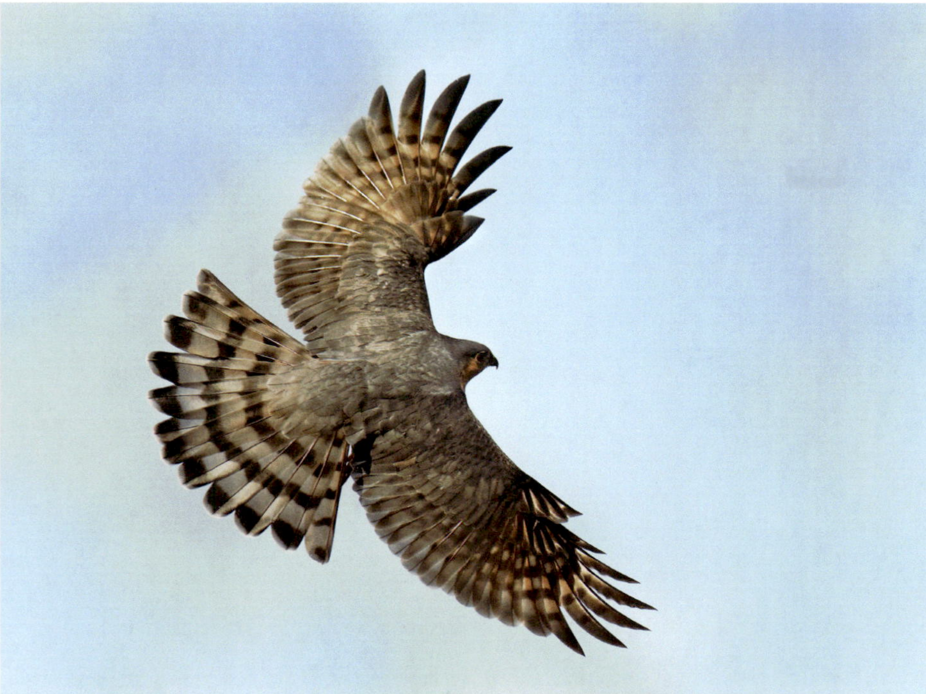

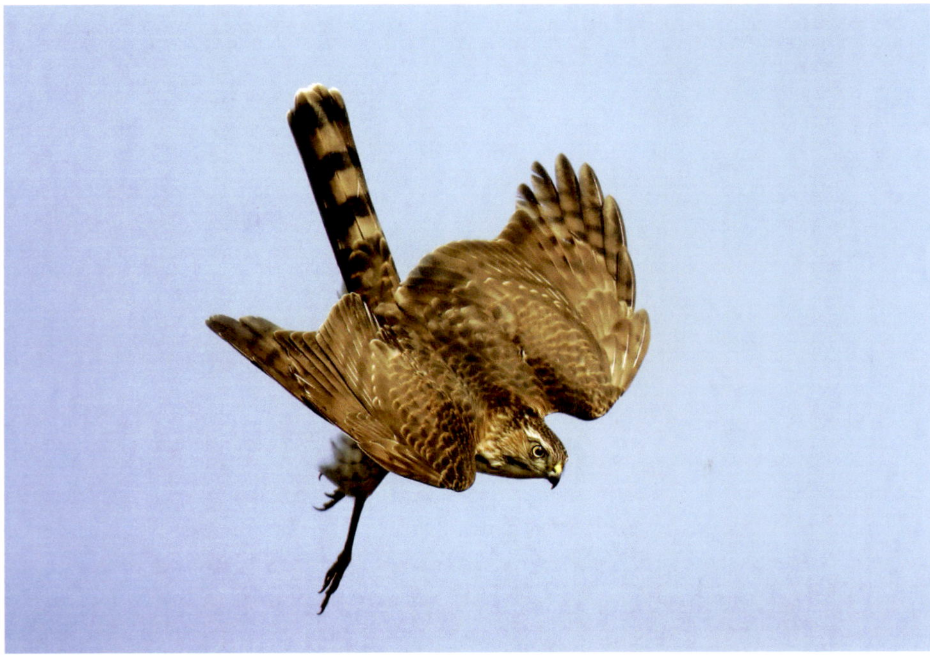

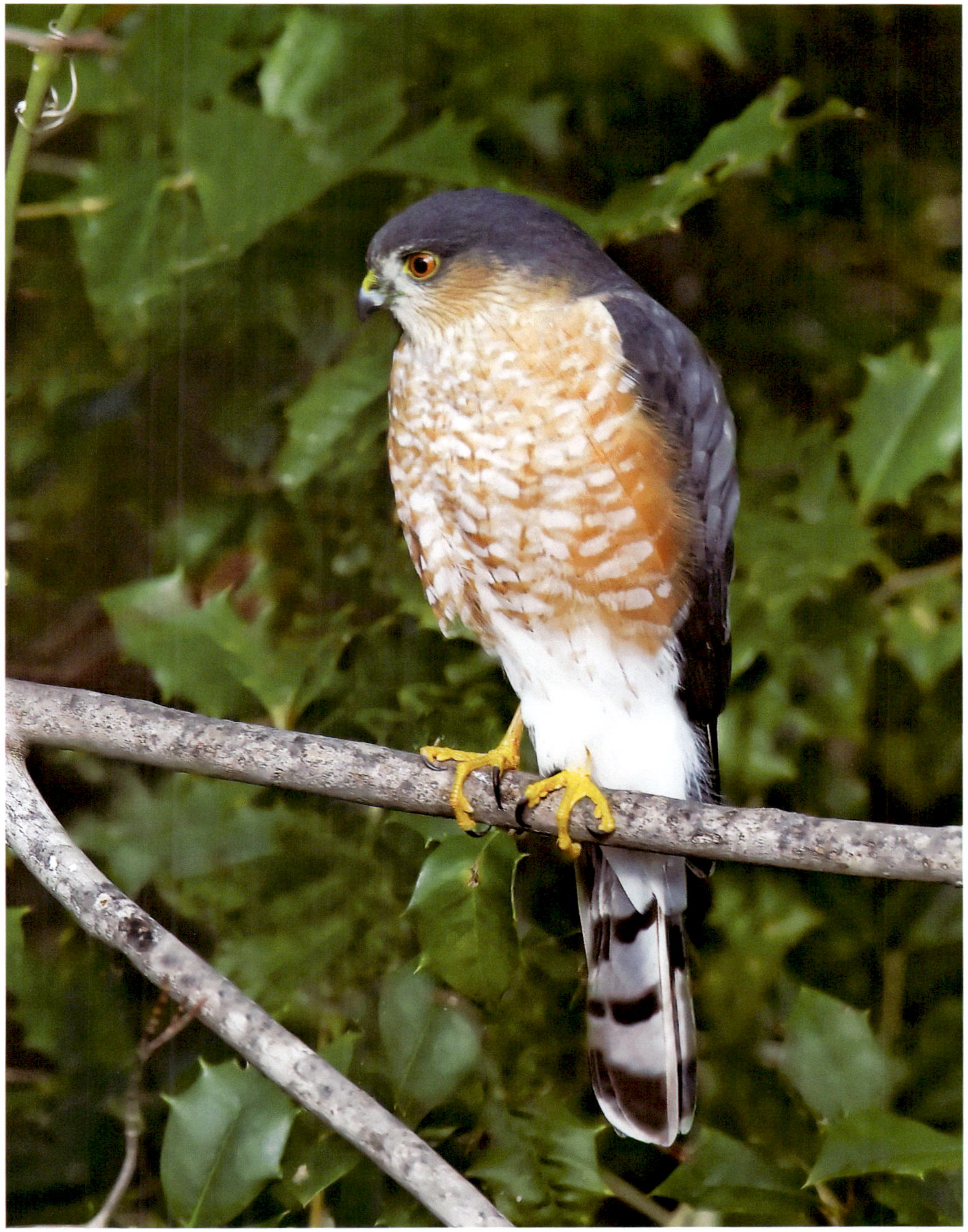

Sharp-shinned Hawks are small birds of prey that fly with incredible agility as they pursue birds through forested areas. Adult males (above) are a rich blue color, while females (upper left) are a bit paler gray. Immature birds (lower left) are brownish. *Photos by Kevin T. Karlson*

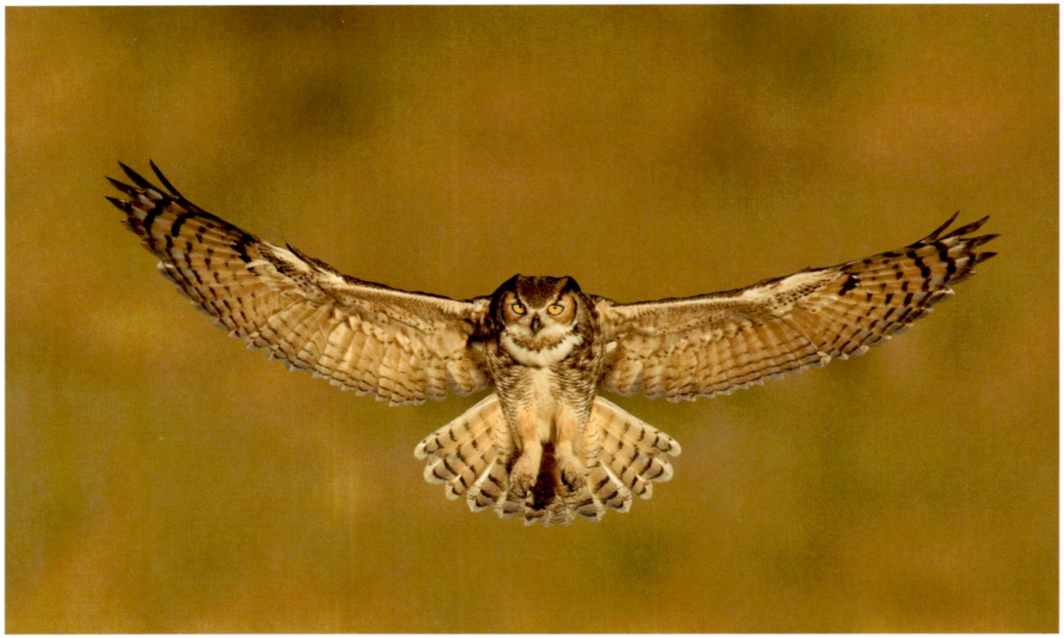

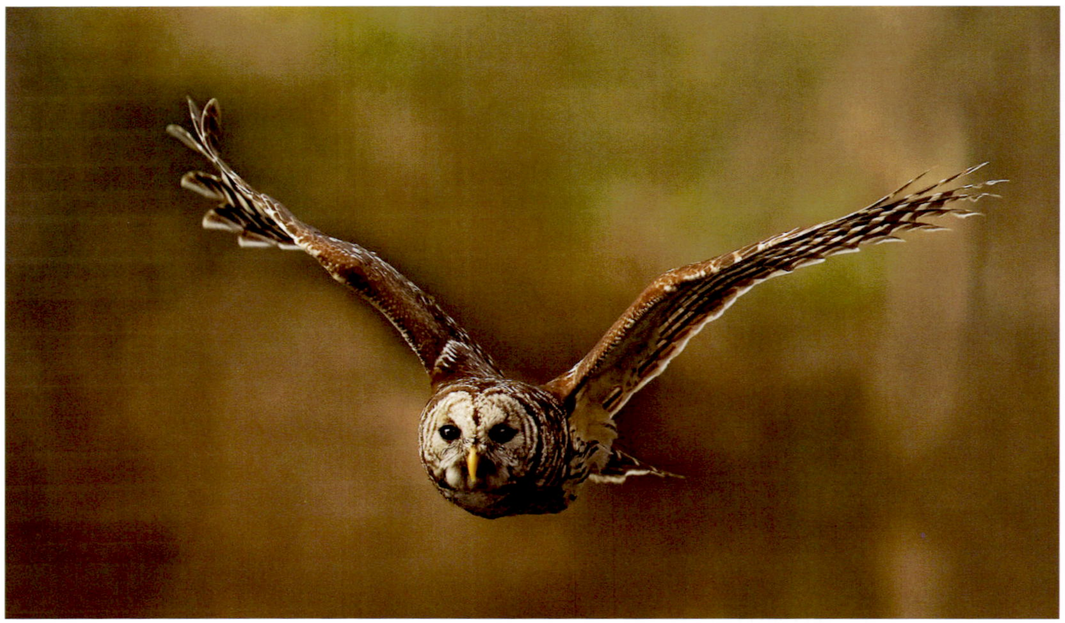

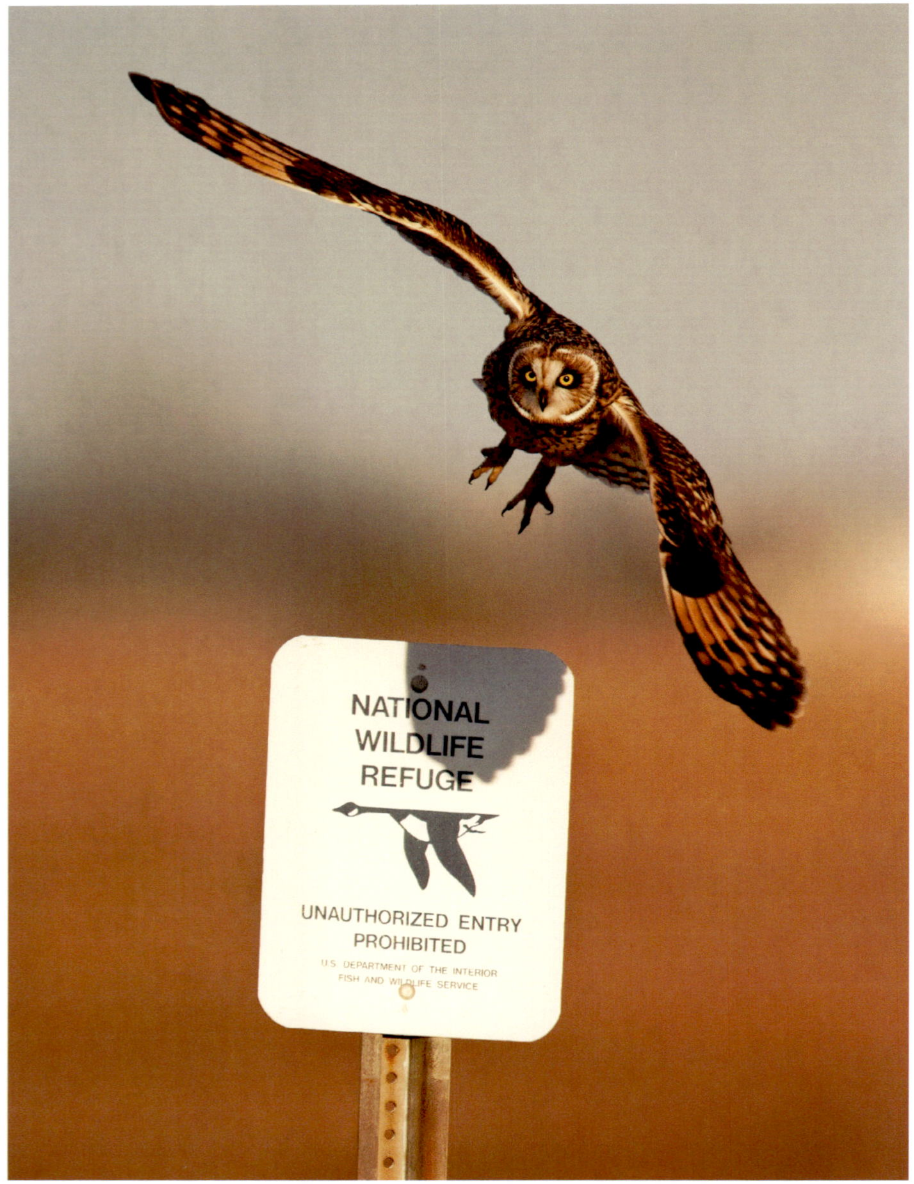

Owls have always fascinated humans because of their secretive lifestyle and nocturnal habits. These images show three owls in head-on flight, which highlight their facial discs and penetrating eyes. *Photos by Scott Elowitz (Great Horned Owl, upper left and Short-eared Owl, above) and Kevin T. Karlson (Barred Owl, lower left).*

A foggy sunrise makes for a moody photo filled with sepia tones. Barred Owls are common residents of these forests (inset) and their loud, hooting calls can be heard at all hours of the day. Both photos were taken near Joe Overstreet Road, Florida. *Photos by Kevin T. Karlson*

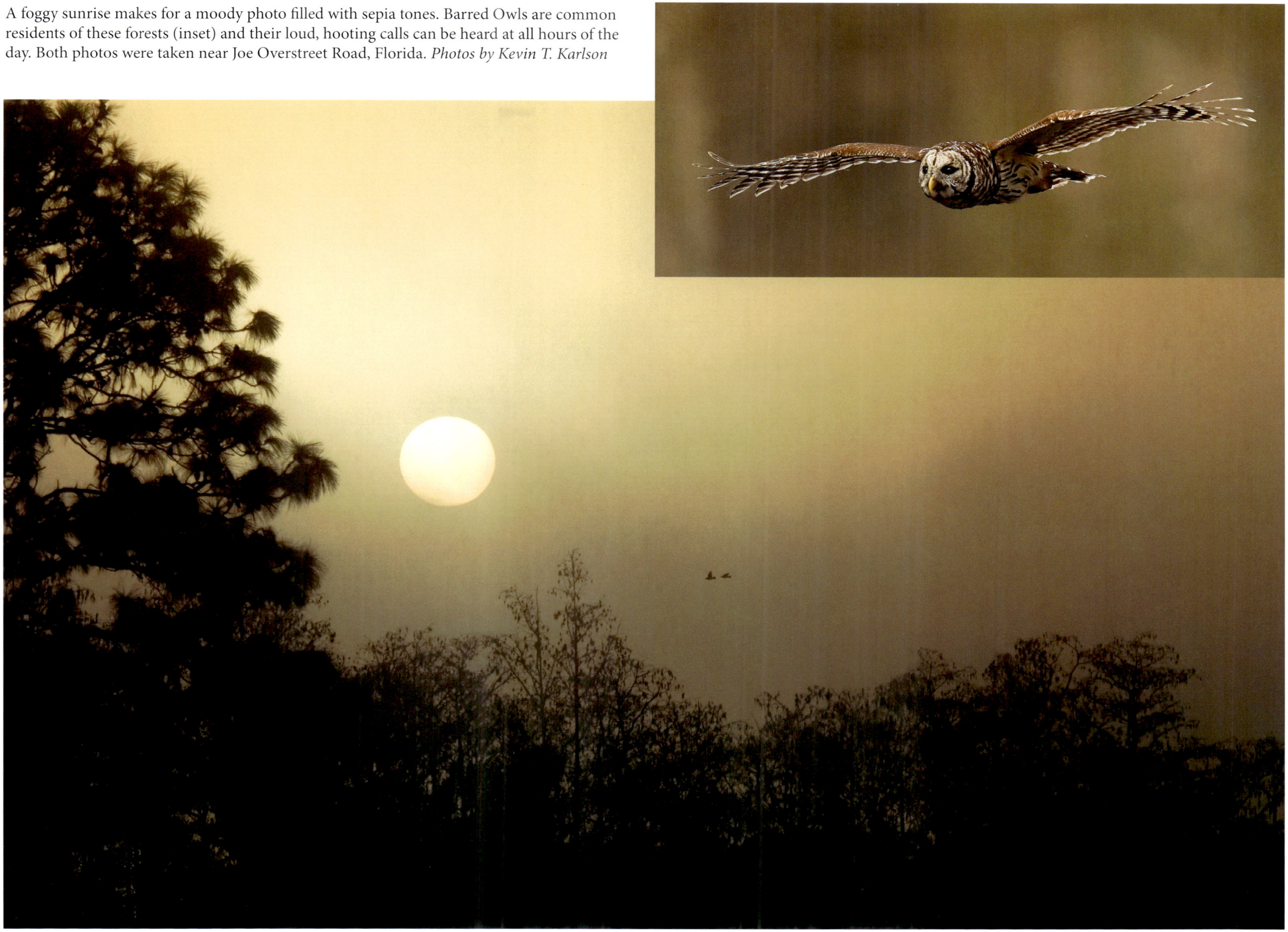

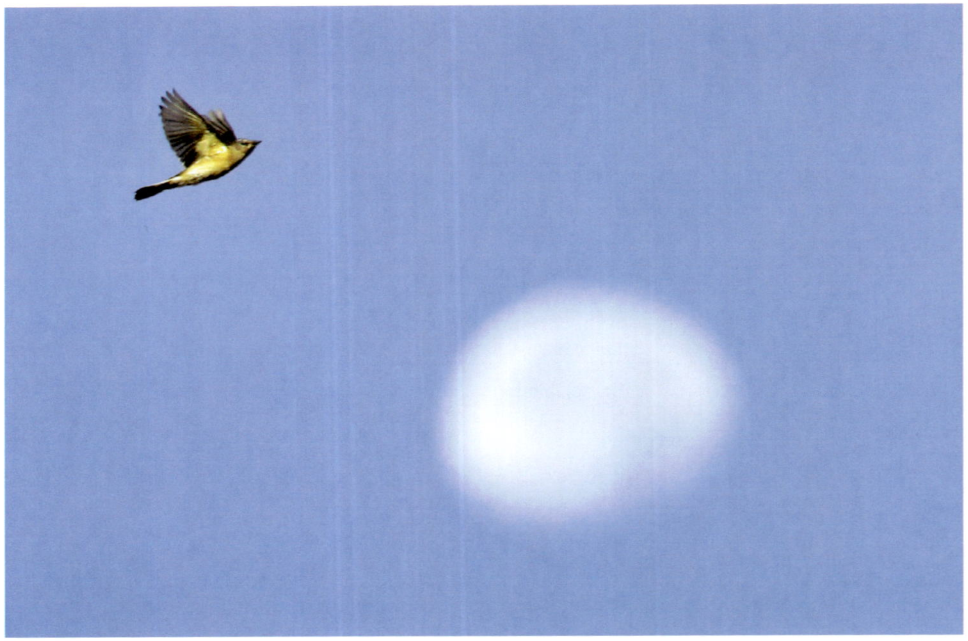

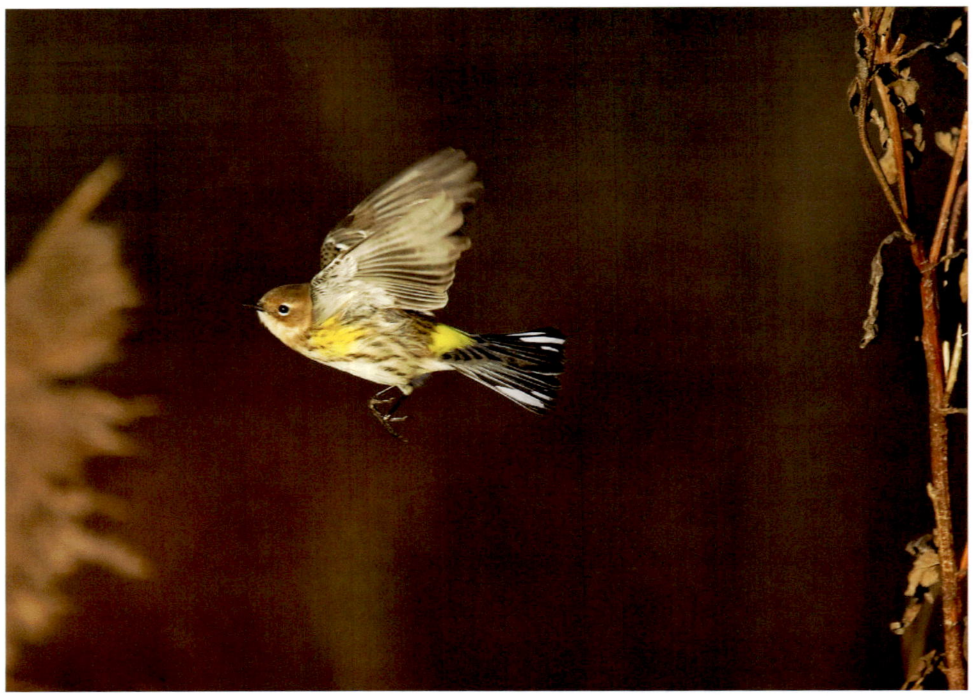

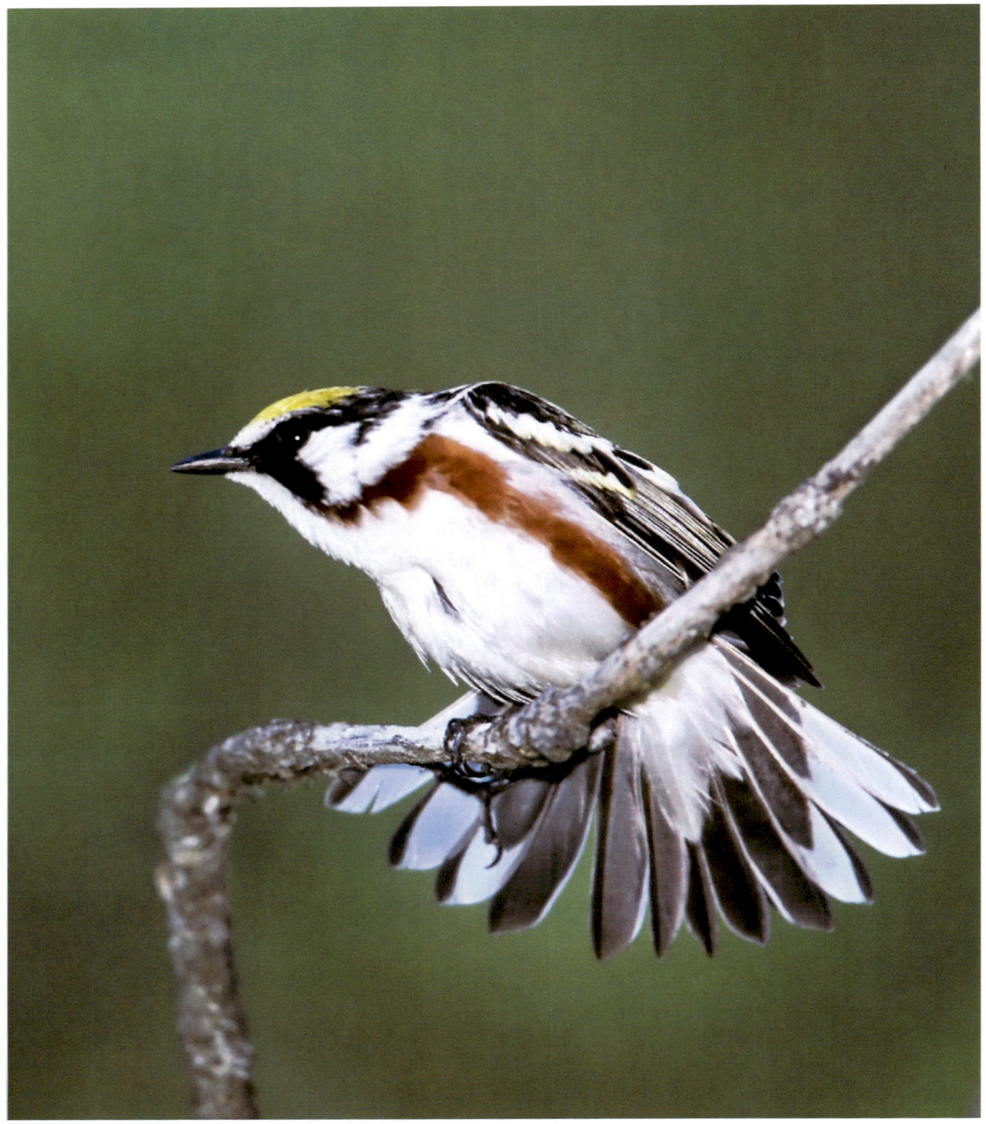

Warblers are small, colorful songbirds that migrate to southern locations for the winter. A female American Redstart (upper left) migrates at dawn against the moon, while a Yellow-rumped Warbler makes a short flight in late fall (lower left). A male Chestnut-sided Warbler stretches before taking flight (above). *Photos by Kevin T. Karlson*

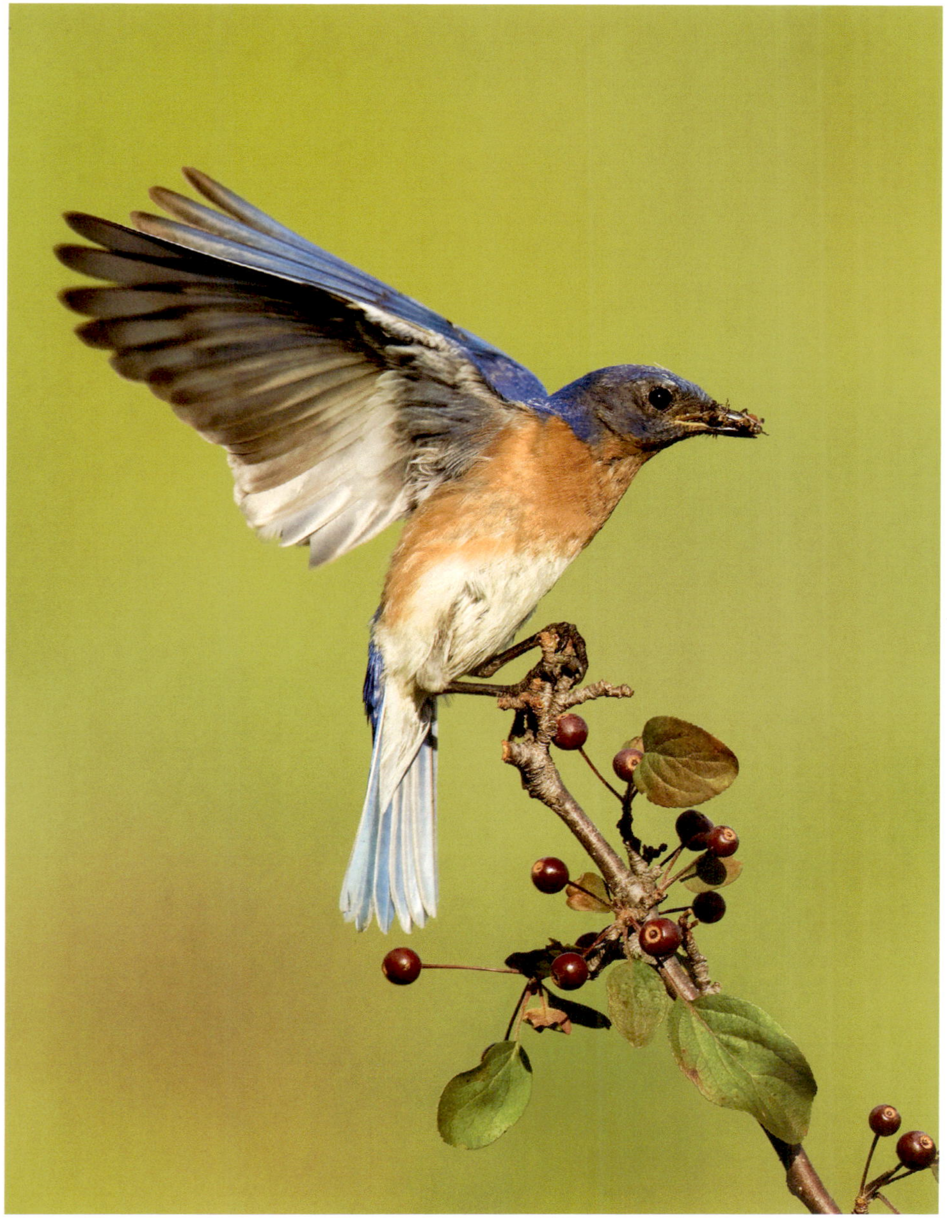

When nature made the bluebird she wished to propitiate both the sky and the earth, so she gave him the color of the one on his back and the hue of the other on his breast.

— John Burroughs

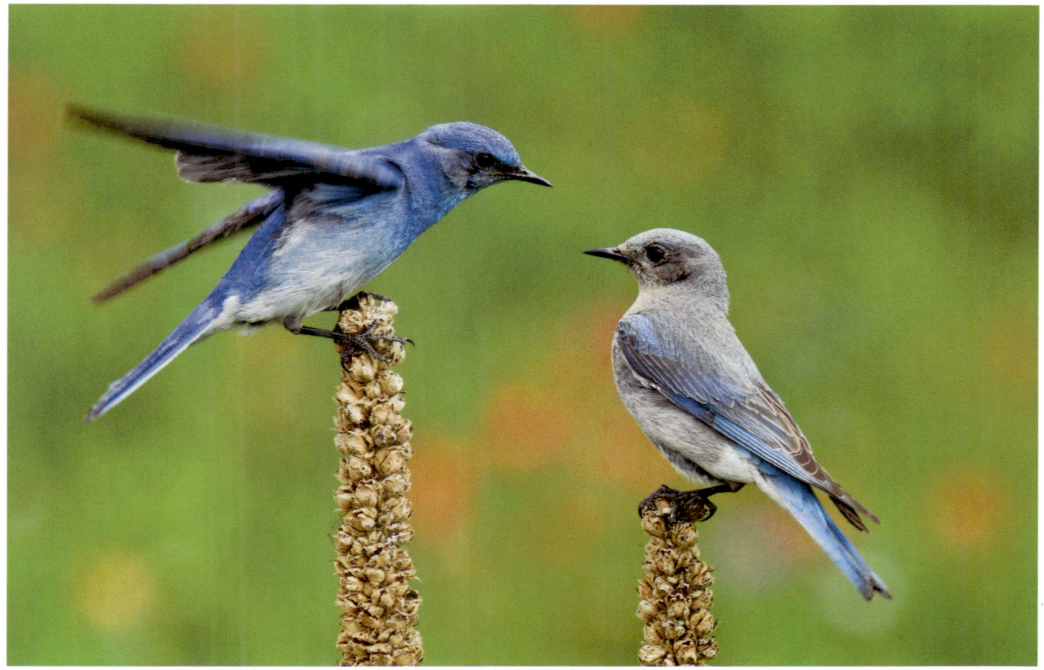

A male Eastern Bluebird steadies himself on a branch (left), while a male Mountain Bluebird lands on a Common Mullein stalk next to his mate (above), taken in British Columbia. *Photos by Scott Elowitz*

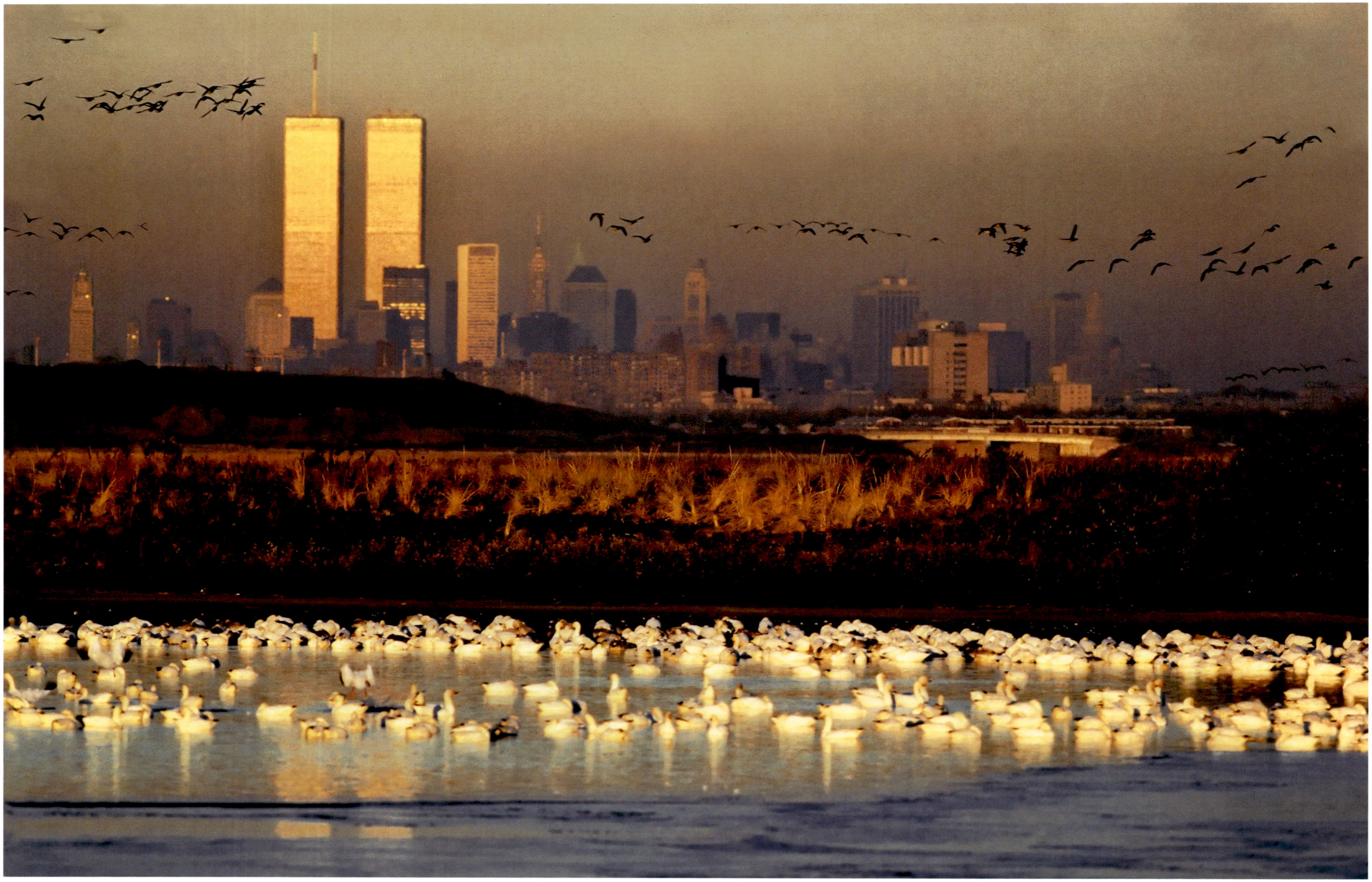

Because of their immense size, the sun would light up the World Trade Centers at dawn before the rest of New York City. In the foreground of this image Snow Geese grace the waters near the Jamaica Bay Wildlife Refuge in Queens, New York and illustrate the value of having natural areas in the heart of metropolitan centers. The World Trade Centers truly bridged the earth and the air as they reached skyward. *Photo by Don Riepe*

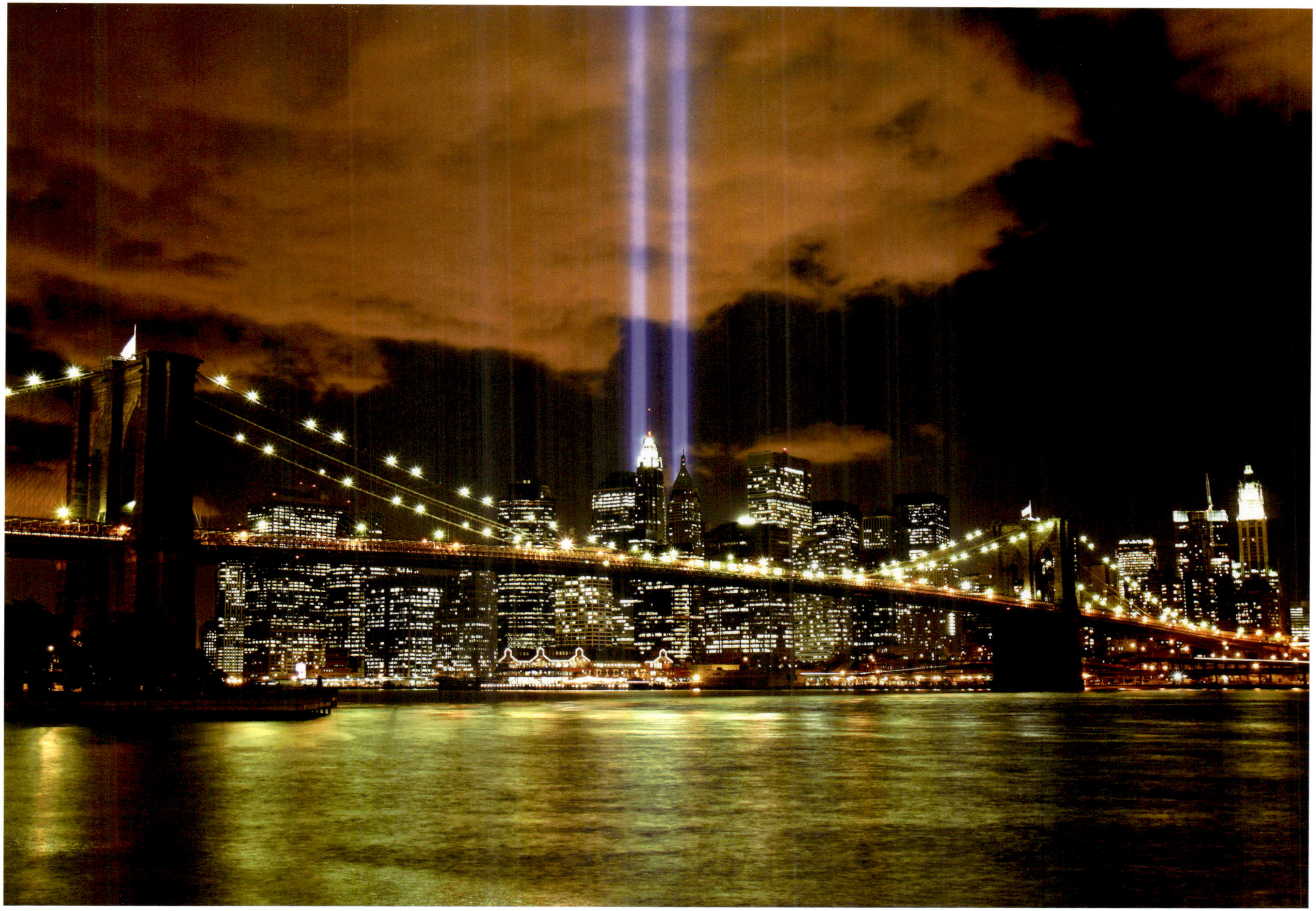

On the fifth anniversary of the World Trade Centers tragedy, two shafts of light were cast into the sky as a tribute to the men and women who lost their lives in this senseless act of terror on September 11, 2001. "We will never Forget." *Photo by Scott Elowitz*

Water

Water gives and sustains life in all living things. It has the ability to awaken a sleeping seed and produce a sprout that will turn into a flower, vegetable, or giant tree. It is mysteriously connected to the cycles of the moon and reacts to lunar events with extreme rises and falls of the ocean tides. Water covers over 70 percent of the earth's surface, although about ninety-seven percent of this is salty. Our bodies are composed of about 65 percent water, and only 0.036 percent is found on the planet as available fresh water in lakes and rivers.

Water replenishes itself in a constant cycle. It evaporates from the ocean and other fresh water bodies, travels through the air as clouds, rains down upon the earth, and then flows back to the ocean or evaporates again. During this cycle, water interacts with the other elements and affects our lives in many ways. Water also changes form when temperatures vary greatly, and the result is snow, ice or steam.

Images in this chapter reflect the ubiquitous nature of water, with some showing water in various forms and others portraying creatures that rely on water for their lifestyles and food. A few even show artwork created by water the artist, either by wave action or ice sculptures in a winter stream. Water is truly a precious resource and element, and one that we desperately need to protect in order to insure the future of our planet.

Wilson's Phalarope is a shorebird that spends most of its time swimming in pursuit of invertebrates and insects. This photo of a juvenile bird perfectly captures its essence, and also shows the miraculous nature of water as a fluid element. *Photo by Lloyd Spitalnik*

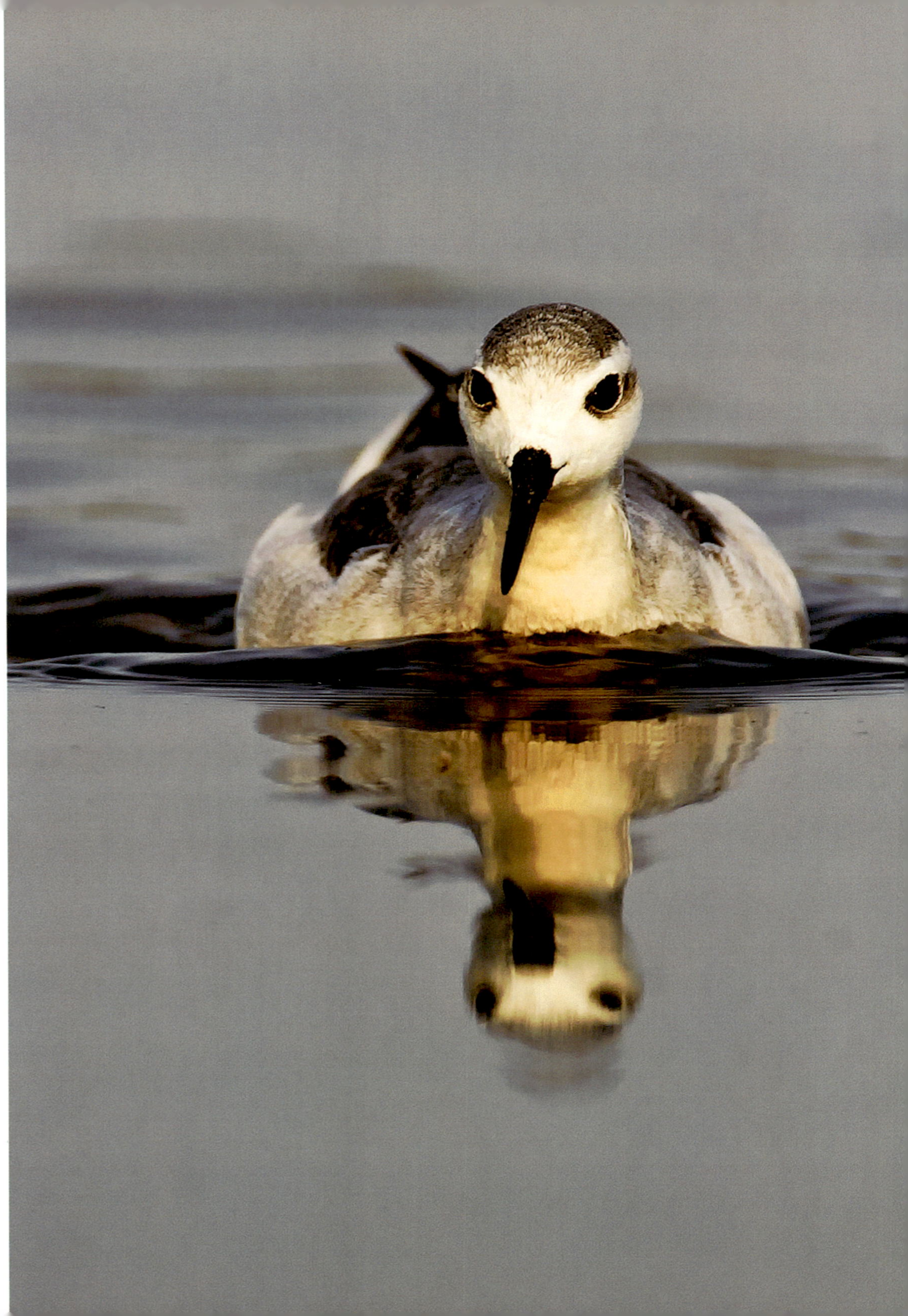

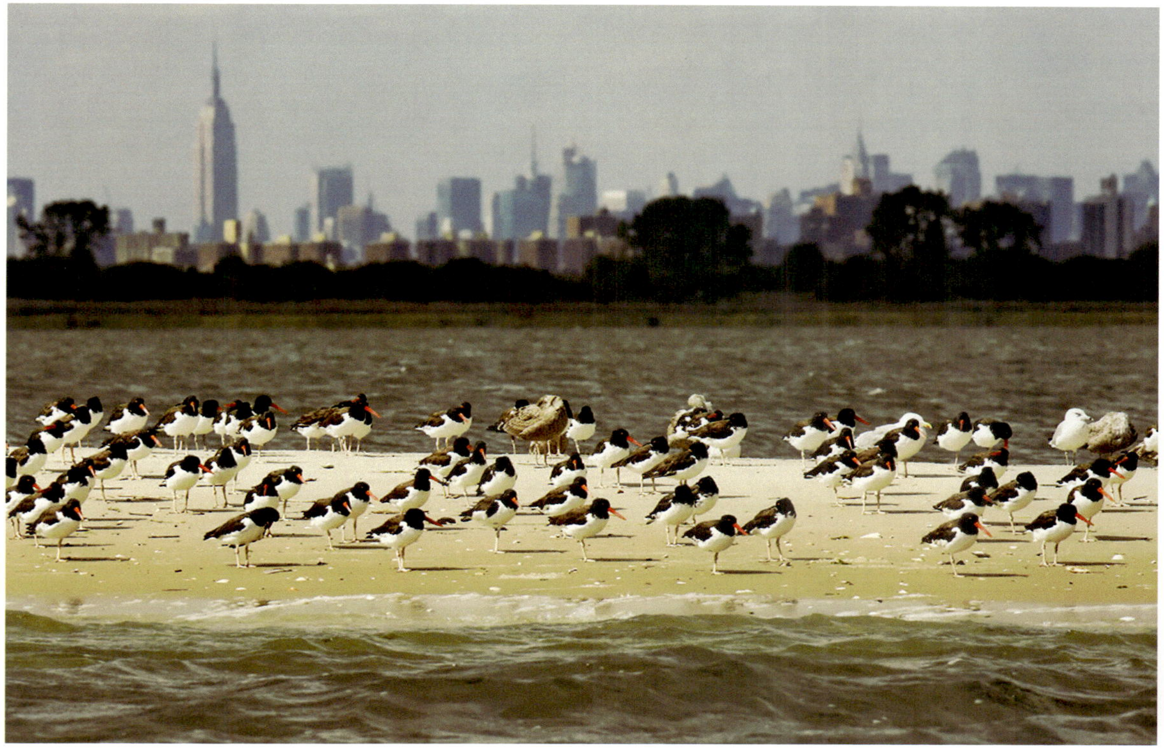

American Oystercatchers live their entire lives adjacent to coastal waters. Large groups gather each fall near Broad Channel, Queens, in the shadow of New York City (left). A cunning Ring-billed Gull steals an oystercatcher's hard earned dinner for the second time (below), but on the third attempt, the oystercatcher flew away with its conch meal. *Photos by Don Riepe (left) and Kevin T. Karlson (below)*

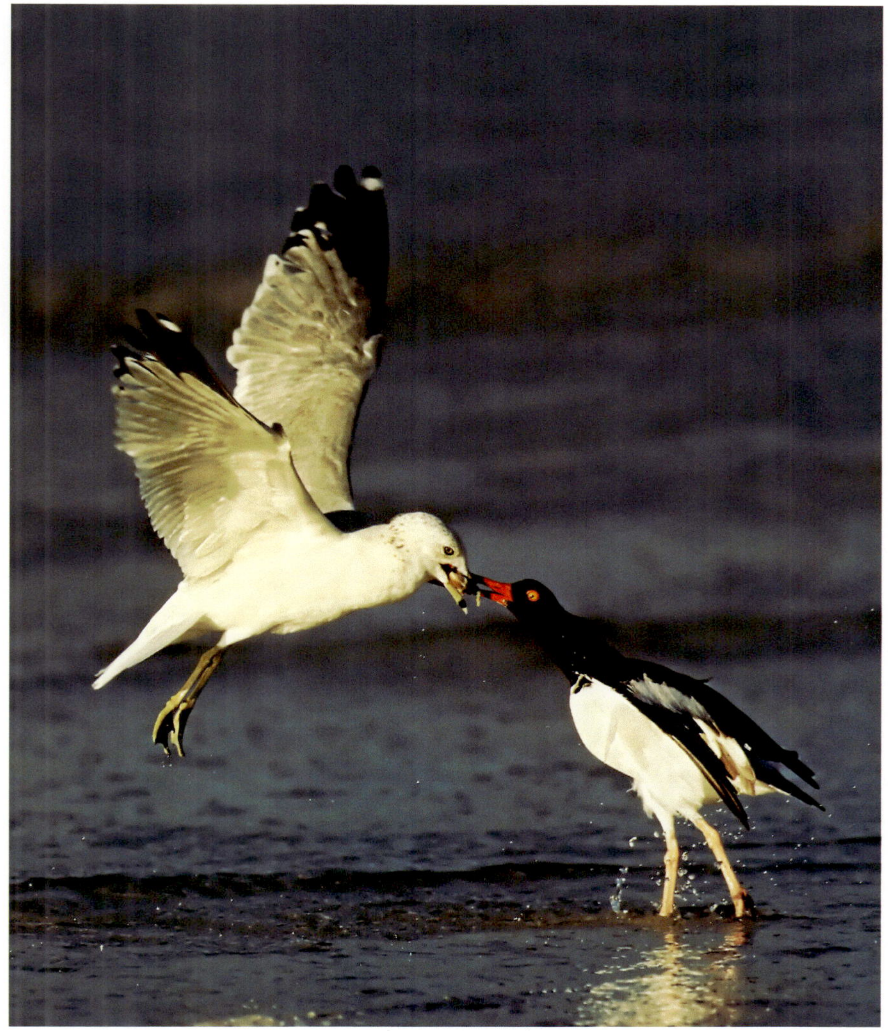

By means of water, we give life to everything.

— Koran

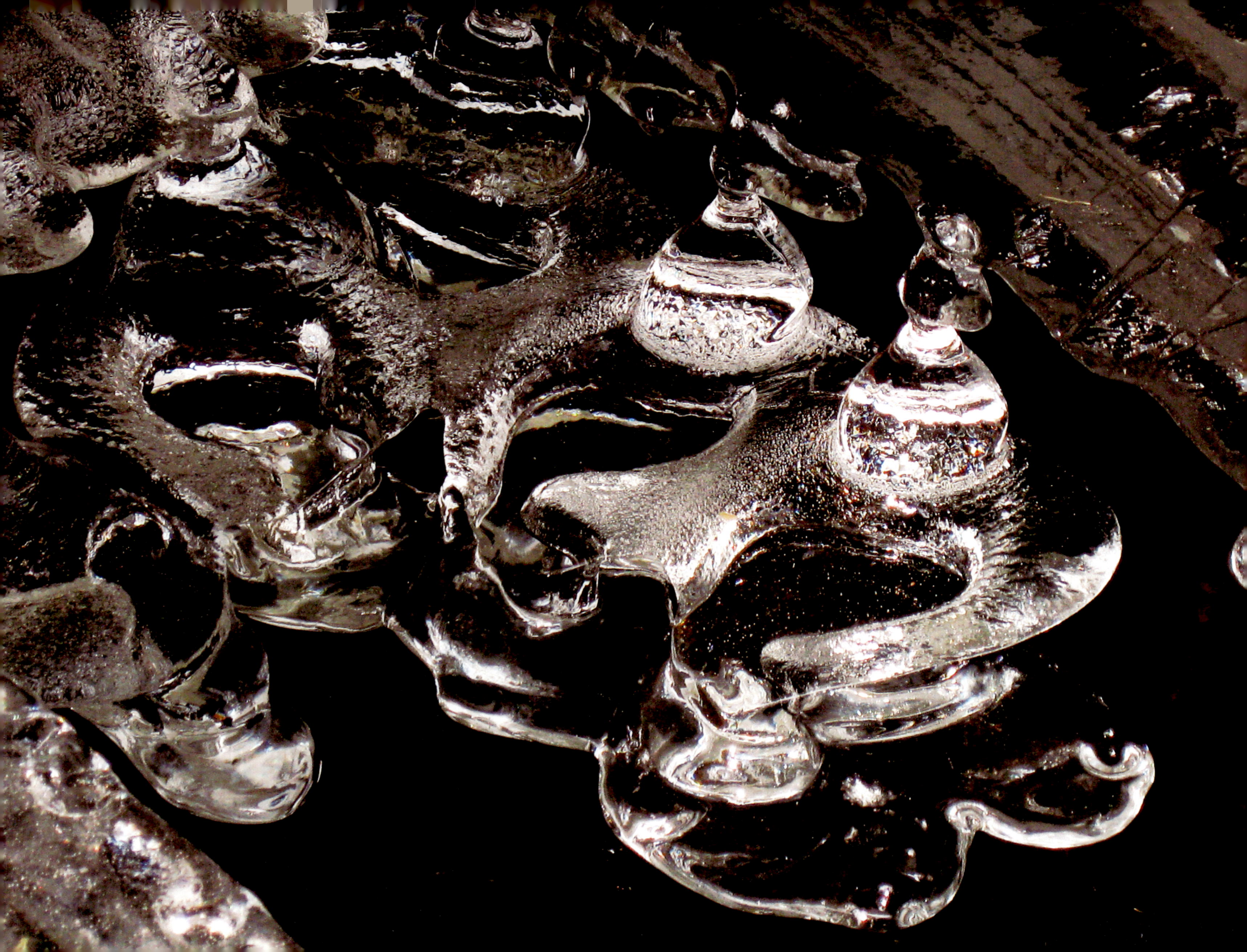

Opposite: A melting ice sculpture in a cold, New Hampshire brook is the work of water and ice interaction, and an artist's eye. *Photo by Dale Rosselet*

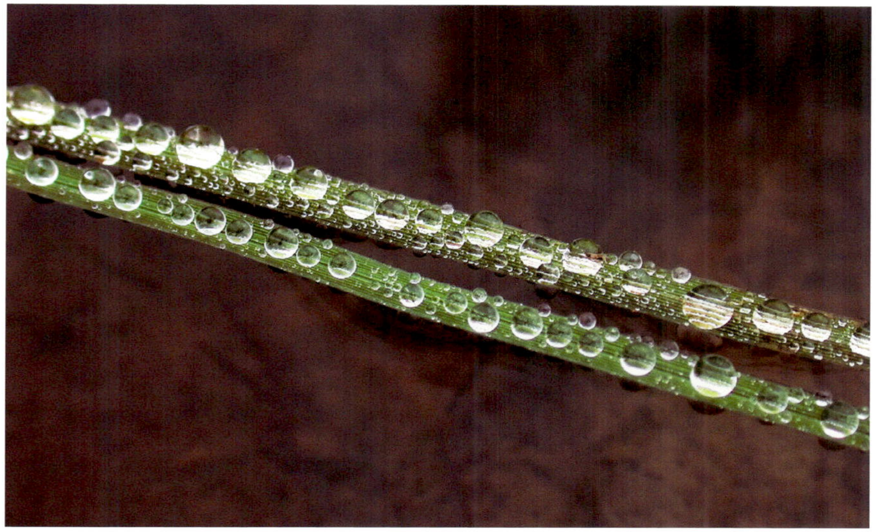

So easy to do and yet so rewarding. Here beads of dew stand proud on two grass leaves floating on a roadside puddle in Norfolk, England. *Photo and caption by Mike Crewe*

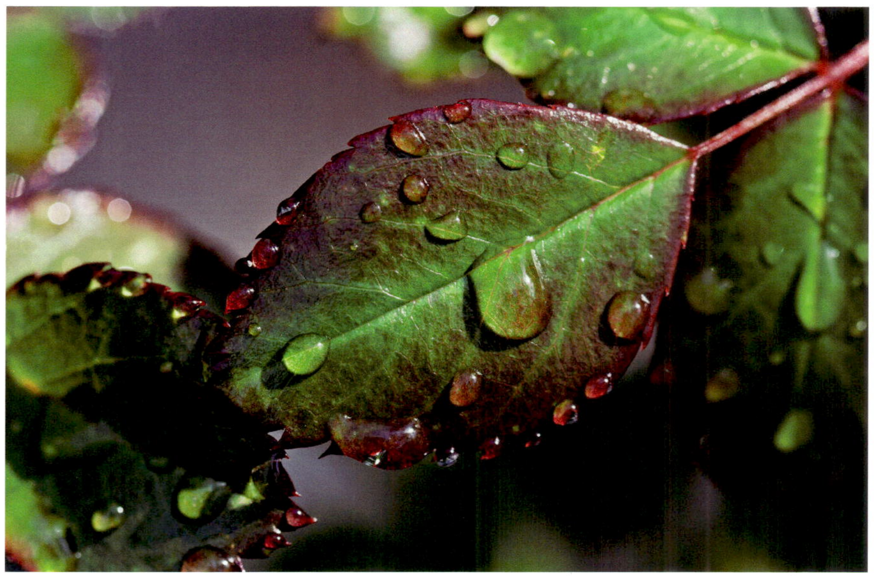

Rain drops on leaves in Central Park reminds us of the beauty in simple things. *Photo by Lloyd Spitalnik*

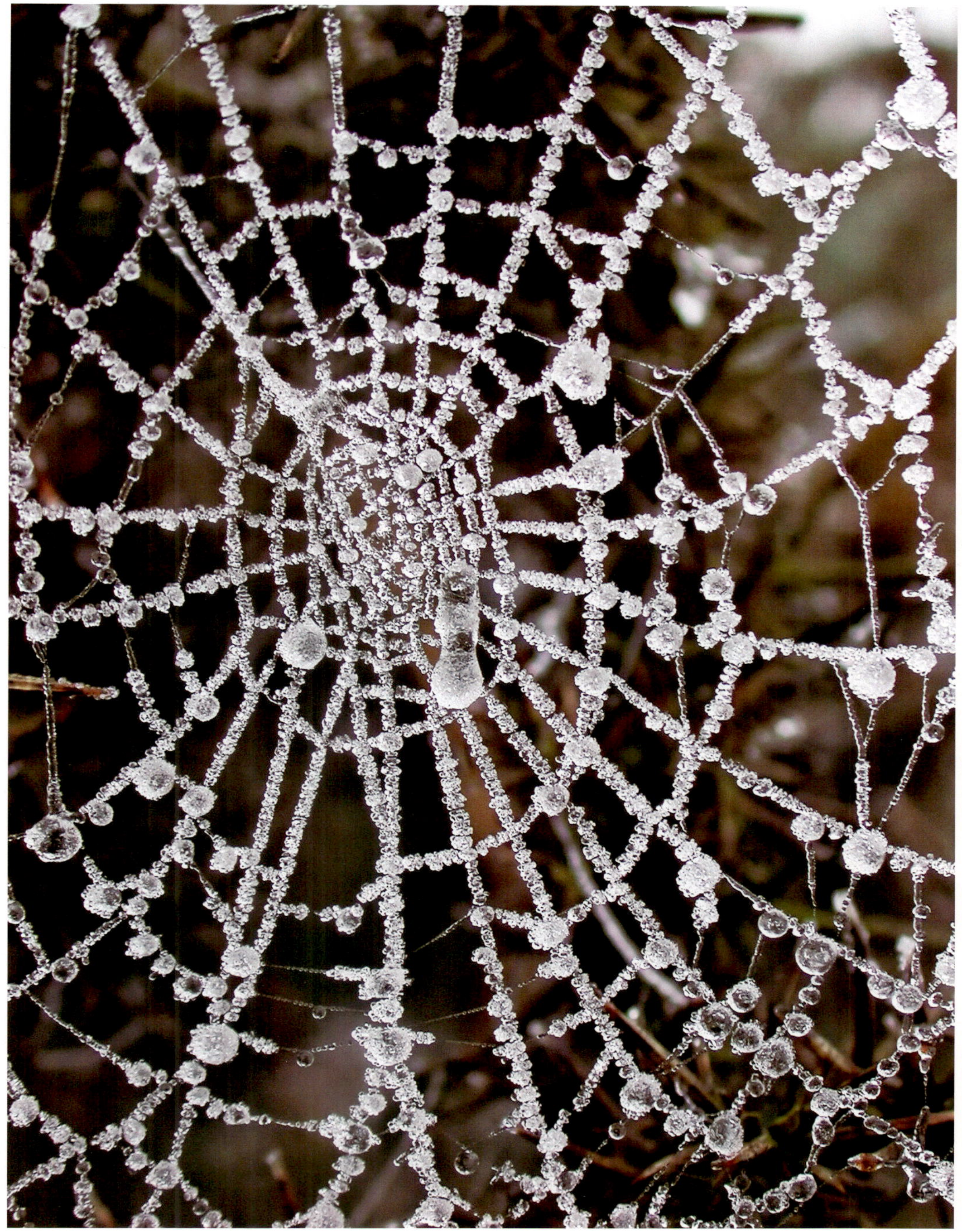

While the first cold and frosty mornings of fall may signal the end of summer, such mornings give endless opportunities to capture the beauty of nature. *Photo and caption by Mike Crewe*

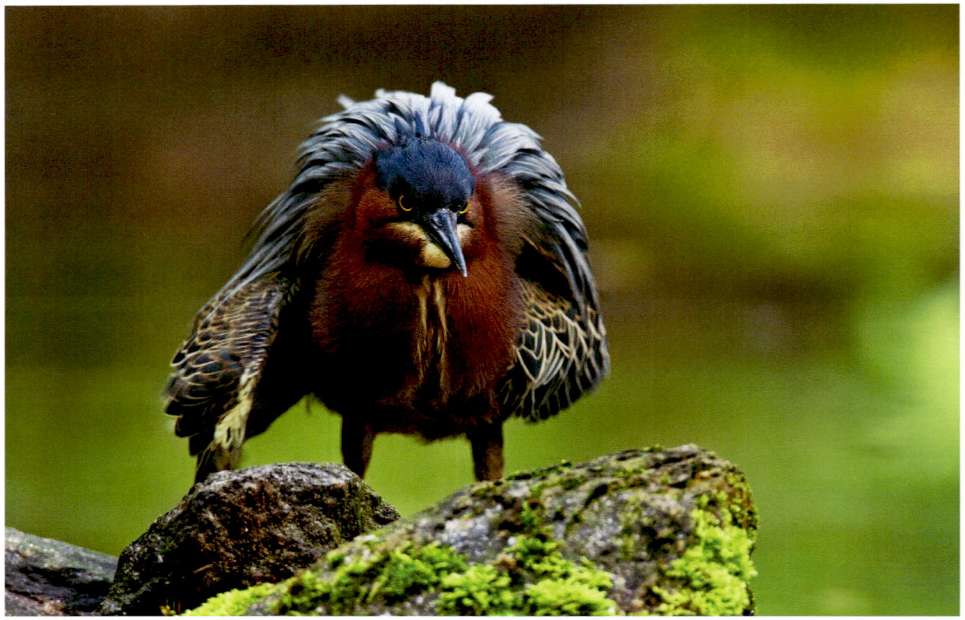

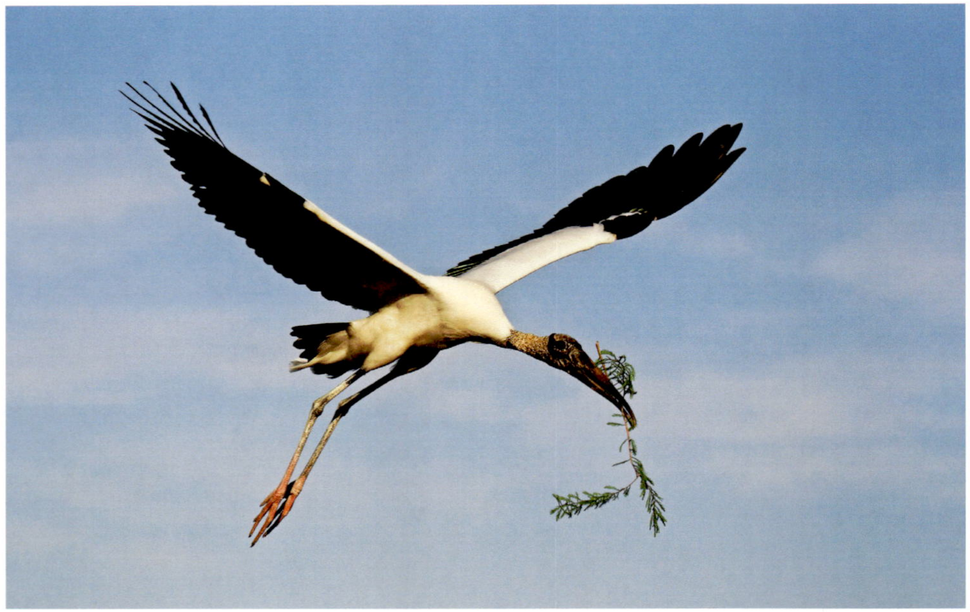

Green Herons (upper left) hunt quietly by the water's edge and wait for small fish to swim by. Wood Stork (above) is a large heron that is shown carrying a branch to its nest. *Photos by Lloyd Spitalnik (upper left) and Kevin T. Karlson (upper right)*

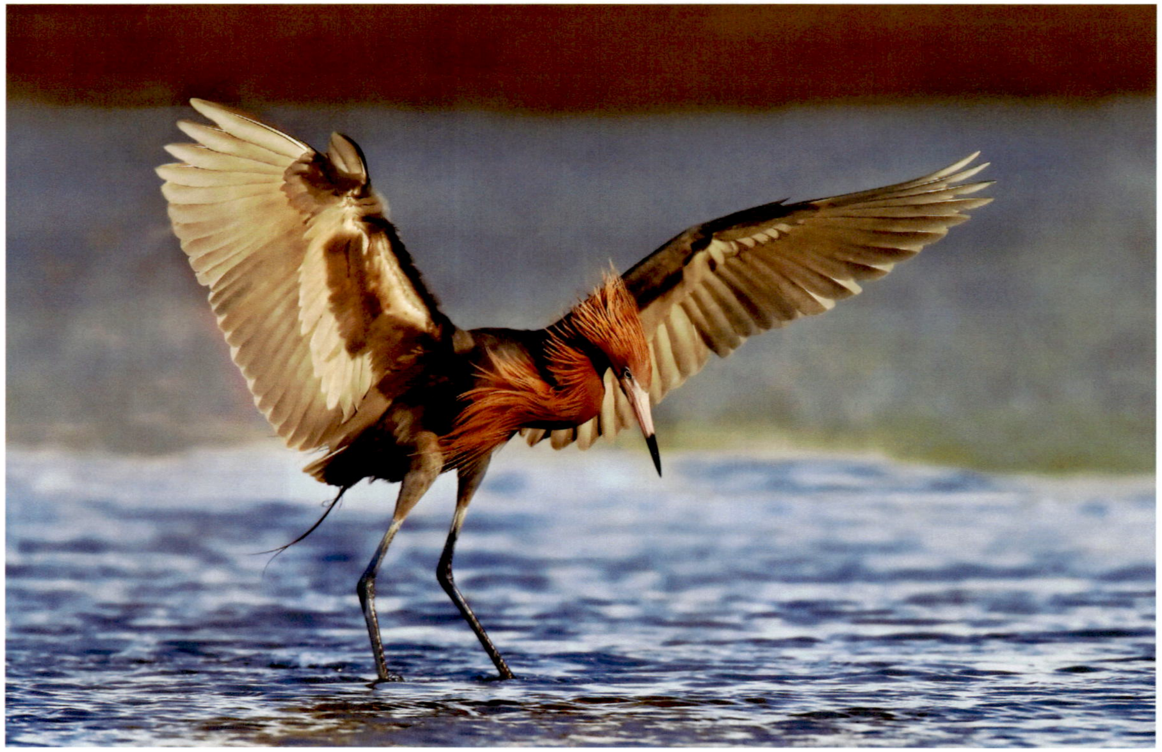

Reddish Egrets are one of the most frenetic and animated of all birds, and often dash about and flash their wings while hunting for small fish in shallow water. *Photo by Kevin T. Karlson*

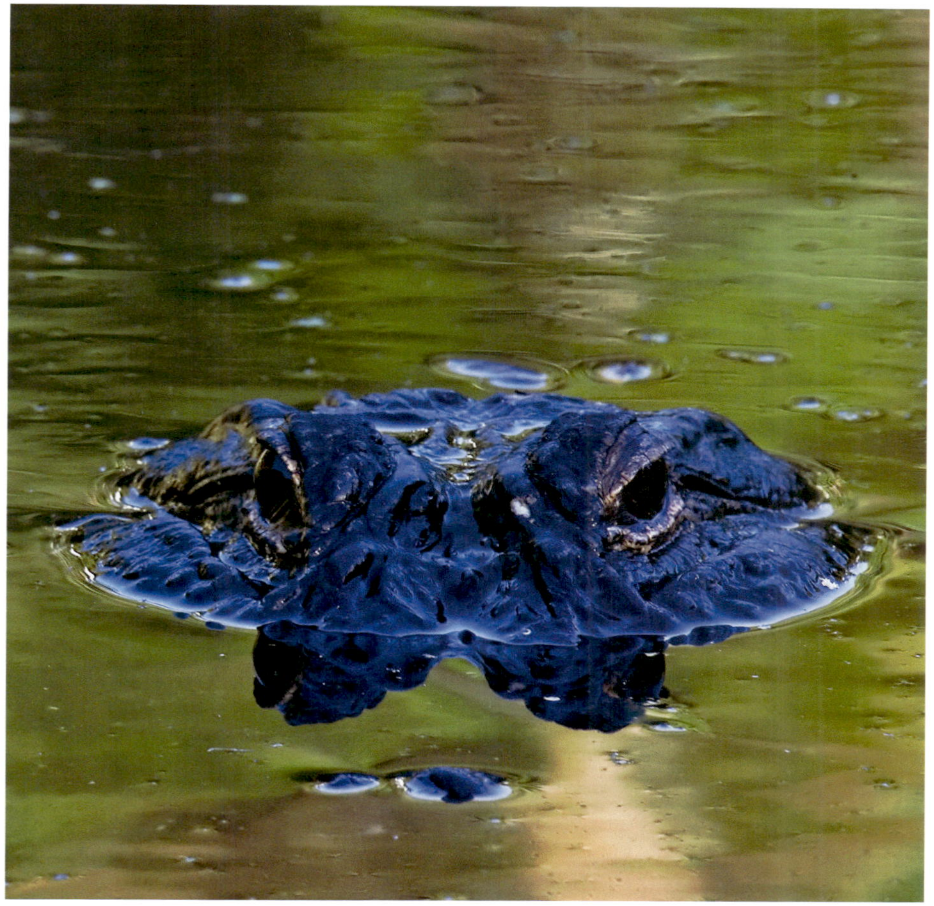

American Alligators are aquatic predators that strike fear in humans because of their reptilian nature and cold, emotion-less demeanor. A large male floats quietly waiting for unsuspecting prey. *Photo by Kevin T. Karlson*

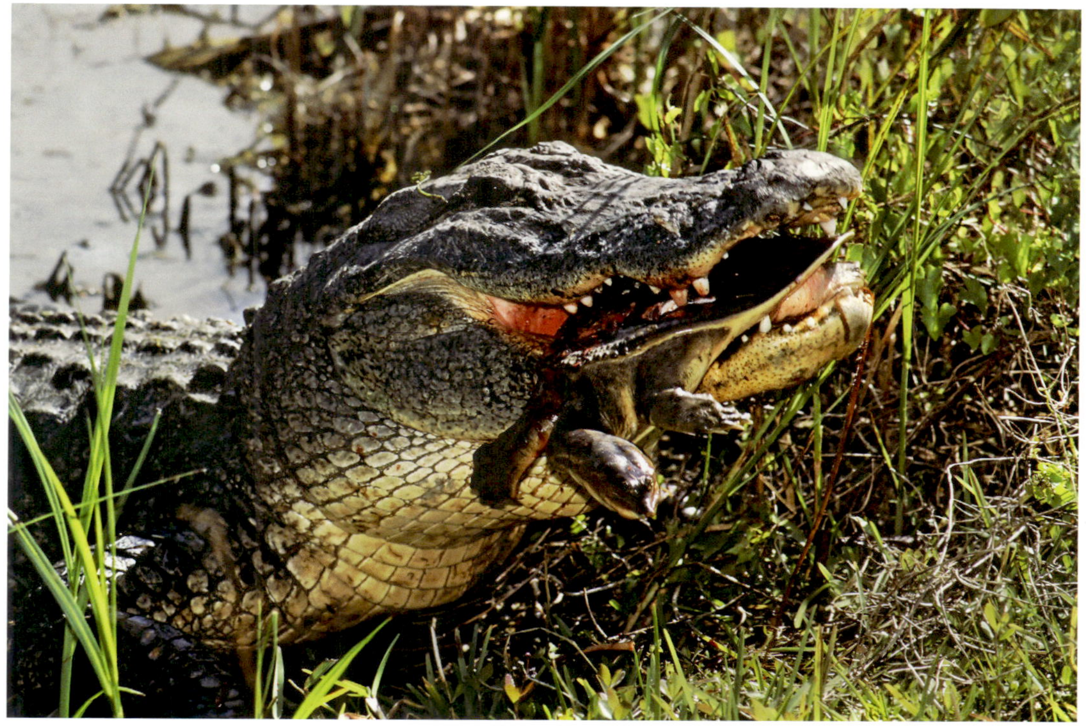

A large Florida Soft-shell Turtle is devoured by a massive American Alligator in the Florida Everglades. *Photo by Kevin T. Karlson*

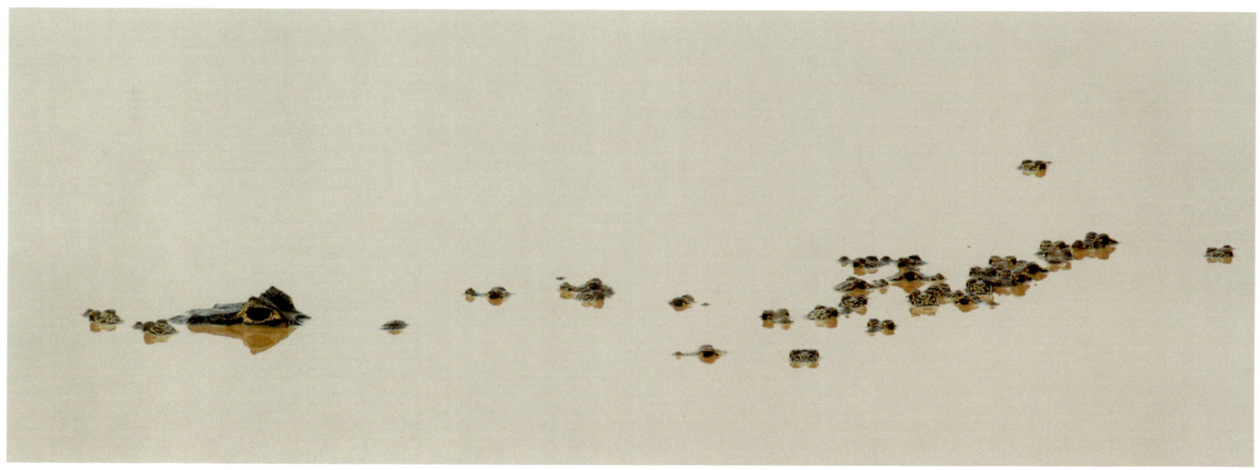

Little bumps of mud stick out of the water in a dry-season pool in the Pantanal, Brazil, creating a pleasing pattern. Then you realize that the largest bump has eyes...and all the little ones have eyes too! A female Yacare Caiman tends her brood in a muddy puddle, making you suddenly realize that you don't need a swim after all! *Photo and caption by Mike Crewe*

Water is the driver of Nature.

— Leonardo da Vinci

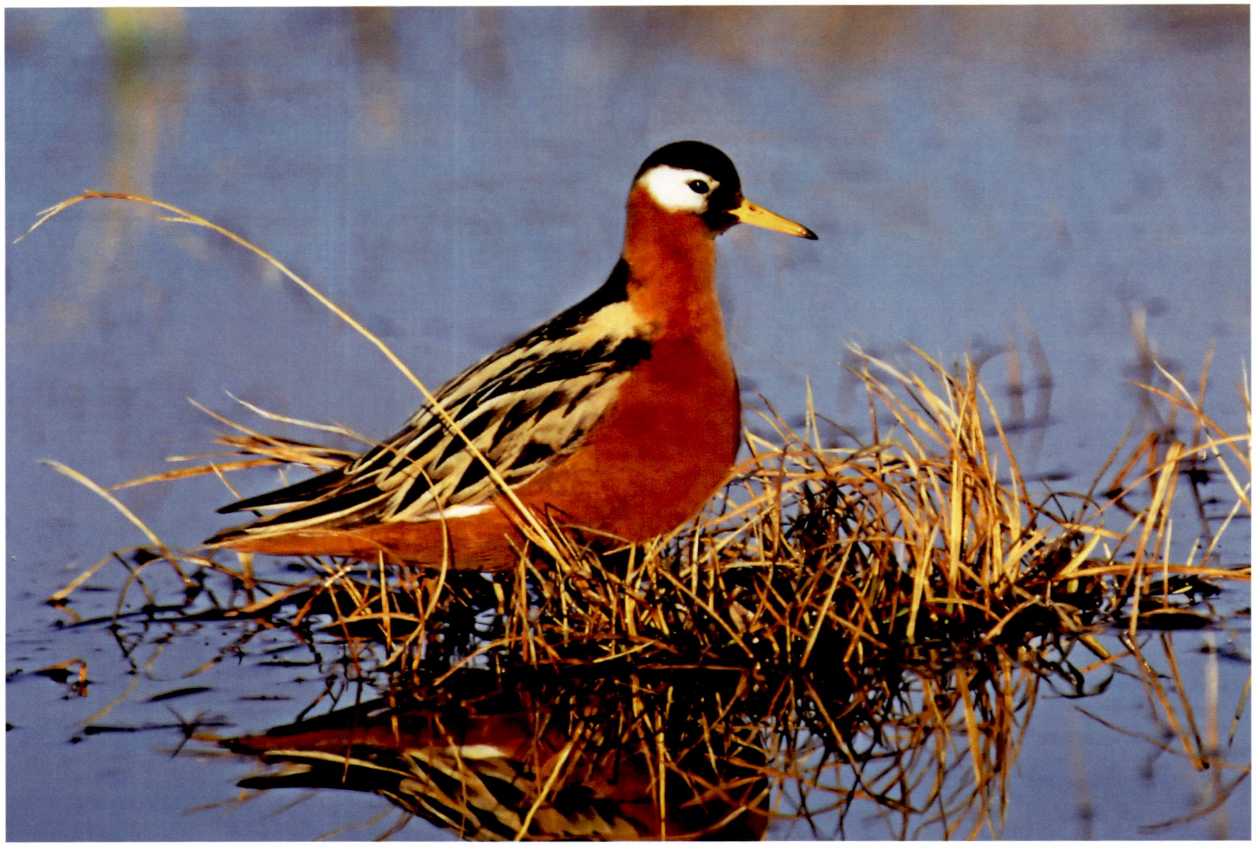

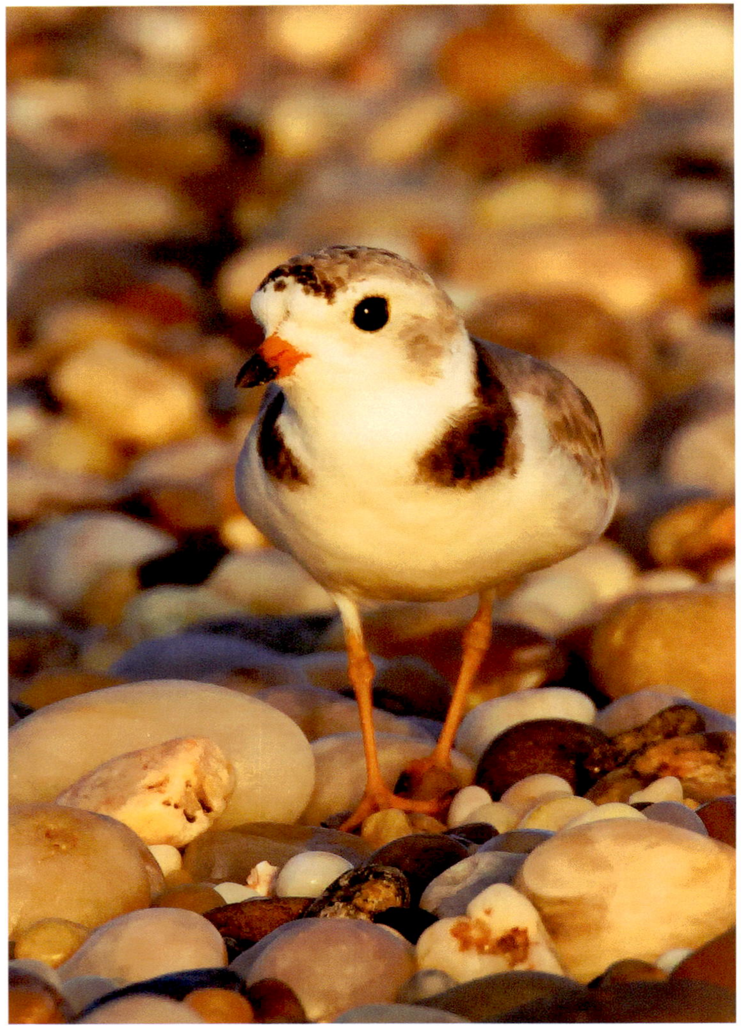

Soft hues set the mood for these images of two small shorebirds, a Red Phalarope resting on a small grass island on the Alaskan tundra (left), and a Piping Plover stepping gingerly among smooth stones on a Long Island beach (above). *Photos by Kevin T. Karlson (left) and Lloyd Spitalnik (right)*

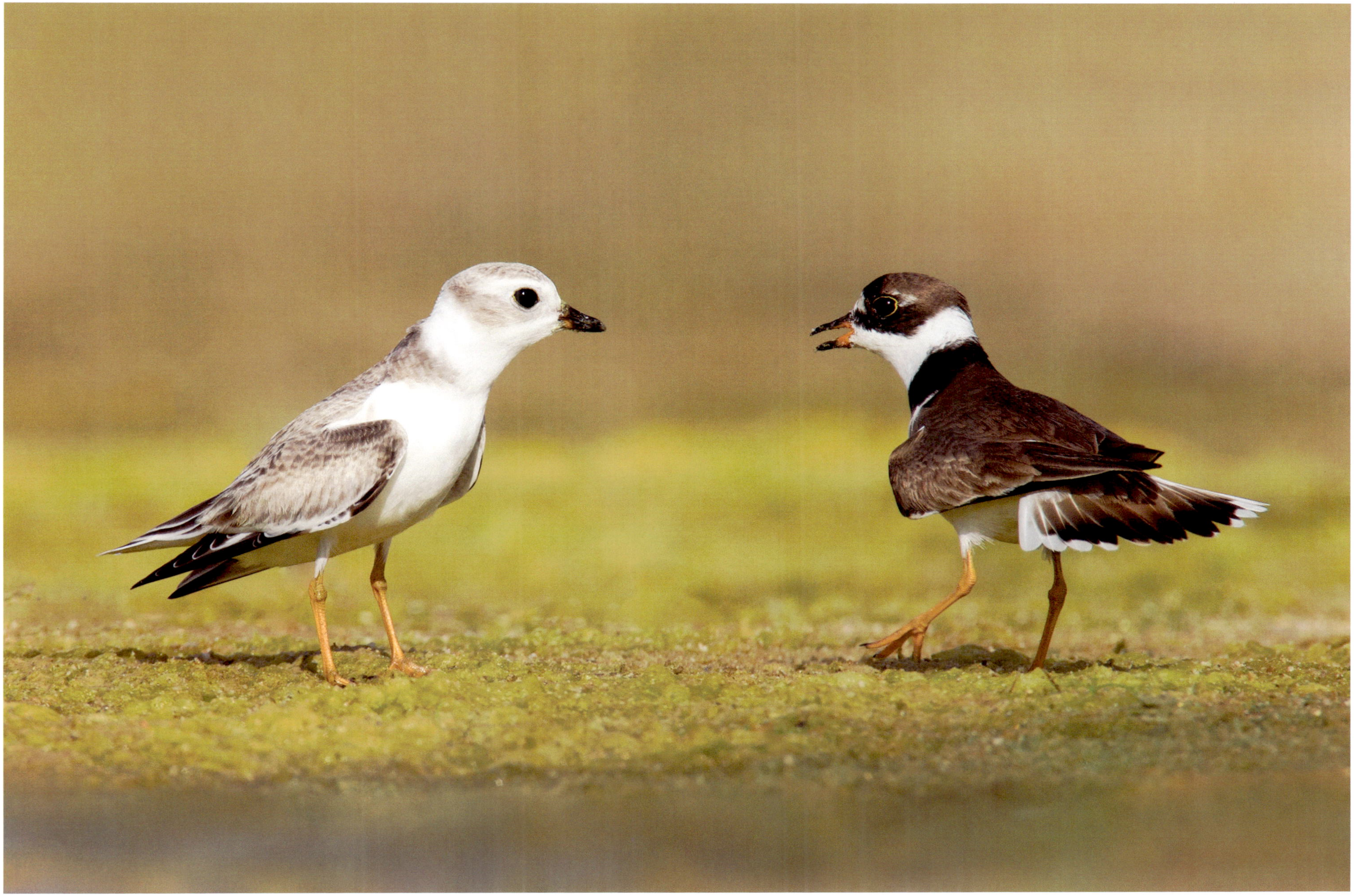

A juvenile Piping Plover (left) is trying to understand the aggression towards it by an adult Semipalmated Plover (right) in a confrontation near Cape May, New Jersey. *Photo by Scott Elowitz*

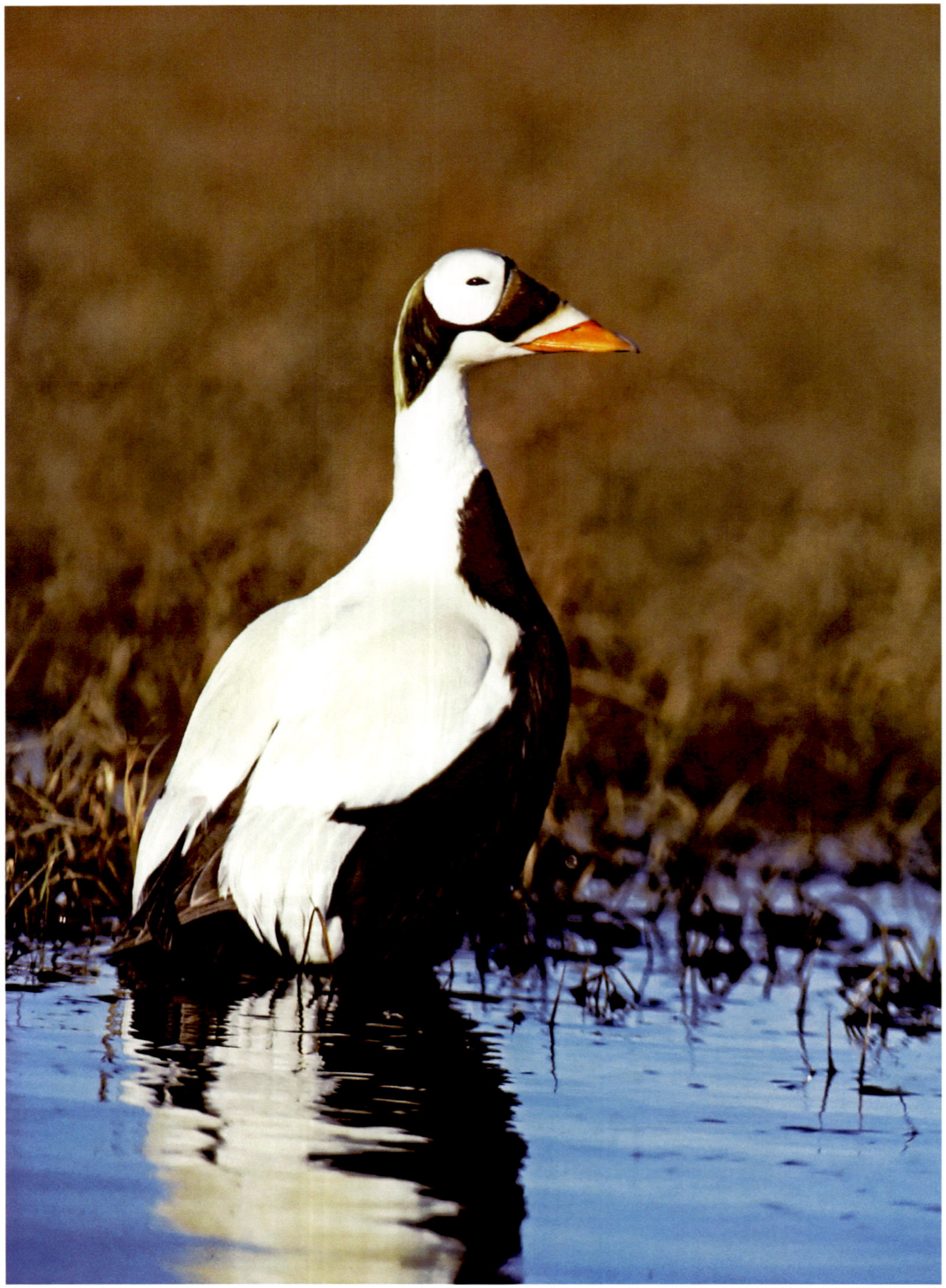

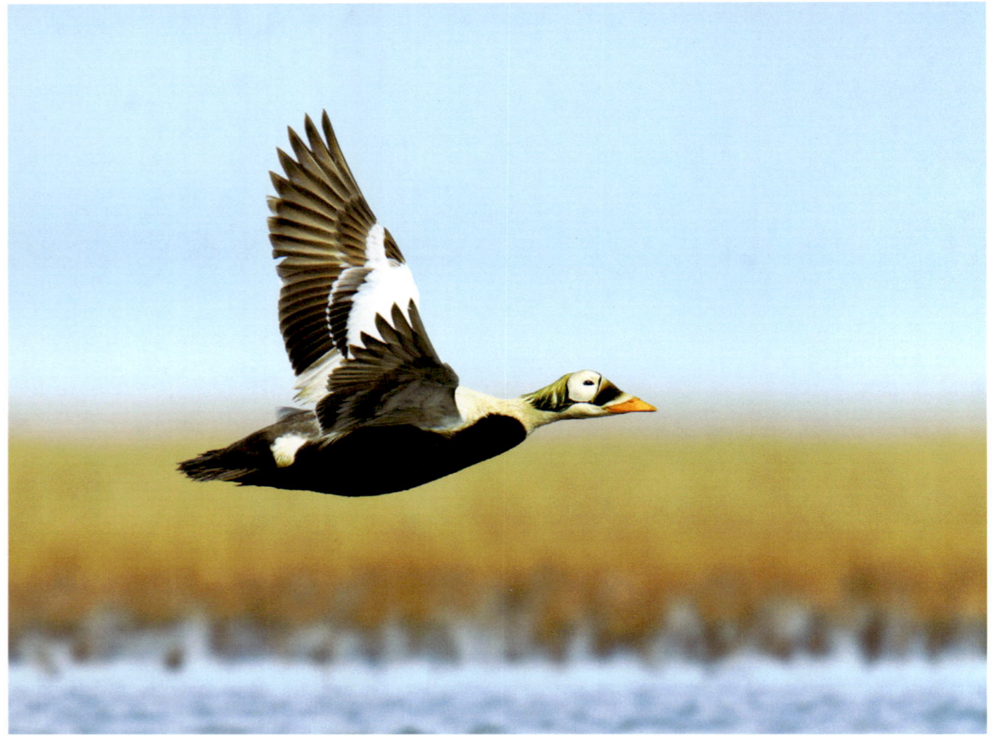

Spectacled Eiders are one of the hardest birds in the world to see because they spend their entire lives in the cold waters adjacent to Arctic regions of Alaska and Siberia. This unusual diving duck is shown here on its Arctic breeding grounds on the North Slope of Alaska, where most of the world's population is found. Males, or drakes, have this odd plumage, while females are a muted brown overall. *Photos by Kevin T. Karlson (left) and Scott Elowitz (right)*

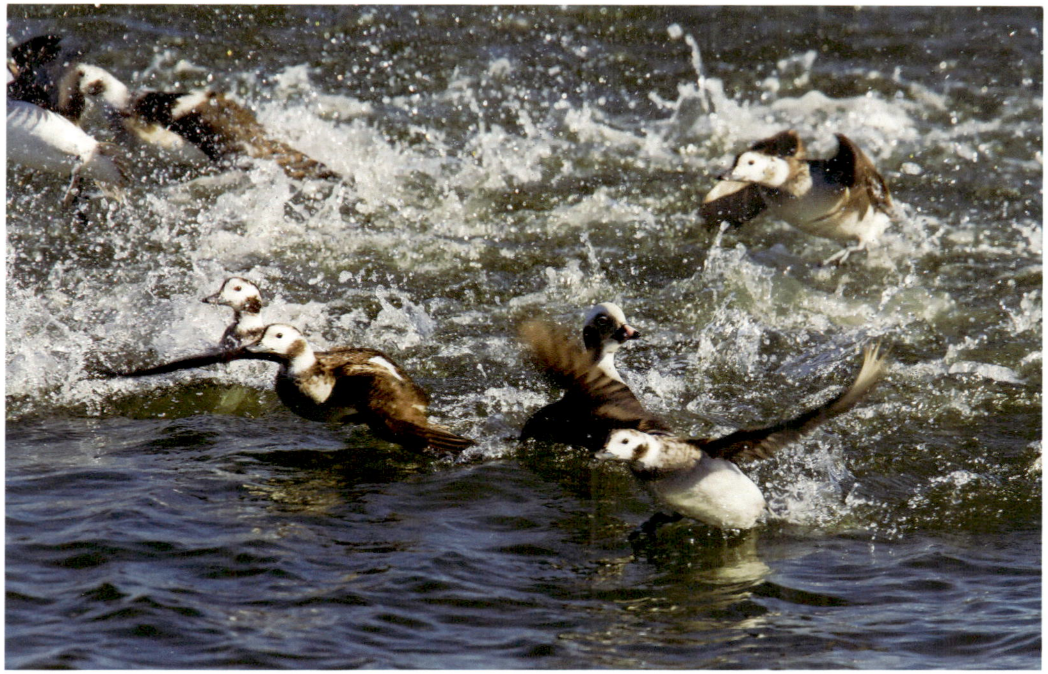

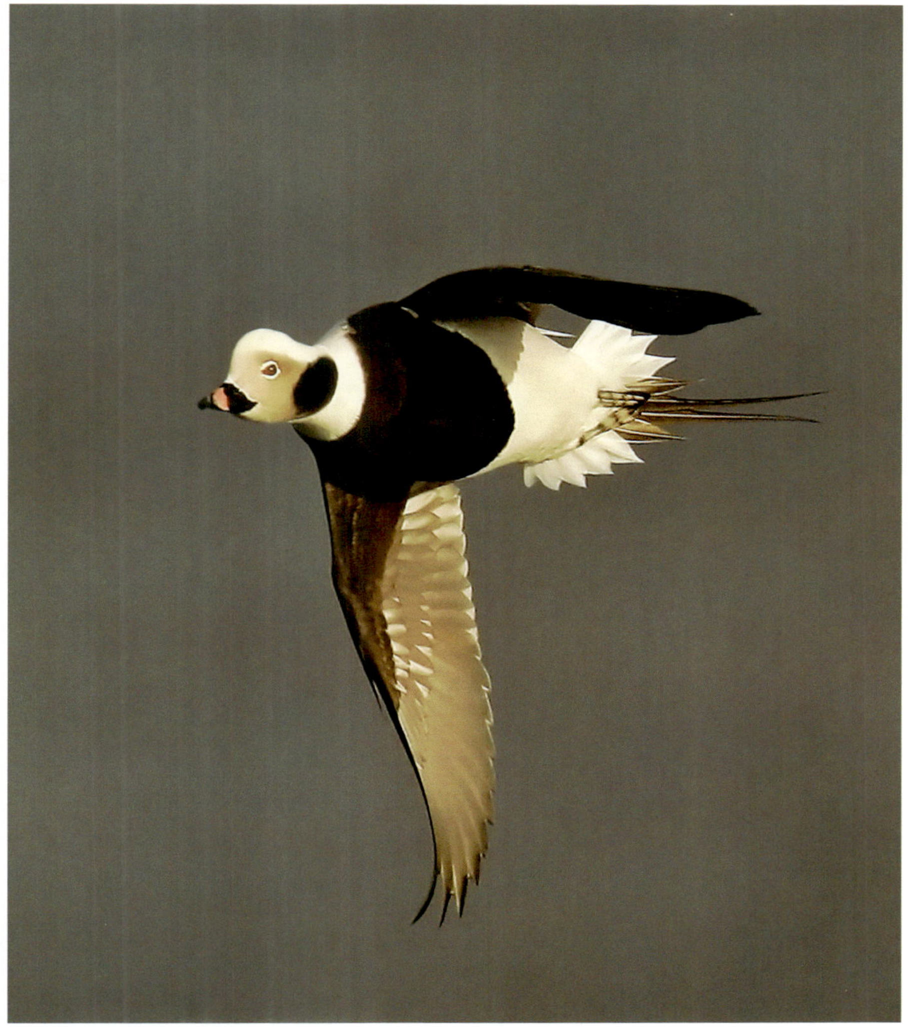

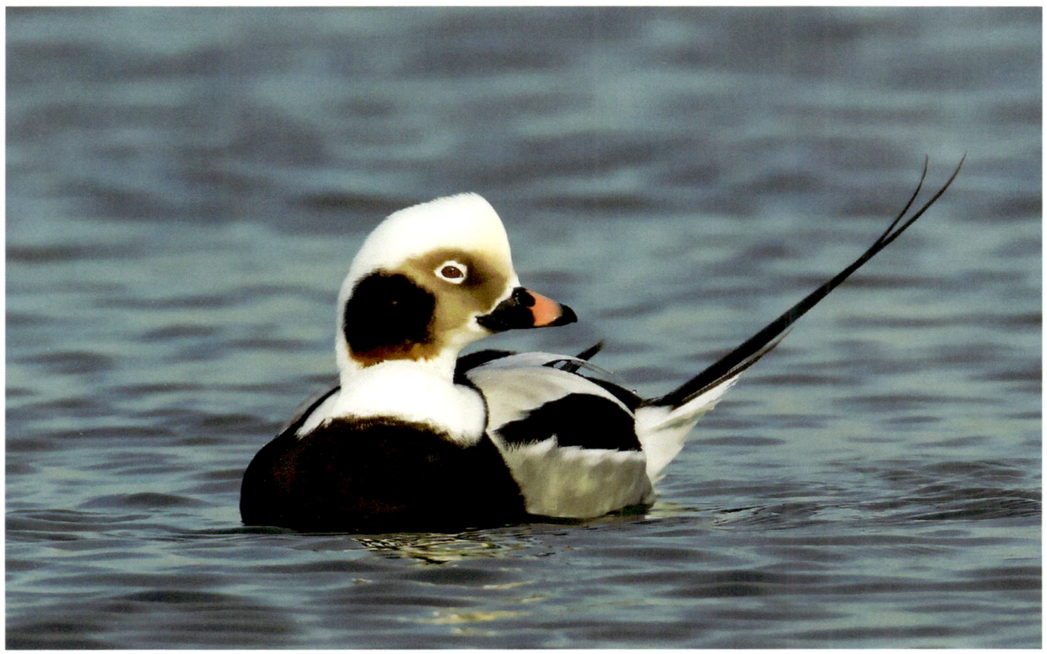

Long-tailed Ducks are small, Arctic-breeding ducks that spend the winter in Atlantic and Pacific coastal waters. Males have a striking black and white plumage pattern with soft, pastel-like shading to the face in non-breeding birds like these. Females are duller with muted patterning (upper left). *Photos by Lloyd Spitalnik (upper and lower left) and Kevin T. Karlson (right)*

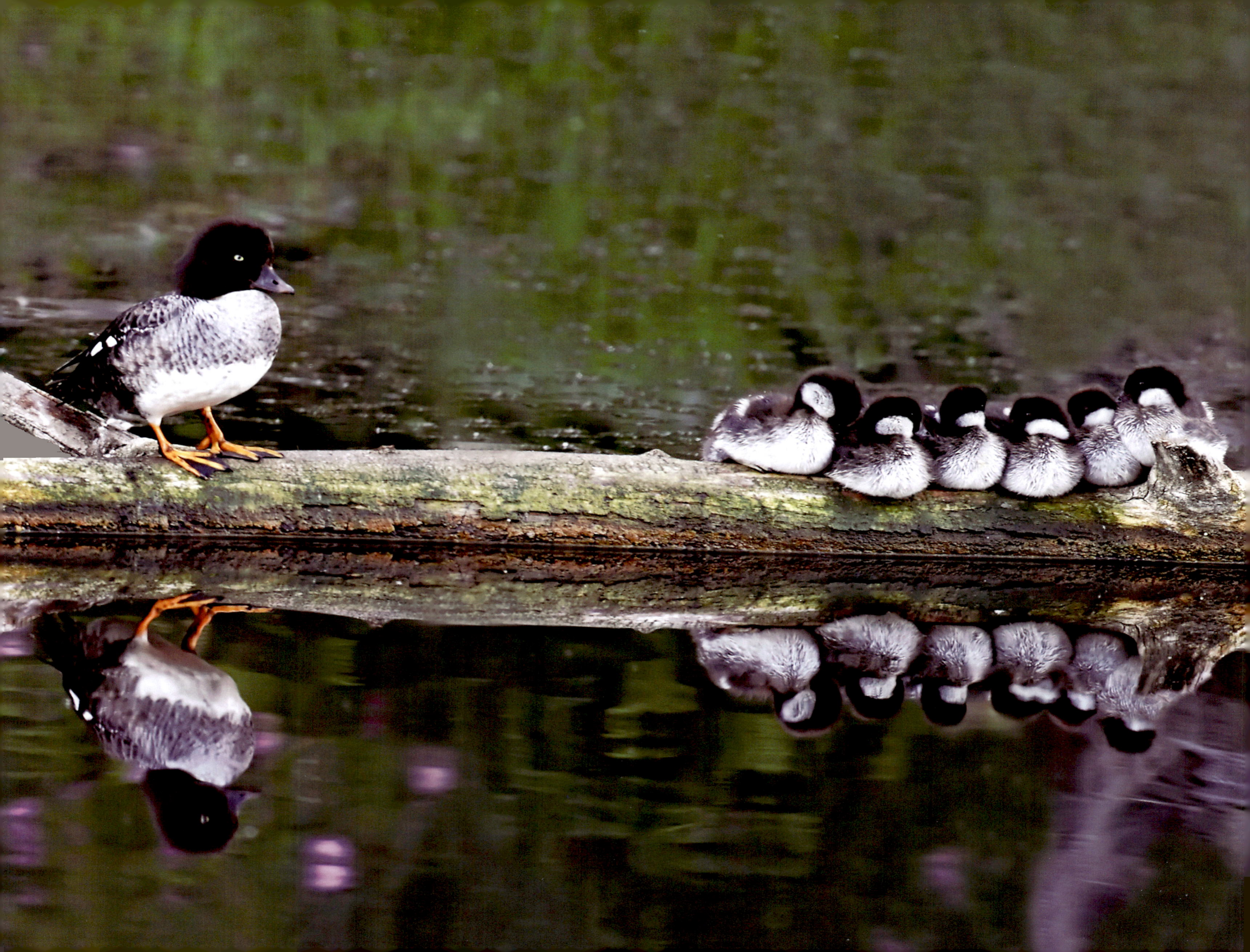

Opposite: A female, or hen, Barrow's Goldeneye puts her brood to bed on a small log in a quiet pool in British Columbia. Kevin rode by this small pond every day at dusk for a week in late June, and watched this scene repeated each night, but this lineup is one of a kind. *Photo by Kevin T. Karlson*

Drake Northern Pintails (right) are stunning ducks, and this flight shot captures their grace and style. *Photo by Scott Elowitz*

A drake American Wigeon (below) performs a wing flap. *Photo by Scott Elowitz*

Two Northern Pintails and a drake Northern Shoveler (lower right) create a tranquil scene in this frozen New Jersey creek. *Photo by Kevin T. Karlson*

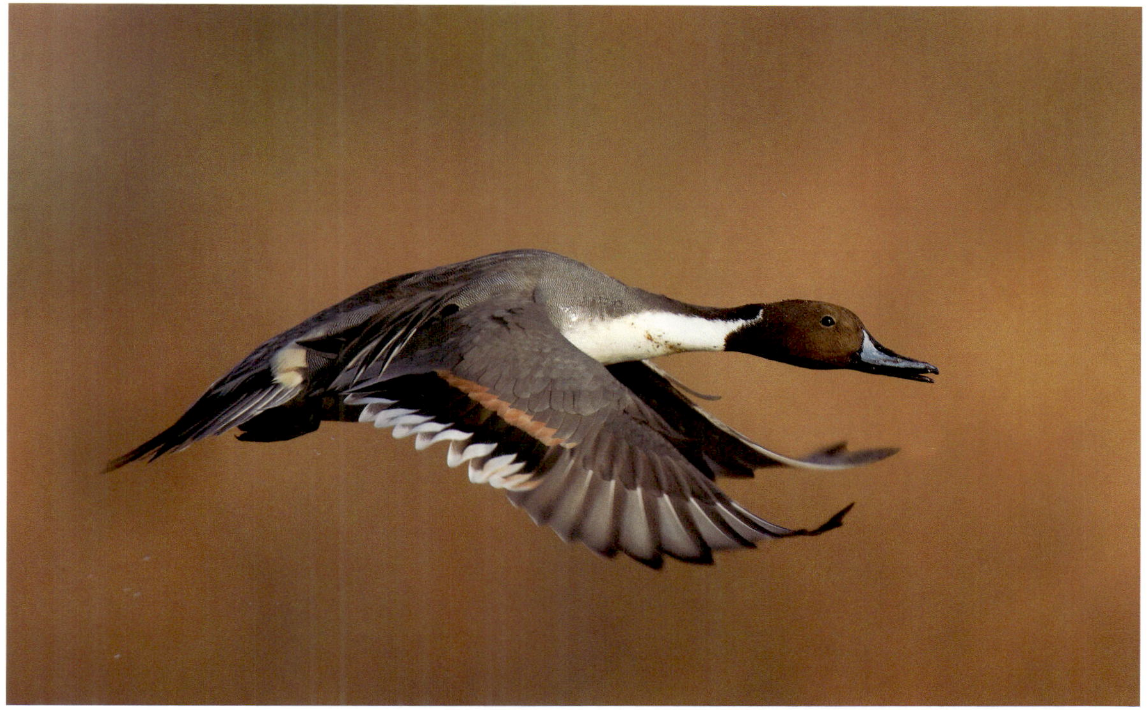

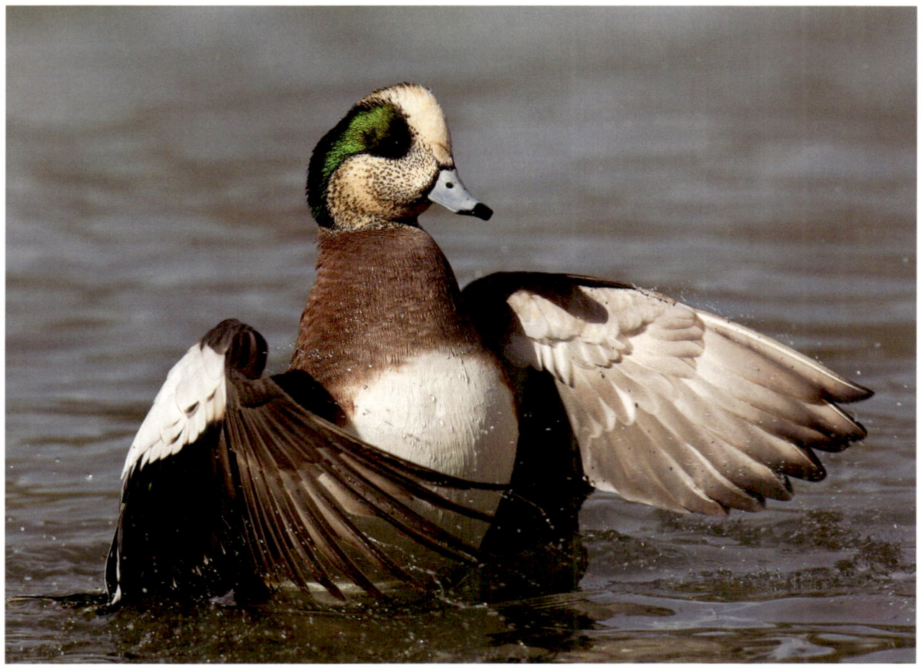

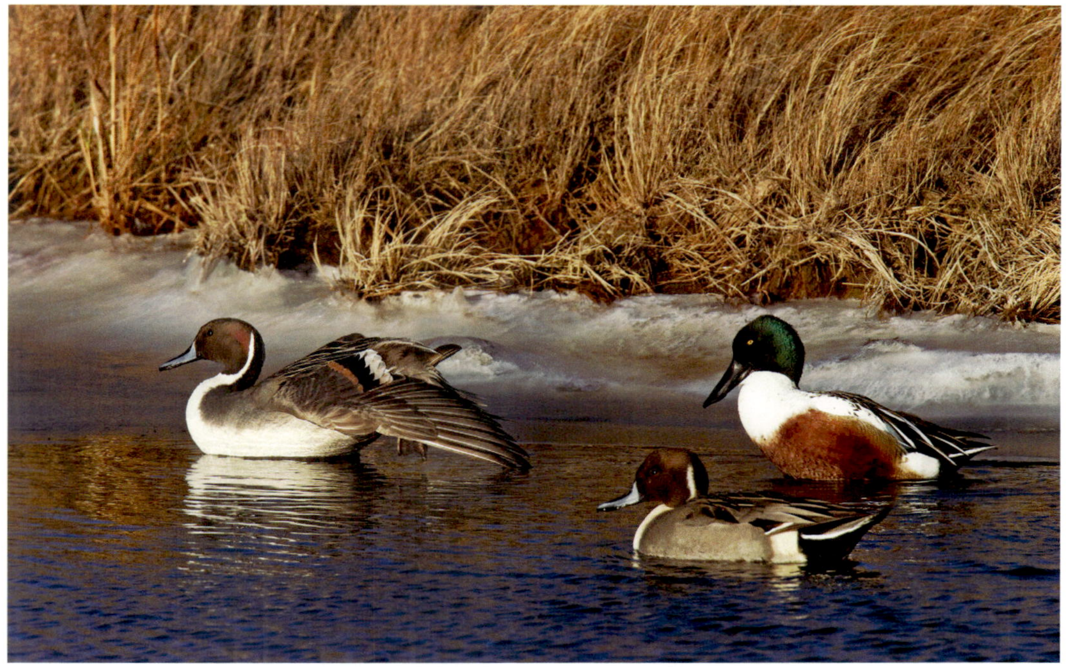

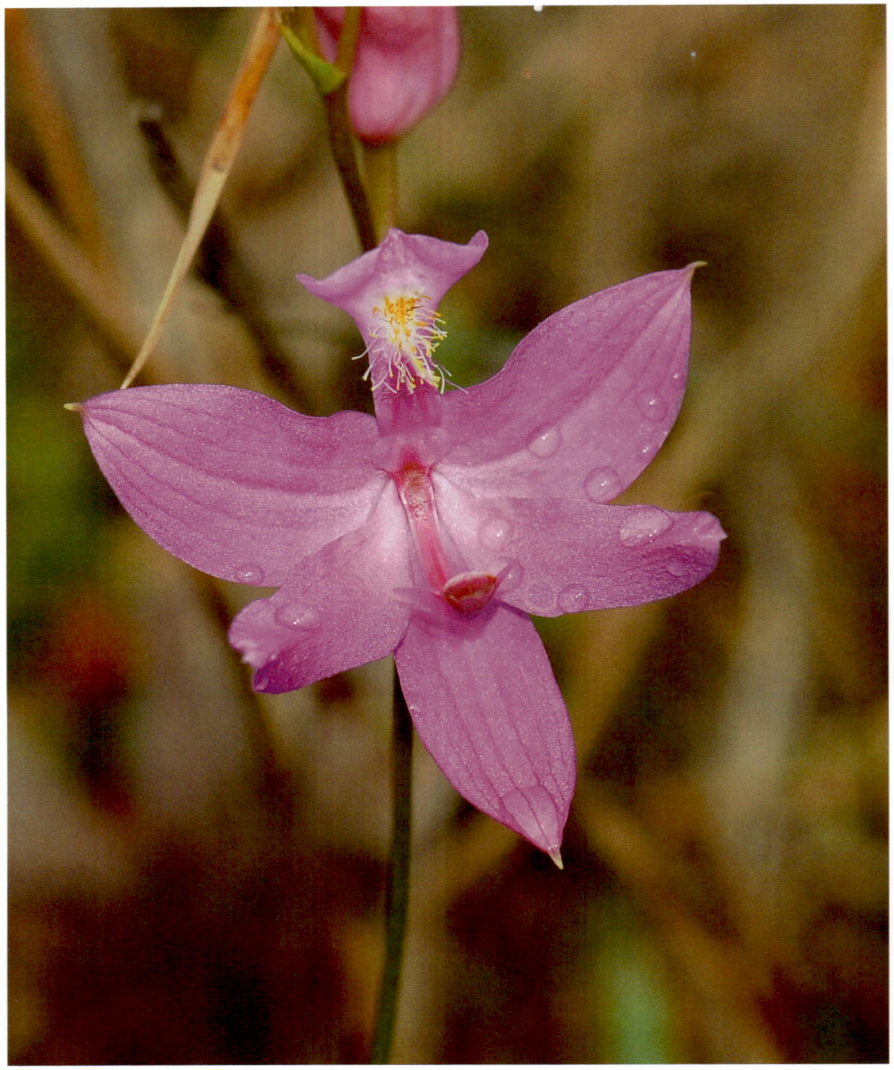

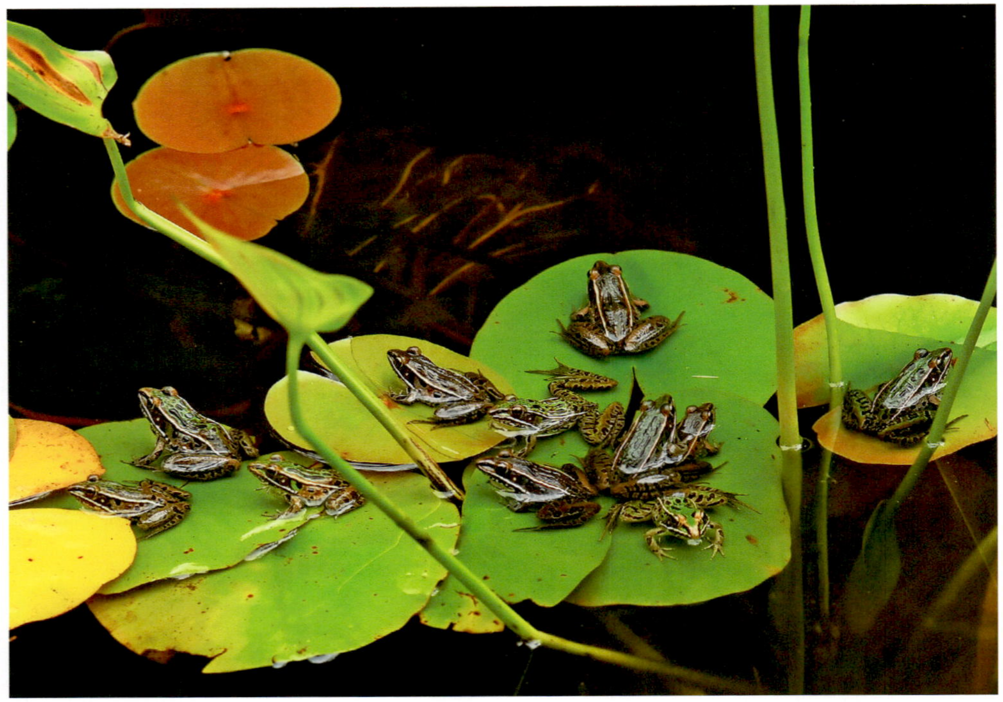

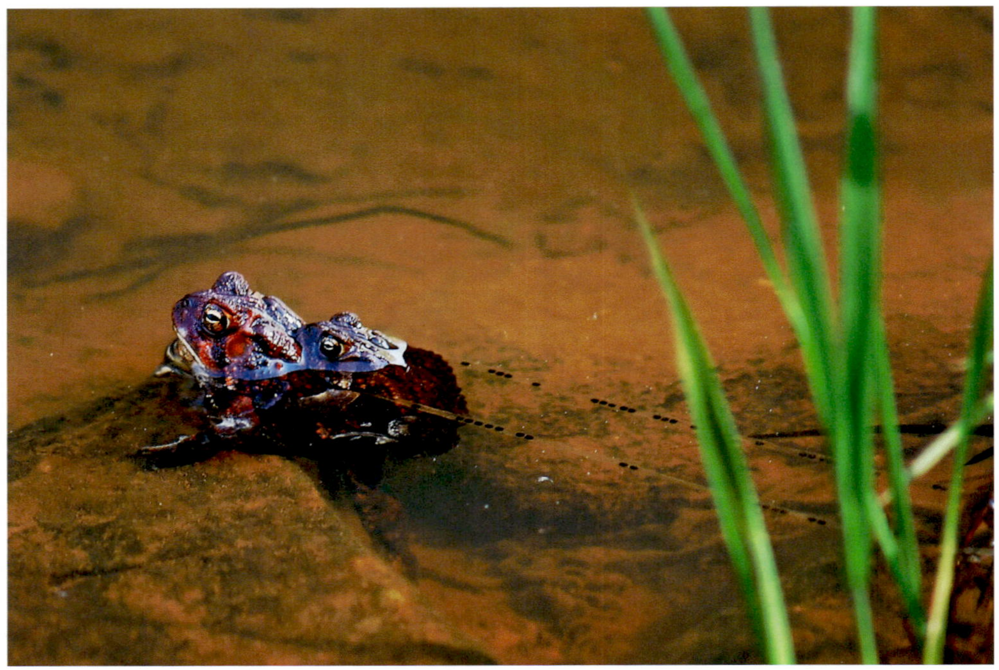

The Grass Pink (above) is a small orchid that occurs in wet bogs.

"Create it and they will come" — eleven of the 83 Leopard Frogs drawn to Pat Sutton's wildlife ponds during a summer drought are shown in this photo from Goshen, New Jersey (upper right).

In Maryland, Pat captured this image of "American Toads in love," trailing their now-fertile eggs (lower right). *Photos by Pat Sutton*

Opposite: "Sunset at Strawberry Avenue" is a fitting title for this soft, pastel-like photo taken in December in southern New Jersey. *Photo by Pat Sutton*

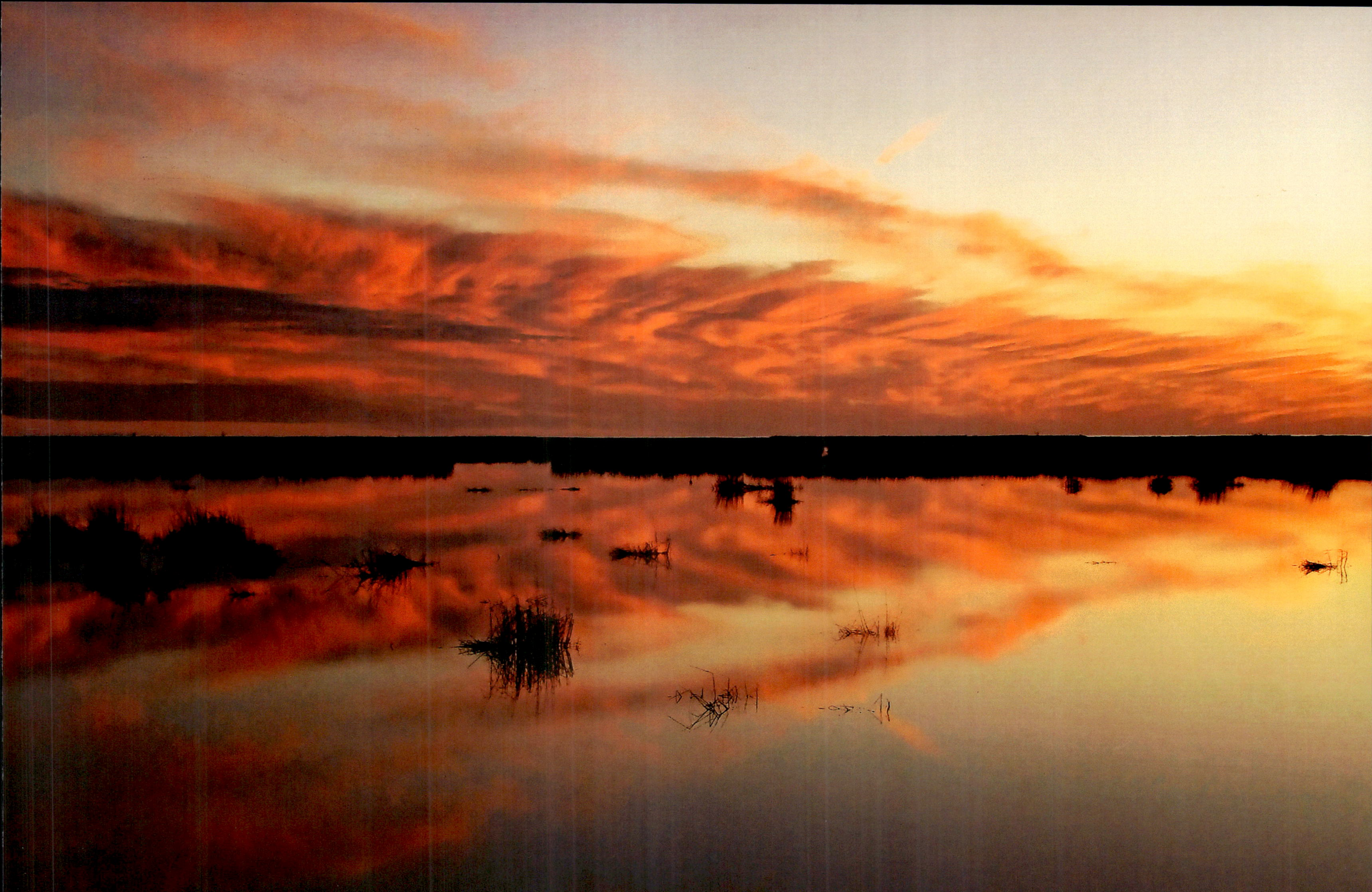

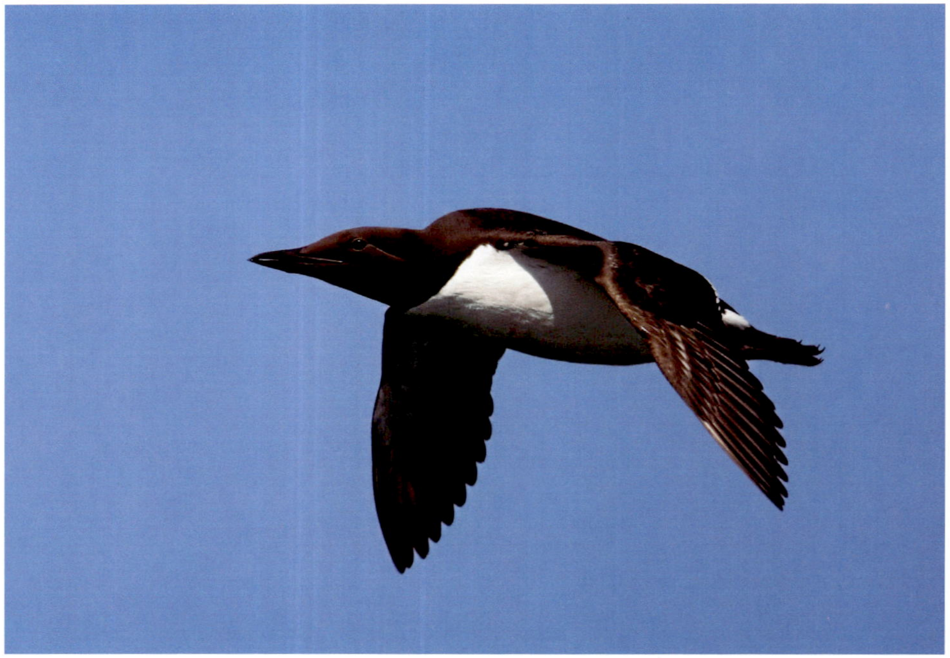

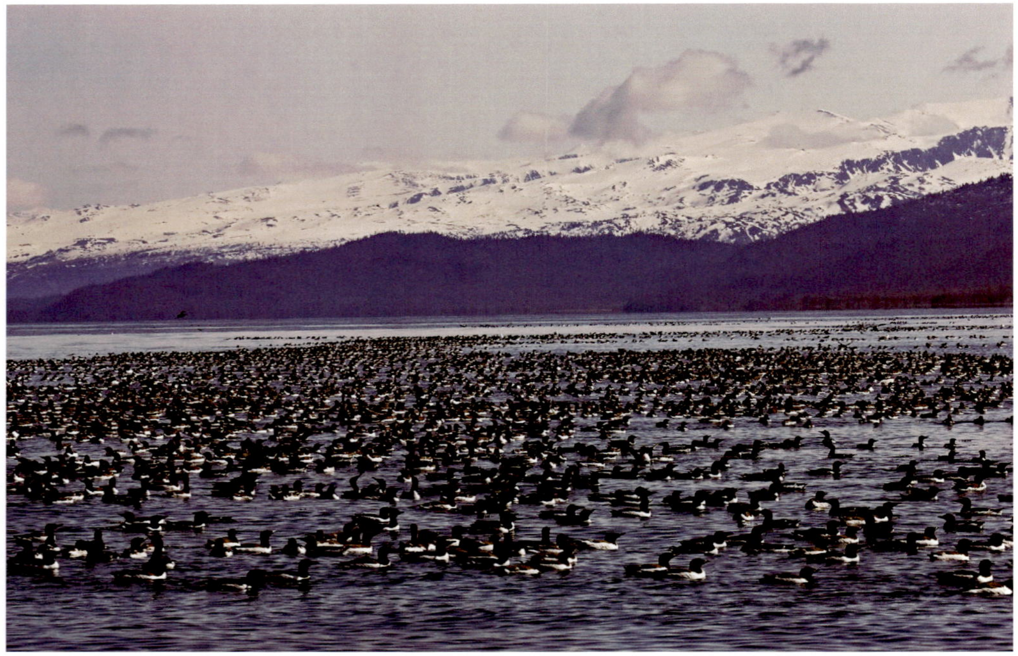

Common Murres (above) are alcids that nest in huge colonies in Alaska. Common Murres stretch to the horizon near their breeding colony in Homer, Alaska (upper right) *Photos by Kevin T. Karlson*

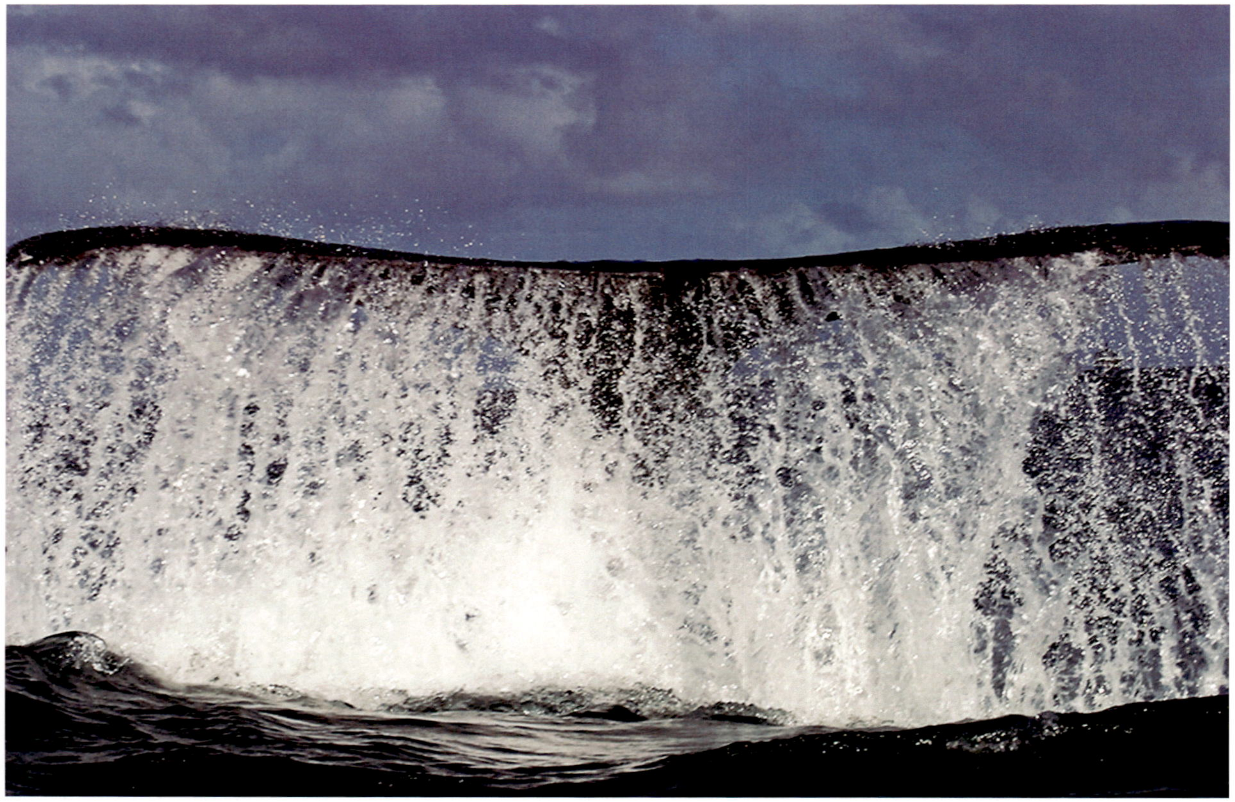

A Humpback Whale's tail leaves the water as it prepares to execute a deep dive. *Photo by Scott Elowitz*

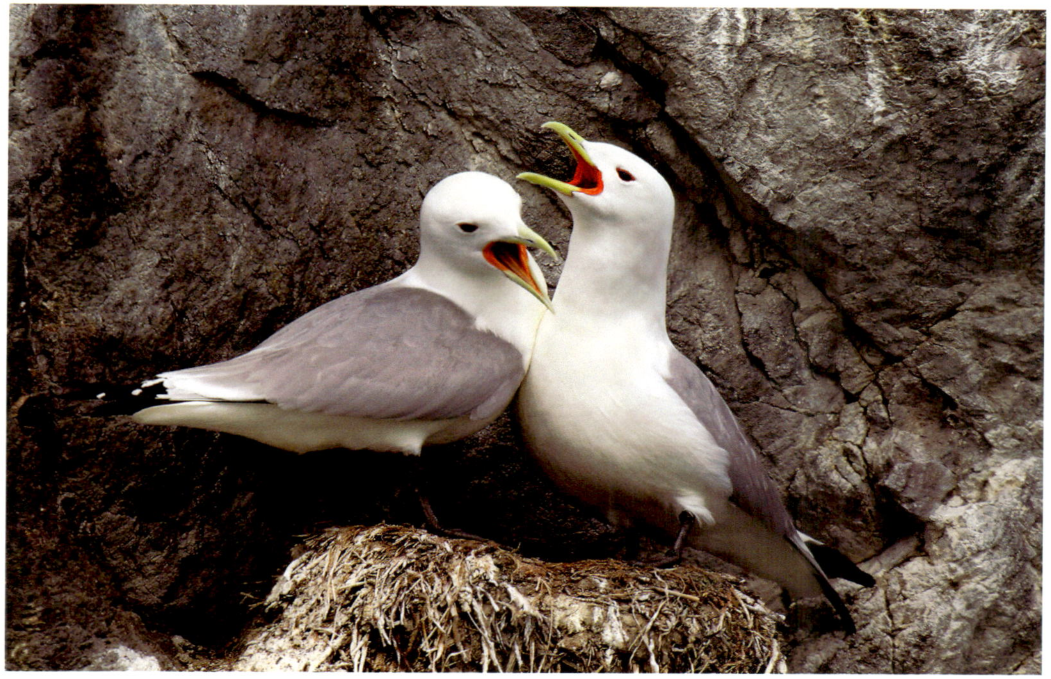

Black-legged Kittiwakes are a small gulls that nest precariously on volcanic stacks in Alaska. At left, a mated pair discusses the finer points of nesting on cliff faces, while a successful fisherman lifts his prize from the water's surface (lower left). A nest colony is a dramatic sight near Cordova, Alaska (below). *Photos by Kevin T. Karlson*

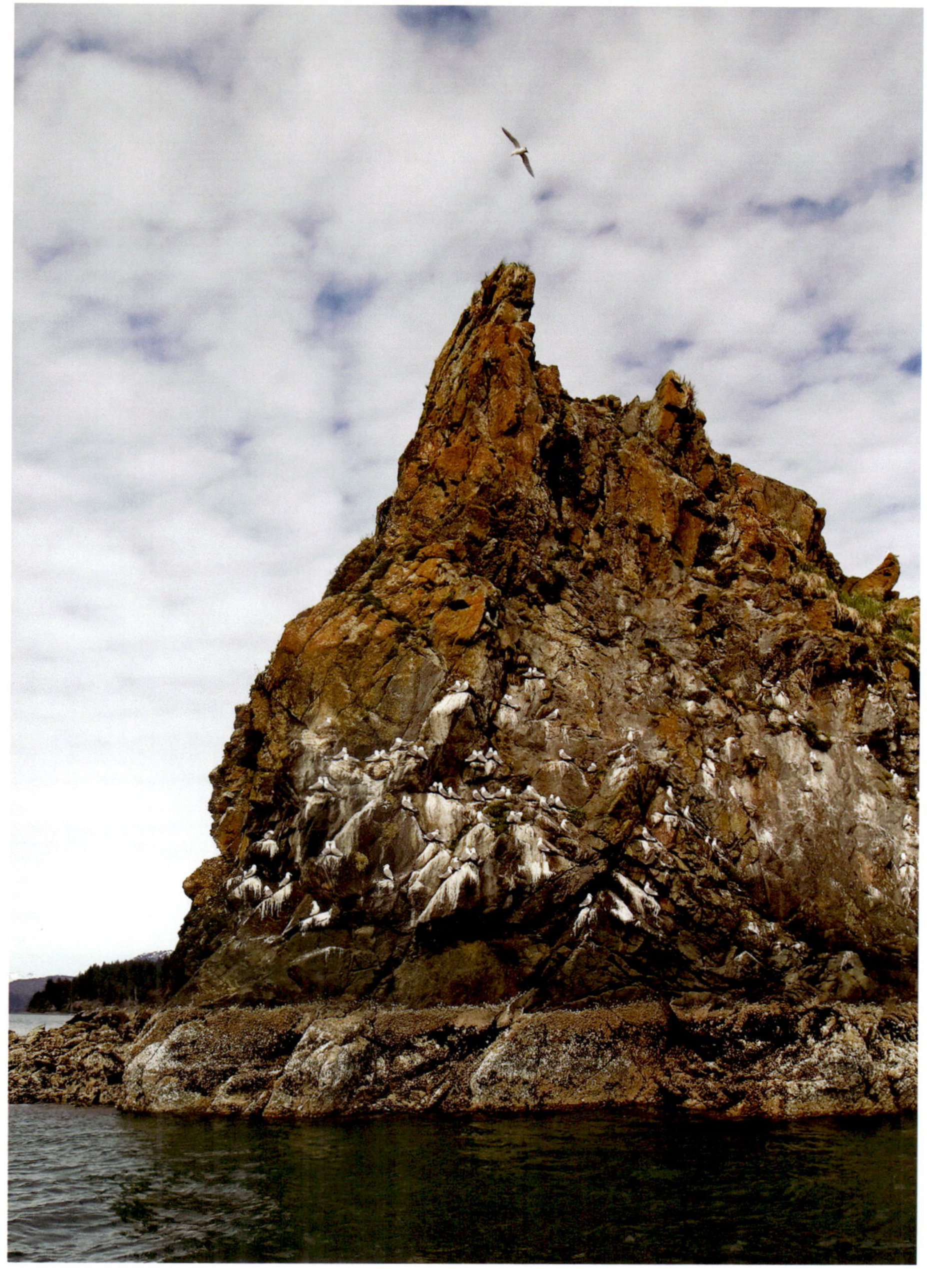

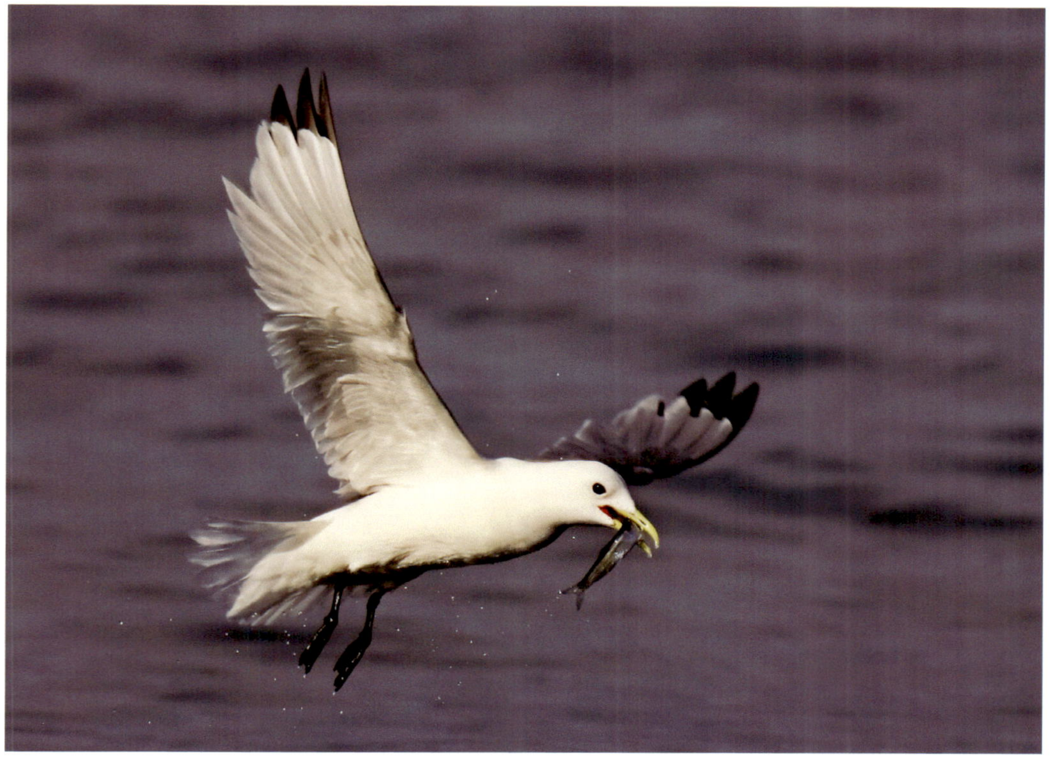

Opposite: Kaaterskill Falls is the highest two-tiered falls in New York state, and this image shows the merging of water and ice. Cold water coats the nearby trees with an icy spray. *Photo by Tina Giaimo*

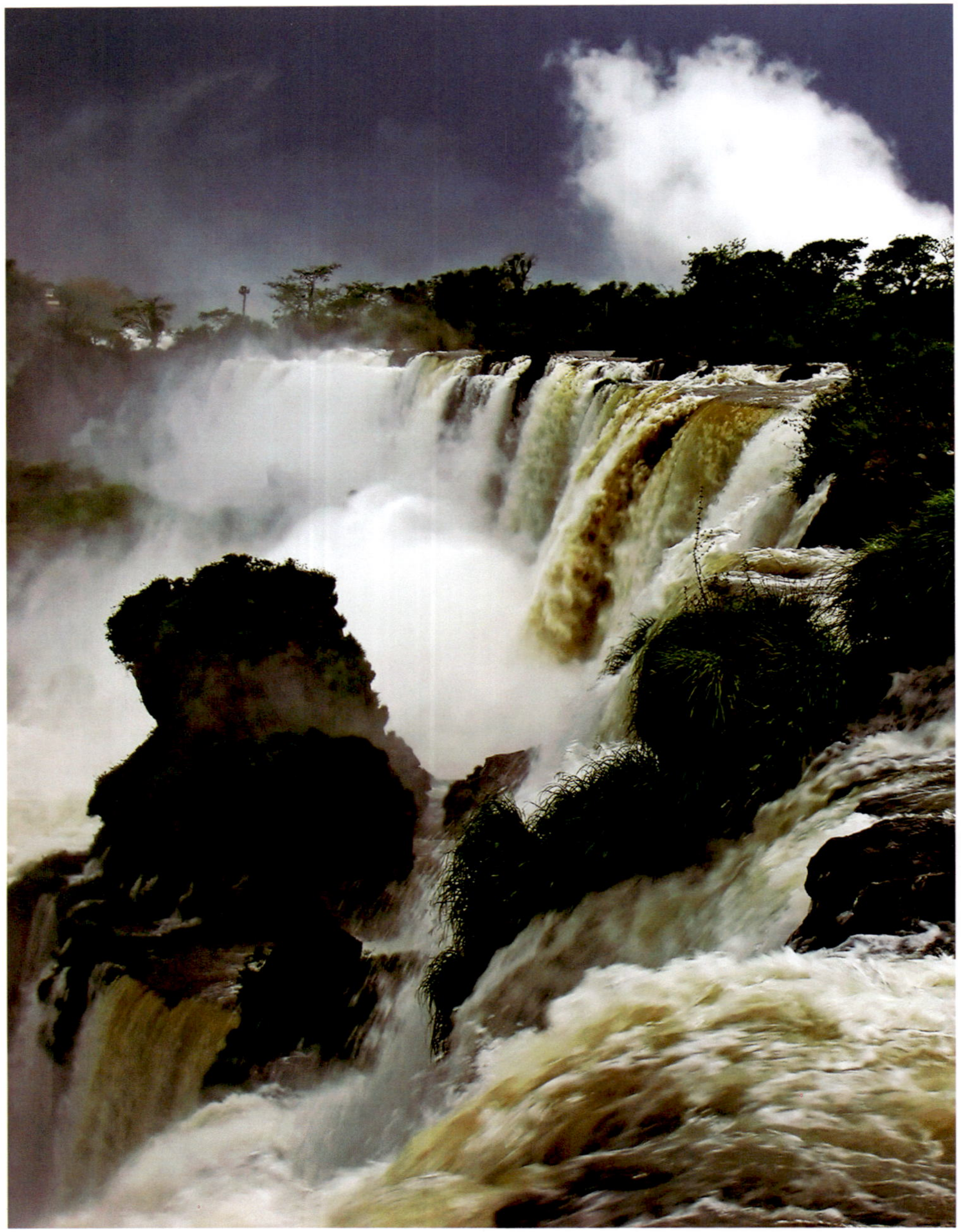

Iguazu Falls on the border of Brazil and Argentina is one of the most spectacular waterfalls in the world and a superb example of the sheer power of nature. *Photo and caption by Mike Crewe*

If there is magic on this planet, it is contained in water.

— Loren Eiseley

The Atlantic Ocean in winter near Avalon, New Jersey, shows wind-driven "whipped cream" waves and foam. *Photo by Pat Sutton*

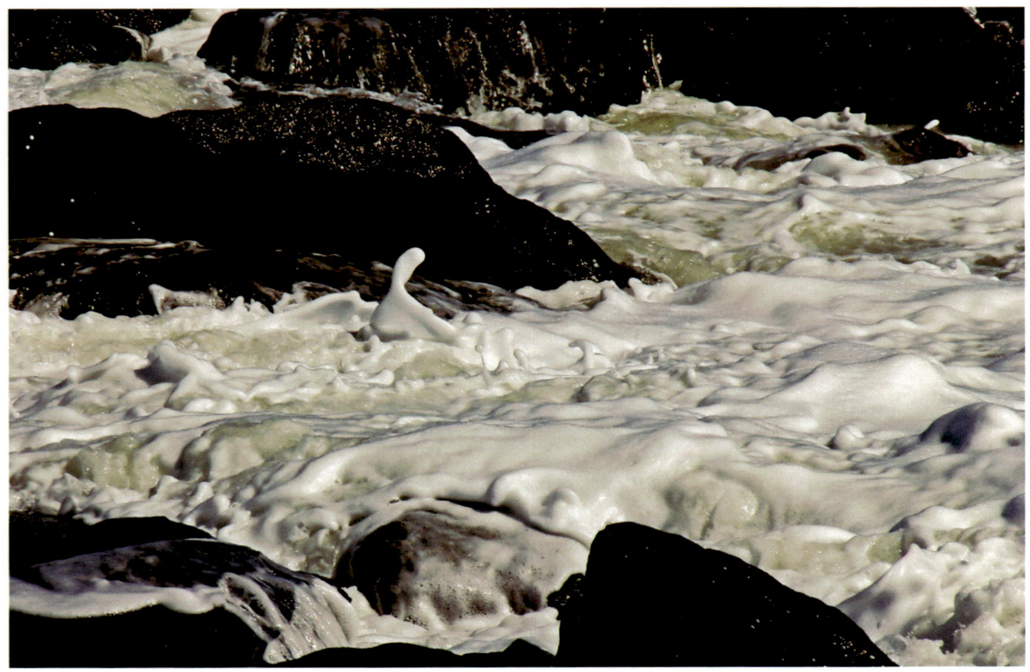

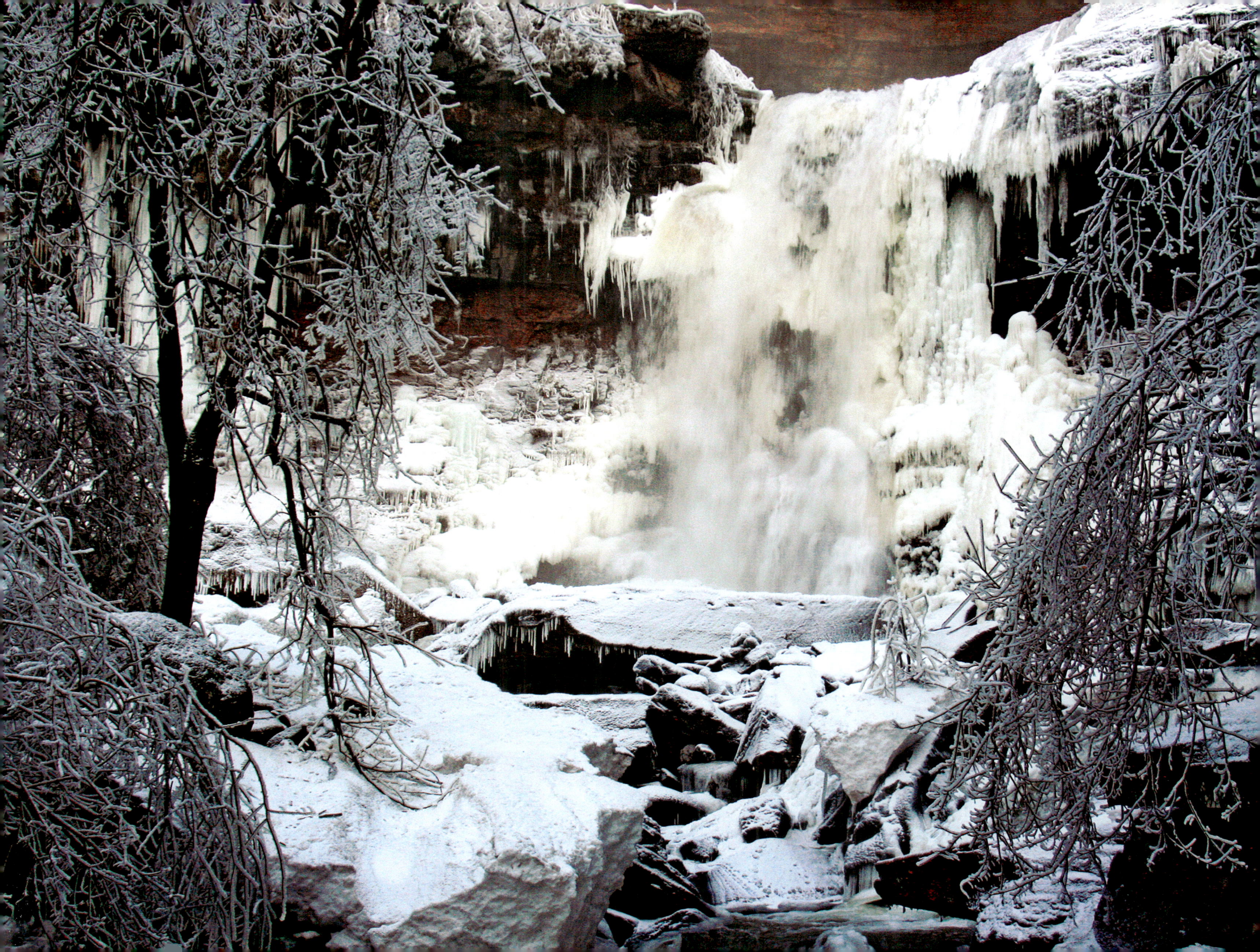

No object is mysterious.
The mystery is your eye.

— Elizabeth Bowen

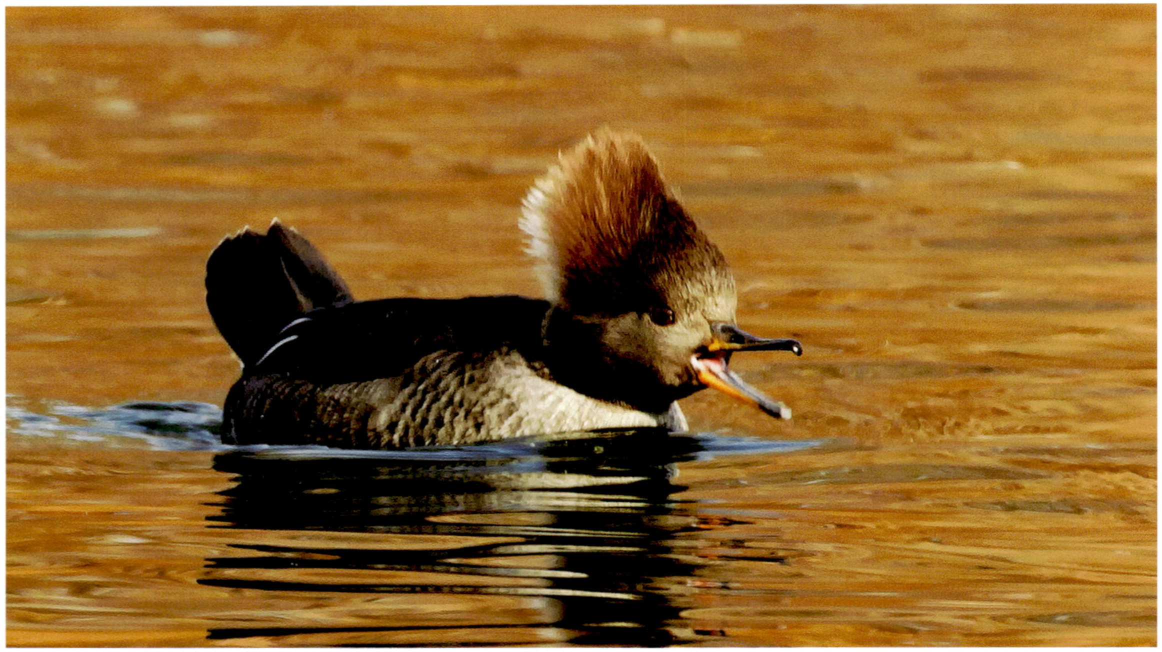

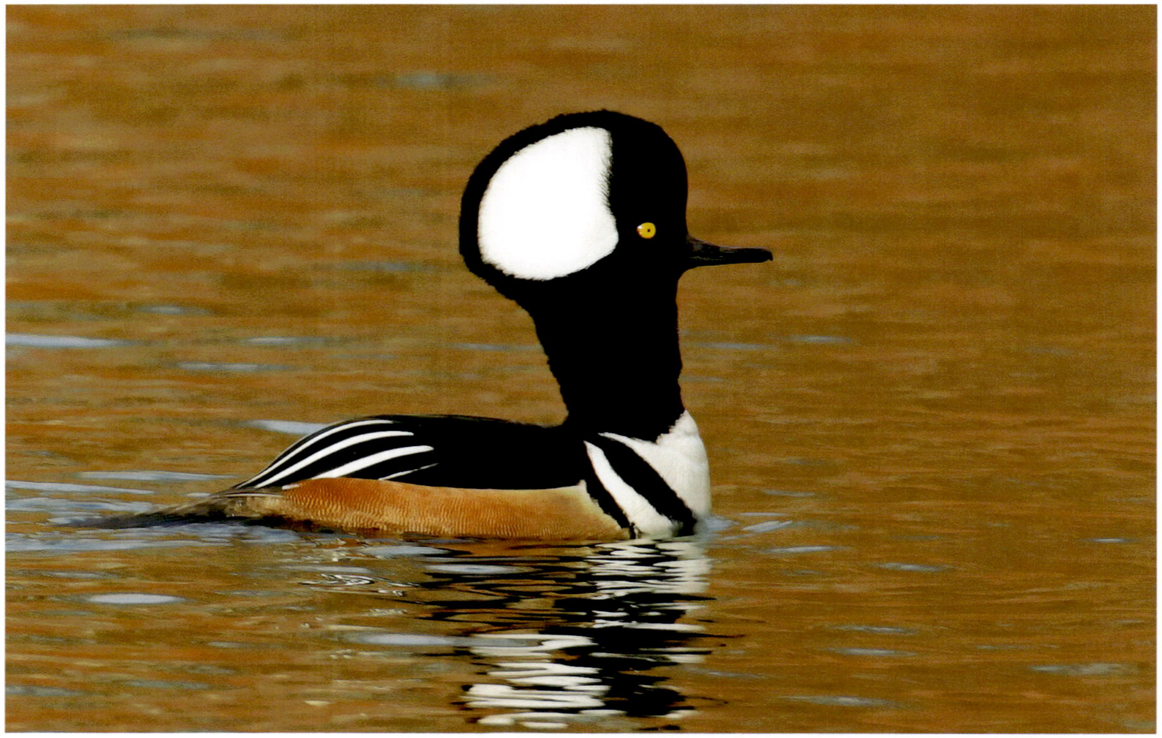

Hooded Mergansers represent some of the most unusual looking ducks in North America. Males show a rich mix of colors and patterns to complement a white head patch that is raised when he is excited or displaying (left).

Females (above) are muted brown in color, but have a similar "bad hair" appearance that spikes when she is excited or disturbed. *Photos by Lloyd Spitalnik*

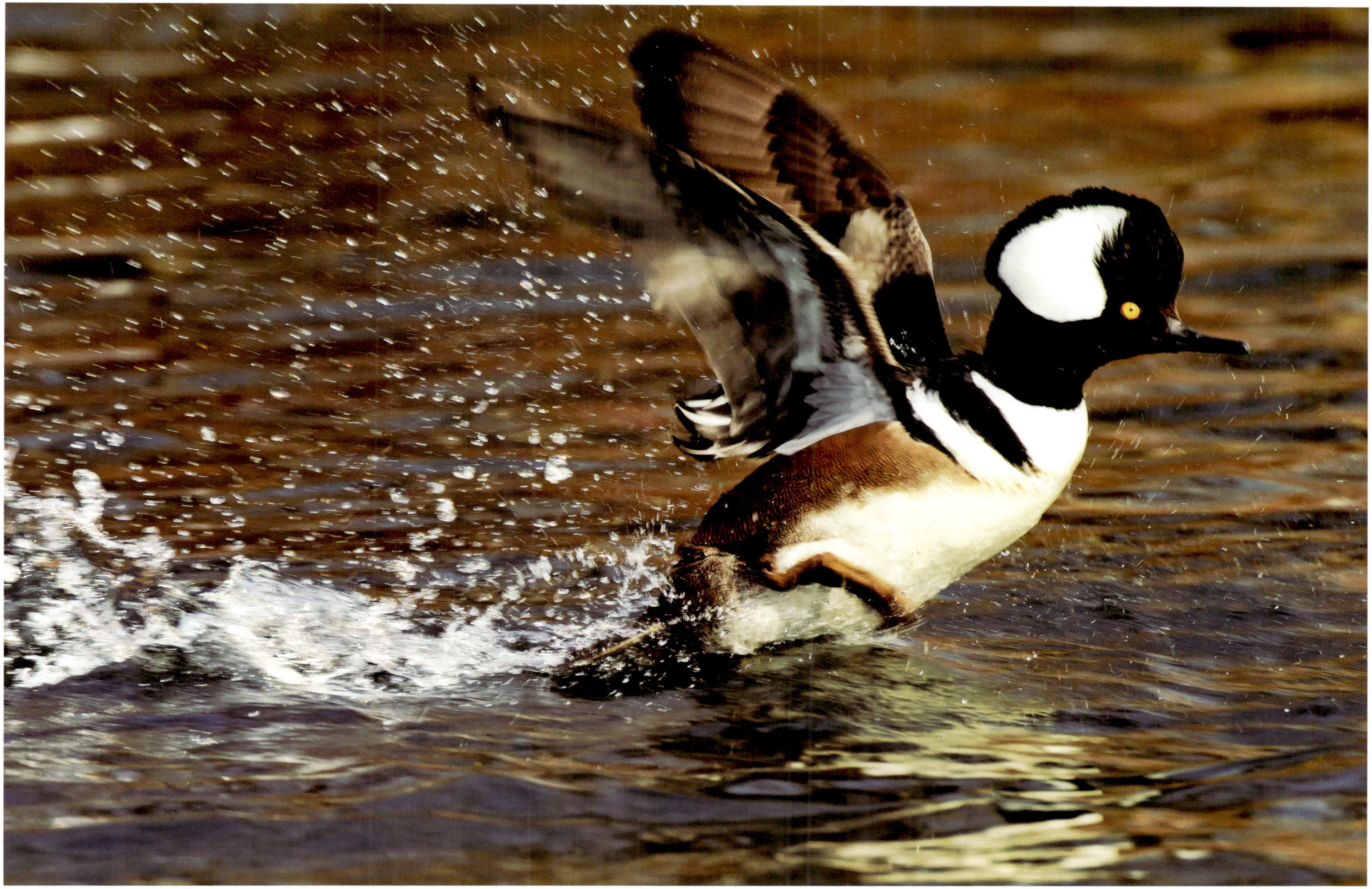

A male Hooded Merganser runs along the water's surface prior to taking flight. *Photo by Lloyd Spitalnik*

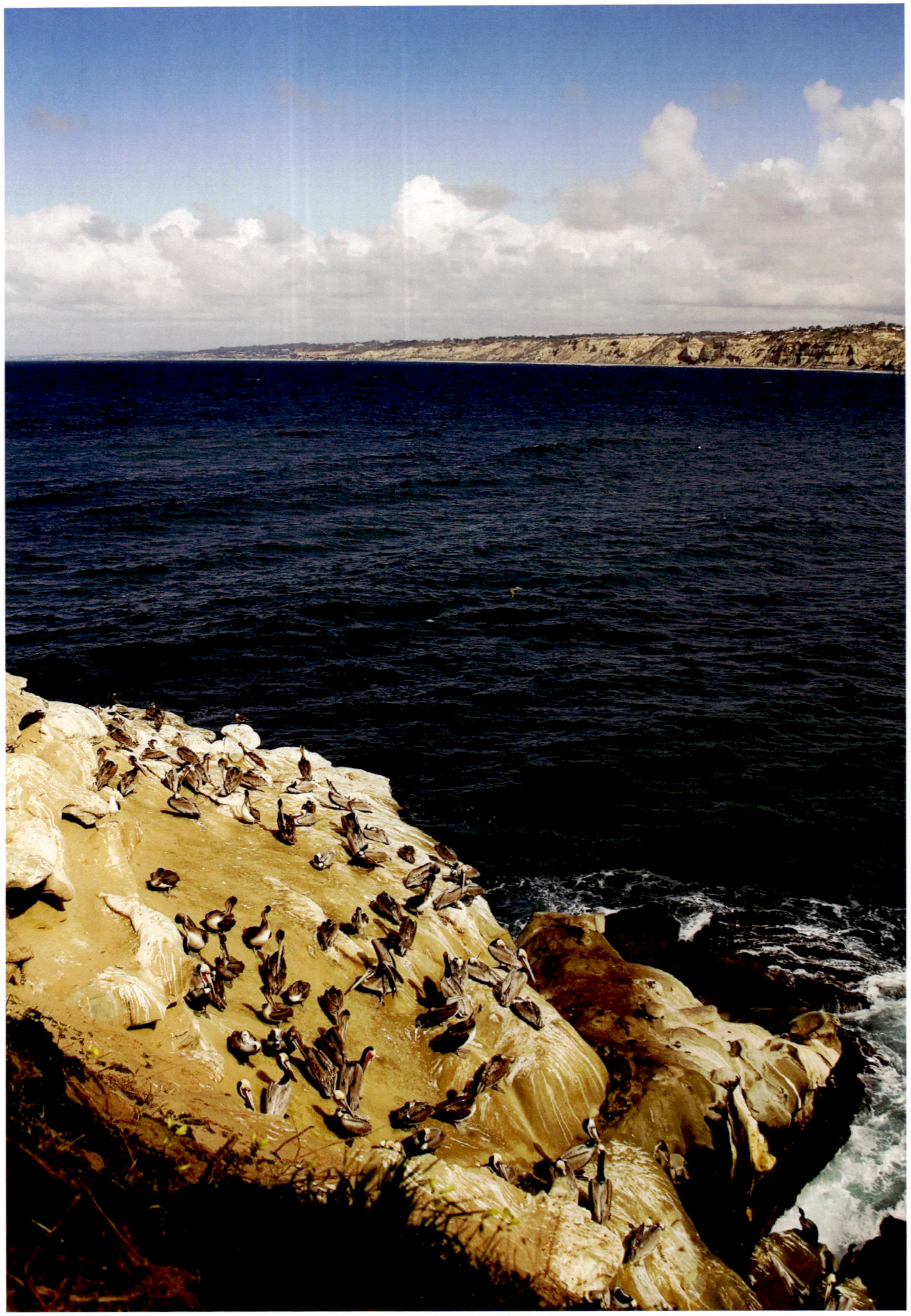

Steep cliffs and rocky ledges at La Jolla, California, make good resting places for Brown Pelicans (left) and California Sea Lions (below). Note how the young pup mimics the aggressive warning posture of his mother as a young bull lion approaches. What a stud! *Photos by Kevin T. Karlson*

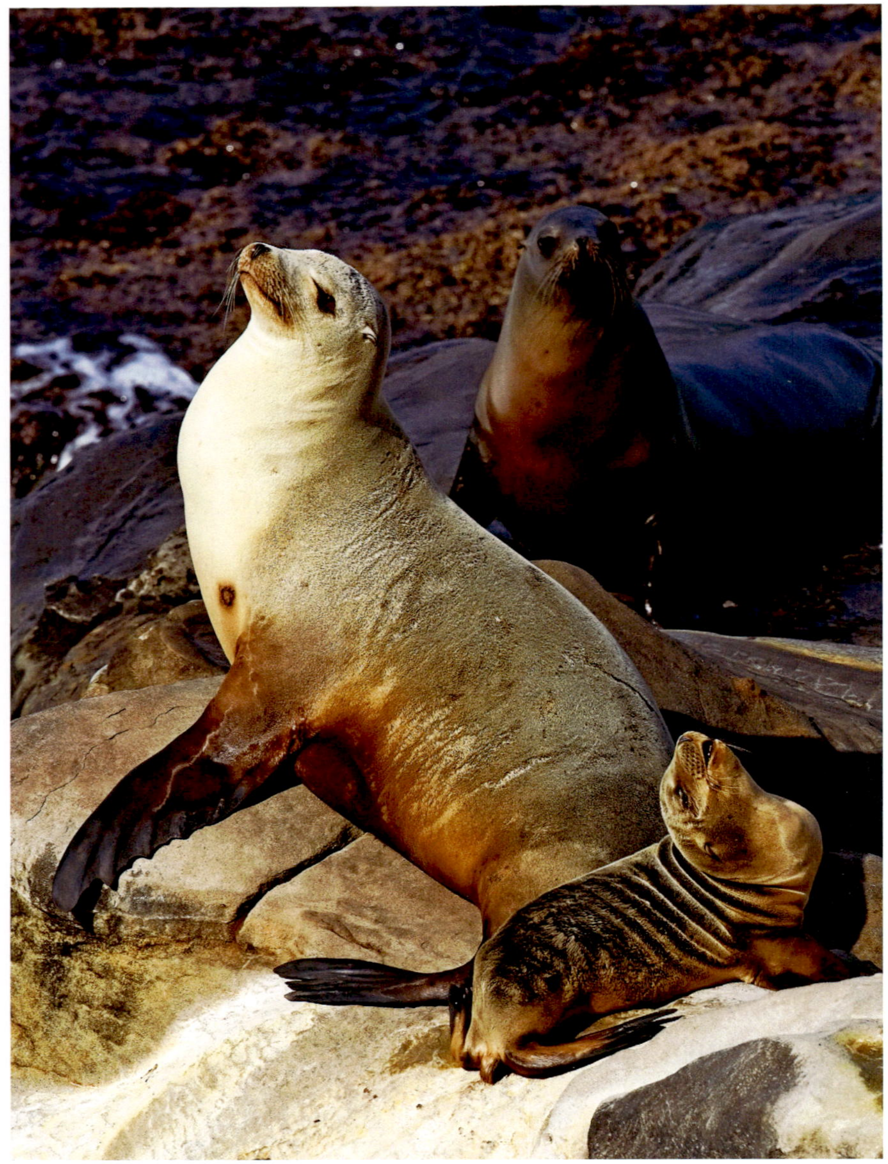

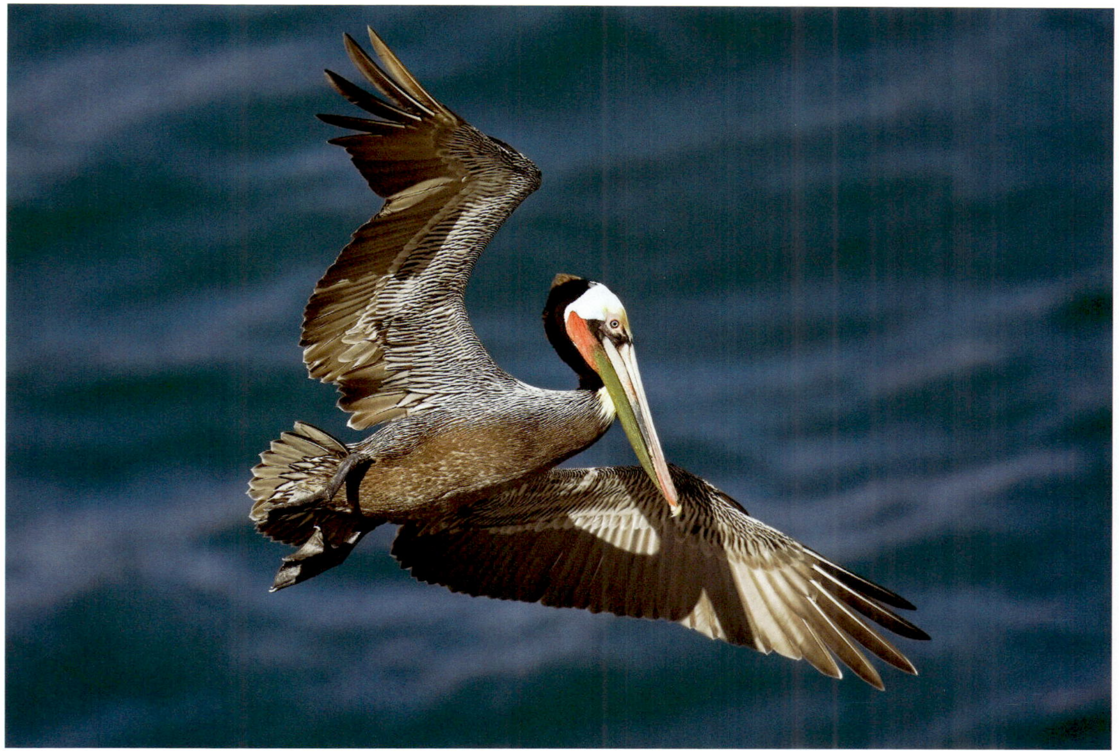

Pacific Brown Pelicans have come back from the precipice of extinction caused by pesticide poisoning, and now enjoy a healthy population in California and other locations. *Photo by Kevin T. Karlson*

This stunning Heermann's Gull nests in Baja California but becomes a common visitor along the Pacific coast after breeding. *Photo by Kevin T. Karlson*

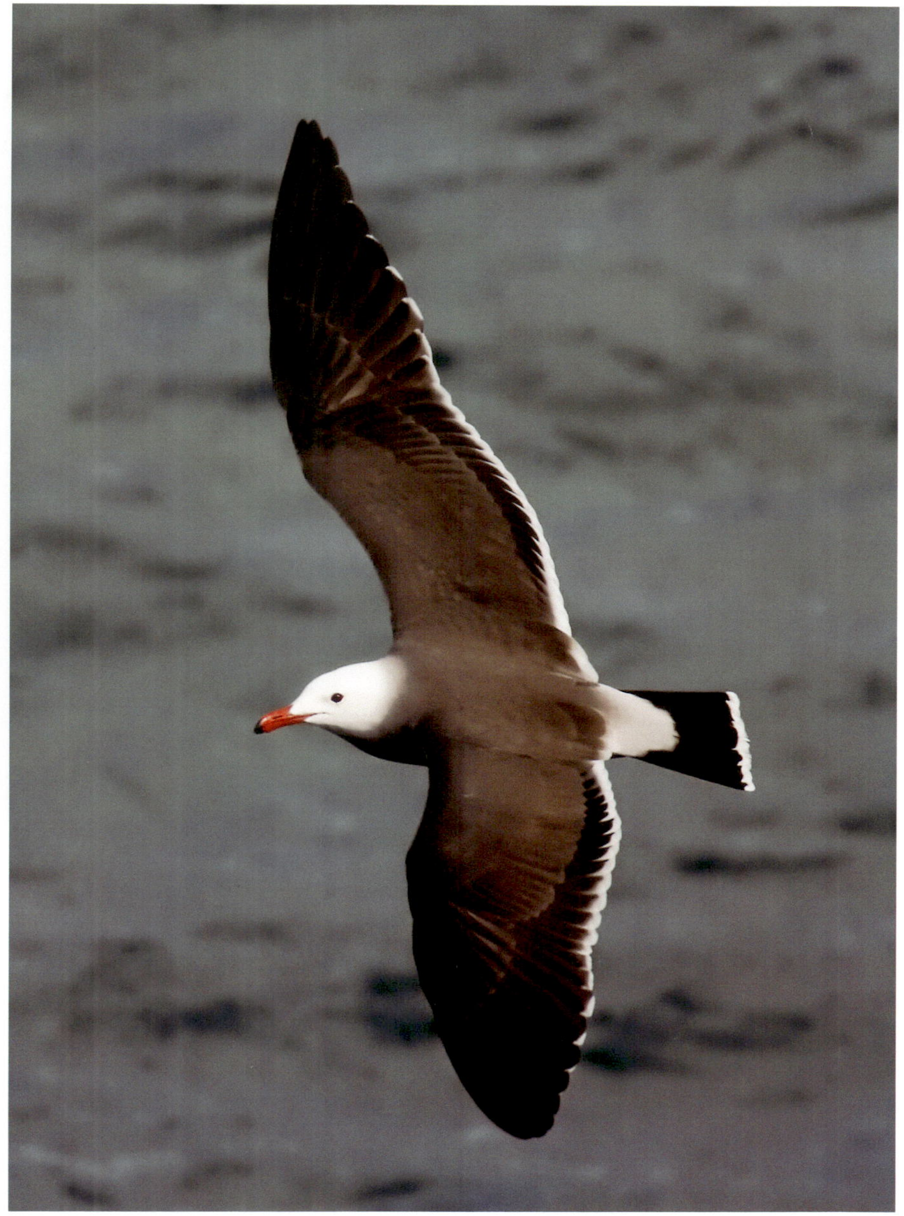

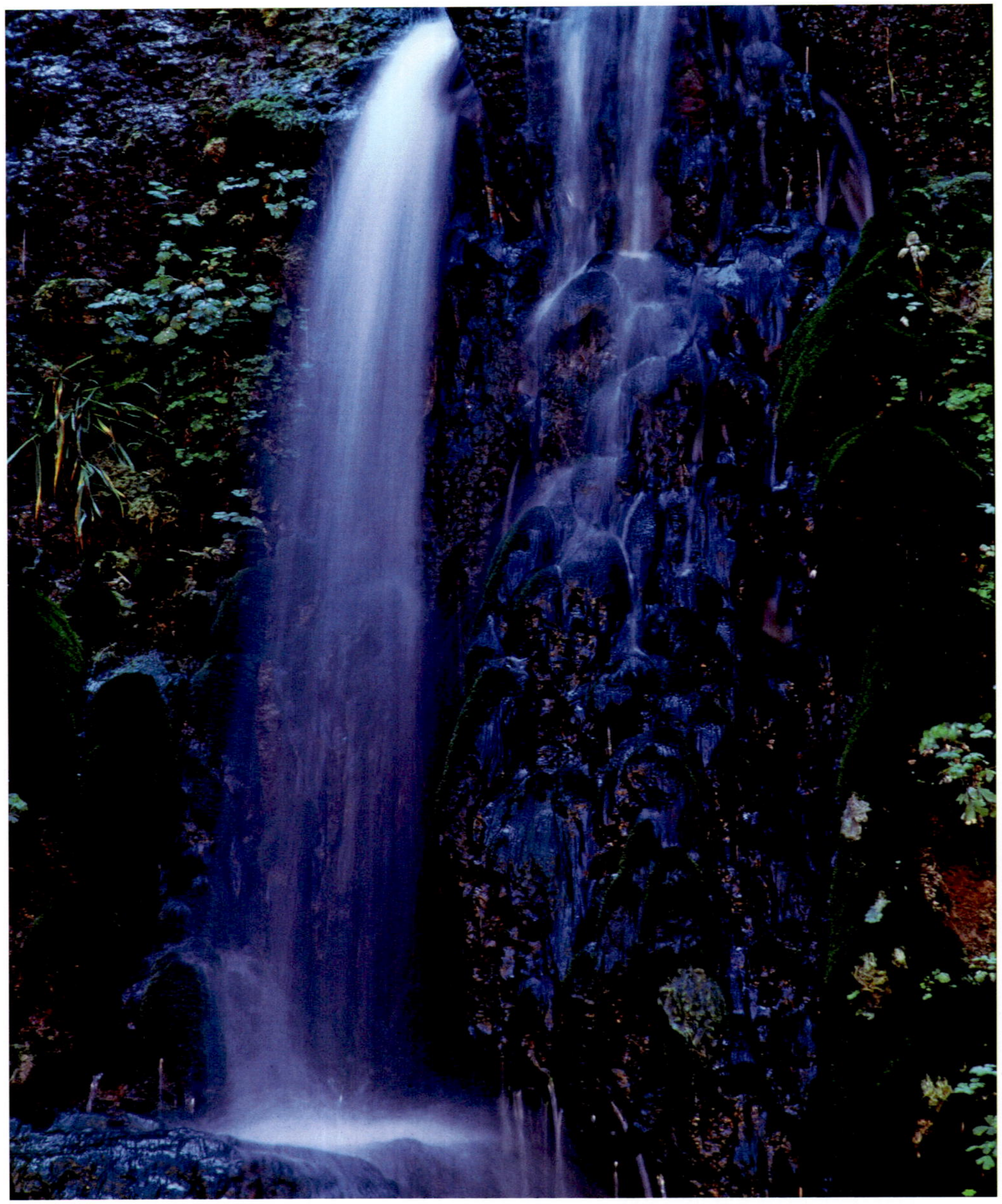

Blue is the mood of this special photo taken with slow exposure at the Hidden Grotto waterfall in Zion National Park in Utah. *Photo by Tina Giaimo*

Tree reflections in a swamp water bayou near Mobile, Alabama, give this image an interesting perspective. *Photo by Don Merwin*

Opposite: Reflections of clouds, sky, and trees give this still water pool a colorful, concentric life of its own. *Photo by Dale Rosselet*

What is seen by the eye is transformed and colored by the vision of the mind.

— Robert Wade

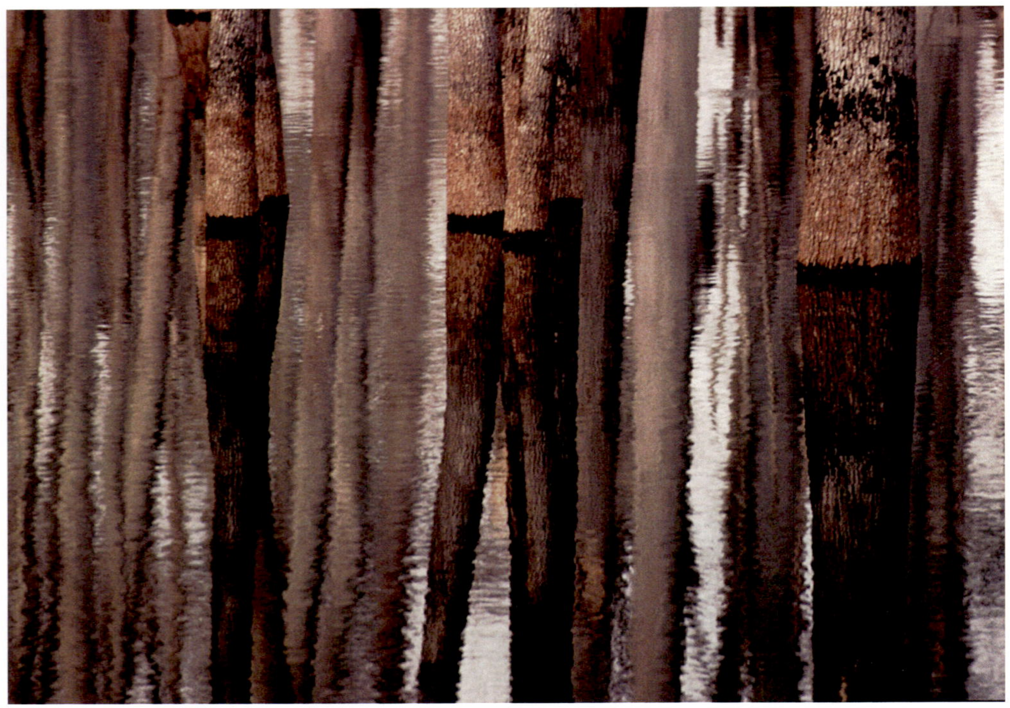

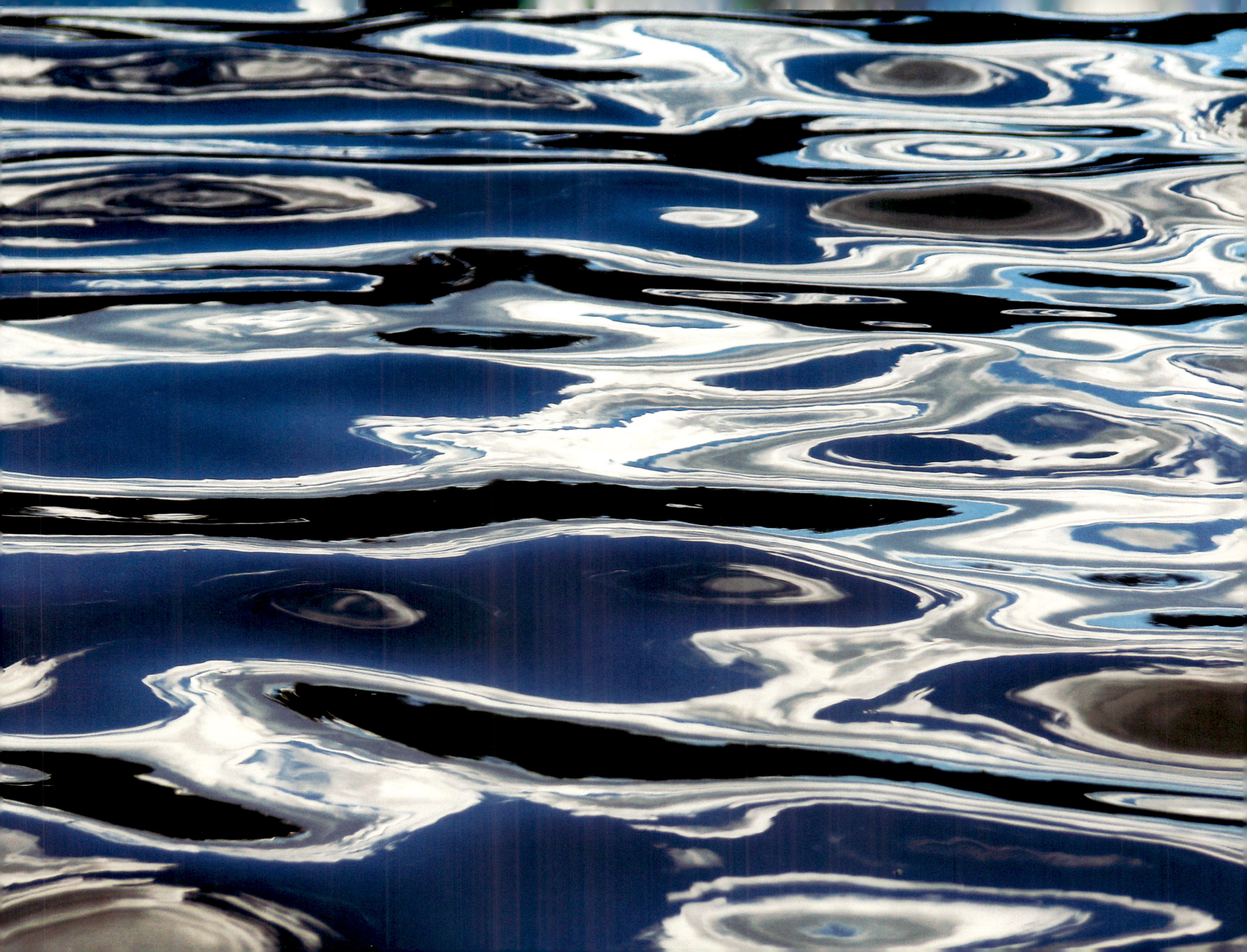

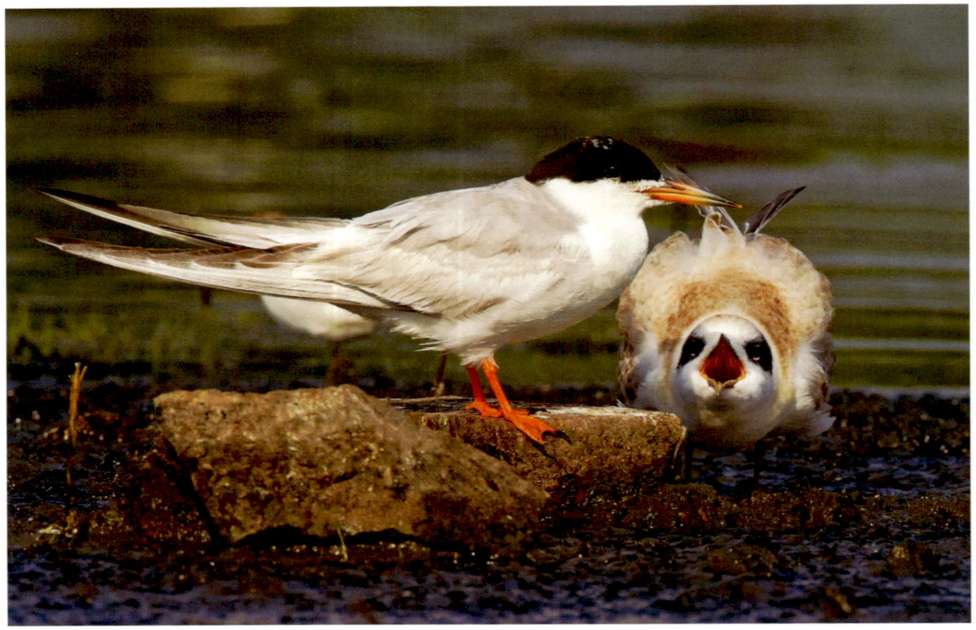

All the birds on these pages rely on water for their survival. A Forster's Tern (left) patiently listens to its begging offspring, while a Herring Gull lifts out of the water to dry its wings after bathing (lower left). An elegant American Avocet is framed by beautiful water and background at the Jamaica Bay Wildlife Refuge in New York. *Photos by Lloyd Spitalnik (upper left), Kevin T. Karlson (lower left) and Scott Elowitz (below)*

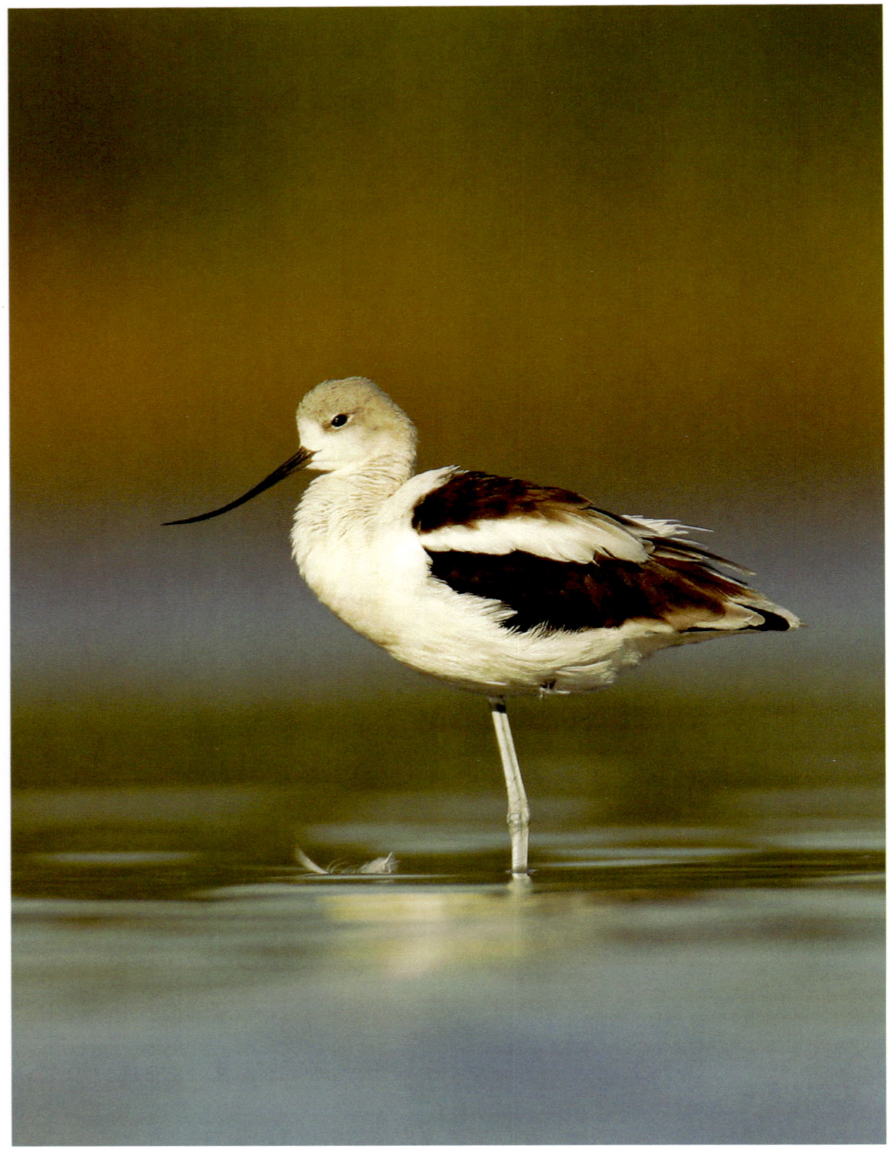

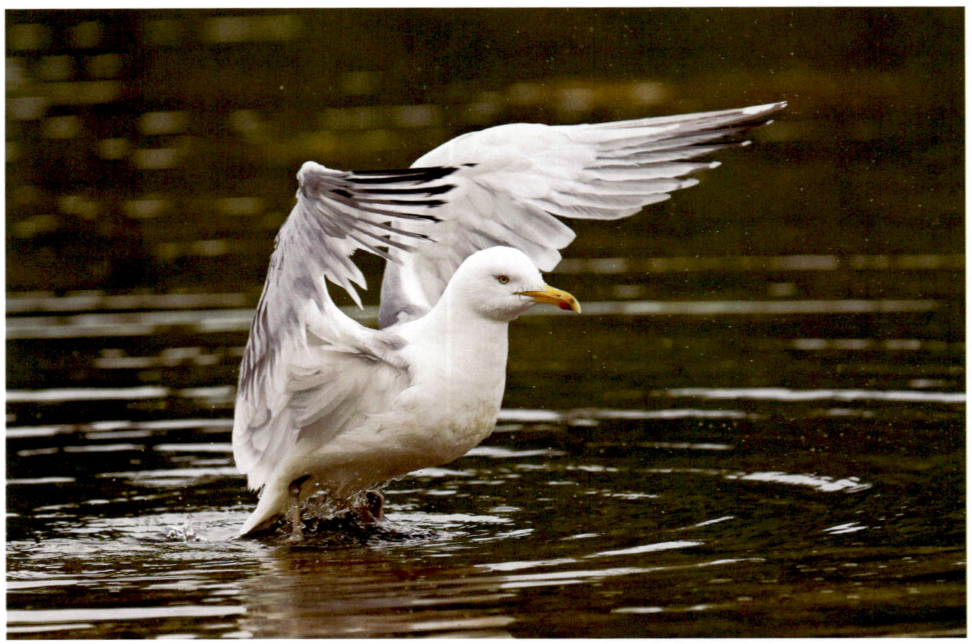

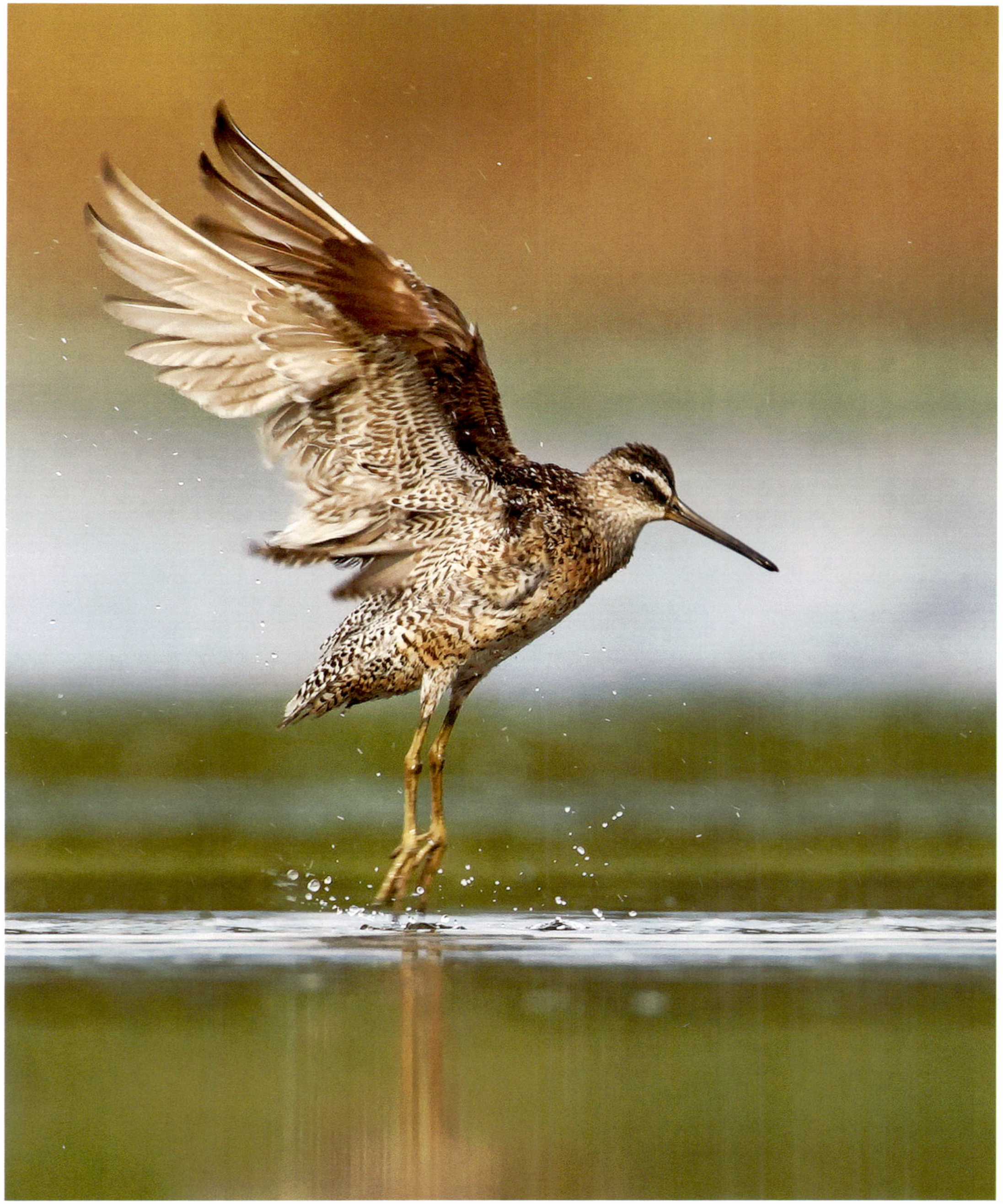

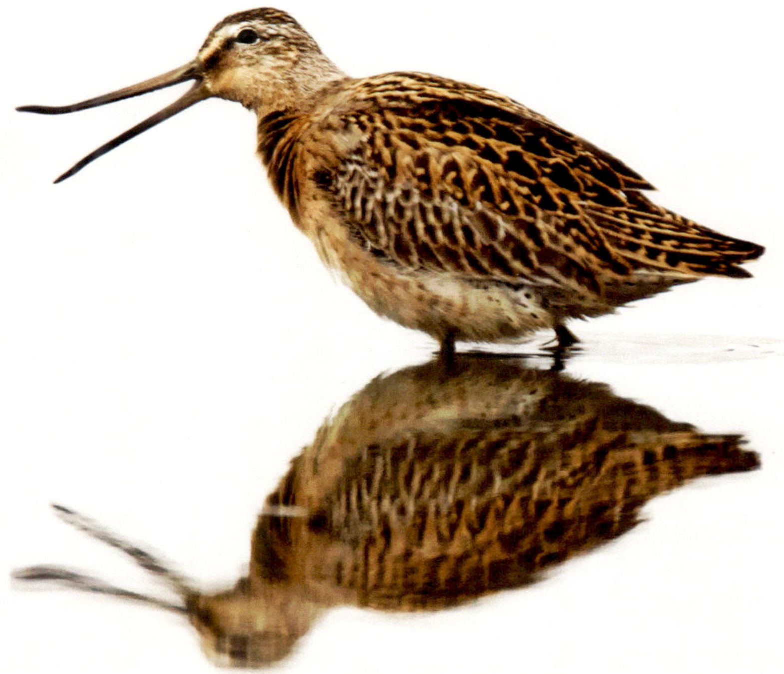

Short-billed Dowitchers are medium-sized shorebirds that live in and around water for all their lives. The long bill probes into the substrate in search of worms and invertebrates, which it locates using the flexible tip of its bill. *Photos by Lloyd Spitalnik*

A sliver moon looks over this peaceful scene at dusk over Lac le Jeune in British Columbia (right). *Photo by Kevin T. Karlson*

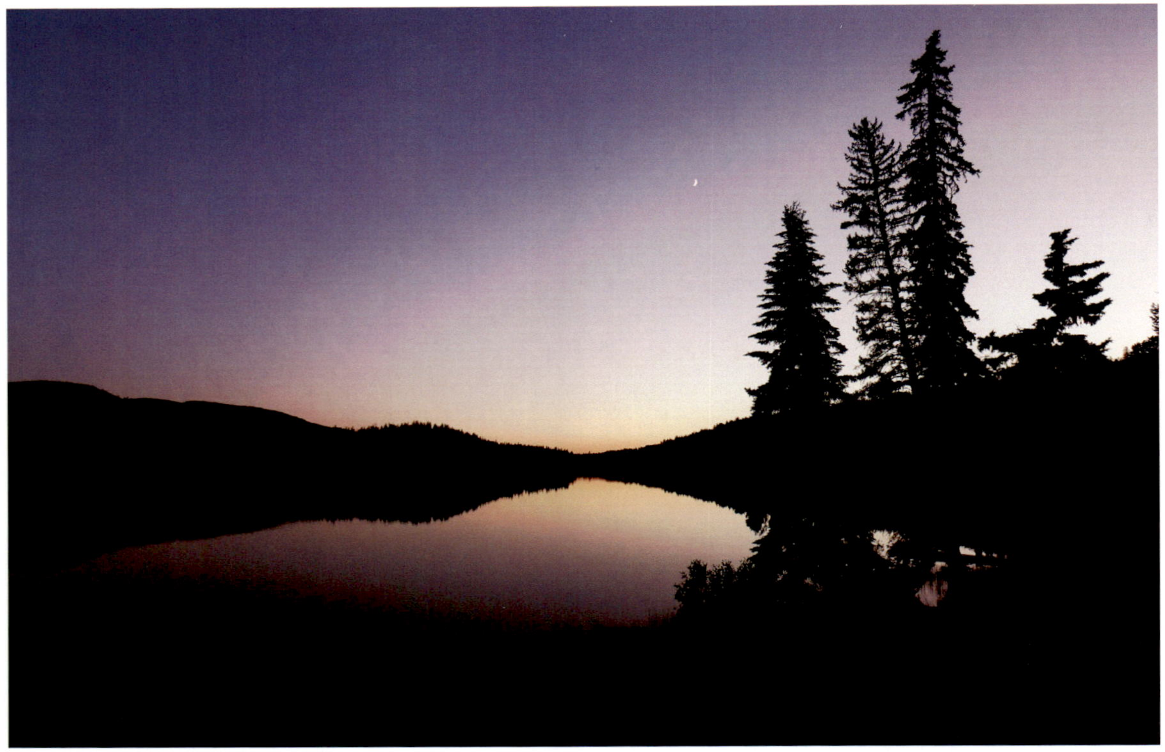

A breeding Common Loon carries two chicks on its back as it floats in a small lake in Lac le Jeune, British Columbia, with colorful reflections of rich, green conifers. *Photo by Scott Elowitz*

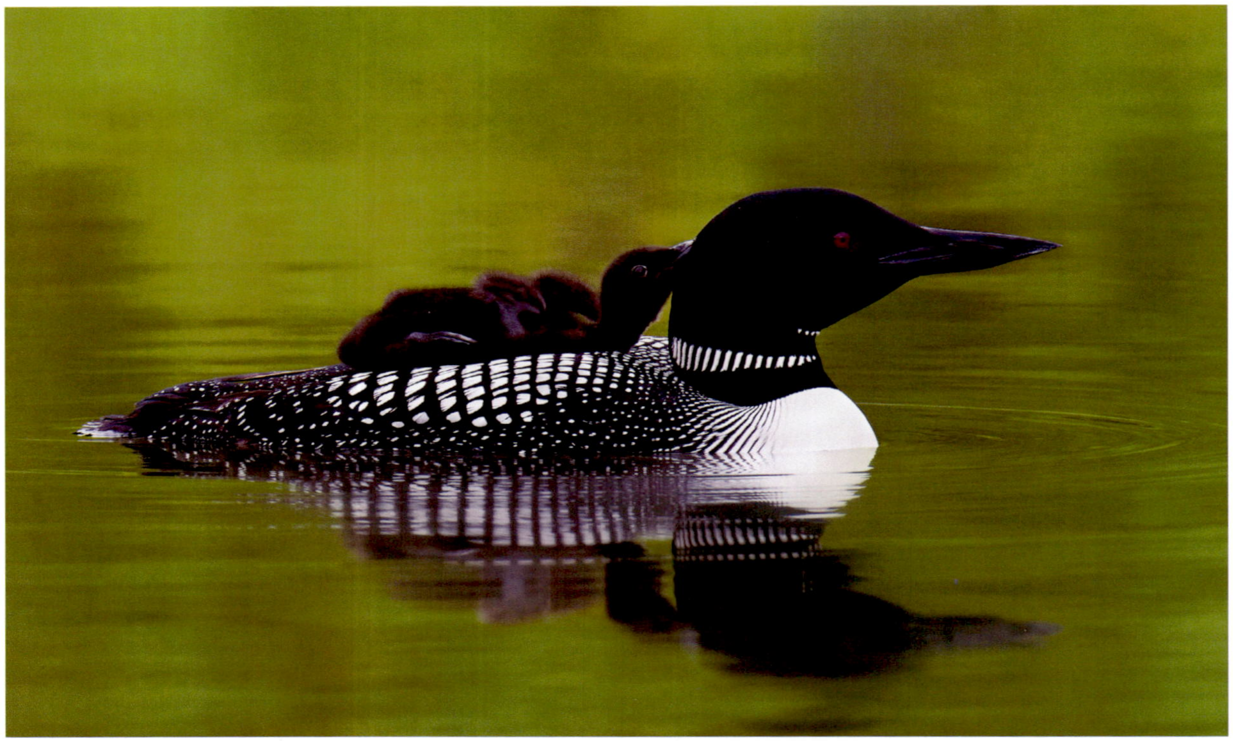

No sadder sound salutes you than the clear, wild laughter of the loon.

— Celia Thaxter

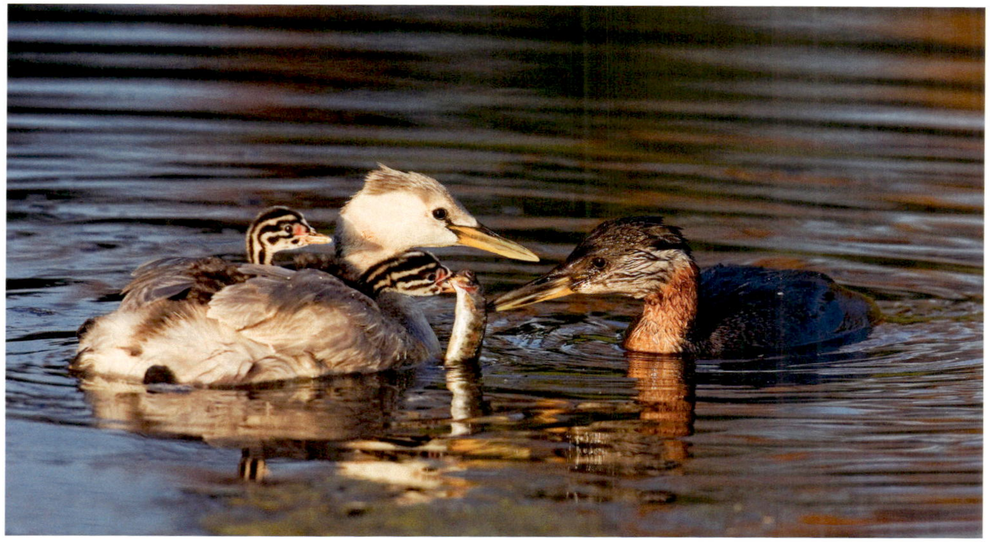

The female of this pair of Red-necked Grebes at Logan Lake in British Columbia lacks the rich, red pigment tones of typical adults. She was so pretty that we nicknamed her "the Angel." Only two chicks remain from their clutch, but a big fish, which took time to swallow, will help these cute young ones grow quickly. *Photos by Kevin T. Karlson*

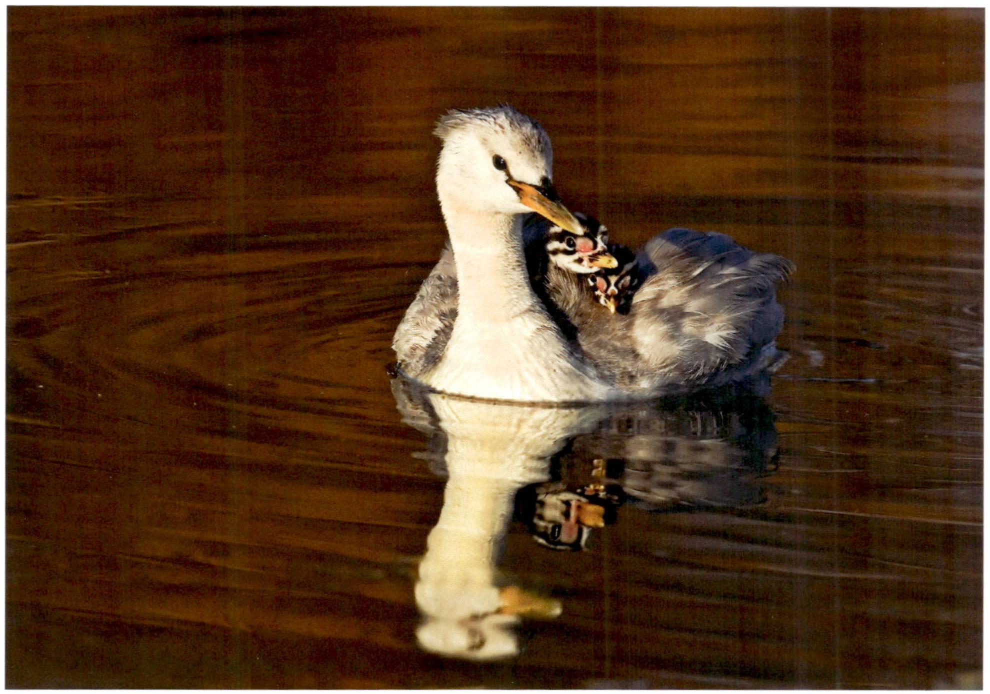

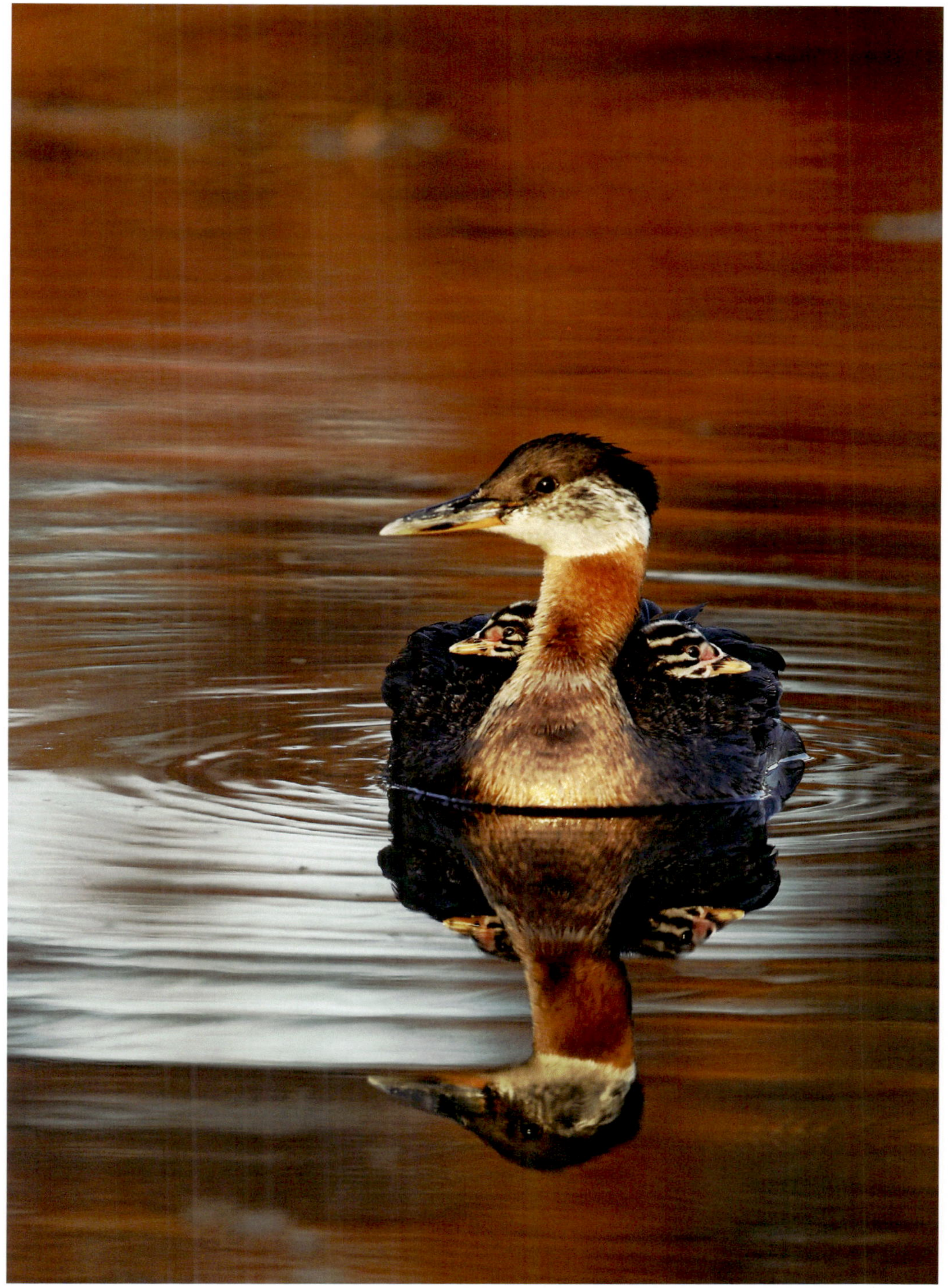

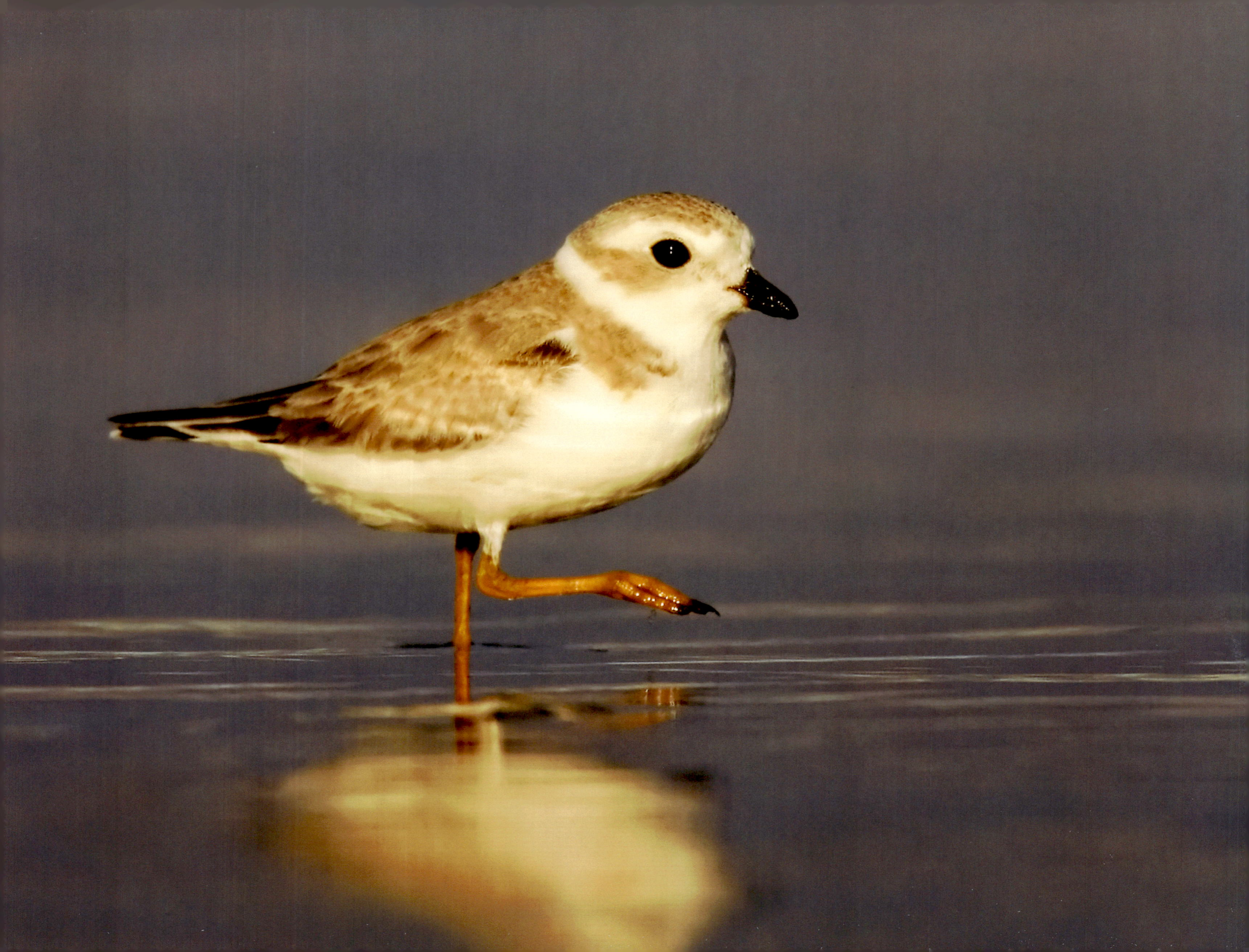

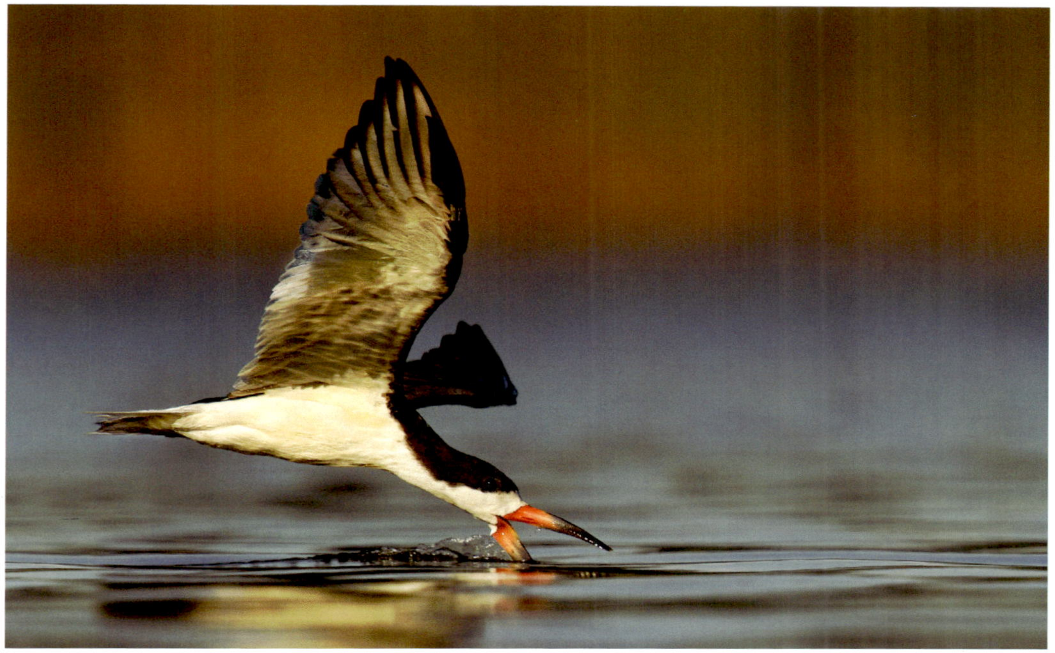

Black Skimmers are unique members of the tern family that have a strange orange and black bill that is used to skim the surface of the water in search of fish (above). A young Black Skimmer chick looks with wonder at the great big world, including its parent in the background (right). *Photos by Scott Elowitz*

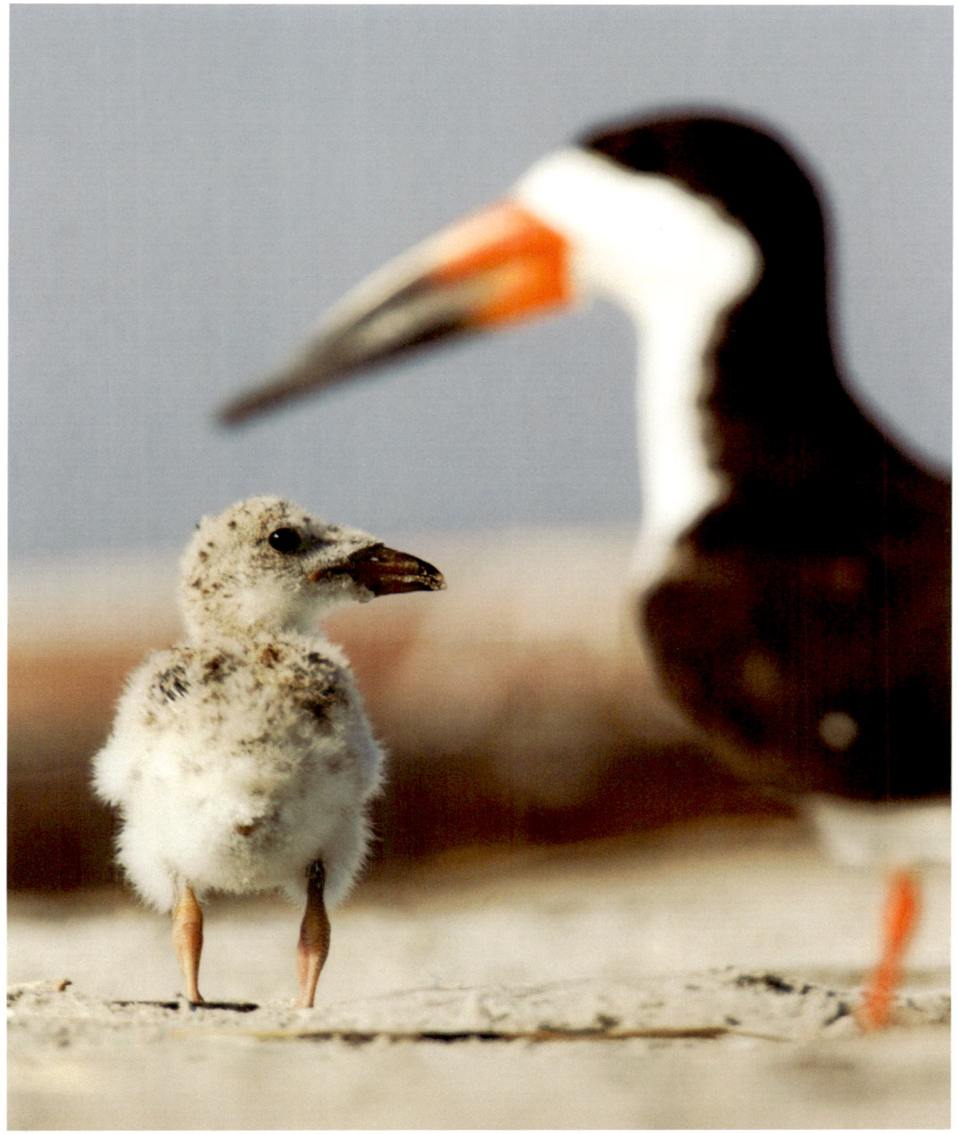

Opposite: A juvenile Piping Plover struts along the Atlantic Ocean tide line in southern New Jersey in search of a meal of marine worms. *Photo by Kevin T. Karlson*

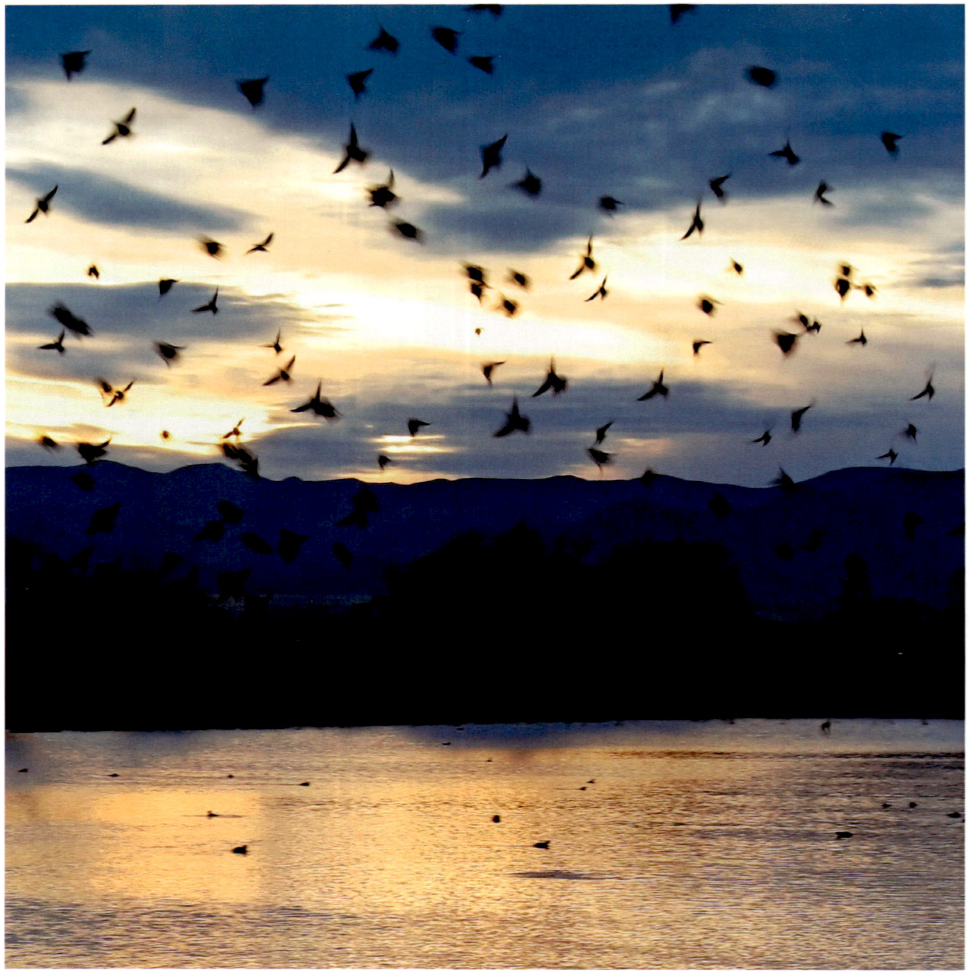

These beautiful days ... do not exist as mere pictures – maps hung upon the walls of memory to brighten at times when touched by association or will ... They saturate themselves into every part of the body and live always"

— John Muir

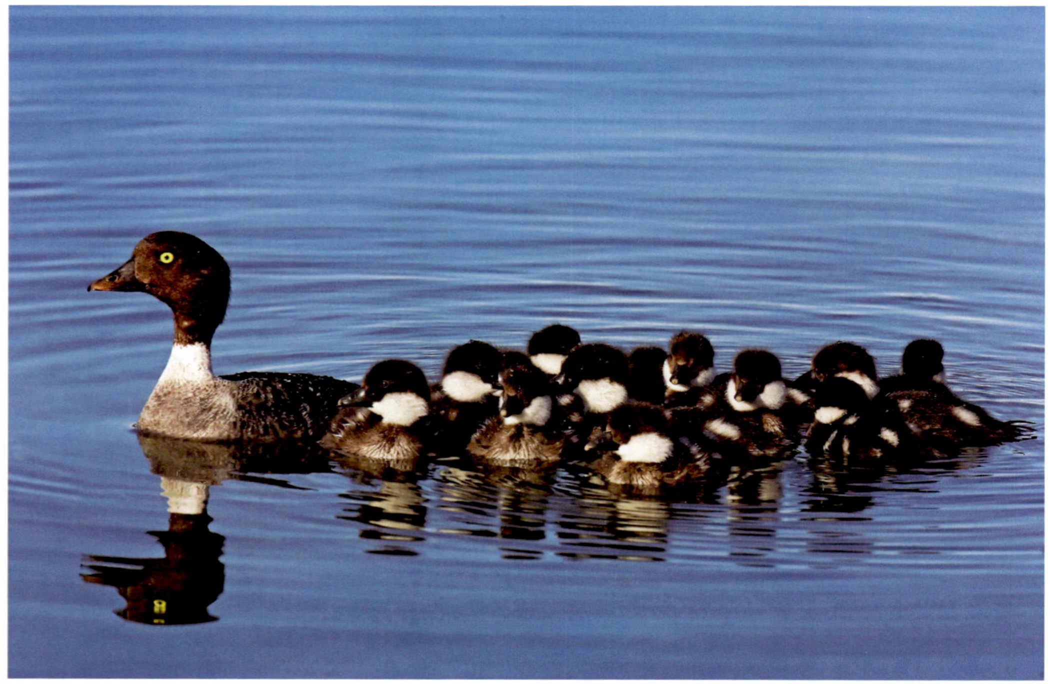

A flock of blackbirds fly above their home near a freshwater lake. Many creatures rely on aquatic habitats for their survival, and these blackbirds spend most of the year near water (above). *Photo by Dale Rosselet*

Barrow's Goldeneyes are common diving ducks that breed near quiet, northern ponds. This mother hen has her hands full with a clutch of eleven ducklings, and must keep a sharp eye out for danger (right). *Photo by Kevin T. Karlson*

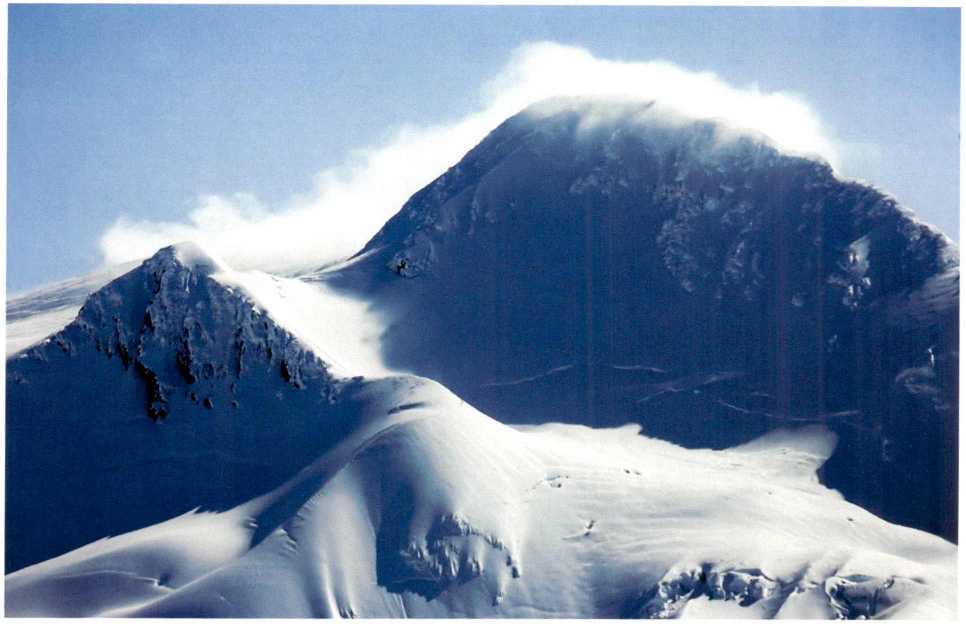

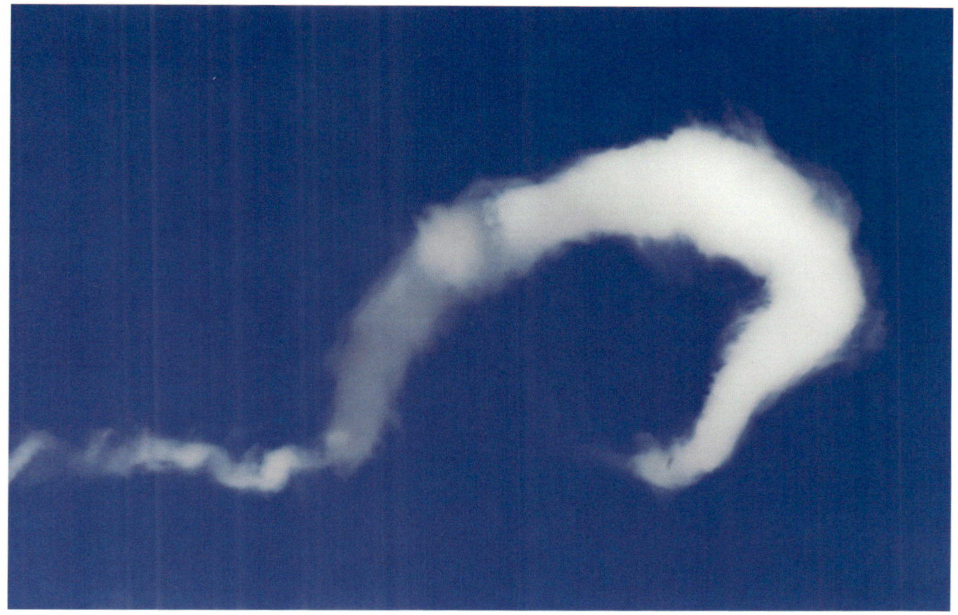

Water is shown in all its forms in these three photos. A snow-covered mountain with perched glaciers and a shroud of fog overlooks the picturesque town of Cordova, Alaska (above).

A very strange natural cloud suddenly appeared above the mountains near Zion National Park in Utah (upper right).

A massive glacier meets the sea near Seward, Alaska (right), in the photo at right. When the water of Resurrection Bay erodes the lower section of the glacier, a huge chunk of ice crashes into the water with a roaring sound (right) *Photos by Kevin T. Karlson*

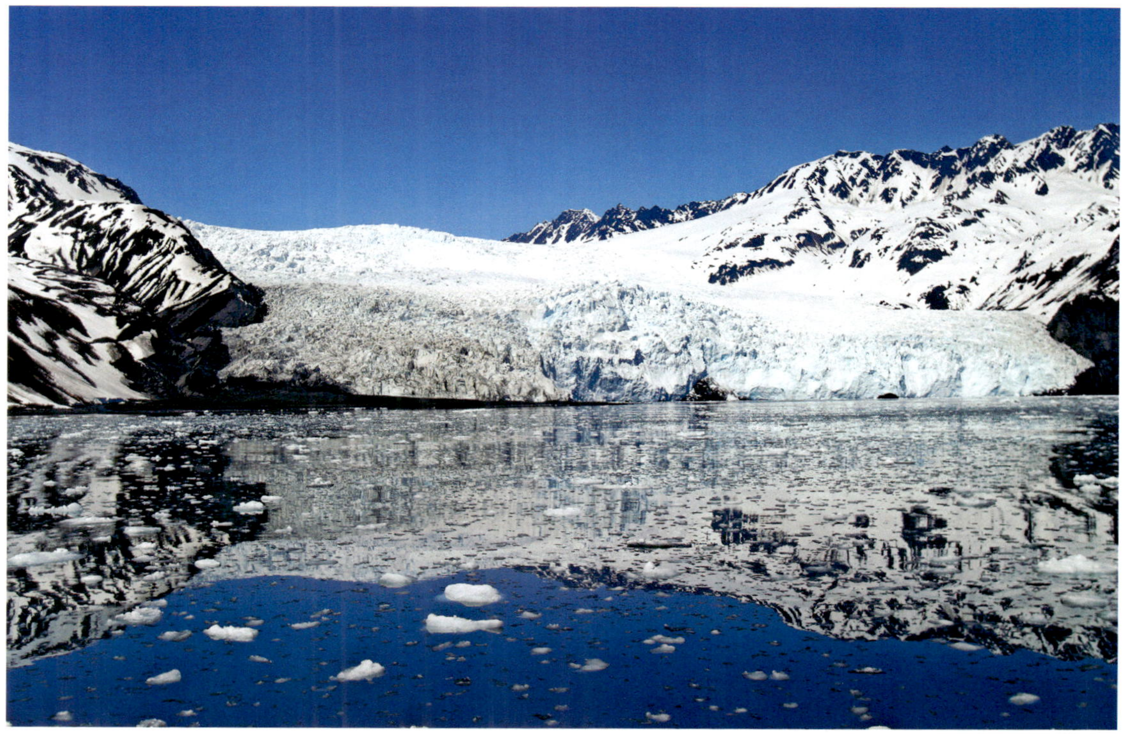

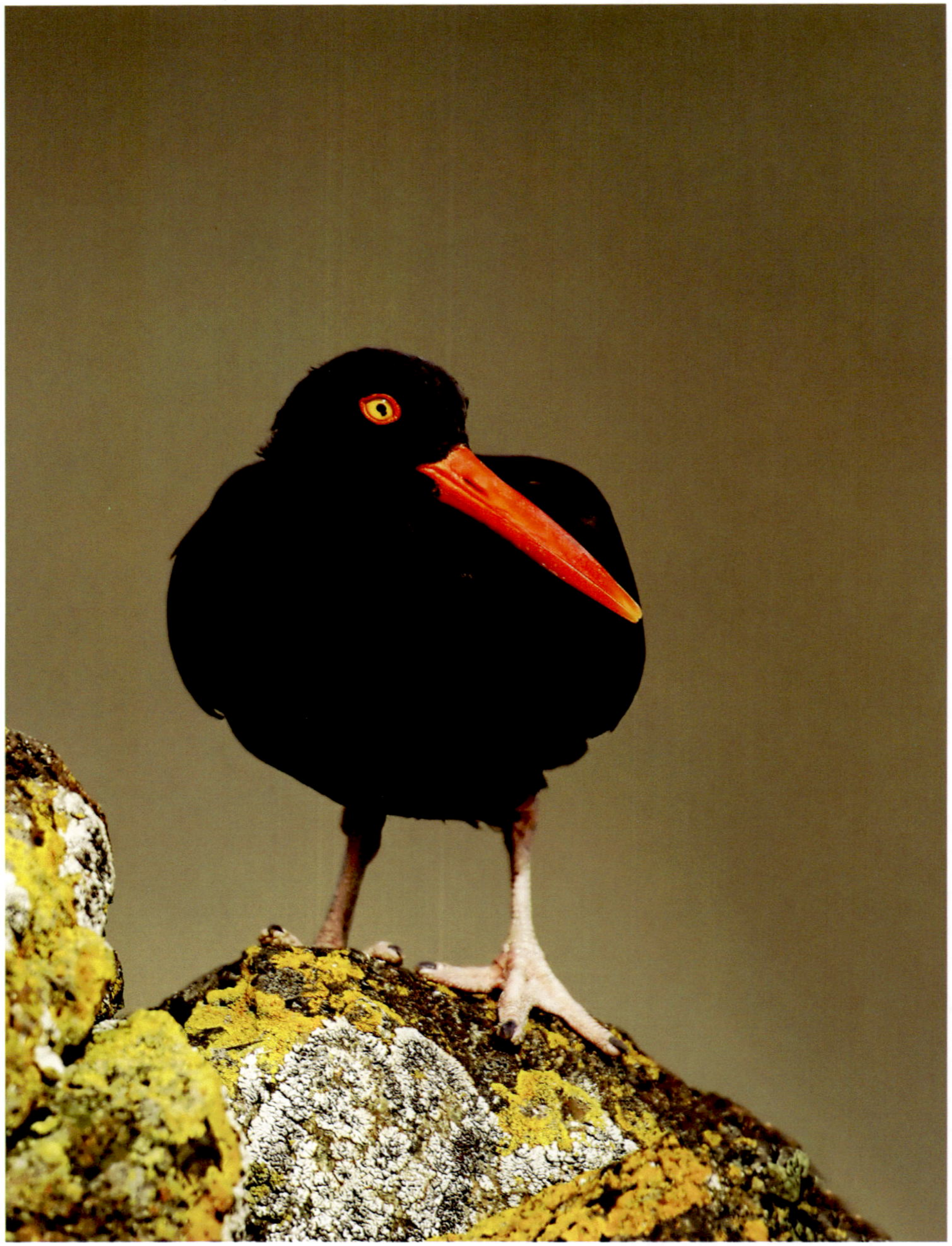

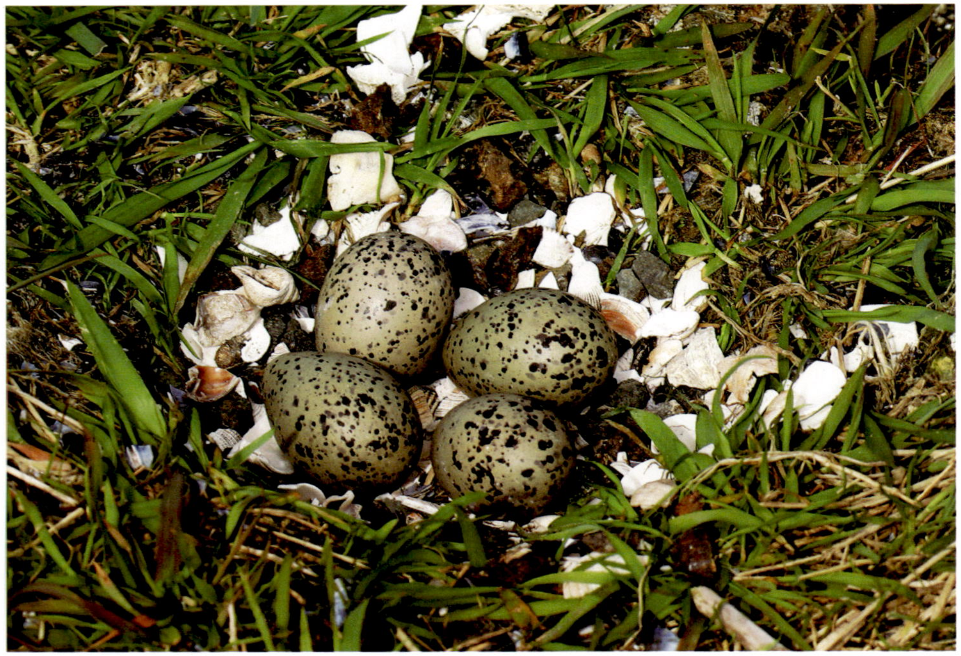

While in Cordova, Alaska a few years ago, Milo Burcham dropped Kevin off at this beautiful location (below) near the mouth of the Copper River. A Black Oystercatcher posed for photos, but only because its nest was located among the rocks (above).

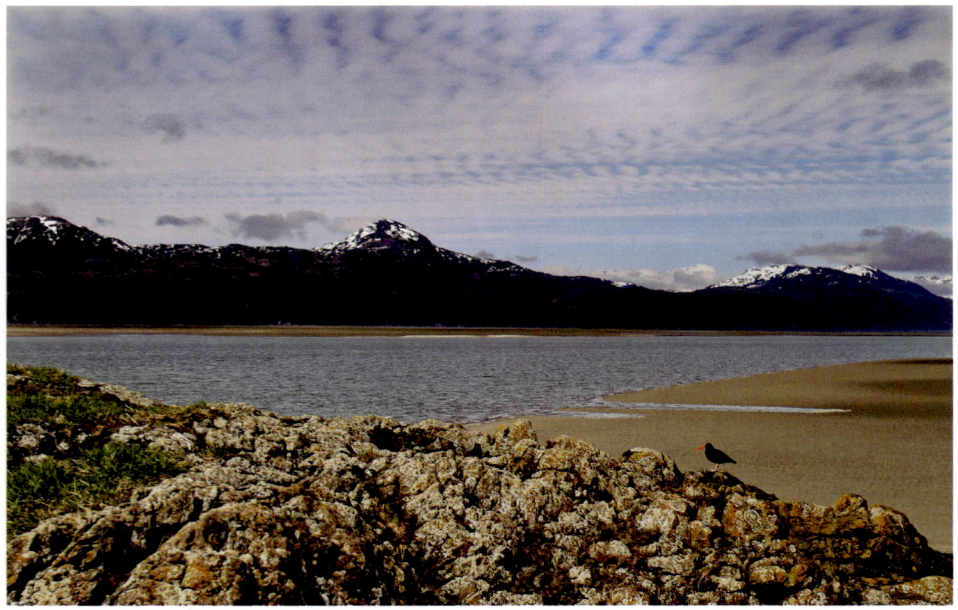

Opposite: Nearby mountains and marsh show some of Alaska's beauty, along with a pair of nesting Trumpeter Swans. *Photos by Kevin T. Karlson*

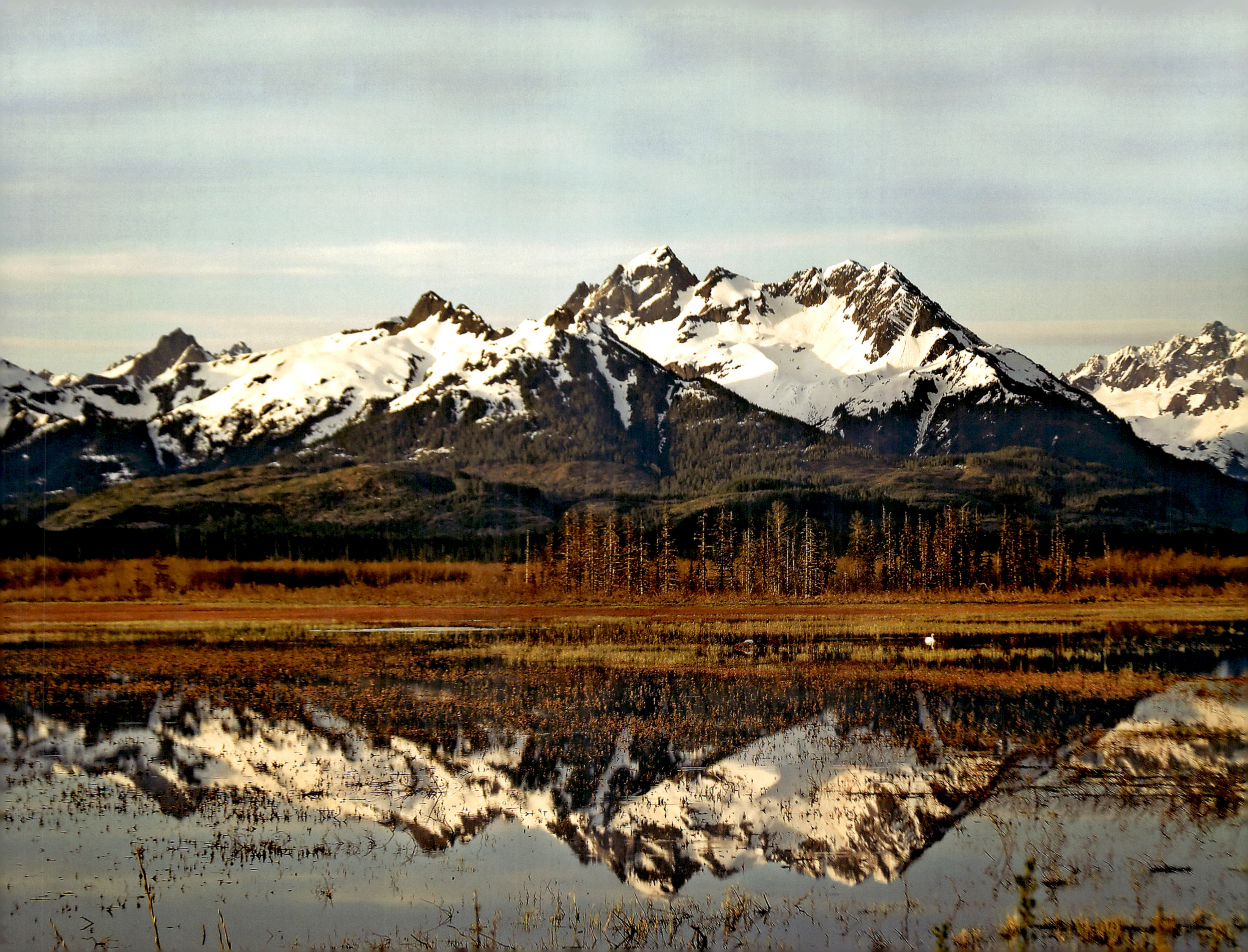

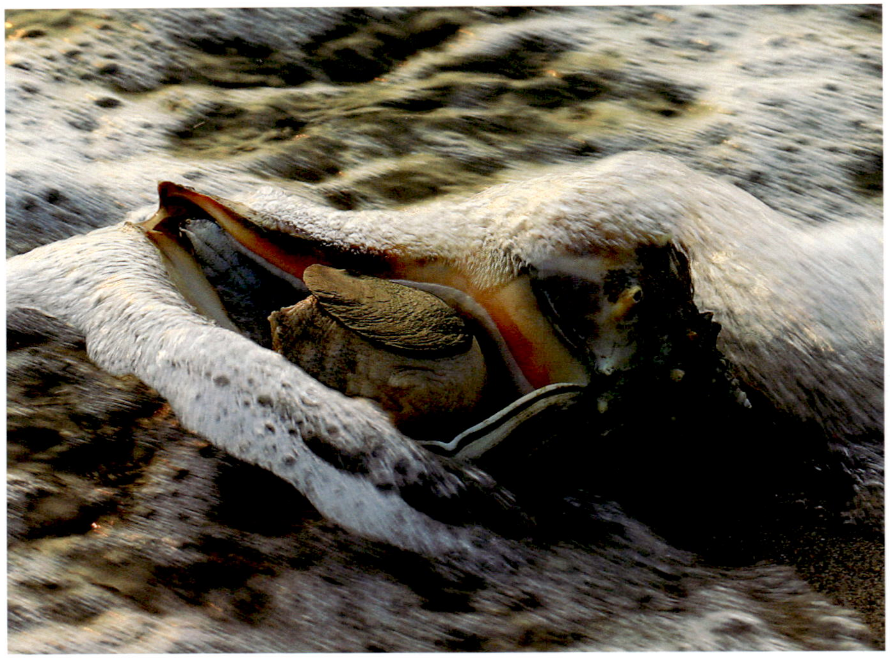

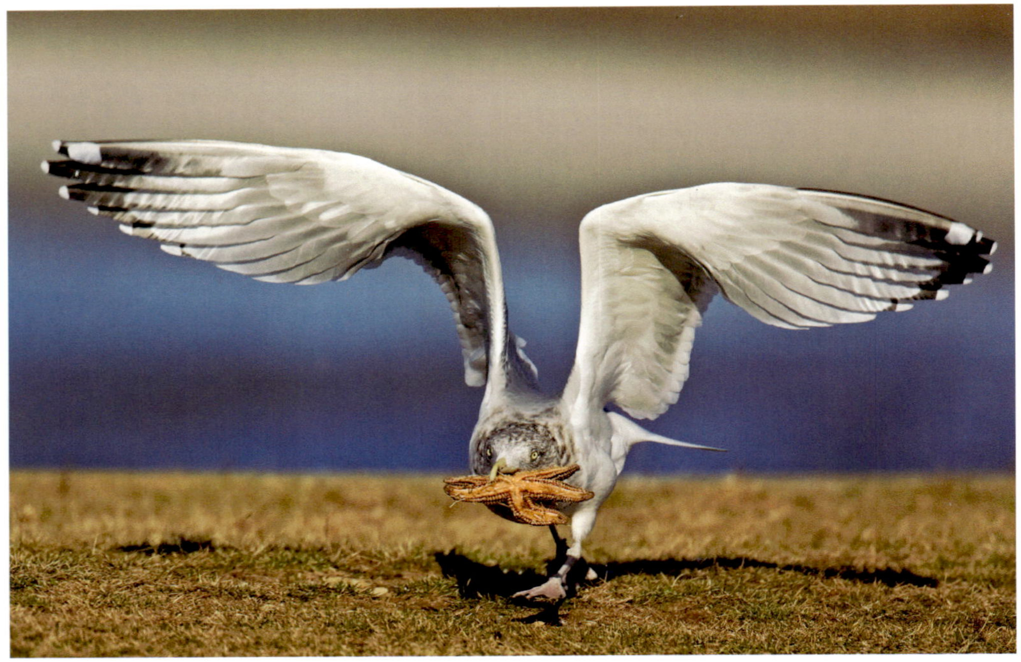

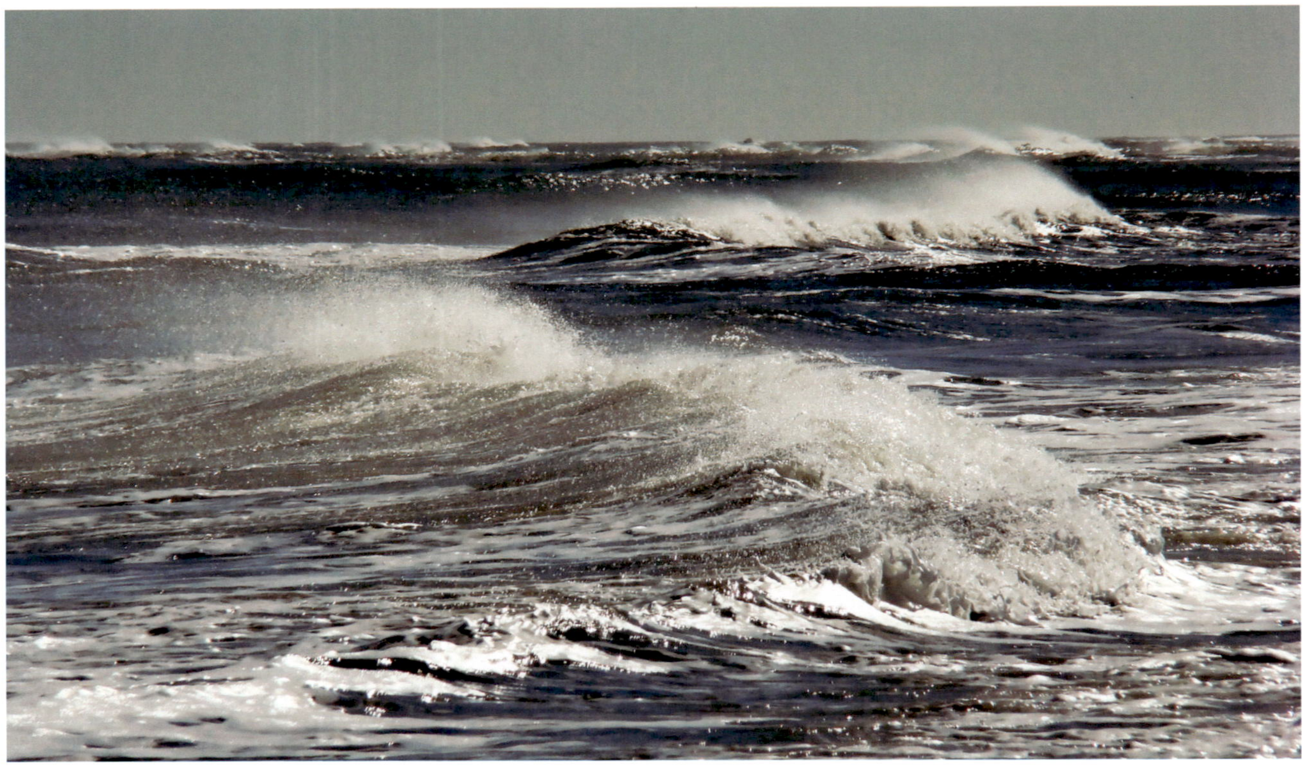

A conch in the waves near Cape May, New Jersey, gives a great perspective of wave action and still life (upper left). *Photo by Don Merwin*

A Herring Gull prepares to eat a meal of unlucky starfish on the shoreline of Long Island, New York (upper right). *Photo by Lloyd Spitalnik*

Winter surf boils with fury near Avalon, New Jersey (left). *Photo by Pat Sutton*

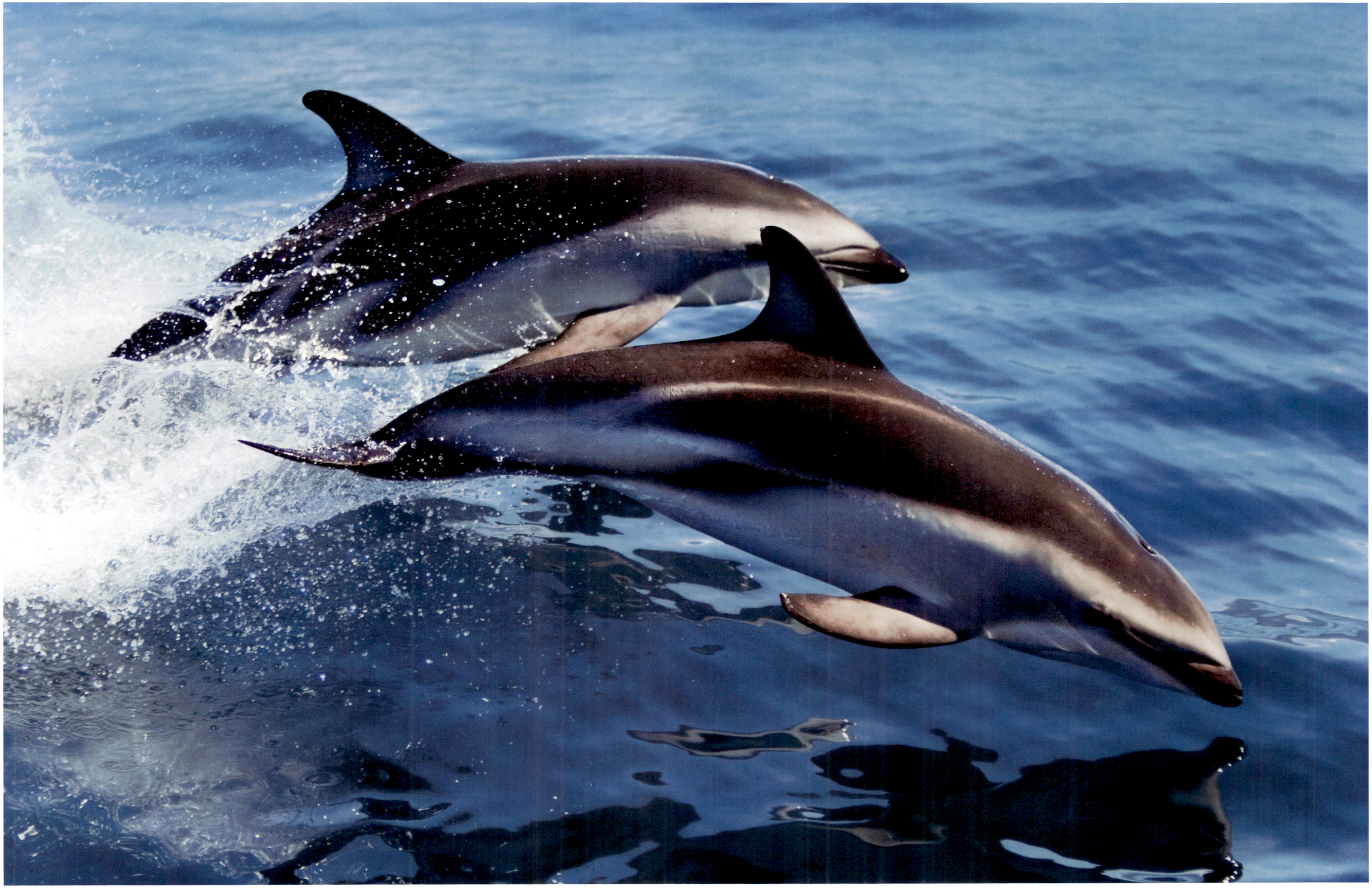

Dusky Dolphins are captured in a playful breach. *Photo by Scott Elowitz*

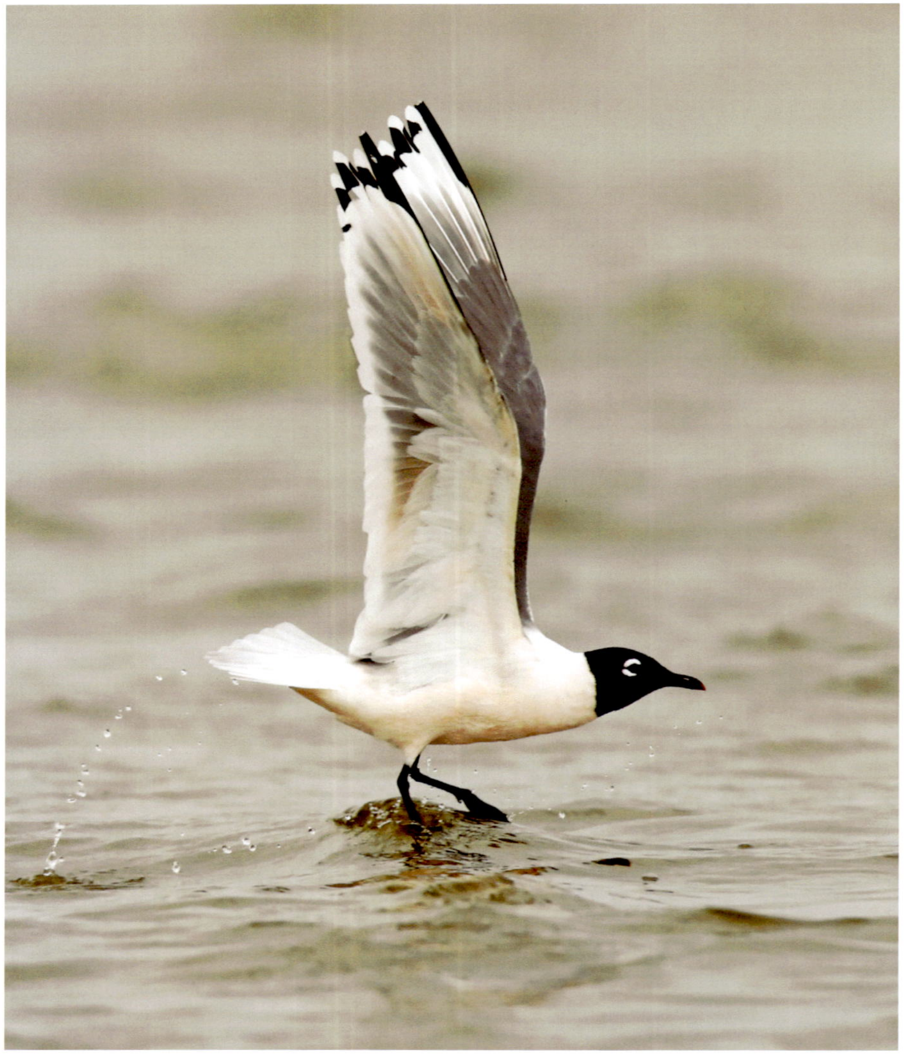

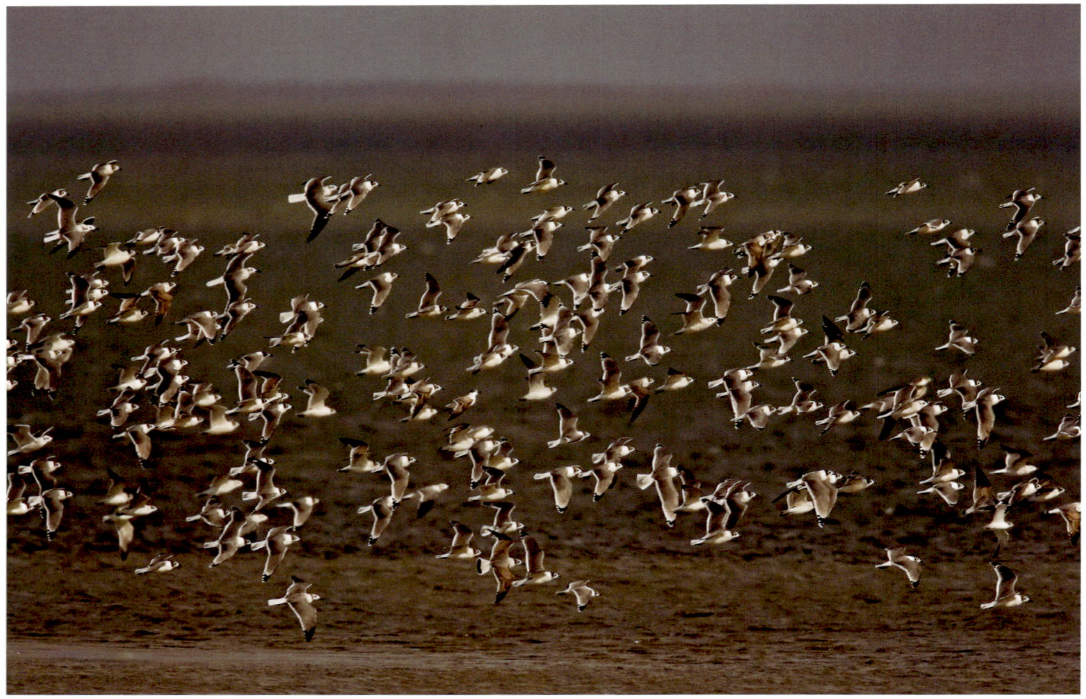

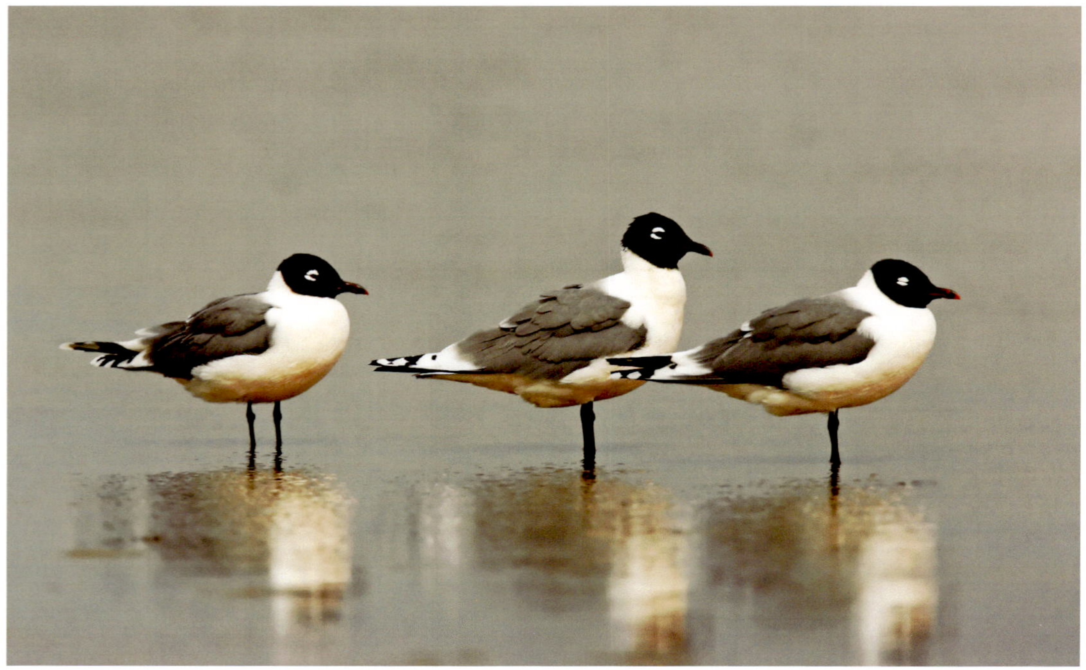

Franklin's Gulls are some of the most striking of all gulls, and a pink chest in spring gives them a soft, warm glow (above and right). Franklin's Gulls spend the winter in South America, and often congregate by the thousands at the Laguna Madre near South Padre Island, Texas, during migration in November (upper right). *Photos by Kevin T. Karlson*

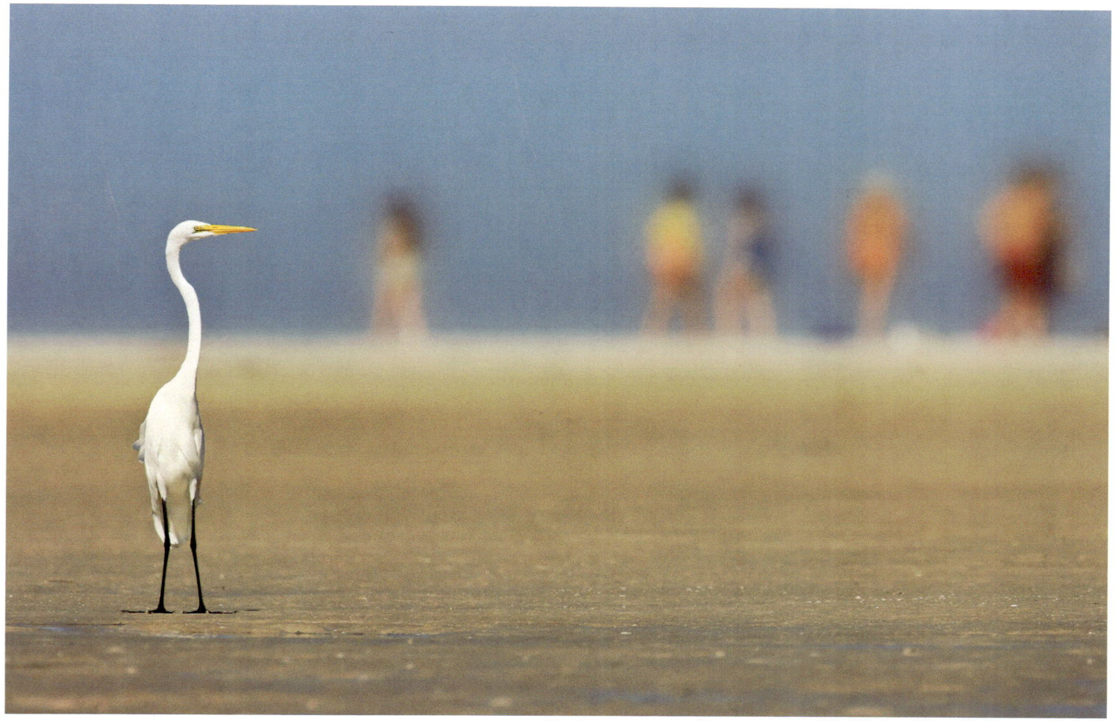

Many birds breed and forage for food near coastal beaches, including the Great Egret at left. Sometimes they have to share this habitat with people, especially during summer months when beaches are crowded with bathers. *Left photo by Scott Elowitz*

Wilson's Plovers are small shorebirds that live their entire lives on sandy beaches and salt flats adjacent to water. An adult female gets ready to incubate her eggs in the lower right image. *Lower left photo by Scott Elowitz; lower right photo by Kevin T. Karlson*

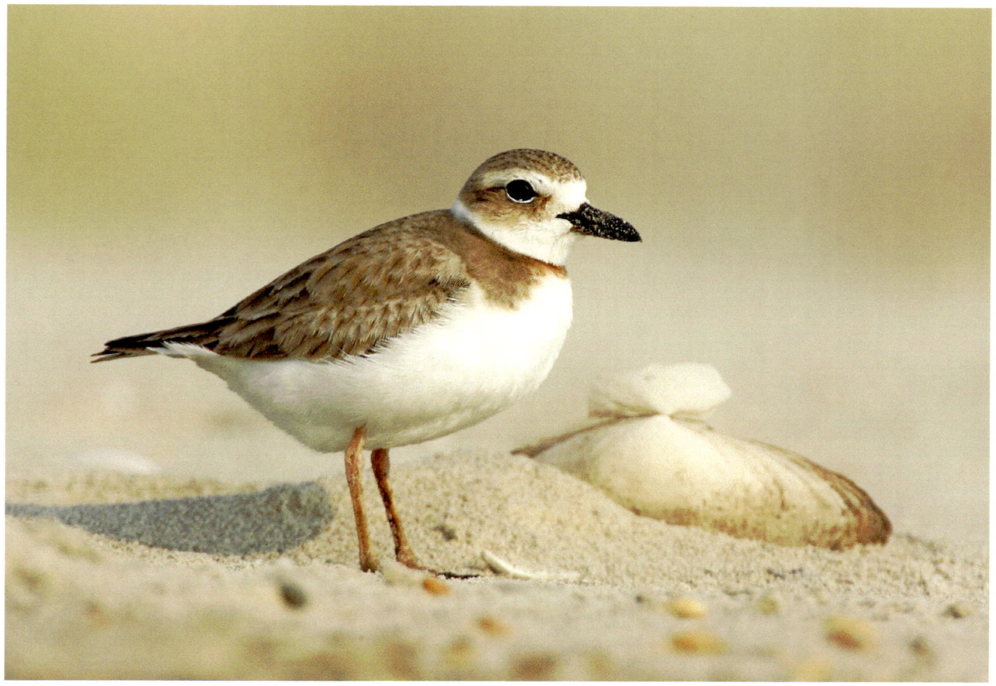

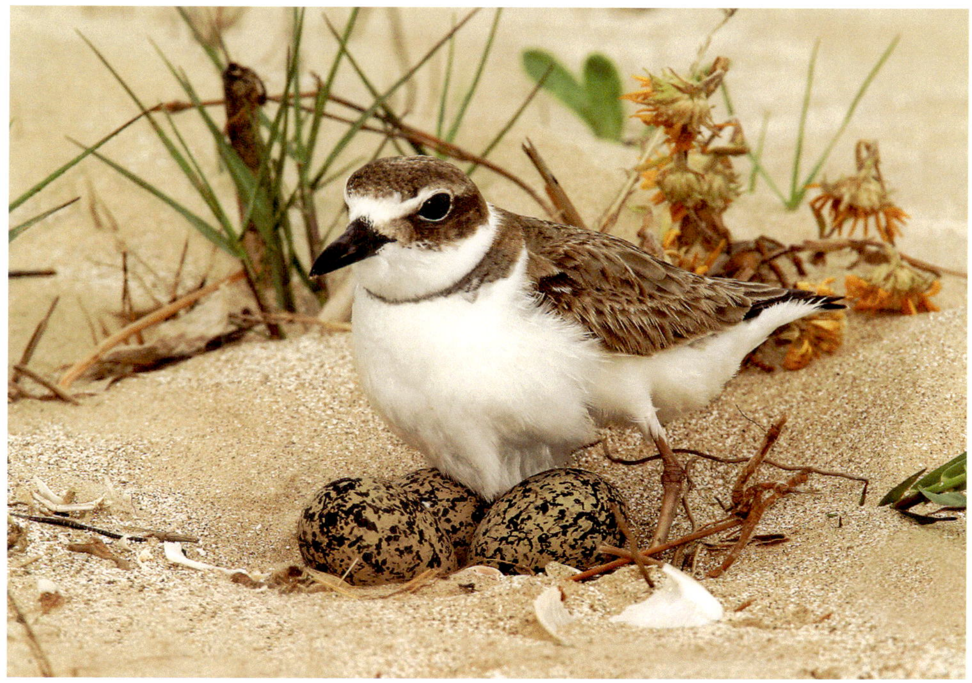

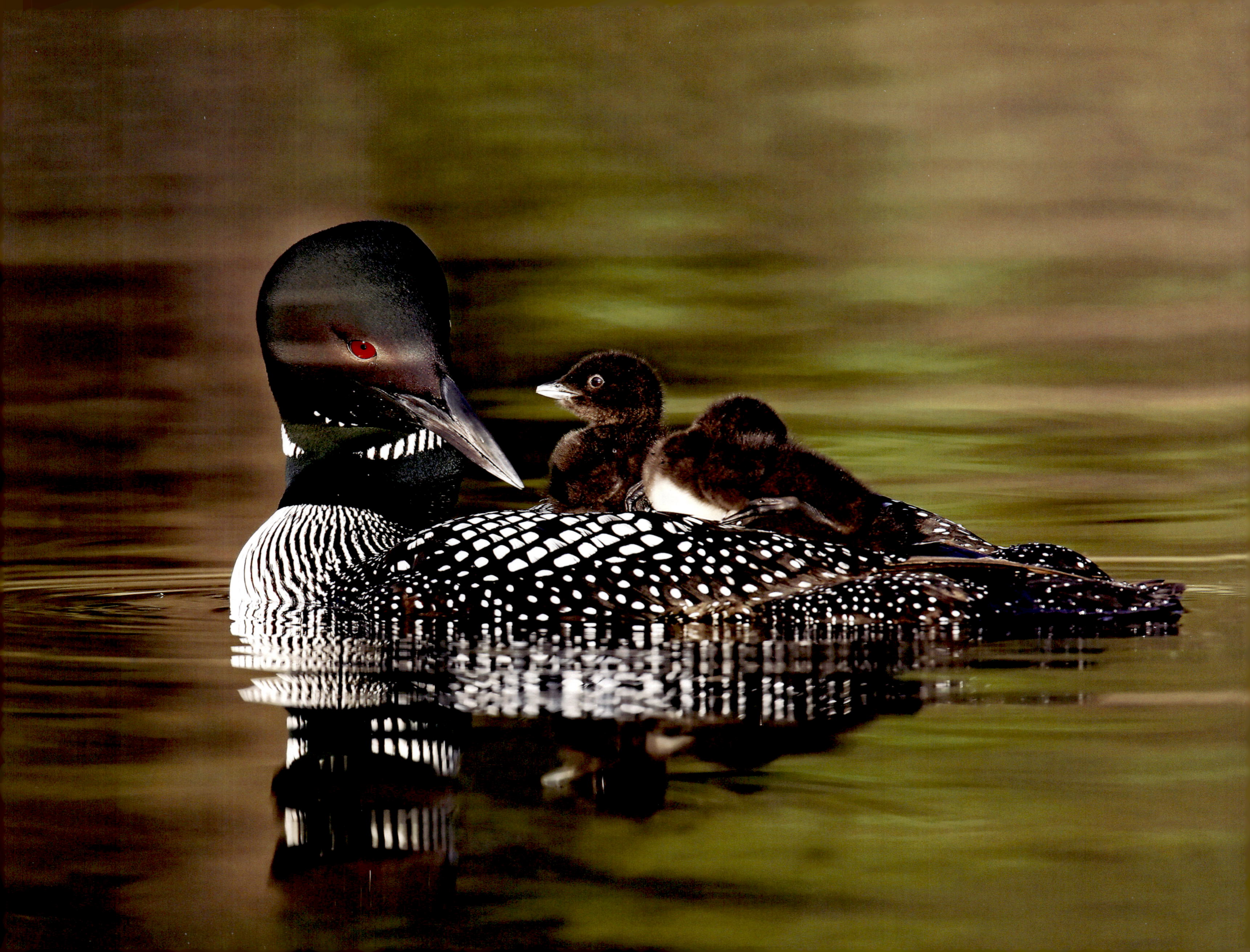

Opposite: An attentive Common Loon watches over its chicks on a calm, summer night in British Columbia while one baby sleeps peacefully. *Photo by Kevin T. Karlson*

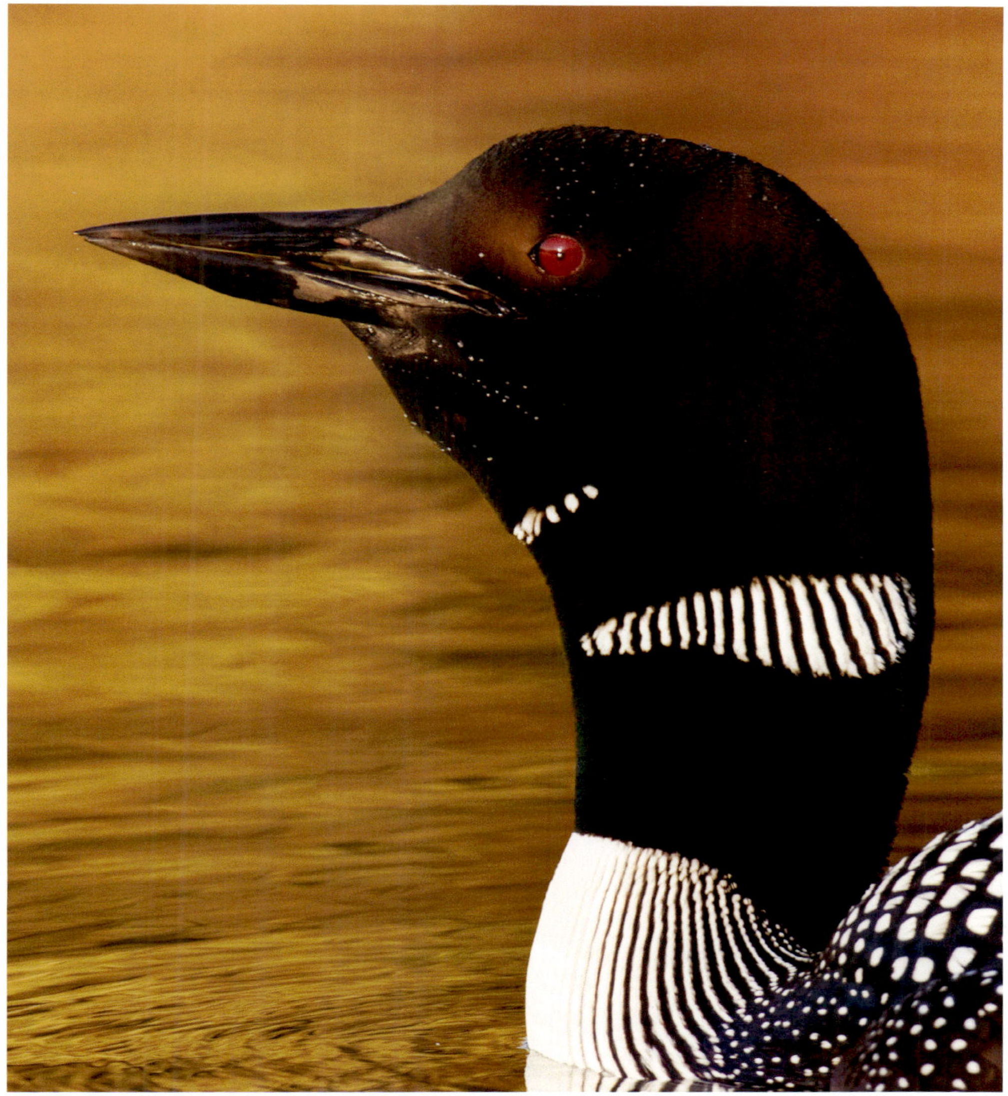

I am no more lonely than the loon in the pond that laughs so loud, or than Walden Pond itself.

— Henry David Thoreau

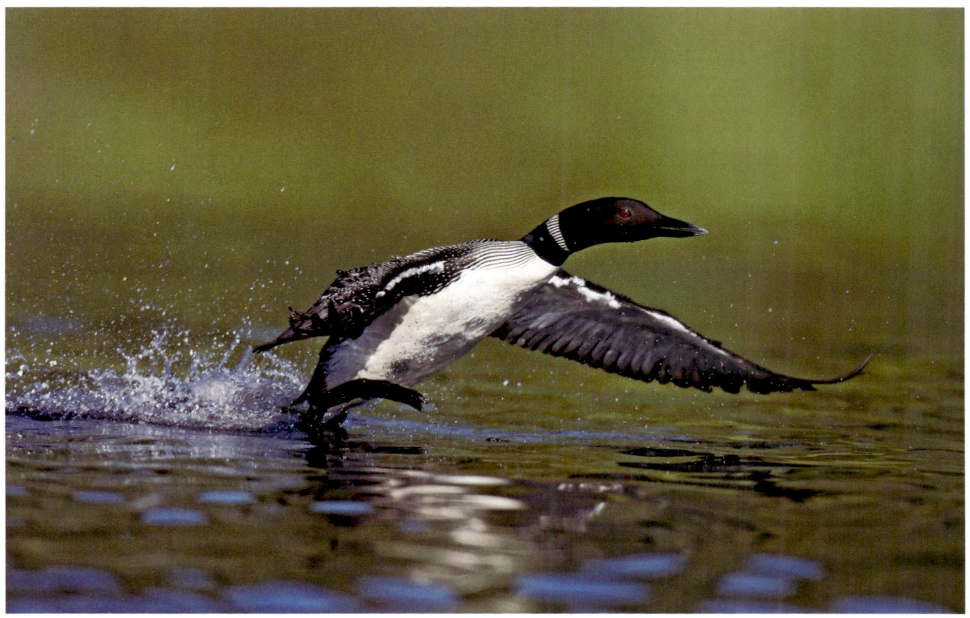

Common Loons are among the most beloved and beautiful birds. They are seen here at Lac le Jeune, British Columbia. A stunning close-up of a loon calling is shown above.

An adult comes in for a landing and uses its big feet to run on the water. *Photos by Scott Elowitz and Kevin T. Karlson (left)*

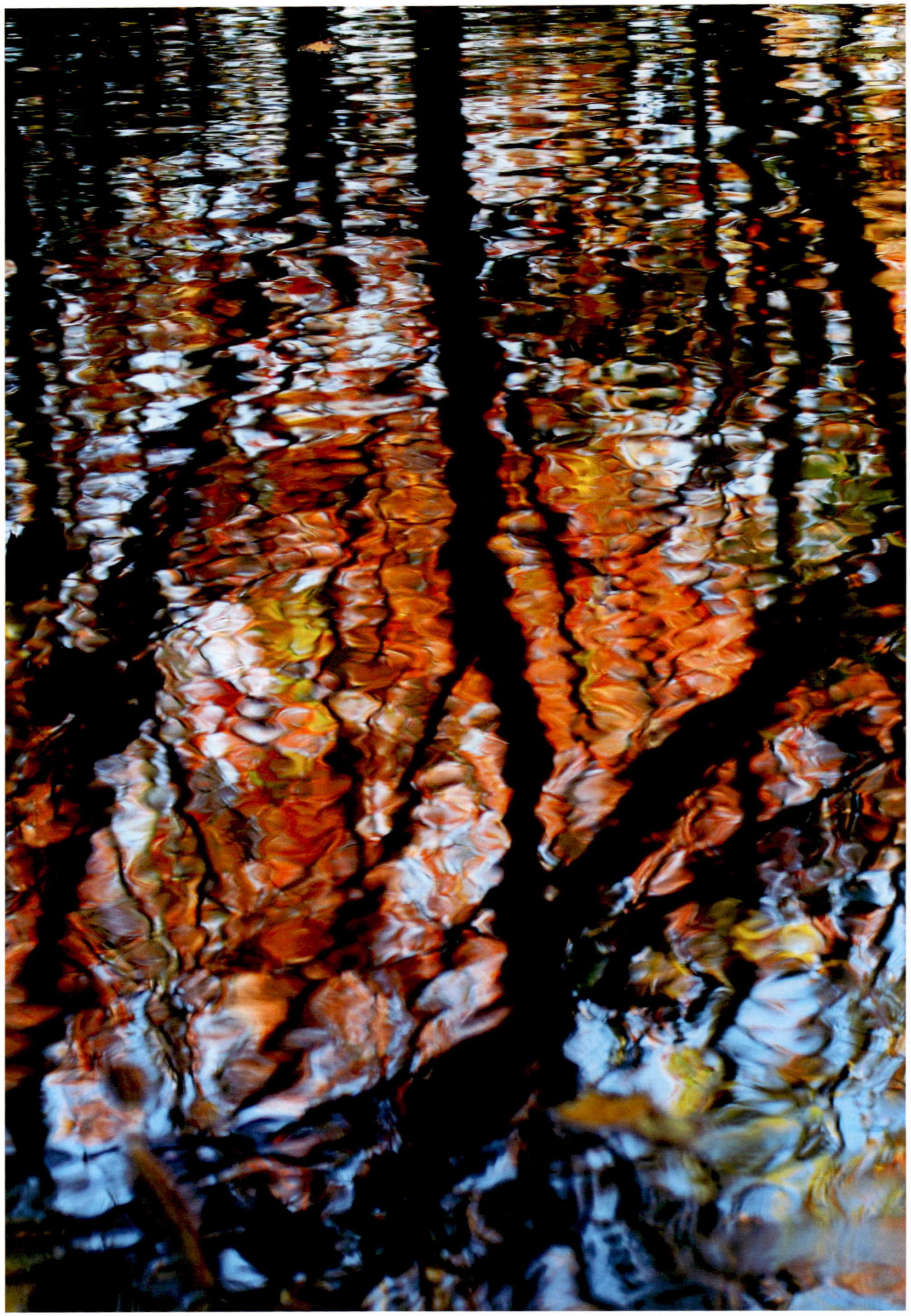

Opposite: Remnants of the previous night's frozen water attached themselves to Phragmites stalks and created this work of art by the artist Nature. Taken on the morning of the Cumberland County Christmas Bird Count, Dividing Creek, New Jersey, Pat Sutton describes this scene as "ice tutus." *Photo by Pat Sutton*

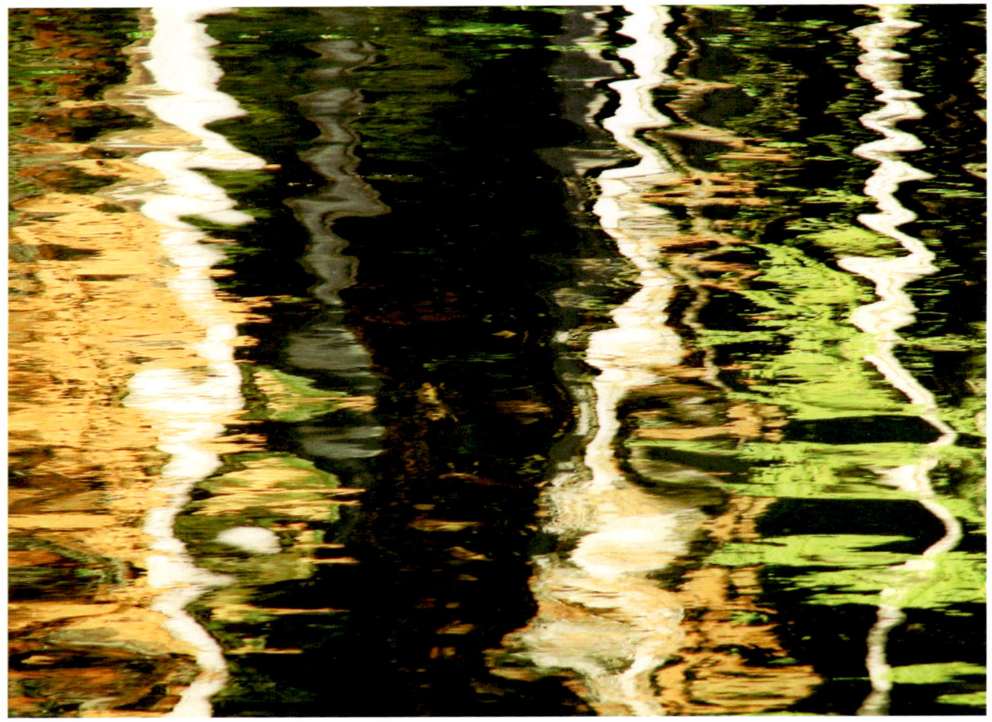

Impressionistic patterns are often found in colors and reflections in water pools, and ripples on the surface further enhance their shapes. An interesting mix of greens, yellows, and white complement the patterns in the image above. *Photo by Dale Rosselet*

Fall colors and water – the perfect combination! Red Maples reflected in a pond provide a perfect opportunity for artistic nature photography in Cape May, New Jersey. *Photo and caption by Mike Crewe*

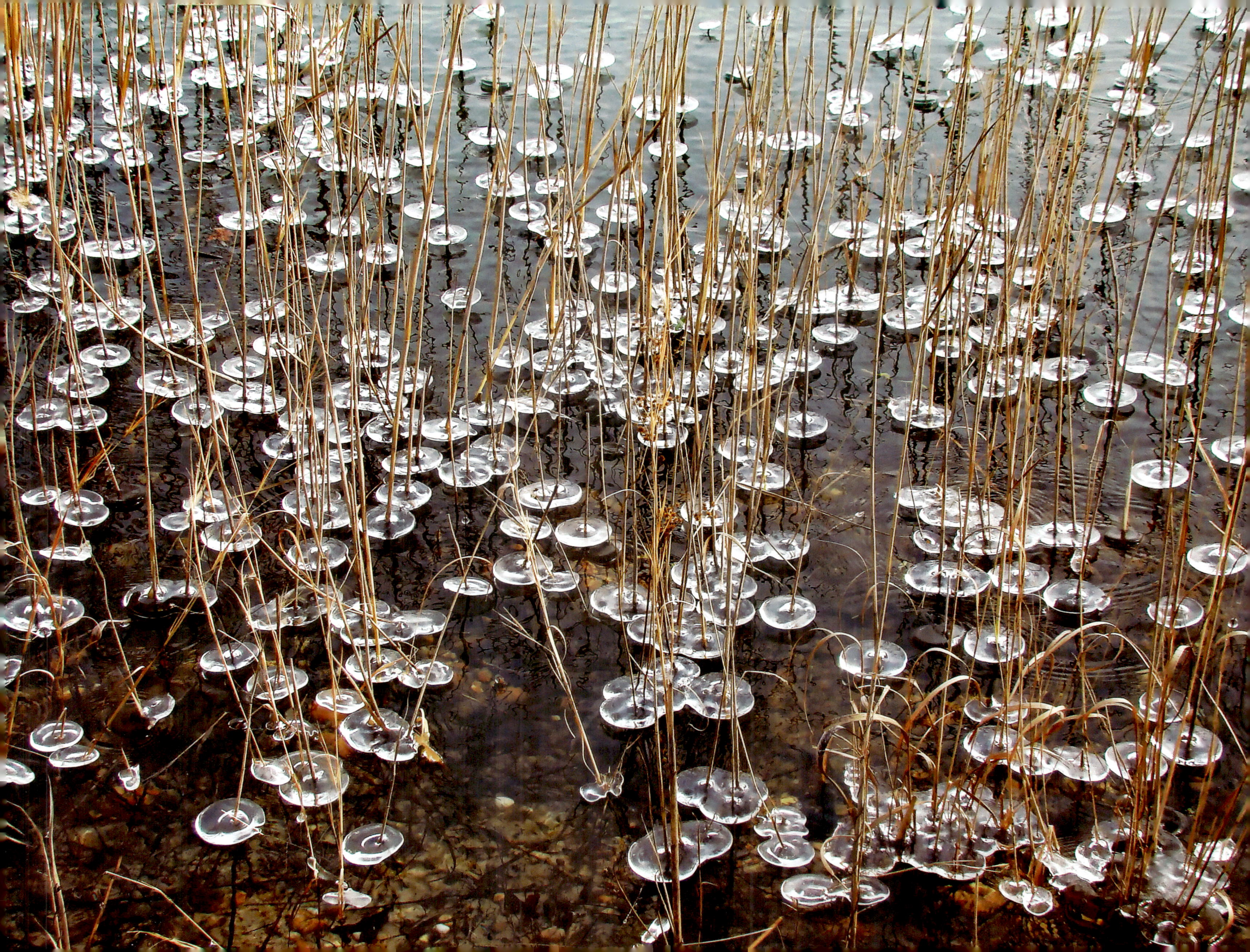

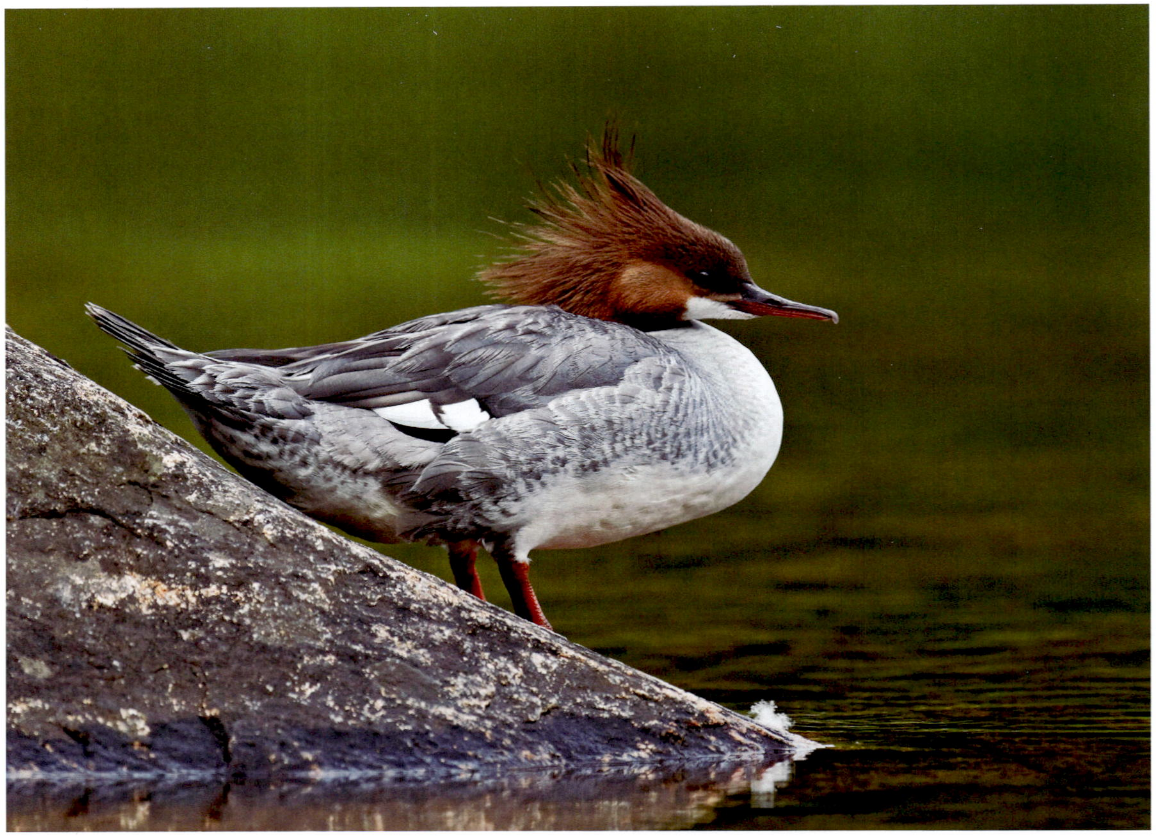

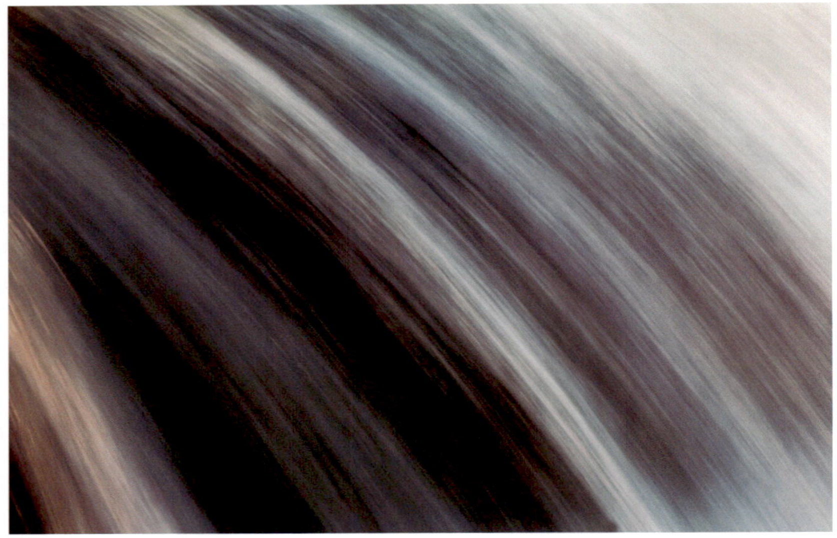

A female Common Merganser sits quietly on a rock at Acadia National Park in Maine (above). These birds breed near lakes and streams, and are totally at home in these habitats.

A 2-second exposure slows down the water in a small waterfall (upper right).

Nobody can deny the soothing quality of a fast-moving stream, and these rapids on the Virgin River in Utah capture some of that mood (right). *All photos by Kevin T. Karlson*

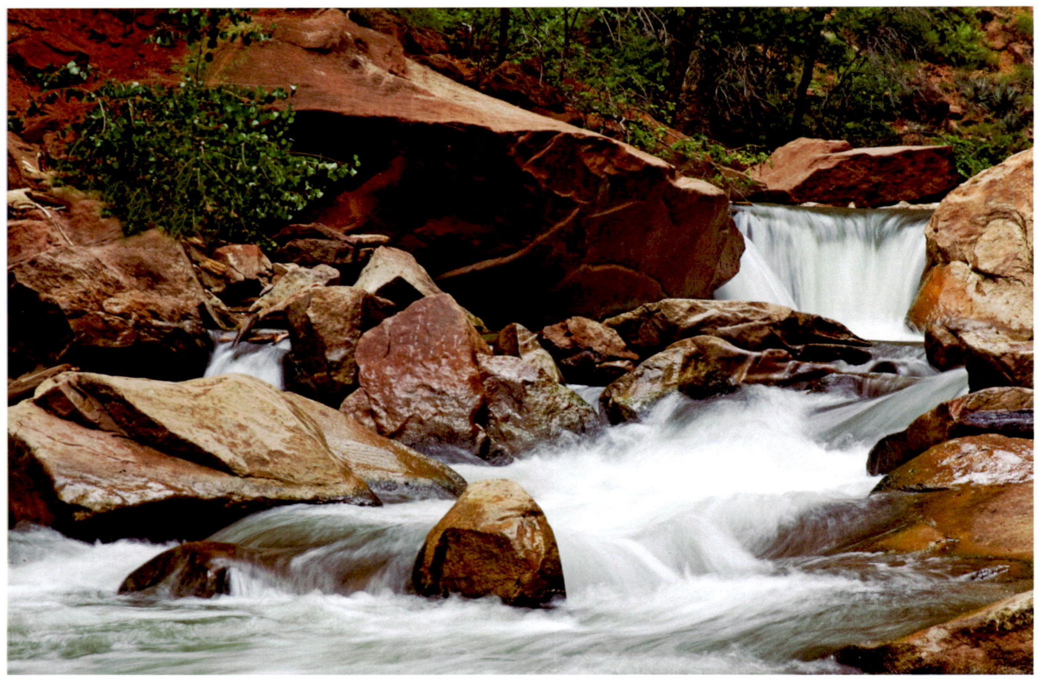

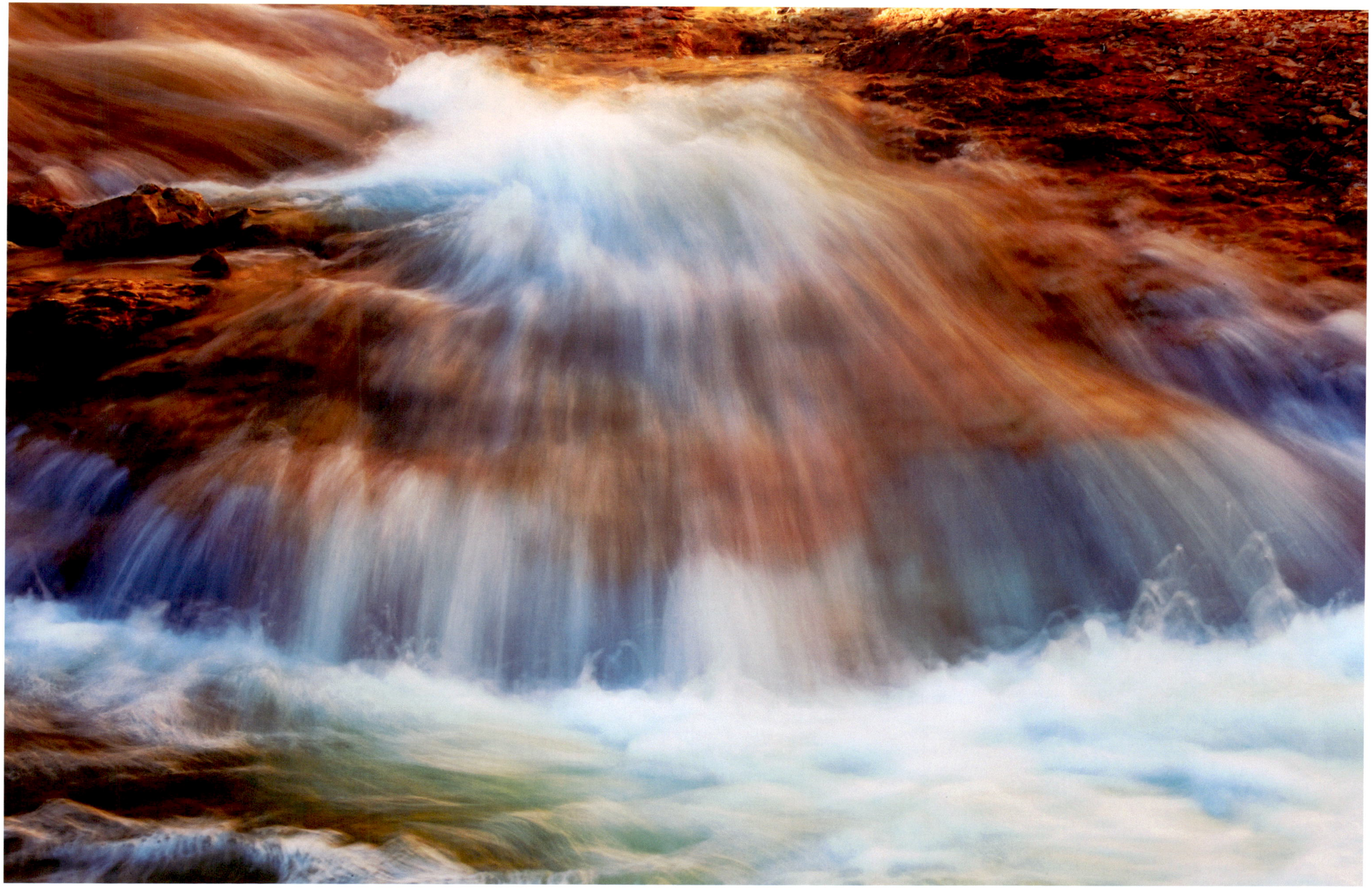

The colors and hues in this rushing waterfall near Bryce Canyon, Utah, reflect the red rock canyons that predominate this area and the blue and green tones of fast moving water. There are no filters used in this image, and this rushing stream kept us entertained for hours. *Photo by Kevin T. Karlson*

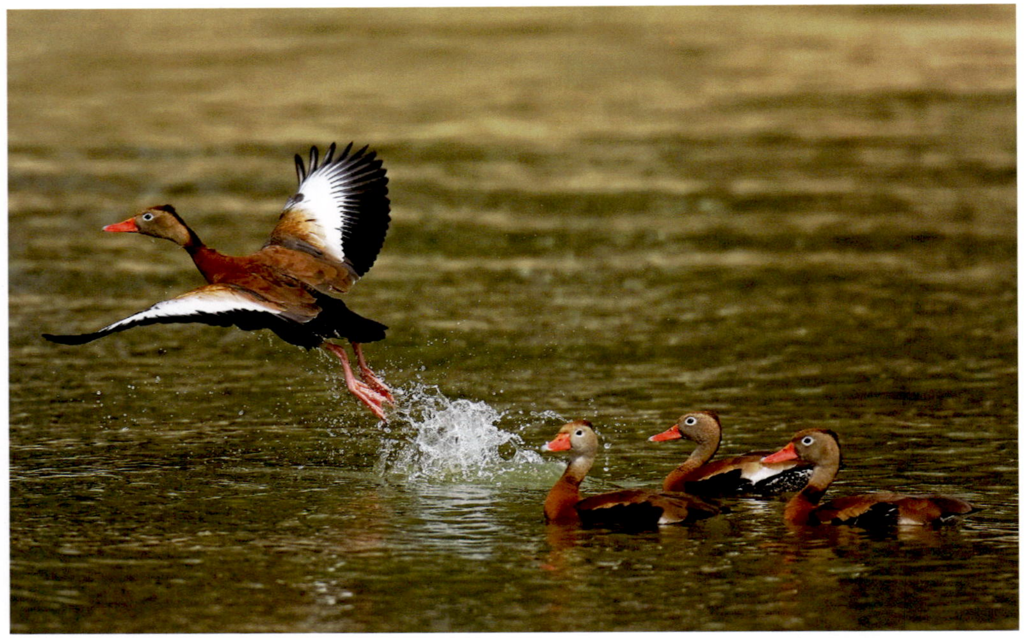

Black-bellied Whistling Ducks are some of the most captivating of all North American waterfowl with a coral bill color and dramatic wing pattern. A quiet mood is shown in the image at the left as these birds rest at dusk. A whistling-duck explodes into flight in the photo above. *Photos by Kevin T. Karlson*

The real voyage of discovery consists of not in seeking new landscapes but in having new eyes.

— Marcel Proust

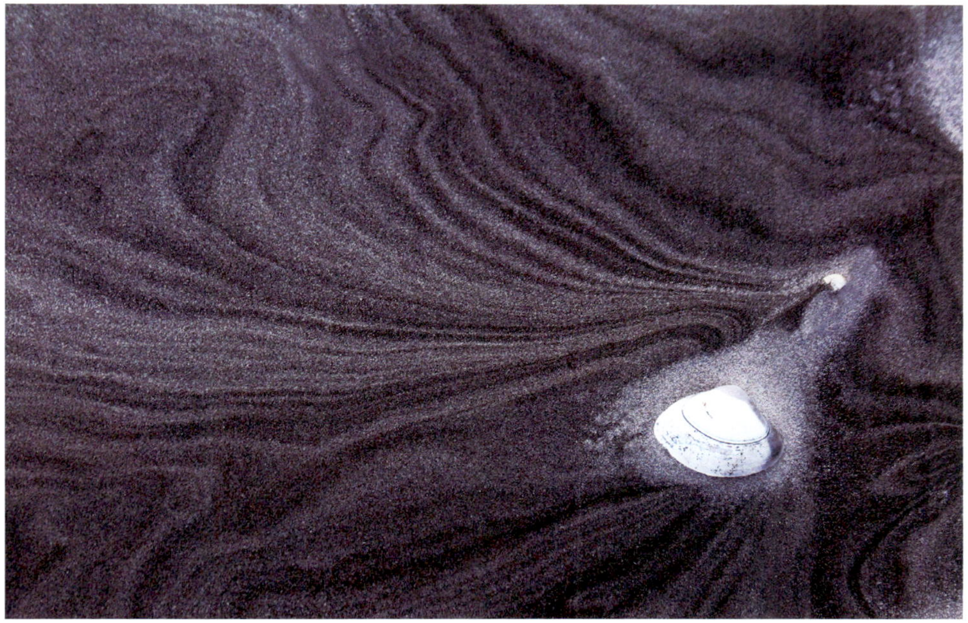

Two artists created the sand patterns on this page: wind and water. These images were taken on New Year's Day near Cape May, New Jersey, at the tide line of the Atlantic Ocean. The various sands were arranged by nature. Everyone seems to imagine a black stallion or dragon in the right image, but did you notice the man's contorted face leaning on the back of the stallion's head! It is truly gargoyle-like. *Photos by Kevin T. Karlson*

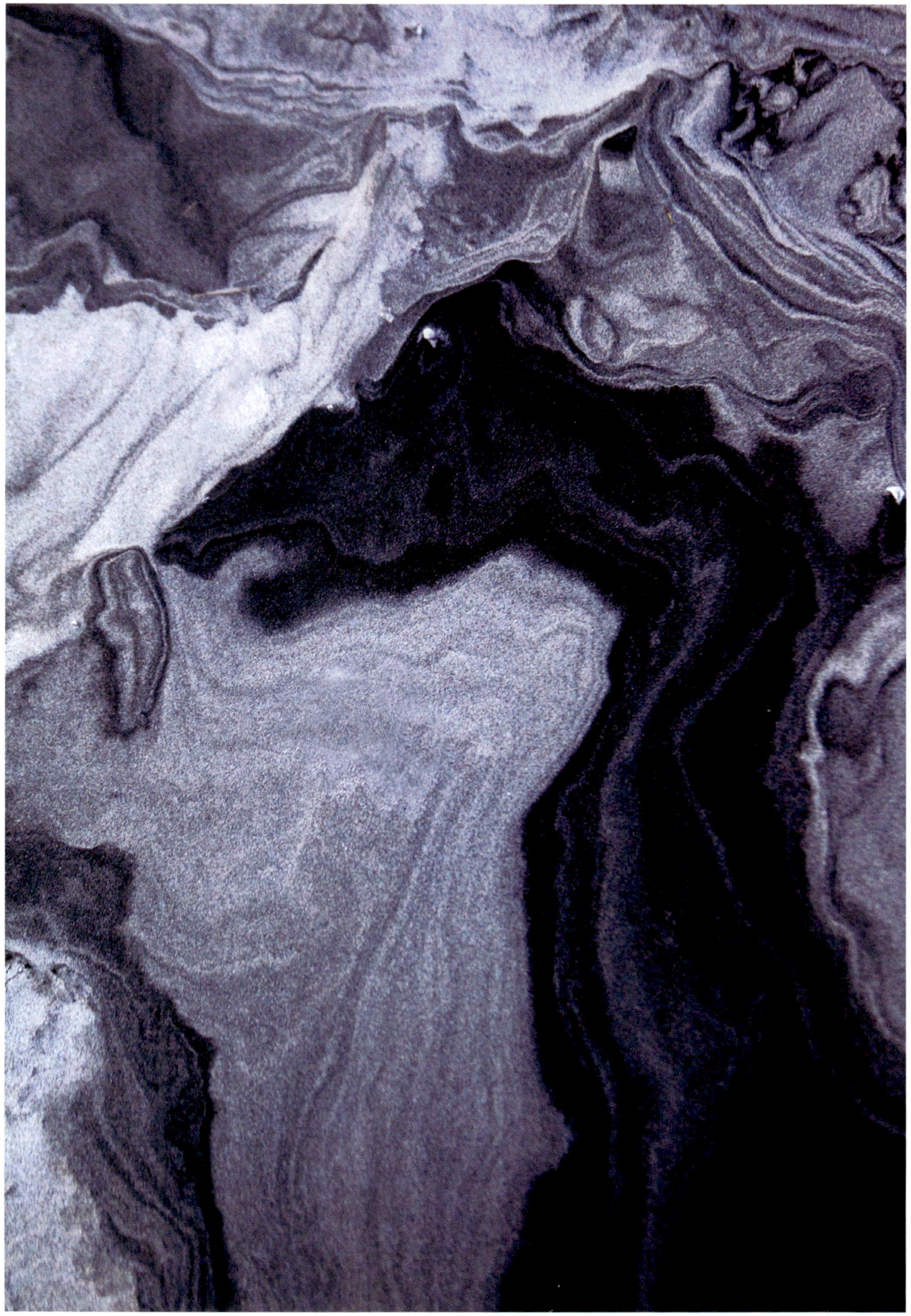

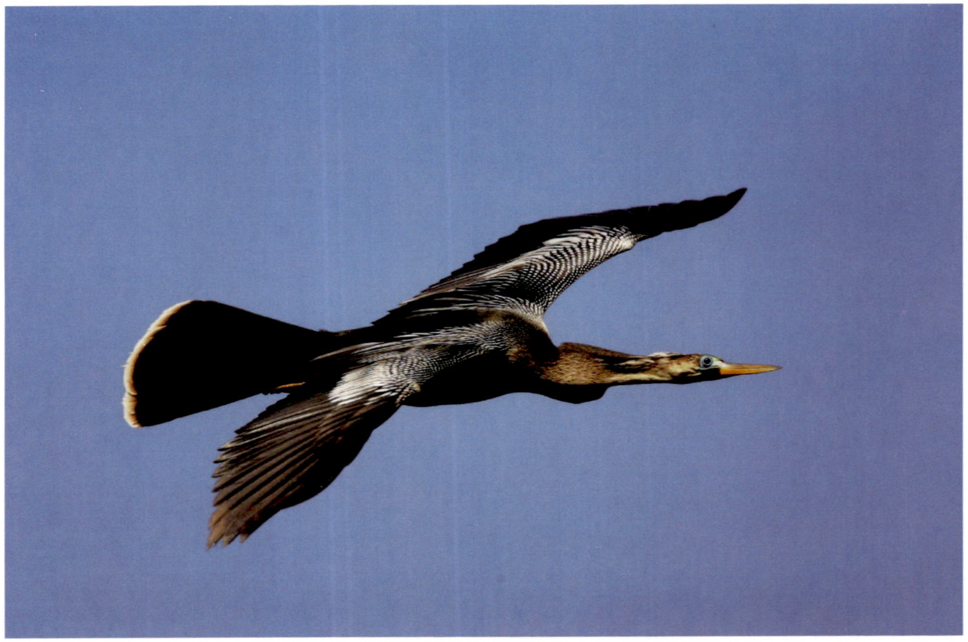

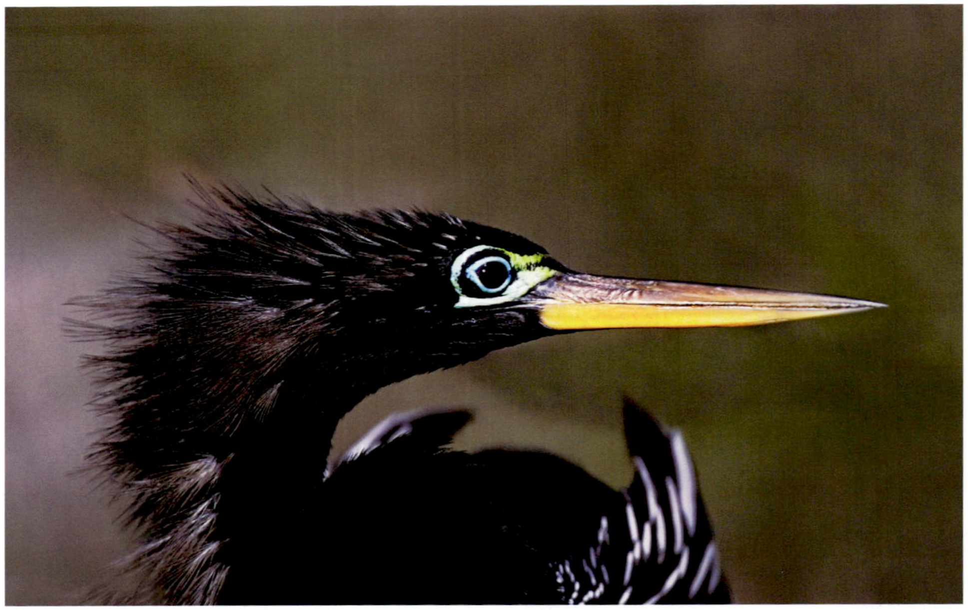

Anhinga are strange water birds that live in freshwater swamps of the southeast United States and other tropical areas. Males are all black, while females and immatures have brownish-buff heads and necks.

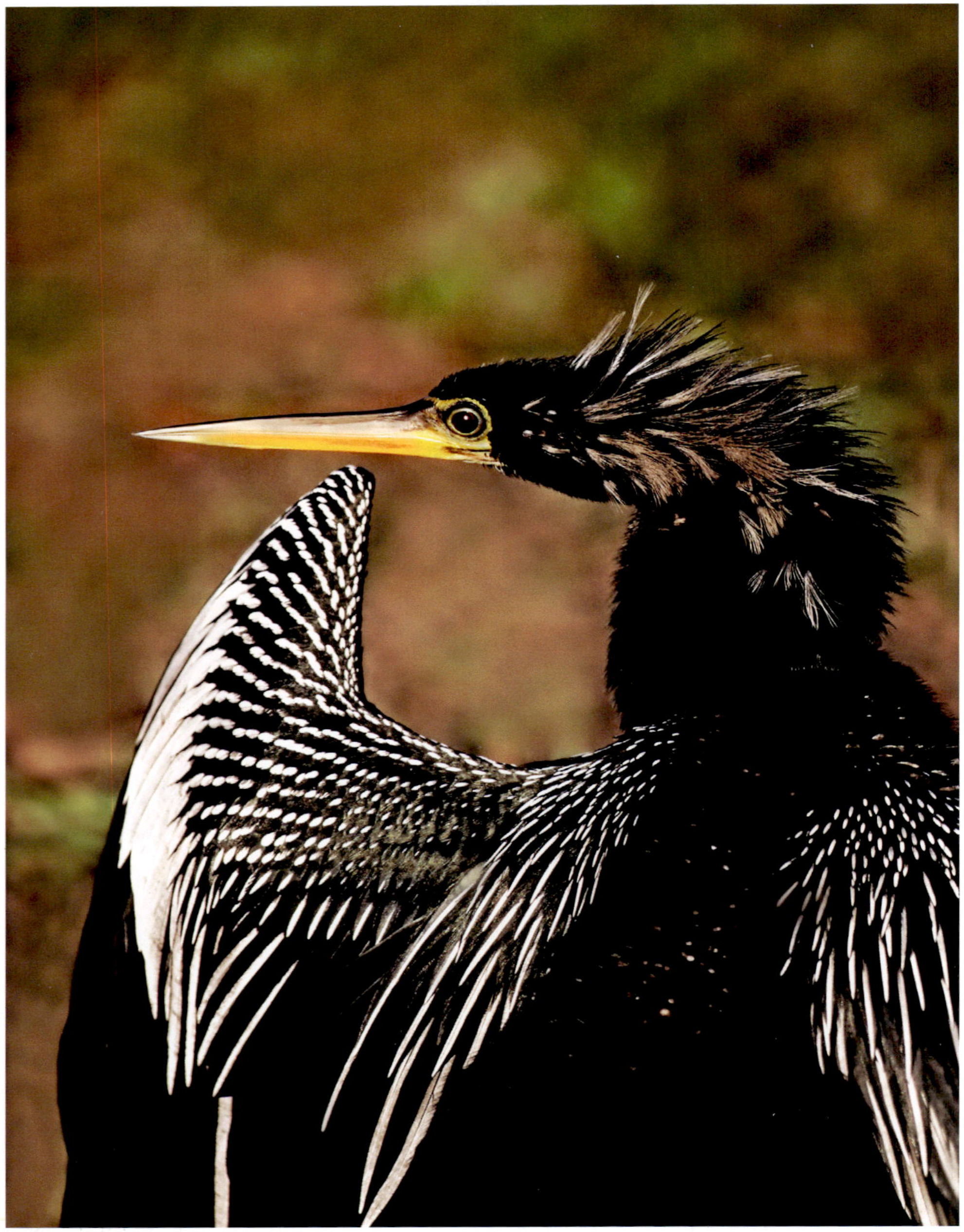

Opposite: The two Anhingas at the nest site on a palm tree formed a heart when they crossed bills. *Photos by Kevin T. Karlson*

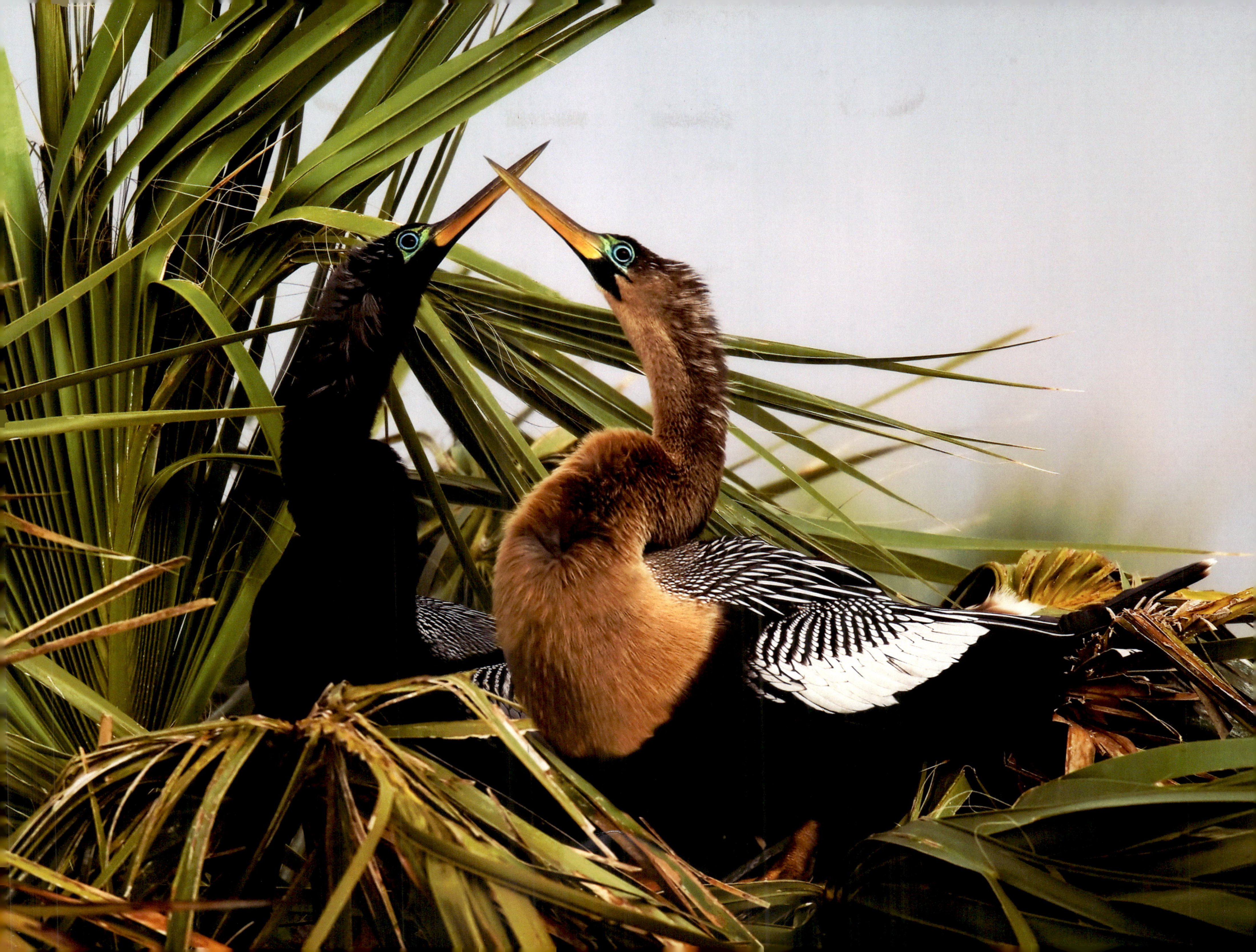

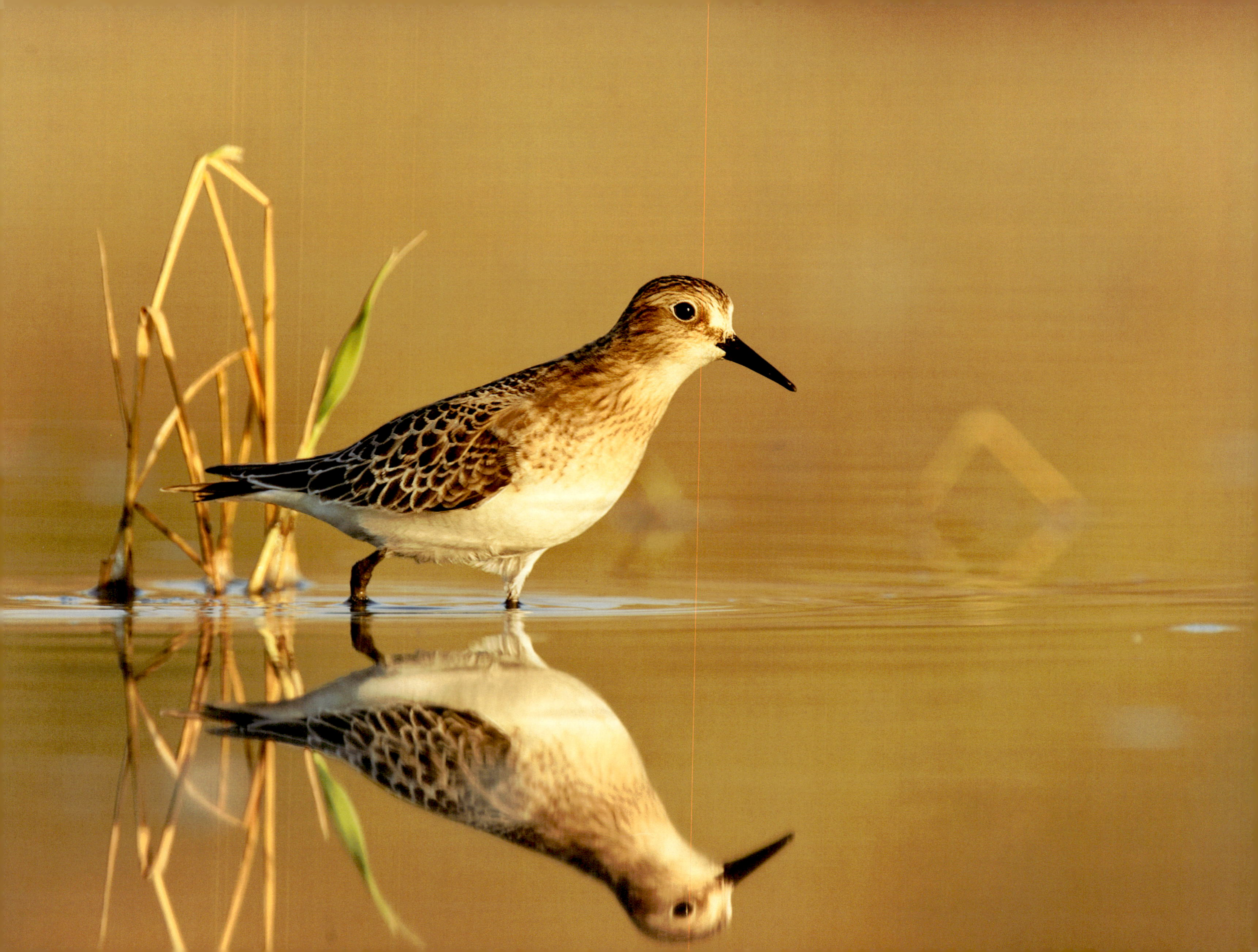

Opposite: A juvenile Baird's Sandpiper casts a beautiful reflection in a shallow water pool (opposite page).

A Least Sandpiper, the smallest sandpiper in the world at just under 5 inches long, fluffs its feathers (below).

Pectoral Sandpipers (right) are long-distance migrants that travel almost 20,000 miles each year. The bird's reflection adds to the mood of this image. *All photos by Scott Elowitz*

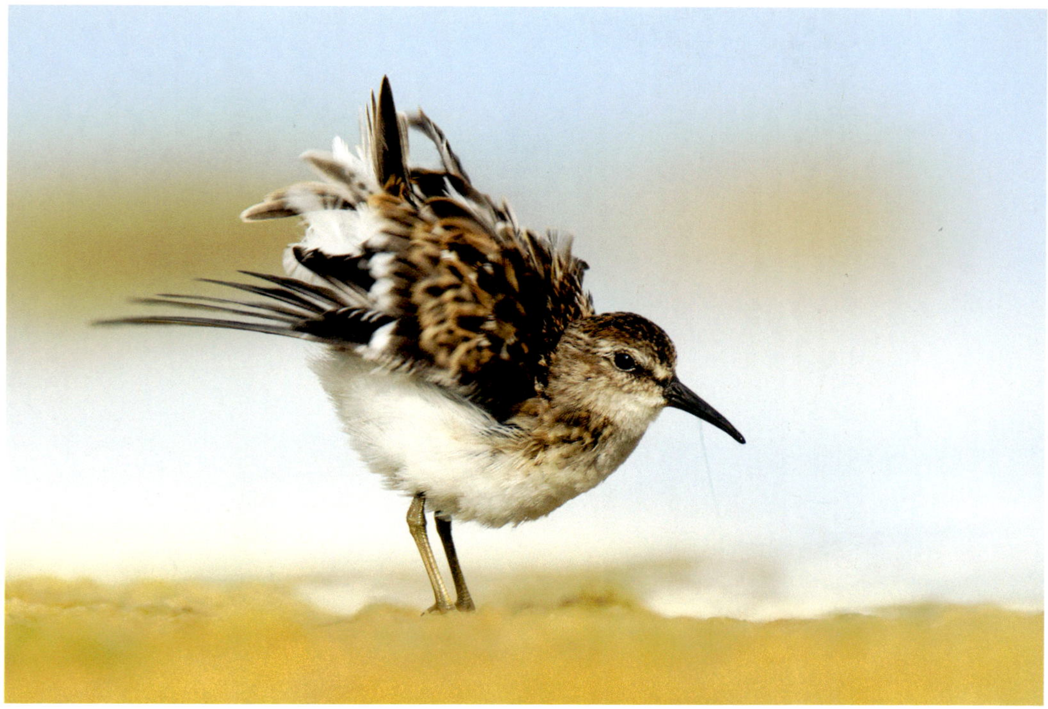

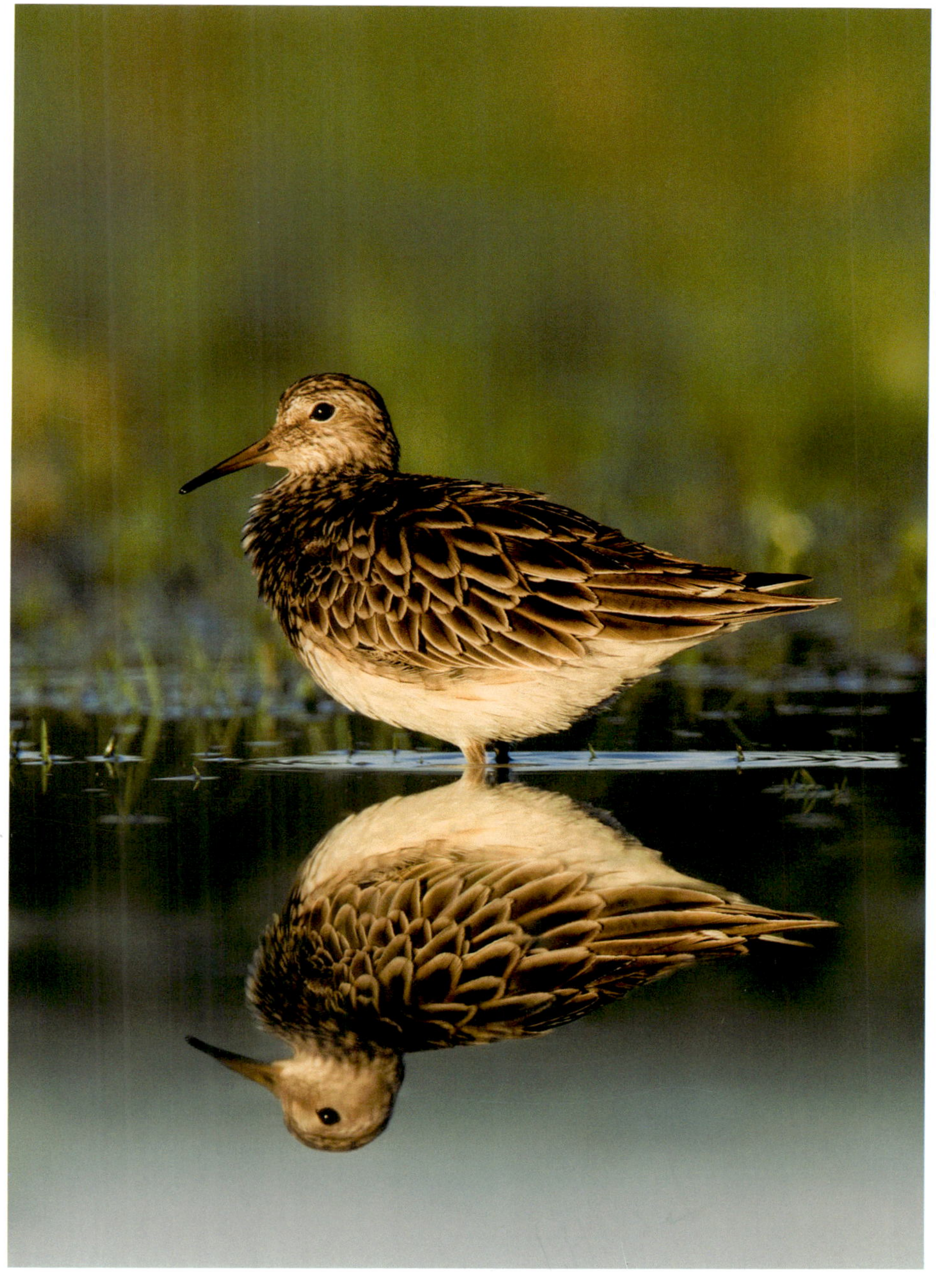

A juvenile Wilson's Phalarope enjoys its aquatic habitat in the photos below and at lower left. A non-breeding Red Knot (left) picks up a rock hoping that it is a small crab. *All photos by Lloyd Spitalnik*

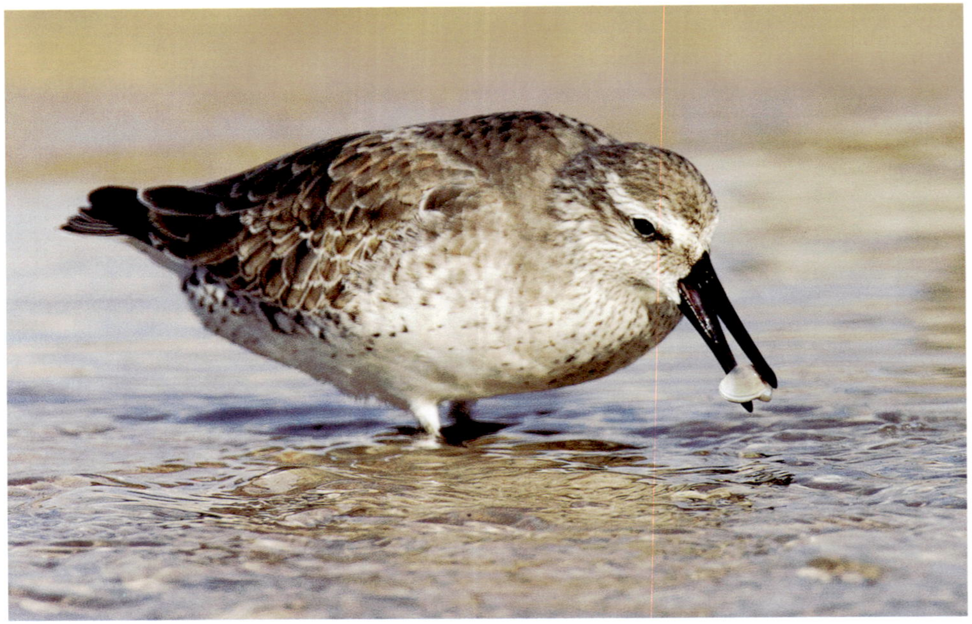

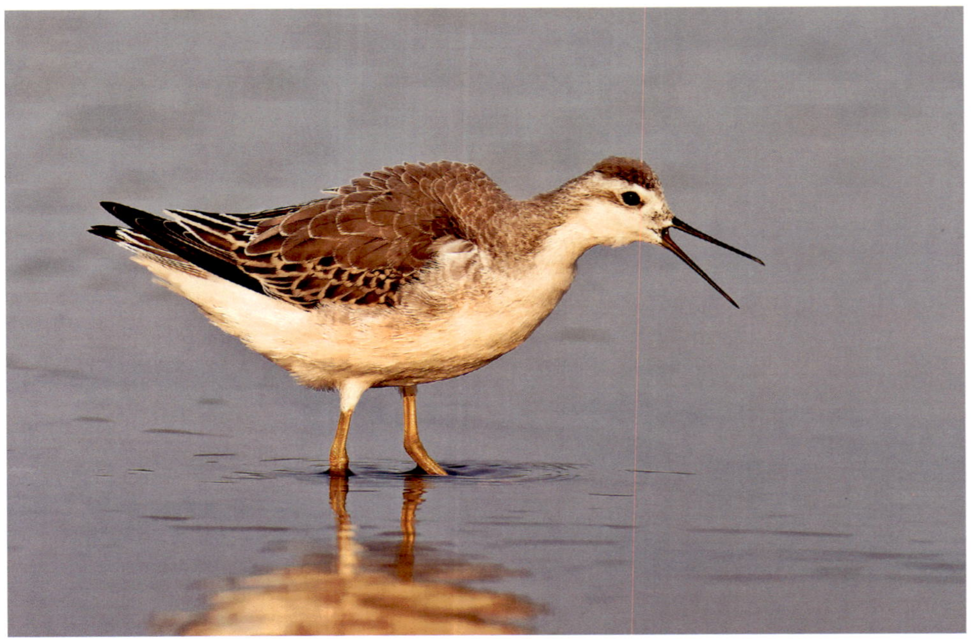

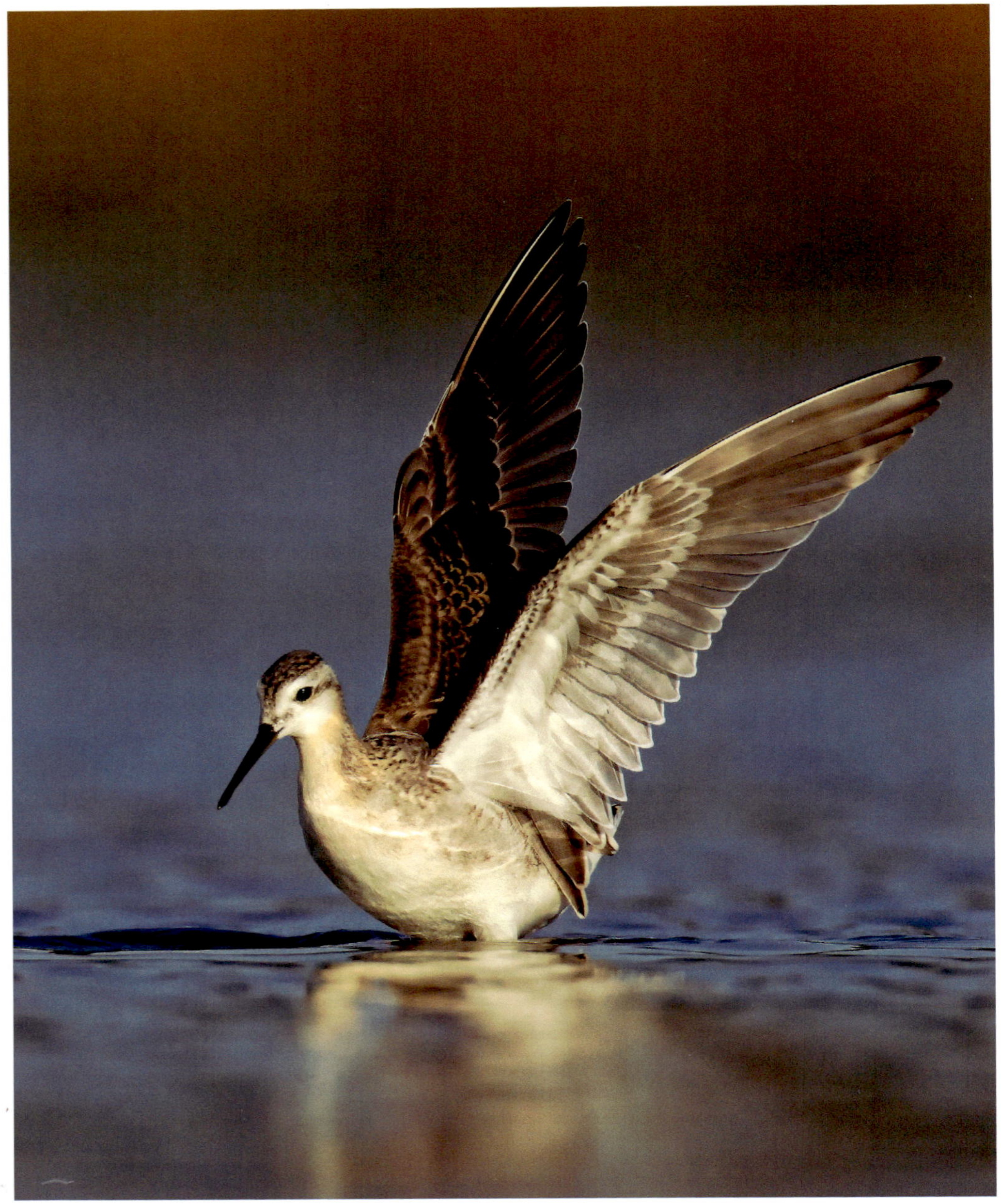

Opposite: An ethereal mood accompanies this eye-level photo of a breeding female Wilson's Phalarope, with fog enhancing the colorful bird. *Photo by Scott Elowitz*

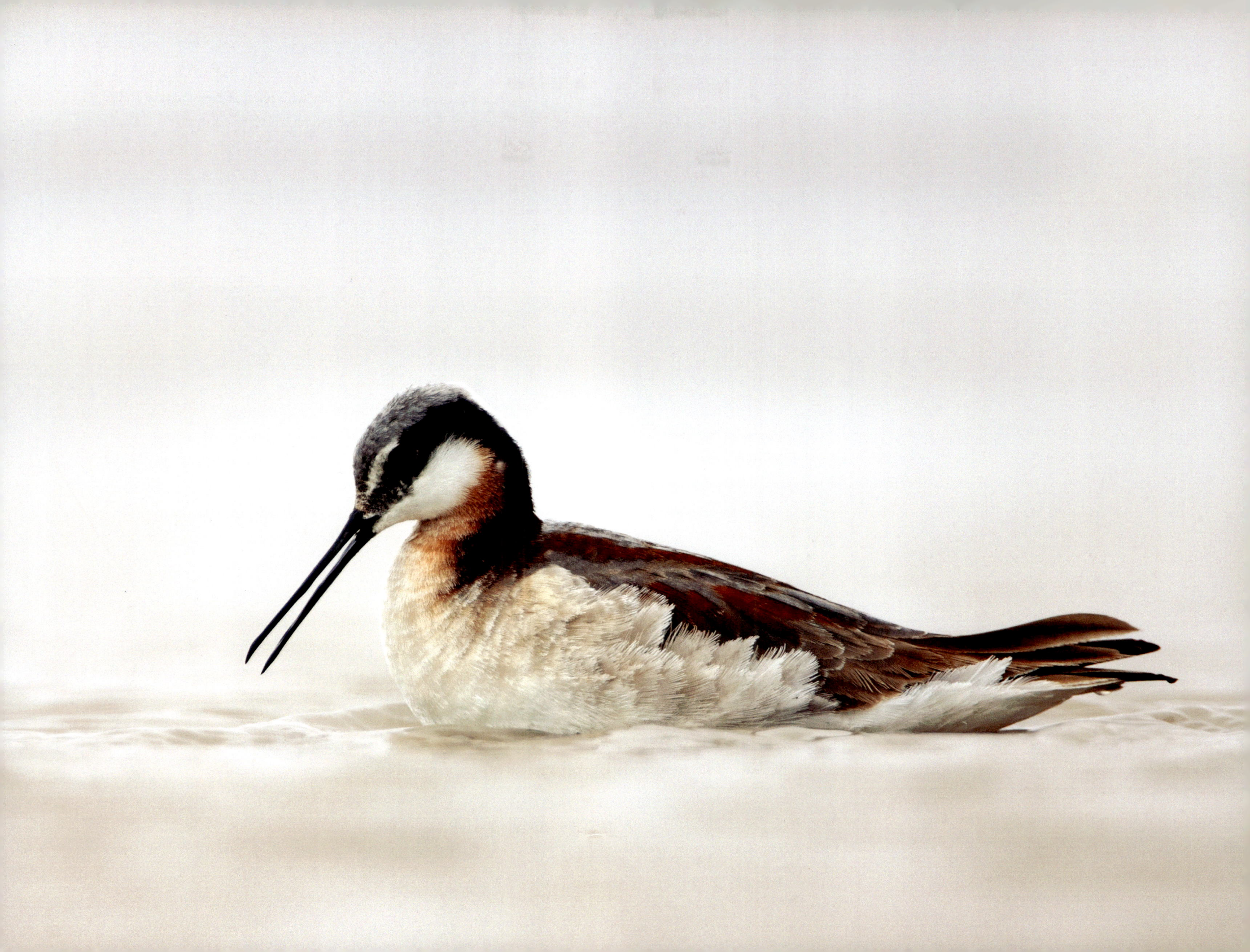

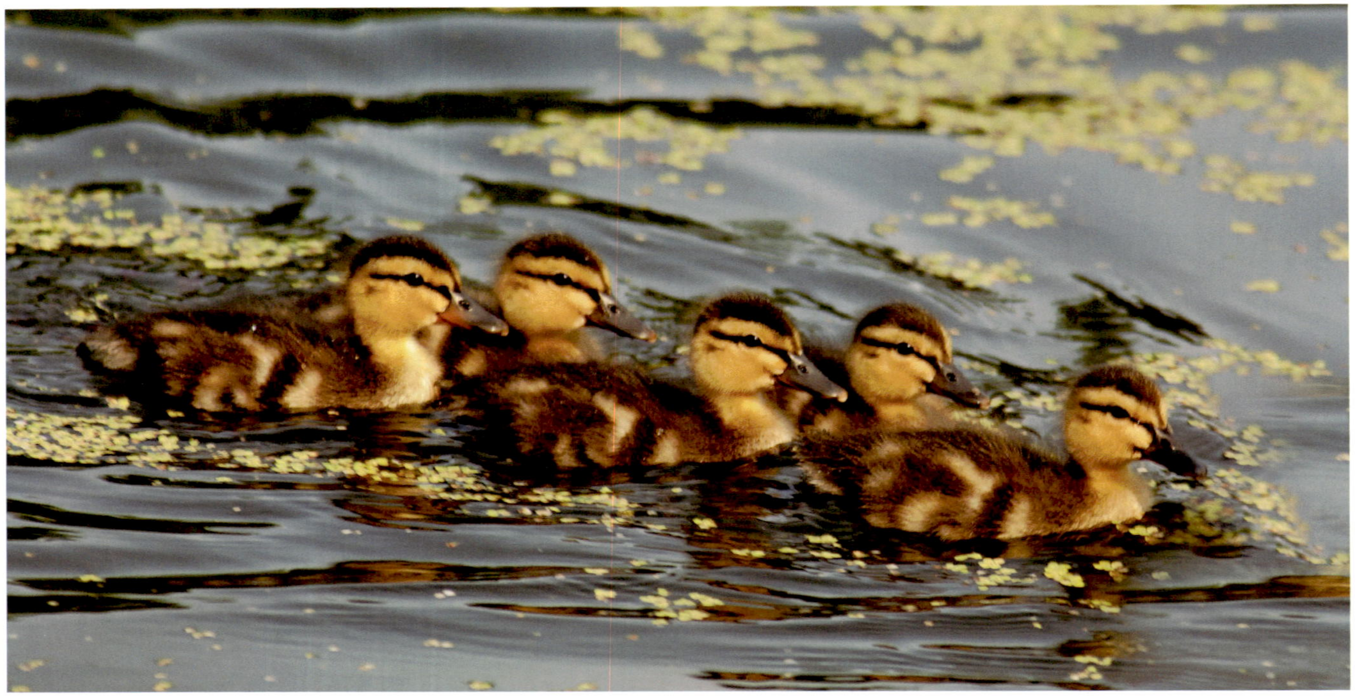

Tiny Mallard ducklings (above) can't help but be cute, but they must watch for danger at every step of their growth.

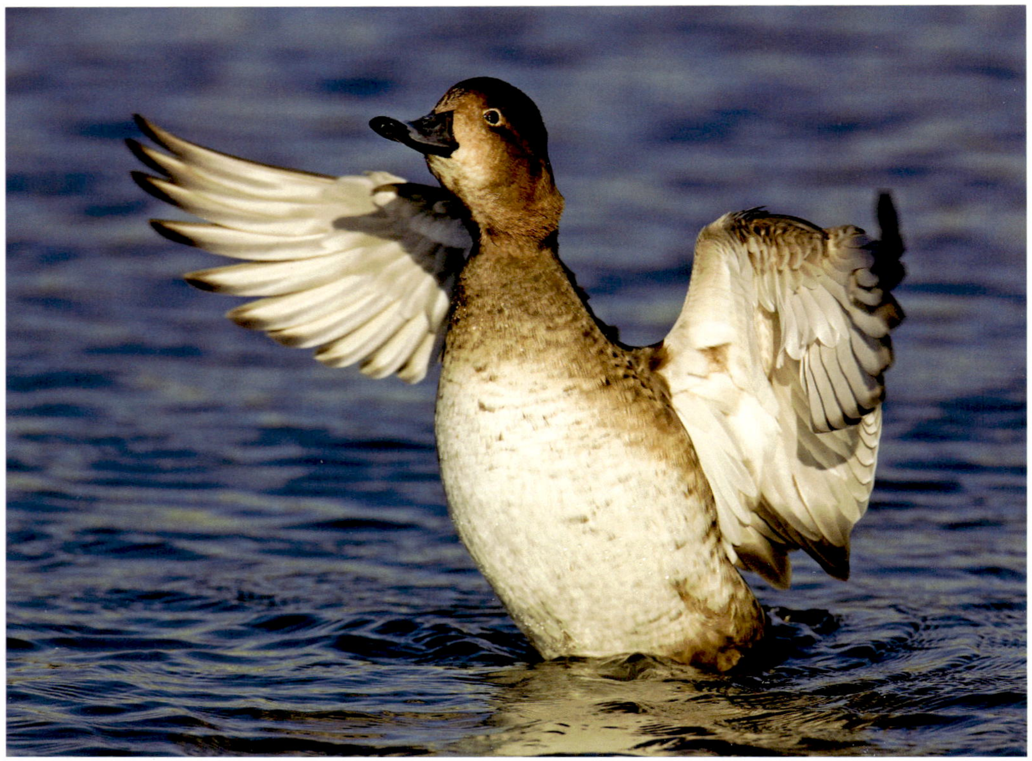

A female Redhead (right) performs a wing flap to exercise her wings and celebrate her love of water. *Photos by Lloyd Spitalnik*

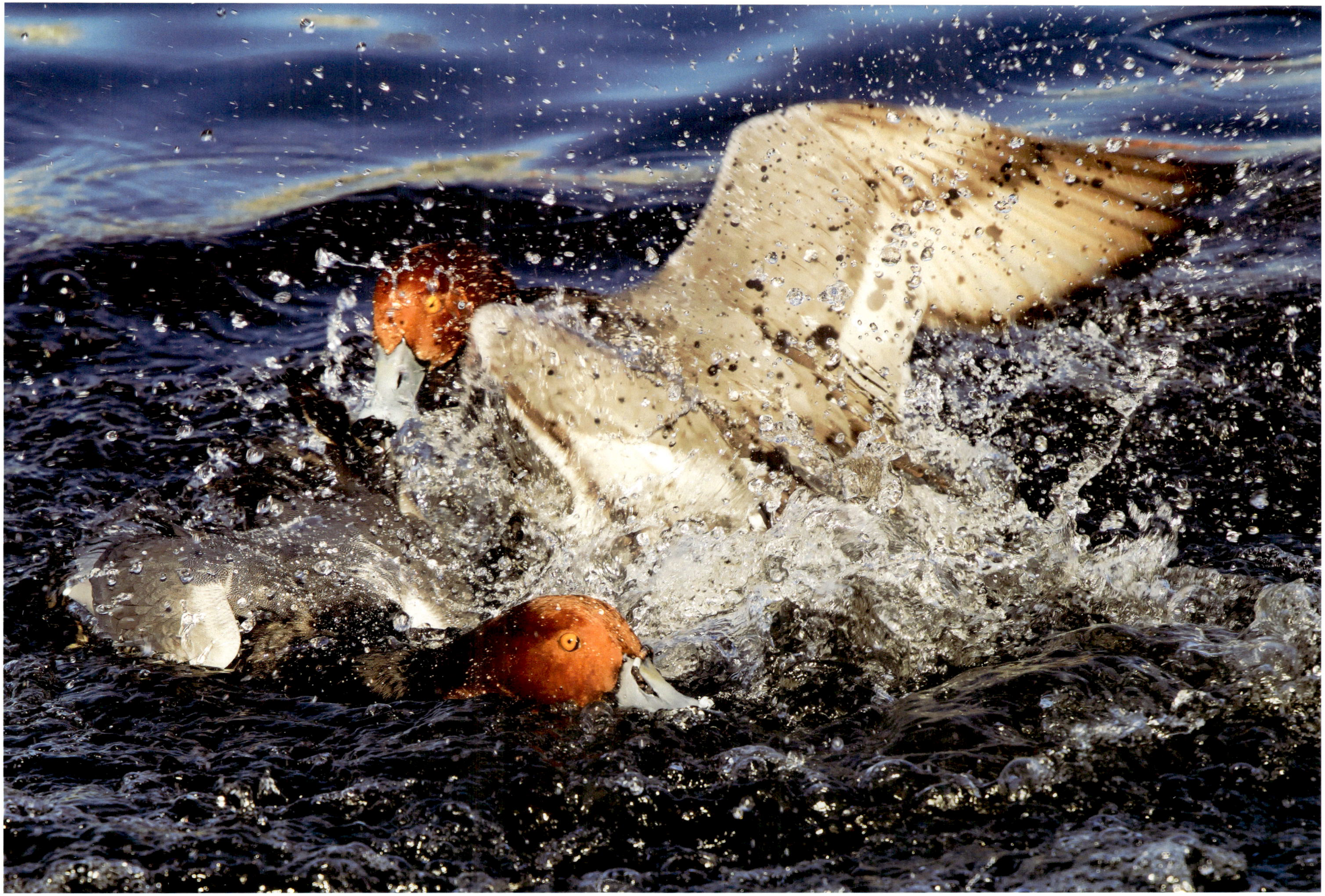

Two drake Redheads settle a difference of opinion by chasing and biting each other. The water is roiling with their intense struggle.
Photo by Lloyd Spitalnik

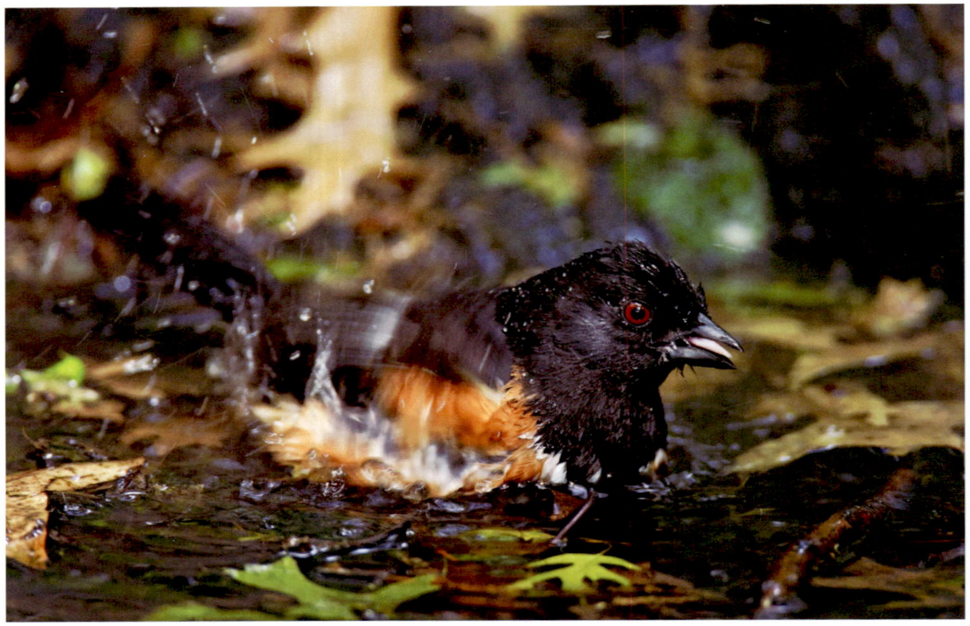

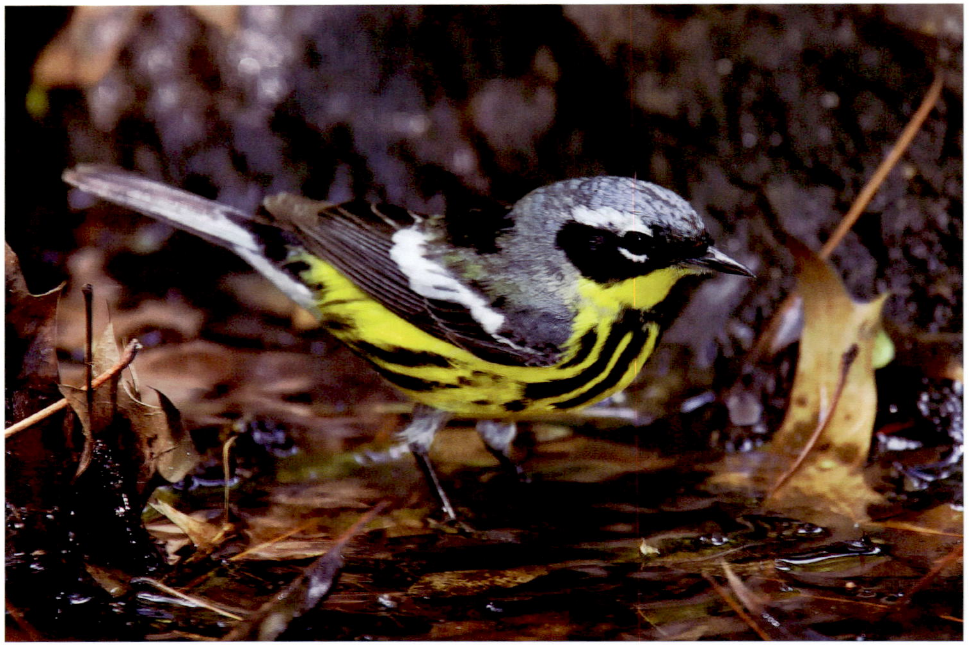

Songbirds are not typically associated with water, unless they are bathing or drinking. A Worm-eating Warbler (below) and Magnolia Warbler (lower left) enjoy a welcome bath, while an Eastern Towhee (left) throws water all around during his invigorating splashing. *All photos taken in Central Park, New York by Lloyd Spitalnik*

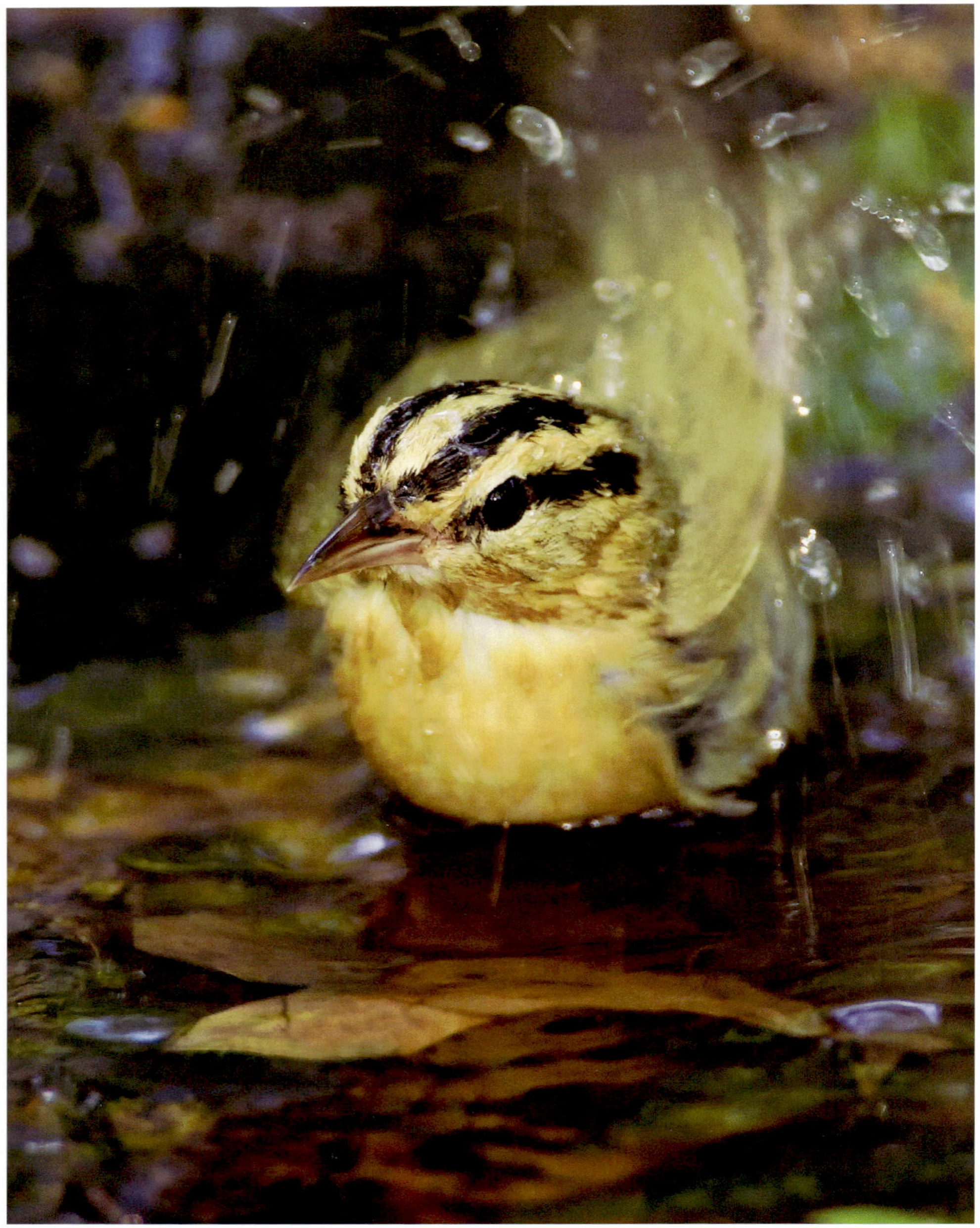

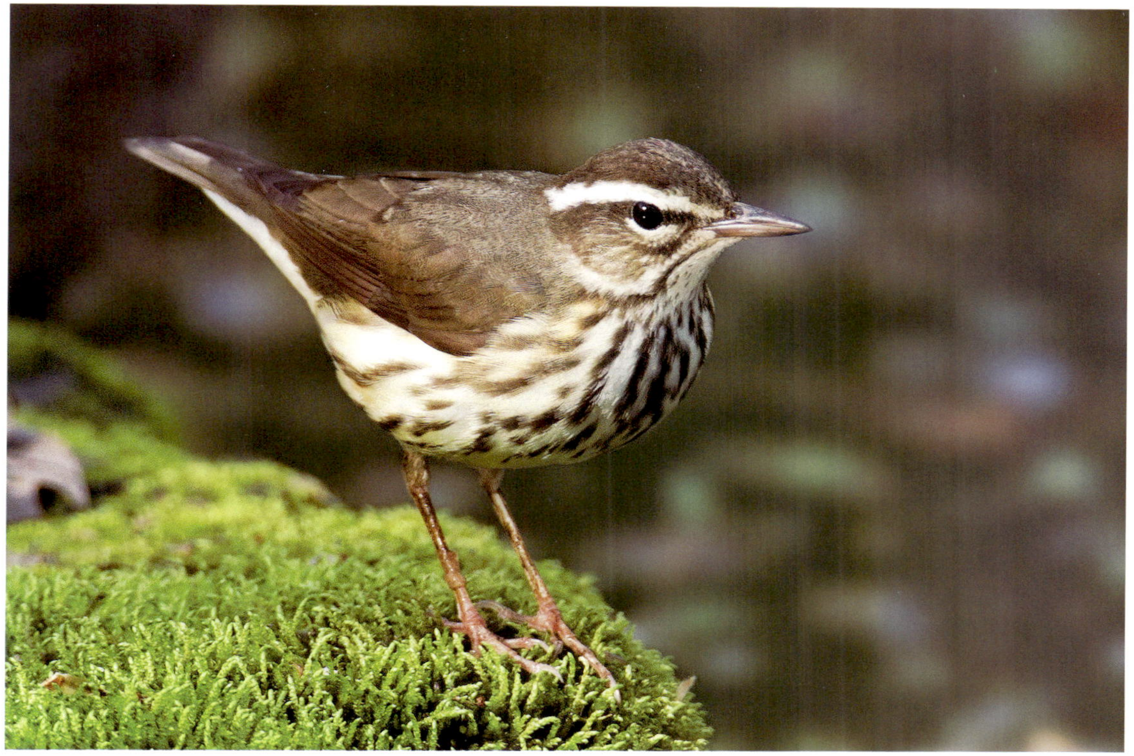

Louisiana Waterthrushes (left) are warblers that live and nest adjacent to fast moving streams. *Photo by Lloyd Spitalnik*

A stunning male Blue Grosbeak (lower left) gets ready to bathe in this image taken in the Dry Tortugas, Florida. *Photo by Kevin T. Karlson*

Four Cedar Waxwings (below) enjoy the cool waters in Central Park, New York. *Photo by Lloyd Spitalnik*

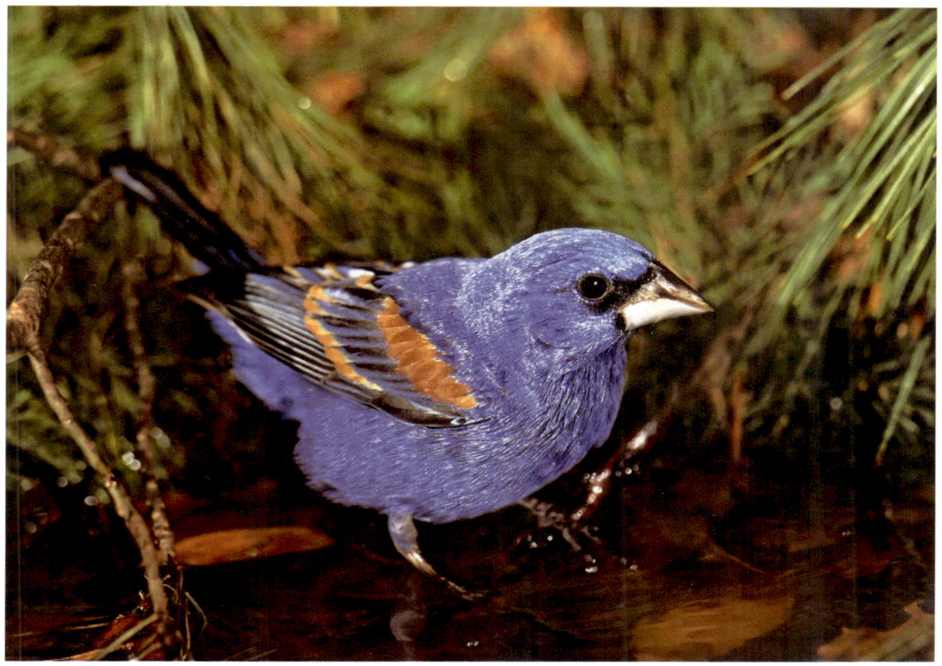

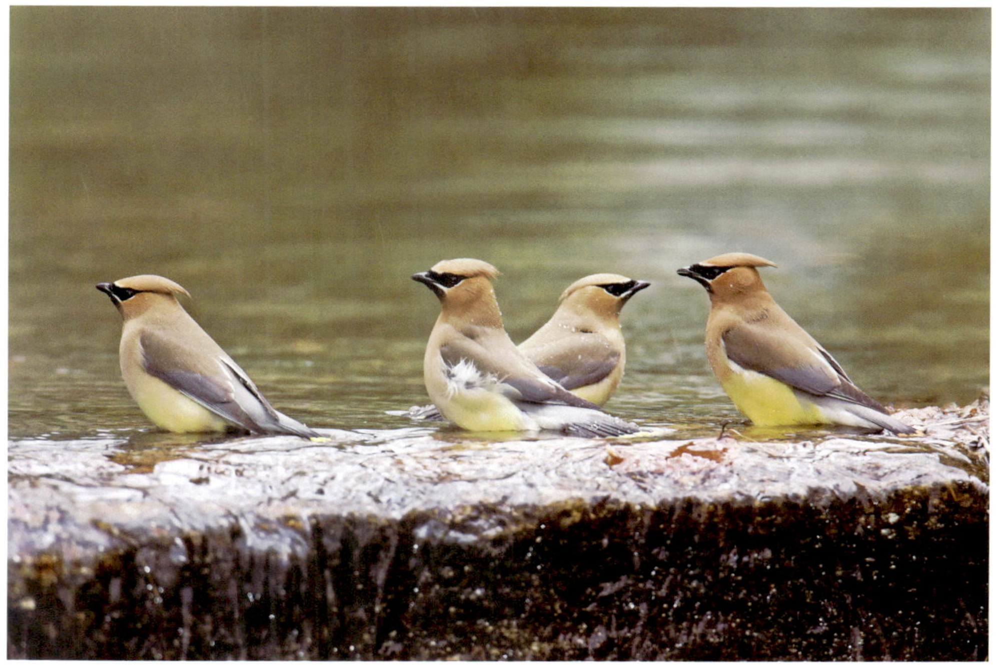

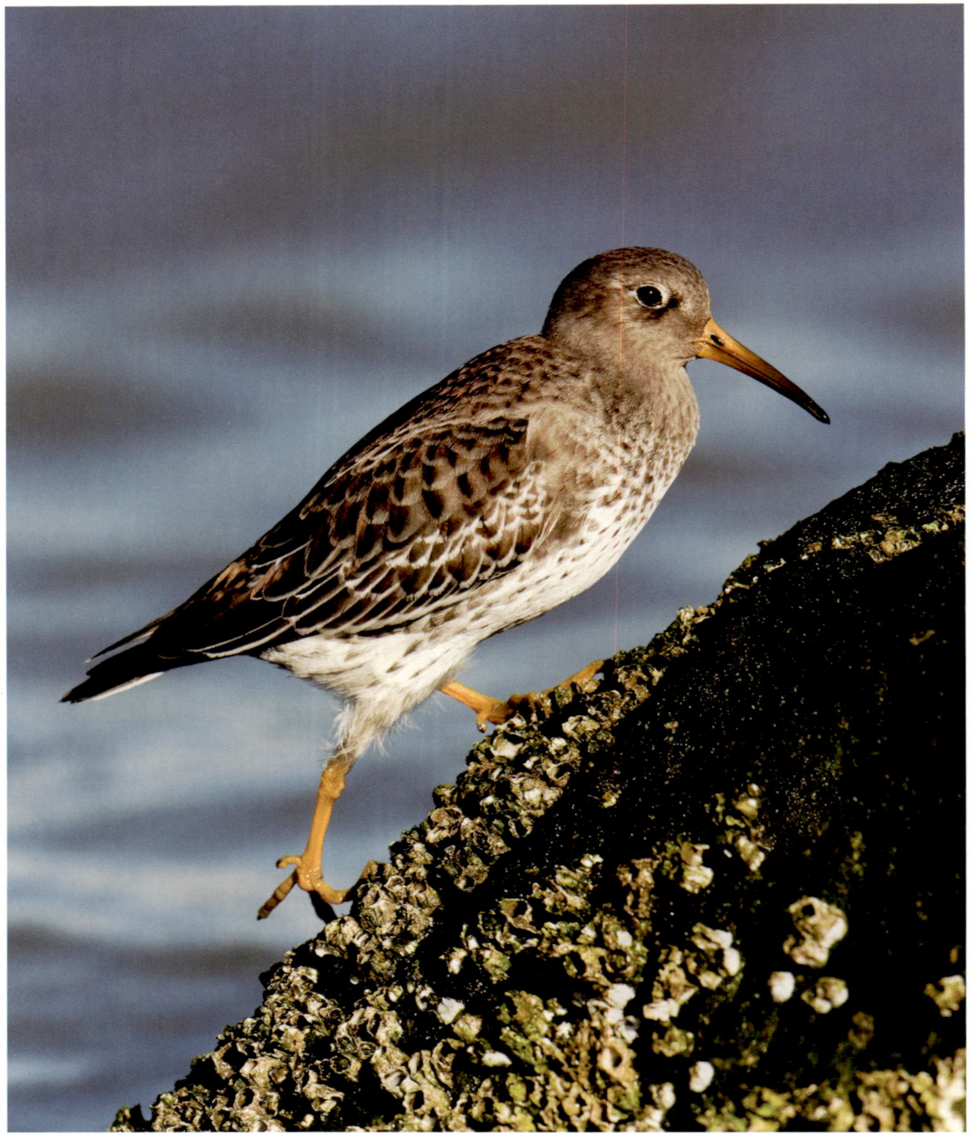

The Purple Sandpiper (above) is a small shorebird that spends the winter on cold, rocky jetties and breakwaters. *Photo by Scott Elowitz*

A juvenile Semipalmated Sandpiper (right) ruffles it feathers in anticipation of a bath. *Photo by Lloyd Spitalnik*

Opposite: Dunlin, Barnegat Light, New Jersey. "Here's looking at you. It's tempting to try and get that perfect 'portrait shot' of a bird, but sometimes photographing them as you see them in the wild gives a different perspective. Dunlins roosting on a stone jetty use the rocks to protect them from the elements and predators. A peeping eye is often all you will see." *Photo and caption by Mike Crewe*

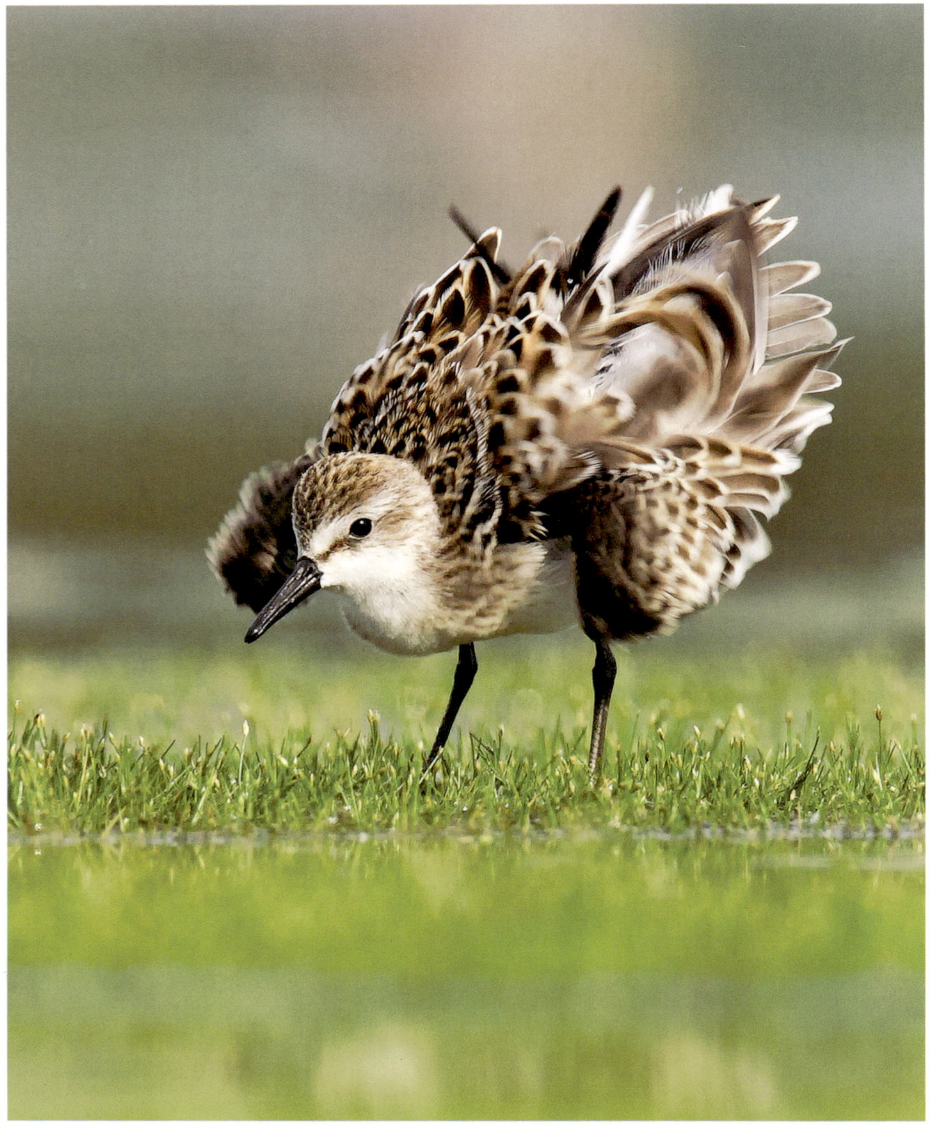

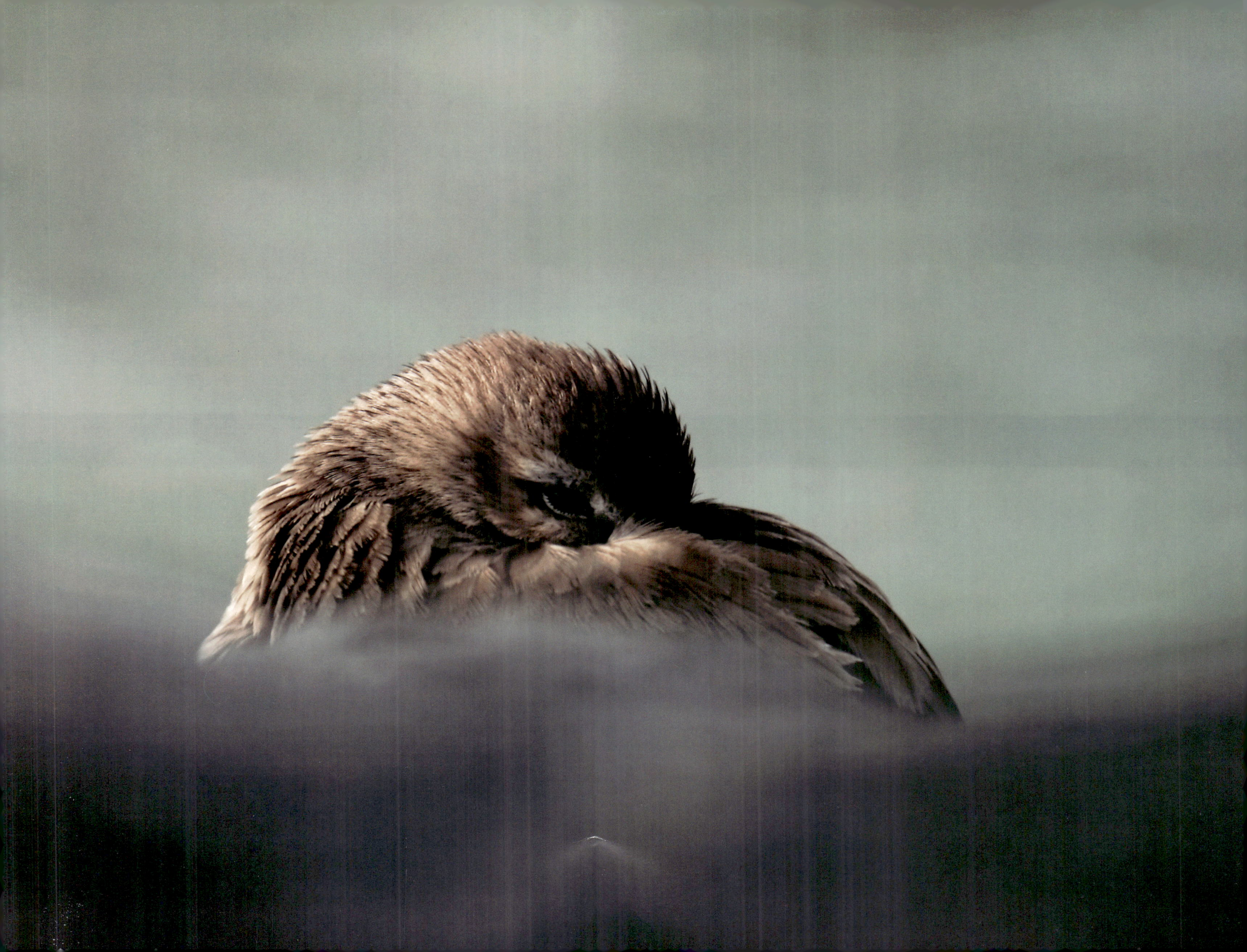

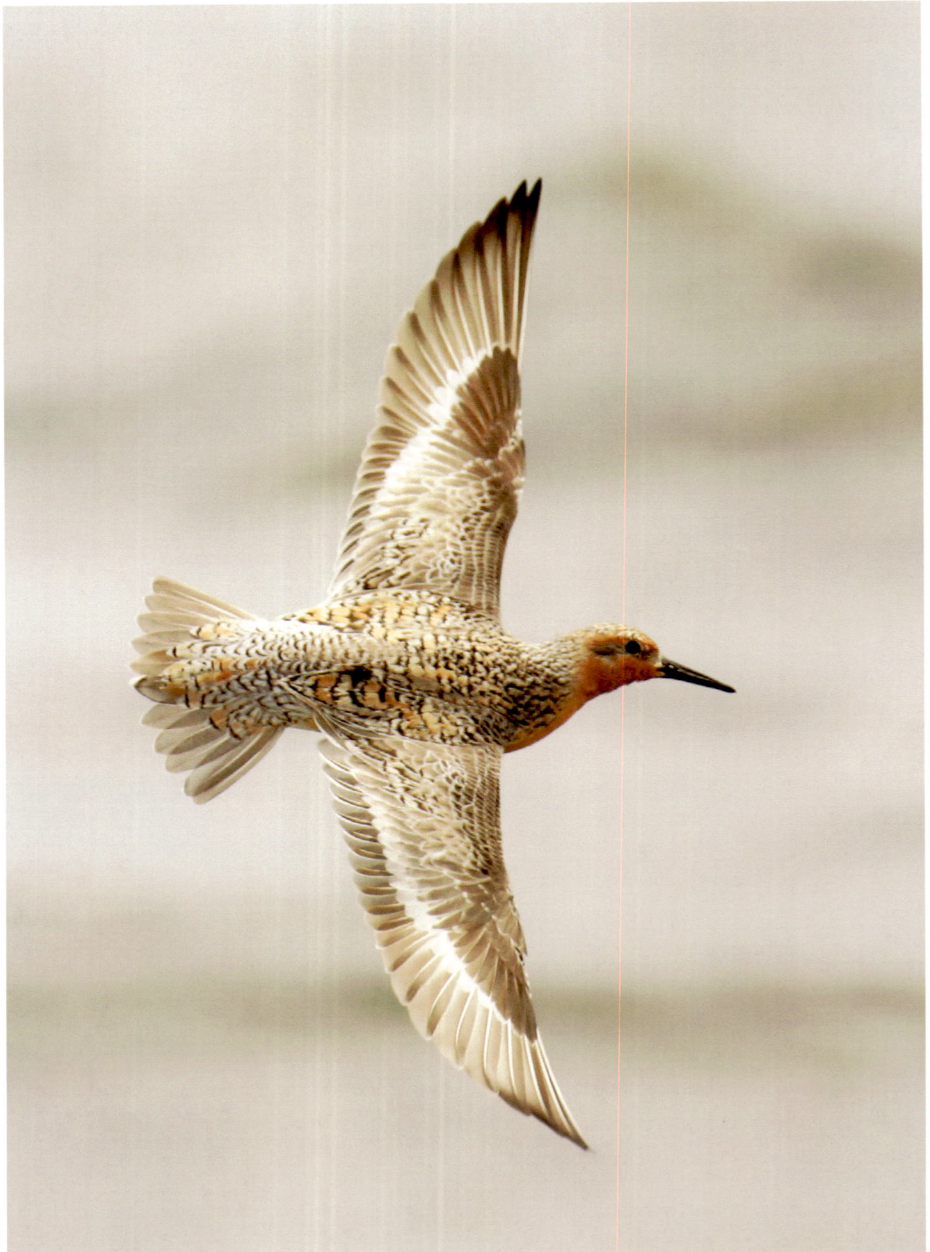

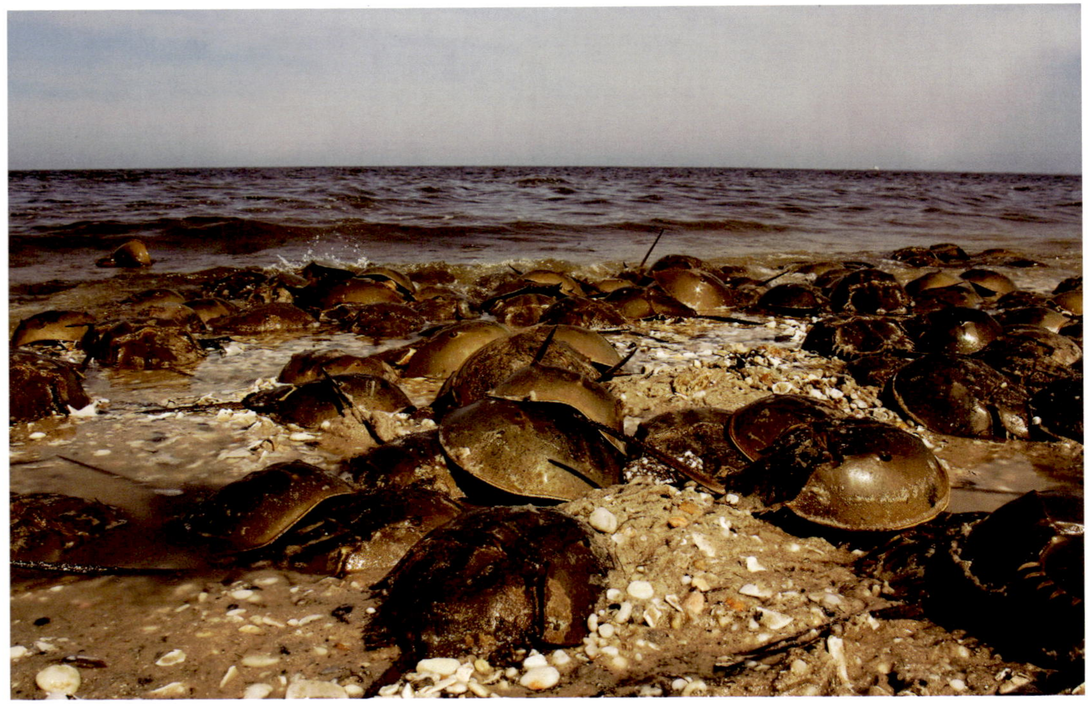

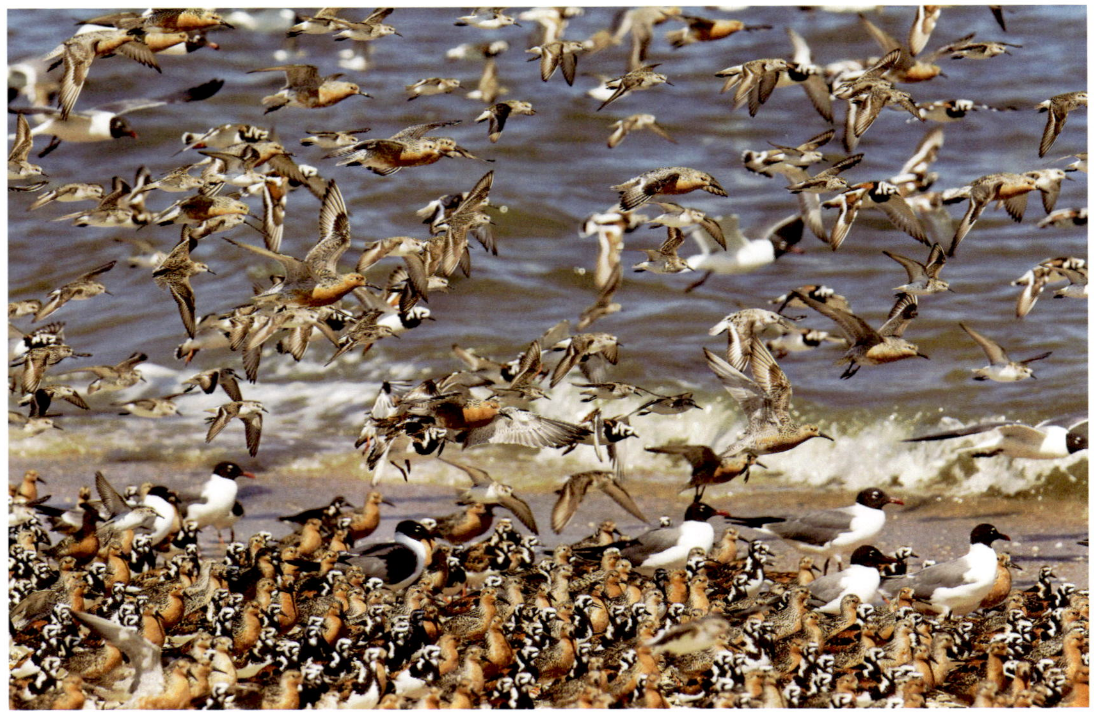

Red Knots and Ruddy Turnstones feed on Horseshoe Crab eggs on the Delaware Bayshore of New Jersey (upper right).

A graceful Red Knot shows its long wings in flight (above), while a large group of Red Knots and Ruddy Turnstones explode from a Delaware River beach (right). *Photo above by Scott Elowitz. Photos upper right and right by Kevin T. Karlson*

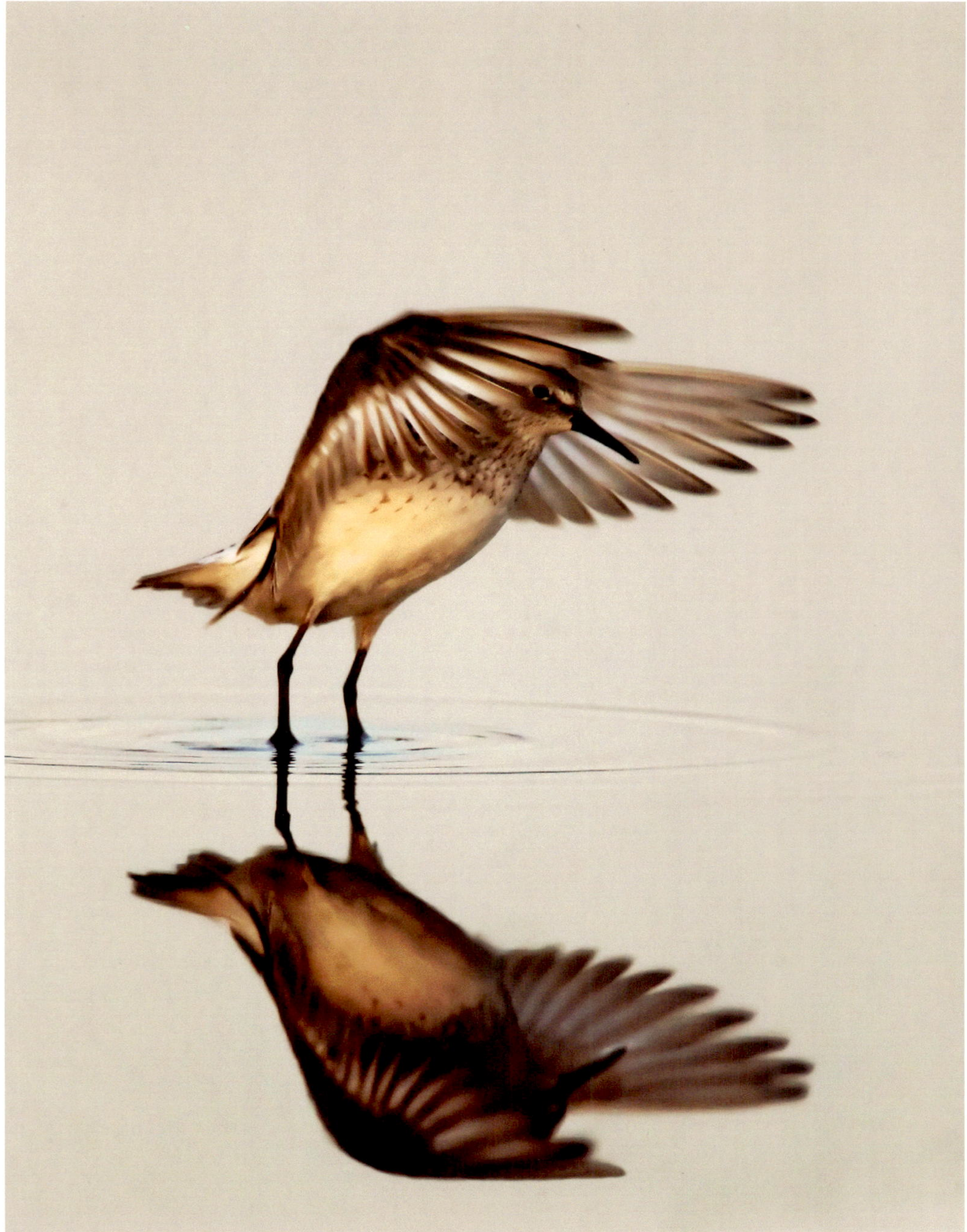

One eye sees, the other feels.

— Paul Klee

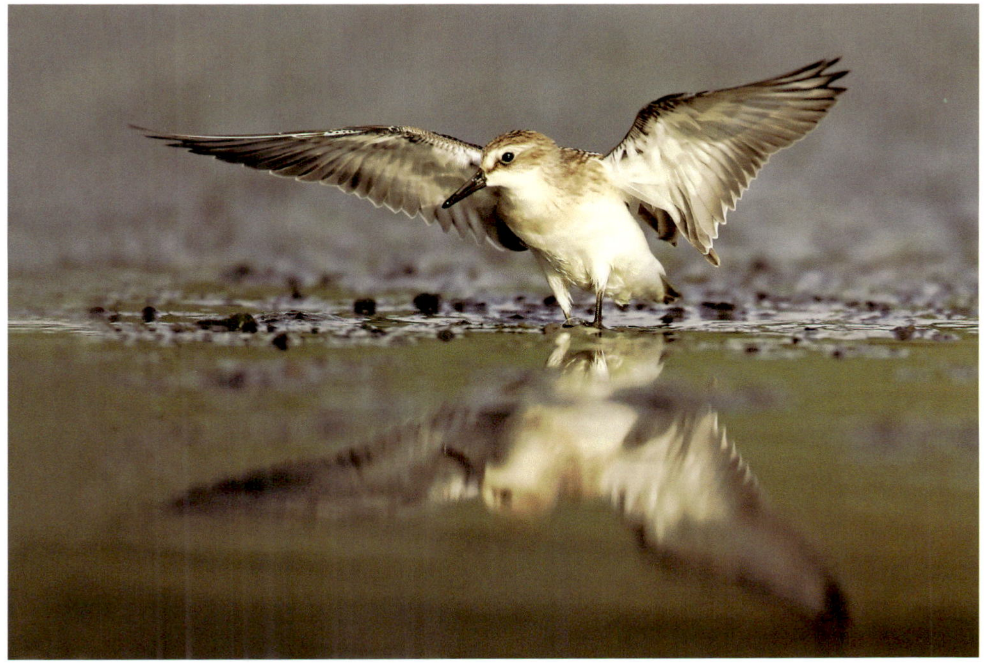

Semipalmated Sandpipers are small shorebirds that breed in Arctic regions. A moody shot taken after sunset in soft grayish-pink light (left) shows a "Semi" lifting from the water after a bath.

Using its wings to keep from sinking in the mud allows this "Semi" (above) to feed in soft mud that would not support him without the benefit of wing flaps. *Photos by Kevin T. Karlson*

Opposite: A drake Lesser Scaup enjoys a vigorous bath. *Photo by Kevin T. Karlson*

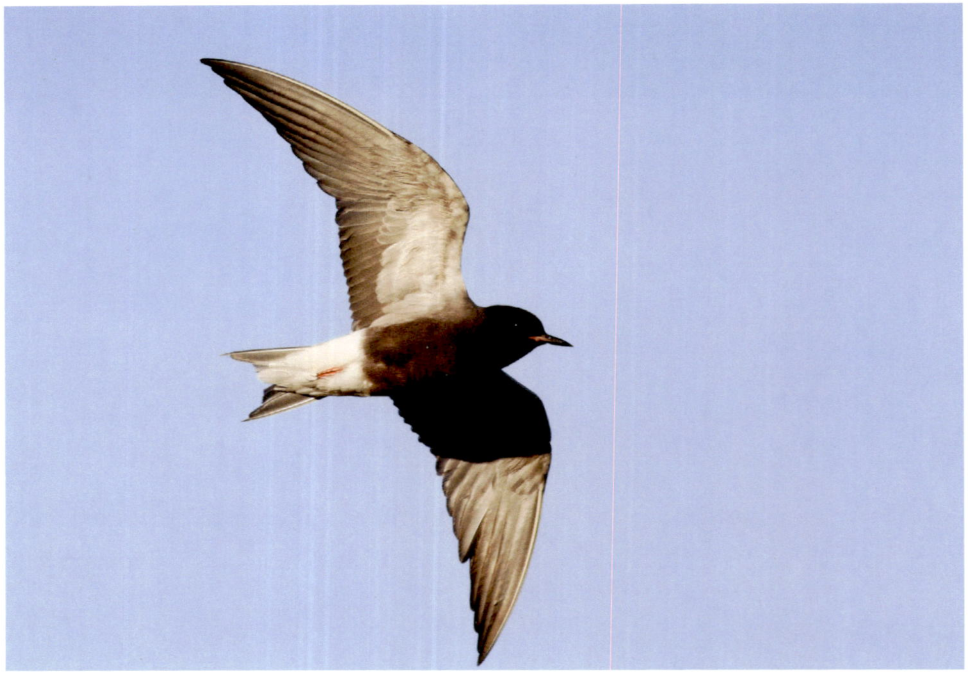

In British Columbia, a Black Tern tenderly cares for her chicks (lower left), while another flies gracefully overhead (left). Meanwhile, in the next pond over, a male Red-necked Grebe cares for a clutch of rambunctious chicks on its floating nest. *Photos by Scott Elowitz*

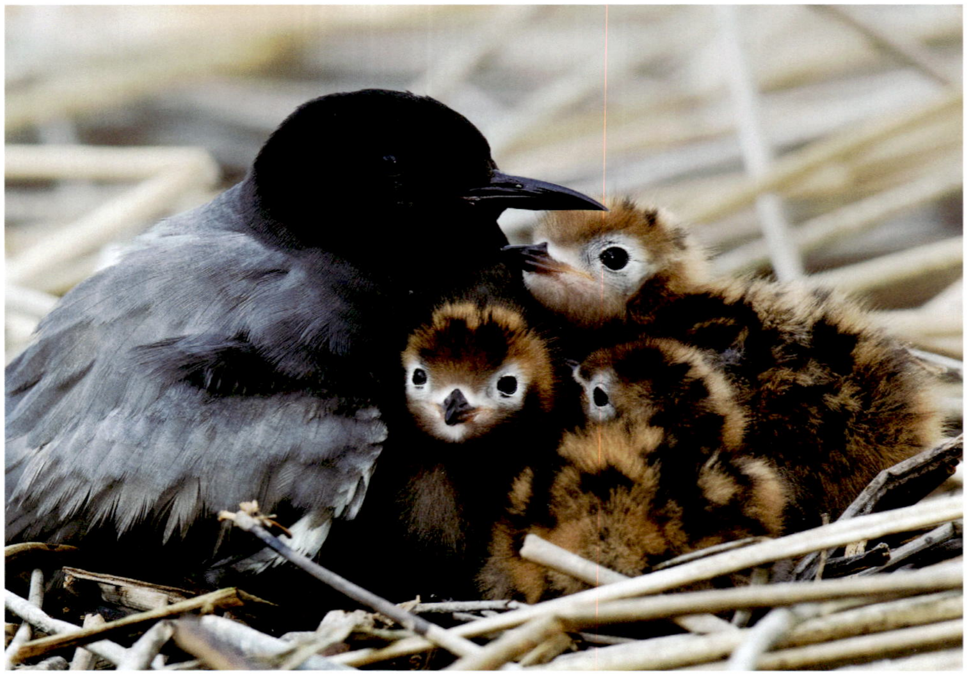

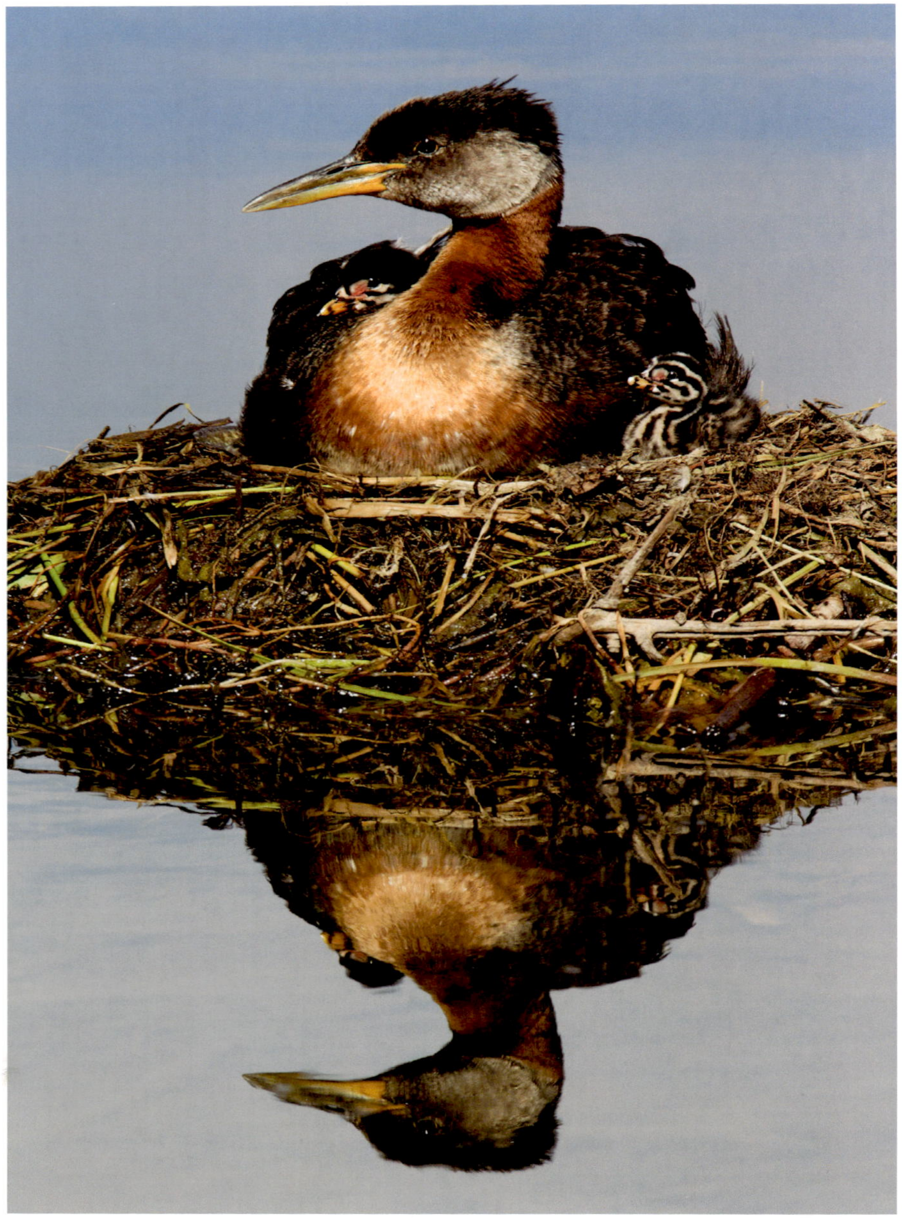

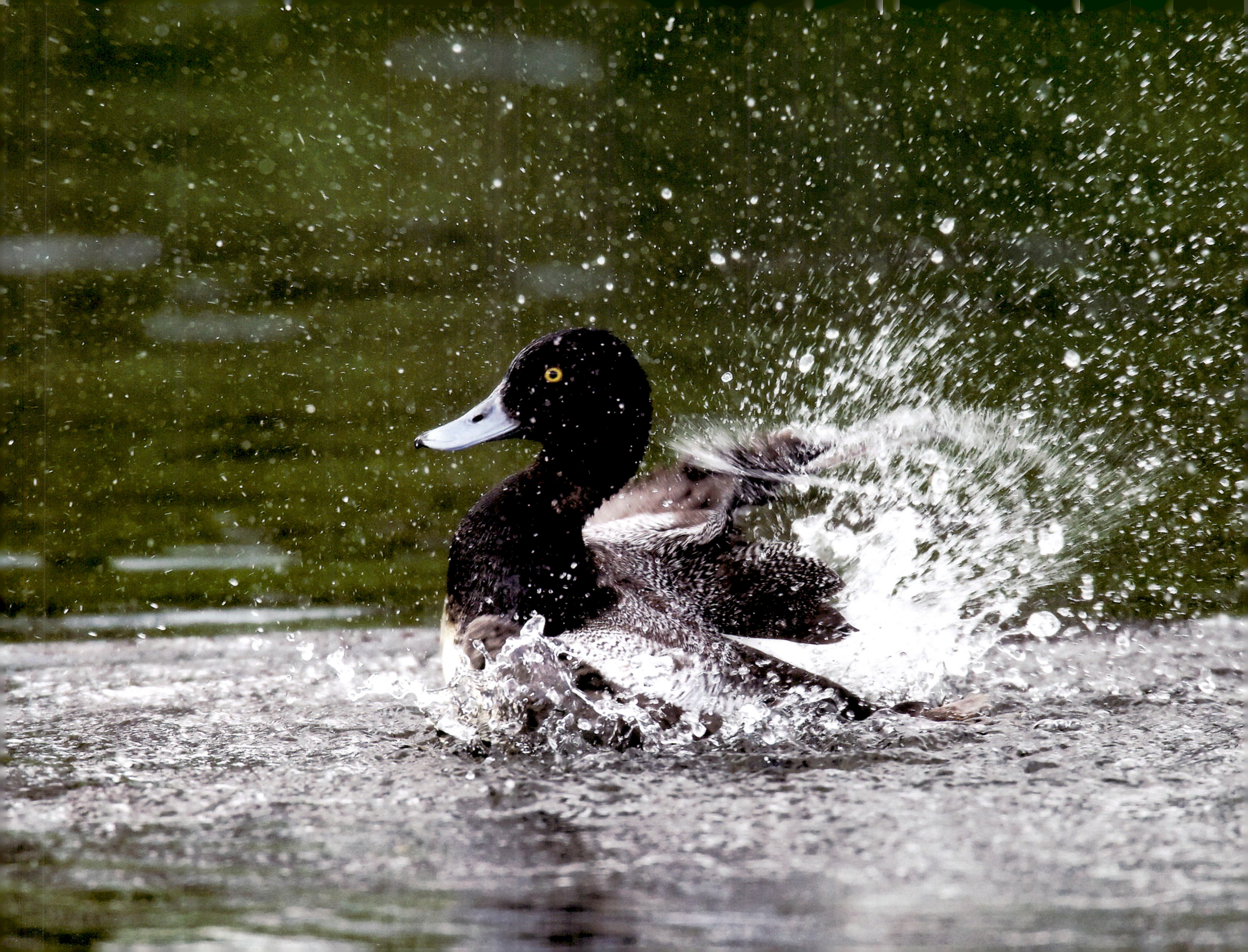

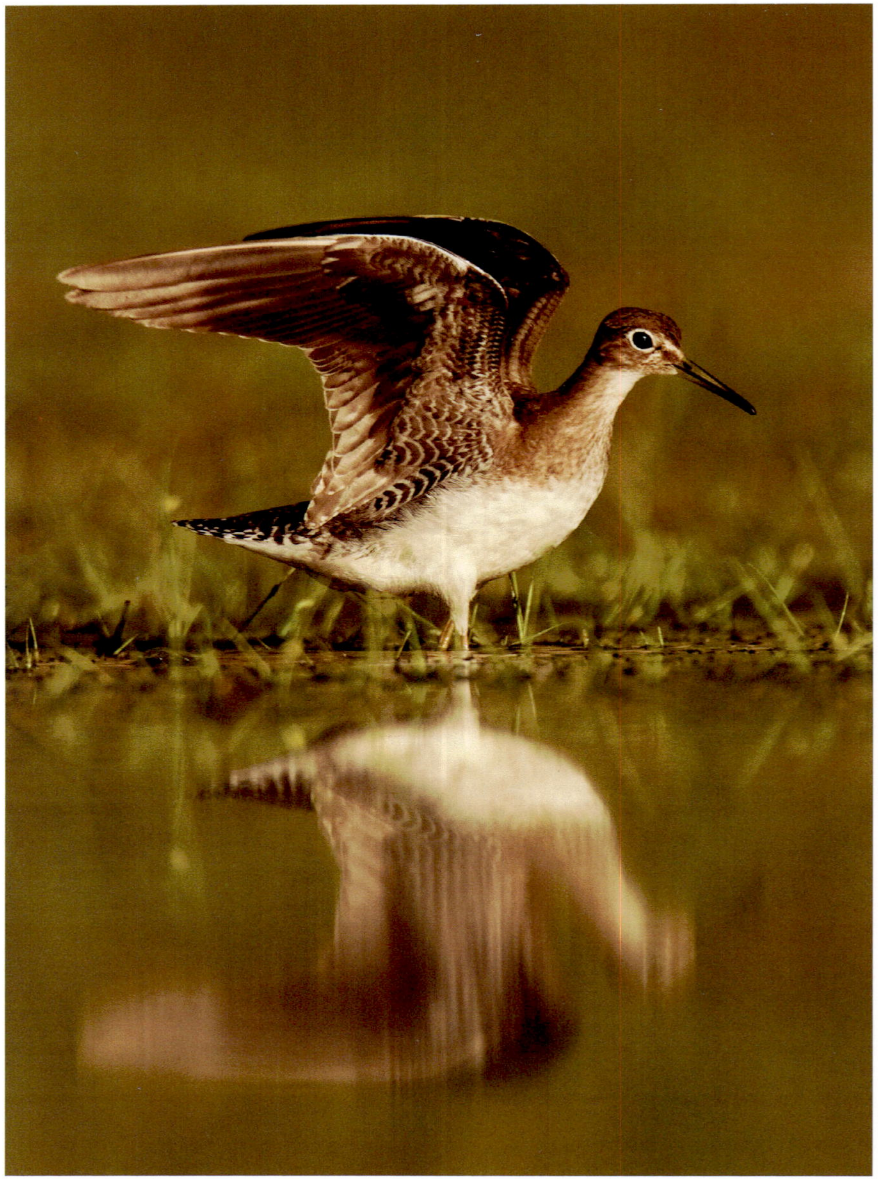

Look at everything as though you were seeing it for the first time or last time. Then your time on earth will be filled with glory.

— Betty Smith, *A Tree Grows in Brooklyn*

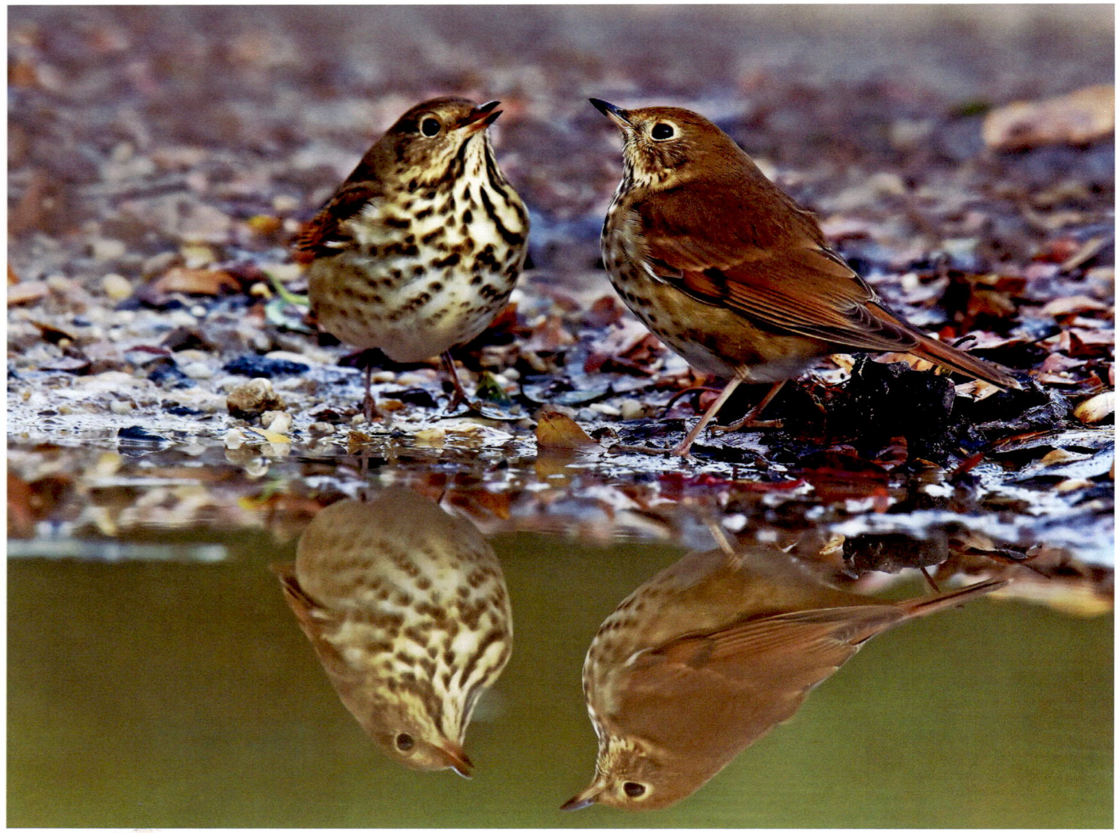

A Solitary Sandpiper (above) feeds on insect larvae and invertebrates in the softened mud in a rain pool, while two migrant Hermit Thrushes take a needed drink during fall migration. You can almost hear the conversation between these two birds, especially in the reflection. *Upper photo by Scott Elowitz; right photo by Kevin T. Karlson*

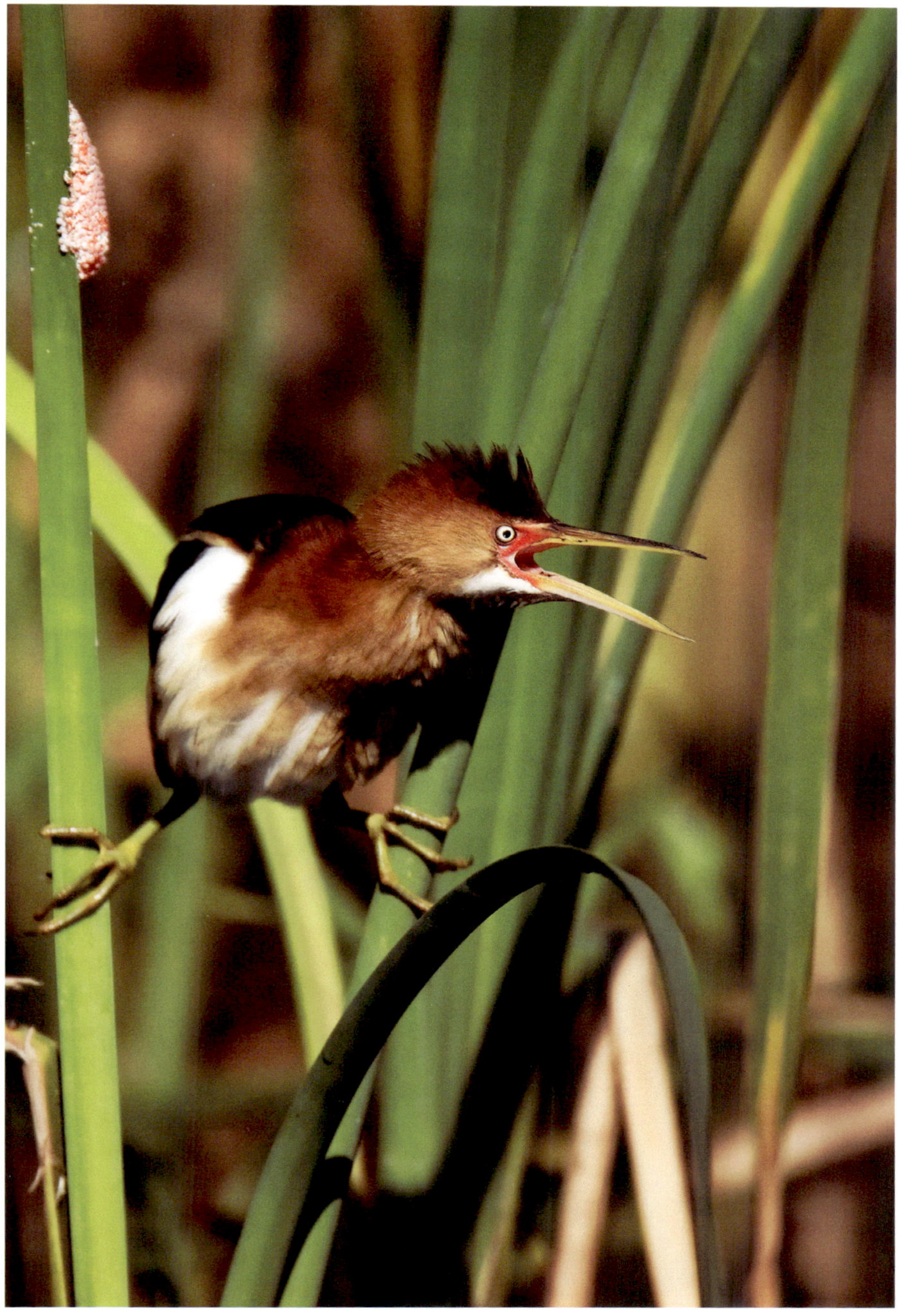

Both birds shown on this page are secretive marsh dwellers that quietly move through the thick wetland grasses. A female Least Bittern (left), which is the smallest heron in the world, protests an intruder to her territory.

An Eastern Clapper Rail (below) stretches its wing and exposes a beautiful symmetrical row of flight feathers, which is further enhanced by warm, soft light. *Photos by Scott Elowitz*

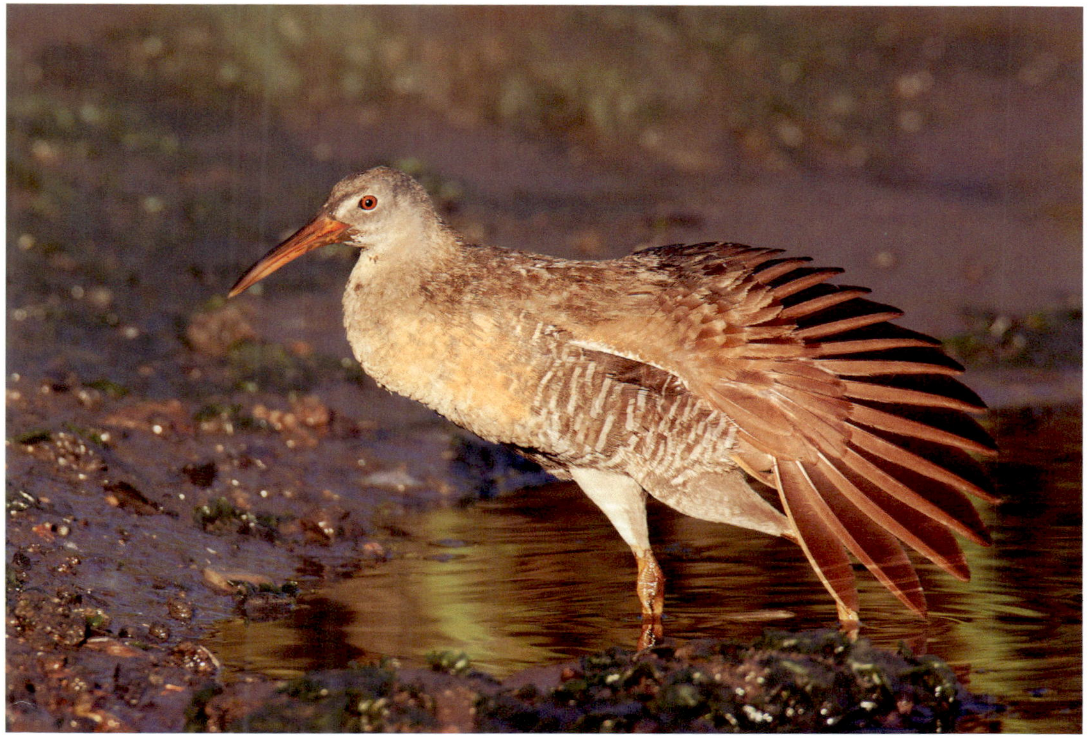

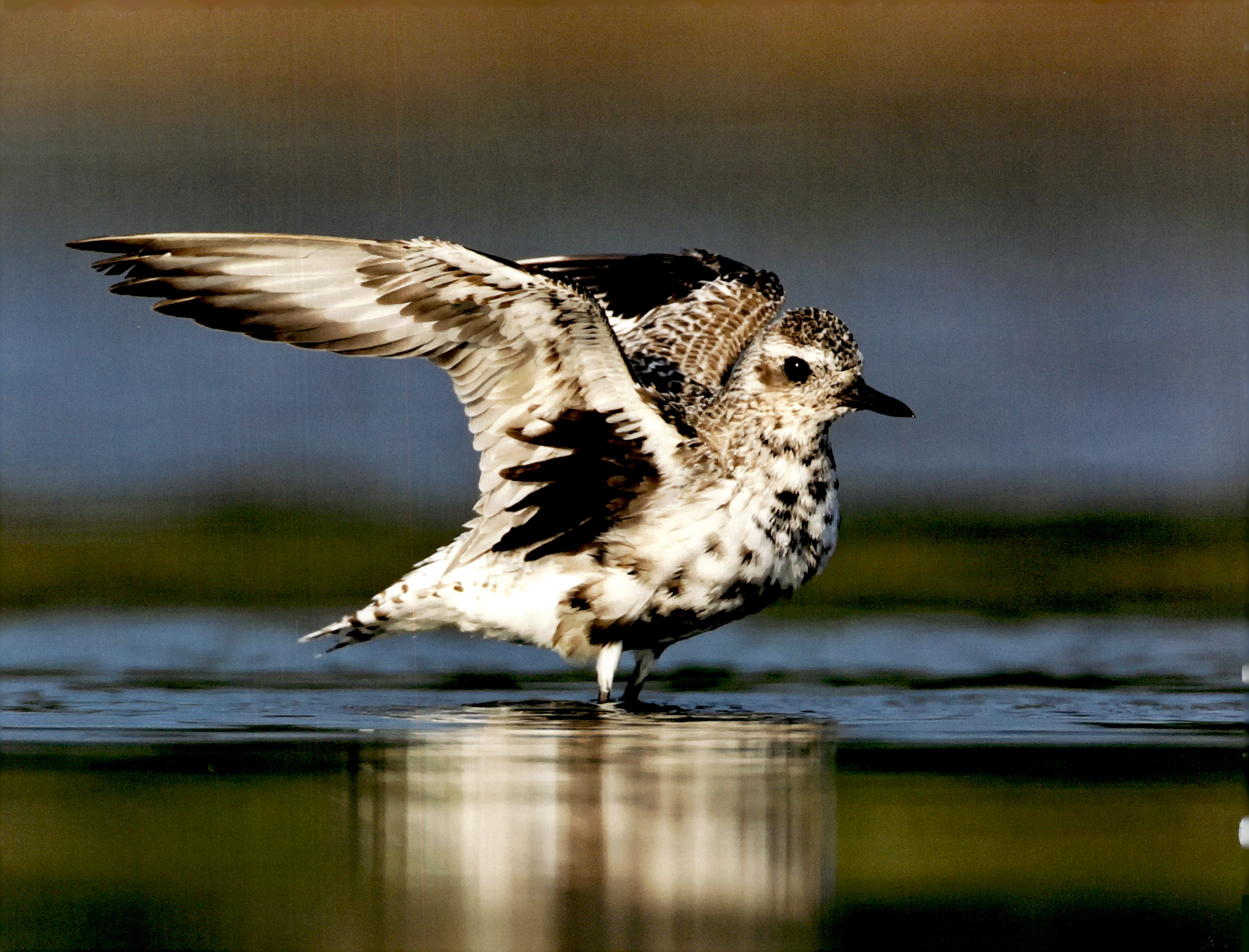

Opposite: A Black-bellied Plover raising its wings. *Photo by Lloyd Spitalnik*

Shorebirds are creatures of watery habitats, but they are also birds of the wind. Shown on this page are Purple Sandpiper (right), Killdeer (lower right), and Semipalmated Sandpiper (below). *All photos by Lloyd Spitalnik*

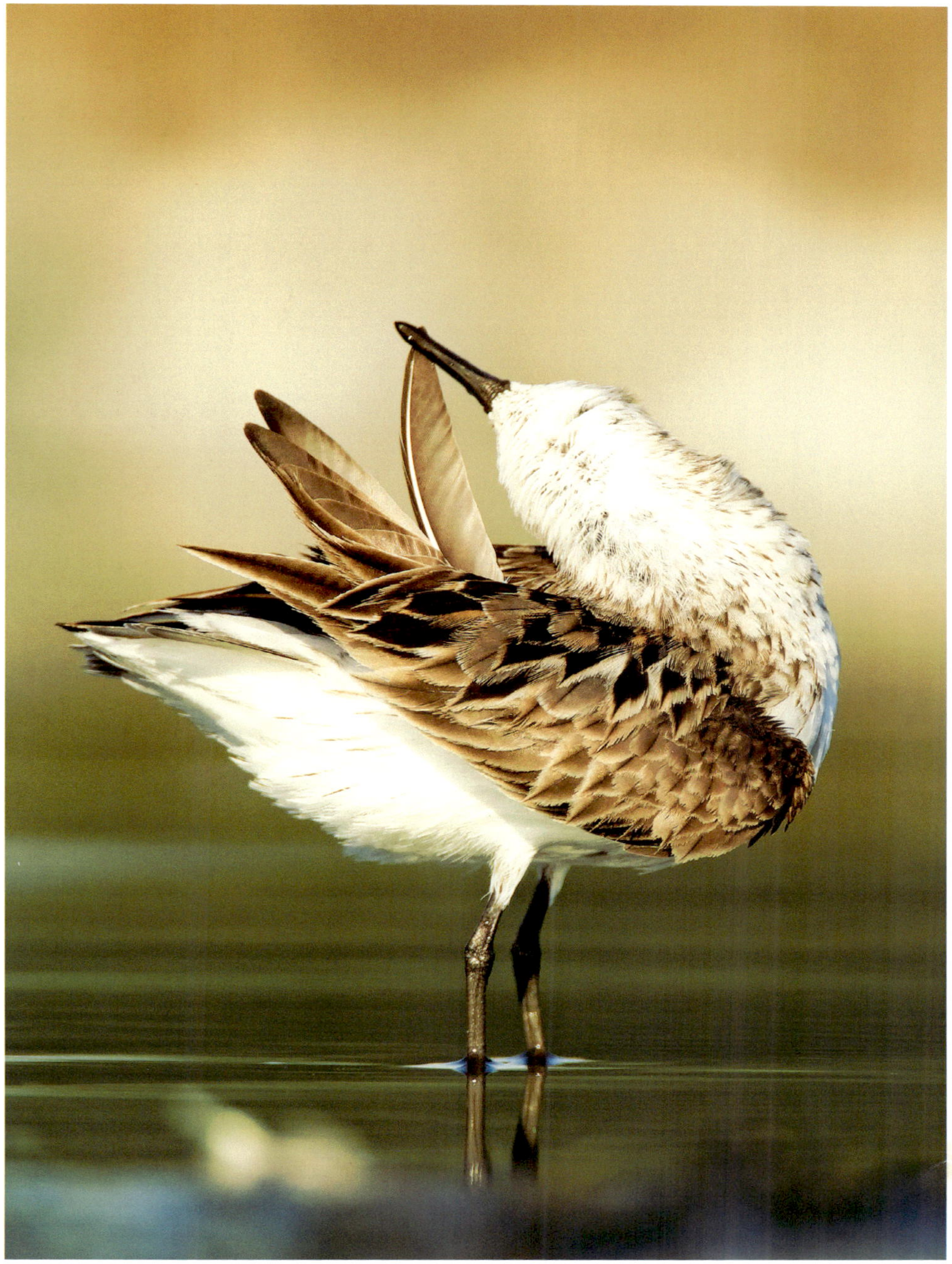

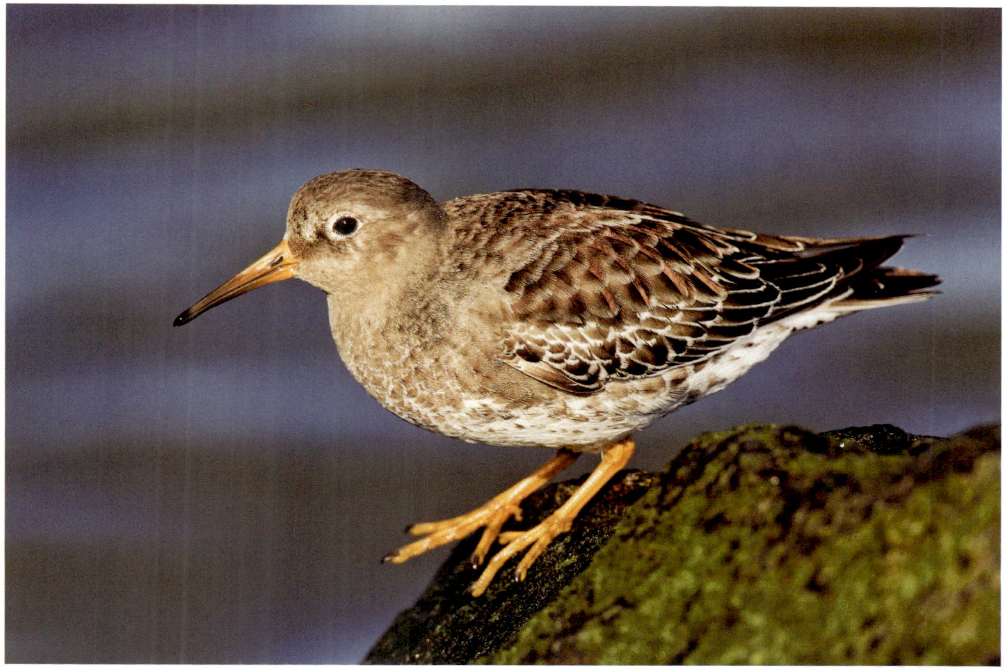

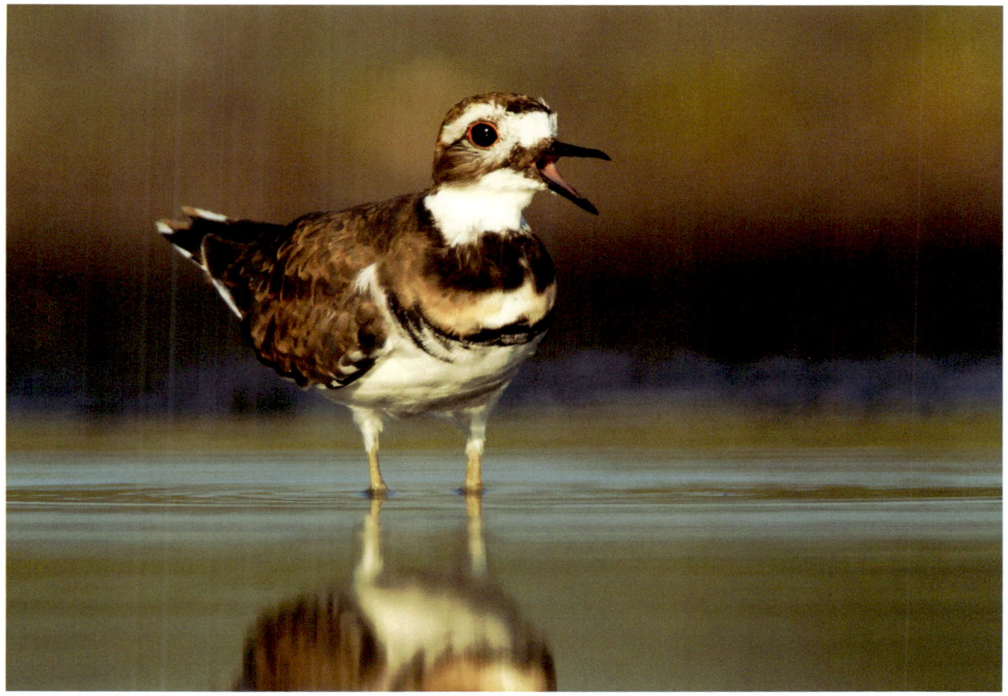

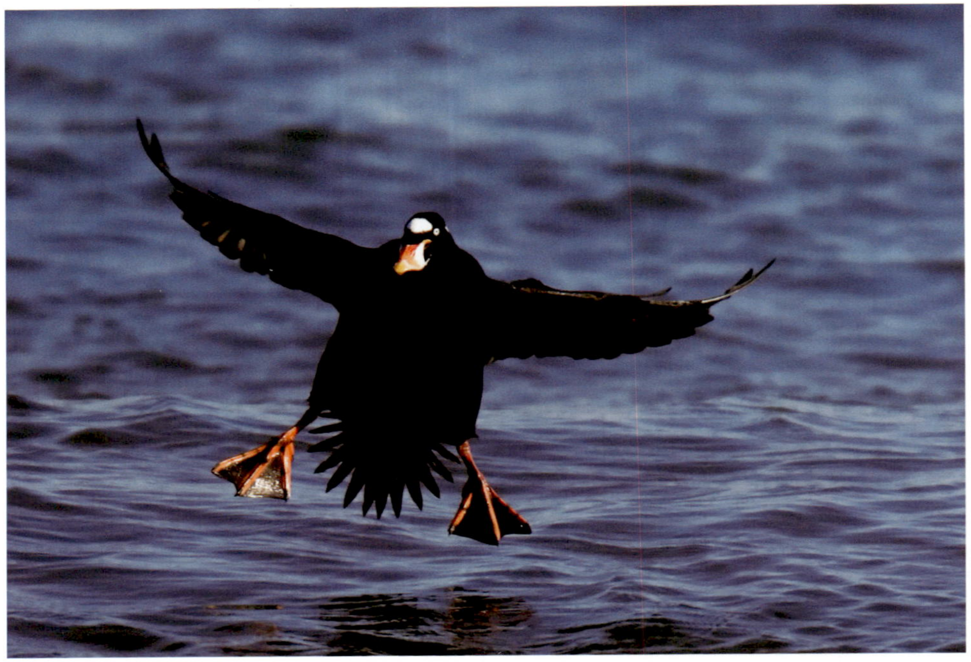

Surf Scoters are large sea ducks that breed near quiet northern lakes and winter on large lakes and coastal ocean waters. Only drakes are shown on this page. At left, a Surf Scoter comes in for a splash-down with its landing gear down. When a Surf Scoter hits the water, it lowers its feet like pontoons and raises its wings for balance, making for a ballet-like landing (lower left). A group of drakes dive underwater at nearly the same time (below), using their wings and feet to enable the dive. *Left and lower photos by Kevin T. Karlson; lower left photo by Lloyd Spitalnik*

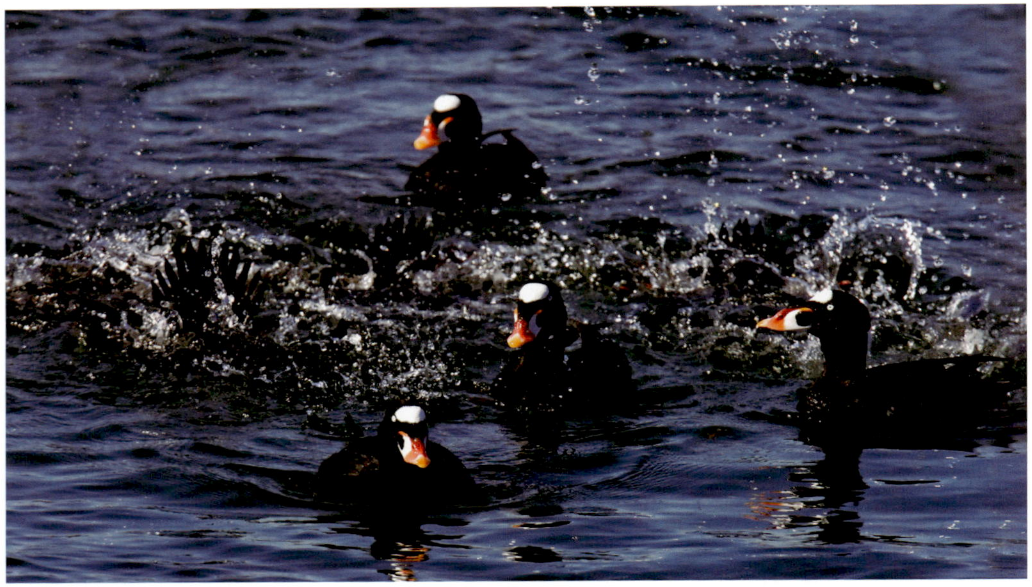

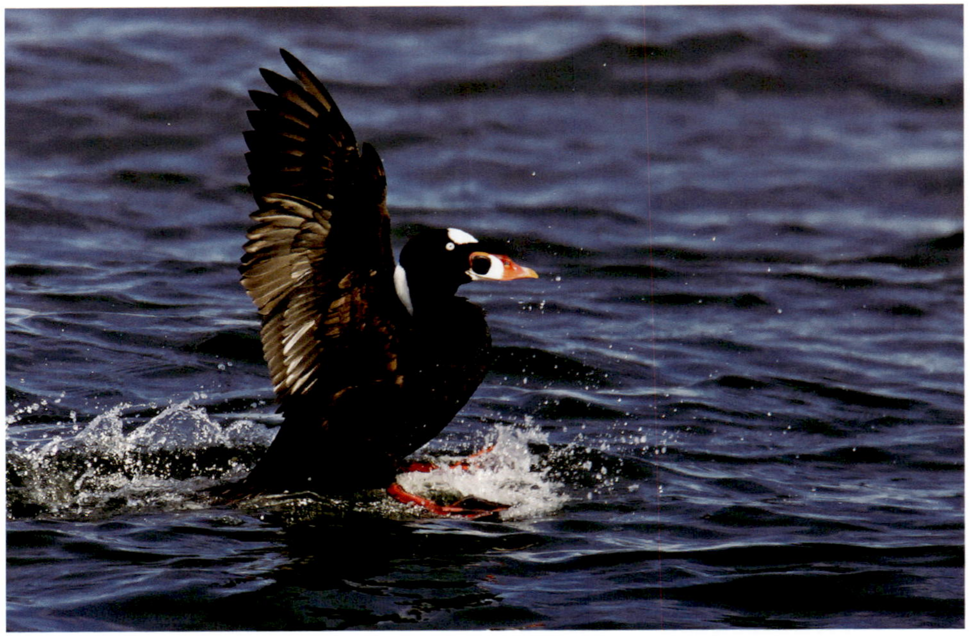

Opposite: Pacific Loons are some of the most beautiful of all birds, and this photo captures the exquisite velvety texture of their feathers. The soft background and stunning bird create the visual impression of a painting, which is a comment many people make. *Photo by Kevin T. Karlson*

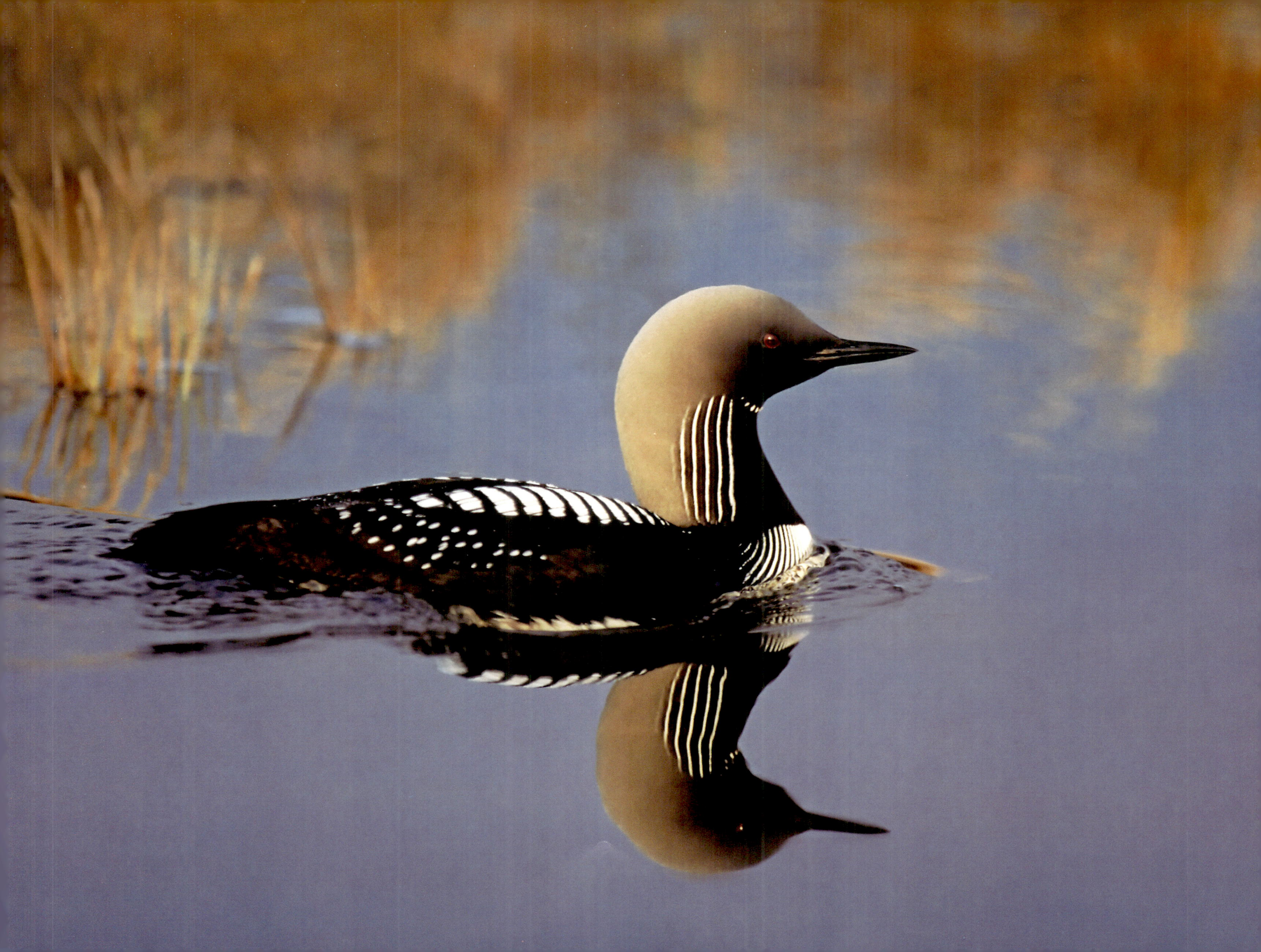

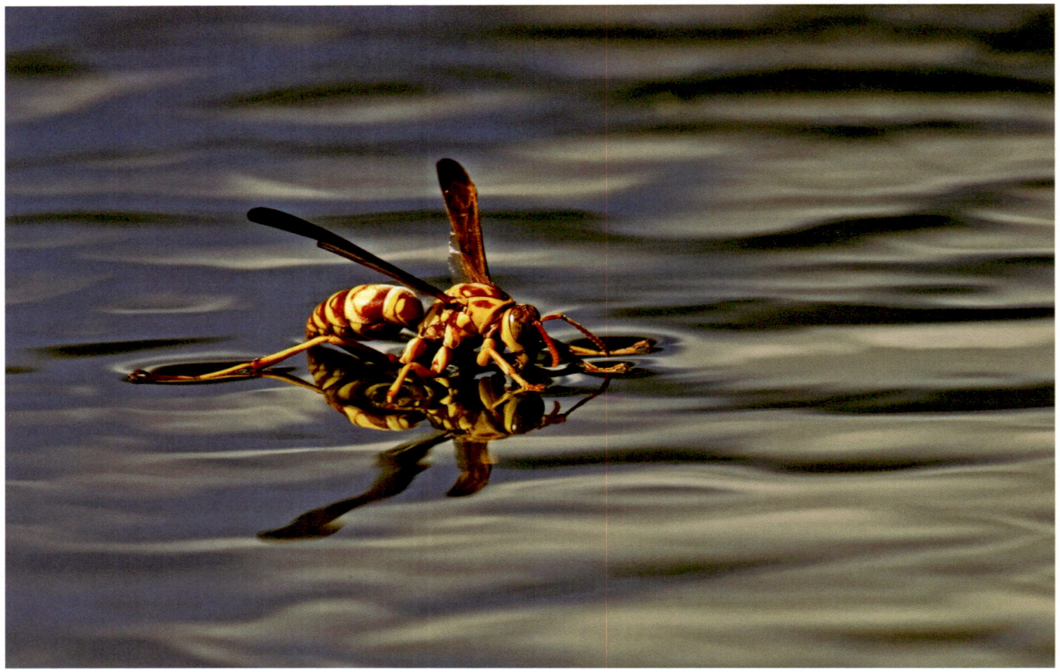

Opposite: Limpkins are members of the rail family that live in freshwater habitats in the southeast U.S. and other tropical areas. This dorsal shot shows the graceful flight and intricate feather patterns of this bird, and the large snail that it captured for dinner. *Photo by Scott Elowitz*

Water is crucial to the survival of these two creatures. Mike photographed this Paper Wasp gathering water (above) by floating his camera on a boogie board in Starr County, Texas.

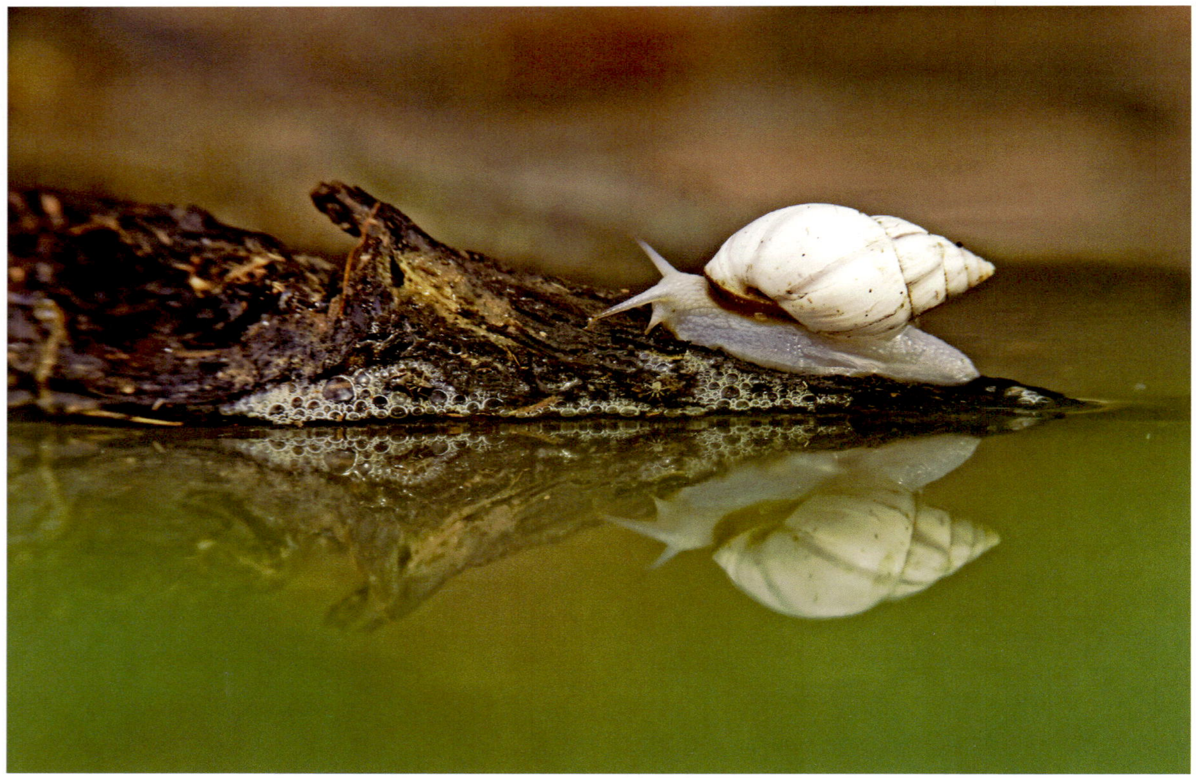

Rabdotus snails are common in the ranch country of south Texas, as long as there is water nearby to keep them moisturized (right). *Photos by Mike Hannisian*

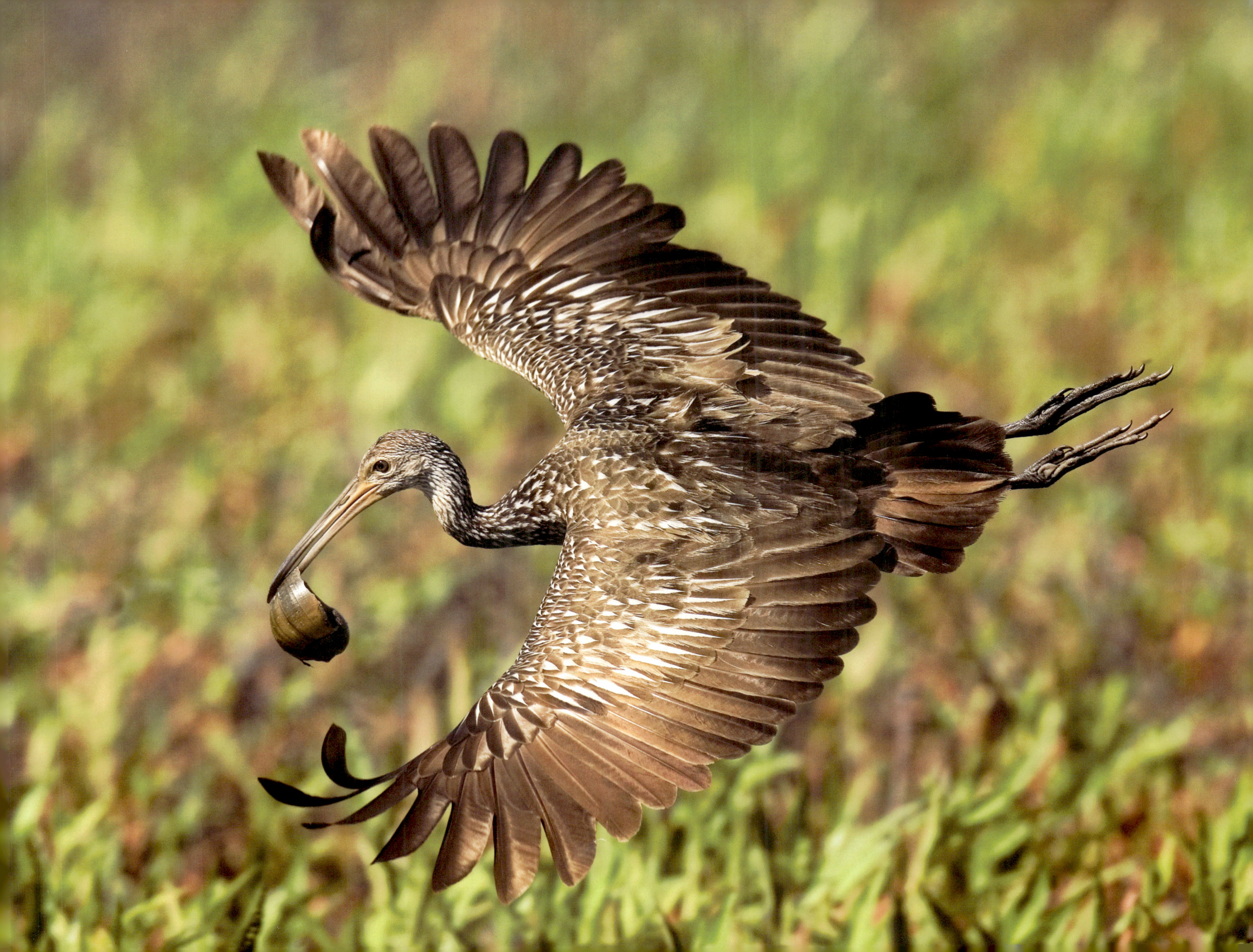

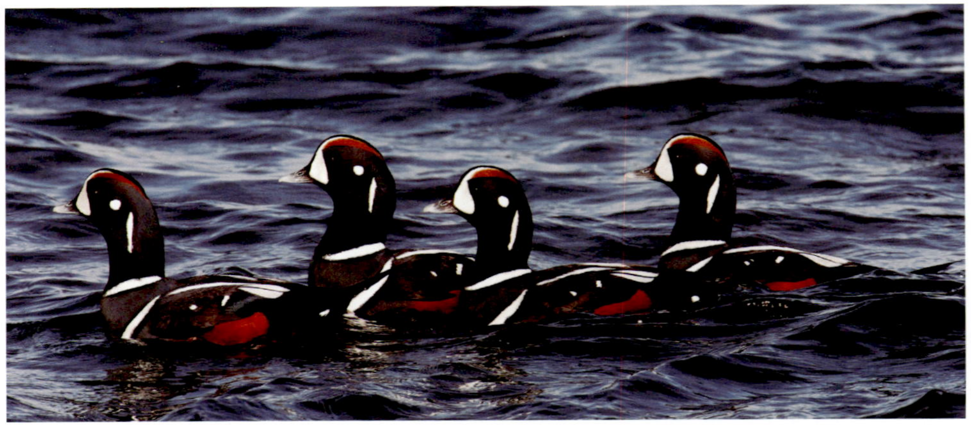

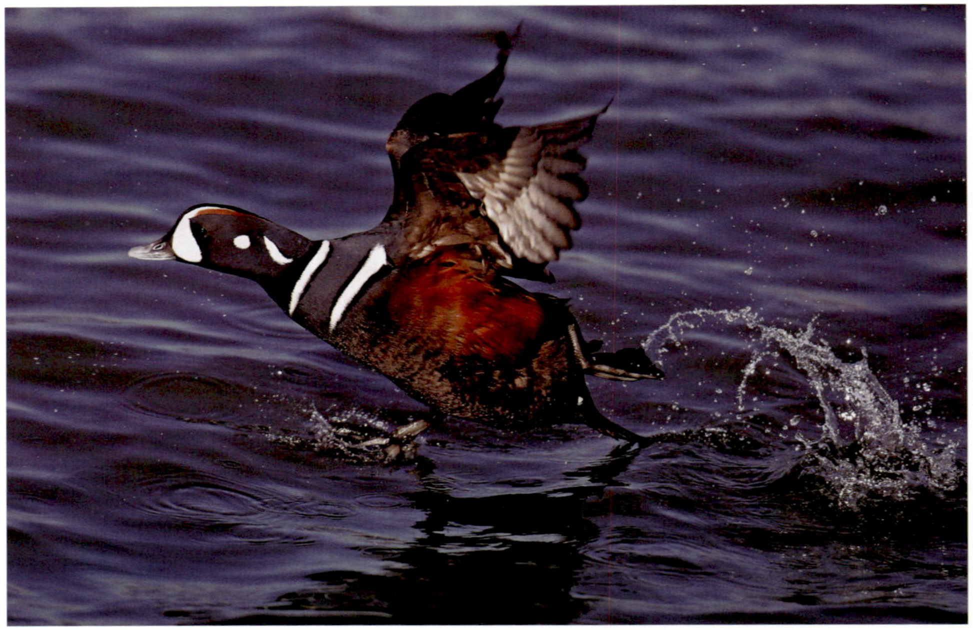

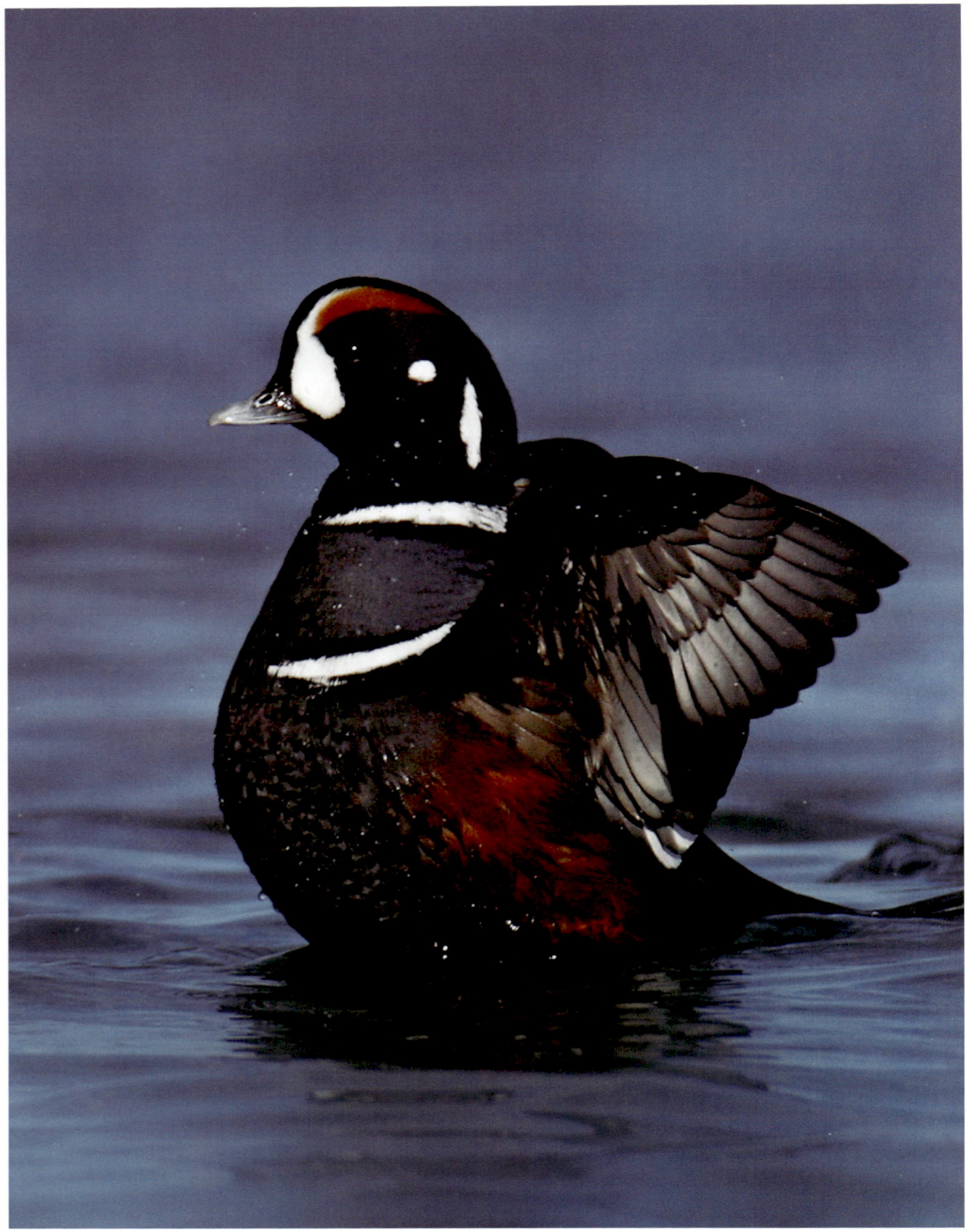

Harlequin Ducks have one of the most striking and bizarre plumage patterns of any bird, and these drakes near Barnegat, New Jersey, in winter are a magnificent sight. *Photos top and right by Scott Elowitz; lower left photo by Kevin T. Karlson*

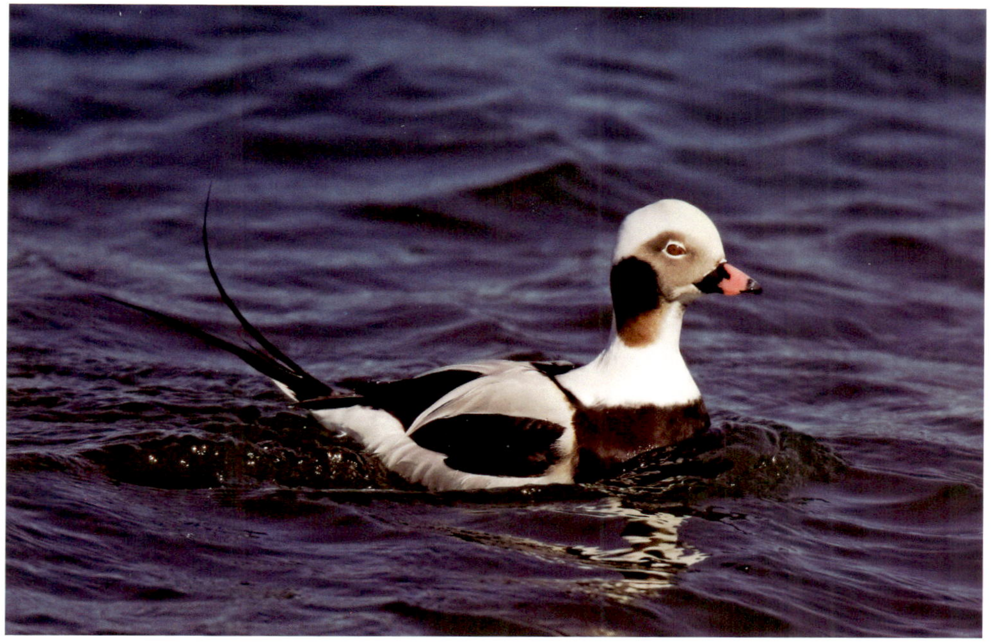

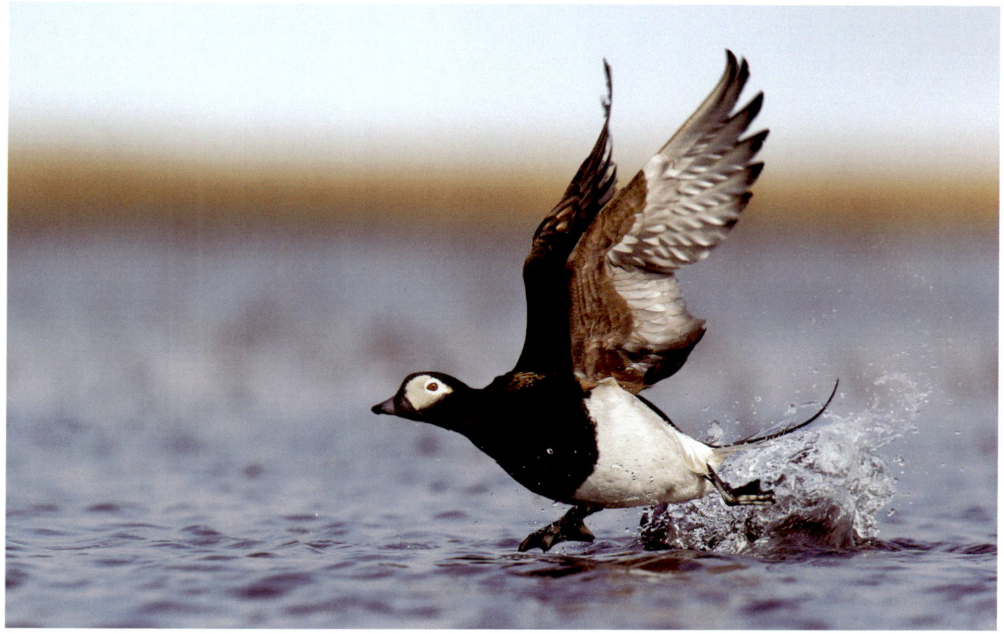

Long-tailed Ducks show a very different plumage in winter (above) than their breeding plumage (above right). These small diving ducks breed in Arctic tundra habitats and migrate to coastal locations for the winter months. *Upper photo by Kevin T. Karlson, upper right photo by Scott Elowitz*

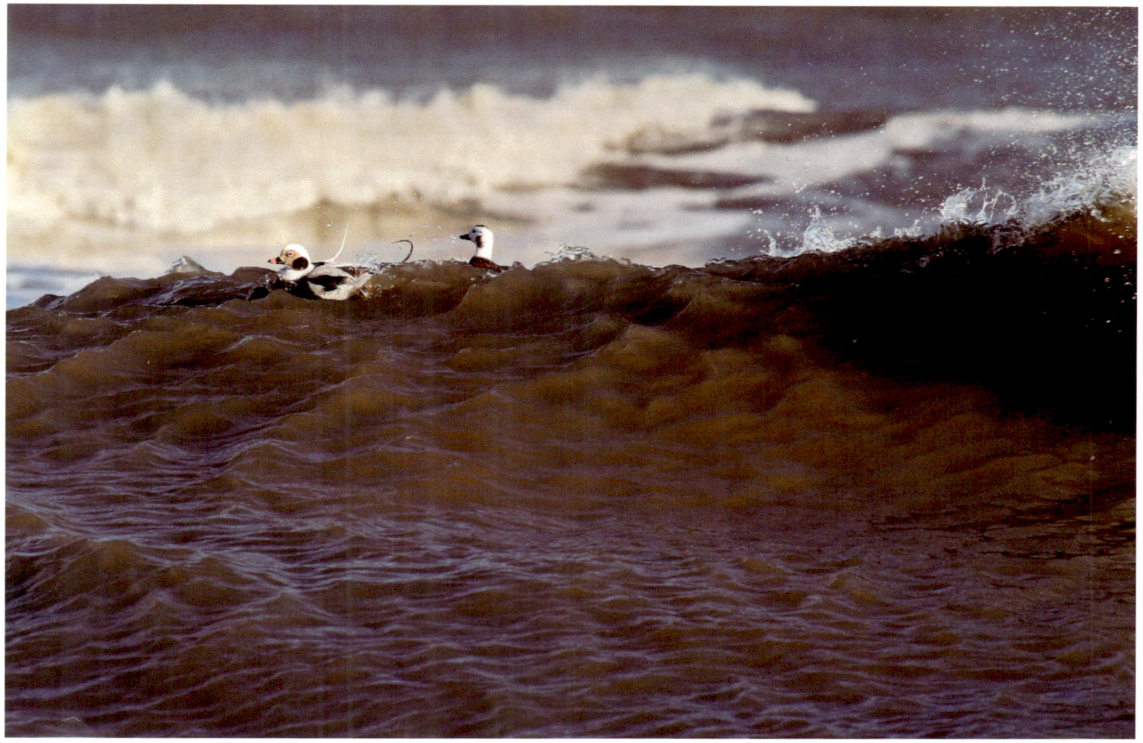

"Sometimes we need to experience what other animals go through to really understand how supremely adapted to their environment they truly are. I took this photo standing in the frigid water in winter in New Jersey, and had to run quickly for the shore. And yet these Long-tailed Ducks charm us all winter as they ride the white horses that race toward the beach" (right). *Photo and caption by Mike Crewe*

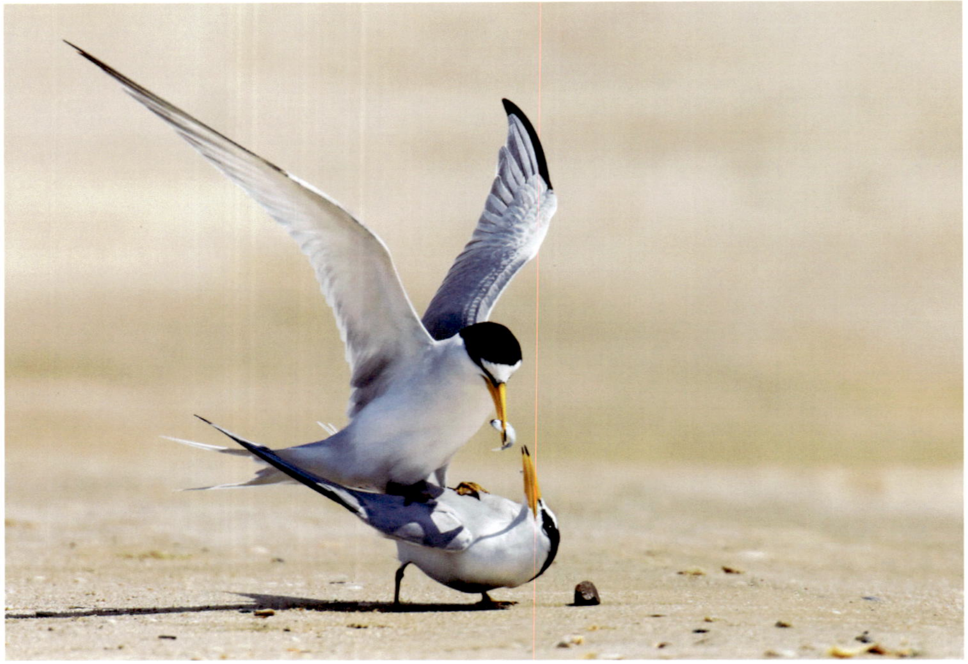

Opposite: A tiny Least Tern chick seeks the comfort of its parent's breast, as the setting sun is reflected in the eye of the adult. *Photo by Kevin T. Karlson*

Eternity is the Absolute present.

— D. T. Suzuki

Least Terns are one of the smallest terns in the world at just over 8 inches long. These frenetic birds are a constant ball of energy from the time they arrive on their breeding grounds to their departure in late summer. A male Least Tern holds the equivalent of a dozen roses in front of the female while copulation takes place (above). After he is finished, he will give her the fish.

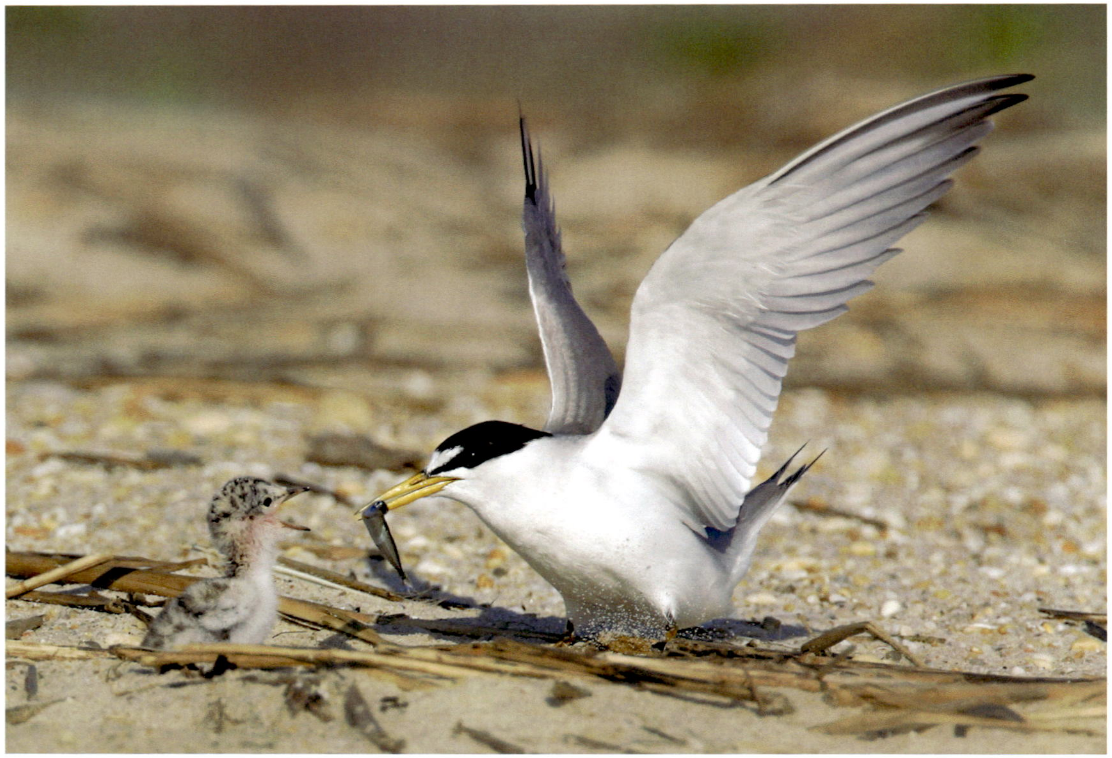

An adult Least Tern tries to feed a small fish to a tiny chick, who is not sure how to manage such a large meal (right). *Above photo by Kevin T. Karlson; right photo by Scott Elowitz*

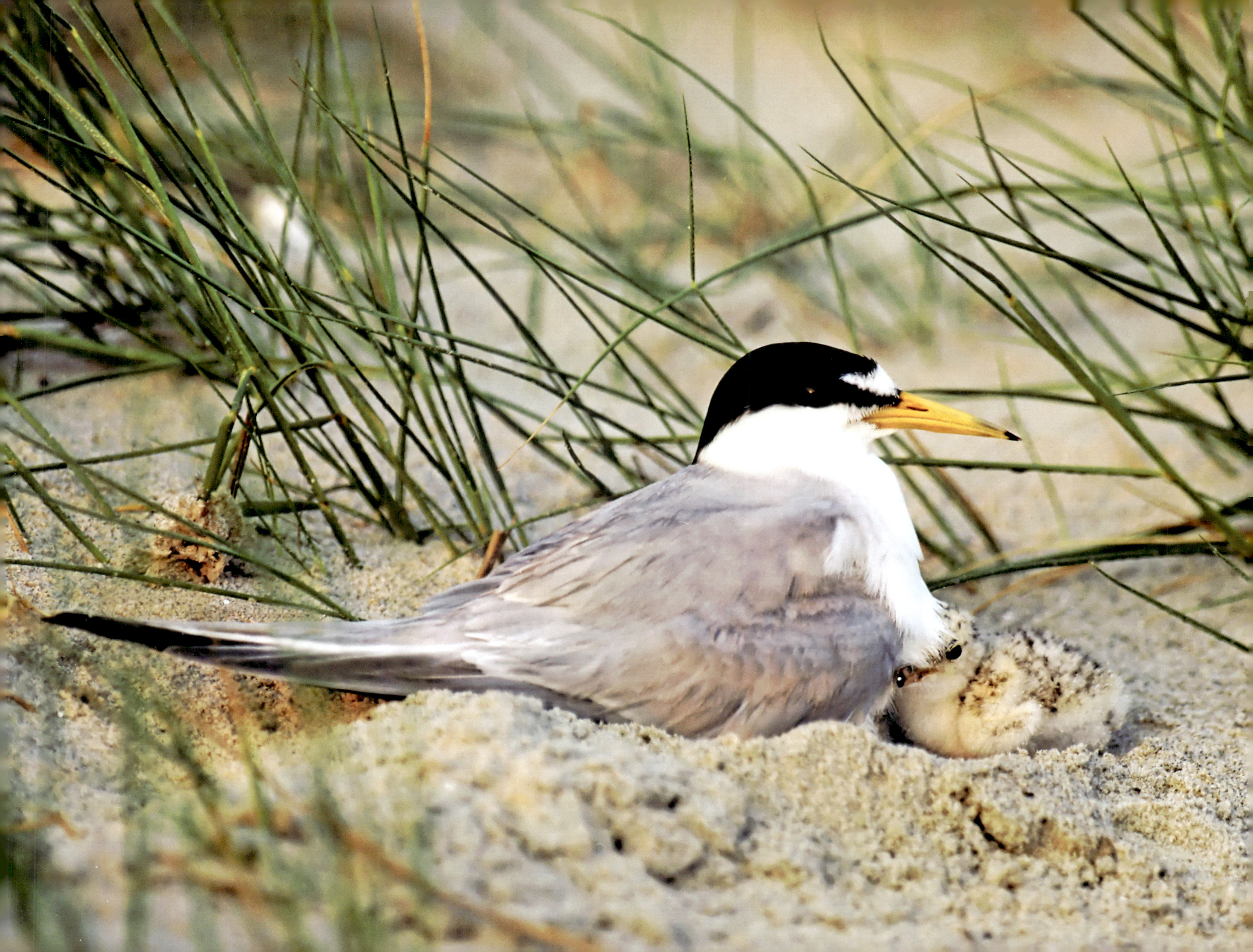

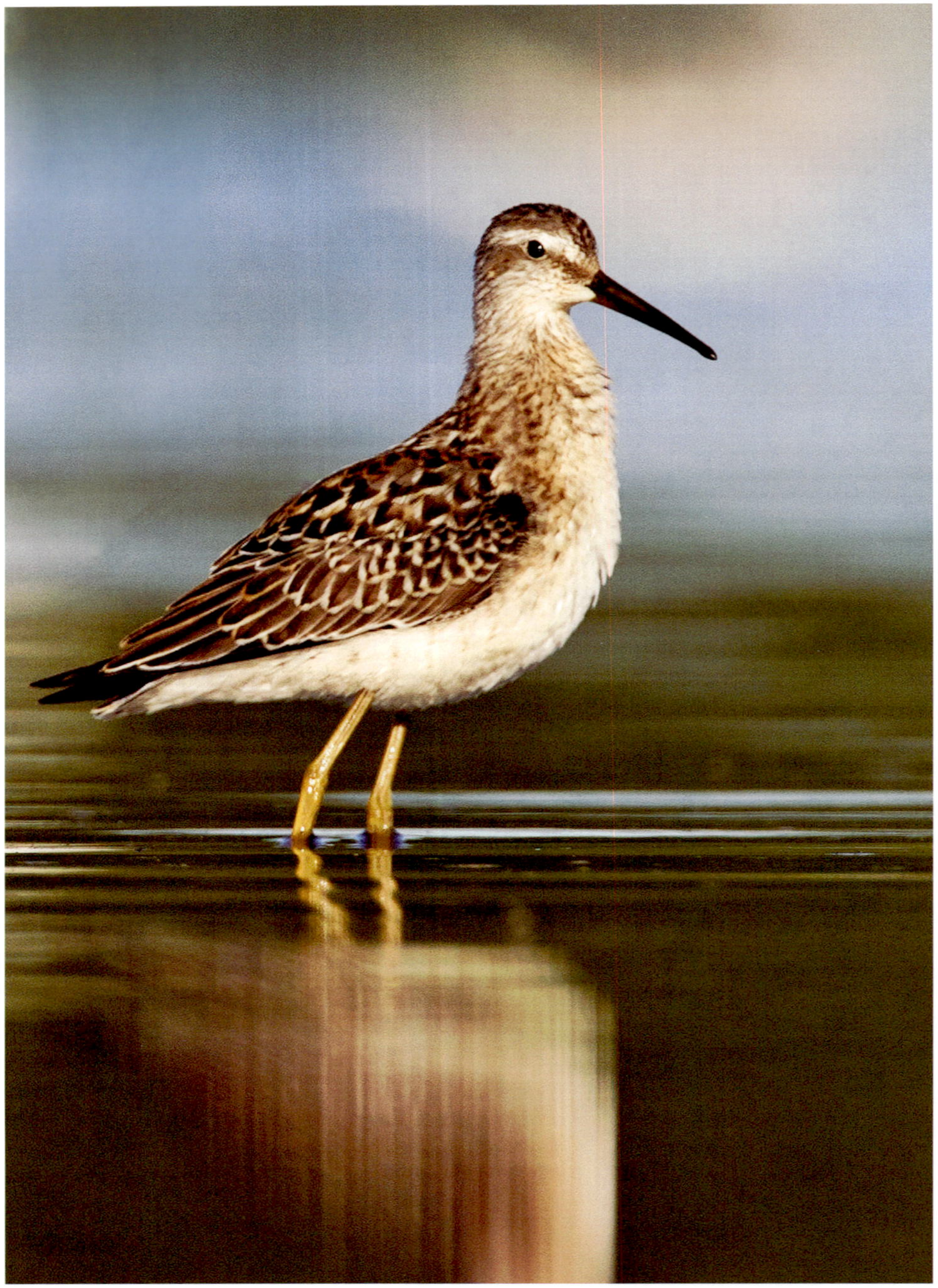

A juvenile Stilt Sandpiper is a picture of grace as it poses for the photo above. A tiny Least Sandpiper walks through still, shallow water in the photo at right. *Photos by Lloyd Spitalnik*

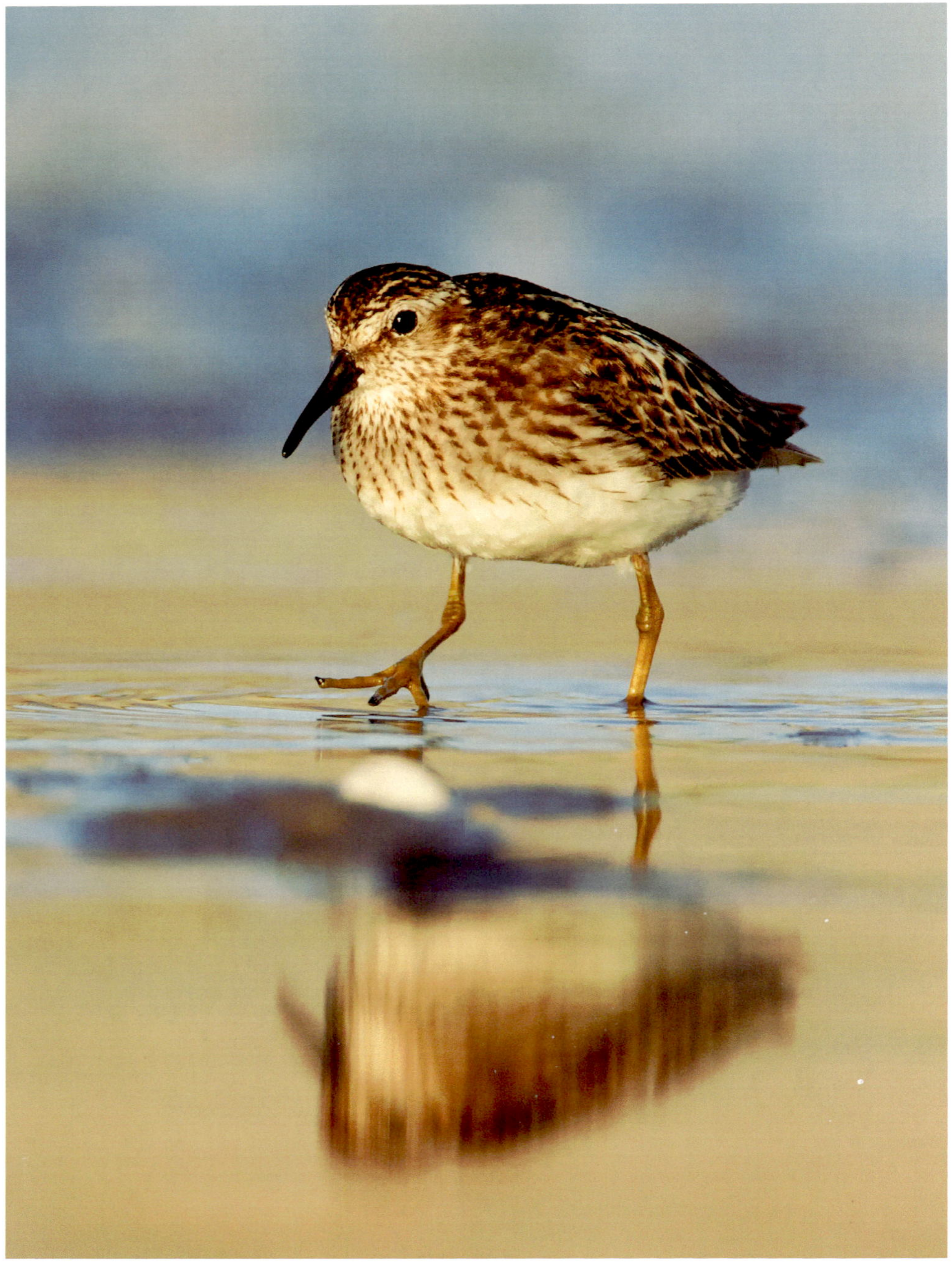

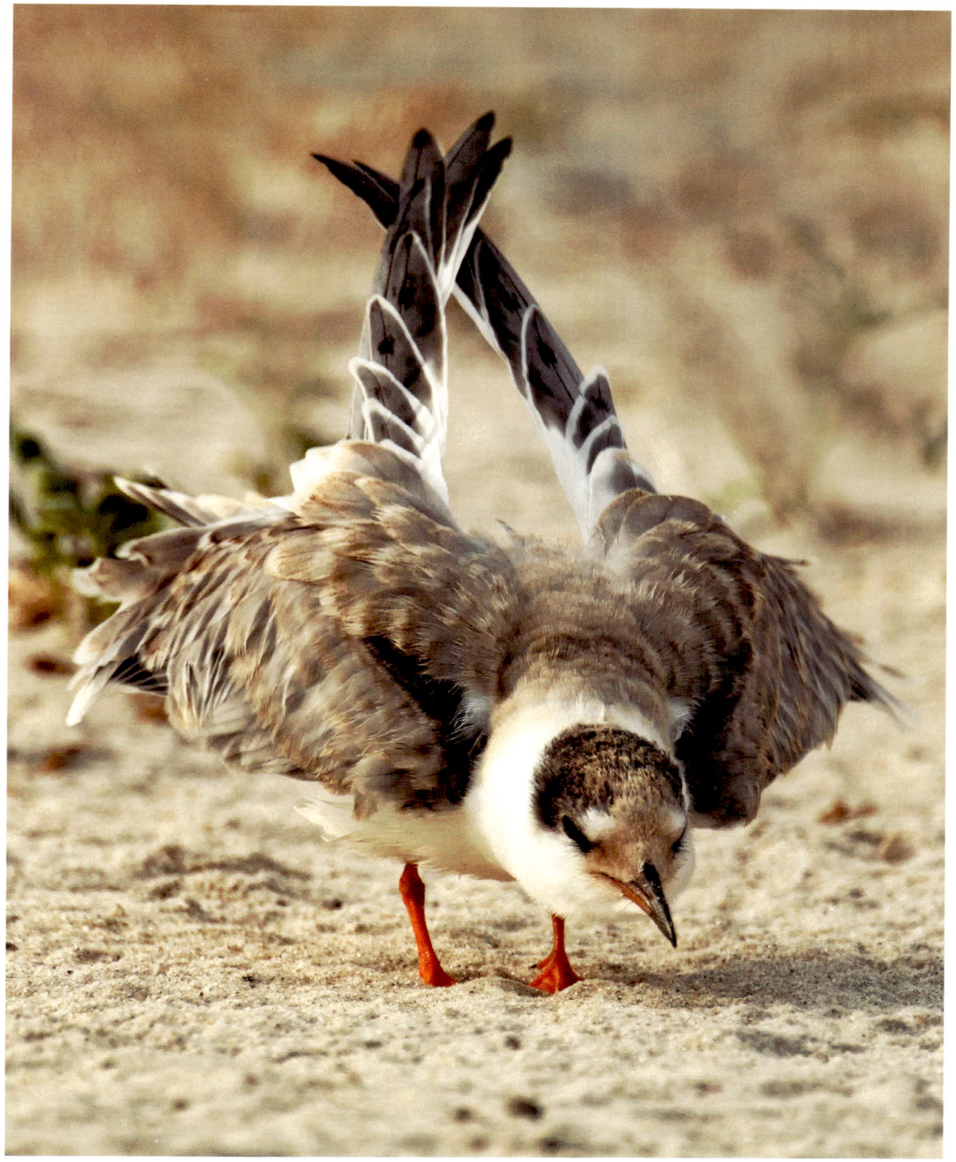

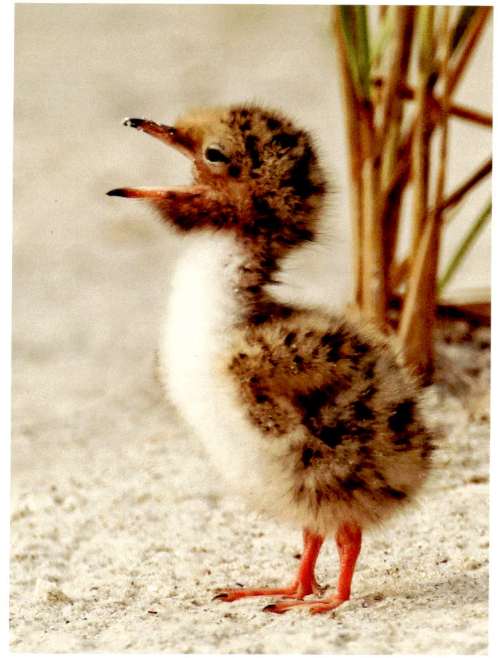

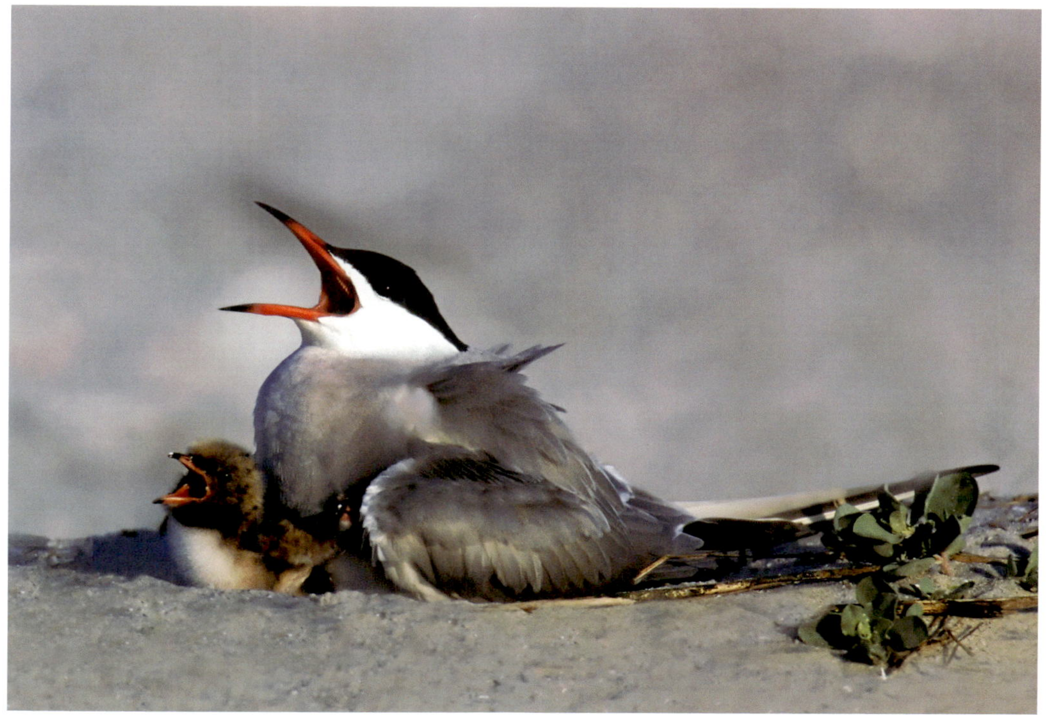

A fledgling Common Tern (above) fluffs its feathers and stretches its wings while forming a symmetrical feather design.

Meanwhile, a very young Common Tern chick (above right) cries out for its parents.

A protective parent warns an intruder not to venture near its nest with two young chicks (right). *Photos above by Lloyd Spitalnik; right photo by Kevin T. Karlson*

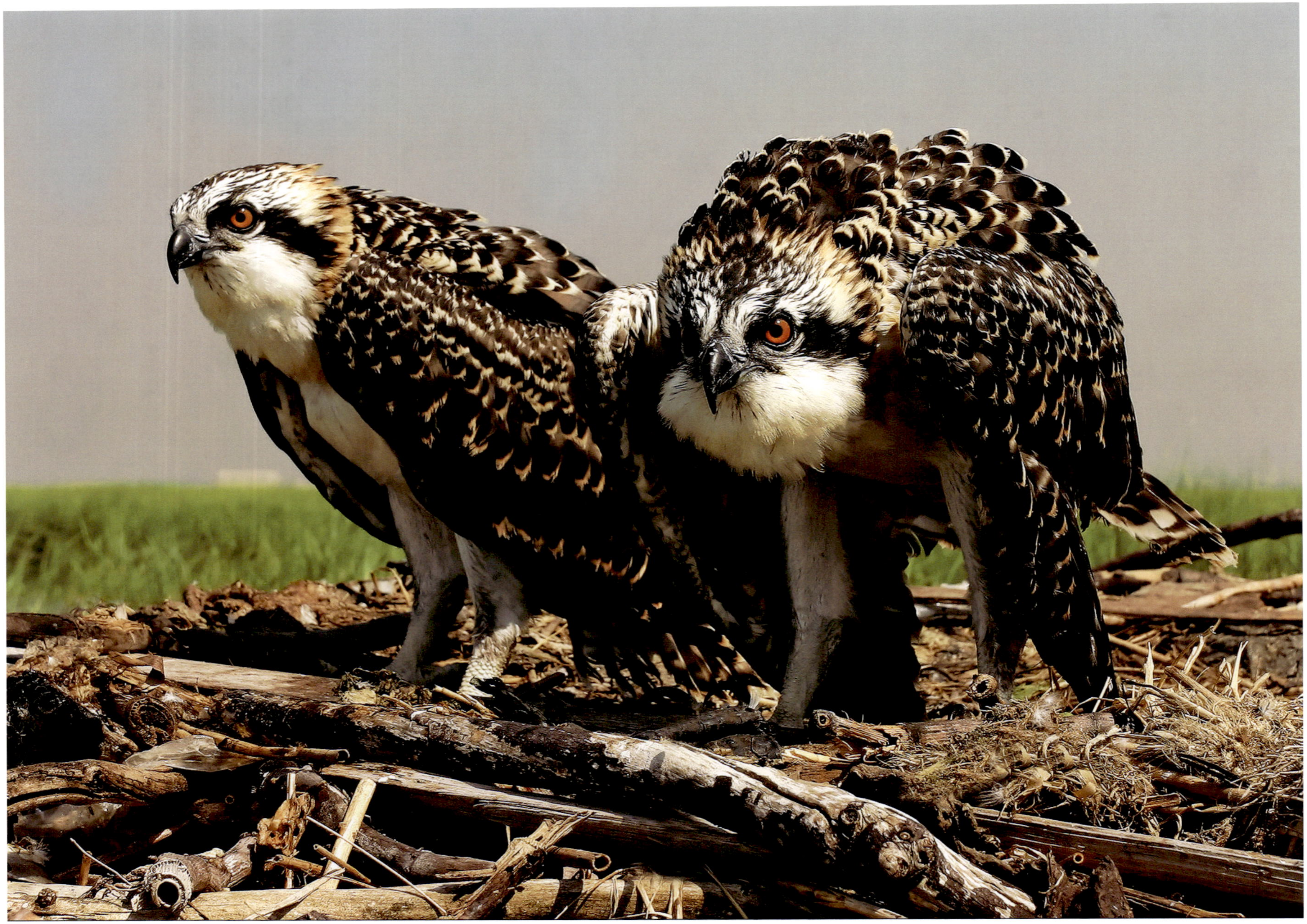

Two fledgling Ospreys in a nest near the Jamaica Bay Wildlife Refuge in Queens, New York. Don captured this special image by photographing a nest built on a low dock, and the chicks fledged successfully. *Photo by Don Riepe*

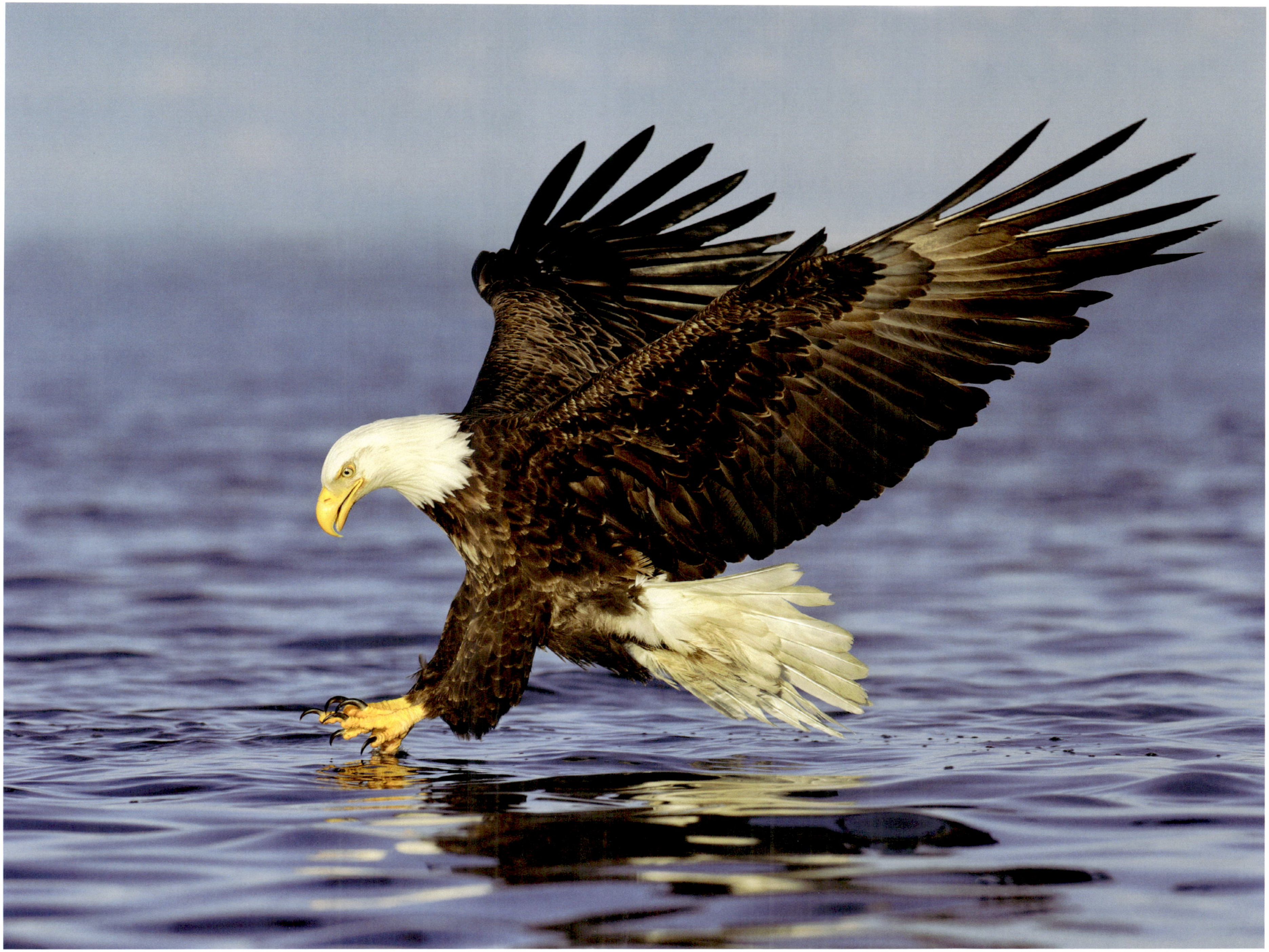

This majestic Bald Eagle is about to plunge into the water to catch a fish with its strong toes and razor sharp talons.
Photo by Scott Elowitz

Personal Epitaphs

We would like to pay tribute to a pair of very special people who passed away recently, and who touched the lives of countless others with their grace, charm, and bright life force.

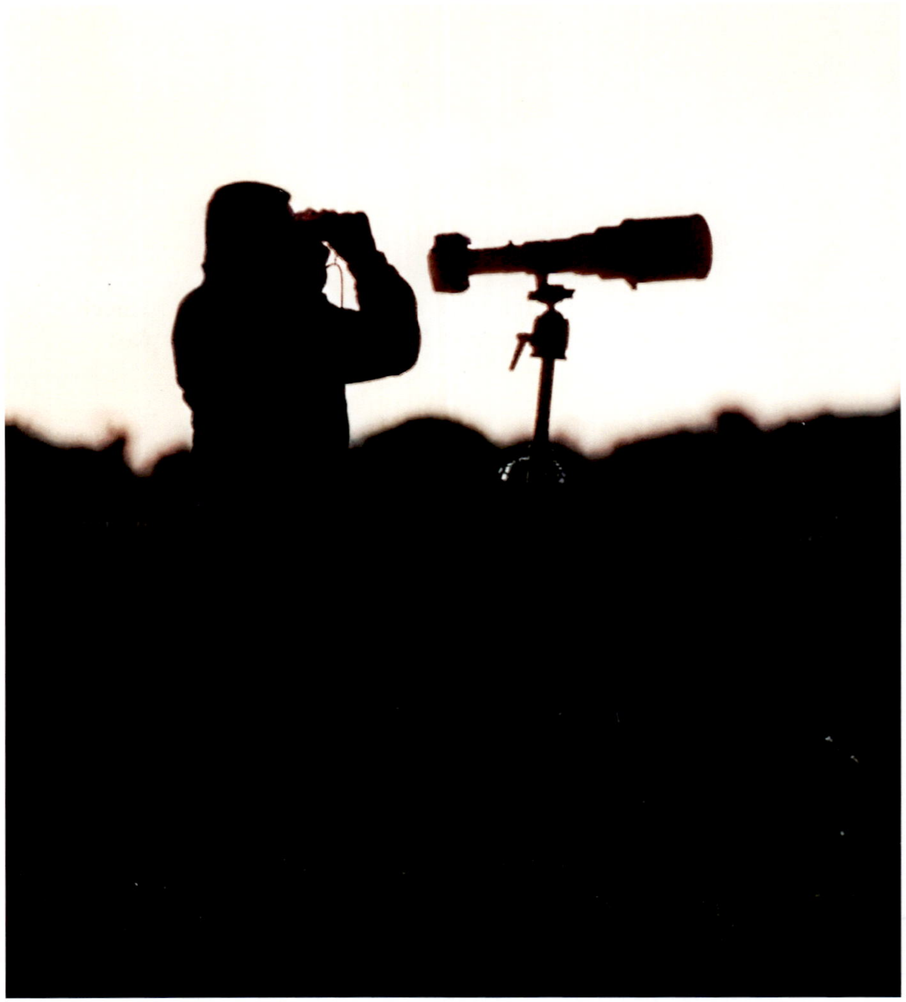

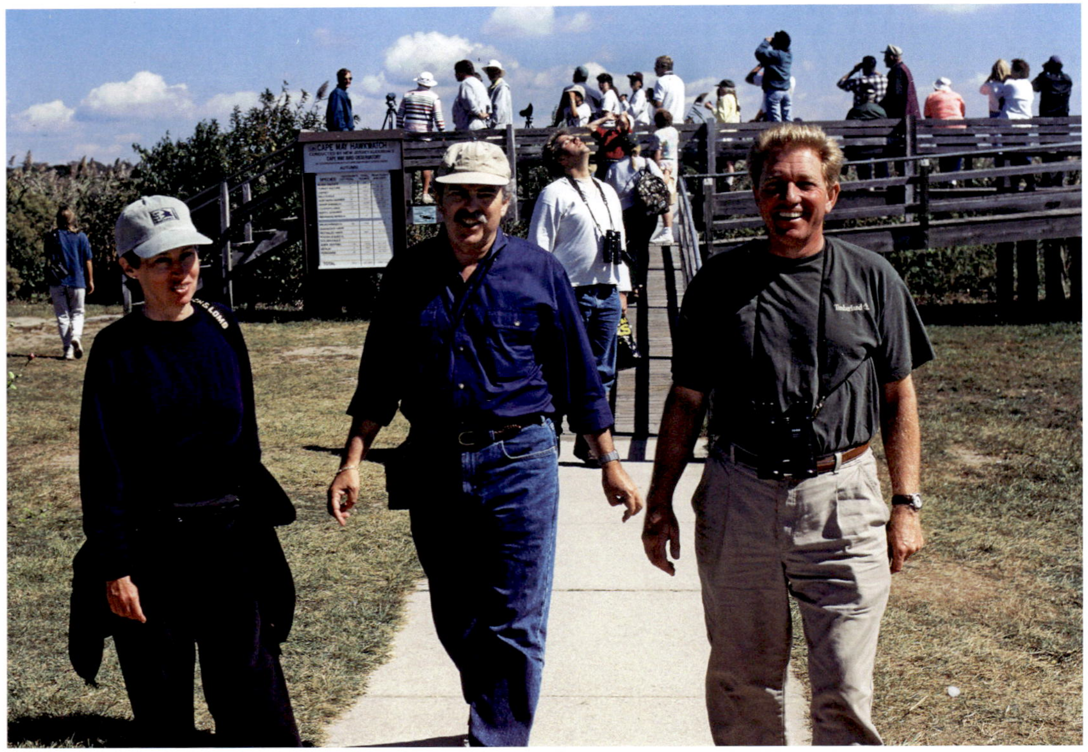

Tom Vezo

Tom Vezo was a close personal friend of the three authors. His talents as a photographer were near the top of his field. He had an artist's eye for beauty and composition, and his images inspired many photographers. Tom died in 2008 while returning from a photo shoot at the young age of 62. His passing left a hole in the national wildlife photography community and in the hearts of his family and close friends. His wife Dorothy and all his close friends miss Tom very much.

Above: Tom, right, is shown with his dear friends Lloyd and Sandy Spitalnik in Cape May New Jersey, in 1998.

Left: Kevin took this moody shot of Tom at one of his favorite photo locations, Jones Beach, New York, in 1989. He was moved by Tom's dedication to keep shooting after the sun had set, and loved the recognizable silhouette of Tom and his camera.

It is like clouds rising in the sky: suddenly there, gone without a trace.
And it is like drawing a pattern on water: it is neither born nor passes away.
This is cosmic peace and eternal rest.

— Ma-tsu

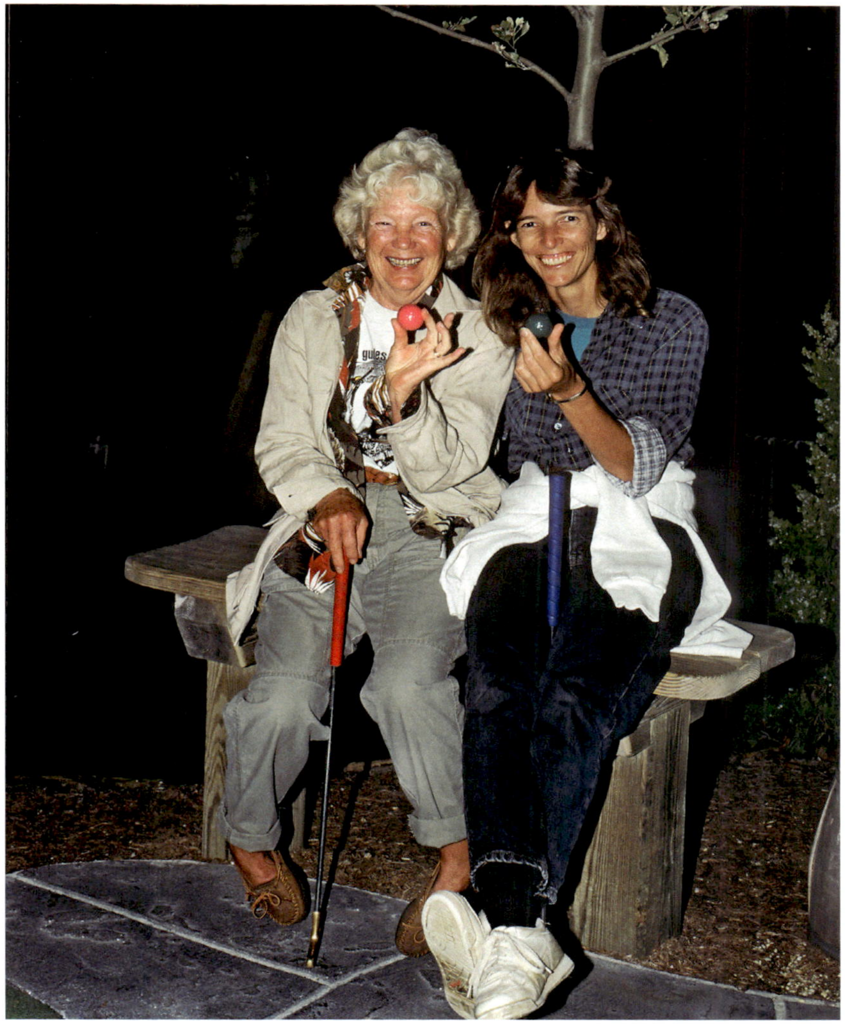

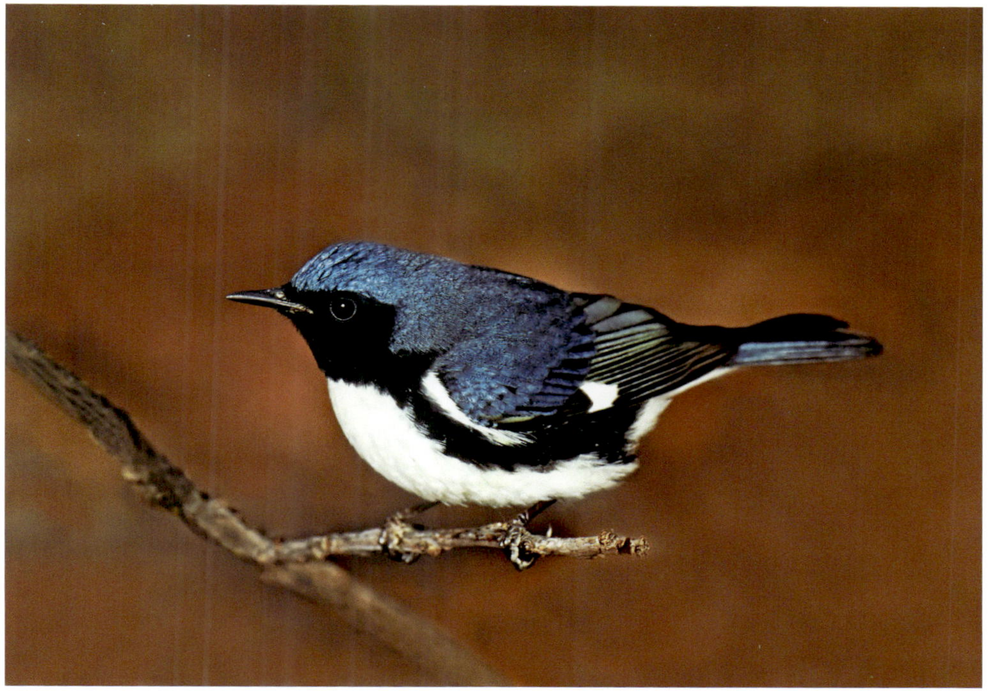

Above: It is hard to say what Kate's favorite warbler was, since she loved them all so much, but Kate always had a soft spot for male Black-throated Blue Warblers, and once asked Kevin for a picture of one.

Kate Brethwaite

Kate Brethwaite was one of the most enthusiastic and beloved members of the Pennsylvania and Cape May, New Jersey, bird communities. She exuded joy and unbridled happiness every time she looked at birds, and her child-like demeanor and frequent giggles lit up the world. She was like a second mother to Kevin Karlson and Dale Rosselet. Her love for warblers resonates even after her death in 2010. Kate was living proof that although you can grow old and raise a family with dignity and honor, it is possible to retain youthful enthusiasm and "giggles" until the day you die. Peter Pan had nothing on you, Kate. We all miss you immensely.—Kevin T. Karlson

Left: Kate with her "adopted" daughter, Dale Rosselet during a fun game of miniature golf.

Closing Words

We hope you have enjoyed your journey through our visions as much as we enjoyed sharing our images with you. For us, birds and nature are not a pastime; they are a passion and driving force of our lives. Our world is changing so rapidly that many people are losing sight of the importance of staying connected with the natural world, which is the foundation and life force of all human existence. Expanding technology provides countless artificial distractions, and it takes a great deal of effort to stay focused on what really matters in our lives. The images in this book touched upon many parts of our natural world, and hopefully fanned the flame of your personal visions of birds and nature.

— Kevin T. Karlson

Man's heart away from nature becomes hard.

— Standing Bear

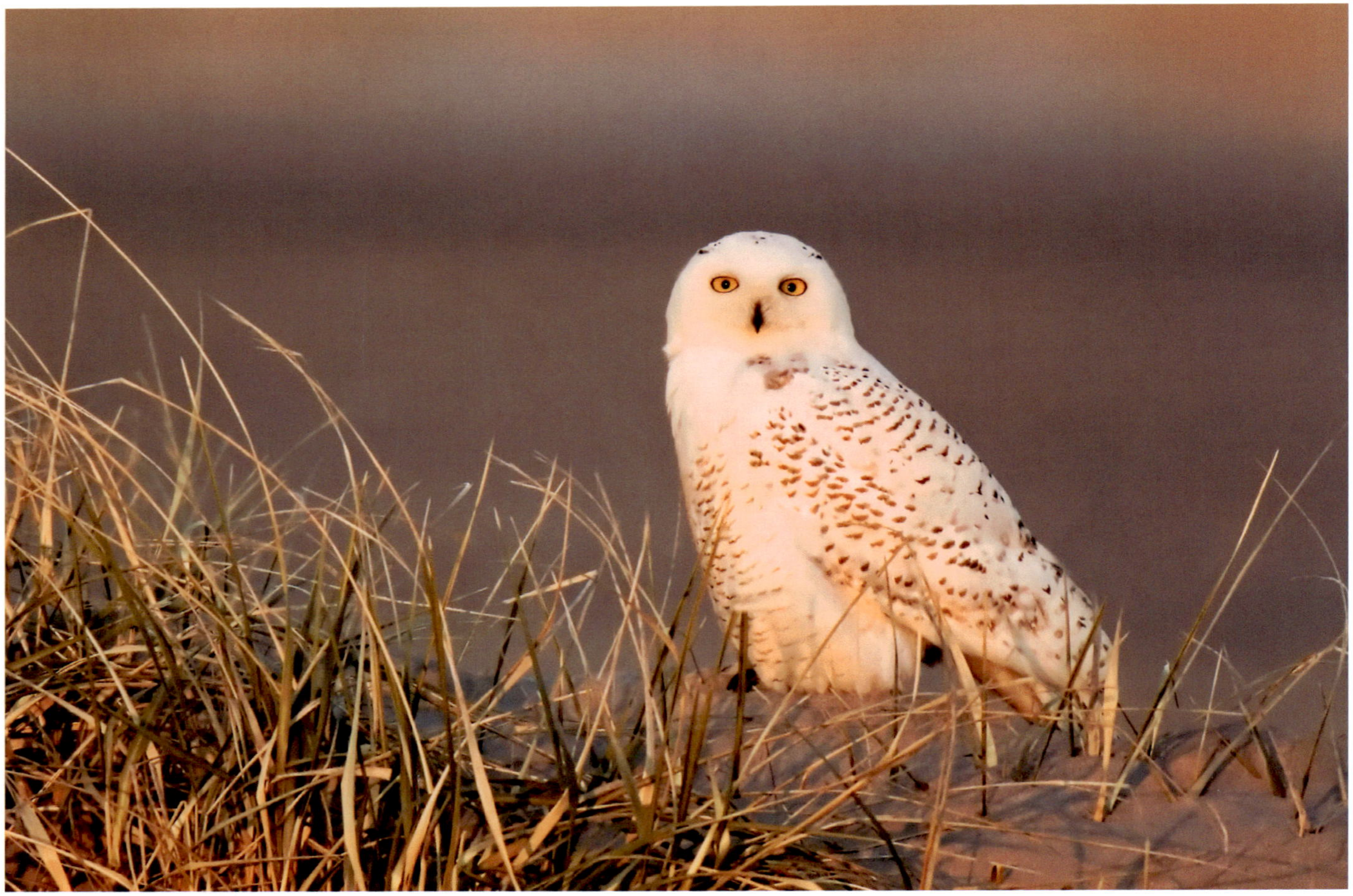

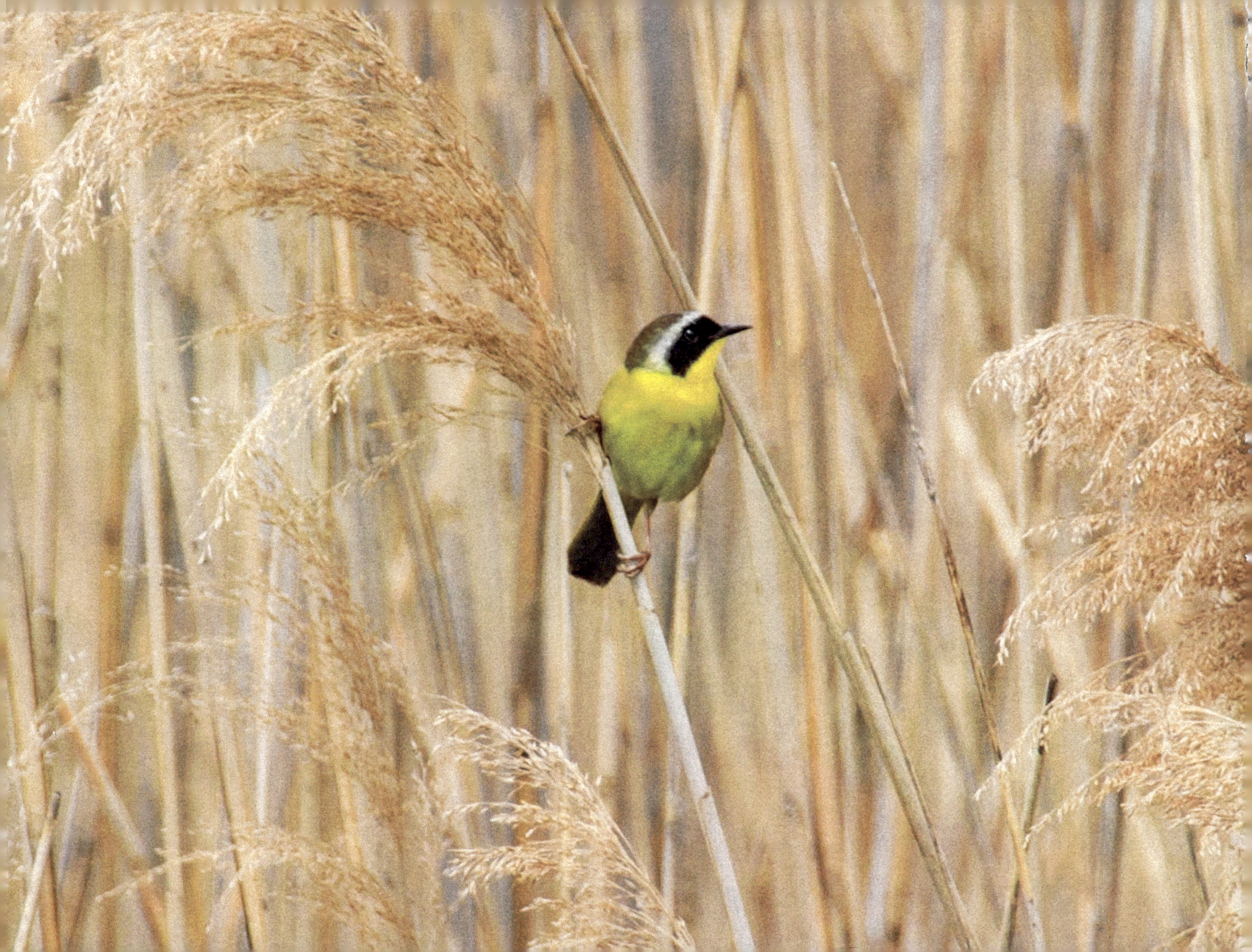